WOODROW WILSON CENTER SERIES

The state and social investigation
in Britain and the United States

Other books in the series

The state and social investigation in Britain and the United States

Edited by
MICHAEL J. LACEY and MARY O. FURNER

WOODROW WILSON CENTER PRESS

AND

Published by the Woodrow Wilson Center Press and
the Press Syndicate of the University of Cambridge
The Pitt Building, Trumpington Street, Cambridge CB2 1RP
40 West 20th Street, New York, NY 10011 4211, USA
10 Stamford Road, Oakleigh, Victoria 3166, Australia

First published 1993

Printed in Canada

Library of Congress Cataloging-in-Publication Data

The State and social investigation in Britain and the United States /
ed. by Michael J. Lacey and Mary O. Furner.
p.   cm. — (Woodrow Wilson Center series)
Includes index.
ISBN 0-521-41638-8
1. Great Britain—Social policy—History.   2. United States—
Social policy—History.   3. Welfare state—History.   I. Lacey,
Michael James.   II. Furner, Mary O.   III. Series.
HV248.S78   1993
361.6'1'0941—dc20   92-41255
CIP

A catalog record for this book is available from the British Library.

ISBN 0-521-41638-8 hardback

WOODROW WILSON INTERNATIONAL CENTER FOR SCHOLARS

The Center is the "living memorial" of the United States of America to the nation's twenty-eighth president, Woodrow Wilson. The U.S. Congress established the Woodrow Wilson Center in 1968 as an international institute for advanced study, "symbolizing and strengthening the fruitful relationship between the world of learning and the world of public affairs." The Center opened in 1970 under its own board of trustees, which includes citizens appointed by the president of the United States, federal government officials who serve ex officio, and an additional representative named by the president from within the federal government.

In all its activities the Woodrow Wilson Center is a nonprofit, nonpartisan organization, supported financially by annual appropriations from the U.S. Congress, and by the contributions of foundations, corporations, and individuals.

WOODROW WILSON CENTER PRESS

The Woodrow Wilson Center Press publishes the best work emanating from the Center's programs and from fellows and guest scholars, and assists in publication, in-house or outside, of research works produced at the Center and judged worthy of dissemination. Conclusions or opinions expressed in Center publications and programs are those of the authors and speakers and do not necessarily reflect the views of the Center staff, fellows, trustees, advisory groups, or any individuals or organizations that provide financial support to the Center.

Woodrow Wilson Center Press
Editorial Offices
370 L'Enfant Promenade, S.W., Suite 704
Washington, D.C. 20024-2518
telephone: (202) 287-3000, ext. 218

Contents

vii

Part II. Empiricism and the new liberalism

Foreword

This volume is a result of a Woodrow Wilson Center project on the growth of knowledge and the rise of the modern state. It is a companion collection to the essays contained in *The State and Economic Knowledge: The American and British Experiences* (1990), edited by Mary O. Furner and Barry Supple. The project began with the recognition that of all the activities undertaken by the modern state, the most neglected as a subject of study is the subtle and multifaceted role played by government institutions in helping to elicit, organize, assess, augment, employ, refine, and conserve in many fields the knowledge base on which contemporary life has come to depend. Those of us who have worked with the project hope that these volumes will deepen understanding of the processes behind the development of knowledge itself, the diffusion of knowledge, and the effects of that knowledge on social and cultural life. We also hope that these studies will highlight once again the usefulness of a historical approach to public affairs and encourage closer collaboration between those who are concerned with the history of ideas and those who work on the political and administrative history of public institutions.

A word of thanks is due to those former fellows and advisers at the Wilson Center who began the conversations that resulted in the symposium in which preliminary versions of most of the chapters presented here appeared. We were particularly fortunate to have as keynote speakers at the symposium Senator Daniel Patrick Moynihan, who knows as much as anyone in public life about the nexus between investigation and policy, and Professor Edward Shils, a distinguished student of the relationship. The late Warren Susman, a gifted historian and interpreter of emerging trends in scholarship, was especially helpful in getting things started, as was the late Jack L. Walker, whose death deprived us of a rare source of wisdom and insight into American politics and institutions.

The editors wish to thank all those who participated in the symposium where most of the chapters were first presented, as well as those who gave us chapters subsequently that helped illustrate more fully the themes that came up in discussions at the symposium and in the later stages of planning for this volume. The contributors were tolerant and cooperative in their responses to editorial suggestions, and as patient as could be hoped for in the face of delays in the production of the book. The Woodrow Wilson Center gratefully acknowledges the support of the Ford Foundation, the Shell Oil Company Foundation, and the Exxon Education Foundation for helping to make the work possible.

MICHAEL J. LACEY

Part I

Knowledge and government

Part I

1

Social investigation, social knowledge, and
the state: an introduction

MICHAEL J. LACEY and MARY O. FURNER

A passage in Hugh Heclo's study of the rise of the welfare state points
to the main concern of this book—the historical development of the
knowledge base on which, however precariously, the public policies of
modern governments depend. "Politics finds its sources," Heclo observes,
"not only in power but also in uncertainty—men collectively wondering
what to do." Uncertainty arises when accustomed ways of proceeding
with the public business no longer seem to fit the situation. Doubt incites
inquiry, and during inquiry, often pressured by crisis, issues begin to take
shape. Not all issues are equally mature, nor are all difficulties equally
matters of public concern. To find a place in the working vocabulary of
public affairs and to attain the culturally distinctive status of a "public
policy problem," with all the pervasiveness and persistence that such
problems call to mind, the issues must be in principle tractable, which
requires that the circumstances in which they are rooted must be perceived
and intelligible.

Finding feasible approaches to such problems begins with gauging the
direction and force of the political currents actually at work in society,
but judgments of feasibility draw on something more than prudential
calculations of this sort. The search also involves an intellectual quest
for hypothetical possibilities, conceivable solutions, of a different kind.
"Governments not only 'power' (or whatever the verb form of that approach might be)," Heclo insists, "they also puzzle. Policy making is a

The authors acknowledge with gratitude the generous and insightful criticisms of this
chapter provided by Donald Winch. We also benefited greatly from suggestions provided
by Robert D. Cuff, Hugh Heclo, John L. Thomas, James Kloppenberg, and Martin Bulmer.

form of collective puzzlement on society's behalf; it entails both deciding and knowing."[1]

In drawing attention to the point that the life of government depends on inquiry as well as edict, intelligence as well as will, Heclo highlights a neglected feature of the modern state: its pervasive reliance on a changing store of social knowledge, including information and ideas about what social problems are, what is known about such problems, what further data are needed to improve comprehension of them, and what might be done about them. To a degree that would have been unimaginable in earlier times, the cultural atmosphere within which modern government proceeds is composed of vast amounts of stylized evidence on social and economic conditions and trends. The collective puzzlement to which Heclo refers is not a quiet, carefully focused intellectual exercise that follows rigid rules. Rather, shaped by the insights and oversights of past puzzlers and conducted by adversaries as well as collaborators, the necessary reflection takes place in a busy public setting, in a swelling, information-rich environment fed continually by many interested parties, all intending to have some bearing on the activities of government.

In keeping with this milieu, the rhetoric of political leadership and policy debate has come to be an empirically grounded style of argument and exhortation. Claims and counterclaims about what the public good requires, assertions about what the government ought to do or undo, are bolstered by favored bits of information plucked from the vortex of testimony, studies, reports, and just-released data that swirls around the institutions of the state. For modern governments, selecting, justifying, and implementing policies of any sort means finding workable grounds for them. This search is a complex historical undertaking, a reflexive process that draws on all the capacities of public office and all the relevant linkages between government and the private, voluntary, or civil sector of society. In the search for workable grounds, none of the special powers with which officials are equipped is more important than the power to look into things. The power to investigate, inherent in the modern state, furnishes the sensorium of the public. The evolution and elaboration of the central operations of today's governments are inconceivable without its exercise. Even allowing for the fact that legislators sometimes legislate first and justify afterwards, lawmaking cannot be divorced from processes

---

[1]Hugh Heclo, *Modern Social Politics in Britain and Sweden: From Relief to Income Maintenance* (New Haven, Conn.: Yale University Press, 1974), 305.

of legislative inquiry; nor can administrative development and direction be divorced from bureaucratic processes of inquiry and report, or adjudication from processes of review and reasoned deliberation.[2]

Taken together, this set of cultural circumstances constitutes the knowledge base that government draws on for whatever general sense of direction and legitimacy it enjoys. Unless the metaphor of a "knowledge base" is carefully deployed, it may suggest a solidity and mass to the grounds for policy that are belied by reports on the political uses of social knowledge. Both participants and scholars cite, in case after case, the inadequacy and ambiguity of such knowledge and the neglect, distortion, or misuse of whatever relevant information may exist by parties to the conflicts that make up policy history. But use of the metaphor need not imply hidden assertions regarding either certitude or consensus with respect to the grounds of policy. When the phrase is broadly conceived, so as to allow for a measure of incompleteness, ambiguity, and disputed meaning, there yet remains a usefulness to the metaphor that alternatives, whether more specific or more general in connotation, do not possess. The "knowledge base" concept points to the fact that in modern societies there are reasons for policies. Above all else, policies are intentional patterns of action. Correct or incorrect, wise or unwise, each was once conceived as an answer to a problem.

Reasons must be distinguished from opinions. It is true, to be sure, that governance takes place within a climate of prevailing opinion. In the writing of political history, reference to such climates and to changes within them is typically a way of describing, in shorthand form, complicated shifts of viewpoint and evaluation regarding the duties of the state on the part of those political elites most closely and continuously engaged with the affairs of government. Yet because the "climate of opinion" metaphor is a shorthand device, it may scant the *reasons* that people give for their opinions, and fail altogether to detect any connection between changing opinion, on the one hand, and a changing context of knowledge, information, and argument on the other.

---

[2]For a discussion of the central importance of information-gathering and -monitoring activities of civil administration in Britain during its emergence as a world power, see John Brewer, *The Sinews of Power: War, Money and the English State, 1688–1783* (Cambridge, Mass.: Harvard University Press, 1990). William R. Brock, *Investigation and Responsibility: Public Responsibility in the United States, 1865–1900* (Cambridge: Cambridge University Press, 1984), provides a comparable account of investigations bearing on social-policy questions at the state level of government in the United States during the last third of the nineteenth century.

In contrast, to ask about the knowledge base for public policy is to invite attention to the specific, documented reasons invoked for changes of viewpoint and evaluation; to be alert to the kinds of evidence cited by contemporaries as factors at work in the process; and to inquire not simply into the structure of conflicting interests involved in struggles over policy, but into the arguments and supporting proofs used by adversaries to make their case as well. The task requires that, in thinking about the history of governance, one take notice of the appearance from time to time of new kinds of evidence and styles of formulating it; new types of expertise thought to be relevant for understanding public problems (e.g., economics, social work, demographics, forecasting, polling, regional planning); new practices intended to elicit pertinent testimony; and new kinds of institutions with functions that are intended to alter in some way the climate of knowledge within which informed opinion takes shape and the struggle for directive control of government goes on. Perhaps most important, the task requires a sensitivity to the discourse of public policy, to changes in the vocabulary and concepts that people have employed in their attempts to make sense of social problems and government's changing role in connection with them.[3]

To the extent that questions of this sort can be asked and answered, it is clear that the knowledge-base metaphor points to a complex and elusive reality in politics and governance. The complexity of it reflects the diversity of perspectives on social questions. No one person commands a holistic view. The central institutions of government are themselves complex and of different kinds. Legislatures, courts, executive agencies—each has a different task, each is subject to different societal pressures, and each represents a different milieu of knowledge and tradition, a different vocabulary and style of reasoning. A similar but greater diversity exists among the many nongovernment bodies that engage in social investigation. Within and between these different knowledge sub-

---

[3]In connection with the possibilities of new scholarly approaches to the discourse of politics and public policy, see Terence Ball, James Farr, and Russell L. Hanson, eds., *Political Innovation and Conceptual Change* (Cambridge: Cambridge University Press, 1989). This collection of essays on political language explores the implications for historical analysis of the fact that politics is conceptually and communicatively constituted. It provides "conceptual histories" for a number of key terms in political discourse. On the issues of method involved, see particularly James Farr's chapter, "Understanding Conceptual Change Politically," 24–49. See also in the same vein Daniel T. Rogers, *Contested Truths: Keywords in American Politics Since Independence* (New York: Basic Books, 1987), and the discussion of the meanings of monopoly and labor in Chapter 5 of this volume.

cultures, knowledge claims, as applied to policy, are routinely disputed. The public interplay of assertion and refutation contributes to the ongoing drama of politics.

The knowledge base is not composed exclusively or even largely of expert information and theory, though the cross-examination of expertise is, in fact, one of the processes that feed into it. Rather, the knowledge base is compound, in the sense that it draws on at least three different kinds of knowledge: (1) disciplinary and professional knowledge; (2) informed opinion of the sort necessarily possessed by elites in politics, government, the media, and active interest groups; and (3) those general forms of cultural beliefs and values, widely shared, that shape civic culture, providing a sense of propriety and impropriety that is called on in evaluating the nature of social problems and proposed remedies to them.[4]

The knowledge base is compound in a temporal sense as well, reflecting the accretion of layers of new data and new ordering principles. A historical phenomenon, it bears the markings of the relevant institutional innovations of the past. Stratigraphy within the base would reveal the presence of government institutions of several varieties, including both those concerned with central statistical operations designed for gathering general intelligence on social and economic conditions (e.g., census bureaus) and more specialized investigative bureaus serving the purposes of the special departments (e.g., Treasury or Defense). In addition, reflecting the development over time of a complex social structure, there would be evidence that a variety of private or voluntary institutions had contributed to shaping the base as well. To cite one instance, the modern university, with its roots in cultural changes of the late nineteenth century, has from the first provided an institutional home for the social scientific disciplines that have played a major role (as sources of theory, criticism, ferment, challenge, reinforcement, and personnel) in the ongoing cultural effort to bring social and political problems under intellectual control. The philanthropic foundation, essentially a twentieth-century institution, has played a large part in the organization and patronage of research relevant to public affairs. So have the research arms of interest-group lobbies and,

---

[4]For a discussion of a typology, suggested by Robert Cuff, that distinguishes professional, practical, and cultural forms of knowledge with reference to economic beliefs, see Mary O. Furner and Barry Supple, "Ideas, Institutions and the State in the United States and Britain: An Introduction," in the volume they edited, *The State and Economic Knowledge: The American and British Experiences* (Cambridge: Cambridge University Press, 1990), 11–14.

especially in the United States, the public policy "think tanks," which are of similar vintage to the foundations and often dependent on them.[5]

The complexity of the knowledge base should not be confused with its adequacy to its many tasks. Contemporary governments are everywhere beset by skepticism about the social knowledge foundations of their policies and pressed to demonstrate the necessity for many of the social and economic roles that they have had in the past. The deepest of all assumptions about the value of democratic government—deeper even than those that stress the importance of participation—is the belief that there are good and sufficient reasons, based ultimately in objective, impersonal, discursively communicable knowledge, for the laws and policies that issue from its proper functioning. Therefore such skepticism represents a more general challenge to the future of governance than is typically acknowledged by political parties or by writers in the various ideological traditions of social criticism. Even as capitalist democracy triumphed as a social form, its premises as a civic system were and continue to be challenged by a pervasive, ubiquitous, and frequently well-warranted cynicism regarding the sources of political action.

To understand better the challenge to today's liberal democratic state, it is necessary to glance backward in time on the development of the knowledge base that grew up in dynamic relation to it and to historicize the connections between them, seeking deeper insight into the interplay of social thought, political institutions, and public policy. The chapters that follow are intended as contributions to that effort. A product of an ongoing Wilson Center project on relations between the forms and capacities of government and the growth of knowledge, this volume is a companion study to *The State and Economic Knowledge: The American and British Experiences*. The editors hope that, like the essays in its companion volume, those presented here will help to demonstrate the mutuality of influence that links the state and social investigation, and that they will register the point, simple and yet far-reaching in its implications, that when the knowledge base on which the operations of

---

[5] On the history and politics of the think tanks, see Chapter 7 in this volume. See also James A. Smith, *The Idea Brokers: Think Tanks and the Rise of the New Policy Elite* (New York: Free Press, 1991); Joseph G. Peschek, *Policy-Planning Organizations: Elite Agendas and America's Rightward Turn* (Philadelphia: Temple University Press, 1987). On the role of philanthropic foundations in generating the knowledge base for public policy, see Barry D. Karl and Stanley N. Katz, "The American Private Philanthropic Foundation and the Public Sphere, 1890–1930," *Minerva* 19, no.2 (Summer 1981): 236–70, and idem,"Foundations and Ruling Class Elites," *Daedalus: Journal of the American Academy of Arts and Sciences* 116, no.7 (Winter 1987): 1–40.

public policy depend is considered, the active, ongoing knowledge-generating activities of the various agencies and components of government itself must be taken into account. Governments must know in order to act. If the kind of knowledge they require is readily available, they make use of it. If not, they do what they can, directly or indirectly, to bring it into being. Both the efficiency and the legitimacy of government operations in the long run depend on their doing so. In their efforts to secure the grounds for legitimate political agency, governments have been producers as well as consumers of social knowledge, mobilizers as well as mobilized.

THE GROWTH OF KNOWLEDGE AND THE HISTORIES OF STATES

A state, Woodrow Wilson wrote, is "a people organized for law within a definite territory."[6] Wilson's terse definition captures one of the essentials of our organizing idea: that governments are the deliberate, purposeful organizers of states. What Wilson's definition fails to capture is the dynamic relationships, changing over time and from context to cultural context, between the roles and functions of states. The tasks assigned to government—be they social or economic regulation, population planning, poor relief, or whatever—interact in complex ways with the forms and functions of knowledge, on the one hand, and the institutions of social inquiry engaged in the making of government policies, on the other.

To help recapture this connection between the state and social knowledge, this chapter offers a sketch of the history of Anglo-American social investigation and suggests something of the meaning of the enterprise for those involved in shaping it. It stresses the importance of the rise of social empiricism in the nineteenth century, and its influence on the formation of the new liberalism from the 1880s onward. It discusses major examples of twentieth-century social investigation, describes its contemporary context, and comments on the challenge to processes of inquiry into the public and its problems posed by the growth of various forms of skepticism regarding the links between knowledge and policy. The chapter closes with some suggestions for new lines of research.

Gianfranco Poggi has made an important start on the job of historicizing the state in a way that invites attention to the changing knowledge base on which it depends. Writing in the tradition of comparative his-

---

[6]Woodrow Wilson, *The State: Elements of Historical and Practical Politics*, rev. ed. (Boston: D.C. Heath, 1909), 8.

torical sociology, Poggi identifies three developmental processes in the rise of the state and its connection with science since early modern times. All have to do with the phenomenon of rule. First, the state expanded and consolidated its authority in a "centralization of rule," taking place over centuries that was most evident in the dynamics of nineteenth-century nationalism. Second, the state took on new duties; this process was intimately bound up with the growth of government in the nineteenth century and, on an increasingly massive scale, in the twentieth. The growth of government was neither steady nor uniform, but over the long stretch it reflected what Poggi calls the "functionalization" of rule, a process through which the more advanced states were increasingly engaged as instruments for attaining wider social purposes. Max Weber, from a different perspective, associated this trend with the inertial complexities of the modern bureaucratic state.[7]

Third, and throughout, there were changes in the cognitive aspects of governance, a process Poggi calls the "rationalization" of rule. This process reflected the ongoing effort to base the exercise of social power not on custom, which Enlightenment thinkers rejected as a guide, or on the arbitrary will of hereditary rulers, but—particularly with the appearance of democratic and republican ideas calling for representative government—on the application of an appropriate body of knowledge and procedure. In contrast to the first two processes, the third is little understood and has been relatively neglected as a subject of study. As a subject it is coextensive with the historical development of what we have been calling the knowledge base of public policy. That development begins, for all practical purposes, with the gradual historic shift from a framework of beliefs that centered on ideas of *rights to rule* existing within providential conceptions of political order, enjoyed by hereditary rulers, to new social and political conventions that centered on *the duties of rule,* which began to take shape in the era of the Enlightenment. Poggi argues that the shift stimulated an attempt at the "scientization" of politics, the search for new kinds of knowledge, different from inherited juridical forms, to guide officials and to justify the actions they took to fulfill their growing repertory of functions. As the gradual rise of mass democracy was channeled through the workings of representative political institutions, and as new bureaucracies and regulatory regimes were

---

[7]Gianfranco Poggi, "The Modern State and the Idea of Progress," in Gabriel A. Almond, Marvin Chodorow, and Roy Harvey Pearce, eds., *Progress and Its Discontents* (Berkeley: University of California Press, 1982), 337–60, passim.

devised in response to public problems, rather inexorably the state took on its contemporary guise, and came to be seen as a "container" of social processes and a "facility" through which society could exercise leverage on itself.[8]

THE MEANING AND TYPES OF SOCIAL INVESTIGATION

Poggi is especially alert to the importance of the cognitive components of state action and to the ways in which the development of these components stimulates the growth of new kinds of knowledge in the surrounding society. In early modern times, to the extent that there was a discourse of public policy that foreshadowed the discourse of later days, the language of statecraft was juridical language. It was rooted in traditions of jurisprudence, particularly natural jurisprudence. With the rise of the modern state, however, nonjuridical forms of knowledge, those rooted in the histories of the natural and the social sciences, for example, came to play an increasingly significant part in the life of governance.[9]

Discussion of the historical development of the knowledge base for the administrative and regulatory activities of the state—the attempted "scientization of politics," to use Poggi's formulation—involves special difficulties of terminology and focus. We have found it useful in confronting this problem to employ a heuristic device of some generality. Thus the category *social investigation* is used, not in the narrow sense, to refer to this or that particular inquiry (or method of inquiry) into poverty, for example, or into the conditions of life for the working classes, although these are included in its scope, but in a broader sense, to refer

[8]Ibid., 341–8. See also Gianfranco Poggi, *The Development of the Modern State* (Stanford: Stanford University Press, 1978), and idem, *The State: Its Nature, Development, and Prospects* (Stanford: Stanford University Press, 1990). The first book is concerned mainly with the rise of the state in continental Europe and devotes the bulk of its discussion to developments prior to the twentieth century; the second volume deals in large part with controversies surrounding the liberal democratic state of the twentieth century.

[9]In *The State: Its Nature, Development, and Prospects*, Poggi observes with respect to the growing significance of nonjuridical forms of knowledge, "Even where law was taken most seriously, its application to concrete circumstances called for sound knowledge and reliable information concerning factual conditions, not just legal norms. Thus, from relatively early on in the development of the state, efforts were made by individual states to collect data on demographic and economic conditions (the term 'statistic' bears witness to this) and to keep themselves abreast of developments in the material and organizational technology of production. Of course, states also sought, more or less successfully, to develop and apply know-how relevant to their two overriding (and overlapping) concerns—the collection of taxes and the organizing, equipping, and deploying of armies and navies" (p. 32).

to an ongoing *process* of public inquiry into social conditions, especially problematic ones, with the intention of bringing knowledge to bear on the decisions and functions of governance. Public social investigation is conducted by the knowledge-generating agencies of government, but many of the investigative processes of "private" bodies, located, strictly speaking, in civil society, are public in the sense that the offices of state and public opinion are their intended object and audience.

In considering the types and history of social investigation understood in these general terms, one is dealing not only with specific individuals, problems, and methods of investigation, but with a broader phenomenon, traceable through the public records, that issues in the cultural history of the modern state. The precise origins of the trend toward an inquiring, would-be problem-solving style of governance remain obscure, but certainly social investigation as an ongoing process of public inquiry into social problems was under way in both Britain and the United States by the 1830s. Gaining authority, social investigation engaged the attention and the energies of a great many people on both sides of the Atlantic in the late nineteenth and early twentieth centuries, and, later in the twentieth century, it became a permanent, though increasingly problematic, feature of the context of thought and action through which politics shapes government. In the contemporary situation, the forms and methods of bringing knowledge to bear on public policy have become so numerous, so routinized in both state and civil society, so specialized, so inaccessible as expert policy talk, and so frequently challenged as partial, deceptive enmeshed in schemes for domination, or irrelevant that the usefulness of such knowledge for purposes of public guidance and legitimation is undermined by a growing popular skepticism, and by philosophically grounded attitudes of relativism regarding the grounds for law and policy.

Before we address the contemporary problem, it is useful to consider the meaning of social investigation when the cultural practice itself was in its heyday, its participants confident and forward-looking, in the late nineteenth century. In one of the most celebrated autobiographies of the period, Beatrice Webb wrote:

Now, without pretending to sum up the influence of the time-spirit on the social activities of the last quarter of the nineteenth century, what is clear is that upon me—in 1883, a woman of twenty-five—it led to a definite conclusion. From the flight of emotion away from the service of God to the service of man, and from the current faith in the scientific method, I drew the inference that the most hopeful form of social service was the *craft of a social investigator* [emphasis added]. And some such conclusion seems to have been reached by many of my contemporaries. For detailed descriptions of the life and labour of the people in all its various aspects, sensational or scientific, derived from personal observation or statistical calculation, become a characteristic feature of the publications of the period, whether newspapers or magazines, plays or novels, the reports of philanthropic organizations or the proceedings of learned societies. It may be said that this novel concentration of attention on the social condition of the people was due neither to intellectual curiosity nor to the spirit of philanthropy, but rather to a panic fear of the newly enfranchised democracy. But this is looking at the same fact from another standpoint. For even the most fanatical socialist asserted that his hopes for the future depended on a deliberately scientific organization of society, combined with the growth among the whole body of the people of a desire and capacity for disinterested social service.[10]

In justifying her life's work, Webb spoke of the craft of social investigator as a vocation, not simply as a scientific specialty. For her and for many others, the vocation was part of a thriving, middle-class subculture devoted to public service and social reform. Its members, including a talented cadre of educated women in both Britain and the United States, were drawn from the modernizing, knowledge-bearing occupations and professions. As William Leach and others have shown, there were strong affinities between feminist ideology, which many men, of course, shared, and the new ways of conceiving the social problem and its resolution. In addition, studying the lives of the poor, particularly those of poor women and children, extended the nurturing role assigned to women and conformed to the assumed capacities and limitations of gender.

This educated, middle-class, feminist, science-and-social-reform subculture, as a number of the chapters in this volume remind us, had been present and growing since the 1830s. In addition to the example provided by British and American abolitionists who documented the conditions of slave life, we can easily note others among those who sought improvement in the care of prisoners, the indigent, and the insane. In the United States, Dorothea Dix and the landslide of reports she pushed on state legislatures in the 1840s, seeking humane care of the mentally ill, are illustrative of the pattern and the investigative subculture in which it flourished. Those who lived within it were involved in cultivating the various nonjuridical forms of knowledge we have mentioned, relating to

[10]Beatrice Webb, *My Apprenticeship* (London: Longmans, Green, 1926), 150–1.

public health and safety, for example, or public education, or, as Webb points out, to empirical social description of different kinds.[11]

As Webb indicates, many of her contemporaries shared her feelings about the general aims of social investigation and its relevance to politics and public policy, among them, in America, Jane Addams, Florence Kelley, John Dewey, and W. E. B. Du Bois. In that subculture, what counted was not so much one's status as a government insider or a critic outside government, but rather a general spirit of optimism regarding the possibilities of the new knowledge as a basis for policy that transcended differences among participants regarding the proper objects or methods of public inquiry and assistance, and united public and private investigators.[12]

Jane Addams, in her autobiography, discussed the permeability of boundaries separating public and private so far as social investigation was concerned. Detailing the early activities and investigations undertaken by the residents of Hull House, she remarked that "the best results are to be obtained in investigations as in other undertakings by combining our researches with those of other public bodies or with the State itself." In both Britain and the United States, in other words, the investigative community that nurtured the new, politically relevant forms of nonjuridical knowledge cut across the boundaries of conventions and roles separating the public world of officialdom from the private world of church, family, school, work, and philanthropy. Just as Jane Addams and W. E. B. Du Bois were acquainted with the investigations directed

[11]William Leach, *True Love and Perfect Union: The Feminist Reform of Sex and Society* (New York: Basic Books, 1980); Linda Gordon, ed., *Women, the State, and Welfare* (Madison: University of Wisconsin Press, 1990); Helen E. Marshall, *Dorothea Dix: Forgotten Samaritan* (1937; New York: Russell and Russell, 1967); and Linda Gordon, "Social Insurance and Public Assistance: The Influence of Gender in Welfare Thought in the United States, 1890–1935," *American Historical Review* 97, no.1 (February 1992): 19–50. This last explores the activities, thought, and impact of women welfare reformers from the beginnings of the progressive era through the passage of the Social Security Act of 1935.

[12]An excellent example of such differences among female social empiricists is presented in Jane Lewis, "The Place of Social Investigation, Social Theory, and Social Work in the Approach to Late Victorian and Edwardian Social Problems: The Case of Beatrice Webb and Helen Bosanquet," in Martin Bulmer, Kevin Bales, and Katherine Kish Sklar, eds., *The Social Survey in Historical Perspective, 1880–1940* (Cambridge: Cambridge University Press, 1991), 148–69. See also Mary Jo Deegan, *Jane Addams and the Men of the Chicago School, 1892–1918* (New Brunswick, N.J.: Rutgers University Press, 1988), and Katherine Kish Sklar, "Hull House Maps and Papers: Social Science as Women's Work in the 1890's," in Bulmer et al., eds., *The Social Survey in Historical Perspective*, 111–47.

under government auspices in Washington by Carroll D. Wright (as was he with theirs), so Beatrice Webb was well acquainted with the work directed by Wright's counterpart in Whitehall, Llewellyn Smith (as was he with hers).[13]

Notice should also be taken of Webb's point about the motives that animated social investigators. It mattered little, as she argued, whether the people engaged in these activities were inspired by "panic fear" of the newly enfranchised masses, by some sense of religious duty, or by hopes for egalitarian socialism. Whatever the motive, they shared an assumption that new knowledge could provide new grounds for policy. Knowledge itself was real, not illusion or pretense. Even the most fanatical socialist among them, as she pointed out, placed his hopes for the future not simply in the power of his ideals, but rather in some combination of science and disinterested social service—in the assumption, in other words, that there were grounds for law and regulation and objective standards of application and eligibility—impersonal, discursively communicable grounds that could be developed as a foundation to orient the policies of the modern state.

We have suggested that the generation of Beatrice and Sidney Webb and Jane Addams, Llewellyn Smith and Carroll Wright, marked the heyday in the history of social investigation, considered as a practice of public inquiry into social problems aimed at building up and refashioning a knowledge base appropriate to the needs of the modern state. To establish a framework for discussion along these historical lines, the remainder of this chapter calls attention to some of the most important changes that have occurred in the context of social investigation over time. To highlight the broad changes in context, we consider (1) the Enlightenment and its effects on the Anglo-American heritage of governance; (2) the growing nineteenth-century hopes for an empirically grounded science of politics and government and the gradual transformation of the premises of public policy-making that took the form of the new liberalism, which gave birth to the bureaucratic-regulatory state; and (3) the mid–twentieth century attitude regarding the state and social investigation, and some of the challenges to that connection that are posed by various forms of skepticism about the reliability of social knowledge.

---

[13]Jane Addams, *Twenty Years at Hull House* (New York: Signet Classic, New American Library, 1961), 214.

ENLIGHTENMENT BEGINNINGS

So deeply ingrained in contemporary thought is a historicist sensibility—the notion that humans make themselves through their institutions and that each historical situation differs from every other—that it takes some effort to recall a time when this was not so, when knowledge of the variable, the contingent, the merely historical, was less esteemed than was philosophical and theological knowledge that aimed at immutable truths. The cultural ferment of the Enlightenment gave birth to this new historicism, and to hope about the manifold possibilities of new kinds of knowledge that it allowed. The rise of the Enlightenment represented the complicated and fruitful shift of horizon that we associate with the proximate origins of a distinctly modern consciousness. The Enlightenment project—to establish a new, historically oriented science of man and society along naturalistic lines—gave birth not only to the modern social sciences, but to new ways of thinking about the public interest and the role of government in society.

So far as governance and relations between society and the state were concerned, that project originated not only within and in opposition to absolutist monarchies, but, as well, within and in opposition to an inherited framework of mercantile state policies. Beginning in the late seventeenth century and on into the eighteenth, England (after 1707, Britain), through its growing military prowess and increasingly far-flung commercial interests, became a major power and a potent new factor in world history. John Brewer points, in his study of the hidden sinews of power that made these operations possible, to the administrative institutions at the heart of the fiscal-military state and to the importance of the kinds of information being pulled together by the clerks. He identifies those "pale and shadowy figures who have never received their due" as a neglected group of official intelligence-gatherers whose significance to state development foreshadows that of another neglected group of investigators, the so-called statesmen in disguise of the mid-Victorian period, whose activities paved the way for the growth of government in that time. In the former case, Brewer shows that while rivalry, warfare, and the threat of it provided the need, the work of the clerks provided the knowledge base on which new schemes of public finance, taxation, public administration, and military organization depended.[14]

[14]See Brewer, *The Sinews of Power*. For the argument that the emergence of the once-

Brewer's account of the remarkable capacity of the eighteenth-century British state—small in comparison with its adversaries but no less powerful, more intelligent in certain respects, relatively unobtrusive at home— is especially sensitive to the relationships between knowledge and policy and between developments within government and those within civil society. He presents the thesis that "a growth in state power is usually accompanied—either as cause or effect—by changes in either the extent or the nature of a government's hold on social knowledge." He also outlines the political dynamics behind the proliferation during this period of such terms as *public knowledge* and *public information,* novel phrasings that indicated a widespread and growing desire within British society to push out into the public sphere kinds of social and economic information that had previously been considered closed or private.[15]

Four different constituencies, each with different needs and interests, pressed for greater access to the stores of information under the care of the clerks. These different sources were (1) ministers of the Crown, given their needs for an overall view of government policy; (2) Parliament, given its needs as both a legislature and a watchdog of the executive; (3) occupational groups and special interests affected by state policies and anxious to have the grounds for them; and (4) the general public, which developed an appetite during the Enlightenment for a new type of information, "useful knowledge"—generally data on population, society, and the economy that only the state at this period could provide.

Brewer demonstrates how the interplay of these needs and interests generated not only new kinds of data, but new ways of thinking about government and the public. For example, he shows how, when the com-

neglected investigators of early and mid-Victorian England marked an underlying movement of the national mind more important than the surface politics of the period, see G. M. Young, *Portrait of an Age: Victorian England* (2d ed. 1936; New York: Oxford University Press, 1983). Young pointed to the importance of the empirical mentality in the 1830s. In Parliament, he argued, "It was the business of the thirties to transfer the treatment of affairs from a polemical to a statistical basis, from Humbug to Humdrum" (p. 28). Oliver MacDonagh's *Early Victorian Government, 1830–1870* (London: Weidenfeld and Nicolson, 1977) is a wide-ranging account of social and administrative reform. On the statesmen in disguise, see the original article by G. Kitson Clark, "Statesmen in Disguise: Reflections on the History of the Neutrality of the Civil Service," *Historical Journal* 2 (1959): 19–39; for subsequent developments, see the review article by Roy M. MacLeod, "Statesmen Undisguised," *American Historical Review* 78 (1973): 1386–1405, together with the discussion of the theme in Chapter 3 of this volume.

[15]Brewer, *The Sinews of Power,* 221. For a discussion of the emergence and changing meanings of public opinion, see J. A .W. Gunn, "Public Opinion," in Terrence Ball et al., eds., *Political Innovation and Conceptual Change* (Cambridge: Cambridge University Press, 1989), 247–65.

mercial lobbies pressed their case for information on parliaments and ministries, the economic arguments so characteristic of special interests were "opened up to elaborate a general picture of the economy, or at least to consider the impact of one special interest upon the polity as a whole." When the commercial lobbies failed in Parliament or the ministries, they did not fall silent, but rather helped to invent a sense of public interest by invoking and addressing the public in a new kind of pamphlet literature. In their efforts to excite sympathy and win the support of a broader audience, the lobbies made their arguments more general, and in doing so they helped to create a new climate of knowledge and information that would gradually undermine the thought world of mercantile state policy.[16]

No one was more influential in undermining that world than Adam Smith, who was especially critical of the trends regarding the politics of information that were developing in the eighteenth century. As Smith pointed out, "the clamour and sophistry of merchants and manufacturers" were effective because they had a "superior knowledge of their own interest." The contribution of the philosophies of the Enlightenment was to shape the growing sense of a modern public sphere and to introduce new ways of thinking about the relationship between government and society.[17]

There were many different national enlightenments, not simply one, but the Scottish Enlightenment was especially significant in terms of the themes of this volume. There, with Francis Hutcheson as its pioneer in

[16]Brewer, The Sinews of Power, 246. The concluding chapter of his study, which traces the dynamics generating the new knowledge and illustrates the reciprocities of concern that linked civil administration and the lobbies, is entitled "The Politics of Information: Public Knowledge and Private Interest," 221–49.

[17]Quoted in ibid., 248. The pertinent literature on the Enlightenment thought in its bearings on governance is vast. See, in addition to Chapter 2 in this volume, Istvan Hont and Michael Ignatieff, eds., Wealth and Virtue: The Shaping of Political Economy in the Scottish Enlightenment (Cambridge: Cambridge University Press, 1983); Donald Winch, Adam Smith's Politics: An Essay in Historiographic Revision (Cambridge: Cambridge University Press, 1978); Knud Haakonssen, The Science of a Legislator: The Natural Jurisprudence of David Hume and Adam Smith (Cambridge: Cambridge University Press, 1981); Duncan Forbes, Hume's Philosophical Politics (Cambridge: Cambridge University Press, 1975); Gladys Bryson, Man and Society: The Scottish Inquiry of the Eighteenth Century (Princeton, N.J.: Princeton University Press, 1945); C. B. A. Behrens, Society, Government, and the Enlightenment: The Experience of Eighteenth Century France and Prussia (New York: Harper and Row, 1985); Drew McCoy, The Elusive Republic: Political Economy in Jeffersonian America (Chapel Hill: University of North Carolina Press, 1980); and James T. Kloppenberg, "The Virtues of Liberalism: Christianity, Republicanism, and Ethics in Early American Political Discourse," Journal of American History 74 (June 1987): 9–33.

his writings on moral philosophy, with David Hume and Adam Smith as its commanding central figures, with Lord Kames, Thomas Reid, Adam Ferguson, John Millar, Dugald Stewart, and others intricately linked through their works and personal relations, an especially consequential, multifaceted inquiry into man and society took shape. A distinctive element of historicity was introduced into social thinking that marked an important departure from the social contractarian views of earlier times. Unlike the rationalism of the French philosophies or the rigid, ahistorical utilitarian first principles of the English philosophic radicals, Scottish thinking had a subtle, open-ended quality that accounts for the fact that its leading writers continue to command such strong contemporary interest from scholars around the world.[18]

No tradition of thought has been more influential in shaping the knowledge base for public policy than political economy. As Donald Winch points out in the second chapter of this volume, the essentially modern version of the science of political economy was born of this Scottish enterprise, but represented only a part of it. That part was tightly connected in the minds of its creators to other parts—to moral philosophy and natural jurisprudence, for example—in such a way as to result in a more open-ended view of relations between society and government than has been normally appreciated, despite the best efforts of specialists to demonstrate that the classical political economists did not dogmatically adhere to their laissez-faire positions.

Laissez-faire dogmatism—deductivist arguments about the functioning of a system of natural liberties—in fact did play an important role in public policy discourse. But recent historical scholarship on the Scottish Enlightenment has made clear how misleading and incomplete a view of

---

[18]On different Enlightenment traditions, see Roy Porter and Mikulas Teich, eds., *The Enlightenment in National Context* (Cambridge: Cambridge University Press, 1981). For an elaboration of the argument that an expressly articulated political science emerged in the Scottish Enlightenment as part of a politics of moderation whose tasks included the critique of religious enthusiasm, see James Farr, "Political Science and the Enlightenment of Enthusiasm," *American Political Science Review* 82, no. 1 (March 1988): 51–69. On American connections with the Scottish Enlightenment there are several surveys of the literature, but see Daniel Walker Howe, "Why the Scottish Enlightenment Was Useful to the Framers of the American Constitution," *Comparative Studies in Society and History* 31 (1989): 572–87, and R. B. Sher, "Introduction: Scottish American Studies, Past and Present," in Sher and J. R. Smitten, eds., *Scotland and America in the Age of the Enlightenment* (Princeton, N.J.: Princeton University Press, 1990), 1–27. See also Knud Haakonssen, "From Natural Law to the Rights of Man: A European Perspective on American Debates," in Michael J. Lacey and Knud Haakonssen, eds., *A Culture of Rights: The Bill of Rights in Philosophy, Politics, and Law—1791 and 1991* (Cambridge: Cambridge University Press, 1991), 19–61.

it is conveyed by those who emphasize laissez-faire to the exclusion of all else. The Scots were very much engaged in working out sociocentric views of life as opposed to state-centered views. Indeed the discovery, some would say the invention, of the idea of civil society itself as an object of analysis and historical study was the focus of their attention. Development of the notion that there were unintended consequences at work in social affairs—the idea, as Winch puts it, that "although the social order was the result of human action, it was not necessarily the result of human design"—was clearly at the heart of the Scottish contribution.

This insight did not inspire quietism, however, but rather a search for explanations that would comport more satisfactorily with the social order as they experienced it. It led to the search for theories of spontaneous order in society that were more far-reaching than those that focused on market mechanisms alone. The doctrine of unintended consequences opened up questions in morals, politics, and law as well as economics. More important than any particular finding it might produce, it suggested a method of connecting individual behavior with social outcomes, revealing the mechanisms, but also the limitations, of an invisible hand, the workings of which, and not merely through markets, could be disclosed by the methodological program that underpinned the study of man and society and gave birth eventually to the modern social sciences.[19]

What was distinctive about that program was its style as a philosophical psychology that worked along naturalistic lines and sought to make use of the insights that could be derived from the rapidly expanding historical and anthropological literature of the day. Compared with their predecessors, Scottish observers had a far broader knowledge of non-European societies and forms of government accessible to them. They had witnessed the emergence of large European monarchies and their own perplexing absorption into the British union, accepted in exchange for military security and the advantages promised in the way of commercial development. The Scots were less interested in reflecting on the historical or anthropological particulars of the accumulated experience

---

[19]For a discussion of the speculations of the Scottish Enlightenment thinkers as they relate to ideas of a spontaneous social order, see Ronald Hamowy, *The Scottish Enlightenment and the Theory of Spontaneous Order, Journal of the History of Philosophy* monograph series (Carbondale: Southern Illinois University Press, 1987). For insight into the subsequent development of these tendencies, see Stefan Collini, Donald Winch, and John Burrow, *That Noble Science of Politics: A Study in Nineteenth-Century Intellectual History* (Cambridge: Cambridge University Press, 1983).

of states than in using those particulars to form generalizations that would shed light on "the common bent of mankind" and the psychological "springs" of human action. Scottish skepticism about utopian schemes of social engineering is well known. One of the distinctive strains in Scottish thought was, in fact, impatience with utopianism, and an interest instead in noncoercive forms of mutual interaction, with the attempt to understand why established mores and manners work the way they do.

The interest in establishing a richer context for understanding the common bent of mankind was expressed in a novel type of historical writing intended to provide an account of the rise and functioning of civil society—as distinguished from political society and the state—as an intelligible subject in its own right. In Adam Smith's *Inquiry into the Nature and Causes of the Wealth of Nations,* as in other texts of the period, this effort took the form of sequential, "stage" theories of historical development, with hunter-gatherer societies appearing at one end of the spectrum and contemporary civilization based on commerce and the intricate division of labor in agriculture, trade, and manufacturing at the other. The new historical consciousness reflected in these theories of patterned evolution clearly foreshadowed later developments in social and political thought. Questions arose about relationships among different aspects of society and culture. Because modes of subsistence, types of society, legal rules, and forms of government could be considered as an *ensemble,* sets of problems could be inspected not only by political economists but also by historical sociologists, legal anthropologists, and other scholars concerned with progressive agencies in history. Stage theories of history provided the context within which Smith presented the outlines of "the science of the legislator," which his contemporaries deemed of fundamental importance in the education of those who would serve the state and inform public opinion.[20]

The influence of the Scottish heritage on British and American thinking about governance is a complicated problem taken up by Winch in his survey of thinking about the grounds for public policy from Smith's *Wealth of Nations* in 1776 (along with Robert Malthus, who appears

---

[20]For discussion of the contents and context of the science of the legislator, see Chapter 2 of this volume. See also Knud Haakonssen, *The Science of a Legislator: The Natural Jurisprudence of David Hume and Adam Smith* (Cambridge: Cambridge University Press, 1981). On the traditions of stadial history, see Ronald L. Meek, *Social Science and the Ignoble Savage* (Cambridge: Cambridge University Press, 1976), and idem, *Smith, Marx, and After: Ten Essays in the Development of Economic Thought* (London: Chapman and Hall, 1977).

here in his capacity as a teacher of Smith's science of the legislator to budding civil servants), through Jeremy Bentham, and on up to the next comprehensive attempt at theoretical reflection on the same scale as Smith's, the mid-Victorian synthesis produced by John Stuart Mill generations later. Winch demonstrates the subtlety of the differences in theories of the Enlightenment regarding questions of political agency and the role of the state by examining two different ways in which the science of the legislator was conceived in the period: (1) the method of Smith, who, in keeping with the revisions wrought by recent scholarship, appears not as the doctrinaire exponent of laissez-faire but as the public-spirited man who understood the need in principle for a continuously active state lest the character of the people be corrupted; and (2) the method of Bentham, who represented the "man of system" interested not so much in the relationship between policy and the character of the people as in the need to place government on a more rational (and therefore publicly accessible) footing.

In Britain, where the utilitarian tradition had far greater influence than it did in America, the two currents of thought represented competing but complementary sources of expertise available to lawmakers engaged in making Parliament a genuine governing body (rather than an institutional watchdog focused on the Crown) and attempting to base state policies, such as those relating to trade and the social consequences of the early industrial revolution, on new grounds. In the United States, as Drew McCoy and others have made clear, Scottish work was a major influence on the political thought of the founding generation, but there were competing influences, including both Lockean liberalism and a powerful strain of civic republicanism.[21]

[21]On the American context, see McCoy, *The Elusive Republic*; Kloppenberg, "The Virtues of Liberalism: Christianity, Republicanism and Ethics in Early American Political Discourse"; and Isaac Kramnick, *Republicanism and Bourgeois Radicalism: Political Ideology in Late Eighteenth Century England and America* (Ithaca, N.Y.: Cornell University Press, 1990). See also for more broad-ranging historical treatments Henry F. May, *The Enlightenment in America* (New York: Oxford University Press, 1976); Donald H. Meyer, *The Democratic Enlightenment* (New York: Capricorn Books, 1976); Gordon H. Wood, *The Creation of the American Republic, 1776–1787* (Chapel Hill: University of North Carolina Press, 1969); Bernard Bailyn, *The Ideological Origins of the American Revolution* (Cambridge, Mass.: Harvard University Press, 1967); and Forrest McDonald, *Novus Ordo Seculorum: The Intellectual Origins of the Constitution* (Lawrence: University of Kansas Press, 1985). Of the many pertinent studies on the development of British economic and social thought in the era of the industrial revolution, see Stefan Collini et al., *That Noble Science of Politics;* William Thomas, *The Philosophic Radicals: Nine Studies in Theory and Practice, 1817–1841* (Oxford: Clarendon Press, 1977); Boyd Hilton, *Cash, Corn, and Commerce: The Economic Policies of the Tory Governments,*

Complications and refinements to the side, however, the developing tradition of inquiry in political economy, a tradition that was in some respects narrowed rather than enlarged by David Ricardo and other followers of Smith, was an important new presence. The most significant legacy of the Enlightenment with respect to social investigation and the evolving knowledge base for public policy was the emerging discourse of classical political economy, the "dismal science" that accounted for growth and change but also forecast inevitable decline.

THE EMERGENCE OF SOCIAL EMPIRICISM AND THE GROWTH OF GOVERNMENT

Although blended currents of evangelical Christianity, political economy, and, particularly in Britain, utilitarianism shaped reflection on governance in the nineteenth century, the most notable change of the period with respect to our subject concerned the emergence, diffusion, and institutionalization, both within and outside government agencies, of new styles of empirical social description. As Winch points out, with the exception of Malthus, the classical political economists from Smith onward were never enthusiastic about political arithmetic or statistical inquiry for its own sake. The empirical sensibility seems to have been more closely associated with the needs of administrative life and legislative advocacy than with the search for general laws and principles, and it was connected philosophically, in the United States, with the justifications of republican government. Although the precise beginnings of the trend toward social empiricism are obscure, from the 1830s onward in both Britain and the United States inquiries rapidly proliferated—into a host of discrete social conditions relating to pauperism and dependency, conditions of labor, public health and sanitation, and education, among others. A new style of literature took form, and new types of evidence

1815–1830 (Oxford: Oxford University Press, 1977); Raymond G. Cowherd, *Political Economists and the English Poor Laws: A Historical Study of the Influence of Classical Economics and the Formation of Social Welfare Policy* (Athens: Ohio University Press, 1977); and Gary F. Langer, *The Coming of Age of Political Economy, 1815–1825* (Westport, Conn.: Greenwood Press, 1987). See also William Lubenow, *The Politics of Government Growth: Early Victorian Attitudes Towards State Intervention, 1833–1848* (Newton Abbot, Eng.: David and Charles, 1971); and Philip Corrigan and Derek Sawyer, *The Great Arch: English State Formation as Cultural Revolution* (Oxford: Basil Blackwell, 1985).

were introduced into the deliberations of governance and the formation of public opinion.[22]

Officials produced "blue books" and statistical reports, while private individuals and voluntary societies also participated in the essentially public business of surveying social conditions. The social empiricists developed a body of work and practice that remains both influential and problematic. They can properly be faulted for the naiveté of their Baconian faith that "the facts" would somehow speak for themselves—for operating with an undeveloped or, perhaps more accurately, an implicit hermeneutics, to use the contemporary jargon. As numerous studies have made clear, humanitarian and evangelical motives that enlisted their sympathy for the poor contended in the empiricists' consciousness with bourgeois inclinations. They came predominantly from what have been variously described as bourgeois, gentry, or respectable backgrounds and carried into their work an ideological orientation and a set of assumptions about political economy that usually affirmed the structural elements of liberal society—market economy (though not strictly laissez-faire), representative government (often with elitist overtones), and an evangelical Protestant ethic.[23]

[22]Malthus's studies of population were an important point of origin for this empiricist turn in Britain and their influence reached the United States. See Gerald Grob, ed., *The State and Public Welfare in Nineteenth-Century America: Five Investigations* (New York: Arno Press, 1976). The historical literature on the empirical tradition and the statistical movements in both countries is substantial. On the British side, see Michael J. Cullen, *The Statistical Movement in Early Victorian Britain: The Foundations of Empirical Social Research* (New York: Barnes and Noble, 1975); Raymond A. Kent, *A History of British Empirical Sociology* (London: Gower, 1981); Donald A. MacKenzie, *Statistics in Britain, 1865–1930: The Social Construction of Scientific Knowledge* (Edinburgh: Edinburgh University Press, 1981); Philip Abrams, *Origins of British Sociology: 1834–1914* (Chicago: University of Chicago Press, 1968); and Martin Bulmer, ed., *Essays on the History of British Sociological Research* (Cambridge: Cambridge University Press, 1985). On the American side, see Robert C. Davis, "Social Research in America Before the Civil War," *Journal of the History of the Behavioral Sciences* 8 (1972): 69–85; James H. Cassedy, *Demography in Early America: Beginnings of the Statistical Mind* (Cambridge, Mass.: Harvard University Press, 1969); Patricia Cline Cohen, *A Calculating People: The Spread of Numeracy in Early America* (Chicago: University of Chicago Press, 1982); and Margo J. Anderson, *The American Census: A Social History* (New Haven, Conn.: Yale University Press, 1988). For a collection of studies of the social and political forces behind the nation's statistics in the twentieth century, see William Alonzo and Paul Starr, eds., *The Politics of Numbers* (New York: Russell Sage Foundation, 1988).

[23]For an example of such criticisms, see Thomas Haskell, *The Emergence of Professional Social Science: The American Social Science Association and the Nineteenth Century Crisis of Authority* (Urbana: University of Illinois Press, 1977); and, as an introduction to the entire issue of social control on the British side, A. P. Donajgrodski, ed., *Social Control in Nineteenth Century Britain* (Croom Helm; Totowa, N.J.: Rowman and Littlefield, 1977).

While citing all these criticisms of the biases reflected in their work, we can also credit the social empiricists with introducing a note of realism and objectivity into discussions of social problems. Self-evidently, the usefulness of empirical information is, in its bearing on normative reflection, a relationship impossible to measure. The new genres were novel elements of language that entered the communicative system of politics and public policy, and the social empiricists produced evidence in their investigations that confounded existing theories, including those described in the versions of classical economics that held sway in Britain and the United States until the mid-nineteenth century. On this point, as Lawrence Goldman discusses in Chapter 3 of this volume, Marx and Engels discovered that only in England was it possible to locate authentic, impartial sources for the study of the proletariat. In his preface to *Das Kapital,* Marx acknowledged his debts to "men as competent, as free from partisanship and respect of persons as are England's factory inspectors, her medical reporters on public health, her commissioners of inquiry into the exploitation of women and children, into the conditions of housing and nourishment and so on."[24]

In response to social upheaval and economic crisis, the industrial transformation in the nineteenth century became the primary focus of social investigation, preoccupying political elites and investigators from humbler backgrounds in both countries for generations. Closely bound up with the gathering political responses to industrialism in both societies, the rise of social empiricism was very much a transatlantic phenomenon. In its heyday in Victorian Britain, as already noted, it was the work of an organized investigative community composed of members of an emerging "professional class" brought into regular communication with one another through participation in the same few "private," nongovernment institutions devoted to science and social improvement.[25]

In the United States, where federalism and the constitutional separation of powers reserved for police powers and responsibility for most areas of general welfare to the several states, the empirical trend was first

---

[24]Quoted in Chapter 3 of this volume.
[25]Ibid. See also O. R. McGregor, "Social Research and Social Policy in the Nineteenth Century," *British Journal of Sociology* 8 (1957):146–57; MacDonagh, *Early Victorian Government, 1830–1870*; and especially S. E. Finer, "The Transmission of Benthamite Ideas 1820–1850," in Gillian Sutherland, ed., *Studies in the Growth of Nineteenth-Century Government* (London: Routledge and Kegan Paul, 1972), 11–32. Harold Perkin, *The Rise of Professional Society: England Since 1880* (London: Routledge and Kegan Paul, 1989), treats professionals as a social type.

registered in argument over public problems at the state and local levels. Americans lagged behind their British counterparts in converting knowledge about bad conditions into effective public control, as the slow progress toward a national public health system indicated. Even so, as much recent scholarship has shown, in the Jacksonian era a loose commitment to laissez-faire was no serious impediment to social legislation against a wide range of evils. As in Britain, so in the United States, the case for regulatory legislation was frequently carried first by dogged individuals such as Dorothea Dix, Horace Mann, and Charles Sumner, who lobbied the state and national governments incessantly on behalf of the mentally ill, the poor and ill-educated, and the blacks, and by voluntary associations, technically private in that they operated outside the machinery of government, but committed to reforming public policy.

Typically these self-mobilized reformers would inquire into the dimensions of a problem, petition the local or state authorities, disseminate their findings to arouse public sentiment, recommend philanthropic relief or legislation, and maintain pressure on lawmakers until a satisfactory response was obtained. Once mobilized, legislatures would often create a board or commission to investigate and report. Even the courts, despite a well-deserved reputation for weighing in on the side of accelerated capitalist development, upheld a wide variety of extensions of public authority over private action, invoking the ancient republican principle *salus populi*.[26]

Between the 1830s and the outbreak of the Civil War, state legislatures in the most populous states received detailed narrative and statistical reports on dependency, delinquency, crime, and conditions of the poor. Sometimes these data were used to buttress arguments for *reducing* pro-

---

[26]On these points see William Nelson, *The Roots of American Bureaucracy, 1830–1900* (Cambridge, Mass.: Harvard University Press, 1982); and William Brock, *Investigation and Responsibility: Public Responsibility in the United States, 1865–1900* (Cambridge: Cambridge University Press, 1984). A rich sample of state-level public investigations into dependency can be found in Grob, ed., *The State and Public Welfare*. On the slow growth of provision for public control of disease prevention, see John Duffy, *The Sanitarians: A History of American Public Health* (Urbana: University of Illinois Press, 1990). See also Marshall, *Dorothea Dix: Forgotten Samaritan*; Dorothea Dix, *On Behalf of the Insane Poor: Selected Reports* (New York: Arno Press and New York Times, 1971); idem, *Prisons and Prison Discipline*, 2d ed. (1845; Montclair, N.J.: Patterson Smith, 1967). On the role of the courts in this regard, see William J. Novak, "Intellectual Origins of State Police Power: The Common Law Vision of a Well Regulated Society," Legal History Program Working Papers, Series 3, University of Wisconsin Institute for Legal Studies, June 1989.

vision for the indigent and disabled, a course justified by references to British precedent in the revision of the Poor Laws. In other cases the reports supported arguments about the need to regulate such matters as the hours and working conditions of labor, methods of payment, or the quality of goods offered for sale, and to provide more humanely for people who were unable to look out for themselves. This "republican empiricism" relied less on the claims of science and disinterested expertise than on the democratic and humanitarian impulses associated with moral reform, which also drove the antislavery crusade; on the political mobilization of groups directly affected by the problems in question; and on the good offices of social and commercial elites who, seeking both uplift and social control, took a more expansive view of the state's role in social and economic development than the laissez-faire orthodoxy of the period might have indicated. In all these efforts, but particularly in those in which social investigation buttressed humanitarian reforms, female reformers played a vital part in extending and reshaping the sphere of concerns connected with what polite society recognized as womanly duties, and, at the same time, stretching the boundaries of state responsibility. Denied the vote, American women based a bid for power over social conditions on converting issues to moral questions, where their credentials were deemed superior to those of men.[27]

From the 1830s onward, a variety of organized groups, both benevolent and reformist, pressed for greater access to government information and for more rapid development within the state itself of the capacity to gather intelligence relevant to the construction of a knowledge base for addressing the problems of a commercial and, in growing pockets, an industrial society. By the 1850s the United States harbored a congeries of middle-class experts in public health, sanitation, law, education, and other fields, similar in aim and outlook to those in Britain. Under the nationalizing influence of the Civil War these groups were taken in organizational terms into the international social science and statistical movements of the mid-Victorian period that Goldman examines in Chap-

[27]Grob, *ed.*, *The State and Public Welfare*. Timothy Malone coined the phrase *republican empiricism*. On the role of women, see Lori D. Ginsberg, *Women and the Work of Benevolence* (New Haven, Conn.: Yale University Press, 1990); Nancy Hewitt, *Women's Activism and Social Change: Rochester, New York, 1822–1872* (Ithaca, N.Y.: Cornell University Press, 1984); and Leach, *True Love*. For a perceptive analysis of changes in female reform during the first half of the nineteenth century, see Anne M. Boylan, "Women in Groups: An Analysis of Women's Benevolent Organizations in New York and Boston, 1798–1840," *Journal of American History* 71 (1984): 497–523.

ter 3. In 1865 the American Social Science Association (ASSA) was established, influenced by the achievements of the wartime Sanitary Commission and modeled on the British National Association for the Promotion of Social Science, but distinguished from it by the greater prominence of commercial elites, reform-minded women, and academics in its membership.[28]

Like its British counterpart, ASSA can be conceived at one level as a clearinghouse for information, maintained by the progressive bourgeoisie, in which members compared notes on rising social problems and monitored the results of various efforts in reform. Its departments of education, public health, jurisprudence, finance, and social economy provided a point of focus for the interests of those who advocated diffusion of an empirically informed, scientific approach to social affairs, transcending the political corruption of the era and promoting efficiency. But ASSA was a more diverse organization than this picture suggests. It attracted a broad range of members, including capitalists who were primarily interested in promoting sound finance; avant-garde lawyers, doctors, ministers, and teachers who sought to upgrade their professions; and middle-class reformers, such as the long-time ASSA secretary, Franklin B. Sanborn, who fused the older moralism of humanitarian reform with the new scientific spirit. The diversity of ASSA's membership set up tensions between genuinely reformist and more conservative impulses that committed the different departments of ASSA to different and sometimes conflicting agendas. For example, its finance department hewed pretty closely to classical liberal economics, with a preference for fiscal and monetary soundness and a small state. But the social economy department attracted reformers such as Sanborn, once a backer of John Brown's raid on Harpers Ferry, who advocated an expanded state presence in behalf of all classes of dependents. The militantly feminist Carolyn Healy Dall, a founding member of ASSA who established its special library of government and philanthropic reports on poverty and dependency from several countries, a data bank that she believed provided the only reliable basis for reform, was also a moving spirit in the department. As William Leach has shown, Dall recruited other women, including Abby May, Zena Fay

---

[28]On ASSA, see Mary O. Furner, *Advocacy and Objectivity: A Crisis in the Professionalization of American Social Science, 1865–1905* (Lexington: University of Kentucky Press, 1975), chaps. 1 and 13; Haskell, *The Emergence of Professional Social Science,* passim; and Leach, *True Love,* esp. chaps. 11 and 12.

Pierce, and Mary S. Parkman, into ASSA and prodded the organization into taking feminist positions.[29]

In addition, ASSA enlisted the service of two other groups. First, a cadre of new-style public officials such as Carroll Wright, Francis Amasa Walker, and John Eaton held important leadership roles in ASSA while also being involved in the early stages of creating state-level and federal information structures equipped to reorient social and industrial policy in response to the economic and social problems of the 1870s and 1880s. As Michael Lacey shows in Chapter 4, these social science–oriented officials were every bit as interested in building new state capacities as were the "statesmen in disguise" (Edwin Chadwick, John Simon, and James Kay-Shuttlesworth) Goldman discusses. This participation of public officials in the organizational life of private, voluntary associations for the cultivation of social knowledge occurs frequently in the history of social investigation in both countries, and suggests that the boundary separating the public from the private has functioned more like a membrane than a wall.

Second, ASSA attracted a group of left-liberal academics, described in Chapter 5 by Mary Furner. Caught up in the early phases of social science professionalization and influenced by the republican heritage and German historicism, these academics embarked on a revision of liberal economic and social theory in response to the crisis of laissez-faire. As with Walker and Wright, their awareness of the obstacles to achieving social and communal objectives through voluntarist, market-driven processes often led them in bureaucratic, statebuilding directions.

Although ASSA played a role in the professionalization of the social sciences, and its education department promoted a college curriculum on social welfare issues, ASSA's ethos was not predominantly academic. Oriented toward producing a more harmonious, progressive society, its guiding spirits were suspicious of the attitude of detachment reflected in arguments for academic specialization, which often called for a rigid separation of knowledge and reform. Rather, in line with their interest in a merit-based civil service, they fell in historically with those who endeavored to build a bridge from social science to government by professionalizing and centralizing government's statistical capacities, or by setting up special schools within the universities to provide broad, prac-

---

[29]On Carolyn Healy Dall and the role of women in ASSA, see Leach, *True Love* 263–346. See also, on American women's reform and social science, Sklar, "Hull House Maps and Papers," in Bulmer et al., eds., *The Social Survey in Historical Perspective*.

tical training for public administrators. Although ASSA encouraged the development of social research, its aim was not scholarship per se but the application of the best available information and practice to the amelioration of social problems. Its distinctive concern was for civic education, conceived as an ethical and theoretical training for citizenship. Its immediate legacy was registered more clearly in the establishment of voluntary associations for social service professionals in social work and public health than in the modern social science disciplines and the societies for professional social scientists who took advantage of ASSA's meetings and prestige to form their own distinctive groupings. Concerns about amateurism and reformism, as distinct from professionalism and objectivity, were not theirs.[30]

In retrospect, the most important institutional legacy of social empiricism in both Britain and the United States was the creation of new state capacities, embodied in public agencies such as the improved census in the United States and the labor bureaus in both countries, which were charged with monitoring the conditions of various segments of the populace, recommending preventive or protective legislation, and eventually administering social welfare legislation. As Roger Davidson demonstrates in Chapter 6, such agencies were often slow to break through the barriers of ideology, class, and personal inclination of government officials that shielded traditional methods and institutions from criticism. Often the agencies were hostile to radical change and sought to conserve rather than fundamentally reconstruct social relations. Yet in the long run, improvements in population, health, and labor statistics, and more precise measures of economic performance, among other categories of inquiry, laid the basis for modern trend analysis, demographics, and indicative planning. And whatever their biases, the investigative processes involved were public ones: the more obvious distortions in them could be detected by those adversely affected and exposed.

The most difficult problem in the tradition of social empiricism, identified in Davidson's account of inquiries into British labor studies and in Barry Supple's description of investigations of social and economic problems between the wars (see Chapter 9), was the ad hoc nature of many investigations; they emphasized report rather than analysis, and they failed to identify and direct attention to larger, structural problems that

---

[30]On ASSA's opposition to narrow specialization and the compartmentalization of knowledge, see Furner, *Advocacy and Objectivity,* 313–20, and Leach, *True Love,* 324–46.

called for more than temporary or palliative solutions. Empiricism permeates the environment of collective puzzlement but does not provide the theoretical orientations and ideological premises required for law and regulation. And yet, as Furner and Supple also make clear, a succession of investigations and reports often had cumulative effects of two types. One led to identification of underlying weaknesses in market processes that could not be cured by settling particular strikes; by isolating pockets of trouble, such as those designated between the wars as "sick industries" or "derelict areas"; or by blaming the victims. The second was a reorientation of political thinking and policy discourse generally, gradually laying the basis for theoretical breakthroughs that contradicted received wisdom.

Along the same line, Chapter 10, by Robert Cuff, provides an example of efforts on the part of defense planners to transcend the ad hoc by establishing special agencies in government with ties to arms producers and universities that could conserve the memories of lessons learned in World War I and incorporate improvements in management theory into the strategies to be invoked in future wars. Such results were precisely what were anticipated by the constructivist rationale for social empiricism laid down by its most articulate proponents, such as Lester Ward and Carroll Wright in the United States. Although their conceptions of the character and sources of social knowledge were often naive, they assumed that their work informed a process of social learning through politics. In the social science associations and elsewhere, their efforts contributed to the processes of criticism and theoretical and methodological innovation that paved the way for a new liberalism, firmly grounded in social empiricism.

SOCIAL INVESTIGATION AND THE NEW LIBERALISM

From the 1830s onward, as the social evils and crises of industrialism accumulated or at least became more visible, a pattern of inquiry that had started as ad hoc empiricism generated so much information in so many domains of inquiry as to change the atmosphere of knowledge and information within which policy was formulated. In both Britain and the United States the mounting evidence on social conditions and problems challenged the outlook of the dominant strand in the inherited political culture, the old liberalism, with its presumptions in favor of a natural system of liberties and limited government. Along with, and as aids and catalysts to, the pressures exerted by labor and other disaffected groups, the mere existence of these kinds of documents invited revisions in the discourse of public policy and helped to force a modernization within the liberal tradition. Because of demands in many quarters for state protection or intervention, the question of what accounted for legitimate political agency hovered over the period. For academic theorists and for many investigation-oriented officials in the last decades of the century, the nature of the state and the grounds for its changing functions became a central problem of inquiry. By the 1880s in both countries a new framework of public thought had begun developing in the form of a new liberalism that was collectivist in orientation.[31]

What we want to emphasize here is not the existence of the specific issues and evils lumped together in both countries as "the social question," but rather the way in which social empiricism was indispensable to and present at the birth of a new liberalism. As Furner, Davidson, and Supple demonstrate (Chapters 5, 6, and 9), investigations pertinent to "the social question" challenged settled cultural patterns and beliefs. They described a set of unaccustomed, cruel realities, visited mainly upon members of the new industrial wage-earning class. As social documents they also opened up the problematic "discovery" and interpretation of these conditions, both by their victims (whose spokesmen represented the developing institutions of the working class), and by socially conscious members of the middle classes. The latter group included the social empiricists whose special concern was to document these developments accurately and to have the problems they reflected dealt with in the arena of domestic politics.[32]

---

[31]Chapters 4, 5, 6, and 9 in this book focus on the new liberalism. See also Michael Freeden, *The New Liberalism: An Ideology of Social Reform* (Oxford: Clarendon Press, 1978), and idem, *Liberalism Divided: A Study in British Political Thought, 1914–1939* (Oxford: Clarendon Press, 1986); Stefan Collini, *Liberalism and Sociology: L. T. Hobhouse and Political Argument in England, 1880–1914* (Cambridge: Cambridge University Press, 1979); John Allett, *New Liberalism: The Political Economy of J. A. Hobson* (Toronto: University of Toronto Press, 1981); James T. Kloppenberg, *Uncertain Victory: Social Democracy and Progressivism in European and American Thought, 1870–1920* (New York: Oxford University Press, 1986); and Furner and Supple, eds., *The State and Economic Knowledge*. While, strictly speaking, there are no U.S. studies parallel to those of Freeden, Sidney Fine's *Laissez-Faire and the General Welfare State* (Ann Arbor: University of Michigan Press, 1956), though dated, remains useful. See also Jeffrey Lustig, *Corporate Liberalism: The Origins of Modern American Political Theory, 1890–1920* (Berkeley: University of California Press, 1982), and Dorothy Ross, *The Origins of American Social Science* (Cambridge: Cambridge University Press, 1991).

[32]Such was the case with the labor bureaus that appeared in the United States from the 1860s and in most European countries, including Britain, by the 1890s. On American

As Lacey (Chapter 4) shows, this latter group also included a group of theorists inside the research-oriented public bureaucracies, some of whom were not engaged directly in the day-to-day fieldwork of social empiricism, but whose more philosophical inclinations led them to criticize and reformulate the premises of the old liberalism. For Lester Ward, John Wesley Powell, and Carroll Wright, the social question was problematic because it comported so badly with the various "individualist" emphases of inherited traditions of political thought, whether derived from classical political economy, utilitarianism, Mill's synthesis of the two, or the Americanized version of Ricardian economics that served as the economic orthodoxy of the entrepreneurial classes. Contemporary social description revealed patterns of facts that fit uncomfortably with the republican ideals that occupied a prominent place in American political culture, particularly its doctrine regarding the supremacy of the public interest over private interests—ideals that had coexisted uneasily with the more extreme expressions of economic liberalism even before the runaway industrialization of the Gilded Age. In the late nineteenth century, public discussion of the social question exacerbated those contradictions, and new political currents—among them discrete varieties of Marxian and non-Marxian socialist and social democratic thought— placed the laissez-faire tradition under siege from without.

Liberals responded in a variety of ways. Some, such as Herbert Spencer (who spoke scornfully of blue-book sociology as the work of careerist meddlers), or William Graham Sumner, the champion of the "forgotten man" who looked after his own affairs and sought nothing from the state, bent their energies mainly toward defending self-reliance of the old type and refurbishing the old liberalism. But it was increasingly unlikely that one could find their viewpoints confidently espoused by the most experienced people in politics and government. For Ward, Powell, and Wright, and for the architects of the British welfare state described by Roger Davidson, social empiricism pointed the way toward assumptions about the relationships between knowledge and politics, between information and policy, that can be characterized as a liberal-positivist outlook.

"Liberal" in this context emphasizes the social empiricists' understanding and acceptance of the traditions of representative government

---

leadership in this movement, see Furner, "Knowing Capitalism," in Furner and Supple, eds., *The State and Economic Knowledge*, 246–7.

and individual rights that gave political expression to liberal values. "Positivist" refers to their understanding of the new science as a cumulative force in history, and to the fact that they were alert to the ways in which the one challenged the other. As bureaucrats and civil service reformers, they had confidence in the directive capacities of a state well armed with statistics gathered and processed by experts in civil intelligence. As evolutionists, they expected the forms and functions of political institutions to change, in relationship to the developing patterns of economic and social organization—to change, in fact, in order to preserve certain fundamental values of liberal culture. Devout believers in human agency, they drew attention to the many deficiencies of individualism and competition as social philosophies under new conditions, and proclaimed a new age of altruism and cooperation in which positive state guidance would take its place alongside voluntary benevolence in identifying and eradicating the problems of an emerging industrial order.

On both sides of the Atlantic, social empiricism and liberal positivism (the latter sometimes, especially in Britain, heavily influenced by the Comtian model) were necessary if not sufficient elements in the emergence of a new liberalism. While not altogether anti-individualist, those searching for a new understanding of liberalism were concerned to distinguish the "old" and now discredited individualism, which was focused on claims to autonomy and noninterference, from a "new" individualism, which acknowledged a higher social or collective interest that remained compatible with, and even dependent on, the liberal values of individual responsibility and self-fulfillment. The main difference between the old and the new was the latter's focus not on the abstract individual, but on the individual in community, in associations, in society, and on those aspects of human action that emphasized altruism, fellow feeling, cooperation, and subordination of private ambition. This focus gave a collectivist cast to new liberal thinking and led to such now familiar distinctions as that between negative and positive rights and between freedom and effective freedom, the latter requiring institutional reinforcements and interventions of various kinds.[33]

There is no better example of the influence of social empiricism in slowly eliciting a new liberal point of view than the case of Charles Booth,

---

[33]See, for example, John Dewey and James H. Tufts, *Ethics* (New York: Henry Holt and Co., 1908); John Dewey, *Individualism Old and New* (New York: Capricorn Books, 1962); and Herbert Croly, *The Promise of American Life* (1909; Indianapolis: Bobbs Merrill, 1965).

whose massive, multivolume project, *Life and Labor of the People in London* (1889–1903), was the most influential model of social investigation in its day. Beatrice Webb's vocation as a social investigator began with her participation as a staff researcher in what she called Booth's "grand inquest into the condition of the people of London." It should be noted, incidentally, that two others who later went on to hold influential positions inside the world of government social investigation and advocacy were also apprentices on the Booth project, Hubert Llewellyn Smith and Ernest Aves, thus demonstrating again the permeability of the boundary separating public and private with respect to the history of social investigation.

In her autobiography, Beatrice Webb, a Fabian socialist, noted the importance of the findings of the project in changing viewpoints, in this instance the viewpoint of Booth himself: "It is surely significant that this wealthy captain of industry, by this time Conservative in politics and strongly anti-Socialist in temper and economic views, should have come out of his prolonged study with proposals the very reverse of individualist." The proposals she had in mind encouraged state intervention in various domains, among them compulsory education at public expense and old-age pensions. Webb argued that Booth's investigation into the conditions of the aged poor throughout England and Wales, together with his incessant propaganda, was the most important factor among the many at work in passage of the Old Age Pension Act of 1908. On the transformation of political belief that was being wrought by the heritage of social empiricism, Webb quotes Booth's own formulation of the role of the state in poor relief:

Our Individualism fails because our Socialism is incomplete. In taking charge of the lives of the incapable, State Socialism finds its proper work, and by doing it completely, would relieve us of a serious danger. The Individualist system breaks down as things are, and is invaded on every side by Socialistic innovations, but its hardy doctrines would have a far better chance in a society purged of those who cannot stand alone.[34]

What was most important about the emerging new liberalism, as this example and many others illustrate, was its consciousness of the need to overcome hostility to the very idea of the interventionist state. For some, the impetus for this type of thinking came from a renewed interest in evolutionary processes at work in the development of society and gov-

[34]Webb, *My Apprenticeship*, 253–5, passim.

ernment, and from a concern with positive methods for giving guidance or direction to those processes. Linking history, evolution, and institutions, these ideas were central to the activities of those on both sides of the Atlantic who were most deeply engaged in the effort to fashion new instruments within government for civil intelligence gathering—and directed their thought to problems of law, bureaucracy, and economic and social regulation.[35]

For others, the catalyst was a more practical recognition of the futility and injustice of state policies that simply repressed workers' collective actions by reinvigorating or reinterpreting old liberal categories such as free contract. In either case, the attempt to define a public sphere of oversight and competence exposed deficiencies in the classical outlook and undermined confidence in the self-regulating market and in the open-ended, undirected impetus of civil society. Administrative nihilism was under fire. The premises of public thought were changing, not simply in response to bureaucratic or academic discontent, but in response to the pressures generated by the stresses and instabilities of advancing industrial capitalism itself, and especially to the organized protest of the working class.

Social investigation as a process of public inquiry into social problems played its role in the form of reports on the hazards of life in capitalist society that documented and publicized problems—thus shifting the premises of public thought and actions away from individualist categories of thought toward those of group life and collective order. Sustained by such information, the new liberals regarded laissez-faire arguments as antique; yet their own views allowed room for conflict and competition as well as cooperation. Although many of them sympathized with socialist moral criticisms, they were hostile not to capitalism itself, some of whose fundamental institutions they located among the progressive agencies of history, but to untutored, unregulated capitalism, which in its recently developed forms appeared to threaten a new slavery.[36]

[35]See Chapters 4, 5, and 6 of this volume. For orientation regarding the literature of the new liberalism, see note 31 above.

[36]Examples of the complexities of the new liberal position on socialism would be, for the American side, such texts as Henry Carter Adams, "The Relation of the State to Industrial Action," *Publications of the American Economic Association* 1 (1887): 465–549, and E. R. A. Seligman, *The Economic Interpretation of History* (New York: Macmillan, 1902). On the British side, the best indications would come from a comparison of early liberal positivist writings, such as those by Frederic Harrison and John Ingram, and the later, more fully developed posture evident in the works of new liberals who eschewed Fabianism, such as Hobson and Hobhouse.

The need for regulation laid the basis for an evolving expression of the new liberalism, in which investigation led to institutional development or reform. Just as the Scots philosophers were critical of the notion, derived from the image of the lawgiver in classical mythology, that the lawgivers' pronouncements fixed the correct social order once and for all, so the new liberal consciousness was critical of once-and-for-all dogmatism, aware of the need to rethink and refashion relations between state and society in a continuous fashion. The result was the modern state—in Britain, the modern welfare state, and in the United States, ultimately a less developed welfare state, but initially the apparatus of modern economic regulation and stabilization.

Any discussion of the origins of the welfare state immediately confronts questions of the motives, timing, and extent of the reforms that went into it, and of the way in which supporting or resisting it intersected with traditional political thinking and practice. In a complex assessment of the forces that drove construction of a state response to the labor question in Britain, Davidson (Chapter 6) shows that social collectivism arose as much from the efforts of those who desired to conserve the social order and protect the mechanisms of capitalism as from the actions of those who sought more far-reaching, structural reform. Davidson's analysis is particularly instructive with respect to weighing the claims of social reform against social control, as well as for its appreciation of the many kinds of constraints that hemmed the boundaries of social investigation and correspondingly limited the reach of the new liberalism.

Britain had powerful institutional and ideological constraints, beyond the limitations imposed by the social characteristics of the various groups within the investigative community. These constraints stemmed from the inertia of the central bureaucracy, and particularly from the stinginess of Treasury support for any but the most routine and minimal investigations; from resistance on the part of manufacturers and local community elites who took the inquisitiveness of Whitehall for unwarranted meddling in their affairs; from opposition on the part of large segments of the public to the growth of government that social empiricism inevitably encouraged; from shortcomings and inconsistencies in existing investigative technology, including statistical methods; from a general lack of expertise and a resistance to change in many of the departments that administered social programs and policies; and from ideological commitments held by people who *did* have the requisite skills—commitments that prevented these people from challenging the fundamental soundness of the existing system and encouraged them to define as local or episodic problems that were in fact permanent and structural. Supple's account of inquiries into social dislocation and economic performance during the interwar period shows the persistence of these kinds of constraints.

In the United States, as the chapters by Furner, Brownlee, and Cuff (Chapters 5, 8, and 10) demonstrate, many of these difficulties were compounded by the division of responsibility and authority among branches of government and among the several levels of the federal, state, and local government systems. In addition, there were further impediments: the tradition of small government enshrined in both republican and liberal traditions; the lack of a mass-based working-class political party, which had been a catalyst to social empiricism and new liberalism in Britain; the late and incomplete development of a professional civil service; the extraordinary power that conservative business interests exerted over political parties and public policies; and the independence of the judiciary, which often served as a barrier to investigative invasions of private rights or overruled legislative enactments supported by statistics on poverty, unemployment, and other industrial evils.

As Furner (Chapter 5) shows, corporate influence, combined with traditions of voluntarism and aspects of the new social science that supported them, conflicted with the more radical and critical traditions, producing a division within the new liberalism by the 1890s. One school, closer to the republican origins of American public discourse, was more statist than the other in its approach to social reform and economic regulation, and sought more democratically derived outcomes. The other school, closer to classical liberal roots, preferred the agency of voluntary collective action on the part of autonomous, self-organized social groups, and accepted the principle of social hierarchy as intrinsic to capitalism. This bifurcation of the new liberalism occurred much earlier than the corresponding split in British new liberalism that came between the wars.[37]

The effort to recover through historical study something of the scope, content, and efficacy of the new liberalism is a controversial area in recent scholarship. In the 1960s and 1970s, in an atmosphere informed by the emergence of a new corpus of social history and radical political theory,

---

[37]For an account of a split within the new liberalism in Britain, see Michael Freeden, *Liberalism Divided: A Study in British Political Thought, 1914–1939* (Oxford: Clarendon Press, 1986).

there was abundant academic criticism both of Britain's new liberals and their "lib-lab" descendants, and of America's progressives and their New Era, New Deal, and later progeny. The limits of their horizons, the purity of their motives, and the extent of their achievements were all called into question.

Our concern is not to downplay the social and economic origins of the new liberalism, however, but to call attention to its indebtedness to the process of social investigation, and to the subtle ways in which that process changed the context of politics. In both Britain and the United States the spur to interventionism was provided not simply by the push of crisis and the clash of newly powerful interests, but also by the pull of a transformation in the perception of social and economic realities. And that perception was fed by processes of inquiry, assessment, and report that took root in both countries in the heyday of social empiricism. The process of investigation was a hurly-burly affair with a politics of its own, initially dominated by more privileged social and professional classes.

There was, of course, a strong political dimension to the construction of a knowledge base for the new liberalism. The politics of public investigation turned on which questions were asked, whose voices were invited to answer, what kinds of expertise were marshaled to make sense of public problems, and what kind of interventions on the part of the state were envisaged as appropriate. The failure to recognize the fundamentally political nature of social investigation leads to contradictions both in theory and in institutional and bureaucratic practice. Chapter 7, by Donald Critchlow, shows, for example, the disintegration of the progressive era's ideal of nonpartisan policy research institutions independent of government in the United States, and their replacement by ideologically driven, competing think tanks bent on influencing social and economic policy. Similarly, Chapter 10, by Robert Cuff, discloses the technocratic, turf-protecting impulses that complicated construction of a knowledge base for management of the most basic of national functions, defense.[38]

---

[38]For critical analyses of the politics involved in sponsoring and orienting social research, see Guy Alchon, *The Invisible Hand of Planning: Capitalism, Social Science and the State in the 1920's* (Princeton, N.J.: Princeton University Press, 1985); Donald T. Critchlow, *The Brookings Institution, 1916–1952: Expertise and the Public Interest in a Democratic Society* (DeKalb: Northern Illinois University Press, 1985); Roger Davidson, *Whitehall and the Labor Problem in Late Victorian and Edwardian Britain* (London: Croom Helm, 1985).

Yet, as Barry Supple (Chapter 9) argues, however flawed, myopic, or conservatively oriented single episodes of investigation might have been, taken together and cumulatively they transformed accepted ways of seeing conditions and envisaging solutions. They armed social constituencies and officials who were prepared to expose errors in existing estimates of the seriousness of the need for intervention, and inspired them to imagine and propose, pragmatically and experimentally at first, solutions that would add up, eventually, to a significant reorientation in accepted ways of thinking about relations between state and market. Every student of this transformation is left to consider which is more striking, the extent to which new ways of thinking differed from traditional assumptions, or the continuity between the old liberalism and the new.

EXEMPLARS: THEORETICAL AND DESCRIPTIVE

One method of conducting such an assessment might involve reflecting on what seem to be the most characteristic products of the union between social empiricism and new liberalism from the standpoint of social description, on the one hand, and social theory, on the other. Social theory is no more unchanging than social description, and we have tried to emphasize the interplay between them over time. From the historical standpoint they move together, perhaps not in tandem, but as part of the same general movement. In concluding this discussion of social investigation and the new liberalism, we wish to mention briefly what seem to us to be the outstanding twentieth-century examples of new liberal theoretical reflection and comprehensive social description. As it happens, both came to fruition in the 1930s, one in Britain and the other in the United States: John Maynard Keynes's *General Theory of Employment, Interest, and Money* (1936) and *Recent Social Trends in the United States: Report of the President's Research Committee on Social Trends* (1933), an empirically based overview of social and economic conditions produced by the largest group of social investigators ever called together in a single project.

The overriding theoretical problem for those concerned with the knowledge base for public policy was the need to provide some systematic justification for the role of the state in the management of the economy, particularly with respect to recurrent problems of unemployment. The manifold "pre-Keynesian" insights and pragmatic adjustments to policy that are now known to have developed in both Britain and the United

States *before* the publication of Keynes's theoretical treatise can be taken as illustrative of the way in which changing conditions and knowledge based on new assumptions paved the way for a new synthetic theory that was at once descriptive and prescriptive. Whatever its deficiencies, *The General Theory* can be taken as the outstanding example of theoretical achievement produced in the new liberal tradition.[39]

Keynes's book advanced both political and economic insight by its ingenious suggestion that there were new ways to conceive closer relations between the private and public sectors that fatally threatened neither one of them. By breaking completely with even the most technically refined inherited "neoclassical" notions that the behavior of private individuals—particularly with respect to savings, consumption, and investment—could be counted on to generate an order acceptable to the modern public and its problems, Keynes recast the terms of debate in social and economic policy. His arguments purported to explain some, at least, of the connectives at the heart of the inherited "social question," particularly chronic unemployment and industrial stagnation, in structural terms. By the same token, Keynes offered new theoretical justification for an expanded and yet minimally intrusive government role in the ordering of the economy, one that promised to dissolve the social threat of unemployment and its nest of affiliated grievances and push them off the public agenda.[40]

As a theorist, Keynes was fully aware of the heritage of social empiricist writings on poverty and unemployment and of the links between economic theory and social thought. In making the theoretical case for new government functions with respect to macroeconomic realities, he fashioned his arguments in terms of the political values of the new liberalism. As he put the essential point:

Whilst, therefore, the enlargement of the functions of government, involved in the task of adjusting to one another the propensity to consume and the inducement to invest, would seem to a nineteenth-century publicist or to a contemporary American financier to be a terrific encroachment on individualism, I defend it, on the contrary, both as the only practicable means of avoiding the destruction of existing economic forms in their entirety and as the condition of the successful functioning of individual initiative.[41]

[39]Some do not identify Keynes with the new liberalism. For a discussion of the reasons why he should be so identified, see Peter Clarke, *The Keynesian Revolution in the Making, 1924–1936* (Oxford: Clarendon Press, 1988), 78–83 and passim.

[40]On Keynesianism in this light, see Clarke, *Keynesian Revolution in the Making;* see also Furner and Supple, eds., *The State and Economic Knowledge.*

[41]John Maynard Keynes, *The General Theory of Employment, Interest, and Money* (1936; New York: Harcourt, Brace and World, Harbinger Book, 1964), 380.

To turn from theory to comprehensive social description in its most fully developed form, we must first emphasize that the composition and methods of social description were extremely varied. Thus, its forms range from massive census compilations of data on population, agriculture, manufacturing, and social life in many domains through the sociological surveys and anthropological community studies of the modern academic tradition. The forms of patronage that brought the different types of social description into being also varied—some were governmental, some private. Two of the most famous and influential examples of social investigation undertaken for public purposes were Booth's *Life and Labor of the London Poor,* and Gunnar Myrdal's *An American Dilemma: The Negro Problem and Modern Democracy,* both of them large, collaborative undertakings that were privately financed.

In terms of sheer scope and comprehensiveness, *Recent Social Trends in the United States: Report of the President's Research Committee on Social Trends* was perhaps the outstanding example of new liberal social description. Although the survey project was technically privately funded, staffed mainly by academics outside government, it was undertaken in 1929 at President Hoover's behest. The report, nearly 1,600 pages in length, represented the outcome of an effort begun some years earlier by Hoover as secretary of commerce to generate studies on the problems of economic performance—to achieve higher productivity, sustain economic growth, and reduce class antagonism through systematic investigation, analysis, and dissemination of data useful to industry and government for planning. A "progressive" and an engineer who looked to nonpartisan, technocratic solutions for social problems, Hoover sought to achieve social and economic efficiency through cooperative planning by government, business, and, in appropriate areas, labor. His administration was a seedbed for the nurture of mediating institutions intended to link in voluntary relations the public and private institutions that were bound up in the processes of economic production and the distribution of goods.[42]

---

[42]On Hoover's voluntary corporatist ideology, see Ellis J. Hawley, "Herbert Hoover, the Commerce Secretariat, and the Vision of an 'Associative State,' 1921–1928," *Journal of American History* 61 (1974): 116–40. For an account of the recent social trends project, see chap. 11, "The Social Sciences and Mr. Hoover: Recent Social Trends," in Barry Karl, *Charles E. Merriam and the Study of Politics* (Chicago: University of Chicago Press, 1974). For a critical account of the project that emphasizes the differences between the assumptions and methods of social science today and during the early New Deal period,

In keeping with his views about the detachment and superior credibility of privately financed researchers, Hoover arranged for the Rockefeller Foundation to fund the survey project. It was organized by a committee of the nation's leading social scientists, chaired by Wesley Mitchell and Charles Merriam, with the research program administered by William F. Ogburn and Howard Odum. It drew on the assistance and advice of several hundred institutional and individual collaborators. The committee was charged with surveying the social changes that had taken place in the major domains of American life between 1900 and 1930, with an eye to detecting, in Hoover's words, "where social stresses are occurring and where major efforts should be undertaken to deal with them constructively." It was understood that these ameliorative efforts might well be conducted by private, nongovernment bodies, but also that the appropriate state agencies would take an interest in these efforts, prodding and facilitating as needed.[43]

Considered simply as a literary document in the tradition of descriptive sociography, nothing produced before or since, in Britain or the United States, rivals *Recent Social Trends* in scope if not in depth. It illustrated better than any previous or subsequent study the attempt to organize the entire panoply of available knowledge for public purposes. As an effort in modern civic education, it represented social empiricism at its apogee. The result of more than three years of work, during which the researchers had the advantage of special access to the information available in scores of government bureaus and agencies, the book provides a carefully focused image of how life in the United States had come to be organized in the first third of the twentieth century.

That image reflected the working of the new liberal mentality and its institutions. The report was designed not merely to present evidence on separate trends but to draw attention to the relationships and frictions among the trends observed. The result was a detailed depiction of the inescapable collectivism of modern life, its historicity, and the extent to which individualistic explanations of causation and prescriptions for social action had lost cogency. *Recent Social Trends* portrayed the pervasive

see Neil Smelser, "The Ogburn Vision Fifty Years Later," in Neil J. Smelser and Dean R. Gerstein, eds., *Behavioral and Social Science: Fifty Years of Discovery* (Washington, D.C.: National Academy Press, 1986), 21–35.

[43]President's Research Committee on Social Trends, *Recent Social Trends in the United States* (New York: Whittlesey House, one-volume edition, 1934), v.

organizational revolution and changing structure of group life that had occurred to distinguish twentieth-century America from its nineteenth-century predecessor.

In his concluding chapter to the report, the committee's vice chairman, Charles Merriam, focused on changes in the relationship between government and society that had taken place between the turn of the century and the Great Depression. In his review of findings Merriam noted approvingly that while public adherence to doctrines of liberty, equality, and democracy had been maintained in the face of social and economic trends in conflict with them, "widespread abandonment of the earlier doctrines of individualism" had occurred. Government at all levels had grown dramatically and taken on a wide variety of new service and regulatory functions, but the changes had been piecemeal and uncoordinated. They had not reached the basic institutional structures of governance, nor had they been accompanied by the adoption and diffusion among the people of any new theory of the role of the state in modern culture.[44]

Further documenting the difficulty of reform in government, Merriam noted that prevailing political attitudes had been "non-theoretical and intolerant towards other systems than our own, and non-experimental in the field of governmental structure, especially if constitutional change were involved." This institutional conservatism stood in sharp contrast to trends in civil society, Merriam pointed out: "In business and in mechanical enterprise the general attitude has been that of free and welcome experiment, but the opposite has been true in governmental affairs, where the weight of tradition has been more heavily felt and where proposals for change have been identified with treason to the state." One of the trends reported was an accentuation of intolerance toward opposing ideas of social and economic organization and behavior, a development especially worrisome because it arose in tandem with new techniques in mass communication, advertising, and propaganda. Merriam observed,

This is not merely the result of preoccupation with expansive interests or of a special American type of mentality, but grows largely out of the identification of the present industrial situation with the preservation of the status quo in constitutional arrangements, and the fear that change might jeopardize existing property interests. The same situation helps to explain the extensive business

[44]Ibid., 1535.

boycott of government, except where special favors are concerned, and the theory that the worst government is best.[45]

The president's committee chafed under the restrictions imposed by the design of the project. The authors of the report pointed out in their preface that a "pervasive limitation of the following chapters is that the authors and collaborators, in their researches, have not been free, as is the everyday citizen, to pronounce upon social ills and to prescribe remedies." While acknowledging that participants in the work had strong individual views, some of them as advocates for certain reforms, the authors of the report emphasized the efforts that had been taken to ensure freedom from bias: the extensive documentation, the examination of all known government and nongovernment evidence, the development where necessary of new data, and the submission of the preliminary drafts of the individual chapters for criticism by many experts. "In so far as this effort has succeeded," the authors remarked, "and no human being can be quite impartial, or is equally alert to all values—the findings can be used by women and men of widely divergent opinions." At various points in the text, the authors (some of whom were later involved in the work of the New Deal planning agencies) commended planning—then a vogue word in both Britain and the United States—as a political tool. Yet they emphasized, in a spirit of ironic detachment, that planning was a social need rather than a social capacity, and they gave a great deal of attention to the problems of fragmented government, confused jurisdiction, and contested relations between public and private authorities that confronted any would-be planner.[46]

For the first time in a semiofficial text intended for wide distribution, the committee's presentation of social trends in their interrelation opened up for inspection the agenda of public policy problems that would face the United States in the following decades. It also introduced much of the language that would long be used to describe policy issues. The report chronicled the changing fortunes of the labor movement during the period, the rise in technological unemployment, the emerging pattern of "deskilling," the collapse of the industrial democracy movement after World War I, and continuing grievances over the use of injunctions against labor. It emphasized the problems of the relationship between business and government and the need for expanded oversight and reg-

[45]Ibid., 1534.
[46]Ibid., xciv.

ulation. It discussed the circumstances of racial and ethnic minorities and called attention to the "social discrimination, injustice, and inequality of opportunity" that blocked "the path of adaptation" for the groups in question, pointing to the need for more sympathetic interpretation and protection of their legal rights. It called attention to the poverty that had persisted even during the unprecedented boom period of the 1920s, noted its spread and intensification with the onset of depression, and speculated that "after this crisis is over the first task will be to regain our former standards, inadequate as they were. The longer and greater task, to achieve standards socially acceptable, will remain."[47]

The report marshaled the evidence on changing family structure, divorce, and the problems of children. Extensive attention was devoted to the changing role of women in the culture as increasingly they moved out of the home and into full- or part-time employment. Alice Hamilton of the Harvard Medical School faculty, a physician with extensive experience as a Bureau of Labor investigator of problems of occupational health and safety, was a member of the six-person committee, and scores of women were among the social investigators who collaborated on the project. Women were depicted in the report as "newcomers into the outside world hitherto mainly the sphere of men," whose appearance was correlated with the other trends under study. "The tradition lingers," the report observed, "that woman's place is in the home and the social philosophy regarding her status has not changed as rapidly as have the various social and economic organizations. The problem of changing these lagging attitudes amounts in many cases to fighting for rights and against discrimination."[48]

Although the committee refrained from making specific policy recommendations, it floated many general notions that became part of the storehouse of statist new liberal public policy ideas. Among them was the idea of a national minimum standard in income, health, and education, which might be developed through the public administrative mechanism of grants in aid from the federal government. The committee traced the growth of the modern medical profession, its infrastructure and institutions, and outlined the emerging rationale for a national health care program. They took special pains to establish the data base and policy arguments out of which the Social Security Act of 1935, the prin-

[47]Ibid., xxxv.
[48]Ibid., xlvi.

cipal legislative foundation for the federal government's social welfare programs, would arise.

On this subject they commended the general principle of social insurance, pointed to its successful adoption in Britain decades earlier, and discussed the inadequacy of attempts, short of compulsory provision, to deal with the problems involved, thus slighting the welfare capitalism approaches preferred by President Hoover himself. They spoke of the idea of social insurance as a political invention, arguing that its institutionalization was a way of distributing, through government, the costs of economic progress, and suggesting the reasons why a new institutional mechanism in this field could be expected to force a longer-term process of social learning upon the polity:

The Committee is aware of the numerous objections urged against these schemes of social insurance, and of the heavy costs which they impose upon society; but it is also impressed with the inarticulate misery of the hundreds of thousands or millions of breadwinners who are deprived of their livelihoods through no fault of their own. To put the cost of unemployment squarely upon those who remain at work, upon employers and upon the public purse makes everyone conscious of the difficulty and focuses attention upon the need of devising more constructive methods for dealing with it.[49]

The major contribution of the report, however, was in the mass of the details through which it depicted the new organizational society and the group basis of the polity. Various chapters emphasized the breakdown and increasing futility of political institutions based on ideas of territorial representation (state and federal legislatures, for example) with the rise of organized groups representing many other kinds of shared interests. In reviewing the evidence on elections, the committee pointed to the beginnings of a decline in voter participation, linked it with the rise and proliferation of voluntary associations and interest groups of many kinds, and, without locating its structural and political causes, spoke of a growing political apathy throughout the society as a whole.

In his chapter on government and society, Merriam emphasized the observed proliferation of interest groups, their formation of alliances, and their employment of professionals, press agents, and scientific experts. He argued that relations between the emerging interest-group system, on the one hand, and legislatures and bureaucracies, on the other, had become "the very essence of politics under modern conditions."

[49]Ibid., xxix.

Merriam depicted the upward thrust of organized social groupings and their often dominating relation to traditional governments as "the most striking of all governmental trends, and perhaps the most significant." While lobbies had from the beginning been a legitimate feature of representative democracy, Merriam contrasted the old lobbying techniques (personal interviews, social pressures, money contributions) with the more sinister new capacities and methods. These involved, he pointed out,

> highly organized campaigns of letter-writing, telegraphing, and telephoning, and the assembly of delegations in person for demonstrations of various types. They include organized educational campaigns on an elaborate scale throughout a special district, a state, or at times an entire nation. They extend to inquiry and even research in special fields, the organization of materials and the formulation of measures for incorporation into law or administration.[50]

Recent Social Trends marked the culmination of a century-long tradition of social empiricism. As a specimen of the genre, it was distinguished from other examples not only for its comprehensiveness but for its method—which linked historical, descriptive, and narrative styles of reporting likely to reach a wider audience than merely statistical reports with a commitment to exploring the possibilities of social planning. Problems detected in the survey of trends would be addressed by mediating agencies in society and the state. Social developments unfolding spontaneously would be steered and guided. Thus the connection between social knowledge and social control, which had been latent in many of the ad hoc reports of the previous generation, became the basis of policy.

Yet while the report represented the fullest development of social empiricism in this sense, it marked the limits of the genre as well, a point about which committee members were quite sensitive. Authors of the report conceded that the narrative suggested many questions of cause and interpretation that were not addressed or answered. They reported empirical trends; they did not offer systematic public philosophy or political doctrine. The committee and its collaborators bridled under the demands placed upon them and the need to submerge their differences. Knowledge of social trends is one thing, they recognized, and social action is another.

The report pointed to the significance of the work that had been

---

[50]Ibid., 1514. Merriam's remarks on trends in relation to organized groups and government are on pp. 1511–15, passim.

generated in previous decades both within government agencies and in the private sector—in universities, foundations, and, increasingly, through privately funded think tanks—which had made it possible for the committee to range so widely in its own efforts. The committee noted that this institutionalization was itself an underlying trend of considerable importance, and raised the question of its natural limits. The committee asked whether "more widely in the future than in the immediate past we may expect the growth of thinking about the meaning of the great masses of social data which we have become so expert and so generous in assembling," and whether it was possible that "there is a radical inconsistency between the industrious and precise collection of material and the effort to utilize what has been found out." Concerns of this type reflected not only the societal pressures of the preceding generation, which had penalized radicalism in academe and politics, but also the efforts, understandable in light of professional canons, to achieve a scientific detachment that was as free as possible from contamination by individual biases or interests. Many of the individual reports were grounded in specific theories, such as those of institutional economics or the sociology of groups, yet, in the report as a whole, the only general theory, set forth after much struggle and disagreement, to serve as a structure of explanation for users of the report was a theory of cultural lag which questioned the rate, but not the overall direction, of social change.[51]

In addressing themselves to the probable future relationship between the development of knowledge and policy, the committee looked to "important contributions from individual thinkers with a point of view" who did not operate under the restraints of institutional collaboration. But, again, the committee emphasized the group and institutional context of likely future trends: "It is also to be anticipated that the initiative in a wide variety of emerging problems will be assumed by research centers, groups, bureaus, institutes and foundations, devoted in some instances to more specialized and in others to more general treatment of social data." While the most recent phase of American development in the social field had been "the recognition of the necessity of fact-finding agencies and equipment, and their establishment, the next phase of advance," the committee suggested, "may find more emphasis upon interpretation and synthesis than the last."[52]

[51]Ibid., lxxii.
[52]Ibid. On the reception of *Recent Social Trends* by the intellectual and policy community, see Karl, "The Social Sciences and Mr. Hoover: Recent Social Trends." The reception as

THE POSTWAR CONTEXT OF SOCIAL INVESTIGATION

In both Britain and the United States, from the onset of the Great Depression through the end of World War II, governments were preoccupied with the politics of economic recovery, the urgencies of mobilization for war, and finally with the problems of social resettlement in the postwar era. In both countries, until the outbreak of the second war, the unemployment problem festered as the central issue. As Barry Supple (Chapter 9) demonstrates, the interwar situation in Britain with respect to social investigation and policy innovation was both striking, in terms of the increased expenditures for social provision and the exercise of control over certain industries, and superficial and unsystematic.

In both countries the end of World War II set the stage for the greatest phase of growth in government functions and activities that either had experienced—fueled by the demands of postwar reordering of the domestic and international economies, increasingly administered along Keynesian lines. In Britain, in the wake of the Beveridge report of 1942 (a document that bears comparison with relevant portions of *Recent Social Trends,* published a decade earlier) and other influences, the Labour government ushered into being the contemporary welfare state in a fashion that could hardly be considered unsystematic or superficial. It filled the gaps in prewar social services and institutionalized concepts of national minimum standards in health care, education, and social security.

In the United States, formal changes in the role of the state were less focused and systematic, in part because of the structure of federalism, which obscured the question of which levels of government were responsible for basic social policy, and, more important, what failure to act on the part of lower levels meant for the higher ones. But the passage of the Employment Act of 1946 secured a continuing role for the federal government in macroeconomic management (although the watered-down

judged by reviews was overwhelmingly favorable, although some leading academic figures registered basic criticisms. Charles Beard regarded the report as a monumental achievement that marked "an epoch in the history of social thought in the United States—and perhaps the end of an epoch." He spoke then of a coming crisis in the empirical method as applied to social thought. Dewey defended the report against those who complained of its emphasis on objectivity. To those who complained of its empiricism, Dewey replied that "the facts are presented—sometimes implicitly, sometimes explicitly—so as to make *problems* [italics in original] stand out, and that, in my judgment, is the proper function of statements of facts. Hence the volumes are an arsenal. And I would rather have an arsenal of authoritative knowledge than such a premature firing-off of guns as would make a lot of noise and emit great amounts of smoke." Quoted in Karl, 221–3, passim.

version of the bill which became law did not provide for the stronger federal role in job creation sought by many advocates). With the Social Security Act of 1935 assured of continuing bipartisan support, the United States, too, began to address many of the problems of education, housing, civil rights, and welfare that had not been faced during the New Deal.[53]

In both countries, of course, powerful conservative reactions against the expanding state emerged, and conservative governments devoted to rolling back the scope of the state's activities and to criticizing the principles on which it operated achieved power in the 1980s. With government expenditures as a proportion of gross national product in both countries at an all-time high, the conservative movements on both sides of the Atlantic obviously have not achieved the attempted rollback. Decades of criticism of the premises on which the core of modern social policy resides have put all who argue for new forms of state intervention on the defensive. Yet in neither country is there a serious, comprehensive attempt to reinstate the legislative and institutional arrangements that prevailed before the post–World War II political economy took shape. Keynesian fiscal theory, which provided the public doctrine for economic management under which new liberal social policies were woven into the routines of institutional life, has been stalemated but not superseded.

In both countries, opposition to further state intervention brought home the limits to the long-term developmental processes of the modern state. The long period of growth driven by what Gianfranco Poggi had called the functionalization of rule—assumption of new tasks and responsibilities by government—ran out of impetus. Bureaucratic gigantism, institutional immobility, massive deficits, and soaring costs in the fixed, nondiscretionary areas of government provision challenged the thinking of political reformers in both nations. Impulses toward "the defunctionalization of rule" took shape, and new attempts at devolution and privatization were introduced. The related process Poggi had described as the attempted rationalization of rule—the search for scientific grounds for public policies as opposed to the exercise of arbi-

---

[53]For relevant studies see Paul Addison, *The Road to 1945: British Politics and the Second World War* (London: Jonathan Cape, 1975); Patricia Thane, *Foundations of the Welfare State* (London: Longman, 1982); Furner and Supple, eds., *The State and Economic Knowledge*; and Michael J. Lacey, ed., *The Truman Presidency* (Cambridge: Cambridge University Press, 1989).

trary rule—also faced a host of difficulties. The twentieth century spawned various forms of a sociology of opposition to science, technology, and technocracy that cast suspicion on empirically oriented traditions of social research. In addition, neoclassicism in economics experienced a renaissance, and theories of public or rational choice buttressed claims for the social-ordering capacities of the market.

The contemporary context for relations between social investigation and the state is marked by three features: (1) a rapidly increasing trend toward organizational pluralism, as new knowledge-generating and knowledge-brokering institutions, both within the state and outside it in civil society, came into being; (2) a gradual politicization of organizational life that accompanied the breakdown of the Keynesian new liberal consensus on the postwar expansion of government's role in social and economic affairs; and (3) a growing popular skepticism about the claims of expertise and a relativistic attitude regarding social knowledge generally.

In his comparative study of patterns of mutual influence between government and social science in Britain and the United States in the postwar era, Martin Bulmer sets out the main lines of development since the period of *Recent Social Trends* and calls attention to the key points of contrast and comparison between the two countries. In British universities, the social sciences, which had been far less securely institutionalized and developed as academic disciplines than had been the case in the United States, were firmly rooted from the 1960s onward. In the United States, too, social science departments shared in the explosive expansion of mass higher education and increased support for research. In both countries, Bulmer notes, social research expanded substantially "in non-academic settings, some of it within government, some of it 'outhouse.' The scale of the latter—in independent institutes, research contracting firms, 'think tanks,' and partisan intellectual groups—was far in excess of what was carried on twenty-five years before."[54]

As *Recent Social Trends* had indicated, and as the chapters by Critchlow, Brownlee, Supple, and Cuff in this volume show, in different ways, this growth in knowledge-producing and -brokering institutions was part of a long-term trend. Over time the process of social investigation has been opened up, if not to all comers (for the unorganized are without

---

[54]Martin Bulmer, "The Social Sciences in an Age of Uncertainty," in the volume he edited, *Social Science Research in Government: Comparative Essays on Britain and the United States* (Cambridge: Cambridge University Press, 1987), 346.

voices in a world of organizations), at least to a bewildering array of groups able to mount and finance special inquiries of various kinds. Organizational mass and density are the primary features of the environment in which contemporary social research and policy argument go on.

The world of policy analysis and advocacy in contemporary Washington illustrates the situation. By the late 1980s there were an estimated 1,200 nongovernment think tanks of various descriptions, various focuses on social and economic issues, and various sources of funding at work in the United States, roughly 10 percent of them in Washington alone. Hugh Heclo has described the institutional context of contemporary policy analysis in the capital, and pointed out that by the late 1970s the number of personal and committee staff of the Congress exceeded 11,000, with another 20,000 persons responding to the information needs of the legislature from other institutional locations in the Congressional Budget Office, the Office of Technology Assessment, and the General Accounting Office. The executive branch, of course, commands far greater numbers. No reliable census exists of interest groups at work in the city, but Heclo notes that by 1977 there were 1,800 trade and professional organizations headquartered in Washington with 40,000 employees, a number that did not include those working for the new style "public interest" groups in the areas of environmental policy, consumer affairs, civil rights, and others.[55]

The patronage for social research, as has been noted, comes from private as well as public sources, but by the late 1970s the scale of spending by the federal government was massive. Washington was spending about $2 billion annually on the acquisition and "application" of research on social conditions. Funding was routed through an estimated 180 bureaus and agencies, and no one could comprehend the complexities of the system as a whole. The vast majority of the offices involved were "mission agencies," and the research they sponsored or undertook themselves was typically limited in range and strongly influenced by their interpretation, broad or narrow, of the mission itself. The vast activity under way included a mixture of "in house" research conducted by career

---

[55]On the think tanks, see James Allen Smith, *The Idea Brokers: Think Tanks and the Rise of the New Policy Elite* (New York: Free Press, 1991). For a discussion of the institutional environment of contemporary policy argument and action, see Hugh Heclo, "Issue Networks and the Executive Establishment," in Anthony King, ed., *The New American Political System* (Washington, D.C.: American Enterprise Institute for Public Policy Research, 1978), 97–100, passim.

civil servants, and a larger body of work conducted by outside parties via grants and contracts, some of it on a "for profit" basis, and some of it on a "not for profit" basis, some of it by university-based scholars, some by professionals in the commercial research and development industry. It has been estimated that about a third of the activity supported by the federal government is aimed at the needs of the federal government, and the remaining two-thirds authorized for state and local governments, school systems, hospitals, police forces, industrial and agricultural groups.[56]

All those in Congress and the executive agencies involved in the funding and management of these activities (not necessarily in the actual conduct of inquiry itself) are caught up in bureaucratic, legislative, interest-group politics. Although some of the work produced meets high standards, the "routinization" and bureaucratization of inquiry impair the quality of work and its links to administration, policy development, or political argument. Agendas for research projects are sometimes set reactively and quickly shift with changes in public and political opinion. Attention may be devoted to the individual project of the moment, but seldom to its predecessors or contemporaries. Work proliferates but does not cumulate or "add up." Funding agencies may devote more attention to attempting to ensure equity in spending research monies than to assessing the results.

A deep presentist bias, reinforced by the dominant styles of academic social science and public administration, accompanies the decentralized, mission-oriented character of the work. Observers complain that the "longitudinal" needs of social investigation, a euphemism for the requirements of historical depth, are slighted. Rapid turnover in the upper echelons of the research-oriented bureaucracies and in the congressional staffs that control them is associated with frequent changes of managerial focus and rhetoric, which are said to have trivializing effects on the work. Dissemination of results is practically and politically problematic, and there are no general policies governing behavior. The central political authorities of the day may well be suspicious and critical of "self-serving" reports flowing from the agencies, and leery about subsidized distribution and controversial findings.

Public policy is not made without controversy and public argument,

[56]Details are from National Academy of Sciences, Study Project on Social Research and Development, *The Federal Investment in Knowledge of Social Problems* (Washington, D.C.: National Academy of Sciences, 1978).

however, and in the private sector in recent decades a new institutional pattern of ideological polarization has appeared. As Critchlow shows in Chapter 7, when measured by the history of the Brookings Institution, the progressive era's ideal of the nonpartisan, privately supported public policy research agency devoted to the public interest and existing above the political fray was tested over time in the real world of Washington politics. The institution went through a number of different eras, its impartiality questioned by New Deal liberals at one point and by Nixon administration conservatives at another. With the emergence in the post-war era of competing, ideologically oriented think tanks on the left and the right—there was a similar upsurge of partisan allegiance in Britain on the part of social scientists associated with politically committed groups such as the Fabian Society, the Tawney Society, the Bow Group, and the Institute for Economic Affairs—it is clear that the need for mediating institutions devoted to the interpretation and criticism of all the arguments and evidence that help form the knowledge base for public policy has taken root. These institutions reflected both the existence of competing paradigms in social theory, including Marxism as well as liberal pluralism, and the disaggregation of the liberal tradition, begun in the 1880s, into distinct variants.

The same ideal of nonpartisan commitment to developing socially useful knowledge suggested the rationale for "scientific philanthropy" at the turn of the century and inspired foundations to support social inquiry in the hope that the root causes of social problems might be illuminated. And although the need for nonpartisanship and impartiality is no less evident than it ever was, an ideological patterning within the world of philanthropic foundations occurred in the 1970s and 1980s as well. The archives of some of the major American foundations have been opened in recent years, and a study by historians who examined the development of American philanthropy with special reference to foundation support for social inquiry relevant to public problems concluded:

What seems clear—in an area where little is transparent—is that between foundations and government, between foundations themselves with very different policy interests, and among groups concerned with the direction and purpose of government-funded policy programs, an intense ideological debate is going on; it is increasingly difficult to describe the elites who manage this debate. That such elites exist is incontestable, but their relations to one another, the institutions they serve, and the general public's influence with them is [sic] not equally clear.[57]

[57]Barry D. Karl and Stanley N. Katz, "Foundations and Ruling Class Elites," *Daedalus:*

Given the mass and density of the organizational context, the pluralism of knowledge-producing and knowledge-brokering institutions, public and private, and the increasing polarization of agencies for the patronage of social investigation, it is no wonder that skepticism prevails toward knowledge claims addressed to policy issues. Those closest to the policy-making process are fully aware of the "hyphenated" quality of much of the argument and evidence introduced into political and policy discussion on the part of those who speak for different sectors of the bureaucracy and different elements of the system of interest groups, foundations, and think tanks. Policymakers are confronted not simply with scientific evidence, but with AFL-CIO (American Federation of Labor and Congress of Industrial Organizations) evidence, National Association of Manufacturers evidence, NAACP (National Association for the Advancement of Colored People) evidence, Heritage Foundation evidence, Brookings Institution evidence, and so on.

FOCUSING PLURALISM

The vast size, complexity, and expense of the system of social investigation should not be taken as a sign that the system is working well. On the contrary, complaints abound from every quarter. The most recent occasion to ventilate such complaints in the public record was provided in 1985, in the hearings of a U.S. House of Representatives task force on science policy that investigated the effects of the social and behavioral sciences on government at a time when a suspicious, conservative administration, anticipating severe budget problems, was cutting back on expenditures in most areas of government. The three main groups represented in testimony were the academic community, the private philanthropic foundations engaged in support of social and public policy research, and the private, for-profit research and consulting firms.[58]

Academics spoke for the most part not as individuals or as citizens, but as representatives of academic disciplines. They sought increased government funding, and pointed to new trends in social science research

---

Journal of the American Academy of Arts and Sciences 116, no. 7 (Winter 1987): 38. See also by the same authors, "The American Private Philanthropic Foundation and the Public Sphere, 1890–1930," Minerva 19, no. 2 (Summer 1981).

[58]U.S. House of Representatives, Committee on Science and Technology, Task Force on Science Policy, Hearings Before the Task Force on Science Policy, vol. 2, The Role of the Social and Behavioral Sciences (Washington, D.C.: U.S. Government Printing Office, 1986).

(e.g., theories of decision making, cognitive science, and the psychobiology of learning and memory). Foundation executives, overwhelmed by increasing demands to reprogram their own funds and spend more money on practical problems and less on inquiry, emphasized to elected officials their own shrinking resources and expressed the hope that government would pay more attention to the overall need for institutional continuity and stability in the field of social investigation. Representatives of the commercial research sector spoke of the need for more efficiency in the research and development "market" which government dominates, and sought easier access to research funding, less red tape, and a better competitive position vis-à-vis civil servants and academics.

With one important exception—James Coleman—no one discussed the broader meanings or central tendencies of this system as a whole; the need for greater focus, clarity, and relevance in social inquiry; or the political and programmatic implications of social inquiry. Coleman, a sociologist at the University of Chicago, in many respects America's most experienced social investigator, was invited to testify by virtue of his experience as the director of a number of large-scale government-supported inquiries into race and educational achievement, a body of research that shaped the context of public discussion on issues of equality of opportunity and race relations from the mid-1960s onward.

In view of our emphasis throughout this survey of the history of social investigation on the permeability of the boundaries separating private and public in the Anglo-American experience, it is important to note that Coleman's work was stimulated by public debate and legislation. Under the provisions of the 1964 Civil Rights Act, the U.S. commissioner of education was instructed to conduct a study on the extent to which America's racial minorities were deprived of equal educational opportunities in the nation's public schools and to report back to Congress and the president within two years. The commissioner appointed Coleman the principal investigator of the project, and Coleman superintended preparation of *Equality of Educational Opportunity* (1966), popularly known as the Coleman Report, a massive, technically complex, statistically based inquiry into the empirical circumstances that gave legislative and administrative impetus to subsequent attempts to integrate public education.

Appearing before Congress some twenty years later, after decades of participation in often acrimonious debate about the bearing of social science on public policy and opinion, Coleman testified that the challenge facing members of Congress in this area of policy was the need to understand that they were dealing not simply with discrete topics and the miscellaneous needs of ad hoc inquiry, but with a maturing system, with the workings of a "new kind of information-generating activity" that had become an essential adjunct of governance, fundamental to the legitimacy of political action generally.

Veteran of many battles, Coleman was aware of the controversies that begin when research findings on sensitive topics are worked over in the public arena by the news media, interest groups, dissenting scientists, and academic critics. He was careful to point out that the basic aim of large-scale social investigation was *not* a more orderly and rational decision-making process by a government agency, a commonly encountered technocratic rationale, but "rather an upgrading of the knowledge base on which policy issues are fought—perhaps even an increase in the likelihood of conflict over policy, as more consequences of policy become known."[59]

If the public is to benefit from conflict over policy, however, the ongoing argument over social and economic evidence and its interpretation must contribute to a process of social and political learning. The drift of popular attitudes toward relativism undermines this process. Plainly, attitudes of skepticism and group distrust in the face of expert knowledge claims are not irrational. This distrust has not appeared overnight, but has emerged as the system of social investigation itself has developed. The main difference between today's investigators and those of the past lies in self-consciousness regarding the limits of social empiricism—the recognition by contemporaries of the difference between facts and the meaning of facts. "Social policy research is not value free," Coleman remarked to the House committee, sounding the contemporary note.

The limits of social empiricism are one thing; the abandonment of social empiricism is another. Public discourse cannot proceed without reference to social facts. One practical aspect of the problem, therefore, is the need to respond to currents of group suspicion and to alter the practices of social investigation accordingly. Coleman spoke of the need to "strengthen democratic pluralism" with respect to large-scale social investigation by disaggregating the process and opening up, politically and administratively, different phases of it. The nub of the problem, in Coleman's view, was the need for ways to ensure "that the information

---

[59]Ibid., 100.

obtained is relevant to the interests of all parties who are affected in a given policy area." He distinguished between the process of conducting research, which plainly requires that information be sought and compiled in an impartial and unbiased manner, and the fashioning of the terms of reference and aims of the inquiry, which requires participation of all who are likely to be critics unless their particular information needs are met. Coleman spoke, therefore, of the principle of "pluralism in design" and its corollary, "open access to results," as innovations that might improve the usefulness of inquiry into public problems in the future.[60]

AGENDA FOR RESEARCH

In closing, we wish to suggest some topics for future research that might help strengthen scholarship on the links between government and society, ideas and institutions. During the 1980s, powerful criticisms of the dominant styles of research and writing about public problems began to appear within both policy-making and academic circles. The criticisms have focused on the lack of philosophical depth not only in recent neo-conservative writings but also in earlier approaches, including pluralist, interest-group theories, and Marxist and New Left theories. Although these approaches are very different in their premises, they have in common a suspicion regarding the reasons for government intervention in society and the economy. All of them explain public policy almost entirely as a function of the needs and interests of private groups, and underestimate the extent to which public officials operate independently and provide the leadership and continuity required to shape the course of public policy.

Many of the criticisms have pointed out the unfortunate neglect of historically oriented, institutional studies, particularly the institutions of government. Variously called the "return to the state" movement and "the new institutionalism," criticisms have been unusually wide-ranging, touching most of the major schools of analysis that have developed in American universities in recent decades. In addition to familiar complaints about narrow specialization and the fragmentation of research, criticisms venture into basic questions of method and theory and stress the deficiencies of "institution free" approaches to social and economic issues. They complain of the shallowness of the traditions of behavioral

[60]Ibid., 98–102, passim.

research and of the meager yield of cost-benefit analysis, systems research, public choice theory, and other fads in policy analysis of the 1970s and 1980s. They focus, too, on the disregard by much New Left scholarship of the role of the state, on the lack of concern with fundamental problems of equality and justice, and on the neglect of overriding public interest issues that hover over much of the writing in the tradition of pluralist, interest-group theory and research.[61]

The critics mainly call for renewed attention to the relations, in all their dynamic complexity, between public policy and public thought. The recent turn to political history and the evident growth of scholarly interest in the history of social, economic, and cultural policy reflect this concern. Rather than to focus, as in earlier days, on elections and voting, the new approach would distinguish between politics and government, and focus more specifically on the connection between politics and the growth and functioning of government-in-society. It would address the history of governance—the collective act of governing itself—which has entailed the construction of the modern state and all the capacities and policies and programs that it comprises.

Some of the issues that arise in approaching the modern history of governance are dealt with in this volume, which emphasizes the development of the knowledge base for state action. In assembling this text we have come to recognize how much remains to be done in this particular vein—how rudimentary is our understanding of this cognitive dimension in the history of law, bureaucracy, regulation, and social welfare. There is an urgent need for work on the agents—individuals and institutions— that have contributed to the knowledge base for public policy, in order to recover the broader meanings and relationships to traditions of political thought involved in their struggles over public policy and its proper grounds. Although it is possible, as some of the chapters in this volume show, to identify for past eras the communities of persons who were

---

[61]For a sample of recent scholarly discussion on these matters, see James G. March and Johan P. Olson, *Rediscovering Institutions: The Organizational Basis of Politics* (New York: Free Press, 1989); Rogers M. Smith, "Political Jurisprudence, the New Institutionalism, and the Future of Public Law," *American Political Science Review* 82, no. 1 (March 1988): 89–108; Peter B. Evans, Dietrich Reuschmeyer, and Theda Skocpol, eds., *Bringing the State Back In* (Cambridge: Cambridge University Press, 1985); Gabriel Almond, "The Return to the State," *American Political Science Review* 82, no. 3 (September 1988): 853–74; Eric A. Nordlinger, Theodore Lowi, and Sergio Fabbrini, "The Return to the State: Critiques," *American Political Science Review* 82, no. 3 (September 1988): 875–901. For a critical analysis of Marxist theory and scholarship on the state, see Axel van den Berg, *The Immanent Utopia: From Marxism on the State to the State of Marxism* (Princeton, N.J.: Princeton University Press, 1988).

involved in providing the grounds for public action and to recover their intentions and the context of their thought, the closer we come in time to the present day the more difficult the task becomes without new research. Plainly, identifying and tracing the "policy networks" that have been active in policy innovation and change in different domains of state life are priorities.[62]

One aspect of the emphasis on bringing the state back into research and theory is the need to get inside the state, historically speaking, in a way that is too seldom attempted. Neither in Britain nor in the United States, for example, has the historical mapping and exploration of the units within government devoted to social and economic investigation of various kinds been done satisfactorily. The need, of course, is not simply for maps, but for some sense of what the sites they indicate have had to do with the process of puzzlement, the questioning and answering that goes on as the essential background to the official and political conversations that drive public policy. This problem is pressing with respect to executive institutions; for example, there is no useful history of the U.S. Treasury Department; nor is there an adequate account of the historical evolution of the tax code, though changes in it not only have fueled the operations of the nation-state but also have functioned as a major arena of nonbureaucratically administered social and economic policy. The difficulty is equally pressing with respect to legislatures; very little work has been done on congressional thought—on the way in which ruling ideas arise, succeed one another, and give way to new ones— as opposed to congressional politics and the vagaries of party opinion, for example.

The regulatory agencies of government were conceived in controversy as answers to divisive social and economic problems. Their history, particularly their intellectual history, is another important area to be investigated. On what theories do the operations of regulatory institutions operate? How are the theories related to the values of the political traditions in which they function? How do they relate to democratic thought? How are the theories tested? What do regulators need to know to make judgments in their areas of responsibility, and what do legislators

---

[62]The notion of "policy networks" was presented in Heclo, "Issue Networks and the Executive Establishment." Heclo was describing the contemporary scene. The network idea has not been systematically worked out, tested, and applied to the historical development of policy.

need to know to make judgments about regulators? And in what instances has the characteristic thrust of regulation—as prevention—been an obstacle to more constructive positive forms of public (or private) management?

If law is justly considered the *language* of the state, what has it been saying? What are the grounds in thought for the legitimacy of administrative action, and how is administrative action controlled? With the rise of the administrative state in the twentieth century, the field of administrative law and regulation has come to loom large in the day-to-day scheme of things. What are the intellectual sources of administrative law? What is the status in legal theory of administrative law in all of its domains, and how has legal theory, a twentieth-century academic enterprise, been influenced by developments in the social sciences and other academic fields, such as philosophy?

The study of interest groups and, where possible, of class structure, might also be more useful to the themes under study here if more attention were paid to the arguments and evidence such groups use to influence policy, and the arguments and evidence their adversaries employ. The patronage of investigation, public and private, is another topic that needs more study. Finally we mention the importance, as a historical topic, of the sociology of opposition to science, technology, and the expanding state. Groups left and right have resisted the growth of the state, some as invasive, repressive, or punitive, others as merely irritating, superficial, and palliative. Historically, how did such groups participate in the ongoing argument about the changing roles of the state? What were their understandings of policy and the grounds for policy? How did they position themselves with respect to long-term trends of social empiricism, social investigation, and political argument? What policy ideas and institutions did they advocate? If knowledge of the history of groups in opposition to the state could be expanded to recover this aspect of their experience, the new knowledge might not only contribute to our grasp of the past, but provide resources for thinking about the future as well.

2

The science of the legislator:
the Enlightenment heritage

DONALD WINCH

In 1817 the East India College at Haileybury, an establishment that had been created in 1805 to educate those destined for government service in India, was ridiculed by one of its opponents for aiming to send out what he described as a "little army of Grotiuses and Pufendorfs" to weigh tea, count bales, and measure muslins. In his reply to this and other criticisms, Robert Malthus, the well-known author of the *Essay on Population* who held a chair at Haileybury with the imposing title of "professor of general history, politics, commerce, and finance," denied the narrowly mercantile requirements of the task but accepted the "happy image" of the little army by suggesting that nothing far short of a training in Grotius and Pufendorf, or rather their modern legislative counterparts, would do for those citizens of a "free constitution" who were destined to discharge the duties of statesmen on the Indian subcontinent.

Malthus's own teaching of the most novel part of the Haileybury syllabus, the "branch of the science of a statesman or legislator" that had been vitally refurbished if not created by Adam Smith's *Wealth of Nations,* was, in fact, the first of its kind in England. And after twelve years of teaching experience Malthus was convinced that the experiment was a success: The subject was neither too difficult nor too dull for sixteen- and seventeen-year-olds to grasp.[1] When combined with evangelical Christianity and Benthamite utilitarianism, political economy was certainly to play a large part in the way India was ruled.[2]

[1]See *The Pamphlets of T. R. Malthus* (New York: Kelley Reprints, 1970), 69–70, 308–9.
[2]See E. Stokes, *The English Utilitarians and India* (Oxford: Clarendon Press, 1959); W. J. Barber, *British Economic Thought and India, 1650–1858* (Oxford: Clarendon Press,

63

Haileybury was a by-product of reforms in the governance of India begun in the Cornwallis-Wellesley era at the end of the eighteenth century. The fact that the new anglicizing and reforming spirit was channeled through an ancient and partly discredited instrument, the East India Company, illustrates a British habit of using indirect means of achieving administrative ends, whereby "government devolved and permitted, rather than initiated and controlled."[3] It is also a reminder that the need for education and expertise in performing the functions of government was never a purely domestic affair—that a great deal of legislative talent in Britain during the nineteenth century was employed on "imperial" duty. Haileybury epitomizes, therefore, albeit in minor educational form, one of the essential themes underlying this volume: the recognition that new branches of knowledge were essential to the performance of the tasks of government, where this included a knowledge of societies and peoples over whom government was to be exercised.

As befitted the Scottish origins of political economy, Malthus had been preceded by Dugald Stewart, professor of moral philosophy at Edinburgh, who had given a separate course on the subject from 1800 to 1810 as part of a successful plan to educate a new generation in the achievements of this essentially modern science, which had been established during the second half of the eighteenth century. The success can be judged largely through the careers of his pupils, and more especially through the pages of the *Edinburgh Review,* which was to become the main arena for reviewing works on the closely related sciences of politics and political economy, and hence one of the main channels through which the influence of what we now call the Scottish Enlightenment was exerted on a wider British public.[4]

Stewart's course at Edinburgh complements Malthus's teaching at Haileybury by illustrating the knowledge of government that was regarded as essential for persons destined either to become domestic legislative experts, or to be called on, as leading citizens, academics, and

1975); and S. Ambirajan, *Classical Political Economy and British Economic Policy in India* (Cambridge: Cambridge University Press, 1978).

[3]See N. Baker, "Changing Attitudes Towards Government in Eighteenth-Century Britain," in A. Whiteman et al., eds., *Statesmen, Scholars and Merchants* (Oxford: Clarendon Press, 1973), 203.

[4]See "The System of the North: Dugald Stewart and His Pupils," in S. Collini, D. Winch, and J. Burrow, *That Noble Science of Politics; A Study in Nineteenth-Century Intellectual History* (Cambridge: Cambridge University Press, 1983); and B. Fontana, *Rethinking the Politics of Commercial Society: The Edinburgh Review, 1802–1832* (Cambridge: Cambridge University Press, 1985).

educated commentators, to judge the conduct of others in this field, and thereby to form the climate of opinion within which governments described as enjoying "free" constitutions operated.

By the early 1800s, of course, Stewart and Malthus were merely *re*-affirming the opportunities for bringing enlightened principles to bear on the problems faced by legislators, but they were doing so in a political climate, dominated by the French Revolution and the Napoleonic Wars, that was frequently hostile to the application of any general principles to human affairs. This atmosphere also gave rise to new, more urgent problems that required significant modification of established principles. As a result, Stewart and Malthus became transitional figures in the process by which eighteenth-century ideas on the science of the legislator were transmitted to the nineteenth century. They mark a kind of midpoint in the period to be surveyed here. Both were strongly conditioned by the pre- and postrevolutionary Enlightenment, and both also wrote largely before the 1830s and 1840s when, as G. M. Young pointed out, a novel weight of "disinterested intelligence" was brought to bear on British society and institutions.[5]

The early 1800s also saw the transformation of parliamentary business from control over an executive toward legislation based on extensive social investigation and implemented through bureaucratic modes of intervention—the period of significant growth in government in Britain and the point at which the other contributions to this volume begin. The task of this chapter is to provide a prologue to these changes, and the first step is to consider the concept of the legislator as it appears in two influential eighteenth-century approaches to the science or sciences thought to be essential to the conduct of his duties.

For the sake of simplicity, the two approaches will be identified with Adam Smith and Jeremy Bentham, respectively, although both have longer Enlightenment ancestry that includes Grotius, Pufendorf, Montesquieu, and Hume in Smith's case, and Condillac, Helvetius, and Beccaria in Bentham's. As an extra complication, Hume and Smith can also be added to Bentham's lineage, though not on ground of some putative "liberal" tradition connecting Locke with John Stuart Mill, thereby inevitably, in good Whig fashion, including Hume, Smith, and Bentham en route. For some purposes it makes sense to speak of a journey *from* Smith *to* Bentham, so long as, first, this does not become an excuse for over-

[5]See *Portrait of an Age* (London: Oxford University Press, 1936), chap. 8.

looking the diversity of an Enlightenment heritage that always encompassed the variations which they epitomize; and, second, this does not lead to an underestimation of the open-endedness, adaptability, and hence durability of some of Smith's most general conclusions.

ROLE OF THE LEGISLATOR

Let us begin with a unifying commonplace: the underlying aim of many philosophers who adopted naturalistic approaches to man in society during the Enlightenment was to construct a science of the legislator capable of doing for their own generation what Aristotle and Machiavelli had done earlier, but to do so on a fresh foundation that incorporated an improved Newtonian methodology of observation and experiment; access to more cosmopolitan historical and anthropological evidence; and a more profound understanding, as they saw it, of the psychological "springs" of human action. The priority accorded to historical experience or psychological observation and introspection might differ, and the nature and range of empirical evidence considered relevant might vary; so, too, might the primary focus on jurisprudential, constitutional, penal, and economic issues. But the foregoing generalizations would apply to many philosophes in various countries and can be taken as evidence of widespread agreement on the importance of placing government on a rational, efficient, equitable, and humane footing—making it, in short, the proper subject of a science capable of serving as the foundation for practical improvements in the art of government.

All this can also be described in terms of the emergence of "society," and more precisely, of "civil society," including the process by which it was understood to change or progress, namely "civilization," as the primary object of inquiry during the eighteenth century—the discovery and celebration of the fact that society represented a more or less autonomous realm of existence subject to its own laws of development. In this form one can speak of "society" (and its possible underpinnings in "economy") as separate from "polity," and of the resulting situation as involving the "erosion of the distinctively political."[6] Alternatively, one can speak of "an antipolitical animus"—of a belief that because the caprice of rulers had been one of the main barriers to progress in the past, the success of modern states in the future would depend on their

[6]See Sheldon Wolin, *Politics and Vision* (Boston: Little, Brown & Co., 1960), chap. 9.

ability to make the activities of government the subject of objective rules that could be taught, tested impartially against experience, and given institutional embodiment.[7]

Enlightenment cosmopolitanism—acceptance of the challenge posed by the increasing evidence of diversity in the social forms known to eighteenth-century observers—also entailed some separation of the social from the political. The inherited classical tradition with its triad of pure constitutions—monarchy, aristocracy, and democracy—together with their corrupted counterparts, no longer seemed capable of explaining the complex differences of degree and kind revealed by comparisons of social stages and states across time and space. Civilization and civil liberty might advance together but have little connection with the degree of political liberty conferred by the various constitutional variants. As Montesquieu argued in a sustained piece of what would later be called sociological relativism, laws and constitutions might best be judged not so much by reference to their external features, internal coherence, and intrinsic merits as in terms of their appropriateness to complex social *states*. Others such as Adam Smith, Adam Ferguson, and John Millar added the concept of historical *stages*. The wise counselor in this emerging tradition begins to look more and more like the well-informed sociologist or anthropologist, faithfully recording and interpreting social similarities and differences but offering little positive advice to legislators beyond an injunction to respect established social mores.

The classical idea of the all-powerful legislator as lawgiver and founder of states was indeed an obvious casualty resulting from the naturalistic approach adopted during the Enlightenment. Scottish historians of civil society in particular made extensive use of the doctrine of unintended consequences—of the idea that although the social order was the result of human action, it was not necessarily the result of human design—as a means of explaining social change.[8] And when attention is narrowed down to the materialist foundations of the four stages of development that often appear in such histories, an essentially society-centered picture emerges. This picture is antagonistic not merely to the legislator as found-

[7]See G. Poggi, *The Development of the Modern State: A Sociological Introduction* (Palo Alto, Calif.: Stanford University Press, 1978), 77–86; and "The Modern State and the Idea of Progress," in G. A. Almond, M. Chodorow, and R. H. Pearce, eds., *Progress and Its Discontents* (Berkeley: University of California Press, 1984).

[8]See especially Duncan Forbes's introduction to Ferguson's *History of Civil Society* (Edinburgh: Edinburgh University Press, 1966), xxiv; and his pioneering article "Scientific Whiggism: Adam Smith and John Millar," *Cambridge Journal* 7 (1953): 643–70.

er but to any developed notion of political agency as a means of achieving social goals. When topped off with a laissez-faire image best expressed in a slogan taken from one of Smith's earliest lectures ("Little else is requisite to carry a state to the highest degree of opulence, but peace, easy taxes, and a tolerable administration of justice; all the rest being brought about by the natural course of things"),[9] a fairly deterministic view of the economic basis of civil society appears to emerge. The result is a science of the legislator that leaves the lawmaker with precious little to do other than to contemplate "natural" processes and to issue pious warnings about "artificial" impediments and expedients.

In recent years, however, historians have been discovering just how misleading this image is, just how significant, in another guise, the role of the legislator was to the Enlightenment. The intimate if over-sanguine relationship of many philosophes to actual legislators, usually absolute monarchs, is well known, with Turgot, Louis XVI's minister of finance, however briefly and unsuccessfully, coming closest to occupying the role of philosophe-king. And Smith, in quieter fashion, ended his days as a commissioner of customs, with his expertise at the disposal of Pitt, North, and Shelburne. Bentham was a member of Shelburne's coterie, teetered on the brink of serving an apprenticeship with Catherine the Great, and eventually offered his services as legislative expert to all and sundry in Europe and the Americas, North and South, and even entertained hopes of becoming "the dead legislative hand of India."[10]

But neither actual legislators nor the lingering attractions of the legislator seen as sole founder seem as important to the Enlightenment as the idea of the legislator, in J. H. Burns's words, as a "continuously active figure, modifying, regulating and sustaining the dynamic structure of political life."[11] The legislator as molder or *machiniste* might have no more historical veracity or concrete existence than the founder figures of ancient myth, but he provided a vehicle for expressing various ideals or principles. By contrast with Smith's politician, "that insidious and crafty animal" whose councils were guided by the "momentary fluctuations of affairs" and hence by the more clamorous pressure groupings in society,

[9]As reported by Dugald Stewart in a lost manuscript: see Stewart's *Account of the Life and Writings of Adam Smith*, as reprinted in *Essays on Philosophical Subjects, The Works and Correspondence of Adam Smith*, (Oxford: Clarendon Press, 1980), 322.

[10]*The Works of Jeremy Bentham*, edited by J. Bowring (Edinburgh: William Tait, 1838–43), vol. 10, 450.

[11]See Burns, "The Fabric of Felicity: The Legislator and the Human Condition," Inaugural Lecture, University College, London, 1967.

the deliberations of the legislator were "governed by general principles which are always the same."[12]

STATE AND CIVIL SOCIETY

By serving as an ideal location to which contributions to knowledge or science could be addressed, this concept of the legislator also provided a flexible way of speaking about that other major abstraction, the state, and of dealing with its relationship to civil society. The Scottish Enlightenment vision of the relationship was, for example, more flexible than later Hegelian and post-Hegelian usages of the state/civil society dichotomy permitted, because it allowed for noncoercive forms of mutual interaction. It did not require rigid assumptions of autonomy, primacy, or parasitism—that is, complete freedom of action by an impartial agency possessing exclusive powers of coercion, a state-centered view of the world, on the one hand, or a derivative and conspiratorial view of the state as the agent of the dominant economic forces in society, on the other. The new conception of the legislator licensed inquiry into a range of institutions capable of mediating between state and civil society, operating in the large space separating the sphere of law from that of manners, the realm of "perfect" and legally enforceable rights from that of "imperfect" obligations and social duties. Less abstractly, it conformed with the devolved and permissive features of the British style of limited government.

As an illustration of the permeability of the categories represented by state and civil society, consider the following (rare) programmatic statement by Smith:

Upon the manner in which any state is divided into the different orders and societies which compose it, and upon the particular distribution which has been made of their respective powers, privileges, and immunities, depends, what is called, the constitution of that particular state. Upon the ability of each particular order of society to maintain its own powers, privileges, and immunities, against the encroachments of every other, depends the stability of that particular constitution.... That particular constitution is necessarily more or less altered, whenever any of its subordinate parts is either raised above or depressed below whatever had been its former rank and condition.[13]

[12]Adam Smith, *Wealth of Nations*, as reprinted in the Glasgow edition of the *Works*, edited by A. S. Skinner and R. H. Campbell (Oxford: Clarendon Press, 1976), 468.
[13]Smith, *Theory of Moral Sentiments*, in the Glasgow edition of the *Works*, edited by D. D. Raphael and A. L. Macfie (Oxford: Clarendon Press, 1976), 230–1.

In terms that are more kinetic than organic, Smith describes state and civil society as being almost interchangeable. "Constitution" has a sociological rather than legal foundation, a corporatist rather than an individualist basis. Smith's approach opens inquiry into the interaction between government and society in a manner that should be expected of someone whose lectures on jurisprudence were designed to show how law and government not only "grew up with society" but represented "the highest effort of wisdom and prudence."[14] The rejection of earlier rationalistic accounts of the origins of government, such as those embodied in the social contract, enabled Smith to forge links between political institutions and broader social and pyschological phenomena such as deference within a society of ranks and the "powers, privileges, and immunities" of the "different orders and societies" that compose any state. It also made questions connected with the climate of "opinion," whether expressed through representative structures or not, an important aspect of the life of legislators.

With the advent of less proleptic and deterministic readings of Smith's work, and a new appreciation of the uncompleted "history and theory of law and government" contained in his lectures on jurisprudence, has come greater recognition of the positive role that Smith assigns to political agency in general and the legislator in particular.[15] Smith's legislator embodies the virtues of the man of "public spirit" when compared with the "man of system." The latter seeks "to erect his own judgement into the supreme standard of right and wrong," and

is often so enamoured of the supposed beauty of his own ideal plan of government, that he cannot suffer the smallest deviation from any part of it. He goes on to establish it completely and in all its parts, without any regard either to the great interests, or the strong prejudices which may oppose it. He seems to imagine that he can arrange the different members of a great society with as much ease as the hand arranges the different pieces upon a chess-board. He does not consider that the pieces upon the chess-board have no other principle of motion besides that which the hand impresses upon them; but that, in the great chess-board of human

---

[14]See Smith *Lectures on Jurisprudence*, in the Glasgow edition of the *Works*, edited by R. L. Meek, D. D. Raphael, and P. Stein (Oxford: Clarendon Press, 1978) 1489.

[15]For some of the work that has produced this result, see D. Forbes, "Sceptical Whiggism, Commerce and Liberty," in T. Wilson and A. S. Skinner, eds., *Essays on Adam Smith* (Oxford: Clarendon Press, 1976); D. Winch, *Adam Smith's Politics* (Cambridge: Cambridge University Press, 1978); K. Haakonssen, *The Science of a Legislator* (Cambridge: Cambridge University Press, 1981); and D. Winch, "Science and the Legislator: Adam Smith and After," *Economic Journal* 93 (1983): 501–20.

society, every single piece has a principle of motion of its own, altogether different from that which the legislature might chuse to impress upon it.

The wise legislator, however, accommodates

his public arrangements to the confirmed habits and prejudices of the people; and will remedy as well as he can, the inconveniences which may flow from the want of those regulations which the people are averse to submit to. When he cannot establish the best system of laws, he will not disdain to ameliorate the wrong; but like Solon, when he cannot establish the best system of laws, he will endeavour to establish the best that the people can bear.[16]

The two stereotypes presented here could stand for Bentham and Smith, respectively, although the "man of system" passage underestimates Bentham's understanding of the "principle of motion," and the pragmatic stance, even contemplative world-weariness, of the description of the wisdom of Solon conveys little idea of Smith's achievement in giving his legislative vision both a philosophical basis and a practical cutting edge that required the active attention of the legislator as well as the impartial judge. And whereas Smith would have been guilty of the utopian arrogance of the "man of system" if he had believed that his own "system of natural liberty and perfect justice" was capable of overcoming all at once the powerful interests and inertial forces, legitimate and illegitimate, that stood in its way, readers of the *Wealth of Nations* could have no doubt that Smith's system contained a coherent set of critical principles and a detailed and fairly radical program of demolition and positive innovation. Withdrawal of government from spheres in which its knowledge or practical competence was suspect, and in which the scope for creating unjust privileges was growing, was quite compatible with, and may even have required, strong government, certainly flexible, efficient, and probably expanding government. Adaptation as well as accommodation was involved, and, in the changing circumstances that were a major feature of life in commercial societies, adaptation was an active process, calling for new ways of dealing with both inefficiency and injustice.

In some respects, Smith's conception of the legislator's role is close to what J. H. Burns has termed "circumstantial empiricism—a cautious and in the end an essentially conservative approach to social institutions."[17] Within the Benthamite tradition, however, the position adopted is rather

[16]Smith, *Theory of Moral Sentiments*, 233–4.
[17]See Burns, "The Fabric of Felicity," 12.

different. In those versions of the science of the legislator that are most closely related to the one Bentham was to spend most of his life articulating, the legislator appears less as circumstantial empiricist and more as *machiniste* or technocrat with potentially unlimited powers of intervention, and the capacity to remodel both individual men and institutions by means of an artificially created system of rewards and punishments. Bentham criticized Montesquieu and Blackstone for their conservatism and failure to stress the "censorial" and "ought" side of any treatment of laws; and he extended the same criticism to Smith on matters of political economy.[18]

This aspect of Bentham seems most relevant to an understanding of the interventionist and collectivist features of his thought. It accounts, too, for the hostility which he has aroused in ultraliberal circles, and for the attempts to separate the Benthamite and Smithian strands of individualism.[19] But having noted some of the more obvious distinctions, I want to close this section by looking at other ways in which the two approaches could converge if not unite. For Bentham was in some respects a self-confessed successor to Hume and Smith. His thinking contains elements drawn from many eighteenth-century sources. He was not always to be found occupying the intemperate, nonempirical, and unpragmatic stance. And Smith's categories were sufficiently open-ended to allow for some of Bentham's later developments.[20] Moreover, early nineteenth-century students of the science of the legislator were not

---

[18]See *Jeremy Bentham's Economic Writings,* edited by W. Stark (London: Allen and Unwin, 1952), vol. 1, 193–4, 223–5.

[19]This tendency in modern assessments can often be traced back to Hayek's association of Smith and Bentham with what he called "true" and "false" individualism, respectively, where the latter essentially entailed the use of constructive types of rationality for the illiberal purpose of planning others' lives; see F. A. Hayek, *Individualism and Economic Order* (Chicago: University of Chicago Press, 1948), 1–32. There are, of course, more profound and precise philosophical reasons for the differences between Smith and Bentham. They can be found, for example, in their divergent attitudes toward natural law and jurisprudence, legal positivism, the role of utilitarian criteria in explaining and judging institutions, and in the value attached to comparative-historical evidence in constructing their respective sciences. As a result of the recent discovery of Smith's lectures on jurisprudence, we are now in a better position to state these divergences without undue political tendentiousness. Knud Haakonssen's work *The Science of a Legislator,* for example, has greatly helped clarify the differences between Hume and Smith on one side and Bentham on the other, largely by emphasizing the priority attached to the negative principle of pain-avoidance rather than the positive injunction to maximize happiness, and the different kinds of knowledge which these priorities entailed.

[20]See J. H. Burns, "Scottish Philosophy and the Science of Legislation," Royal Society of Edinburgh, Occasional Papers, 2–6, 1985; and L. J. Hume, *Bentham and Bureaucracy* (Cambridge: Cambridge University Press, 1981), esp. 9–11 and chap. 2.

always so ideologically anxious or so tidy-minded as some of their twentieth-century counterparts. And whereas the failure of Benthamism to establish roots in the United States is legendary, certainly when compared with the influence exerted by Scottish thinkers, British devotees of Smith's political economy were often utilitarians of one kind or another, including, of course, in the case of David Ricardo and James and John Stuart Mill, the Benthamite strain in fairly virulent form. Thus it seems to be the duty of the historian, as opposed to that of the ideologue, to consider how accommodation, probably falling short of fully self-conscious logical reconciliation, could be achieved.

MACHINERY VERSUS MEN

To see how the two approaches might overlap in some particulars, consider the likely attitude of Smith and Bentham toward a vision of the legislator that we now understand, largely as a result of the work of John Pocock, as that of Machiavellian virtuoso playing variations on perennial cycles of virtue and corruption.[21] Pocock and those influenced by him have shown just how attractive this classical republican model continued to be to eighteenth-century Anglo-Americans, among them Scottish contemporaries of Hume and Smith.[22]

Faced with this alternative, Hume, Smith, and Bentham could be ranged on the same side, the one emphasizing that in matters of law and government it was safer to rely on effective machinery than on good men, and on private "interest" rather than on virtue or public spirit. Their skepticism regarding virtue is part of the depersonalizing process that has been associated with eighteenth-century "constitutionalism," especially of the "mixed" government and American Federalist variety, and treated as antagonistic to any genuine conception of politics.[23] The key statement here is Hume's maxim "that in contriving any system of government and fixing the several checks and balances of the constitution, every man ought to be supposed a *knave*, and to have no other end, in

---

[21]See especially J. G. A. Pocock, *The Machiavellian Moment* (Princeton, N.J.: Princeton University Press, 1975).

[22]For the most recent Scottish interpretations, see the contributions by N. Phillipson and J. Robertson in I. Hont and M. Ignatieff, eds., *Wealth and Virtue: The Shaping of Political Economy in the Scottish Enlightenment* (Cambridge: Cambridge University Press, 1983); and J. Robertson, *The Scottish Enlightenment and the Militia Issue* (Edinburgh: John Donald Publishers, 1985).

[23]See Wolin, *Politics and Vision*, 388–93.

all his actions, than private interest." James Mill cited this maxim as part of the defense of Benthamite utilitarianism in the 1830s.[24] It captures a common feature in the work of Smith and Bentham: their efforts to expose and overcome antisocial proclivities and to harness self-interest to the public good, although Smith's view of individual motivation was less uniform and possibly less narrowly pecuniary.[25]

Smith also appears to have had less confidence than Bentham in the possibilities for making corporate institutions, including joint stock companies and bureaucratic bodies, "knave-proof." Both men were alert to the ways in which all groups, including those possessing knowledge or expertise, could become enervating, self-serving monopoly interests, but Bentham seems to have had more faith in his capacity to design institutions embodying procedural rules for ensuring "interested diligence," accountability, and "uniformity of method." Bentham was also more prepared to depart from market solutions when he thought them inadequate.[26]

But Smith never depicted the choice between machinery and men as a simple binary one, any more than he felt it necessary to choose between a commercial society based solely on strict rules of commutative justice as opposed to one based on beneficence. Indeed, if public spiritedness was totally absent, it is difficult to see where *any* contribution to an understanding of "principles that should always be the same," including his own, could be addressed. It might be hard to find legislators in a world dominated by politicians, but there had to be possibilities for encouraging the legislator's point of view, if only through the slow processes of educating "opinion." Although there is, to my knowledge, only one explicit statement by Smith to this effect, his whole enterprise depends on this assumption.[27]

---

[24]See Collini et al., *That Noble Science*, 113.

[25]See N. Rosenberg, "Some Institutional Aspects of the *Wealth of Nations*," *Journal of Political Economy* 68 (1960): 557–70, for an account of Smith's recognition of conflicting motives and his proposals for institutional expedients designed to cater for them.

[26]See C. F. Bahmueller, *The National Charity Company* (Berkeley: University of California Press, 1981), 105–7 and chap. 6 for remarks on this subject.

[27]The explicit statement is as follows: "Nothing tends so much to promote public spirit as the study of politics, of the several systems of civil government, their advantages and disadvantages, of the constitution of our own country, its situation, and interest with regard to foreign nations, its commerce, its defence, the disadvantages it labours under, the dangers to which it may be exposed, how to remove the one, and how to guard against the other. Upon this account political disquisitions, if just, and reasonable, and practicable, are of all the works of speculation the most useful. Even the weakest and worst of them are not altogether without their utility. They serve at least to animate the

Bentham, too, as Ross Harrison has shown, had difficulties in settling on a mode of address to legislators. The greater commitment to "ought" questions meant that his work had to go beyond an appeal to the dispassionate observer, to disinterested reason and posterity. Rulers had to be persuaded that their duty coincided with the public interest defined according to objective utilitarian methods. But would prejudice, solidified into "sinister interests" and sometimes taking the form of unconscious and repressed beliefs, yield to mere information? Doubts on this score could explain the compulsive search for ways of associating duty and interest which pervade Bentham's bureaucratic theory and plans. Such doubts could also explain the espousal of the cause of democratic government in Britain, for, unlike their rulers, the people at large were thought to have no interest in bad government. The legislative expert now becomes a shoemaker, using his skills to prepare a choice of wares and relying on the people to decide on the correctness of fit.

But democracy only shifts the problem of persuasion to another level: in whose interest will it be for democracy to be adopted? In answer, Bentham and his lieutenant, James Mill, ultimately had to rely on a fiercer form of an argument traditionally associated with Whigs, namely that timely reformation will make wholesale renovation unnecessary. Threat of disorder and total collapse supplies an interest in action that disinterested appeal to public good does not; and once rule by the "subject many" is established, it always sets in motion a learning process capable of finding the right solution.[28]

Neither Hume nor Smith treated the British form of government with Blackstonian reverence. Yet Smith seems to have been *reasonably* content with the "mixed" constitution and cannot be described as a democrat, whatever benefits he might associate with representative institutions when putting forward his "imperial" solution to the problems created by the American Revolution.[29] Bentham's irreverence toward established institutions is legendary, but there is considerable truth in the view that his science of legislation, even after the conversion to democracy, remained

---

public passions of men, and rouse them to seek out the means of promoting the happiness of the society." Smith, *Theory of Moral Sentiments*, 186–7.

[28]See R. Harrison, *Bentham* (London: Routledge and Kegan Paul, 1983), chap. 8. For James Mill's use of fear as a political tactic, see J. Hamburger, *James Mill and the Art of Revolution* (New Haven, Conn.: Yale University Press, 1963).

[29]For an argument centering on this issue, see J. Robertson, "Scottish Political Economy Beyond the Civic Tradition: Government and Economic Development in the *Wealth of Nations,*" *History of Political Thought* 4, no. 3 (Winter 1983): 451–82.

essentially agnostic with respect to forms of government. Although Hume and Smith were not indifferent to the constitutionalist "checks and balances," they shared with Bentham a belief that the benefits of commercial or civilized society did not depend on *forms* of government, free or otherwise.[30]

Another distinguishing feature of the science of the legislator remains, and it can best be understood in terms of the ancient responsibility of the legislator to maintain or preserve the "character" of his people. The "civic" qualities of Smith's diagnosis of the effects of the division of labor on the mass of society, and of his educational and other remedies for dealing with it, clearly demonstrate his unwillingness to discard "republican" or "civic humanist" values and categories, even when his work on commercial society showed their increasing irrelevance.[31] Smith's residual concern with citizenship may also explain why he was not prepared to excuse the legislator entirely from the duties of enforcing or enjoining other "imperfect obligations," to revert to the language of natural jurisprudence usually preferred by Smith.[32] Although in recent work much has been made of Bentham's interest in popular participation,[33] civic virtue does not figure in his writings. Egoism does not exclude altruism; the secret ballot may focus attention on public rather than private interest, but the rational spirit of reform replaces patriotism as a binding agent. It certainly seems significant that the civic justification for education forms no part of Bentham's Chrestomathic schemes or those designed for pauper children, even if the more enthusiastic "social control" interpretations of his intentions appear to be optional.[34] Malthus was a more orthodox follower of Smith on this matter; although Malthus saw education for the poor largely as a means of encouraging moral restraint, he consistently tied education to the spread of civil and political liberties.[35]

A further difference between Bentham and his Scottish predecessors concerns what might loosely be described as the everyday realities of

[30]On this, see Duncan Forbes's reference in note 15 above.
[31]See Winch, *Adam Smith's Politics*, esp. chap. 5.
[32]See *Theory of Moral Sentiments*, 81.
[33]For defense of this aspect of Bentham's political thought, see F. Rosen, *Jeremy Bentham and Representative Democracy; A Study of the Constitutional Code* (Oxford: Clarendon Press, 1983); and D. Lieberman, "From Bentham to Benthamism," *Historical Journal* 28 (1985): 218.
[34]See, for example, Bahmueller, *National Charity Company*, 174–86.
[35]See *An Essay on the Principle of Population*, edited by P. James for the Royal Economic Society (Cambridge: Cambridge University Press, 1989), vol. 2, book 4, chaps. 6 and 7.

political life and behavior. Smith's interest in the pervasive phenomenon of deference to established authority within a society of ranks seems to be matched in Bentham only by vague references to "habits of obedience." Apart from a fairly crude conspiracy theory centering on "sinister interests," there is no Benthamite equivalent to Hume's analysis of political parties, and little positive appreciation of the role played by "influence," management, and ambition in activating political elites within "free" governments. Government entailed "politics" in a significant sense that made it more than a matter of legal and rational administrative procedures supplemented by a democratic franchise system. The trivial fact that Bentham preferred to speak of a science of legislation, rather than of a science of the legislator, could therefore reflect a subtle shift of focus.

NEW CHALLENGES AND CHANNELS OF COMMUNICATION

From the beginning of the nineteenth century, the science of legislation was increasingly shaped by a series of new economic and social challenges that were particularly acute in Britain. Although it is true that many of the distinctive features of Bentham's fundamental position can be traced to earlier Continental authors, notably Helvetius, it is nonetheless obvious that environmental changes connected with the French Revolution, the war with France, and rapid industrialization and population growth in Britain encouraged the movement away from the more skeptical eighteenth-century forms of circumstantial empiricism, with their anti-utopian emphasis on criticism and explanation, toward the more confidently urgent, practical, and reforming accents of philosophic radicalism. Thus a good case can be made for believing that war, increasing concern over pauperism, and the difficulty of obtaining secure and cheap subsistence significantly influenced the agenda and shape of the science of legislation and political economy in the quarter-century after 1795. Indeed, these problems could be held responsible for the fact that political economy, the subordinate branch of inquiry in the middle of the eighteenth century, began to assume dominance during the early part of the nineteenth. The passing reference given so far to Malthus, that practitioner of the "dismal science" who dominated the scene in the first decade of the new century, does little more than signal the existence of a question that needs closer consideration.

But first a further word about those modes of address and channels of communication which provide some clues to the changing function of knowledge, argument, and factual inquiry by reminding us of the new arenas in which expertise was called for and displayed. In a well-known study of Benthamite methods of influencing legislation, S. E. Finer used such terms as permeation, suscitation, and irradiation to describe some new practices and official avenues open to peddlers of legislative expertise.[36] Whereas it would be wrong to underestimate the use made of investigative commissions and expert advice by late eighteenth-century legislators, there can be no gainsaying the increased importance of royal commissions and select committees from 1800 onward.[37] Nor can one underestimate the shift toward giving Parliament a legislative role, rather than one designed simply to check the executive. For Smith and his generation the mechanisms for transmitting influence were rather different. Despite one or two shrewdly Machiavellian confidential policy memorandums directed to statesmen, Smith, like the good academic he was, relied upon broad diffusion of his ideas and took responsibility for contributing to the formation of "opinion" in a general, more "civic" (as opposed to "technocratic") sense—one that was carefully distanced from party politics.

As the example of Dugald Stewart and the *Edinburgh Review* shows, there were early nineteenth-century standard-bearers for the Scottish version of the science of the legislator. Thus Stewart and his prize pupil Francis Horner attempted to maintain the neutral scientific stance on politics, though with growing difficulty in the highly charged world of the early 1800s. But a closer examination of their activities tends to confirm what has been said so far about the change of setting, tone, and direction. Stewart certainly attempted to uphold the civic role of the university teacher under difficult postrevolutionary circumstances; and he was fortified in this by a "perfectibilist" assumption, not shared by Hume or Smith, that educated opinion was inexorably moving in an enlightened direction. Because he also believed that the history of civil society and its political institutions could engender political skepticism— that is, a retrospective or spectatorial view of human affairs—Stewart stressed future standards rather than a purely adaptive view of legislation.

[36]See Finer, "The Transmission of Benthamite Ideas, 1820–50," in G. Sutherland, ed., *Studies in the Growth of Nineteenth-Century Government* (London: Routledge and Kegan Paul, 1972).

[37]According to Brian Harrison, 7 volumes of Parliamentary Papers in 1801 had grown to 24 in 1824; the annual average grew to 60 or 70 after 1850; see "Finding Out How the Other Half Live: Social Research and British Government Since 1780," in his *Peaceable Kingdoms* (Oxford: Clarendon Press, 1982), 264.

This approach accords well with the Benthamite position. Before Bentham's espousal of parliamentary reform along democratic lines—the issue that brought philosophic radicals (Bentham and James Mill) and philosophic Whigs (James Mackintosh and Thomas Babington Macaulay) into conflict—Stewart's belief, that "the happiness of mankind depends, not on the share which people possess . . . in the enactment of laws, but on the equity and expediency of the laws that are enacted," corresponded with Benthamite priorities, providing a basis for close collaboration on matters of legal reform (with Samuel Romilly, James Mackintosh, and Henry Brougham) and education (Lancasterian schools, the Society for the Diffusion of Useful Knowledge, and University College, London).[38]

Arguments of a different kind could be advanced to explain convergence. The open-ended character of Smith's categories for government action has been mentioned, and insofar as reforms in the nature and competence of the state were successful, partly as a result of Benthamite and other pressures, a major obstacle to intelligent and uncorrupt intervention had been removed. "Opinion" in some general eighteenth-century sense employed by Hume and Smith, especially when discussing the climate in which "free" governments operated, gradually hardened into "public opinion," an entity normally attached to the middle classes and increasingly invoked by political commentators. It may not have always been "enlightened" in Stewart's sense, but it was a more potent force to be appealed to and actively formed through clubs, societies, newspapers, and the periodical press.

By some eighteenth-century standards, Smith was peculiar in not publishing a single topical pamphlet and in publishing only a couple of learned reviews (in his youth). Reviews, pamphlets, newspaper and encyclopedia articles were the lifeblood of his early nineteenth-century Whig and radical successors. Bentham needed editorial midwives to put his views before the public, and it is not surprising that someone who wrote ten or twenty pages a day for sixty years left a mass of unpublished

---

[38]See Collini et al., *That Noble Science,* 25–61, 93–9. For other recent studies of the fate of the Scottish approach in nineteenth-century Britain, see the work by Bianca Fontana cited in note 4 above, and a series of articles by K. Haakonssen, including "From Moral Philosophy to Political Economy: The Contribution of Dugald Stewart," in V. Hope, ed., *Philosophers of the Scottish Enlightenment* (Edinburgh: Edinburgh University Press, 1984); "The Science of the Legislator in James Mackintosh's Moral Philosophy," *History of Political Thought* 5 (1984): 233–66; "John Millar and the Science of a Legislator," *Juridical Review* (1985):41–68 and "James Mill and Scottish Moral Philosophy," *Political Studies* 33 (1985:628–41).

papers behind him. Smith burned most of his papers just before his death. Given Bentham's belief that he was solving future as well as current legislators' problems, it would have been inconceivable for Bentham to have followed suit, and it might have been a major fire hazard if he had tried to do so.

With regard to political economy and the system of natural liberty, of course, Smith's general authority remained high, whereas Bentham had difficulty in convincing even his most faithful disciples that his opinions on this subject were "sound."[39] But Smith's system needed to be considerably recast by Malthus, Ricardo, and other aficionados of the science to give it purchase on the new issues thrown up by the Napoleonic Wars, notably currency instability, rising taxes and national debt, scarcity of food, a growing dependence on foreign markets for manufactured exports and food supplies, and increasing conflict along class lines, punctuated by sporadic popular unrest. Political economy became a narrower discipline as it was tailored to fit more urgent specifications.[40]

The 1830s and 1840s have received the most attention in the growing body of secondary literature on the growth of government. But the entire Napoleonic War period was at least as crucial in producing, if not a growth in government responsibilities, a fundamental reassessment of those responsibilities and the first articulate demands for the relevant information on which a mature national judgment could be formed. The implications of this reassessment for state/civil society relationships are best illustrated by Malthus's writings in general and by his contributions to debates on the Poor Laws and the Corn Laws in particular. Thus his writings on population from 1798 onward bring together a postrevolutionary reconsideration of the more visionary claims for an Enlightenment science of society (as articulated by the Marquis de Condorcet and William Godwin); a renewed concern with public order and the stability of British constitutional arrangements; and the rapid growth of pauperism connected with serious grain scarcity (1795, 1799, and 1802). In holistic shorthand, British society did not suddenly need to call on an active state to restore or redirect its powers of motion; instead the "natural" course on which it appeared to be embarked—abetted by "artifi-

---

[39]See T. W. Hutchison, "Bentham as an Economist," *Economic Journal* 66 (1956): 288–306.
[40]See R. D. C. Black, "Smith's Contribution in Historical Perspective," in T. Wilson and A. S. Skinner, eds., *The Market and the State* (Oxford: Clarendon Press, 1976), 42–8; and Winch, "Science and the Legislator," 511–17.

cial" stimulants connected with war—no longer seemed as unproblematic as it had to Smith.

Malthus struck the new note in his first *Essay* when he criticized Smith's "hitchless" theory of growth by querying whether the process of capital accumulation, particularly when applied in an unbalanced manner that favored manufacturing over agriculture, might not produce a situation in which national "wealth" was in conflict with the "happiness and comfort" of the mass of society.[41] Here was a case in which the conclusions of political economy, not merely the population principle, might have to give way to higher considerations derived from the science of politics and morals.[42] Much of Malthus's career can be described as an attempt to give substance to his fears on this score. It underlies his agrarian bias, his belief that life in manufacturing towns and occupations was "unwholesome" and unstable, his doubts on the subject of excessive capital accumulation and general gluts during the postwar depression, and his act of apostasy in supporting agricultural protection in 1815— an act that separated him from his Whig friends on the *Edinburgh Review* as well as his radical friend Ricardo.

In making the case for the abolition of the statutory right of relief under the English Poor Laws, Malthus was less isolated from his fellow experts. He had been preceded by Joseph Townsend and Sir Frederick Morton Eden in raising the alarm about a commitment by the state, which, although administered locally, threatened, under conditions of periodic grain scarcity, to generate a new form of dependency, an inability to preserve the line between poverty and pauperism, and a check to that emulative spirit on which so much of the Smithian system of natural liberty relied.[43] Malthus is still best known as an abolitionist and as a stern apostle of the gospel of self-help (notably through his support for "moral restraint" as the chief long-run solution to the problem). Nevertheless, it is important to stress that his version of the science of the legislator (based on a Christian interpretation of the principle of utility) led him to defend the allowance system and public works for their short-term benefits during every period of scarcity and public disorder, and to

---

[41]See the first *Essay,* chaps. 16 and 17. See also G. Gilbert, "Economic Growth and the Poor in Malthus' *Essay on Population,*" *History of Political Economy* 12 (1980): 83–96.

[42]See Collini et al., *That Noble Science,* 65–89.

[43]On the whole question, see J. R. Poynter, *Society and Pauperism; English Ideas on Poor Relief, 1795–1834* (London: Routledge and Kegan Paul, 1969); and a more recent study by G. Himmelfarb, *The Idea of Poverty* (New York: Alfred Knopf, 1984).

make education of the poor a precondition for abolition.[44] Far from drawing unequivocal policy conclusions in the manner of Ricardo and his followers, Malthus was ultrasensitive to what Ricardo dismissed as "temporary inconveniences" (delays and breakdowns in the efficacy of purely market processes of adjustment). Because he upheld a "doctrine of proportions," he was more reliant on moral and empirical assessments of the wider circumstances surrounding legislative action.[45]

Outside the popular literature, at least, it has always been recognized that classical political economists did not dogmatically adhere to laissez-faire positions. That Malthus (once thought to be the chief architect of the view that "the essence of social policy is that there should be no social policy")[46] could simultaneously espouse legislative action to protect agriculture and long-term abolition of existing legislative responsibility under the Poor Laws is a further indication that the issue of laissez-faire versus state intervention often serves to divert attention away from what the protagonists saw as the main issues in the late eighteenth and early nineteenth century.

MALTHUS AND STATISTICS

In their works devoted to general principles, neither the political economists nor the Benthamites relied significantly on statistical evidence. In his capacity as population theorist, of course, Malthus was a far more avid user of statistical material than were most other contemporary economists. And the agenda that Malthus set forth in the first *Essay* for the collection of empirical evidence bearing on the everyday life of the mass of mankind, requiring "the constant and minute attention of an observing mind during a long life," certainly describes his own career, despite the fact that many of his leading ideas were formulated before there was any official census to show what was actually happening to population trends.

Malthus apart, the orthodox successors to Smith's mantle during the first half of the nineteenth century are not normally noted for their sen-

[44]See P. James, *Population Malthus; His Life and Times* (London: Routledge and Kegan Paul, 1979), 126–36.

[45]See J. Pullen, "Malthus and the Doctrine of Proportions and the Concept of the Optimum," *Australian Economic Papers* 21 (1981): 39–54; and for further justification of these conclusions, D. Winch, *Malthus* (Oxford: Oxford University Press, 1987).

[46]The conclusion of H. L. Beales in D. V. Glass, ed., *Introduction to Malthus* (London: Frank Cass, 1959), 22.

sitivity to historical and empirical evidence. Moreover, whether or not there was an actual divorce between theory and fact in their work, as is sometimes alleged, it must be admitted that the relationship was by no means without marital strain.[47] Indeed, even Malthus has been criticized for confusing moral and scientific categories and thereby propounding a theory that was inherently tautological, incapable of being falsified by the mass of historical, statistical, and ethnographic material he assembled.[48] Now that more evidence has emerged to show that Malthus reacted open-mindedly to census findings that conflicted with his predictions and we have come to realize that the measurement of "moral" variables can be separated from "moralizing," a more tolerant attitude seems to be emerging—one that recognizes, as Malthus himself claimed, that there were genuine epistemological differences between his own work and that of Ricardo on such matters.[49] It was not accidental that Malthus was a founder of the Statistics Section of the British Association for the Advancement of Science in 1833 (along with Charles Babbage, Adolphe Quetelet, and Richard Jones) and of the London Statistical Society.[50]

Nevertheless, even Malthus was reluctant to join forces with William Whewell and Richard Jones in constructing a thoroughgoing inductive and anti-Ricardian version of political economy.[51] At an earlier stage of his career he had supported other economists in defending theory and the use of deductive methods from the ignorance of "practical men" and the spokesmen for special interests or causes—bankers, merchants, and landowners as well as social visionaries such as Robert Owen.[52] Moreover, despite his interest in the assembly of accurate population

---

[47]For an indication of the issues at stake here see M. Blaug, *Ricardian Economics* (New Haven, Conn.: Yale University Press, 1958), 182–8. For a response to this, see N. B. de Marchi, "The Empirical Content and Longevity of Ricardian Economics," *Economica* 37 (1970): 257–76.

[48]Here again Mark Blaug has been one of the leading critics; see his article on Malthus in the *International Encyclopaedia of the Social Sciences;* and K. Davis, "Malthus and the Theory of Population," in P. F. Lazarsfeld and M. Rosenberg, eds., *The Language of Social Research* (Glencoe, Ill.: The Free Press, 1955), 540–53.

[49]See, for example, the work by John Pullen cited in note 45; and E. A. Wrigley, "Elegance and Experience: Malthus at the Bar of History," in D. Coleman and R. S. Schofield, eds., *The State of Population Theory; Forward from Malthus* (Oxford: Clarendon Press, 1986), 46–64.

[50]See James, *Population Malthus*, 443–9; and L. Goldman, "The Origins of British 'Social Science': Political Economy, Natural Science and Statistics, 1830–1835," *Historical Journal* 26 (1983): 587–616.

[51]See N. B. de Marchi and R. P. Sturges, "Malthus and Ricardo's Inductivist Critics: Four Letters to William Whewell," *Economica* 40 (1973): 379–93.

[52]See Malthus, *Essay*, book 4, chap. 13.

statistics, it seems unlikely that any political economist with a general commitment to the system of natural liberty would have supported the kind of patriotic or "Tory paternalist" interpretation that John Rickman gave to his case for collecting the nation's vital statistics.[53] Political economists from Adam Smith onward were never greatly enthusiastic about statistical inquiry for its own sake. Smith was not enamored of political arithmetic, and statistics was regarded as a quite separate enterprise by J. R. McCulloch, the only political economist who was active in this field.[54] The real devotees of numerical and other forms of direct inquiry into society, whether undertaken with official blessing or not, appear to have belonged to a thought-world different from that of the orthodox school of economists throughout the nineteenth century, one strain of which eventually emerged during the last third of the nineteenth century as an attempt to create ethicohistoricist alternatives to economics.[55]

How then can the undoubted connections be explained between Benthamism and social investigation of the Chadwick or Kay-Shuttleworth variety in the 1830s and 1840s? Close parallels between this and the methods of political economy should not be expected. Even when there were personal and political alliances between the two groups, different activities as well as people were often involved. To oversimplify the matter, those wishing to promote a new form of legislative activity, and later to take part in administering it, have a much greater need for statistical and other information than those who are expounding or even applying general principles. That arch-deductivist James Mill would not have been a very effective civil servant at East India House without detailed knowledge of the empirical information required to carry out his everyday duties.

[53]See the statement concerning the "glorious superstructure [which] might be raised by a Government anxious for the good of its subjects" in J. Rickman, *Thoughts on the Utility and Facility of Ascertaining the Population of England,* as reprinted in D. V. Glass, *Numbering the People,* (Farnborough: Saxon House, 1973), 108. One of the motives behind the operation was to calm discontent by revealing that population and hence prosperity had grown, an un-Malthusian conclusion; see M. J. Cullen, *The Statistical Movement in Early Victorian Britain* (New York: Barnes and Noble, 1975), 12.

[54]See L. Goldman, "The Origins of British 'Social Science'; Political Economy, Natural Science and Statistics," *Historical Journal* 26, no.3 (1983): 611–12.

[55]For earlier studies of this see T. W. Hutchison, *Review of Economic Doctrines, 1870–1929* (Oxford: Oxford University Press, 1953), chap. 1; and A. W. Coats, "The Historist Reaction in English Political Economy, 1870–90," *Economica* 21 (1954): 143–53. For studies of the challenge to orthodox economics in the latter half of the nineteenth century, see A. Kadish, *The Oxford Economists in the Late Nineteenth Century* (Oxford: Clarendon Press, 1983); and J. Maloney, *Marshall, Orthodoxy and the Professionalisation of Economics* (Cambridge: Cambridge University Press, 1985).

Statistics were, of course, only one of the forms in which information about society could be collected and disseminated. Political economy and Benthamite utilitarianism come closer to each other when seen as two sources of expertise, two ways of organizing information, that were increasingly being called upon by parliamentary select committees. For example, Francis Horner served on the Bullion Committee (1810), and Ricardo, along with Huskisson, served on the Select Committee on Agriculture (1821). Malthus was one of the main expert witnesses before the Select Committee on Emigration in 1826, and James Mill before the Select Committee on the Affairs of the East India Company in 1831–32, thereby setting ample precedent for his son's appearances later before a wide variety of official inquiries.

The parliamentary career of political economy has given rise to a large body of literature charting the influence of economists on policy-making over a wide field which includes "imperial" responsibilities in Ireland, India, Canada, and such "new" countries as Australia and New Zealand.[56] Dedicated pragmatists are no more likely to be impressed by this literature than they have been by the literature on Benthamite contributions to the Victorian administrative state. But if influence is treated as secondary to the question of what language and forms of knowledge are called on in the conduct of public life at any given period, the evidence is almost as impressive as the extent of the secondary literature suggests.[57]

ANGLO-AMERICAN COMPARISONS

Anglo-American comparisons could be helpful at this juncture. The first observation has already been made in passing, namely, that Benthamism made little headway in America.[58] The second is that the eighteenth-

[56]In addition to the literature cited in note 2 above, see B. J. Gordon, *Political Economy in Parliament, 1819–23* (London: Macmillan, 1976), and *Economic Doctrine and Tory Liberalism, 1824–30* (London: Macmillan, 1979); F. W. Fetter, *The Economist in Parliament; 1760–1868* (Durham, N.C.: Duke University Press, 1980); L. Brown, *The Board of Trade and the Free Trade Movement* (Oxford: Clarendon Press, 1958); R. D. C. Black, *Economic Thought and the Irish Question, 1817–1870* (Cambridge: Cambridge University Press, 1960); D. Winch, *Classical Political Economy and Colonies* (Cambridge, Mass.: Harvard University Press, 1965); and A. W. Coats, *The Classical Economists and Economic Policy* (London: Methuen, 1971).

[57]Boyd Hilton's *Corn, Cash, Commerce: The Economic Policies of the Tory Governments, 1815–30* (Oxford: Clarendon Press, 1977) is an example of work that is sophisticated in its treatment of the way in which ideas and interests actually affected cabinet decisions.

[58]On the comparative failure of Benthamism to strike root in North America, see Paul A. Palmer, "Benthamism in England and America," *American Political Science Review* 35 (1941): 855–71.

century Scottish agenda for the science of the legislator, as expounded in the style of Hume and Smith, continued to be far more visible in the United States than in Britain during the early nineteenth century. With respect to the responsibilities of government in the economic field, the questions raised by the science of the legislator in the larger Hume-Smith (and, more surprisingly, perhaps, Malthusian) sense seem far more important than any differences arising from mere forms of government and the divergent courses taken by ideas on representation in the two countries.[59] The continuing role played by the Scottish Enlightenment in American public life during the pre- and postrevolutionary period and well into the nineteenth century—in the *Federalist Papers,* in public debate generally, as well as in the curricula of colleges and universities—has either become a commonplace, or, through exaggeration, the subject of counterclaims.[60]

An understanding of "republican" problems, whether or not they were likely to be outdated by developments in commercial society, was a prominent feature of the work of Hume and Smith. There is much evidence that Smith in particular shared the American colonists' view of themselves as living in a land-abundant society unencumbered by such feudal remnants as primogeniture and other "oppressive" relationships between ranks and orders, a society where political and economic liberty might thrive together in a way that was not possible in Europe.

American legislators were sufficiently under the sway of the eighteenth-century versions of political economy to believe that its diagnoses applied to them and would require measures to delay or prevent any corrupting consequences of developments predicted by the science.[61] Their worries on this score form a kind of mirror image of those questions of population and subsistence that have been sketched for Britain during the first two decades of the nineteenth century. Jefferson and Malthus shared the same anxieties about the corrupting effect on the "happiness and virtue" of the populace of the growth of manufacturing occupations at the expense of agricultural ones. For Malthus, as for Smith, the United States had an

---

[59]On the divergence see J. R. Pole, *Political Representation in England and the Origins of the American Republic* (London: Macmillan, 1966).

[60]See, for example, A. Haddow, *Political Science in American Colleges and Universities, 1636–1900* (London: D. Appleton-Century, 1939); D. Sloan, *The Scottish Enlightenment and the College Ideal* (New York: Columbia University Press, 1971); D. Adair, *Fame and the Founding Fathers,* edited by T. Colbourn (New York: Norton, 1974); and G. Wills, *Inventing America* (New York: Doubleday, 1978).

[61]See D. McCoy, *The Elusive Republic: Political Economy in Jeffersonian America* (New York: Norton, 1980).

ideal combination of circumstances; it was a place where the population could expand at its maximum pace without *as yet* giving rise to pressure on standards of living or resorting to "unwholesome" occupations in which the worker was exposed to uncertainties arising from "the capricious taste of man, the accidents of war, and other causes"—what Jefferson referred to in his *Notes on Virginia* as "the casualties and caprice of customers."

But the crucial phrase has been italicized, for Malthus also held that America could not expect to escape indefinitely from the principle of population. A man "might as reasonably expect to prevent a wife or mistress from growing old by never exposing her to the sun or air."[62] Jefferson and Madison were well aware of the Malthusian diagnosis and, like Malthus, accepted the idea that although "perpetual youth" could not be sustained, it might be possible, through wise policies, to stave off "premature old age," especially if the concern was not simply about "wealth" but, more important, about the need of the legislator to protect "virtue" or "character" as well.[63]

The absence of a subsistence issue and all the divisive questions surrounding the Poor Laws, the Corn Laws and rent, and urban and factory conditions in a crowded island constitutes a major difference between the United States and Britain in the first third of the nineteenth century, one that had clear implications for the way in which the agenda and instrumentalities of the state developed. But the established findings of a science of the legislator still offered promise of explaining developments in both countries. It was not until Britain had to square up to the problems of settlement and land disposal in Australia, Canada, and New Zealand in the 1830s and 1840s that a new variation on these themes appeared, and this variation is primarily associated with another Benthamite-inspired undertaking, the movement for colonial reform led by Edward Gibbon Wakefield.

Contradicting the Smith-Malthus diagnosis, Wakefield suggested that

[62] See *Essay on Population* (1798), as reprinted in facsimile by Macmillan for the Royal Economic Society (London, 1966), 343.

[63] This would be one of my reasons for rejecting the conclusions of Joyce Oldham Appleby on this subject, notably her belief that although Smith provided "a blueprint for a society of economically progressive, socially equal, and politically competent citizens," the same ideas were employed in Britain's class-bound society for purely technocratic, amoral purposes of optimum generation of wealth. See Appleby, *Capitalism and a New Social Order* (New York: New York University Press, 1984), 60, and 14, 50 for other comparative remarks; and D. Winch, "Economic Liberalism as Ideology: The Appleby Version," *Economic History Review* 38 (1985): 287–97.

new countries that adopted a policy of cheap land disposal were unlikely to reap the benefits of "concentration," international specialization, and, ultimately, civilization. This was Wakefield's explanation for such expedients as the American tariff, and, more important, for the survival of slavery as a means of overcoming the drawback of a labor force dispersed by ease of acquiring land. The risk was no longer premature aging so much as prolonged infantilism. Wakefield, it might be said, was invoking the Hamiltonian bogeyman as a counter to the Jeffersonian preference for agrarian independence.[64]

Wakefield's influence on British colonial policy was controversial, extensive, but short-lived. His ideas and reputation would chiefly be known to specialists in the history of colonial administration if it were not for the fact that one of his staunchest supporters was John Stuart Mill. Mill, in fact, endorsed Wakefield's land disposal policy as an illustration of an exception to the general rule of laissez-faire in book 5, "On the Influence of Government," of his *Principles of Political Economy*.[65]

JOHN STUART MILL'S SYNTHESIS

The Benthamite and Ricardian conceptions of the science of legislation meet and mingle in Mill's midcentury synthesis. His *Principles* was the first attempt since 1776 to write a comprehensive work along the lines of the *Wealth of Nations,* including a treatment equivalent to Smith's lengthy discussion of "the duties of the sovereign" with respect to defense, justice, education, and public works. A detailed comparison of the two works, concentrating on the functions assigned to government and on the grounds for so doing (or not doing), would reveal much about continuity and change during the period with which this and other chapters in this volume deal.

Mill's *Principles,* taken in conjunction with *Considerations on Representative Government* and *On Liberty,* remains a classic statement by the joint heir to Bentham and Ricardo, as well as to a host of other early nineteenth-century influences that were antagonistic to their ideas. But it is not simply as the consummate representative of philosophic radicalism in its later guise that Mill can legitimately be used as the closing point for this survey. He had participated in most of the attempts to implement the policy conclusions of Bentham and Ricardo regarding

[64]See Winch, *Classical Political Economy and Colonies,* 96–9.
[65]See book 5, chap. 11, para. 12.

government policy at home, in Ireland and India, as well as in the countries of new colonization. Apart from his daily duties as a civil servant at East India House, Mill was also heavily committed to what subsequently emerged as the Northcote-Trevelyan reforms of the British civil service along meritocratic lines.

Much of the interpretative comment on Mill has taken the form of assessments of how far, in what respects, and under what auspices Mill retained or departed from the views of his mentors.[66] It seems generally agreed that he remained a faithful Benthamite in associating "good government" with knowledgeable and efficient government. Legislation was still to be prepared by skilled shoemakers before being passed on for fitting to a democratically elected assembly. Hence Mill's enmity to the leisured aristocratic view of the legislator, his enthusiasm for meritocracy, and his antagonism to the breakup of the East India Company in 1858 and the dispersal of the expert means by which Britain had exercised the role of benevolent despot in India.

But Mill was also aware of a problem that is not readily apparent in Bentham's elaborate committee structures, with or without popular participation. On a mundane level this awareness features in Mill's appreciation of the dangers of extending centralization too far at the expense of local government. At a higher level of generality, this awareness is demonstrated in Mill's increasing concern about the possibility that the state might have an enervating influence precisely because it was more efficient, more capable of engrossing national legislative and administrative talent. That is why extension of what Mill called the "authoritative" functions of government in the *Principles* needed strong reasons and why it had to be avoided altogether in certain purely self-regarding spheres. It also explains why he regarded *any* increase of government activity as likely to endanger the "habit of spontaneous action for a collective in-

---

[66]For a sample taken from the most recent literature, see A. Ryan, "Utilitarianism and Bureaucracy: The Views of J. S. Mill," in G. Sutherland, ed., *Studies in the Growth of Nineteenth-Century Government* (London: Routledge and Kegan Paul, 1972), "Two Concepts of Politics and Democracy: James Mill and John Stuart Mill," in M. Fleisher, ed., *Machiavelli and the Nature of Political Thought* (London: Croom Helm, 1973), and *J. S. Mill* (London: Routledge and Kegan Paul, 1975); and S. Collini's criticism of the last of these in "Liberalism and the Legacy of Mill," *Historical Journal* 20 (1977): 237–54; D. F. Thompson, *John Stuart Mill and Representative Government* (Princeton, N.J.: Princeton University Press, 1976); J. H. Burns, "The Light of Reason: Philosophical History in the Two Mills," in J. M. Robson and M. Laine, eds., *James and John Stuart Mill: Papers of the Centenary Conference* (Toronto: University of Toronto Press, 1976); and B. Semmel, *John Stuart Mill and the Pursuit of Virtue* (New Haven, Conn.: Yale University Press, 1984).

terest," and therefore why he was eager to find ways in which the state could act in an advisory or regulatory fashion that left scope for collective action without further state involvement.

The acknowledged sources (by Mill and others) of this concern with potential stagnation or "Chinese stationariness," and with the preconditions for the survival and development of "individuality," were Coleridge, von Humboldt, and, above all, Tocqueville. But this concern can also be expressed, as Mill himself expressed it, in terms of the "character" of a people, and therefore as a revival of ideas that were prominent in those versions of the eighteenth-century science of the legislator that were not exclusively wedded to the *machiniste* concept. The revival was not, of course, self-conscious: it provides another example of the way in which Mill frequently attributed novelty and a Continental origin to non-Benthamite ideas which were eighteenth-century commonplaces in the work of Montesquieu, Hume, Smith, and others.[67] Tocqueville was more aware of his affinities with Montesquieu.[68]

There may be differences of tone and content between the use of the concept of character in the late eighteenth and mid-nineteenth centuries. Mill sounded a more strenuous moral note in wishing to *raise* character, free it from hidebound Victorian constraints, and generally prepare it for a higher and later role; earlier exponents would have been content with the *preservation* of character (warts and all).[69] But when Mill states that "the only security against political slavery is the check maintained over governors by the diffusion of intelligence, activity, and public spirit among the governed," and firmly ties this need to fears of "despotism," he could well be echoing one of the more enthusiastic eighteenth-century "Machiavellian moralists," Adam Ferguson.[70]

More strain could be involved in equating Mill's "necessary" and "optional," or his "authoritative" and "non-authoritative" categories for state intervention, with the earlier distinction between "perfect" and "imperfect" obligations, between "law" and "manners"; but it would not be a foolhardy exercise. Clearly, however, a tradition that accorded mutuality to relations between civil society and state was continually

---

[67] On this see Collini et al., *That Noble Science,* 132–3.
[68] See M. Richter, "The Uses of Theory: Tocqueville's Adaptation of Montesquieu," in M. Richter, ed., *Essays in Theory and History* (Cambridge, Mass.: Harvard University Press, 1970).
[69] See S. Collini, "The Idea of 'Character' in Victorian Political Thought," *Transactions of the Royal Historical Society,* 5th series, vol. 35, 1985.
[70] Mill, *Principles of Political Economy,* book 5, chap. 11, para. 6.

open to the idea of building bridges between the two realms, beginning from either side, and solving problems as much by stimulating "good offices" between the members of society as by requiring an efficient state to act authoritatively as the sole means of overcoming the deficiencies and contradictions of civil society.

Part II

Empiricism and the new liberalism

3

Experts, investigators, and the state in 1860: British social scientists through American eyes

LAWRENCE GOLDMAN

"England is the country, and this is pre-eminently the age, of social inquiries. Probably more men devote themselves without desire of reward to questions connected with the physical and moral improvement of their fellows than are induced by the richest prizes to study other departments of knowledge."[1] So judged *The Times* of London in September 1860. Six years later the *Daily Telegraph* concurred: "The distinctive feature of modern society is not so much its material triumphs as its spirit of inquiry."[2] The spirit was so strong, so prevalent, and so distinctive in Britain that it won the attention and praise of diverse foreign observers. Taine's *Notes on England*, compiled in the 1860s, made continual reference to the national preoccupation with information and investigation and drew from it a political moral: it helped form "a more enlightened public opinion on great subjects, less incompetent in political matters, more sensible, nearer the truth, more open to good counsel."[3] In other words, it helped consolidate the political pluralism and stability that Taine admired in mid-Victorian Britain when he compared it with his native France.

Even writers not otherwise noted for their admiration of British institutions made an exception when it came to this "spirit of inquiry." It is inconceivable that Marx could have written *Capital* in the form that it took without the preceding research of British social investigators, and in the preface to the first edition he duly expressed his appreciation of

---

[1] *The Times*, 26 September 1860, 8.
[2] *Daily Telegraph*, 3 October 1866, 4.
[3] Hippolyte Taine, *Notes on England* (London, 1873), 203.

"men as competent, as free from partisanship and respect of persons as are England's factory inspectors, her medical reporters on public health, her commissioners of inquiry into the exploitation of women and children, into the conditions of housing and nourishment and so on."[4] As Engels had observed in the first German edition of the *Condition of the Working Class in England* (a work based, as its subtitle explains, on "authentic sources" as well as "personal observation"), "only in England is adequate material available for an exhaustive enquiry into the condition of the proletariat."[5]

Such testimony leads to the essential point of departure for any remarks on mid-Victorian social investigation: that the sudden proliferation of information from the 1830s was, in Brian Harrison's words, an "event in its own right,"[6] deserving of historical attention. The social investigators did more than merely provide a later generation of historians with raw data. They were themselves actors in an important drama—the attempt, however piecemeal and incoherent, to understand the transformations in the first industrial society.

Recognition of this fact has produced a growing literature on social investigation and an accepted chronology of its development in which certain key texts, primarily concerned with "how the poor live," as George Sims's investigative classic of 1883 was entitled, stand out.[7] Curiously, although Marx specifically praised factory inspectors, medical reporters, and commissioners of inquiry—men employed by the state on official investigations—the literature on nineteenth-century social research has tended to concentrate on the projects of persons outside government: on Engels in Manchester, Henry Mayhew and Charles Booth in London, and Seebohm Rowntree in York. It may thus have the virtue of reminding us how much of Victorian intellectual and cultural activity was undertaken by "amateurs." But in so doing it has missed a more appropriate focus, whether judged in terms of the volume of investigative material produced or the wider influence of inquiry on government and opinion—the infamous blue books, the fruit of official investigation, and the people who compiled them.

[4]Karl Marx, *Capital,* vol. 1 (Harmondsworth, 1976), 91.
[5]F. Engels, *The Condition of the Working Class in England,* translated and edited by W. O. Henderson and W. H. Chaloner (Oxford, 1958), 3.
[6]"Finding Out How the Other Half Live: Social Research and British Government Since 1780," in Brian Harrison, *Peaceable Kingdom: Stability and Change in Modern Britain* (Oxford, 1982), 272.
[7]George R. Sims, *How the Poor Live* (London, 1883).

This is not to contend, of course, that Engels's *Condition of the Working Class in England* or Charles Booth's *Life and Labour of the People of London* are without interest, or that the research of social investigators outside government was not important. Indeed, this chapter emphasizes just how relatively well informed many of these "amateurs" were and how useful they could be to the state. Rather, it is to question the individualized image of the investigator that the existing historical literature frequently presents—an image that fails to take account of the existence of an organized investigative community in mid-Victorian Britain and makes the history of social investigation into a series of unconnected projects in different locations undertaken by different sorts of people—journalists, men of leisure, philanthropists, officials—for varied (indeed, often conflicting) reasons. This image also generally presents the investigator as a traveler in the slums, essentially concerned to describe the conditions of urban poverty and reproduce for a middle-class audience variations on *The Bitter Cry of Outcast London*.[8]

The history of social investigation conceived in this way remembers Dr. James Phillips Kay (later Sir James Kay-Shuttleworth) as the author in 1832 of *The Moral and Physical Condition of the Working Classes Employed in the Cotton Manufacture in Manchester,* a forerunner to Engels's similar study in 1844. Yet, between 1839 and 1849, Kay-Shuttleworth was also secretary to the Committee of Council for Education that was charged with establishing and supervising a team of inspectors of schools whose regular reports were extensive exercises in social and institutional research, and who frequently interpreted their role as being the provision of information on public instruction to further the campaign for a full-scale commitment from the state to elementary education.

In other words, social investigation in the nineteenth century was something more than those few celebrated poverty surveys that periodically captured public attention. In the mid-Victorian period, social investigation became a part of bureaucratic routine that was integral to the processes of constructing, implementing, and regulating social policy, and a continuing obligation on the state if legislation was to keep pace with changing social conditions. It was an integral part of the so-called nineteenth-century revolution in government—the process by which

[8]The pamphlet *The Bitter Cry of Outcast London: An Inquiry into the Condition of the Abject Poor*, published anonymously in October 1883, was written by the Reverend Andrew Mearns, secretary of the London Congregational Union.

Victorian social administration was professionalized and "the greatest political achievement of nineteenth-century Britain."[9]

It is a strength of the literature on the growth of the Victorian state that it has paid some attention to the background of, and the influences on, the great civil servants like Edwin Chadwick, John Simon, William Farr, and Kay-Shuttleworth, who led the "revolution." If discussion has been sidetracked into the sterile debate on the role of Bentham's ideas and of Benthamite lieutenants with positions in the bureaucracy, it has also yielded much information on the intellectual and social imperatives that drove Victorian administrators—information that has helped to explain how and why the "revolution" took place. Hitherto, work on the history of social investigation in Britain has tended to concentrate on the investigated rather than the investigators, on whether or not the descriptions of life in the alleys and courts of Manchester and the "rookeries" of London were accurate evocations of the realities of working-class existence at the time. Thus there may be some scope for an approach drawn from administrative history, which tries to understand Victorian social investigation by examining the milieu of the investigator; this approach can concentrate on the many inquirers who were employed or financed or activated by the state. These were the "middle class professional people" whom Paul Smith refers to; "the type," he writes, "who were in the nineteenth century the driving force of social investigation and the formulation of social policy."[10] They were the civil servants in the departments of state in London and "the factory inspectors and inspectors of schools, the chief constables of counties and the medical officers of health"[11] in the provinces, all of whom, in the course of their duties, depended on and added to the stock of accurate social research. They were drawn from the "forgotten Middle Class" of "lawyers, doctors, public officers, journalists, professors and teachers"[12] who occupy a marginal place in the written history of the Victorian period, overshadowed by the commercial and industrial bourgeoisie in its wider conflicts with the working class below and the aristocracy above. But this group's increasingly important role in an expanding bureaucracy and their rise in status to the recognized position of "experts" in Victorian society is a distinctive feature of nineteenth-century social development.

[9]H. J. Perkin, *The Origins of Modern English Society, 1780–1880* (London, 1969), 270.
[10]P. Smith, *Disraelian Conservatism and Social Reform* (London, 1967), 30.
[11]John Roach, *Social Reform in England 1780–1880* (London, 1978), 163.
[12]Perkin, *The Origins of Modern English Society*, 252.

Their expertise—a word that seems to have entered the language in the 1860s[13]—depended to a large extent on their knowledge of society, their wide experience of social problems, and their skills, particularly statistical skills, of investigation. And it may therefore prove possible to approach the history of social investigation and its interconnections with the state by examining the social milieu of the men who provided the investigative skills on which government increasingly depended—their social background, training, career structure, collective values, esprit de corps, and political outlook.

THE MILIEU OF MID-VICTORIAN SOCIAL INVESTIGATION

A fitting point of departure for an investigation of the investigators is the picture of them preserved in the private records of a trip to Britain in 1860 undertaken by Dr. Edward Jarvis of Dorchester, Massachusetts. Jarvis, born in Concord, Massachusetts, in 1803 and educated at Harvard (1822–6) was, by midcentury, in the words of his recent biographer, "a figure of considerable eminence. He ranked among the leading three or four American psychiatrists of the period." He was

a contributor to and publicist for the young public health movement; he helped lay the foundations of the modern federal census as a source of data and an instrument of policy; he stimulated the movement to preserve vital statistics in order to shed light on the conditions of health and disease; and he wrote extensively on social and medical issues.[14]

Jarvis was a consultant to the federal censuses of 1850, 1860, and 1870, and his *Report on Insanity and Idiocy in Massachusetts* in 1855 was one of the most sophisticated social surveys of the century.[15] Moreover, as President of the American Statistical Association, founded in imitation of the Statistical Society of London, between 1852 and 1884, he was "one of the best known members of a growing scientific and scholarly community" in the United States.[16] Such intellectual and professional engagements are analogous to those of the statisticians, physicians, and sanitarians who led the public health and statistical movements in mid-Victorian Britain. Jarvis was familiar with British writings on social med-

---

[13]Donald Read, *England 1868–1914* (London, 1979), 133.
[14]Gerald N. Grob, *Edward Jarvis and the Medical World of Nineteenth Century America* (Knoxville, 1978), 7.
[15]*Report on Insanity and Idiocy in Massachusetts, by the Commission on Lunacy, Under Resolve of the Legislature of 1854*, Massachusetts House Document 144, 1 March 1855.
[16]Grob, *Edward Jarvis*, 107.

icine.[17] He organized an exchange of books and periodicals with the Statistical Society of London,[18] and he began corresponding with two of the most important investigator-bureaucrats, Farr and Chadwick, in 1850 and 1853, respectively.[19]

In 1860 when Jarvis spent five months in Britain, he delighted in the exchange of views with fellow investigators who shared his interest and outlook. Ostensibly accompanying an American merchant taking the water-cure at Malvern in Worcestershire, Jarvis arrived in Liverpool on 20 March 1860 and engaged in what may be termed a professional tour of Britain. He visited government departments, learned societies, asylums, hospitals, prisons, schools—institutions of all sorts—exchanging views and information and making new intellectual contacts. He was at home in the world of political economists, statisticians, sanitarians, educationalists—the new experts of mid-Victorian society. Feted by his peers, Jarvis discovered the extent of his eminence on the other side of the Atlantic. He wrote to his wife:

I have been the especial subject of interest and kindness from the men who were engaged in the three great matters that have occupied me most—insanity, mortality and statistics. I found that I was known to them in advance and they received me as an old friend, as one with whom they had before communed freely, and whose principles and life, whose wishes and sympathies, they understood and knew how to meet and were desirous to gratify.[20]

The tour climaxed at the Fourth International Statistical Congress in London in July 1860. The idea for such periodic meetings to link together an international community of investigators had taken shape in London during the Great Exhibition of 1851, and the first congress was held in Brussels two years later. In all, nine meetings were organized in European

[17]See his lengthy review article on the British public health movement, "Sanitary Reform," *American Journal of Medical Sciences* 15 (April 1848): 419–50.

[18]Jarvis to Edward Cheshire, assistant secretary of the Statistical Society of London, 5 May 1854, Jarvis Collection, Letterbooks, vol. 3, B. Ms. b. 56. 4.3 fol. 224–6, Francis A. Countway Library of Medicine, Harvard Medical School, Boston, Massachusetts.

[19]Jarvis to William Farr, 10 June 1850, Jarvis Collection, Countway Library, B. Ms. b. 56. 4.1 fol. 133–4; and Jarvis to Edwin Chadwick, 10 June 1853, Jarvis Collection, Countway Library, B. Ms. b. 56. 4.3 fol. 15–20.

[20]Edward Jarvis to Almira Jarvis, 11 August 1860, Edward Jarvis Papers, European Letters, vol. iii, fol. 289, Concord Public Library, Concord, Massachusetts. The three volumes of "European Letters" are transcriptions of all Jarvis's letters sent to his wife during the five months in Europe. Written almost daily, they present a detailed record of all his personal and professional experiences. See, in addition, the section devoted to Jarvis's visit to Britain in his manuscript autobiography held in the Houghton Library, Harvard University, Ms. Am. 541, pp. 253–321. This appears to have been written in late 1873.

capitals between 1853 and 1876, each under official government auspices. Among the first international conferences concerned with a single discipline—in this case, social statistics—the congresses promoted official statistical research, the claims of investigative experts to government employment, and the international standardization of categories and procedures of analysis.[21]

In London in 1860 the week-long congress divided into sections concerned with judicial, sanitary, industrial, and commercial statistics; the census; and statistical methods. Here Jarvis met with "scientific men, statisticians, philanthropists and political economists" to discuss questions of "sickness, insanity, mortality, crime, pauperism, population, business, finance, agriculture—all the interests of humanity came under their review."[22] The International Statistical Congress, spanning the years of the great mid-Victorian economic boom, fittingly exemplified the great confidence of the period in the reformative power of scientific method allied to numbers.

Jarvis, who delivered three papers,[23] considered the congress, as he told William Farr, "the crowning pleasure of my European visit."[24] He met the earl of Shaftesbury, who presided over the sanitary section of the congress;[25] Lord Ebrington, a prominent member of the influential Health of Towns Association during the 1840s, who invited him "to a party at his house where was a large collection of sanitarians";[26] Matthew Davenport Hill, the judicial reformer, with whom he discussed "the means of repressing crime";[27] and Charles Babbage, the Cambridge mathematician famous for the construction of a mechanical "calculating en-

[21]On the International Statistical Congress, see Harald Westergaard, *Contributions to the History of Statistics* (London, 1932), chap. 14; T. N. Clark, *Prophets and Patrons: The French University and the Emergence of the Social Sciences* (Cambridge, Mass., 1973), 133–4.

[22]Jarvis, Autobiography, Houghton Library, Harvard University, 295–6. For a full record of the London Congress compiled by William Farr, secretary to the meeting, see *Report of the Proceedings of the Fourth Section of the International Statistical Congress, Held in London, July 16, 1860 and the Five Following Days* (London, 1861).

[23]"On the Laws and Practice of Registration in America"; "On the Crimes of Males and Females"; "On the Further Inquiry in the Census as to the Personal Health and Power of Each Person." For all his contributions, see ibid., 51–5; 176; 264–7; 271–2; 277–83; 446–7; 497–9.

[24]Jarvis to Farr, 25 November 1860, Jarvis Letterbooks, Countway Library, B. Ms. b. 56. 4.6. fol. 141–4.

[25]Jarvis, Autobiography, 306.

[26]Jarvis, European Letters, iii, fol. 192, 22 July 1860.

[27]Ibid., iii, fol. 180, 19 July 1860; and Jarvis, Autobiography, 302.

gine"—the first computer—and a founder of the Statistical Society of London.[28] Jarvis discussed Anglo-American cooperation with Prince Albert, president of the congress, at Buckingham Palace,[29] and at "the grand party at Lord Palmerston's" at Cambridge House to which "all the Congress were invited," Shaftesbury introduced Jarvis to the prime minister.[30]

When in London, Jarvis at various times visited the General Register Office, the Poor Law Commissioners, and the Office of the Commission on Lunacy.[31] At the Privy Council Medical Office, the center of the rudimentary public health bureaucracy, "Dr. Simon, the head, received me as others had, seemed glad to talk with me" and "offered me all the reports of the office."[32] On three occasions Jarvis breakfasted at the home of Florence Nightingale, where he sat with "the elite of the philanthropists, the men of higher culture of England and of Europe."[33] He frequented the offices of the Statistical Society of London in St. James's Square and dined with the society's council. At one of their meetings he first met in person Chadwick, Farr, and the statistician and economist William Newmarch.[34] And he was encouraged by Newmarch to compose the paper "On the System of Taxation Prevailing in the United States and Especially in Massachusetts," which was delivered to the Statistical Section, Section F, of the 1860 meeting of the British Association for the Advancement of Science at Oxford.[35]

Jarvis also met with the founder and president of the British Medical Association, Sir Charles Hastings.[36] He spent considerable time with Sir Charles's son George Woodyatt Hastings, who was the secretary and organizer of the Social Science Association, founded in 1857 to bring together all the new specialists on social questions into a single organization promoting the new synthesis of "social science."[37] And Jarvis twice visited Lord Brougham, president of the new and celebrated association

---

[28]Jarvis, European Letters, iii, fol. 196, 22 July 1860.
[29]Jarvis, Autobiography, 297–8.
[30]Jarvis, European Letters, iii, fol. 203, 23 July 1860.
[31]Jarvis, Autobiography, 275, 300.
[32]Jarvis, European Letters, iii, fol. 76, 22 June 1860.
[33]Ibid., iii, fol. 209, 28 July 1860.
[34]Jarvis, Autobiography, 277–9; Jarvis, European Letters, iii, fol. 55–6, 22 June 1860. Chadwick "was very cordial and from that time forth treated Dr J. like a brother, and seemed to feel as if he were responsible for his comfort and happiness in England."
[35]The paper was published soon afterward in the *Journal of the Statistical Society of London* 23 (September 1860): 370–8.
[36]Jarvis, Autobiography, 263; Jarvis, European Letters, i, fol. 260–1, 11 April 1860.
[37]Jarvis, Autobiography, 312; Jarvis, European Letters, iii, fol. 133, 5 July 1860.

and a living embodiment of an earlier period of social reform.[38] Impressed by what he had seen and heard of the Social Science Association in its role as a central clearinghouse for social research and the discussion of social policy in Britain, Jarvis returned home enthusiastic about the idea of an American Social Science Association.

FEATURES OF THE COMMUNITY OF EXPERTS

In the summer of 1860, therefore, Dr. Edward Jarvis was the guest of the British social science community—a community he described at length as a distinct intellectual and administrative elite. His letters and diaries are a prolonged exposition of the influence, sophistication, and professionalism of this community, whose high profile and acknowledged place in national life so impressed him. His effort to organize an American Social Science Association after the Civil War was an attempt to foster a similar community in the United States. And as chairman of the Committee of Arrangements, he presented the motion in the State House in Boston on 4 October 1865 that brought ASSA into being.[39]

Certainly the statisticians and "social scientists" in mid-Victorian Britain met some of the criteria enumerated by sociologists of science to define mature intellectual disciplines: journals for publication, regular meetings, a place in the public eye, a publicly recognized function, and a place in a wider international community of scholars and practitioners. And to complement their more specialized publications and societies they could rely on a large middle-class constituency; hundreds attended meetings of the Social Science Association and thousands subscribed to popularizing journals like *Meliora*, which discussed questions of public health, moral reform, temperance, and statistical investigation.[40]

Certain features of this community stand out in Jarvis's narrative and deserve closer scrutiny. A first feature concerns the central role played

[38]Jarvis, Autobiography, 291; Jarvis, European Letters, iii, fol. 132, 5 July 1860; fol. 145, 8 July 1860.
[39]Lawrence Goldman, "The Social Science Association, 1857–1886: A Context for Mid-Victorian Liberalism," *The English Historical Review*: 1 (1986) 95–134. On the founding of ASSA and its connections with the Social Science Association in Britain, see Lawrence Goldman, "A Peculiarity of the English? The Social Science Association and the Absence of Sociology in Nineteenth Century Britain," *Past and Present* 114 (February 1987): 133–71.
[40]*Meliora: A Quarterly Review of Social Science in Its Ethical, Economical, Political, and Ameliorative Aspects* was published quarterly in twelve volumes between 1858 and 1869.

by a few learned forums in intellectual interchange; in chronological order these were the Statistical Section of the British Association, which was founded in 1833; the Statistical Society of London, which dated from the following year and was one of several statistical societies organized in British cities in the 1830s;[41] the Social Science Association, which was active between 1857 and 1886; and the more specialized organizations that attracted practitioners from a single discipline—for example, the British Association of Medical Superintendents of Insane Asylums, whose conference Jarvis attended in June 1860.[42]

A second notable feature was the role played by the professions in this investigative and administrative community. Lawyers and physicians are the most noticeable groups, but Jarvis also met with civil engineers, medical officers of health, specialists in the treatment of the insane, actuaries—experts in new areas who were in the process of "professionalization" during the mid-Victorian period. Of the list of eighteen key civil servants active from the 1830s to the 1860s, who were singled out by Lord McGregor in 1957 as collectively composing the "greatest range of masterful talent ever assembled in the public service" in Britain,[43] six were barristers (James Booth of the Board of Trade, Tom Taylor of the Home Office, Sir James Stephen and Herman Merivale of the Colonial Office, H. S. Tremenheere of the education and mines' inspectorates, and the ubiquitous Chadwick) and five were physicians (Thomas Southwood Smith, Neil Arnott, James Kay-Shuttleworth, William Farr, and John Simon).[44] The legal knowledge and the analytical skills of lawyers had obvious relevance to administration and investigation. The part played by medical men in all aspects of Victorian social reform also is not hard to explain. The medical profession had a long tradition of local investigation connected with efforts to improve the conditions of the poor. Physicians, especially those affiliated with dispensaries, were frequently the first professional people to gain extensive and direct experience of the lives of the poorest classes of the cities. And from the late eighteenth

[41]On the origins of the "statistical movement" in the 1830s, see Lawrence Goldman, "The Origins of British Social Science: Political Economy, Natural Science and Statistics, 1830–1835," *Historical Journal*, 26, no.3 (1983): 586–616.
[42]Jarvis, Autobiography, 287–8.
[43]O. R. McGregor, "Social Research and Social Policy in the Nineteenth Century," *British Journal of Sociology* 8 (1957): 150.
[44]The remaining seven outstanding civil servants were James Deacon Hume and G. R. Porter of the Board of Trade; Sir Henry Cole of the Science and Art Department; Frederic Hill, the prisons inspector; Rowland Hill, his brother, from the General Post Office; Henry Taylor of the Colonial Office; and Arthur Helps, clerk to the Privy Council.

century the incidence of fever in the poorest areas encouraged local surveys and attempts at control on the part of individual doctors and ad hoc, voluntary "boards of health."[45]

For example, James Phillips Kay, on leaving Edinburgh University in 1827, settled in Manchester and became medical officer of the Ancoats and Ardwick Dispensary in a poor, overcrowded district of the city. During the cholera epidemic of 1832 he served as secretary of the local Board of Health and took part in its survey of the extent and spread of the disease. This direct, professional experience of the slums—quite different in motivation from the journalistic forays of later investigators—gave rise to his study *The Moral and Physical Condition of the Working Classes.*[46]

In other words, and as Jarvis's career in the United States also demonstrates, physicians had more than merely medical skills. They also had access to data—"vital statistics"—that were reliable, verifiable, and profuse; thus they took a large part in the "statistical movement" of the 1830s and 1840s, which was above all else committed to the reform of public health.[47] In addition, with access to information and experience in using it, they not only came to dominate reformist institutions of all sorts but also found their way into a bureaucracy otherwise lacking in such skills.

A third feature that stands out in Jarvis's descriptions is the lack of any clear division between governmental and extragovernmental research, between "professionals" in the employ of the state and "amateurs" inquiring for themselves—a state of affairs different from that at the end of the nineteenth century. Jarvis met William Farr at the General Register Office where he was "Compiler of Abstracts"; he also met him at the International Statistical Congress and the Statistical Society of London, where men like Farr had perfect freedom to express their opinions, present their data, combine with others in investigation, and at the same time take back to Whitehall the results and ideas of other members of the social science community.

Amateur research was never irrelevant or insignificant. In various fields, indeed, it clearly surpassed the inquiries of the state, as three

[45]J. M. Eyler, *Victorian Social Medicine: The Ideas and Methods of William Farr* (Baltimore, 1979), 30.
[46]Frank Smith, *The Life and Work of Sir James Kay-Shuttleworth* (London, 1923), 20–8.
[47]See M. J. Cullen, *The Statistical Movement in Early Victorian Britain: The Foundation of Empirical Research* (Hassocks, 1975).

examples drawn from the history of the Social Science Association suggest. The detail on the provision of local sanitary facilities across the
country, which was presented in two papers delivered to the association
in 1866 by Edward Jenkins, a barrister and member of Parliament, and
a physician, Alexander Stewart, and which was republished as *The Medical and Legal Aspects of Sanitary Reform,* was far in advance of anything
an embarrassed government could provide.[48] In fact, Stewart related that
he had applied to the Conservative Home Secretary, Gathorne-Hardy,
for official figures on the number of medical officers and nuisance inspectors, among other things, and was told that such information not
only was unavailable but could not be obtained by the rudimentary public
health bureaucracy: "that the Government could not get such a return;
that, in the second place, if it were possible to get it, it would be so
inaccurate as to be wholly worthless; that, in the third place, it would
be enormously voluminous; and that, in the fourth place, it would be
immensely costly."[49] Similarly, the Webbs later adjudged the association's
extensive investigation of trade unions in Britain, published in 1860 as
Trades' Societies and Strikes, as "the best collection of Trade Union
material and the most impartial account of Trade Union action that has
ever been issued," and "as a source of history and economic illustration
... far superior to the Parliamentary Blue Books of 1824, 1825, 1838
and 1867–68."[50] And the SSA's Quarantine Committee, established in
1858 to review British regulations and procedures in comparison with
those of other nations, had its research, reports, and recommendations
published as official parliamentary returns in recognition of the services
of an eminent group of investigators on an important subject.[51]

In each of these cases the association, exploiting its many links with
government, was acting more as an unofficial arm of the state than as

[48]Edward Jenkins, M.P., "The Legal Aspect of Sanitary Reform"; Alexander P. Stewart,
M.D., "On the Results of Permissive Sanitary Legislation; or the Medical Aspects of the
Laws Relating to the Public Health," *Transactions of the National Association for the
Promotion of Social Science* [hereafter *Transactions*] (1866), 478–94, 494–569; see
M. W. Flinn, ed., *The Medical and Legal Aspects of Sanitary Reform* (Leicester, 1969).
[49]See Henry W. Rumsey, *On State Medicine in Great Britain and Ireland* (London, 1867),
50; Royston Lambert, *Sir John Simon and English Social Administration* (London, 1963),
399n.
[50]Sidney and Beatrice Webb, *The History of Trade Unionism* (London, 1920 ed.),
227–8n.
[51]See "Abstract of Regulations in Force in Foreign Countries Respecting Quarantine, Communicated by the Board of Trade," *Parliamentary Papers* [hereafter *P.P.*], 1860, 60: 155–
385. "Papers Relating to Quarantine, Communicated to the Board of Trade on the 30th
Day of July 1861," *P.P.*, 1861, 58: 225–92.

an independent research agency. The Quarantine Committee included a number of physicians in government service in the armed forces, as well as three members of Parliament and William Farr and Southwood Smith from the central bureaucracy. It was also able to use the good offices of the earl of Shaftesbury and W. F. Cowper, M.P., to bring "the subject at first under the favourable attention of the Foreign and Colonial Ministers of the Crown, and afterwards before the House of Commons."[52] The Committee on Trades' Societies and Strikes included ten past, present, or future Liberal members of Parliament, among them W. E. Forster, Henry Fawcett, Thomas Hughes, and George Shaw-Lefevre, as well as the ever active Farr, Kay Shuttleworth, and Horace Mann from the civil service.[53] And even Stewart and Jenkins began their research by direct inquiry to the home secretary of the day.

The picture presented by these examples and Jarvis's narrative is of a community of experts, some inside and some outside Parliament and the bureaucracy, whose official positions (or lack of them) presented no barrier to their use by government or learned societies for investigation and recommendation. These experts, in effect, formed an unofficial civil service that could be used and co-opted by the state when the necessary expertise inside government was lacking.

The pattern was consistent throughout the 1830–70 period. Cullen, in his study of the statistical movement in early Victorian Britain, has identified a "charmed circle of the Whig-Liberal intelligentsia who were to dominate the parliamentary enquiries and statistical investigations of the 1830s"[54]—men outside government who took temporary positions inside it; men like Joseph Fletcher, a barrister, secretary of the Statistical Society of London, and first editor of its journal, who served as secretary to the Royal Commissions of Inquiry into the handloom weavers and the employment of children, and as an inspector of schools. Philip Abrams saw the Council of the Statistical Society of London in its early years as "a subcommittee of a Whig cabinet,"[55] an external forum where politicians could benefit from contact with experts. Thus Lord Lansdowne

---

[52]*P.P.*, 1861, 58: 234–5.
[53]The full committee is listed in *Trades' Societies and Strikes: Report of the Committee on Trades' Societies, Appointed by the National Association for the Promotion of Social Science, Presented at the Fourth Annual Meeting of the Association at Glasgow, Sept 1860* (London, 1860), iv.
[54]Cullen, *The Statistical Movement*, 21.
[55]Philip Abrams, *The Origins of British Sociology 1834–1914* (Chicago and London, 1968), 15.

(the then lord president of the council) chaired, and Thomas Spring Rice (chancellor of the exchequer from 1835 to 1839) attended, the society's inaugural meeting. The existence of a unitary social science community such as this has important implications for the historian of mid-Victorian social investigation and administration. It makes the study of expert forums like the statistical societies and the Social Science Association indispensable if the processes by which investigations were pursued and social policies made are to be understood, because to a large extent they were pursued and made by members of these organizations acting as, or in alliance with, the agents of the state.

MODUS OPERANDI OF THE STATESMEN IN DISGUISE

Research in the history of social policy has pointed to the crucial position in this social science community of the so-called statesmen in disguise[56]— those few outstanding officials who for three or four decades after the Great Reform Act used the latitude that a haphazardly developing system of government gave them to initiate, restructure, and reform without reference to their nominal political masters. A fourth feature of Jarvis's narrative is his contact with such men—with Chadwick, whose official career ended six years before Jarvis met him, and with Farr and Simon who in 1860 were at their most creative and influential. Chadwick's machinations on the Factory Commission of 1833, the Poor Law Commission of 1834, the Police Commission of 1839, and the Health of Towns Commission of 1844 (the list could be much extended) are so well-known as to require little comment.[57] In the General Register Office, Farr turned the Annual Reports of the Registrar General into "the vehicle for the expression of passionately held personal views, for propaganda directed against the opponents of public health reform, and for agitation for state intervention in a new field to a degree" that, as Michael Flinn puts it, "would send cold shivers down the spine of a modern civil servant."[58]

As for Simon, he "had no qualms at all about identifying himself with overt pressure groups, chairing their meetings, delivering papers, discussing government policy." He "even sometimes amended his own of-

[56]See G. Kitson Clark, " 'Statesmen in Disguise': Reflexions on the History of the Neutrality of the Civil Service," *Historical Journal* 2 (1959): 19–39.
[57]S. E. Finer, *The Life and Times of Sir Edwin Chadwick* (London, 1952).
[58]Edwin Chadwick, *Report on the Sanitary Condition of the Labouring Population of Great Britain* (1842), edited by M. W. Flinn, introduction, 28.

ficial circulars and projected legislative reform with their aid."[59] Simon's
relations with the Social Science Association are instructive in this respect.
Simon was present at the private meeting in July 1857 at Brougham's
house in London where the association was founded and attended its
first congress in Birmingham a few months later.[60] In 1859–60 he served
on one of its committees which inquired into the system of registration
of disease, and in 1862 he chaired an important session of its triumphant
congress in London where one of his medical protégés, E. H. Greenhow,
drawn from the array of talented young physicians he employed in pioneering sociomedical research, led the discussion on the relationship
between occupation and health.[61] Simon brought the association prestige,
the commitment of the medical profession, and a place in the framing
of central health policy which the Social Science Association, in alliance
with the British Medical Association, exploited to the full. In return, the
association deployed its full political influence in Parliament to lay secure
foundations for his official position. In 1858 and 1859, when the continuation of the medical officership—his position—was in some doubt,
SSA sponsored resolutions, deputations, and memorials in his favor and
engaged such imposing political figures as Lords Russell, Shaftesbury,
and Stanley—all of whom were members of the association—to intercede
on his behalf. And there is no doubt that Simon helped orchestrate the
successful campaign.[62]

Senior civil servants did not simply seize opportunities as they arose.
Given the vicissitudes of public opinion, the fact that formal party politics
had not yet begun to concern itself with social policy, and the institutionalized resistance to any extension of government control (by which
is meant not just the ideology of laissez-faire, but also the obstructive
power of vested interests and the sheer incompetence of local officials),
then, in a sense, the responsibility for innovation and initiative could
only rest with the expert in government, who became, sometimes by
default, a "statesman in disguise." Of course, there were legitimate means
by which civil servants could influence policy, but far more important

---

[59]Lambert, *Sir John Simon*, 300.
[60]J. L. Clifford-Smith, *A Manual for the Congress with a Narrative of Past Labours and
Results* (London, 1882), 3.
[61]E. H. Greenhow, M.D., "On the Effect of Occupation on Health," *Transactions* (1862):
670–4.
[62]*Transactions* (1858), xxix–xxx; (1859), xxviii–xxx; (1861) xxxviii; G. W. Hastings to
Edward Henry, Lord Stanley, 13 July 1859, Derby Papers, Nonofficial Correspondence,
Liverpool Record Office. See also Lambert, *Sir John Simon*, 272–5.

were the covert operations—in Richard Johnson's words, "the Chadwick-Simon-Trevelyan-Porter-Hill modus operandi."[63] This modus operandi was possible for two reasons: first, because at this stage there were no developed conventions and codes of conduct that muzzled civil servants in public and ensured that they really did *serve* ministers;[64] second, because many civil servants were not under effective political control.

This was a period of slow movement toward the modern doctrine of ministerial accountability; "when new functions were needed, governments continued for some time to create departments in which there was no minister to take responsibility"[65] or in which responsibility was shared by a number of putative heads. The Poor Law Commission lacked a ministerial chief until 1847; this situation was something of a mixed blessing for such a controversial authority in need of a parliamentary spokesman to defend its corner. Similarly, responsibility for the Committee of Council on Education was divided among the various ministers who were its members. Between 1830 and 1870 the practice and theory governing the behavior of ministers and their civil servants had not been decided, and in such circumstances "statesmen in disguise" had institutional room for maneuver.

And being the men they were, they used it. A feature of Jarvis's account of the investigative community in 1860 is his description of the personal qualities of the leading experts in government:

All these men's comprehensions are broad, and their hearts are warm in their work. They take large views of the interests entrusted to their supervision and they bring great intellectual power and deep philosophy to their work. They are generous and helpful, and aim not only to relieve the present evils, but find and spread such light and influence as will diminish the measure of sickness, insanity, pauperism and crime.[66]

This is hardly a description of the style and motivation of the modern civil servant, and it points to an important aspect of Jarvis's visit—the date. When Jarvis saw the community of experts in 1860, they were perhaps at the height of their influence in the nineteenth century.

Administrative historians have tended to divide the century into three

[63]Richard Johnson, "Administrators in Education before 1870: Patronage, Social Position and Role," in Gillian Sutherland, ed., *Studies in the Growth of Nineteenth Century Government* (London, 1972), 133.

[64]Sir Norman Chester, *The English Administrative System, 1780–1870* (Oxford, 1981), 316–20.

[65]Kitson-Clark, "Statesmen in Disguise," 144.

[66]Jarvis, Autobiography, 276–7.

periods. The first, up to 1830, depicts Britain as a type of ancien regime, although administrative change had been under way since the "economical reformers" of the 1780s, and the eighteenth-century state was never so ineffective and inefficient as nineteenth-century historians have generally supposed. The third period, from the 1870s, is characterized by the relatively swift development of a professional bureaucracy and the resolution of all remaining questions concerning official conduct, propriety, and status so as to severely restrict the scope for initiative. In this period the experts gave way to men who brought no previous training and experience to the job save their Oxbridge degree; who claimed no special competence save the critical facilities instilled by first-class honors in classics; and who were not to be innovators, creating an administrative machine and extending the regulatory functions of the state, but were to administer an already established bureaucracy. A clear differentiation emerged between, in Richard Johnson's terms, "the policy maker/politician" on one side and the "administrator/civil servant" on the other.[67]

Between these two periods, however, came a lengthy interval of transition in which information was amassed, new social policies were introduced, government grew, and the state needed outside expertise to deal with all of these changes but lacked the institutional means to control the experts once they had been co-opted into government. The patronage system was used creatively to bring into Whitehall the very best talent— "it was rare for the permanent head of a department to have started his career as a junior clerk"[68]—and this elite group of officials, once established, used their influence to bring into subordinate positions as many like-minded men—physicians, statisticians, Benthamites—as they could.[69]

This is not to argue that external expertise played no role at all in government in the late nineteenth century: Roger Davidson's study of the Labour Department of the Board of Trade has shown how Llewellyn Smith as commissioner of labor engaged some exceptional specialists from outside the civil service.[70] But it is generally accepted that the status

---

[67] Johnson, "Administrators in Education," 131. Johnson's article is the clearest presentation of this tripartite chronological division.
[68] Chester, *The English Administrative System*, 310–11. On the imaginative use of ministerial patronage, see also Johnson, "Administrators in Education," 113–14.
[69] For an example of Kay-Shuttleworth's use of such influence, see Johnson, "Administrators in Education," 117. On the Benthamites' use of patronage in the civil service see S. E. Finer, "The Transmission of Benthamite Ideas, 1820–50," in Sutherland, ed., *Studies in the Growth of Nineteenth Century Government*, 29.
[70] Roger Davidson, "Llewellyn Smith: The Labour Department and Government Growth,

of the expert declined as that of the permanent official rose in the 1880s and 1890s.[71] The Webbs had to develop a strategy for influencing government, and they coined a new term, *permeation,* to describe it: a half-century before, the state had been far more effectively "permeated" by the sort of men whom Jarvis met on his visit and whose characteristics— notably energy and commitment—so impressed him.

THE ANOMALOUS POSITION OF EXPERTS

Jarvis presents an overall picture of a confident, organized, and powerful community of experts in 1860. Was he correct? There is no doubt that the community as he described it existed, that it had influence, and that it had gained a measure of social recognition. But some qualifications are in order. The first is its transitory nature. As the institutional context in which the community functioned changed, it lost its coherence and its foothold in government. Had Jarvis returned to Britain in the year of his death, the year in which the Social Science Association held its last congress, 1884, he would have had greater difficulty in identifying, let alone securing access to, the dominant policy-making experts.

A second qualification follows from Jarvis's nationality and the particular task he set himself as an American. Given his long-standing intellectual links with Britain and Europe, he conceived his role as the disseminator of the new social scientific wisdom of the Old World in the United States. He identified strongly with the British community of experts he describes, and he sought to develop a similar community on the other side of the Atlantic. He was active in the American Statistical Association and the Sanitary Association that was established in Boston in the late 1850s, and he helped create the American Social Science Association. But all to no avail. The Statistical Association "enlisted but few"; the Sanitary Association "had not much vigour"; and the American Social Science Association, eight years after its foundation, had "a very doubtful title to life" ("The subjects have not attracted the attention of

1886–1909," in Sutherland, ed., *Studies in the Growth of Nineteenth Century Government,* 245.

[71]Emmeline W. Cohen, *The Growth of the British Civil Service, 1780–1939* (London, 1941), 206. Gillian Sutherland, "Administrators in Education After 1870: Patronage, Professionalism and Expertise," in Sutherland, ed., *Studies in the Growth of Nineteenth Century Government,* 264.

the American people as they do that of the people of Britain").[72] Although ASSA revived in the late 1870s, it was never as influential as its British prototype.[73] All three societies fell short of the hopes of their promoters because, as Jarvis judged, "the anthropological questions which employ much attention in Europe, do not find a similar response here.... Our people are as humane and as intelligent as those of Great Britain, but they do not manifest these elements of their character in this way."[74]

Such judgments were, of course, premature. America was not so different, just a little behind the first industrial nation. Had a man similar to Jarvis made a similar visit to Britain thirty or forty years later, he might well have considered that the explosion of interest in sociology and social investigation allied with the new politics of progressivism and urban reform in America gave his own country the intellectual and practical edge. But in 1860, a society consumed for a generation with the issue of slavery and with questions of moral and individual perfectionism might indeed have looked somewhat backward to a man like Jarvis. In the United States he was isolated; in Britain he was among friends and colleagues. As he noted, "These Lunacy Commissioners and the statistical men and the sanitary men and some others seem to take upon themselves the responsibility of making me comfortable and having me obtain what I want."[75] The difference inevitably promoted an uncritical posture.

Amid the praise and the genuine excitement that Jarvis communicates, there is one significant omission—reference to, and analysis of, the relations between the experts and the politicians, between the professional middle class that had been brought into government and the traditional ruling class that still held power in mid-Victorian Britain. When he went to the prime minister's party for the participants in the International Statistical Congress, Jarvis believed he saw "nobles, ministers, men of high degree, ladies noble and great, in their grandest attire"[76] mixing easily with the statisticians. But Benjamin Disraeli, who was also present

---

[72]Jarvis, Autobiography, 238–42. As Jarvis wrote to the secretary of the British Social Science Association in February 1869, "We have an Association on the plan of yours, and we are making some progress, but we fall far short of your success. We have not, as you have, enlisted the best minds of our men of power and influence to cooperate with us." *Sessional Proceedings of the National Association for the Promotion of Social Science* (London) [hereafter *Sessional Proceedings*], 1868–9, 360.
[73]Goldman, "A Peculiarity of the English?" 154–61.
[74]Jarvis, Autobiography, 243–4.
[75]Jarvis, European Letters, iii, fol. M8, 18 July 1860.
[76]Jarvis, European Letters, iii, fol. 202–3, 23 July 1860.

on this occasion, recorded a somewhat different perception. In his view, Lady Palmerston's

crowded salons at Cambridge House were fuller ever than usual, for she had invited all the deputies of the Statistical Congress, a body of men who, for their hideousness, the ladies declare, were never equalled: I confess myself to a strange gathering of men with bald heads, and all wearing spectacles. You associate these traits often with learning and profundity but when one sees one hundred bald heads and one hundred pairs of spectacles, the illusion, or effect is impaired.[77]

This is more than an amusing anecdote. The cruel wit tinged with social snobbery of a man who had recently been chancellor of the Exchequer and thus was very close to the top of the "greasy pole" of politics in 1860 was undoubtedly representative: many Victorian politicians expressed similar distaste for specialists on whose skills they increasingly relied.

Disraeli's comment thus brings into focus the outstanding issue that troubled the investigative community in the mid-nineteenth century (an issue that Jarvis never perceived)—the seemingly vain quest for political recognition of their expertise. The issue was encapsulated by Lord John Russell at the Social Science Congress in Liverpool in 1858 in referring to penal policy: "We may surely presume that the country will always furnish men of ability and energy competent to such a task; it must be left to our responsible rulers to make their ability and energy a title for employment."[78] The skills existed; the question was whether a landed ruling class would recognize the claims to office and preferment of an aspiring administrative class.

Russell himself was something of an exception. Continuously concerned with social questions throughout a long political career, he paid tribute at Liverpool in 1858 to men "who in their several capacities of lawyers, political economists and physicians, have patiently inquired into these subjects, have at a great sacrifice of time (and in the case of the medical profession at a great risk of life and health also) devoted themselves to the improvement of their fellow-creatures."[79]

First as home secretary and then as prime minister, Russell built up an exemplary relationship with Kay-Shuttleworth. According to Matthew Arnold, "Statesmen like Lord Lansdowne and Lord Russell appreciated (Kay-Shuttleworth) justly; they followed his suggestions, and founded

---

[77]Disraeli to Mrs. Brydges Williams, cited in J. Bonar and H. W. Macrosty, *Annals of the Royal Statistical Society, 1834–1934* (London, 1934), 86.
[78]*Transactions* (1858), 15.
[79]*The Times*, 13 October 1858, 12.

upon them the public education of the people of this country."[80] For his part, Kay-Shuttleworth made no secret of his admiration for Russell—a political master infinitely preferable to Peel's home secretary, Sir James Graham[81]—and referred to him in retirement as "that great little man."[82] But this situation was exceptional, not least because on Russell's recommendation, Kay-Shuttleworth had received a knighthood on his retirement in recognition of his services to the state.[83] Others were not so lucky. Simon resigned in despair in 1876, believing that the influence of the Poor Law bureaucracy would set back improvement of the public's health for at least a generation. Chadwick's official career was destroyed in 1854 by an unholy parliamentary alliance of metropolitan radicals, rural anticentrists, and the representatives of vested interests who voted down the General Board of Health. Although Simon was knighted in 1889, the honor came only a year before he died and long after his services to the state had been forgotten.[84] And William Farr was never given the promotion—to registrar general—he wanted and deserved; consequently, he left the General Register Office in January 1880 "in bitter disappointment." When Sir Brydges Henniker, "an ex-captain of the Royal Horse Guards, a brother-in-law of a cabinet member," who possessed neither medical nor statistical qualifications,[85] was appointed instead of Farr, the affair became a cause célèbre in which the medical profession, as one, made loud and sustained protest at what they took as another in a series of political snubs for physicians, but to no avail. As these examples suggest, it was by no means uncommon for an expert to end his career in obscurity and frustration.

Richard Johnson has pointed to the anomalous position of the expert in a society in which only birth and the possession of land conferred power and status. The expert generally held no property but depended instead on "particular knowledge, particular skills, a particular sense of commitment" as his title to employment; these qualities, because they are so alien to aristocratic politics, have always been suspect in British public life.[86] Expertise was needed but distrusted. When Chadwick was

[80]Quoted in Smith, *Sir James Kay-Shuttleworth*, 319.
[81]See the letter of delight that Kay-Shuttleworth sent to Russell when, in December 1845, it looked as if he would form a ministry on Peel's resignation, in ibid., 170.
[82]Ibid., 335.
[83]Ibid., 222.
[84]For an account of Chadwick's demise, see Finer, *Sir Edwin Chadwick*, 453–74.
[85]Eyler, *Victorian Social Medicine*, 190.
[86]Johnson, "Administrators in Education," 122.

driven out of government in the summer of 1854, *The Times,* generally a friend to the mid-Victorian public health movement, led a chorus of protests decrying his "wrong-headed dogmatism." Chadwick and Southwood Smith were men "heated with all the zeal of propagandists and all the intolerance of inquisitors." They were "persuaded of their own infallibility, intolerant of all opposition."[87] The style of the expert and the rigor of the specialist went against the national grain. In addition, they came from the wrong sort of background. As was later made plain to him, despite his work on the Royal Commission, Chadwick was not appointed a member of the new Poor Law Commission in 1834 because the cabinet "considered that his station in society was not as would have made it fit that he should be made one of the Commissioners."[88] As Richard Johnson has described, Kay-Shuttleworth bitterly resented his subordination to a "gossiping dilettante" like Charles Greville, grandson of the duke of Portland, who was clerk to the Privy Council. Although Kay-Shuttleworth married into an old, established family and so gained an estate worth some £10,000 a year and accordingly changed his name, he could not escape the discrepancy between his high private status and income and his lowly public position as a functionary of state.[89]

The problems of an anomalous social position were only compounded for the experts by a constant tension in their relationship with the industrial bourgeoisie. The service middle class held office; the industrial bourgeoisie owned property. The investigators staffed the inspectorates that regulated conditions in factories and mines; the owners complained about the intrusive authority of the state, which the experts represented. The tensions sometimes surfaced at a provincial congress of the Social Science Association, when the metropolitan experts took the trains north to cast their critical eyes over the new industrial cities. At Sheffield in 1865 they antagonized the local bourgeoisie by drawing attention to the appallingly high rates of occupational disease and mortality associated with the local metal trades, to the extensive employment of children in local factories, and to the lack of concern for public health. The builder and architect George Godwin described the River Don as a "black ditch."[90] The indolence, parsimony, and neglect of the local corporation

[87]*The Times,* 11 July 1854, 9.
[88]Earl Spencer to Chadwick, 8 May 1841, quoted in Finer, *Sir Edwin Chadwick,* 109, 199.
[89]Johnson, "Administrators in Education," 123–6.
[90]See, in particular, the paper delivered by J. C. Hall, M.D., the senior physician to the Sheffield Public Hospital, "The Effects of Certain Sheffield Trades on Life and Health,"

were laid bare by the investigators in the course of a week, and in consequence, as the *Daily News* observed, "The town councillors have taken no share in it, and they saw no need for them to do the civil to the social philosophers, who would, as one of the worthy aldermen suspected, be 'poking their inquiries into all sorts of unpleasant things.'"[91]

SCHEMES FOR SECURING EXPERTISE

Neither aristocratic disdain nor middle-class hostility is evident in Jarvis's analysis of the social science community. Fitting so easily into that community, he could not appreciate that it was anomalous in mid-Victorian Britain and that its relations with other social groups were often fraught with difficulties. For the investigators and administrators, the problems of recognition and status seem to have been most acute in the 1850s. A traditional political and legislative chronology depicts the period from the repeal of the Corn Laws in 1846 until the Second Reform Act in 1867—the so-called age of equipoise—as a hiatus, a quiescent period, devoid of important developments in social reform and administration. This situation is largely explained by political instability. The 1850s witnessed six different governments of varying ideological hue—Whig, Tory, and coalition. In a decade when there were five different home secretaries, six presidents of the Board of Trade, and four different chancellors of the Exchequer, it is argued that constructive social legislation, which needs time to gestate and constant attention once implemented, was impossible. It was too large and too difficult a commitment for short-lived ministries dependent on insecure majorities.[92] Moreover, when Palmerston finally imposed some order on Parliament between 1859 and his death in 1865, stability was bought at the expense of innovation.

Consequently, in the early 1860s another American then in Britain, Henry Adams, believed he saw a case of "arrested development." The "British mind" appeared to him "unravelled, at sea, floundering in every sort of historical shipwreck. Eccentricities had a free field. Contradictions swarmed in Church and State."[93] This view was very different from that of Edward Jarvis, although as W. L. Burn has pointed out, Adams prob-

---

Transactions (1865): 382–402. Godwin's comment was reported by the *Daily News*, 7 October 1865, 3.

[91] *Daily News*, 12 October 1865, 4.

[92] Valerie Cromwell, "Interpretations of Nineteenth Century Administration: An Analysis," *Victorian Studies* 9, no. 3 (1966): 254.

[93] *The Education of Henry Adams* (New York, 1931), 193.

ably saw little of the type of men who Jarvis mixed with, "the men investigating the legal and educational systems or local government or taxation and working out, even in Palmerston's lifetime, the changes which were to be made within a decade."[94] For here was the rub: despite political disaggregation, experts inside and outside government carried on with research and investigation—indeed an average of eight royal commissions were appointed annually in the 1850s, the peak period of the nineteenth century[95]—and thereby provided the basis for the burst of administrative and social reform associated with Gladstone's first ministry between 1868 and 1874. But as the politicians fiddled, so the experts chafed in frustration at the constriction of opportunities as compared with the 1830s and 1840s; their reliance on political good-will and their vulnerability to crises of state far beyond their control were all too obvious.

Their frustration expressed itself in various schemes to reorder and redirect the state, schemes that embodied the experts' political program. In the wake of disease and defeat during the Crimean War, the Administrative Reform Association tried a frontal assault on the mismanagements of aristocratic government. Although it had the support of some members of the community of experts—Chadwick wrote its first three pamphlets in 1855 and Newmarch and Babbage were early subscribers—more subtle methods of the "statesmen in disguise" were always likely to prove more effective than outspoken condemnation, which won few friends in the ruling elite.[96] The Social Science Association, less strident in tone but still critical of parliamentary complacency and ministerial incompetence, succeeded in gathering together far more of the community in a so-called amateur Parliament, which was to provide a forum for expertise and gently guide the politicians in the desired legislative directions.[97]

There were some schemes, meanwhile, that linked the experts' claims to recognition with the issue of parliamentary reform when it intermittently surfaced in this period. The aim was to ensure the election to the

---

[94]W. L. Burn, *The Age of Equipoise: A Study of the Mid-Victorian Generation* (London, 1964), 304.
[95]Harrison, "Finding Out How the Other Half Live," 264.
[96]Olive Anderson, "The Administrative Reform Association, 1855–1857," in Patricia Hollis, ed., *Pressure from Without in Early Victorian England* (London, 1974), 270, 273n.
[97]Goldman, "The Social Science Association," 116–7.

House of Commons of men of higher intelligence and moral tone than was usual in mid-Victorian Britain—men capable of appreciating the work of the experts and their schemes. One such idea was the "Educational Franchise," which was sponsored by, if it did not originate among, the members of the Social Science Association and was communicated to Palmerston, the prime minister, in December 1857 shortly after the SSA's first congress in Birmingham.[98] The memorial was signed by "Bishops, Lords, Church dignitaries, masters of public schools, men of science, men of literature, Dissenting preachers and others,"[99] many of whom were members of the association; by leaders of Victorian philanthropy such as Lords Brougham and Shaftesbury; by intellectual leaders such as F. D. Maurice, Charles Kingsley, and John Ruskin; by natural scientists such as Charles Babbage, Richard Owen, and Sir David Brewster; and by statesmen in disguise such as Edwin Chadwick and Arthur Helps. It called for the creation of seventy geographical constituencies, each returning a single member of Parliament to replace an equal number of the smaller boroughs then represented in the House of Commons. In each new constituency the electorate would comprise "those classes who have had the advantage of a liberal education" in the universities and professions. The total electorate represented by these seventy would number about 92,000, made up of "30,000 clergymen and Dissenting ministers, some 17,000 lawyers of all classes, 13,000 medical men, 14,000 officers of the Army, Navy and Indian Service, 12,000 graduates of the universities, 5,000 persons connected with literature, science and art."[100]

The scheme was one of the more fancy (and exclusive) of the "fancy franchises" thrown up for discussion when the question of parliamentary reform was occasionally broached in the 1850s and 1860s, and it gained mostly abuse as a species of special pleading in the interests of a single

[98]See *The Times*, 19 December 1857, 8. See also (Anon.) *The Educational Franchise* (London, 1857). The suggestion of the SSA's involvement is based on only circumstantial evidence, including the facts that the idea came so soon after its inaugural congress, that many of the dignitaries who signed the petition to Palmerston were members of the association, and that the scheme embodied the sorts of principles that the association stood for. Certainly the editors of J. S. Mill's correspondence believe that the Social Science Association was involved. See F. E. Mineka and D. W. Lindley, eds., *The Later Letters of John Stuart Mill 1849–1873* (Toronto, 1972), *Collected Works of John Stuart Mill*, vol. 15, 543, 684. The anonymous pamphlet explaining the scheme, *The Educational Franchise*, was first published in 1853 and then reissued in 1857. It would seem likely, therefore, that the association revived rather than initiated the idea.
[99]*The Times*, 21 December 1857, 6.
[100]Ibid.

class.[101] But the call "for a political recognition of the educated classes"[102] was an interesting example of the political ambitions of the professional middle class and of the group's collective frustration at the inadequacies of a political system that refused to value the principles of intelligence and competence. The aim was to introduce into Parliament "some of the men best fitted for the task of legislation . . . men who have ability, freedom and leisure to devote their thoughts to the difficult problems which the science of Government involves."[103] With their own men in Parliament, their influence could only increase.

One man with leisure enough to devote to the "science of Government" in the later 1850s was Chadwick. After the collapse of the General Board of Health in 1854 he was not unnaturally obsessed with schemes for the reform of institutions of state that would secure the position of officials.[104] During the Crimean War Chadwick suggested to Palmerston that he should be empowered to conduct a Royal Commission of Inquiry into the machinery of government.[105] In 1859 he presented before the Law Amendment Society a paper suggesting radical changes in "the chief methods of preparation for Legislation."[106] Chadwick argued that investigation was an integral part of legislative procedure and that it was best undertaken by "a special Commission of Inquiry" on the model of a Royal Commission—a commission that would go so far as to draft legislation for debate by Parliament. The Privy Council was to oversee all such investigations, delegating them to various standing committees which would use "subordinate inquiry"—assistant commissioners at a local level—for the collection of information.[107] The ad hoc procedures of a Royal Commission were thus to be given a permanent place in British constitutional machinery, and men like Chadwick with the requisite skills were to be assured of constant employment.

The plan was no doubt self-serving, but it appealed to the wider community of experts, among them Sir James Stephen, who, as under secretary of state for the colonies from 1836 to 1847, "literally ruled the

---

[101]Ibid. See also *Daily Telegraph*, 21 December 1857, 3; *The Economist*, 26 December 1857, 1427.
[102]*The Economist*, 26 December 1857, 1427.
[103]*The Educational Franchise*, 5, 8.
[104]Finer, *Sir Edwin Chadwick*, 475.
[105]Chadwick to Palmerston, 5 July 1855, in ibid., 487.
[106]Edwin Chadwick, *A Paper on the Chief Methods of Preparation for Legislation Especially as Applicable to the Reform of Parliament* (London, 1859).
[107]Ibid., 31. Chadwick's scheme is summarized in Finer, *Sir Edwin Chadwick*, 480.

colonial empire"[108] and who chaired the particular session of the Law Amendment Society when Chadwick outlined his scheme. John Stuart Mill, who had recently retired from service in the East India Company,[109] also commended the ideas: "Your paper cannot be too much read or too widely circulated." Indeed, it has been suggested that Mill used the ideas in developing his own schemes for constitutional reform that were published two years later in *Considerations on Representative Government*.[110] Mill's conception of a Legislative Commission, staffed by unelected officials who would draft the bills that Parliament would debate, and his suggestion for ministerial cabinets—councils of permanent, independent advisers, made up of "able and experienced professional men" to guide ministers—are certainly close in spirit to Chadwick's schemes and derive from the same motivation: to improve parliamentary procedures by securing the constitutional position of expertise.[111] But the first of these ideas, at least, had been broached by Mill as early as 1840 when he visualized a "skilled Senate, or Council of Legislation" to perform the specialized function of parliamentary draftsmanship.[112]

MILL AND THE PROBLEM OF SKILLED AGENCY

To mention John Stuart Mill in this context takes the discussion from social and administrative history to the history of political thought. Among the most distinctive themes in Mill's writings on politics was an abiding concern for what has been called the "principle of competence"[113]—the values of intelligence, ability, skill, and expertise that the investigative community sought to establish in the mid-nineteenth century. In consequence, Mill may be read with justification as an exponent of the claims of the new experts in Victorian society—a reading

---

[108] *Dictionary of National Biography,* vol. 54, 163–4.

[109] The meeting of the Law Amendment Society began with Chadwick's reading a letter of support from J. S. Mill who was unable to attend; it ended with Stephen's warm praise for the scheme. See Chadwick, *The Chief Methods of Preparation for Legislation* (London, 1859), 4–5, 33.

[110] See Finer, *Sir Edwin Chadwick,* 480n. As Dennis Thompson points out, there is no evidence to substantiate Finer's contention. Dennis F. Thompson, *John Stuart Mill and Representative Government* (Princeton, N.J., 1976), 122n.

[111] J. S. Mill, *Considerations on Representative Government* (1861; Oxford, 1912), 220, 347.

[112] J. S. Mill, "M. de Tocqueville on Democracy in America," in J. S. Mill, *Dissertations and Discussions,* 4 vols. (London, 1859–75), vol. 2, 82–3 (originally published in the *Edinburgh Review,* October 1840).

[113] Thompson, *John Stuart Mill and Representative Government,* 9–10.

that would certainly fit the biographical facts. Whatever weight we choose to give to the role of ideas in determining social and administrative reform from the 1830s, Benthamism was undoubtedly the most potent of various ideological forces caught up in the "nineteenth-century revolution in government," and Mill was the classic product of the creed. He may have rebelled and rejected his early indoctrination, but utilitarianism— particularly its contempt for the inefficient, the anomalous, and the ignorant—marked him throughout his life.

More to the point, Mill shared the outlook of the experts and officials because he was one of them. For thirty-five years he was a civil servant working in the Examiners Office in India House for the East India Company. He followed his father in the task of supervising "all despatches and instructions sent out to the executive in India." And, like his father, he rose to the head of the department in 1856, that is, to a position of responsibility comparable to that of an under secretary of state in which he was "virtually head of the Indian administration."[114]

The effect of this is not hard to trace. In 1854 he welcomed the Northcote-Trevelyan proposal "to select candidates for the Civil Service of Government by a competitive examination" as "one of those great public improvements the adoption of which would form an era in history."[115] In 1858 his remonstrance to the parliamentary bill that dissolved the East India Company and transferred its functions to a minister of the Crown and an advisory board of fifteen specialists was a defense of the old administration of India suffused with Mill's strong personal loyalty to the company and its officers. He was a member of the community of experts and shared their professional commitments and esprit de corps. He joined the Statistical Society of London and the Political Economy Club; he went to meetings of the Law Amendment Society and the Social Science Association; he knew Chadwick, Arnott, Southwood Smith, Henry Cole, Henry Taylor, and a host of lesser officials in the mid-Victorian bureaucracy. In background and occupation he was part of the milieu that Jarvis described, and his suggestions on the more practical aspects of politics, developed over many years and collected in *Considerations on Representative Government* in 1861, preserve a record of the preoccupations of the professional middle class in government.

Large tracts of *Representative Government* read as a hymn to "the

---

[114]M. St. John Packe, *The Life of John Stuart Mill* (London, 1954), 36.
[115]"Papers on the Re-Organisation of the Civil Service," *P.P.*, 1854–5, vol. 20, 92.

acquired knowledge and practised intelligence of a specially trained and experienced few"—to "skilled labour and special study and experience."[116] Those qualities were sadly absent from the contemporary House of Commons, and Mill spoke for the administrative class in his contempt for this "tribunal of ignorance." To Mill, "the utter unfitness of our legislative machinery for its purpose is making itself practically felt every year more and more"; this was a common judgment on the politics of the 1850s. Procedure was so slow that important measures "hung over from session to session" without being enacted. Despite extensive deliberation and research, no bill could pass "because the House of Commons will not forgo the precious privilege of tinkering it with their clumsy hands."[117]

Generalizing from this, Mill proposed the division between "doing the work" and "causing it to be done."[118] As the task of making law needed the attention of "experienced and exercised minds," legislation should be drafted by a commission "not exceeding in number the members of a Cabinet."[119] Bills so drafted would then be passed back to Parliament, which would retain "the power of passing or rejecting the bill when drawn up, but not of altering it otherwise than by sending proposed amendments to be dealt with by the Commission."[120] Parliament might "watch and control the government"; it might serve as "the nation's Committee of Grievances and its Congress of Opinions," but it should not be allowed a role in expert executive tasks for which its size, composition, and proven incompetence made it unsuitable.[121] No doubt the secretary of the Social Science Association, who saw "Bills shelved or shoved through, not merely without proper consideration, but without the smallest reference to their value in the country" in the summer of 1856, would have agreed.[122]

Having reordered the institutions of state to assure the place—indeed, the predominance—of expertise, Mill, like those members of the Social Science Association who signed the petition for the Educational Franchise, also turned to the reform of the electoral system. Mill had declined to sign

[116]Mill, *Representative Government*, 228, 225.
[117]Ibid., 221–2.
[118]Ibid., 223.
[119]Ibid., 220, 223.
[120]J. S. Mill, *Autobiography* (London, 1873), 265.
[121]Mill, *Representative Government*, 226.
[122]G. W. Hastings to Lord Brougham, 27 June 1856, Brougham Papers, University College, London, B. Mss. 13052.

the petition in 1857 on a question of means rather than ends; he agreed with "the object aimed at by (the) scheme" but disliked the constitutional apparatus suggested.[123] In 1859 he suggested an alternative to the separate representation of the educated classes, a system of plural voting weighted in their favor under which the "ordinary unskilled labourer" might have a single vote and "a member of any profession requiring a long, accurate and systematic mental cultivation" might have five or six votes, with various gradations in between where political influence as measured by the number of votes was proportional to educational attainment.[124]

Very soon afterward Mill was converted to that famous "crotchet" of the 1860s, Thomas Hare's scheme for electoral reform, roughly comparable to the modern system of the single transferable vote, a scheme that Edward Jarvis heard Hare himself explain at a meeting of the Statistical Society of London in June 1860 before an audience of "scholars, mathematicians, political economists, philanthropists."[125] This scheme was attractive not only because "the representation of minorities" that it promised would make Parliament into a more accurate reflection of the varieties of national opinion. By making it possible for an elector to vote for any candidate in any constituency, it also opened the way to the election of especially well qualified men who had previously failed to find a seat in Parliament because they had too few supporters in any one constituency.[126] Under Hare's scheme, "The minority of instructed minds scattered through the local constituencies, would unite to return a number, proportioned to their own number, of the very ablest men the country contains."[127] Thus, in Mill's judgment, "of all modes in which a national rep-

---

[123] J. S. Mill, *Thoughts on Parliamentary Reform* (London, 1859), 22–3n.

[124] Ibid., 20–2.

[125] Jarvis, Autobiography, 227–9; European Letters, iii, 22 June 1860, fol. 55–6. Soon after publication of his *Thoughts on Parliamentary Reform*, Mill received from an unknown barrister called Thomas Hare a copy of his recently published book, *The Election of Representatives, Parliamentary and Municipal* (London, 1859). Mill was quickly converted. As he wrote to Hare, "You appear to me to have exactly, and for the first time, solved the difficulty of popular representation; and by doing so, to have raised up the cloud of gloom and uncertainty which hung over the futurity of representative government and therefore of civilization." Mill to Hare, 3 March 1859, *Collected Works of John Stuart Mill*, vol. 15, 598–9.

[126] See J. S. Mill, *Thoughts on Parliamentary Reform* (2d ed.), Supplement, 26.

[127] Mill, *Representative Government*, 263. For good explanations of Hare's scheme, see Thompson, *John Stuart Mill and Representative Government*, 102–12; Paul B. Kern, "Universal Suffrage without Democracy: Thomas Hare and John Stuart Mill," *Review of Politics* 34, no. 3 (1972): 306–22.

resentation can possibly be constituted, this one affords the best security for the intellectual qualifications desirable in the representatives."[128]

Historians have tended to dismiss Mill's great enthusiasm for Hare's scheme in the last years of his life as a faintly embarrassing and inexplicable aspect of his old age. Certainly the House of Commons could not disguise its amusement when Mill proposed the plan as an amendment to the Second Reform Bill on 30 May 1867.[129] Yet the issue was of great importance to Mill; it "became, after women's suffrage, the greatest practical interest of his life."[130] And in advancing it, Mill was once again articulating the views and interests of the professional community of which he was a part. For Hare's scheme won the support of the experts each time it was explained to and debated by the members of the Social Science Association.[131] To Frederic Hill, the prisons inspector, the principle was "so just and so simple that one would think it only required to be clearly stated to command general concurrence." To one physician who earnestly desired "that professional men should be able to return a certain number of members to represent their special interests and views," it seemed likely that "under Mr Hare's scheme the medical profession would be able to ensure the return of some of their best members" who would "be competent to offer their advice to Parliament on questions upon which it displayed very often the most lamentable ignorance."[132]

Yet Mill must be separated from these men for one significant reason. They latched onto "minority representation" as they had earlier supported the Educational Franchise and Chadwick's plans for reforming the state because they seemed likely to increase the influence of the professional middle class at the expense of an incompetent ruling aristocracy. Mill also was critical of this incompetence, but in the later 1850s and 1860s he be-

---

[128]Mill, *Representative Government*, 257. See also J. S. Mill, "Recent Writers on Reform," *Fraser's Magazine* 59 (April 1859): 502, 506.

[129]*Hansard's* Parliamentary Debates, 3d ser., vol. 187 (1867), pp. 1343–62.

[130]Packe, *John Stuart Mill*, 417.

[131]For Hare's various papers to the SSA on his electoral schemes, see *Transactions* (1862), 110–12; (1865), 163–71; (1866), 202–8; (1879), 218–28. *Sessional Proceedings* (1868–9), 59–67; (1870–71), 215–35. See also the report of a special meeting of the association where Hare read a paper "On such an organization of the metropolitan elections as would call into exercise the greatest amount of the knowledge and judgement of the constituencies, and as far as possible discourage all corrupt and pernicious influences." *The Times*, 11 April 1865, 10. Mill was present at the meeting and spoke in favor of Hare's ideas.

[132]*Sessional Proceedings* (1868–9), 68–70. The physician quoted was a Dr. Stallard.

came committed to wholesale institutional and electoral reform because of the threat to intelligence from what he saw as a greater danger—an uninstructed democracy. All his suggested innovations take as their starting point the challenge of democracy, rather than the inadequacies of the traditional governing class. For if Mill was committed to the "principle of competence," he was also committed to the "principle of participation."[133] He believed that representative government and representative institutions were superior to any other form of political organization and that men and women should participate fully in affairs that touched them.

But as is well known, Mill also believed that "the natural tendency of representative government, as of modern civilisation, is towards collective mediocrity."[134] Democracy threatened society with "class legislation on the part of the numerical majority"; it also threatened "a low grade of intelligence in the representative body, and in the popular opinion which controls it," especially given the shameful state of public education in Britain in 1860.[135] To Mill, therefore, "the great problem of modern political organization" was "the combination of complete popular control over public affairs with the greatest attainable perfection of skilled agency"[136]—"to secure, as far as they can be made compatible, the great advantage of the conduct of affairs by skilled persons, bred to it as an intellectual profession, along with that of a general control vested in, and seriously exercised by, bodies representative of the entire people."[137] The aim was to obtain a "skilled democracy,"[138] and it was in pursuit of this that Mill made his suggestions for institutional and electoral reform.

Representative Government is, in consequence, something more than an eloquent defense of expertise in the context of the 1850s and 1860s, though it is certainly that. It is also a prescient exploration of a series of issues concerning competence and participation in modern societies that have dominated discussion of the role of expertise in our own century. For if in mid–nineteenth century Britain the issues at stake concerned the relationship between the expert and the minister, the significant questions now, a century and more later, concern as well the relationship between the expert, with specialist skills and esoteric knowledge, and the citizen, vainly trying to understand, to license, and to control.

[133]Thompson, *John Stuart Mill and Representative Government*, 9.
[134]Mill, *Representative Government*, 259.
[135]Ibid., 247.
[136]Mill, *Autobiography*, 265.
[137]Mill, *Representative Government*, 236.
[138]Ibid.

4

The world of the bureaus: government and the positivist project in the late nineteenth century

MICHAEL J. LACEY

This chapter outlines the emergence of Washington's late nineteenth-century scientific community, its institutional context and leadership structure. It will also describe the most significant features of that community's outlook on the relations among science, society, and government—a compound of liberal and positivist beliefs that developed in opposition to the laissez-faire individualism of the period and in support of adoption by the federal government of new responsibilities, particularly in the gathering of information pertinent to the understanding of social and economic affairs. While Washington's scientific spokesmen did not advocate big government in the present-day sense of the phrase, they strongly advocated a new style of knowledgeable governance and were among the first Americans to try to work out the premises for the modern regulatory state.

The resulting "liberal positivist" viewpoint was an important if merely transitional one that linked the older republican tradition of public inquiry and direction, dormant in the Jacksonian era, to twentieth-century currents of thought that took the form of pragmatic or instrumentalist social philosophy, institutionalist economic thought, and the search for a sociologically informed jurisprudence. Because these later currents of thought, nurtured primarily in the modern university, constitute the most sophisticated and fully developed sources of argument on the rationale for state intervention along the lines of the "new" or collectively oriented liberalism that dominated public thought in the progressive and New Deal periods, this chapter suggests that recovery of the earlier experience of the late nineteenth-century Washington community, driven as it was by the peculiar exigencies of public service in the United States, contributes as well to developing accounts of the relations between ideas and institutions in modern America.

EMERGENCE OF THE SCIENTIFIC COMMUNITY

Before the Civil War, Washington, D.C., had no intellectual community to speak of. With the exception of the Smithsonian Institution, which opened in 1846, the antebellum capital reflected the kind of institutional impoverishment that resulted from the stalemated sectionalist politics of the period, and most permanent residents viewed the local way of life as appropriate for a northern outpost of southern culture. But in the decades after the Civil War, Washington became a bustling center of activity. An important cultural shift was under way that had to do with the piecemeal conquest of the capital by people who carried with them a developing heritage of political beliefs and values rooted in the northeastern and midwestern portions of the country and were bent on transforming the city into a new outpost for their viewpoints and institutions. Among the many thousands who descended on the city in the postwar years were a steady stream of cultural entrepreneurs and institution builders determined to set up a new infrastructure for the intellectual life of both the city and the nation. They had a beachhead of sorts in the Smithsonian Institution, which frequently served as guide, supporter, and unofficial headquarters as they measured their prospects in the capital.[1]

The newcomers included a few organizers, such as Francis Walker, John Eaton, John Wesley Powell, and Carroll D. Wright, who took the lead in establishing the scientific agencies of a larger, more purposeful, and progressive postbellum government. For these men and others like them the Civil War had been the formative experience in their lives, demonstrating at great cost the reality and resources of the Union as something potentially quite different from the timid governance that had

[1] The standard account of antebellum Washington is Constance McLaughlin Green, *Washington: Village and Capital, 1800–1878* (Princeton, N.J.: Princeton University Press, 1962). Another important study of the early period is James Sterling Young, *The Washington Community: 1800–1828* (New York: Columbia University Press, 1966). For the light it sheds on the sometimes comic situation of a group of elected officials embarked on the construction of a new state yet hobbled by their own antistate reservations and distressed by their sense of isolation from the significant centers of political development in their home districts, see particularly chap. 3, "Self Image: Splendid Torment." The richest source on the Smithsonian Institution in the nineteenth century is George Brown Goode, ed., *The Smithsonian Institution, 1846–1896: The History of Its First Half Century* (Washington, D.C.: Smithsonian Institution, 1897).

issued from a loose federation of distrustful states. Although most came from evangelical backgrounds and maintained in muted form evangelical commitments, they considered themselves men of science—and science, broadly understood, as the politically significant ecumenical movement of the time.

All were advocates for generating knowledge and putting it to use in social and political affairs. Many of them who were concerned with the emerging social sciences were members, frequently in top positions, of the American Social Science Association (ASSA), through which they sought to coordinate discussions of social inquiry and social reform. Whether devoted to the social or the natural sciences, most newcomers moved into the public service, to what they called the world of government science. They created places for themselves, and many became the founders and guiding spirits of those institutions and programs that would host the growth of modern Washington's resident class of scientific and professional civil servants.

By the turn of the century that class was large and active. The government's first detailed report on the composition of the local work force showed a total of nearly 26,000 employees arrayed in a hierarchical pattern that ranged from subclerical personnel and unskilled laborers up through the middle ranks of skilled craftsmen (more than 2,000 printers among them), to an executive class of 558 employees who held, however precariously, career posts as heads of departments, chiefs of divisions or bureaus, officers in charge, "superintendents miscellaneous," and others.

Just below the executive group was a classification composed of "professional, technical and scientific" workers, numbering 3,919 people, some 15.2 percent of the total resident work force. It included architects and attorneys, botanists, chemists and physicists, curators, draftsmen, illustrators and artists, electricians and "dynamo tenders," engineers, engravers, geographers, geologists, paleontologists, and statisticians. A subgroup of nearly 1,100 people was described vaguely as "special agents, experts, and commissioners," while another of some 300 was designated simply as "scientific experts and investigators."[2]

The postwar expansion of this resident civil service work force did much to alter the tenor of local life; the impact was felt in everything from the cost of real estate to the quality of public education and the

[2]Details on the occupational structure are taken from U.S. Bureau of the Census, Bulletin 12, *The Executive Civil Service of the United States* (Washington, D.C.: U.S. Government Printing Office, 1904), tables 72 and 73.

kinds of entertainment that were available. In an 1894 article on the economic development of the District of Columbia, one of the leaders of the new community, Carroll D. Wright, chief of the Bureau of Labor Statistics and director of the Eleventh Census, pointed out that the make-shift and boardinghouse atmosphere that had marked the capital during the first three-quarters of the century had been rooted in part in the insecurities of government service, which had depressed the real estate market, not to mention the government workers themselves. With the growth of new bureaus and the gradual stabilization of employment that followed the passage of the Civil Service Reform Act in 1883, however, real estate had become one of the thriving local industries, to the point that there were jokes about it. Wright observed that by the 1890s there were basically two kinds of people in Washington, "those who were real estate agents and those who were not."

Except at their upper levels, there was little mixing between those who made up the local world of government science and the city's resident but ever-changing social elite. The latter group was dominated by elected officials and top political appointees, who spoke authoritatively on government plans and policies. They were the natural focus of public attention, but as far as the affairs of local institutional life were concerned, they were creatures of divided loyalties and part-time affections. "They spend their money here," Wright observed, "and take a certain interest in the welfare of the city because of their property interests and further, because of their social relations, but they are not influential factors in securing development."

The people with lasting influence were the new government workers, whom Wright considered "safely the most intelligent group of employees that can be found in the United States." Their involvements had caused the city's churches to "flourish" and driven its public schools "to rank with the best in the land." Unlike the world of elected officialdom and wealthy visitors, this group was public-spirited "not in a temporary way, but permanently."[3]

[3]Carroll D. Wright, "The Economic Development of the District of Columbia," *Proceedings of the Washington Academy of Sciences*, vol. 1 (1899), 161–87, passim. For a recent study of the city's "high society" during the period, see Kathryn A. Jacob, "High Society in Washington During the Gilded Age: 'Three Distinct Aristocracies,' " Ph.D. Diss., Johns Hopkins University, 1986. Jacob does not treat the scientific intellectual community, which was made up primarily of long-term civil servants. One of the "aristocracies" she examines, however, was the elected and appointed people who, as the political superiors of the scientific intellectuals, made up "official" Washington. See also Cindy S. Aron, *Ladies and Gentlemen of the Civil Service: Middle Class Workers in Victorian America* (New York:

Government workers played a secondary role in the shaping of national affairs, providing staff to meet the new responsibilities taken on by the national government. In many cases, however, the initiative in establishing new state responsibilities came from the network of those who would in the early phases also fulfill those responsibilities.[4] Here the leadership was provided by the spokesmen for government science, and drew upon the staff capacities of its own developing subculture. Decades in the making, the burgeoning postwar community of government scientists was bound together in a complex structure of institutions, public and private.

The institutional legacy of the postwar generation included, on its public side, the United States Geological Survey; the United States National Museum; the Bureau of American Ethnology; the United States Weather Bureau; the Bureau of Forests (later the United States Forest Service); the Biological Survey of the Department of Agriculture; the Woods Hole Marine Biological Survey; the foundation elements of what became eventually the United States Fish and Wildlife Service; the Department of Education; the Bureau of Labor Statistics; and the components of what became, just after the turn of the century, the permanent Bureau of the Census.

So far as private, voluntary institutions were concerned, by the turn of the century there were nine local scholarly and scientific societies that

---

Oxford University Press, 1987), which develops the argument that Washington's civil service community represented the pioneering members of what C. Wright Mills would later call the nation's "new middle class."

[4] That this point was present in the minds of insiders is evidenced by remarks made by William Healy Dall in his *Spencer Fullerton Baird* (Philadelphia: J. B. Lippincott, 1915), a biography of the secretary of the Smithsonian who was also a founder of the U.S. National Museum and of the United States Fish Commission. The Fish Commission was the first federal agency to undertake large-scale ecological research operations in the nineteenth century. Dall, a long-time colleague of Baird's in the Washington scientific community, observed: "Most persons unacquainted with the interior workings of our executive bureaus have the impression that they are the creation of law, in the sense in which the term 'creation' was formerly used to describe the coming into being of some part of the material universe. It is common to hear arguments from intelligent people, bent on ameliorating government, which tacitly assume that an Act of Congress by some inherent magic will accomplish that which they desire. It is a truism that whole schemes of social reorganization are built on no better foundation, and thousands of earnest reformers work, suffer, and even die for theories erected on this hypothesis.

"Nothing could be more mistaken in its application to the government scientific bureaus. For each and every one of them the world is indebted to some individual. In the majority of cases the man came with his purpose before the law was thought of, and his devotion to his self-imposed mission, his persistence, and his energy were the inciting causes of some lines in an appropriation bill, with all its potentialities, the seed of the present organization" (p. 25).

combined to form the Washington Academy of Sciences, with a total membership exceeding 1,700. The most important components were the Philosophical Society of Washington, the Anthropological Society of Washington, the National Geographic Society, and the Columbia Historical Society. The Cosmos Club was founded in 1878 by the leaders of the community to provide a sense of common membership, together with facilities for dining and accommodations, meeting rooms, and a library.[5]

Most members of the community were engaged in research and publication. The bureau chiefs were de facto managing editors for the output of their agencies, published in decentralized fashion by the government. By the 1890s Washington's bureaucracy had become by far the nation's most active publisher of scientific work, in fields ranging from agronomy and anthropology to geography, geology, education, and social statistics.[6] The *National Geographic* magazine came out of the Washington circle, as did the *American Anthropologist*. For many years *Science* magazine, the period's most important source of reporting on science and civic affairs, was dominated editorially by members of the Washington community; in fact, it was funded by one of them.

During the same period, of course, the major journals of the emerging specialized academic disciplines began to appear, reflecting a competing idea of social science as a professional calling best left to the community of experts in university departments. These experts sometimes dismissed the hortatory rhetoric of the government scientists as the passing enthusiasm of shallow amateurs, bourgeois reformers, and patrician scholars. Revealing his own commitment to social science as something different from professional learning, as a more diffuse and general feature of the cultural equipment of the day, Carroll Wright surveyed the activities pertinent to the field then under way in Washington and concluded that the federal government had become the nation's "chief promoter of social

[5]For an account of the social and institutional context in which the community existed, see James Kirkpatrick Flack, *Desideratum in Washington: The Intellectual Community in the Capital City, 1879–1900* (Cambridge, Mass.: Shenkman, 1975), and Michael J. Lacey, "The Mysteries of Earth Making Dissolve: Washington's Intellectual Community and the Origins of American Environmentalism in the Late Nineteenth Century," Ph.D. Diss., George Washington University, 1979. For a history of the Cosmos Club founded by the community, see Wilcomb Washburn, *The Cosmos Club of Washington: A Centennial History, 1878–1978* (Washington, D.C.: Cosmos Club, 1978).
[6]On the publication of science in this era, see Daniel J. Kevles, J. Sturcio, and P. Carroll, "The Sciences in America, Circa 1880," *Science* 209 (1980): 27–32.

science."[7] As evidence he pointed to the vast literature of social description and reporting produced by government workers to document conditions of life in the midst of the industrial transformation.

LEADERSHIP OF THE WASHINGTON COMMUNITY

With the rise of the graduate schools and the developing scholarly apparatus of the specialized academic disciplines, the locus of intellectual life and expertise in modern America shifted to the university. Although some had connections with the emerging universities, most members of the Washington community were government employees, whose shared experience of public service shaped their thought and action. As was mentioned above, for many among the leaders of that community that service began in the Union Army, where a number of them first became acquainted in the officer corps. The principal leaders of the community during the last quarter of the century enjoyed some contemporary reputation as scientists and scholars, but the central tasks of leadership were institution building, management, and the advocacy of science in the public service that went along with it. Among the important settings for advocacy, beyond the hallways of Congress itself, were the American Social Science Association, the American Association for the Advancement of Science, and the National Academy of Sciences.

The leaders of the community were drawn from its central public organizations. As the Smithsonian Institution was the best established of these, Joseph Henry, the founding secretary and its director until his death in 1878—as well as the president of the National Academy of Sciences and founder of the Washington Philosophical Society—was a seminal figure. Another active and influential member of the group was Spencer Baird, Henry's successor and the chief architect of the U.S. National Museum, which he conceived as the museum of the general gov-

[7]Carroll Wright, "Contributions of the United States Government to Social Science," *American Journal of Sociology* 1, no. 3 (November 1895): 257. Wright's piece provides a historical account of the federal government's data-gathering activities, together with a discussion of the publications programs of the departments, independent agencies, and the Congress. In his *Outline of Practical Sociology with Special Reference to American Conditions* (New York: Longmans, Green, and Co., 1899), he updated his discussion and incorporated information on the publications activities of state-level agencies and on the activities of private groups and scholarly associations as well. Regarding the predominance of the federal government at this point, Wright remarks (p. 17), "When it is known that the United States Government alone expends annually about eight million dollars and employs nearly four thousand people in scientific work, the value of the official contributions will be thoroughly comprehended."

ernment and sought to build up through cooperative relationships with the research and exploration activities of all the other agencies in the government science community. So was George Brown Goode, assistant secretary of the Smithsonian, a naturalist and historian whose scholarship first pulled together in a coherent account the history of American scientific institutions. Otis Mason, the Smithsonian's first ethnologist, founder of the Washington Anthropological Society, was especially active in promoting popular education in anthropology and worked with Baird and Goode to formulate the National Museum's exhibition plan on the theme of scientific progress and the development of modern civilization. The father-in-law of Alexander Graham Bell, Gardiner Green Hubbard, the fiscal and financial wizard behind the development of the Bell empire, was one of the chief figures in the circle and one of its patrons, as was Bell himself.[8]

Another important presence in the community was Ainsworth Rand Spofford, appointed by Lincoln as Librarian of Congress, a position he held for nearly forty years. While his Smithsonian colleagues sought to circumscribe and organize knowledge on the natural history and ethnography of the continent, he sought to do the same for the literature of the world. It was Spofford the "bookman," as he was known, who transformed the Library from a modest working collection for the needs of legislators into a vast collection of resources for the study of world civilization.[9]

John Eaton, who was commissioner of the Bureau of Education for fifteen years, also was an active participant in the Washington community

[8]For biographical information on Henry, see Thomas Coulson, *Joseph Henry: His Life and Work* (Princeton, N.J.: Princeton University Press, 1950). For the gist of his thinking on science, ethics, and society, see Arthur Mollella, Nathan Reingold, and Marc Rothenberg, eds. *A Scientist in American Life: Essays and Lectures of Joseph Henry* (Washington, D.C.: Smithsonian Institution Press, 1980). On Baird, see Dall, *Spencer Fullerton Baird.* On Goode, see Sally G. Kohlstedt, "History in a Natural History Museum: George Brown Goode and the Smithsonian Institution," *Public Historian* 10, no.2 (Spring 1988): 7–26. Goode was virtually the only American scholar in the nineteenth century to have a deep knowledge of the nation's scientific institutions. When A. Hunter Dupree's classic study *Science in the Federal Government: A History of Policies and Activities to 1940* (Cambridge, Mass.: Harvard University Press, 1957) was published, Dupree acknowledged that Goode had provided its one true predecessor. For a collection of Goode's papers on the subject, see "A Memorial of George Brown Goode," *Annual Report for 1897*, Part II (Washington, D.C.: Smithsonian Institution Press, 1901). For Otis Mason, see Curtis M. Hinsley, Jr., *Savages and Scientists: The Smithsonian Institution and the Development of American Anthropology, 1846–1910* (Washington, D.C.: Smithsonian Institution Press, 1981), 84–117; and Lacey, "The Mysteries of Earth Making Dissolve," 70–82. On Bell and Hubbard, see ibid., 82–90.
[9]On Spofford, see John Y. Cole, *Ainsworth Rand Spofford: Bookman and Librarian* (Littleton, Colo.: Libraries Unlimited, 1975).

and in the leadership of ASSA as well. A graduate of Andover Theological Seminary, Eaton had entered the Union Army in 1861 as a chaplain, become a field superintendent of freedmen, and emerged from the war as a brigadier general with close ties to the Freedmen's Bureau. He settled in Tennessee, edited the *Memphis Post,* and served as state superintendent of schools until President Grant called him to Washington to take over the Bureau of Education in 1870.[10]

For many years William Torrey Harris—who followed Eaton as commissioner of the Bureau of Education—also was a member of the group. Harris was the principal expositor of Hegelianism in the United States and the founder and editor of the *Journal of Speculative Philosophy,* which carried the first studies of German philosophy to appear in America. For a time Charles Peirce, Josiah Royce, William James, and John Dewey were among its contributors. Harris also was a leader of ASSA.

Still another influential participant in the circle, especially during the 1870s, was Francis Amasa Walker, an economist and statistician. Like Eaton, Walker had been promoted quickly through the ranks of the Union Army during the war and emerged as a brigadier general. In the late 1860s he was appointed as a special deputy to David Ames Wells, commissioner of revenue in the Treasury Department, and subsequently became chief of the Bureau of Statistics in the department. Walker, too, was a founder and sometime president of ASSA. The first president of the American Economic Association and an important critic of classical economic theory, he was a leading advocate inside and outside government for the creation of permanent, wide-ranging institutional capacities within government for the statistical investigation of social and economic problems. Walker was superintendent of the Ninth and the Tenth American censuses, and from the early 1880s until his death in 1897 he served as president of the Massachusetts Institute of Technology.[11]

Carroll D. Wright, the son of a Unitarian minister, was a sociologist, statistician, and historian who arrived in Washington in 1884 as a Walker protégé to become first commissioner of the Bureau of Labor Statistics (BLS), the federal government's principal statistically oriented investigative agency on industrial problems in the late nineteenth century, a

---

[10]For Harris, see William Goetzman, ed., *The American Hegelians* (New York: Knopf, 1973). On Eaton, see the *Dictionary of American Biography* (New York: Charles Scribner's Sons, 1930), vol. 3, 608–9.

[11]For Walker, see Carroll Wright, "Francis Amasa Walker," *Proceedings of the American Statistical Association,* n.s., 38 (June 1897): 245–75.

position he held for twenty years. By the early 1890s Wright was the most experienced administrator of large-scale social inquiries in the United States. Another war veteran, Wright had left the army with the rank of colonel, served in the Massachusetts state senate, and was appointed chief of the Massachusetts Bureau of the Statistics of Labor (the first agency of its kind established in Europe or America) before moving to Washington. In addition to his work at the BLS he directed the Eleventh Census and was long active in ASSA, serving as its president from 1885 to 1888 and as vice president for several years thereafter.[12]

Lester Frank Ward, one of the principal founders of theoretical sociology in America, was for forty years an active member in the Washington intellectual community. Wounded at the battle of Chancellorsville, he was discharged from the army and settled in the capital, where he found work in the Treasury Department. Ward served for a time as chief of the Division of Navigation, then chief of the Division of Immigration, and for some years as librarian of the Bureau of Statistics. In 1881 he moved over to the United States Geological Survey, which was fast becoming the largest and most active of the scientific bureaus with a wide-ranging program of research on the natural resources of the nation under the direction of John Wesley Powell. Ward remained at the survey until leaving Washington in 1904 to take up an academic appointment at Brown University.[13]

John Wesley Powell was the most prominent spokesman for the community during its heyday in the last two decades of the century. A military

---

[12] On Wright, see James Lieby, *Carroll Wright and the Labor Reform: The Origins of Labor Statistics* (Cambridge, Mass.: Harvard University Press, 1960). See also Joseph Goldberg and William Moye, *The First Hundred Years of the Bureau of Labor Statistics: 1884–1984* (Washington, D.C.: U.S. Government Printing Office, 1985). For a critical view of the early consumption studies of Wright and his staff as reflecting middle-class values unsympathetic to the cultural preferences of the immigrant working class, see Daniel Horowitz, *The Morality of Spending: Attitudes Towards the Consumer Society in America, 1875–1940* (Baltimore: Johns Hopkins University Press, 1985). On Wright's labor studies and ideological formation, see Mary O. Furner, "Knowing Capitalism: Public Investigation of the Labor Question in the Long Progressive Era," in Mary O. Furner and Barry Supple, eds., *The State and Economic Knowledge: The American and British Experiences* (Cambridge: Cambridge University Press, 1990), and Furner, Chapter 5 in this volume.

[13] On Ward's career and its intellectual context, see Lacey, "The Mysteries of Earth Making Dissolve," 130–43 and 168–216. See also Clifford H. Scott, *Lester Frank Ward* (Boston: Twayne, 1976); and John Gillis Harp, "Republican Positivists: The American Comtean Tradition, 1850–1920," Ph.D. Diss., University of Virginia, 1986, chap. 5. Robert Bierstedt provides a fresh and carefully balanced account of Ward's thought in chap. 2 of his *American Sociological Theory: A Critical History* (New York: Academic Press, 1981).

hero, explorer, geologist, anthropologist, and "statesman of science," as his colleagues put it, Powell was the acknowledged if unofficial leader of the circle during the period. Son of a circuit-riding Methodist minister and abolitionist preacher, Powell enlisted in the infantry at the outbreak of the war, soon rose into the officer corps, was badly wounded at the battle of Shiloh (losing his right arm below the elbow as a result), and was discharged with the rank of major. For decades thereafter his associates commonly referred to him simply as "the Major."

Influential behind the scenes in developing the legislation that established the Geological Survey in 1879, Powell served as its director from 1881 to 1894. His principal scientific interest, however, was in ethnology, an interest he attributed to the early encouragement of Francis Walker. Powell was responsible for having the Bureau of American Ethnology (BAE) placed, with the support of Spencer Baird, within the Smithsonian Institution in 1879—an environment more hospitable to the conduct of basic research than other government institutions, where the pull toward applied research often skewed programs. In addition to his leadership of the Geological Survey, Powell served as chief of the BAE from its founding until his death in 1902, during which period the bureau's employees brought to light, as Claude Lévi-Strauss would point out generations later, "most of what will remain known of the American Indian"—their languages, technologies, patterns of social organization and government, mythologies, and religious beliefs and practices. The BAE under Powell was especially concerned with problems of theory in accounting for social evolution. In his survey of the activities of the federal government pertinent to the social sciences, Carroll Wright noted that "no more important contributions to social science have been made under government auspices than those of the Bureau of Ethnology. Striking at the very roots of social science itself . . . it must take first rank in the estimation of social scientists."[14]

[14]The quotation attributed to Wright appears in his "Contributions of the United States Government to Social Science," 269. Claude Lévi-Strauss's assessment of the role played by the BAE in what he called "the golden age" of American anthropology is provided in "Anthropology: Its Achievements and Future," in Paul Oehser, ed., *Knowledge Among Men: Eleven Essays on Science, Culture, and Society Commemorating the 200th Anniversary of the Birth of James Smithson* (Washington, D.C.: Smithsonian Institution Press, 1966), 111–22. For an account of the institutional history of the BAE, see Neil Judd, *The Bureau of American Ethnology: A Partial History* (Norman: University of Oklahoma Press, 1968). The standard biography of Powell is William Culp Darrah, *Powell of the Colorado* (Princeton, N.J.: Princeton University Press, 1951). See also Lacey, "The Mysteries of Earth Making Dissolve," 143–53 and 219–83.

THE NETWORK OF POLITICAL SUPPORT

To be successful, initiatives require collaboration and highly placed collaborators. The government's developing scientific community was dependent on the interest and support of a group of like-minded officials in the dominant but faction-ridden Republican party, embroiled in the politics of Reconstruction and national economic development. During the war years Republican leadership had established the Commission on Agriculture (later the Department of Agriculture) and laid the foundations for the system of public higher education in the United States via the Land Grant College Act. The Pacific Railroad Act coordinated the development of transcontinental rail lines. Wartime tax policies resulted in the establishment of the Bureau of Internal Revenue in the Treasury Department, and a doubling of the size of the Treasury staff. A national currency and the heart of the national banking system were established.

Many people associated with these policy innovations were active in the Washington Philosophical Society, established in 1871 by Joseph Henry in response to a petition submitted to him by more than forty prominent Washingtonians. Membership in the society was drawn from three sectors of activity that generated the city's postwar intellectual elite: heads of prewar research-oriented governmental institutions, such as the Smithsonian, the Naval Observatory, and the Coast Survey; military administrators who rose to national prominence during the war; and a number of the leading officials of the Republican party.

Henry explained that the term *philosophical* had been chosen for the society not to denote "an unbounded field of speculative thought," but to refer in a more restrictive sense to "those branches of knowledge that relate to the positive facts of the physical and moral universe." There were many such branches, and they overlapped with questions of public policy. Topics discussed by the society ranged widely through the natural sciences and mathematics to anthropology and archaeology, geography and exploration, and into current issues in public affairs, among them the silver question, the operations of the national banking system, and the borrowing capacity of the federal government. Members of the Republican political elite within the society included Salmon Chase, secretary of the treasury under Lincoln, an architect of the national banking system, and chief justice of the United States during Reconstruction; Sen. John Sherman of Ohio, younger brother of Gen.

William T. Sherman (also a member); and John Jay Knox, comptroller of the currency.[15]

Perhaps no Republican leader was more important to the fortunes of the government's scientific community, however, than James A. Garfield of Ohio, the first American politician of stature to associate himself publically with the need for a new knowledge base for postwar politics and new institutions to provide it. Garfield was a major force in the Republican leadership of the House of Representatives from his arrival there in the 1860s until his departure in 1880, shortly before beginning his brief and ill-fated presidency.[16]

A lawyer and one-time college teacher, Garfield, too, had come to national prominence during the war. He held the rank of major general when he left the army to take up his congressional post in Washington, and he was personally acquainted with many in the leadership of its scientific circle. He had a reputation as a moderate reformer interested in the newer currents of nineteenth-century thought. Some in the American Association for Social Science spoke of him as "a ready friend and able champion in Congress of all liberal and progressive measures."[17] Garfield soon became a member of the Smithsonian's board of regents, its central governing body, and was a eulogist at the memorial service for Joseph Henry. He was the principal sponsor of the legislation founding the Department of Education (later the Bureau of Education), established in 1866 as a clearinghouse for information on the educational resources and problems of the nation, and its principal protector for years thereafter, working closely with John Eaton. On several occasions in the

[15]The information is derived from the *Bulletin of the Philosophical Society of Washington* 1 (March 1871–June 1874), published in cooperation with the Smithsonian Institution (Washington, D.C., 1874). The quotation attributed to Henry is taken from his presidential address and appears on p. vi. As the society grew, its members came to include Henry Adams; George Bancroft; Benjamin Peirce, the mathematician and superintendent of the U.S. Coast Survey; Charles Sanders Peirce, Benjamin's son, the founder of pragmatism and a sometime employee of the survey; Francis A. Walker; John Eaton; Ainsworth Spofford; John Wesley Powell; and Lester Ward.

[16]For biographical information on Garfield, see Robert Granville Caldwell, *James A. Garfield: Party Chieftain* (New York: Dodd, Mead and Co., 1931); and Allan Peskin, *Garfield: A Biography* (Kent, Ohio: Kent State University Press, 1978). Both books are straightforward political biographies and do not deal in detail with Garfield's intellectual life. Peskin nonetheless sees as the "central contradiction" of Garfield's career that "he was a misplaced intellectual thrown onto the stage of public life, moving restlessly between the worlds of action and introspection, drawing strength from each but feeling at home in neither" (p. 612).

[17]The quotation is from Francis A. Walker, "Some Results of the Census of 1870," presented before the American Social Science Association at its eighth general meeting in Boston, May 15, 1873 (Cambridge, Mass.: Riverside Press, 1873), 71.

1870s Garfield helped arrange support for John Wesley Powell's research; he backed the establishment of the U.S. Geological Survey in 1878, and in 1881, as president, appointed Powell to head the agency.[18] He was an early advocate for civil service reform and abolition of the spoils system, and the leading congressional spokesman for the establishment of a permanent census bureau.

Garfield was chairman of the House Committee on the Ninth Census in 1869. In that role, with the aid of Francis Walker and the advice of Edward Jarvis, president of the American Statistical Association, he surveyed the development of government statistical agencies in Europe and America.[19] In an attempt to bring American practice abreast of the times, his committee advocated a new set of schedules designed to develop an extensive information base on the social and industrial condition of the nation.

Garfield argued that new forms of civil intelligence had become "indispensable to modern statesmanship." While the rather primitive census data of earlier periods were essential in fixing the basis of political representation, far more comprehensive contemporary statistical inquiry promised to go well beyond that point and open up for political inspection conditions of life "in the hovels, homes, workshops, mines, fields, prisons, hospitals, and all places where human nature displays its weaknesses and its strengths," thus providing a "basis for scientific induction" in the process of lawmaking itself. Unlike the founders of the republic, who conceived statecraft as dependent on knowledge of the constants of human nature, Garfield stressed its dependence on a grasp of the variables of the human situation, and thus the need for continuous monitoring of actual social conditions. The modern legislator, he claimed, "must study society rather than black letter learning," and must acknowledge the truth that "statesmanship consists rather in removing causes than in punishing or evading results."

A properly working system of civil intelligence gathering, he suggested, would stimulate both social science and political discourse "by so exhibiting general results that they may be compared with similar data

---

[18]On the relationship between Garfield and Powell, see the index in Darrah, *Powell of the Colorado*. One aspect of the relationship was that when Garfield received the nomination of the party for the presidency, he asked Powell to release his private secretary, Joseph Stanley-Brown, to assist him. Stanley-Brown became Garfield's private secretary and served as a top personal assistant thereafter.

[19]On the relationship among Garfield, Walker, and Jarvis, see Wright, "Francis A. Walker," 261–2. Garfield's census speech was delivered to ASSA before it was delivered in Congress.

obtained by other nations." The stressful, industrializing postwar polity required no less. "Now that the great question of slavery is removed from the arena of American politics," he argued, "the next great question to be confronted will be that of the corporations and their relation to the interests of the people." Garfield pointed to a growing fear that had come to be entertained by "our best men in the national and State legislatures of the Union"—that, by encouraging through new law the rapid growth of corporations, they had unleashed a spirit "which may wield a power greater than that of the Legislatures themselves" and would require new kinds of information to comprehend and control.[20]

Congress in 1869 was preoccupied with the immediate problems of Reconstruction. Garfield's bill passed the House but died in the Senate, where it encountered a combination of skepticism about the need for new schedules and the determined opposition of his Republican colleague, Sen. Roscoe Conkling of New York, who saw in its proposed administrative changes (which required that the enumerations be made "by persons with a special fitness for such work") an emerging threat to the traditions of patronage on which leadership in the party system depended. Some of Garfield's proposals were incorporated a decade later in the Tenth Census, directed by Francis Walker, which marked the origins of the modern American system. No permanent census bureau was established until 1903.

Garfield's rather sudden and unexpected election to the presidency in the fall of 1880 augured well for the fortunes of the local scientific community. His inaugural ball in March the following year was the first major public event held at the Smithsonian Institution's newly opened Arts and Industries Building, then being fitted out for a new type of museum installation designed by George Brown Goode and Otis Mason to illustrate the role of science in the growth of modern civilization. When Garfield died in September 1881 as the result of wounds inflicted on him in July by a deranged and "disappointed" office seeker, only several months into a presidential tenure that had not worked up a program and was mired in factional struggles over patronage, the Washington scientific community lost an important ally. As the president's condition worsened in the summer heat of the city, Powell and others set up in Garfield's

---

[20]All quotations attributed to Garfield are taken from his *Ninth Census: Speech of the Honorable James A. Garfield of Ohio, Delivered in the House of Representatives December 16, 1869* (Washington, D.C.: F. and J. Rives and George A. Bailey, 1869), 1–16, passim.

room at the White House an air-conditioning device, constructed by the Smithsonian, to lower the temperature.[21] Civil service reformers viewed his death as a martyrdom, which contributed to the passage of the Civil Service Reform Act of 1883.

LIBERAL POSITIVISM

The Washington scientific community occupied a unique position in the developing social thought of the era, and the perspective of that community was forged in the experience of accounting for the aims and activities of the institutions its members inhabited. The leaders of the bureaus saw themselves as participants in the multifaceted, transnational, progressive thought of the period, the principal currents of which were evolutionary theory, political economy, and German organicism. In their encounter with these currents of thought the leaders sought to coordinate what they understood to be the two major agencies at work in modern history: the cumulative development of science on the one hand, which they believed to require public support and direction, and the growth of liberty and personal autonomy on the other, which they believed to require reinterpretation in light of the inherent collectivism of industrial life.

Important shared concerns for members of the community included the relationship among science, society, and government; a preoccupation with the problems of industrial history; and a critique of those traditions of laissez-faire individualism in both philosophy and political economy that opponents invoked to limit the role of the state in scientific research and reporting. A large body of writings—books, articles, essays, and lectures—grew out of meetings of the scholarly and scientific associations of the community. The dominant outlook reflected in this work is designated here as "liberal positivism."[22]

---

[21]Details on the efforts of Powell and others in the scientific community to assist in Garfield's recovery are taken from Darrah, *Powell of the Colorado*, 283.

[22]On the intellectual history of the period, see Sidney Fine, *Laissez-Faire and the General Welfare State: A Study of Conflict in American Thought, 1865–1901* (Ann Arbor: University of Michigan Press, 1956); Morton White, *Social Thought in America: The Revolt Against Formalism* (Boston: Beacon Press, 1957); R. Jackson Wilson, *In Quest of Community: Social Philosophy in the United States, 1860–1920* (New York: Oxford University Press, 1970); Edward A. Purcell, *The Crisis of Democratic Theory: Scientific Naturalism and the Problem of Values* (Lexington: University of Kentucky Press, 1973); Robert C. Bannister, *Sociology and Scientism: The American Quest for Objectivity, 1880–1940* (Chapel Hill: University of North Carolina Press, 1987); Jurgen Herbst, *The German Historical School in American Scholarship* (Ithaca, N.Y.: Cornell University Press, 1965);

A convenient point of access to liberal positivism is provided by Lester Ward's major work, his two-volume *Dynamic Sociology* (1883), the first systematic treatise in evolutionary sociology written in the United States. In a long, critical review of it, John Wesley Powell concluded that, despite its shortcomings, the book represented "America's greatest contribution to scientific philosophy," not least because it offered "sufficient warrant for the course pursued by practical statesmen and jurists" in their efforts to deal with the unprecedented social problems that bedeviled the late nineteenth century.[23] Such warrants were provided via a complex treatment of the nature of science, the history of the sciences, the classification of the sciences and their bearings on one another, and finally the relationship of science to society as the key to interpreting the history of human progress—all in such a manner as to develop in extenso, as another reviewer put it, "the startling assertion that positivism is not necessarily indifferentism, nor Manchesterism, nor fatalism."[24]

Nor, it might be added, was this type of positivism a plea for a re-

and Richard Hofstadter, *Social Darwinism in American Thought* (Boston: Beacon Press, 1968).

See also John L. Thomas, *Alternative America: Henry George, Edward Bellamy, Henry Demarest Lloyd and the Adversary Tradition* (Cambridge, Mass.: Harvard University Press, 1983); "The Evolutionary Controversy," in Elizabeth Flower and Murray G. Murphey, *A History of Philosophy in America*, vol. 2 (New York: G. P. Putnam's Sons, 1977); Daniel J. Wilson, *Science, Community and the Transformation of American Philosophy, 1860–1930* (Chicago: University of Chicago Press, 1990); Charles D. Cashdollar, *The Transformation of Theology, 1830–1890: Positivism and Protestant Thought in Britain and America* (Princeton, N.J.: Princeton University Press, 1989); Dorothy Ross, "Socialism and American Liberalism: Academic Social Thought in the 1880's," *Perspectives in American History* 11 (1977–8): 5–79. See also her "American Social Science and the Idea of Progress," in Thomas L. Haskell, ed., *The Authority of Experts: Studies in History and Theory* (Bloomington: Indiana University Press, 1984), 157–75. In the same volume see David A. Hollinger, "Inquiry and Uplift: Late Nineteenth Century American Academics and the Moral Efficacy of Scientific Practice," 142–56; and "Justification by Verification: The Scientific Challenge to the Moral Authority of Christianity in Modern America," in Michael J. Lacey, ed., *Religion and Twentieth Century American Intellectual Life* (Cambridge: Cambridge University Press, 1989), and 116–35.

Finally, for an acute and wide-ranging study of the period's progressive discourse considered as a transatlantic movement of thought in search of the premises adequate for developing a "via media" between classical liberalism and socialism, see James T. Kloppenberg, *Uncertain Victory: Social Democracy and Progressivism in European and American Thought, 1870–1920* (New York: Oxford University Press, 1986). For a contemporary reassessment of the themes first developed in Morton White's early and influential *Social Thought in America*, see Kloppenberg, "In Retrospect: Morton White's Social Thought in America," *Reviews in American History* 15, no. 3 (September 1987): 507–19.

[23] John Wesley Powell, "Ward's *Dynamic Sociology*," *Science: An Illustrated Journal* 2 (July–December 1883): 45–9, 105–8, 171–4, and 222–6. The quotations appear on pp. 226 and 106, respectively.

[24] Albion Small, "Review of *Dynamic Sociology*, Second Edition," *American Journal of Sociology* 3, no. 1 (July 1897): 110.

ductionist scientific method. Ward's book grew out of frustration with what he termed "the essential sterility of all that has thus far been done in the domain of social science"—a sterility rooted in the metaphysical elements of reasoning that lingered most prominently in the individualist traditions of British empirical thought about the nature of society and government and that accounted, in his view, for the essentially premodern qualities of both liberalism and republicanism. These philosophical views, formulated long before the breakthroughs that produced the new evolutionary cosmologies then being established, were at the root of those theories of society that resulted in the reluctance to innovate in government affairs and buttressed the spirit of administrative nihilism. Although a modest stock of "true data of social science" was accumulating in the nineteenth century, lingering attachments to received theories of liberty and natural rights, for example, accounted for the hesitations of those who "not only fail to apply the data when obtained, but persist in teaching that no application of them can be made."[25]

Thus the negativism of the received traditions was to be countered by the positivism of the emerging social sciences. As Ward pointed out, "just as Comte could complain that the philosophy of Hobbes, Locke, and Voltaire was negative, so it may now be maintained that the school of Mill, Spencer, and Fiske is also negative." Ward's book was intended to undermine the rationale for negativism, and his strategy was to construct a broader context of perception that drew selectively on currents of the new evolutionism and made these earlier viewpoints appear narrow and limited in comparison, inadequate in their empirical and historical reference, thus reducing them to moments of a historical phase that had to be assimilated but also surpassed. The goal was to search out the thinking appropriate to "the actively dynamic stage" of contemporary social life in which "social phenomena shall be contemplated as capable of intelligent control by society itself in its own interest." Because "the real object of science is to benefit man" and Victorian social science was weakest in its applied dimensions, it confronted the "danger of falling

---

[25]Lester F. Ward, *Dynamic Sociology; or, Applied Social Science as Based upon Statical Sociology and the Less Complex Sciences,* 2 vols. (New York: Greenwood Press, 1968). This is a reprint of the second edition of 1897. Quotations in this section appear on pp. xxv–xxvii, passim. In his reference to Mill as a member of the "negative" school Ward was in rhetorical flight and was not being entirely fair, as pointed out by Donald Winch in Chapter 2 of this volume. Actually Ward was a well-informed reader of Mill and particularly admired his *August Comte and Positivism,* which made a number of criticisms of Comte that Ward agreed with.

into the class of polite amusements, or dead sciences." Ward's work aimed to "point out a method by which the breath of life may be breathed into its nostrils."

The liberal positivists agreed on a set of major distinctions. The most basic was the distinction between nature and culture, and specifically between the mechanisms that accounted for changes in the natural order, on the one hand, and the processes invoked to account for changes in human social evolution on the other. The liberal positivists' critique of older thinking centered on its failure to make the appropriate distinctions. This failure resulted in a fundamental category mistake—what Ward came to call "the nature worship fallacy"—which confused social thought and worked as a drag upon its refinement and modernization. The Washingtonians argued, for example, that in the works of their leading adversaries, such as Herbert Spencer and William Graham Sumner, category mistakes in the treatment of evolutionary sociology converged with the political rhetoric of laissez-faire economics, thus reinforcing the "negativism" of a once-progressive body of thought that had taken its shape in the preceding century from Adam Smith onward, independent of the reappraisals of social thought provoked by the Darwinian revolution. While developmental theories of many kinds—Scottish, French, English, German, and American—abounded before the *Origin of Species* appeared, Darwin's challenge intensified the criticisms of all received theory. His method of reasoning and identification of natural selection as a mechanism to account for descent with modification spurred the search for a still larger context of inquiry.

The essential principle running through *Dynamic Sociology* was that nonhuman evolution was fundamentally distinct from human evolution. The former is the result of the struggle for existence and involves genetic phenomena; the latter is the outcome of the "struggle for happiness" and involves teleologic phenomena (the workings of mind, the exercise of foresight and calculation). As a philosophical naturalist and a monist, Ward held that the origins of mind resulted from natural selection, representing an extension of the intelligence found in other species, but an extension that gathered force and separated the natural and the human domains in the course of evolutionary time. Human progress was a matter of harmonizing natural phenomena with human advantage, the basic aim of science, and was expressed in the manipulation of the laws governing nonhuman phenomena, as in the case of agriculture, the domestication of animals, the energy mechanics of mill works, or the physics of the steam engine. The manipulation of natural processes gave rise to the arts and industries on which civilization was based. Both arts and industries turned on the regulation of natural laws, which was quite a different matter from adherence to them. Thus Ward described the nature worship fallacy with this maxim: "Observe nature, nothing could be more sound or wholesome. Imitate nature, nothing could be more false or pernicious."[26]

Powell, too, held that the survival of the fittest in the struggle for existence did not apply to mankind. Like Ward, Powell argued that in the study of human evolution it was useful to speak of methods rather than mechanisms, and that the methods involved were those in which psychic activities of invention and choice intervened. The psychic activities were conceived not as being in the tradition of Locke's solitary individual, but as being inherently social and intersubjective, the work not of one person but of many, like language itself. Through these psychic processes, Powell argued, "man has transferred the struggle for existence from himself to his institutions."[27] The evolution of institutions was mediated by language—the medium of knowledge and belief, science, religion, and civic discourse. It had to do with the intellectual and moral processes at work in politics, and proceeded via "the invention and selection of the just."[28] Powell conceived sociology as the science of institutions. He defined an institution as "a rule of conduct which men make by agreement or which is made for them by some authority which they recognize as such."[29] As a field of evolutionary study, sociology was not, for obvious reasons, confined to the present, but essentially amounted

[26]Lester Ward, "The Gospel of Action," in *Glimpses of the Cosmos: A Mental Autobiography, Comprising His Minor Contributions Now Republished, Together with Biographical and Historical Sketches of All His Writings* (New York: G. P. Putnam's Sons, 1918), vol. 6, 59.

[27]John Wesley Powell, "Competition as a Factor in Human Evolution," *American Anthropologist* 1, no. 4 (October 1888): 309. For Powell's other writings on this theme, see his "Human Evolution," *Transactions of the Anthropological Society of Washington* 2 (Feburary 1882–May 1883): 176–208; "From Savagery to Barbarism," *Transactions of the Anthropological Society of Washington* 3 (November 1883–May 1885): 173–96; "From Barbarism to Civilization," *American Anthropologist* 1 (April 1888): 97–123; "Darwin's Contributions to Philosophy," *Bulletin of the Philosophical Society of Washington*, published in the *Smithsonian Institution's Miscellaneous Collections* 25 (1882–3): 60–70; "Outlines of Sociology," *Saturday Lectures of the Anthropological and Biological Societies of Washington* (Washington, D.C.: Judd and Detweiler, 1882), 60–82; "Sociology, Or the Science of Institutions, Pt. 1," *American Anthropologist*, n.s., 3 (1901): 475–509; "Sociology, Or the Science of Institutions, Pt. 2," *American Anthropologist*, n.s., 3 (1901): 695–745.

[28]Powell, "Human Evolution," 207.

[29]Powell, "Sociology, Or the Science of Institutions, Pt. 1," 475.

to an interpretive historical and ethnographic discipline, based on the contrast and comparison of cases, that drew on pre-Darwinian "stage theories" of historical development as well as on contemporary evidence on American Indian cultures then accumulating in the Bureau of American Ethnology under his direction.

When Powell established the Bureau of Ethnology and organized its research program, he relied for basic concepts and categories on the most sophisticated treatment of historical stages developed to that time, *Ancient Society, or Researches in the Lines of Human Progress from Savagery through Barbarism to Civilization* (1877), by his American colleague Lewis Henry Morgan.[30] Powell provided copies of *Ancient Society* to his BAE staff members, so that they could go into the field familiar with its themes and concepts. The special merit of the work, from Powell's standpoint, was that it "laid the foundation for the science of government as it is to be finally erected by the philosophy of evolution."[31] Morgan was credited with cracking the kinship code, one of the fundamental insights in Victorian anthropology, and with establishing kinship relations as the underlying basis of tribal social organization and government. For contemporaries, however, what made the book resonate was its concluding section, titled "Growth of the Idea of Property." Its pages provided an intricate, closely reasoned account of the transition in mores from simple tribal systems, in which most real property was held in common, to complex ones in which private property fixed social relations, government extended over large territories of diverse peoples,

---

[30]Morgan's immediate impact was extensive. Darwin considered Morgan to be the New World's first social scientist, and Henry Adams believed Morgan to have provided the essentials for a more comprehensive style of historical analysis than previously attempted. Friedrich Engels credited Morgan with the independent formulation of the materialist dialectic, rather mistakenly in view of the latter's theism and principled "republican" politics. Powell saw Morgan as the source of the first truly scientific accounts of tribal life given to the world. For the scholarship on Morgan, see Carl Resek, *Lewis Henry Morgan: American Scholar* (Chicago: University of Chicago Press, 1960); Robert E. Bieder, "Lewis Henry Morgan and the Evolution of an Iroquois Scholar," in his *Science Encounters the Indian, 1820–1880: The Early Years of American Ethnology* (Norman: University of Oklahoma Press, 1986), 194–248. For a powerful interpretation of Morgan's intellectual development that focuses on his kinship studies, his education in the tradition of Scottish commonsense realism dominant in America during his youth, and the impact on his thinking of the revolution in concepts of ethnological time wrought by the discovery of fossil man, see Thomas R. Trautman, *Lewis Henry Morgan and the Invention of Kinship* (Berkeley: University of California Press, 1987). For Powell's contemporary appraisal, see his "Sketch of Lewis H. Morgan," *Popular Science Monthly* 18, no. 1 (November 1880): 114–21.

[31]Powell, "Sketch of Lewis H. Morgan," 120.

and legal conventions regulating ownership and inheritance were put in place.

Speculation about the growth of the property impulse, the historical evolution of its forms and meanings, and its elaboration in the social structures that led up to contemporary civilization was the theme of the most famous passage in *Ancient Society:*

> Since the advent of civilization, the outgrowth of property has been so immense, its forms so diversified, its uses so expanding and its management so intelligent in the interests of its owners, that it has become, on the part of the people, an unmanageable power. The human mind stands bewildered in the presence of its own creation. The time will come, nevertheless, when human intelligence will rise to the mastery over property, and define the relations of the state to the property it protects, as well as the obligations and limits of the rights of its owners. The interests of society are paramount to individual interests, and the two must be brought into just and harmonious relations. A mere property career is not the final destiny of mankind, if progress is to be the law of the future as it has been of the past.[32]

GOVERNMENT AND THE STATE

The felt need for intelligence to rise to mastery over property led to the construction of evolutionary positivism and expressed itself in an attempt to conceive the relationship between society and government in terms of a more inclusive scientific perspective than had been available to the founders of the Republic. For Powell, the state had become "the grand unit of social organization."[33] For Ward, the state was "the most important step taken by man in the direction of controlling the social forces."[34] What was novel in this viewpoint was the refusal in principle to recognize as the embodiment of special virtue either government or civil society at the expense of the other; instead, the emphasis was on the combined effects of government and civil society in determining the overall condition of the social order.

Thus both Ward and Powell distinguished between government and the state, the latter being the more inclusive term roughly synonymous

---

[32]Lewis H. Morgan, *Ancient Society, Or Researches in the Lines of Human Progress from Savagery through Barbarism to Civilization,* edited, annotated, and introduced by Eleanor Burke Leacock (Cleveland: Meridian Books, World Publishing, 1963). Quotation appears on p. 562.

[33]Powell, "Outlines of Sociology," 63.

[34]Lester Ward and James Q. Dealey, *Textbook of Sociology* (New York: Macmillan Co., 1921), 293.

with "the social order" and pointing to a complex and compound structure of connections between the public and the private held together by the legal and regulatory operations of the former. In his first paper on the subject, given as a lecture in the Smithsonian's National Museum in April 1882, Powell divided the science of sociology into three parts: "the constitution of the state, the form of the government, and the regulation embodied in the law." When Powell spoke of the constitution of the state, he meant the combination of public and private agencies that made up the organizational structure of society. He argued that in the modern state "two grand classes of organizations are found," those directly related to government and those indirectly related to it. The official agencies of government composed the first of Powell's classes, and he called them organizations of the major class. The private or voluntary agencies of civil society composed his second group. He called these organizations of the minor class; they "do not constitute a part of the government, but they form a part of the state and must necessarily be considered in the plan of the state." Included in this group were all those associations that were organized for religious, charitable, educational, industrial, and other purposes, and "while not a part of government in an important way, they are connected therewith."

The regulation of conduct required for the successful operation of private associations was primarily the concern of the members themselves, whose intentions were expressed in charters, constitutions, by-laws, and rules of order. "But over all these," Powell pointed out, "there is the law of the government with which the rules or laws of the several minor organizations must conform, and for the ultimate enforcement of which the government is to a large extent responsible."

In Powell's evolutionary studies, therefore, the rise of government occurred as a differentiation from the state, which was a more complex idea. It referred not to the mystical unities of German idealism, but to the prevailing social order as a whole, a whole that was presumed to be empirically accessible and subject to directed change through the spread of new ideas. The state had become a vast "plexus of organizations," public and private, organized in a descending series.

Government grew in response to the need for an organized system of regulation: the more complex the society, the greater the number of laws. Government was conceived as the principal sociological organ for the regulation of conduct; the institutions of civil society were subsidiary to it, bound by indirect connections. There were no hard and fast lines separating the public from the private. The long view of social development established by Lewis Henry Morgan and others made it apparent that social conventions were too variable historically to be captured in political, legal, and economic doctrines held to be timeless and invariant, applicable without regard to ever changing circumstances.

With respect to the legitimate functions of government, the lesson drawn from the long view was that the lines separating the public from the private were permeable and indistinct. As Powell put it, "The functions of the two classes of regulation are not clearly and permanently differentiated. A particular system of regulation may be relegated now to the government, and now to a society of the minor class, or the system of regulation may be divided between them." Examples were plentiful in education, exploration and economic development, the support of science, and other important functions of society. "The boundary lines between major [i.e., public] and minor [i.e., private or voluntary] regulation are ever shifting."[35]

This perspective, of course, led to the focus of attention on the roles of government in organizing systems of regulation, on the institutions and conventions involved, and on the broader political processes that accounted for legitimacy or its reverse. Struggling with these matters in the 1880s, the evolutionary sociologists in Washington outlined an approach to fundamentals that characterized the developing viewpoint of liberal positivism. In doing so they emphasized three kinds of problems they believed to be inhibiting further social progress: (1) the need to modernize law so as to bring it into conformity with advancing knowledge; (2) the need to graft onto the inherited institutional structures of the American government new capacities for coordinating knowledge with the discourse of politics; and (3) the need in social theory for new ways in which to coordinate science with ethics.

GOVERNMENT AND LAW

Powell was aware of the possibility of defining sociology simply as the study of law (i.e., rules of conduct that government attempted to enforce), but the study of law was then a rather haphazard craft tradition with its own conventions, inherently conservative because of the nature of law and quite independent of the newer currents of evolutionary thought that suggested the need for a higher viewpoint. Garfield had spoken of the

[35]Powell, "Outlines of Sociology," 60–3, passim.

need for legislators to get away from the traditions of "black letter learning" and to study society itself. Powell agreed, and in his writing chose therefore to "define sociology as the science of institutions rather than as the science of law, because in the term sociology I wish to include a study of the law itself, and also to consider in what manner it originates and by what agency it is enforced, whether by sanctions of interest, sanctions of punishment, or sanctions of conscience." Because institutions were defined abstractly in terms of their cultural content—not as commands but as "rules of conduct which men make by agreement"—the way was opened to broaden the field of inquiry and examine the ideas on which the rules were based.[36]

Powell distinguished several types of law, among them property law, corporation law, government law, international law, military law, ecclesiastical law, and criminal law. The referents of each type but one are obvious. By government law, Powell referred to constitutional law and to what would become the field of administrative law. This field developed because, although government is the key organ of regulation within the state, "the organ itself must be controlled, the conduct of government must be regulated."[37]

Ward made a related point regarding the dynamics of statutory development. Most contemporaries, he said, believed that the executive branch of government merely *administers* national affairs, and "this is a great mistake. A very large part of the real legislation of the country is done by the executive branch." This overlooked form of lawmaking occurred at the level of the operating bureaus of government and was driven not by common-law precedent, but by administrative exigency—the need to interpret new congressional enactments or to reinterpret old ones to bring them into conformity with the problems encountered in practice. It was at the level of practice that administrative officials were exposed to "the popular pulse more sensitively than the legislature." Such officials often became identified (sometimes too closely, as later critics of interest-group liberalism would point out) with the industries involved and were called on by them to adopt specific reforms. As Ward put it,

After stepping to the verge of their legal authority in response to such demands, whereby much real legislation is done not contemplated by those who framed the laws under which these bureaus were established, they finish by making

[36]Powell, "Sociology, Or the Science of Institutions, Pt. 1," 475.
[37]Powell, "Outlines of Sociology," 68.

recommendations of the rest to the law-making power. This latter usually recognizes the wisdom of such recommendations, and enacts them into laws, thus ever enlarging the administrative jurisdiction of government.[38]

Ward went beyond calling attention to neglected developmental processes of this sort, however. In his sociological writings he developed the metaphor of law as an invention, comparable to mechanical inventions, and likened the environment of lawmaking in the Congress to the workshop of the inventor. Garfield had suggested that statesmanship "consists rather in removing causes than in punishing or evading results," and Ward elaborated the point in his work. In *Dynamic Sociology* he distinguished between compulsory legislation, which operated on the basis of sanctions and penalties and accounted for most extant law, and "attractive legislation," seeds of which were present in the nineteenth-century American experience with internal improvements, for example, or certain types of protective tariffs intended to nurse infant industries.

In making the distinction, Ward identified the basic premise of what would become, in the twentieth century, a major development in American social policy, namely, the use of incentives. Two examples are federal matching grants made to the states to encourage the adoption of specific social and economic policies and tax deductions allowed to encourage industrial innovation and investment, charitable contributions, and the formation of philanthropic foundations, homeownership, and other goals. As a concept, attractive legislation foreshadowed a new system of governance. It turned on the deployment of incentives and the removal of obstacles, rather than on punitive sanctions, and it was premised, of course, on the existence of reliable ways of publicly monitoring the actual effects of incentives in achieving social purposes.[39]

---

[38]Lester Ward, *The Psychic Factors of Civilization*, 2d ed. (New York: Johnson Reprint Corporation, 1970), 310–11. Ward was pointing here rather uncritically to a dynamic that would come to be viewed as the "capture problem," the linkage between government agencies and organized private groups. As far as I am aware, there is no criticism of pluralism per se in Ward's writings.

[39]Ward's initial discussion of compulsory versus attractive legislation appears in his *Dynamic Sociology*, vol. 1, pp. 35–45. See also the concluding chapter of his *Applied Sociology* (New York: Arno Press Reprint, 1974). Note that in a laudatory review of John R. Commons's *Distribution of Wealth* in the *Annals of the American Academy of Political and Social Science* IV, no. 5 (March 1894): 818–22, Ward argued that the taxing power was the most important principle of political economy because it was the most amenable to his notion of attractive legislation. At that point there were no federal income taxes, and the federal budget was generated from excise taxes and tariffs. Commons pointed out that taxes could be, and had been, used for a variety of purposes other than revenue, to protect or discourage industries, for example, or to concentrate or diffuse wealth.

As Ward elaborated the comparison between mechanical invention and legislation, the raw materials of social invention were identified as the social forces, psychic in origin, made up of the wants and needs of people. Since these wants and needs were expressed in social conflicts, and conflict was the natural and perhaps irreducible outcome of the diversity of interests in society, the comparison suggested to him not only the importance of incentives but also the possibility of so devising law as not to eliminate competition but to get the social benefit of it in ways not possible under the blanket prohibitions of laissez-faire. So Ward called for the invention of new laws and regulatory conventions that would be largely self-executing, requiring public oversight and administrative supervision, but a minimum of government personnel. In his view, while the government itself "achieves little, it is the condition of all achievement"; thus he emphasized the need for ideas with progressive potentials.[40]

THE RATIONALE FOR GOVERNMENT RESEARCH

Government research and information gathering played an especially important role in establishing the general conditions for social achievement, and the bureau chiefs were among the first to formulate the case for government commitment to the production and analysis of social data. In doing so the bureaucrats sought to convince legislators that expanded federal activities in this area would raise the level of responsible policy debate and contribute directly to an informed citizenry, but would not threaten the structure of federalism itself; the prerogatives of state government bureaus; or the activities of private, voluntary institutions and associations.

That case was difficult to make. The political environment after the Civil War was volatile; the status and standing of the new research bureaus were uncertain. Most bureaus had been born in the form of riders attached to appropriations bills, and might be closed down just as easily. The civil service reforms that had followed the assassination of Garfield were slowly stabilizing the conditions of employment within the bureaucracy, though often, ironically, at the cost of the administrative discretion that had made it possible to assemble the hand-picked teams of researchers on which the bureau chiefs had come to depend.

[40]Ward and Dealey, *Textbook of Sociology*, 292.

Operating without clear constitutional grounding or assured tenure, the bureau chiefs faced special difficulties in establishing and maintaining the long-term research programs that promised order and progress. Plans had to be sold not once but repeatedly, and implementation was easily disrupted. The fact that some state governments were developing their own research agencies sometimes posed thorny jurisdictional issues. Old fears of centralization occasionally surfaced, and, as the Washington community grew, concerns about monopolization of research in the capital grew apace. There was always pressure, now and then severe, to limit the work of the bureaus to matters of immediate, practical importance, and this pressure, if unchecked, encouraged narrow specialization and the formation of alliances with well-organized interest groups, and thus the neglect of overall coherence and depth.

Given the uncertainties of the situation and the absence of much tradition to guide them, the builders of the bureaus attempted to invent a tradition and to defend it. In so doing they worked up new arguments about the rationale for government science. Some arguments were practical, simply stressing the need for sound empirical information to enable the government to carry out its statutory obligations properly. Some arguments, however, went beyond claims of administrative utility to broader assertions about how the work of the bureaus might contribute to the solution of questions of long-term political development, civic education, and the delineation of new functions to be undertaken by government.

In defending the sociological approach to public problems, for example, Powell, Ward, and Wright all made claims about the uses of government statistics that went beyond simple empiricism. Powell spoke of statistics as one of the component methods of sociology, and distinguished between its business or governmental uses as practical information to assist in decision making, on the one hand, and its higher uses in "the verification of sociologic inferences," an activity that occurred not simply in the library, but in public debate and political argument more generally.[41] Ward spoke about the potential usefulness of statistical series in the same light, as "the initial step in state regulation" and as a tool for use in developing and monitoring legislation.[42]

Carroll Wright had more experience in the administration of statis-

[41]Powell, "Sociology, Or the Science of Institutions, Pt. 1," 479.
[42]Ward, "The Province of Statistics," *Glimpses of the Cosmos*, vol. 2, 164.

tically oriented social investigation, and the sometimes heated politics of the process, than any other American in the late nineteenth century. In the tradition of those who conceived statistics as "history in repose," Wright emphasized that statistics was a branch of contemporary history, a response to the need of modern society to "know itself" in the new, collective, scientific context. The practice of statistics required not simply mathematical abilities, he argued, but a comparative, developmental sense, "for the statistician must have the spirit of . . . ethical philosophy, the recognition of the great fundamental law, the principle which governs this world and all things in it, the principle of evolution."[43]

Conscious of the point that government statisticians were generating primary sources of information that would find their way into both political argument and scholarly research, Wright preached to his subordinates and to the officials in bureaus of labor statistics at the state level, as well, about the special moral obligations they were under to guard against bias and inattention in the drudgery of office routine. He argued repeatedly that they had a "sacred obligation" not to mislead legislators and fix a falsehood in the history of the state: "I do not believe there is a man in our membership who would commit so great a crime as to falsify history in this way. If he would, he certainly deserves all the odium that his own community can put upon him." Wright sympathized with the statisticians over the perils that the new profession brought with it and urged them to concentrate on the long view in the midst of political turmoil:

I take the papers; I see what is going on in the different States. My order to the press clippings bureau is to send me everything that relates to each one of the State bureaus as well as to my own office, and I know as well as you that once in awhile some of you are called very hard names. Why within the last six months in my own experience I think I have been called about everything that could come into the catalogue of names that an official would be entitled to. I have been called a rampant free trader, a high protectionist, a blatant labor agitator, a tool of the capitalists, whatever comes handy to the writer's mind to clinch his point.

[43]"Address of Carroll Wright, President of the American Statistical Association, at Its Annual Meeting in Boston, January 17, 1908," *Publications of the American Statistical Association* 11, nos. 81–8 (1908–9): 14. For Wright's discussion of the practice of statistics, see "The Study of Statistics in Colleges," *Publications of the American Economic Association* 3 (1888–9): 5–28; "The Limitations and Difficulties of Statistics," *Yale Review* 3 (1894–5): 121–43.

This, too, will pass, he would say, but the official records would remain, and if history was to be of any use to political understanding, the records would be useful. Composing them was no trivial matter.[44]

The most interesting argument for government science circulating around Washington during this period, however, was a more basic one. It focused not on the uses of statistics, but on the social character of knowledge itself, and on the role of government in increasing and disseminating that knowledge. The most persistent challenge to the legitimacy of the new research programs was the fear that the centralization of information in Washington amounted to the concentration of power there, threatening the prerogatives of other levels of government or of private individuals and institutions. Most of the bureau chiefs were, in fact, strong advocates for local government (Powell, for example, is often cited as the "father" of American regionalism), but they thought that local governments and private institutions were woefully inadequate in generating the knowledge base of modern civilization. They sought not to displace lower levels of government but to energize them; not big government, but more knowledgeable and responsible governance in a federal system.

In dealing with anxieties about collectivism and the concentration of power, the bureau chiefs updated one of the tenets of early republicanism: that the health of the state depended on the intelligence and virtue of the citizenry. They asserted that an overriding public interest was served in providing information on the social and economic conditions with which contemporary intelligence and virtue had to contend. They argued that only the federal government had the right combination of authority, breadth of view, and presumption of continuity to develop knowledge of such conditions on the appropriate scale. They defended the work of the bureaus as contributing impartially to an ongoing civic education of the people as a whole.

Officials in the Department of Education, established in 1867, for example, saw the problem of mounting nationwide inquiries into the postwar situation early on, because the Constitution leaves education to the states and localities and makes no provision for the involvement of the federal government. Under John Eaton's leadership in the 1870s the Office of Education—the name had changed—often produced reports

---

[44]"Address of Carroll Wright, President of the Association," *Proceedings of the Tenth Annual Convention of the National Association of Officials of Bureaus of Labor Statistics in the United States* (Minneapolis, 1894), 12.

that criticized state and local conditions and both private and public agencies, especially with respect to the situation in the South. Some congressional critics voiced familiar complaints about outside influences and the concentration of power in Washington. Eaton responded that the determined diffusion of centralized information worked *against* the grain of concentration of power: "It puts into the hands of everyone who has the intelligence to comprehend the given case all any officer can know, all the whole nation can know. The principle is a grand equalizer, and is essential to the primary ideas of republican, as distinguished from other forms of government."[45]

Eaton's successor at the Office of Education, William Torrey Harris, elaborated on the theme and brought out some of its implications. He pointed out that the preference for local government control of education was based on the belief that local government was closest to the people and thus represented the best context in which to develop the "directive powers" of each citizen. To secure the highest degree of independent activity, however, the "individual must do his own work, but do it in the light of all that has been done and planned in his sphere." The role of the office was to provide that light, thus encouraging voluntary innovation and development. The office's aim was to ensure that each local system should be in a position to benefit from the experience of all. Harris contended that the research program of his office was in conformity with broad principles of political development. "The ideal of this nation is the diffusion of intelligent self direction, not the centralization of it," he explained. "But inasmuch as intelligent directive power implies a general survey of the entire field of operation and the knowledge of whatever has heretofore been attempted in it, it is perfectly clear that there is a necessity for the central Government to maintain national bureaus" charged with the appropriate functions.[46]

Powell spoke in the same vein. In 1885 a joint congressional commission on the scientific work of the federal government launched an investigation into the activities of the Washington scientific community. Because Powell was the unofficial dean of that community and director of the Geological Survey, the largest of the research bureaus and the one most directly concerned with conflicting economic interests engaged in

[45]U.S. Office of Education, *Report of the Commissioner of Education for the Year 1874* (Washington, D.C.: U.S. Government Printing Office, 1875), v.

[46]U.S. Office of Education, *Annual Statement of the Commissioner of Education to the Secretary of the Interior for the Year 1889–1890*, 4.

resource development, the hearings focused on his views of the relationship between science and government. Democrats on the commission, led by Rep. H. A. Herbert of Alabama, a colonel in the Confederate army during the war who would cap a sixteen-year congressional career by entering Grover Cleveland's cabinet in 1893 as secretary of the Navy, mounted an attack on Powell's program. Arguing that laissez-faire doctrine contained all the incentives required for the development and deployment of scientific knowledge, Herbert threatened to abolish the Geological Survey and, failing that, to restrict the scope of its work and "privatize" the publication of its research reports.

While Powell and the other bureau chiefs thought of their work as contributing to a growing system of civic education that took the nation as its audience and aimed for the free or inexpensive distribution of their reports to public libraries in every county, Herbert saw the development of a "wasteful and extravagant" counterculture and suggested that if the Geological Survey were confined to the collection of publicly accessible data, some combination of market mechanisms, private scholars, and publication firms would handle the distribution of knowledge well enough.

Powell was accused, in effect, of running a kind of Tammany Hall for scientists, monopolizing the research enterprise in geology and related disciplines and centralizing scientific authority in Washington. In his long response to the charges, Powell pointed out the collective and public nature of both scientific progress and authority; the sorry record, historically speaking, of laissez-faire principles as applied to scientific work; the foolishness of the hope that the future would be any different; and the inappropriateness, for a social theory that purported to be progressive, of confusing real property with property in knowledge. The following passage reflects his understanding of the political economy of science and recapitulates the rationale of the bureau chiefs for an activist role for government in the development of knowledge and its application to public affairs:

Possession of property is exclusive; possession of knowledge is not exclusive; for the knowledge which one man has may also be the possession of another. The learning of one man does not subtract from the learning of another, as if there were a limited quantity to be divided into exclusive holdings; so the discovery by one man does not inhibit discovery by another, as if there were a limited quantity of unknown truth. Intellectual activity does not compete with other intellectual activity for exclusive possession of truth; scholarship breeds scholarship, wisdom breeds wisdom, discovery breeds discovery. Property may be divided into exclusive ownership for utilization and preservation, but knowledge is utilized and preserved by multiple ownership. That which one man gains by discovery is a gain of other men. And these multiple gains become invested capital, the interest on which is all paid to every owner, and the revenue of new discovery is boundless. It may be wrong to take another man's purse, but it is always right to take another man's knowledge, and it is the highest virtue to promote another man's investigation. The laws of political economy that relate to property do not belong to the economics of science and intellectual progress. While ownership of property precludes other ownership of the same, ownership of knowledge promotes ownership of the same, and when research is properly organized every man's work is an aid to every other man's.[47]

The proper organization of research, of course, was the heart of the matter. Powell insisted that government science did not exclude individuals from the field in any manner, and he distinguished between control and coordination: "Scientific men spurn authority, but seek for coordination." They realize the truth that "no great work can be performed without a proper division of labor, and they are always anxious that their several labors may be fitted into the grand system of scientific operations for the development of knowledge."[48] Fitting the labors of individuals and institutions into a progressive system of operations, however, was an ongoing process of interpretation. It implied the existence of interpreters and institutions where the process was under way. The interpretive problem itself was multifaceted; it required trust, competence, and a large measure of administrative discretion. To secure a public place for the role was the central, practical challenge facing those who would be statesmen of American science. For his part, Powell favored a greater measure of centralization for the government's research bureaus, concentration on long-term issues in both the natural and social sciences, and resistance to any proposed division of labor that would limit government scientists to ad hoc investigations.

Centralization, even of information, and concentration on long-term issues have never been easy for the American government. Intelligent participation in "the grand system of scientific operations" requires high-

---

[47]John Wesley Powell, *On the Organization of Scientific Work of the General Government: Extracts from the Testimony Taken by the Joint Commission of the Senate and House of Representatives to Consider the Present Organization of the Signal Service, Geological Survey, Coast and Geodetic Survey, and the Hydrographic Office of the Navy Department, With a View to Secure Greater Efficiency and Economy of Administration* (Washington, D.C.: U.S. Government Printing Office, 1885), 1082. For an account of the joint commission and its work, see Dupree, *Science in the Federal Government*, 215–31.
[48]Powell, *On the Organization of Scientific Work*, 178.

level understanding of it, and thus a special kind of person within the civil service. It requires an elite group that has broad discretionary powers and is composed not of experts, who are notoriously incapable of transcending mere expertise, but of persons capable of judging and directing experts, persons with an appropriate sense of science and society.

Because, as the bureau chiefs argued, the development of knowledge differs in important ways from the provision of routine administrative services or the fulfillment of the particulars of the law, successful leadership of the scientific community required a measure of independence that was hard to come by. When questioned on this issue by members of the Joint Congressional Commission, Powell pointed out that it was a practical impossibility to direct the course of inquiry by statute. The judgments involved in advancing knowledge were too complex, interdependent, and dynamic to permit specification in congressional directives, even for that matter to capture within the administrative directives of the bureau chiefs themselves: "It is therefore impossible by law to organize such operations, and more, it is impossible for the directors or superintendents of such work to lay out plans of operations which shall be a full guide to their assistants."[49] Getting the job done required giving people who had character and intellectual quality a generous measure of freedom of maneuver. The process of research and interpretation was amenable only to general statutory direction and control by appropriations politics; beyond that point "the several bureaus engaged in research should be left free to prosecute such research in all its details without dictation from superior authority."[50]

[49]Ibid., 24.

[50]Ibid., 26. While the federal government employs many thousands of technical and scientific experts and government research and planning bureaus have proliferated apace, the hopes of the late-nineteenth-century Washington intellectual community for the development of a scientifically competent civil service elite that might play a role in interpreting conditions and helping to shape affairs of state have not been fulfilled. The most sophisticated studies of the character of the American career civil service have been those of Hugh Heclo, who points out that, in contrast to traditions prevailing in England, France, Germany, and Japan, where civil servants are members of a social and intellectual elite, with a place at the center of governance, the American government is "hollow" at its center so far as the continuous, long-term presence of those who represent the experience of the "inside" of government is concerned. Career higher civil servants are not located near the centers of power in the American system; presidents and cabinet officers seldom know their names. The most important functions, political and intellectual, of the higher civil service in the other countries mentioned are performed in America by political appointees. Heclo distinguishes between the de jure higher civil service and the de facto version of same, the latter represented not by career civil servants, but increasingly by those knowledgeable policy brokers loosely called the "in and outers."

The most persistent criticism of government research in all domains over the years

SCIENCE AND ETHICS

The liberal positivists were not systematic moral philosophers, but they were moralists nonetheless, and there was a common pattern of argument to their moralism, one that converged with the primacy accorded in their thinking to historically oriented, empirically rich social description as the proper context for political debate, and the emphasis on law and regulation as the legitimate expression of the evolving intelligence and moral consensus at work within society. The bureaus were attempting to describe the various contexts of "the social question" that resulted from the vast transformation of the industrial polity and to furnish details on economic organization and industrial practice, class conflict, unemployment, poverty, and dependency.

Not all problems were recondite. As Wright put it: "One may know that filthy streets are demoralizing without being absolutely certain as to the nature of the state."[51] Some problems, however, were recondite, and an appropriate moral response to the multifaceted "social question" of the era necessarily engaged beliefs about the nature of the state. Inasmuch as the political aspect of the individualistic ethics of classical liberalism was most strongly expressed in the laissez faire doctrine on the limits to state action and defense of the regime of contract within civil society— the viewpoint developed in such touchstone texts as Spencer's *Social Statics, The Man Versus the State, The Principles of Ethics,* or in William Graham Sumner's *What the Social Classes Owe to Each Other*— the liberal positivists threw themselves into the opposition. Lester

---

has been the want of any "grand system" with historical depth in it, because of the pull of politically driven "ad hocery," and a refusal to concede significant discretionary authority in the relevant operations to career people. Thus there is the aversion of "high flyers" to civil service careers and the importance of quasi official mediating bodies such as the National Academy of Sciences, the think tanks, the foundations, and other institutions as sources of criticism, patronage, and refuge, within the structure of the American political elite. On the civil service and the culture of contemporary policy-making and analysis more generally, see Heclo, *A Government of Strangers: Executive Politics in Washington* (Washington, D.C.: Brookings Institution, 1977); idem, "In Search of a Role: America's Higher Civil Service," in Ezra N. Suleiman, ed., *Bureaucrats and Policy Making: A Comparative Overview* (New York: Holmes and Meier, 1984), 8–34; idem, "The In-and-Outer System: A Critical Assessment," in G. Calvin Mackenzie, ed., *The In-and-Outers: Presidential Appointees and Transient Government in Washington* (Baltimore: Johns Hopkins University Press, 1987), 195–211; and idem, "Issue Networks and the Executive Establishment," in Anthony King, ed., *The New American Political System* (Washington, D.C.: American Enterprise Institute, 1978), 87–124.
[51]Wright, *Outline of Practical Sociology*, 6.

Ward spoke of the engagement, which stretched out over many years, as "Spencer-smashing at Washington."[52]

Several lines of opposition argument were developed, but the most important focused on the ethics of "competition," a term that linked biological and economic theories. As noted earlier, the liberal positivists rejected biological or materialistic premises as inadequate to account for social evolution. Ward's basic contribution to the field was to highlight the importance of psychic factors and thus to call attention to feeling, desire, and aspiration as the potent elements in the process. Although members of the Washington community conceded the usefulness of biological theory as a spur to social theory, they held that "the biological analogy is not now generally admitted to be sound; for if an organism society must have something in it other than the ethical and social relations of men; it would possess parts and functions independent of human relations."[53] The existence of parts and functions independent of human relations would imply the need to deal with something beyond the reach of intention, understanding, judgment, and responsibility. Such a notion was unacceptable, indeed unintelligible, to the members of the Washington community, and thus they rejected as well any functionalist views of evolution that obscured the importance of conscious choice and will—the basic foundations of self-government whether considered in its individual or its social aspect.

Their reading of evolutionary sociology, then, converged on the idea that "we must recognize human thoughts and feelings as well as the propensities which serve to bring individual units into institutional relations."[54] It was the connection between human thoughts and feelings, between ideas and values, the basic stuff of both politics and ethics, that generated the need for government's role in social investigation. The liberal positivists pointed to three sources of informed opinion on social affairs: personal observation, systematic works in social science (then rapidly developing as a new genre of discursive literature), and the records

[52]Ward, "Spencer-smashing at Washington," *Glimpses of the Cosmos*, vol. 5, 109–10. The Washington community's interest in Spencer—and knowledge of Spencerian texts was extensive—highlights the point that the same cultural currents were flowing through Britain and the United States. For a discussion of the argument that British and American intellectual elites were part of a single Anglo-American subculture preoccupied with the same problems regarding science and religion, expertise, and democracy, see David D. Hall, "The Victorian Connection," in Daniel Walker Howe, ed., *Victorian America* (Philadelphia: University of Pennsylvania Press, 1976), 81–94.
[53]Wright, *Outline of Practical Sociology*, 4.
[54]Ibid.

of official inquiries. The third source, they pointed out, represented the bulk of the raw materials available for social analysis. It fueled and encouraged development of the second source, and thus contributed to "the spirit of sociological inquiry," which was understood to be the spirit of responsible citizenship and was marked by certain characteristics. The person who had the proper spirit "is more fond of the inductive than the deductive method of reasoning; he is also the friend of the historical school, ... [and] he welcomes with enthusiasm the efforts of governments everywhere to report the facts relative to the conditions of the people." These interlocking assumptions represented the prevailing view in Washington circles and in ASSA in the final decades of the century, and they could be succinctly stated, Carroll Wright suggested, in the axiom that "men who think alike will act together," the bedrock of a rational politics.[55]

Many people, of course, distrusted the axiom. On the left were emerging groups of Marxists, socialists, populists, single taxers, and utopian reformers of different kinds. The liberal positivists generally lumped these groups together and dismissed them as the carriers of various forms of romantic idealism, which provided new styles of idealist social criticism but were based on an excessively altruistic social psychology. To the liberal positivists, the radicals seemed as unrealistic and suspicious of empiricism in politics as were their opposite numbers in the tradition of liberal individualism. The latter, entrenched in the mainstream, represented the most formidable challenge—in terms of numbers, philosophy, and institutional resources—to any hope of thinking alike and acting together. For polemical purposes liberal individualists were generally lumped together as disciples of the "Spencerian school" who espoused a "gospel of inaction" based on fears derived from faulty analogies, chiefly Spencer's famous phrase about "the survival of the fittest" in the struggle for existence. The Washingtonians believed that the liberal individualists preferred deductive reasoning from dubious first principles, were indifferent to the themes of the historical school, and viewed the government's social investigation as a Trojan horse likely full of misguided volunteers for the construction of a diseased state.

The response of the liberal positivists to those in both wings of opinion—radicals and liberal individualists—was the same. As Ward put it, "Society needs less to be told what it is doing wrong than to be shown

[55]Ibid., 5.

what it is really doing." Empirical monitoring would reveal, he believed, a "schism between theory and practice" that was rooted in faulty analogical reasoning and resulted in a preference for "natural" as opposed to "artificial" regulation.[56] Ward emphasized, as had Thomas Huxley in his famous essay on evolution and ethics (which Ward accused Huxley of having plagiarized from his own work), that social progress was a matter of checking natural selection at every point and substituting for it ethical and political processes. Ward singled out beliefs about competition as the nub of the problem, and suggested that these beliefs, too, would benefit from public, empirical examination. "A new political economy," he argued, "will devote itself not to exhortation about the glories of competition, but to showing how society can secure whatever benefits competition has to offer."[57]

The search to secure the benefits of competition without its destructive ethical and economic effects was a continuing preoccupation of the liberal positivists. None of them doubted the importance of competitive behavior, or thought the competitive impulse itself suspect in ethical terms, because they believed it to be so closely tied to all forms of endeavor and to progress in all departments of culture. Wright's view was representative on this score. He regarded the struggle of labor for better wages and hours and a stronger voice in industrial affairs as an example of the more general and enduring labor problem, considered in its philosophical aspect. "The real labor problem," he suggested, "is the struggle of humanity for a higher standard," a struggle flowing from human nature itself, which he sometimes referred to as a Divinely implanted restlessness that rendered conflict—and the urge to resolve it—a permanent feature of the human condition. "Every step in civilization has been achieved by it, and it is the method of history. It is a conflict which cannot be avoided, and should it be avoided, the result would be not only the death of industry, but the disintegration of society."

The conflict was to be confronted by ethical and political commitment,

---

[56]Lester Ward, "Politico-Social Functions," *Glimpses of the Cosmos*, vol. 2, 335–53. Quoted sentence appears on p. 338. Ward's paper was originally given as an address before the Washington Anthropological Society on March 15, 1881.

[57]Lester Ward, "The Psychologic Basis of Social Economics," *Glimpses of the Cosmos*, vol. 4, 345–66. Quoted sentence is on p. 364. The charge that Huxley plagiarized him is detailed on pp. 348–9. This is one of Ward's most cogent essays on the need to differentiate the meanings of competition and the paradoxes that result from doing so. For other discussions in the same vein in the same work, see his "Political Ethics of Herbert Spencer," vol. 5, 38–66; "Plutocracy and Paternalism," vol. 5, 231–40; "Herbert Spencer's Sociology," vol. 6, 169–77; "Mind as a Social Factor," vol. 3, 361–7.

however, and not by administrative nihilism. To make his point, Wright cited with approval Mill's declaration that "there is not any one abuse or injustice by merely abolishing which the human race would pass out of suffering and into happiness," the lesson being that "yet we can feel with most of those who have any remedy to propose that they may contribute to a softening of the struggle, which, after all, is the real, great question."[58]

The liberal positivists saw this concentration on softening the struggle, which led to progress, without arresting it, which made for decline, as the central problem in the social ethics of the day. This view led to a variety of efforts to sort out the different shades of meaning of competition and to examine their ethical implications, all with an eye to the amenability of favored meanings to legislative and regulatory reinforcement and diffusion. In Powell's case, for example, given his argument that early in the evolutionary process man had transferred the focus of struggle from himself to his institutions, the question arose as to how institutional change was to be conceived. The appropriate principles, he argued, could not be derived from biology, but only from "the canons of justice, for the efficiency of competition itself in human progress depends primarily upon preestablished justice."[59] Justice was preestablished not as a permanent set of precepts to be handed down and applied, regardless of changing circumstances, but as a permanent aim. On this question Powell reflected the continuing influence of "moral sense" philosophies in the United States. He held that conscience was a universal human faculty that made existence of the institutions of community life possible and made change within them possible as well.

With respect to the contemporary situation, Powell distinguished between "emulative" and "antagonistic" competition:[60] "By emulation is meant the strife between men for greater excellence—to perform better service for their fellow men. By antagonism is meant strife in which man endeavors to injure his rival that he may himself succeed." The model for emulative competition turned on continuous learning and was found in the work of creative people in art, science, and scholarship, but it was evident in other sectors of culture as well. Among the professional classes, for

[58]Wright, *Outline of Practical Sociology*, 423–4.
[59]Recorded remarks of Powell in discussion of Ward's "Mind as a Social Factor," which had been presented as a lecture before the Anthropological Society of Washington, *Transactions of the Anthropological Society of Washington* 3 (1885): 36–7.
[60]Powell's discussion of the differences between emulative and antagonistic competition is presented in "Competition as a Factor in Human Evolution." Quotations are from pp. 317–20, passim.

example, both forms of competition existed, and to avoid the evils of the one while securing the benefits of the other, professional associations were formed. "Thus the physicians of a city organize an association to meet and discuss questions relating to the principles and applications of their science, to promote personal intercourse and friendship, and to regulate rates of compensation." In the agricultural sector, given its distant and indefinite markets, one competed not directly with one's neighbor but with the whole body of farmers, and thus in a necessarily emulative fashion: "So farmers organize agricultural societies, and establish agricultural colleges, and support agricultural newspapers, and by every possible agency diffuse knowledge among themselves relating to their vocation; and emulative competition is wholly an agency for progress."

The growing numbers of people caught up in the rise of the new industrial sector, however, which pitted employers against employees, faced a very different situation. Both forms of competition existed among employers, and, to reduce the risks of competition, new forms of organization were rising, most notably the corporations and the trusts. That the trend promised a reduction in wasteful, antagonistic competition was clear, but the possible long-term cost was threatening. As Powell put it, "By organization and consolidation emulative competition is also avoided, for the managers of business corporations no longer compete for business, but distribute business by convention."

Of all the occupational groups, members of the industrial working class had the worst prospects because common-law traditions of individual contract combined with the hostility of employers toward union movements to force antagonistic competition upon workers. To succeed, they had to overcome these obstacles through legally sanctioned organization or be prepared to offer their labor for lower wages than their neighbors did. Powell favored the growing trend toward labor organization because "in all civilized society there is no competition so direful in its results, so degrading to mankind, as that which is produced among the employees of these classes who compete for employment by cheapening their labor, for it results in overwork, which is brutalizing, and in want, which is brutalizing, and the abolition of this form of competition is one of the great questions of the day." Powell was critical of those in the middle class who, having solved the problem for themselves, "stand aloof and deplore the struggle." They should learn this lesson from evolutionary history, he suggested, "that when wrongs arise in any class of society those wrongs must ultimately be righted, and so long as they remain, the conflict also must remain, and when the solution comes not by methods of peace, it comes by war." The immediate problem of the emerging industrial society for those who did not stand aloof was to reduce the range of antagonistic competition by permitting new forms of organization and institutional development; the long-range problem was to keep the spirit of emulative competition alive in a culture that would become increasingly dense in its organizational structure.

Ward followed a similar course of argument in his criticism of Spencer's political ethics. Ward pointed out that although Spencer's sociology laid great stress on processes of social differentiation, it said little about social integration, the realm of politics and government. Spencer was hostile to the latter, Ward believed, because he confused emerging contemporary practices by government officials with the abuses wrought by their predecessors during the long dominance of aristocratic and military rule, the original target of liberalism. As a result, Spencer saw "no bond of mutuality between government and the citizen" and could concede no higher, genuinely representative cognitive functions to democratic rule, but only the democratization of self-interested vice and a general weakening of individual character and incentive. The interferences Spencer complained of, Ward argued, "are not attempts to create or destroy the forces of society, but to direct them." Moreover, Spencer's emphasis on protection as the main function of government failed to allow for a changing meaning of the term in novel circumstances, a failure most evident in Spencer's antilabor rhetoric about "worthless tramps who shuffle from union to union."[61]

Like Spencer, Ward and other liberal positivists put a premium on the value of individual initiative and responsibility, but unlike Spencer they argued that "individualism is not only consistent with true collectivism, it is in fact the only way it can be obtained."[62] Individualism was to be obtained via government activism based on the principle that "unbridled competition destroys itself. The only competition that endures is that which goes under judicious regulation," a process that required institutions to monitor the changing social effects of the pursuit of self-interest in society.[63] In a number of polemical essays Ward elaborated his point of

[61] Ward, "The Political Ethics of Herbert Spencer." Quotations are from pp. 55–65, passim. This essay provides an extensive and careful critical discussion of Spencer's major writings on ethics, evolution, and the role of government in society.
[62] Ward, "Spencer's Sociology," 175.
[63] Ward, "Plutocracy and Paternalism," 235.

view as a series of social and economic paradoxes aimed against the social psychology of laissez-faire: that the artificial is superior to the natural, that free competition can be maintained only through regulation, that private monopoly can be prevented only by resort to the public monopoly of power within the state, that prices fall as wages rise, and so on.[64]

GOVERNMENT SCIENCE AND THE NEW LIBERALISM

The liberal positivists did not intend to replace individualist abstractions with collectivist ones. Their genuine sympathy for the fundamental purposes of the liberal tradition out of which they came was generally strongly reinforced by modernist religious views in which the same felt need to winnow the chaff of dogma from the grain of conviction was much in evidence throughout the course of the evolutionary controversy.[65] But social and political beliefs required modernization no less than religious beliefs, and the members of the government's scientific community were convinced that there was no way to secure the fundamental purposes of those who had built up the tradition of classical liberalism other than by abandoning the dogmatic forms it had taken and searching for new ways to give expression and extension to its enduring values, particularly those of individual responsibility and personal assent to the reigning public philosophy—the basic requisites for a working consensus on social affairs. Social empiricism was a check on dogma, sometimes a solvent for it.

The purposes of the liberal tradition were understood to be permanent, rooted in human nature; the means of achieving them were variable, and therefore subject to criticism, reappraisal, and intentional development. Science promised to be of use here. Its "positive" character was reflected in the cumulative, progressive, diffusible features of its history, which contrasted favorably with the history of metaphysical reasoning. If social

---

[64]See, for example, "Some Social and Economic Paradoxes," *Glimpses of the Cosmos*, vol. 4, 153–65; "Broadening the Ways to Success," *Glimpses of the Cosmos*, vol. 4, pp. 31–43.

[65]These concerns linked the liberal positivists to certain aspects of what became the "social gospel" movement in liberal protestantism. See, for example, Carroll Wright, "Religion in Relation to Sociology," in his *Some Ethical Phases of the Labor Question* (Boston: American Unitarian Association, 1902), 3–24; and Powell, "Sociology, Or the Science of Institutions, Pt. 2," in which he argues (pp. 732–45) for an understanding of conscience as an instinctive impulse to moral conduct and suggests that religion has not to be overthrown but rather perfected with the aid of scientifically generated information on the consequences of collective action.

development was to reflect the same features, an empirically informed sociological viewpoint, generally diffused throughout the culture, promised to be the medium of collective criticism, reappraisal, and continuing political innovation. Only government, the liberal positivists believed, had the right combination of responsibility and legitimacy to generate the required types of social empirical information, and its work was to be open to public criticism and control.

Thus the liberal positivists of the Washington scientific community, with their allies in ASSA and elsewhere, played a part in the transformation of the political tradition and the creation of an American "new liberalism," collectively oriented and based on an evolutionary view of the role of the state as a moral agency in social development. With few exceptions these people were not academic scholars but public servants, and it was public service that attracted them and spurred their thinking. From the debates in which they were engaged in the last decades of the century came the first important body of reflection on the new liberalism and the first specification of its themes and their implications for law, government, and social philosophy.

As a developing tradition of practice, the new liberalism would be expressed in the political controversies of the progressive era, after the turn of the century, and subsequently in the halting rise of the welfare state. As a developing tradition of formal thought, the new liberalism would be entrusted to the universities, the foundations, and to a lesser extent the policy think tanks of the twentieth century. Its themes would be elaborated in three distinct but related "schools" or movements of academic inquiry. First was the "institutionalist school" of economic thought associated with Thorstein Veblen and John R. Commons, with its broadly cultural approach to economics; its sympathy for historical analysis; and its concern with the relationship among economics, law, and administrative life. Second was the movement for a "sociological jurisprudence" associated mainly with the writing of Roscoe Pound, with its emphasis on the need for "team work" between jurisprudence and the other social sciences, its turn to sociopsychological theories of legal obligation, its historical orientation and emphasis on study of the world view of judges and doctrinal writers. Third, of course, was the instrumentalist philosophy of John Dewey and his associates, with its emphasis on education and a more broadly conceived process of communication and social learning as the core, ethically speaking, of the development of authentic democracy; its commendation of "the method of intelligence" as the key to resolving social conflict; its view of the state as the chief instrument for use on the part of an inchoate public in its efforts to achieve progress and forestall decline; its distinction between intermittent and sometimes baseless public opinion and continuous, tested public knowledge; and its insistence that while "there may well be honest divergence as to policies to be pursued, even when plans spring from knowledge of the same facts," it nonetheless remains that "genuinely public policy cannot be generated unless it is informed by knowledge, and this knowledge does not exist except when there is systematic, thorough, and well equipped search and record" of the sort that only an activist government could provide.[66]

[66]John Dewey, *The Public and Its Problems* (Chicago: Swallow Press, 1927), 178–9. For a discussion of the origins of the new liberalism, see Chapter 5 by Mary Furner in this volume. There is as yet no full-scale analysis of the development of the new liberalism in America. See, however, Charles Forcey, *Crossroads of Liberalism: Croly, Weyl, Lippman, and the Progressive Era, 1900–1925* (New York: Oxford University Press, 1965); and R. Jeffrey Lustig, *Corporate Liberalism: The Origins of Modern American Political Theory, 1890–1920* (Berkeley: University of California Press, 1982). Lustig takes a more sinister view of the empiricism in politics theme than the one presented in this essay. For studies of the new liberalism in Britain, where it grew in response to the same currents of thought and in relation to the same social problems, see Michael Freeden, *The New Liberalism: An Ideology of Social Reform* (Oxford: Clarendon Press, 1978), and Stefan Collini, *Liberalism and Sociology: L.T. Hobhouse and Political Argument in England, 1880–1914* (Cambridge: Cambridge University Press, 1979).

The relationship between the liberal positivists and subsequent "schools" of institutionalist economics, sociological jurisprudence, and instrumentalist social philosophy is the subject of the author's current research. Continuities in the intellectual agenda are evident, but the question of direct influence passing from the one generation to the other is unclear. It should be noted, however, that Veblen was well acquainted with Ward's writings and developed some of the same themes in his work. The ten-volume *Documentary History of Industrial Society* (1910–11), edited by John R. Commons et al., was the completion of a project begun by Wright. Dewey shared many of Ward's interests in the problems of working out a philosophy of evolutionary naturalism, and, of course, Dewey did a better job of it than Ward or anyone else, for that matter. He was the most acute contemporary critic of Ward's *Psychic Factors of Civilization* (see Dewey's review in his "Social Psychology," *Psychological Review* 1 [1894]: 400–11). Despite his criticisms, Dewey was sympathetic to Ward's aims and appreciative of his contributions, particularly Ward's emphasis on the contributions that social science might make to directing processes of competition along socially desirable lines. Like Ward, Dewey insisted that "the elimination of conflict is a hopeless and self-contradictory ideal" (ibid., 408). With respect to the history of legal thought, it should be noted that Roscoe Pound in his initial analysis of sociological jurisprudence as a movement of thought ("The Scope and Purpose of Sociological Jurisprudence," *Harvard Law Review* 24 [1911]: 591–619; 25 [1912]: 140–68; 25 [1912]: 489–516) attributed a key role to Ward in breaking up the influence of biological analogies in jurisprudential speculation: "The change of front which involved complete abandonment of that conception begins with Ward" (ibid., 506).

5

The republican tradition and the new liberalism:
social investigation, state building, and
social learning in the Gilded Age

MARY O. FURNER

How to achieve the public good? The question has preoccupied Americans since 1776. Traditionally, discussion of the best means for promoting the general welfare centered on the contrasting methods of social ordering described in the ideological framework inherited from the American Revolution. In the early republic, political argument was shaped by a tension between the republican ideal of a virtuous society as a politically ordered commonwealth and the liberal conviction that the general welfare flowed spontaneously from the self-interested actions of individuals competing in an autonomous natural market.[1] The middle period (ca. 1830–70) defined a kind of accommodation between the two ideals. Liberal means such as free trade and a liberal land policy combined with distributive politics to promote egalitarian social forms that (for white males)

I would like to thank those who helped me shape this essay and the work surrounding it since its inception at the Woodrow Wilson Center in 1982: Michael Lacey, the late Warren Susman, William Leach, John L. Thomas, Robert Cuff, Hugh Heclo, Morton Keller, Robert Kelley, A. W. Coats, Martin Bulmer, James Kloppenberg, John Jentz, Roland Guyotte, Clarence Wunderlin, and Linn Freiwald. I am also grateful to the National Endowment for the Humanities for time stolen from a related project on the new liberalism, which the Endowment supported, to attend to this one.

[1]On republicanism and liberalism as constituent ideologies, and the tensions between them, see Gordon Wood, *The Creation of the American Republic, 1776–1787* (Chapel Hill: University of North Carolina Press, 1969); Drew R. McCoy, *The Elusive Republic: Political Economy in Jeffersonian America* (Chapel Hill: University of North Carolina Press, 1980); Isaac Kramnick, *Republicanism and Bourgeois Radicalism: Political Ideology in Late Eighteenth-Century England and America* (Ithaca, N.Y.: Cornell University Press, 1990); Eric Foner, *Free Soil, Free Labor, Free Men* (London: Oxford University Press, 1970); Daniel Walker Howe, *The Political Culture of the American Whigs* (Chicago: University of Chicago Press, 1979).

approximated a democratized, commercialized version of republican ideals.[2]

The generation that came of age in the 1870s entered a different world. Cycles of economic expansion were punctuated by wrenching depressions and unprecedented social conflict. Self-reliance no longer bore the fruit of personal independence; and in the realm of ideas and principles, the old words failed. Laissez-faire collapsed as a creditable basis for policy, and the failure reopened discussion of the proper role of government.[3]

Identifying the proper sphere of the state in relation to class conflict and monopoly became the focus of public discourse, party politics, and statecraft. These preoccupations, outside the realm of existing theory, placed a premium on applicable social knowledge, reinvigorating and redirecting social investigation. Analysis centered on the fit or lack thereof between the practiced methods of nineteenth-century liberalism and new questions of dependency and distribution. One reaction to the failure of market ordering was a resurgence of republicanism, and particularly of communal and statist strains within it that revived a commonwealth ideal in which individual gain was subordinated to collective purposes, reflected in the will of the majority of the productive members of society. Henry Georgism, greenbackism, Bellamy Nationalism, Populism, the vogue of cooperation, and the persistence of labor republicanism exemplified this trend. Equally important, new types of social investigators searched for empirically based theories capable of dealing with conditions and questions anticipated in none of the inherited ideologies.[4]

---

[2]James Kloppenberg, "The Virtues of Liberalism: Christianity, Republicanism, and Ethics in Early American Political Discourse," *Journal of American History* 74 (1987): 9–33.

[3]Jeffrey G. Williamson, *Late Nineteenth Century Economic Development* (Cambridge: Cambridge University Press, 1974); Harold Vatter, *The Drive to Industrial Maturity: The U.S. Economy, 1860–1914* (Westport, Conn.: Greenwood Press, 1975); Elliot Brownlee, *Dynamics of Ascent: A History of the American Economy* (New York: Alfred A. Knopf, 1974); James Livingston, "The Social Analysis of Economic History and Theory: Conjectures on Late Nineteenth-Century Economic Development," *American Historical Review* 92 (1987): 69–95; and David Montgomery, *The Fall of the House of Labor: The Workplace, the State, and Labor Activism, 1865–1915* (Cambridge: Cambridge University Press, 1987).

[4]The importance of republican values as a source of resistance to industrial capitalism throughout the nineteenth century is a theme in Sean Wilentz, *Chants Democratic: New York City and the Rise of the American Working Class, 1788–1850* (New York: Oxford University Press, 1984); David Montgomery, *Beyond Equality: Labor and the Radical Republicans, 1862–1872* (New York: Alfred A. Knopf, 1967); Leon Fink, *Workingmen's Democracy: The Knights of Labor and American Politics* (Urbana: University of Illinois Press, 1983); Herbert Gutman, *Work, Culture, and Society* (New York: Alfred A. Knopf, 1976); Lawrence Goodwyn, *The Democratic Promise* (New York: Oxford University Press, 1976); Norman Pollack, *The Just Polity: Populism, Law, and Human Welfare*

Under pressure to find ways of addressing contradiction and crisis, state and national governments took the lead. Legislatures refined traditional methods such as committee hearings, and they enhanced their capacities by creating specialized agencies, including an improved census, pathbreaking labor bureaus, special investigating commissions, and regulatory bodies with investigative and administrative functions. In a complementary vein, social scientists claimed a decisive role in the criticism of established theory and the development of new ordering techniques. From their posts in new, research-oriented universities, professionalizing economists in particular helped to reconceptualize both the state and the market. Their investigations provided scientific authority for conflicting assessments of the efficacy of competition and the potential benefits of "state interference," as contemporaries initially designated regulation. In addition, the economists began to inhabit and shape the new investigative agencies, forging relationships between academic investigation and public discourse, and promoting policy prescriptions from within the state.[5]

To shed further light on the connections between the state and development of a knowledge base for social policy in this period, this chapter analyzes in some detail two strategies for investigating what was known as the "social question" during the Gilded Age: (1) legislative investigations by congressional committees and commissions and (2) the parallel and intersecting inquiries of American economists as they confronted the crisis of laissez-faire. The analysis addresses in particular the impact of the social question on what was expected of government; the role of public investigation in the reassessment and revision of nineteenth-century republican liberalism; the uneven penetration into state-based investigations of alternative liberalisms formulated by social scientists;

(Urbana: University of Illinois Press, 1987); and Bruce Palmer, *Man over Money: The Southern Populist Critique of Industrial Capitalism* (Chapel Hill: University of North Carolina Press, 1980), among many others.

[5] Mary O. Furner, *Advocacy and Objectivity: A Crisis in the Professionalization of American Social Science, 1865–1905* (Lexington: University of Kentucky Press, 1975); Lawrence Veysey, *The Emergence of the American University* (Chicago: University Press of Chicago, 1965); and Thomas Haskell, *The Emergence of Professional Social Science* (Urbana: University of Illinois Press, 1977). On the relationship among science, investigation, and policy, see Hugh Heclo, "Social Policy and Political Learning," in his *Modern Social Politics in Britain and Sweden* (New Haven, Conn.: Yale University Press, 1974), 284–322; and Jack L. Walker, "The Diffusion of Knowledge, Political Communities and Agenda Setting: The Relationship of Knowledge and Power," in John E. Tropman, Milan J. Dluhy, and Roger M. Lind, eds., *New Strategic Perspectives on Policy* (New York: Pergamon Press, 1981), 75–96. See also Gianfranco Poggi, "The Modern State and the Idea of Progress," in Gabriel Almond, ed., *Progress and Its Discontents* (Berkeley: University of California Press, 1982), 337–60.

and the relationship of public and academic social investigation to the development in this period of specifically American forms of a new liberalism.[6]

The interaction between congressional and academic investigations is necessarily compared with patterns of social policy and analysis developing contemporaneously in the courts. In every modern society, the various languages that comprise the knowledge base for social analysis contend for influence in the public policy argument. In the 1870s, when the reconstruction of liberalism began, the most authoritative American policy language was the classical discourse of the law, with its characteristic references to legal knowledge as the product of a gradual, incremental process of discovering and perfecting natural laws embedded in human nature and reflected in the constitutional order. In legal discourse, rights were inherent and immutable, the authentic source of correct principles for regulating social relations was the common law, and the arm of government responsible for providing a coherent system of authoritative rules governing matters involving labor and property was the judiciary. The language of the law was often in conflict with the social vocabularies employed in legislative debates, which, in this period, often bristled with republican rhetoric. Legal discourse could hardly fail to be at odds with the developing discourse of the new economics, whose leading figures in this period understood theory as provisional, relative to the current economic and technological order, and defined rights, law, and state forms as cultural creations, shaped by the conditions and needs of a particular historical context and subject to experimentation, growth, and change.[7]

---

[6]There is a rich literature on British new liberalism that is most accessible in Michael Freeden, *The New Liberalism* (Oxford: Oxford University Press, 1978); Stefan Collini, *Liberalism and Sociology: L. T. Hobhouse and Political Argument in England 1880–1914* (Cambridge: Cambridge University Press, 1979); and John Allett, *New Liberalism: The Political Economy of J. A. Hobson* (Toronto: University of Toronto Press, 1981). We have not yet achieved the same degree of consensus on how the American new liberalism should be defined. For an extension into the twentieth century of the approach suggested here, see Mary O. Furner, "Knowing Capitalism: Public Investigation of the Labor Question in the Long Progressive Era," in Mary O. Furner and Barry Supple, eds., *The State and Economic Knowledge: The American and British Experiences* (Cambridge: Cambridge University Press, 1990), 241–86. See also notes 8–10 below.

[7]On the language and theoretical perspectives of American law in the Gilded Age, see Lawrence M. Friedman, *A History of American Law*, 2d ed. (New York: Simon & Schuster, 1985); James Herget, *American Jurisprudence, 1870–1970* (Houston: Texas University Press, 1990). For a more critical perspective that emphasizes ideology, contingency, and contextuality in the law, see Robert W. Gordon, "Critical Legal Histories," *Stanford Law Review* 57 (1984): 57–125; idem, "Legal Thought and Practice in the Age of American

The points of conflict among these various discourses evoke and re-
semble differences between classical liberalism and two new conceptions
of liberalism that began appearing in the Gilded Age. Reflected in the
new social science and government inquiries into the social question,
these variants of new liberalism differed significantly among themselves,
echoing earlier tensions between republicanism and liberalism. Yet although they offered opposing perspectives regarding the proper roles of
state and market, both versions of American new liberalism provided
collectivist alternatives to classical and neoclassical individualism.[8]

One variant of the new liberalism was corporate liberalism, a body
of social theory and policy advice that left economic and social ordering
largely to cooperative arrangements between organized private parties,
agreeing voluntarily among themselves. Keen to preserve the vitality and
integrity of civil society, corporate liberalism relied on state action only
to the extent that the innovative institutional forms that it required, such
as new forms of business association, required legal recognition, and in
those instances in which sources of economic and social instability, such
as those in the banking system, could be reached only by changes in the
law.[9] The other approach, not sufficiently recognized heretofore as a
parallel, alternative form of new liberalism, was a more democratic, statist

Enterprise," in Gerald L. Geison, ed., *Professions and Professional Ideologies in America*
(Chapel Hill: University of North Carolina Press, 1981); and idem, "The Ideal and the
Actual in the Law," in Gerald W. Gawalt, ed., *The New High Priests: Lawyers in Post-
Civil War America* (Westport, Conn.: Greenwood Press, 1984).

[8]The idea that there were important collectivist elements in Gilded Age social thought is
not new. One of the most original works along these lines was James Gilbert, *Designing
the Industrial State: The Intellectual Pursuit of Collectivism in America, 1880–1940* (Chicago: Quadrangle Books, 1972.) See also, for conflicting views of the tendency to collectivism, R. Jeffrey Lustig, *Corporate Liberalism: The Origins of Modern American Political
Theory, 1890–1920* (Berkeley: University of California Press, 1982); Frank Tariello, Jr.,
The Reconstruction of American Political Ideology, 1865–1917 (Charlottesville: University Press of Virginia, 1982); and Richard Adelstein, " 'Islands of Conscious Power': Louis
D. Brandeis and the Modern Corporation," *Business History Review* 63 (1989): 634–5.

[9]The definitive works on corporate liberalism are William Appleman Williams, *Contours
of American History* (1961; Chicago: Quadrangle Books, 1966), esp. "The Age of Cor-
poration Capitalism," 343–450; Martin J. Sklar, "Woodrow Wilson and the Political
Economy of Modern United States Liberalism," *Studies on the Left* 1 (1960): 14–47;
James Weinstein, *The Corporate Ideal in the Liberal State* (Boston: Beacon Press, 1968);
Ellis Hawley, "The Discovery and Study of Corporate Liberalism," *Business History
Review* 52 (1978): 309–20; Lustig, *Corporate Liberalism*; Martin J. Sklar, *The Corporate
Reconstruction of American Capitalism, 1890–1916* (Cambridge: Cambridge University
Press, 1988). See also Samuel Hays, "The Politics of Reform in Municipal Government,"
Pacific Northwest Quarterly (1964): 157–69; Livingston, "Social Analysis of Economic
History," 82–7; and Carl P. Parrini and Martin J. Sklar, "New Thinking About the Market,
1896–1904: Some American Economists on Investment and the Theory of Surplus Cap-
ital," *Journal of Economic History* 43 (1983): 559–78.

collectivism. This latter vision combined social purposes recovered from republicanism with a new, more positive conception of what the state could accomplish without itself becoming a threat to liberty. Specifically, democratic statists assigned responsibility for mediating class conflict, equalizing distribution, and controlling monopolies to an institutionally developed, effective government. The role of the state and other points at issue between these two designs for modern liberalism set the parameters of political discourse from the 1880s through the New Deal.[10]

The first section of this chapter describes the development of the dia-

---

[10]After long deliberation, going back to 1982, I have decided to construct the new liberalism as a discourse between corporate liberalism and democratic collectivism (or democratic statism). Partly, the choice of these terms is a function of the meanings that historiography has given to other terms. Until the 1960s, historians such as Sidney Fine and Harold U. Faulkner, working generally within the framework and assumptions of progressive historiography, discussed late nineteenth-century reform thought in terms of a "decline of laissez-faire" and a rise of "progressivism." In the 1960s New Left historians explained progressive era reform as the product of a coalition of conservative business and political interests. Although later refinements on this idea have properly emphasized the "progressiveness" of corporate liberalism, the category "progressive" lost its former meaning and much of its typological usefulness. As examples of this shift, compare Faulkner, *The Decline of Laissez-Faire, 1897–1917* (New York: Holt, Rinehart and Winston, 1951), and Fine, *Laissez-Faire and the General Welfare State* (Ann Arbor: University of Michigan Press, 1956), with Sklar, "Woodrow Wilson and the Political Economy of Modern United States Liberalism"; Gabriel Kolko, *The Triumph of Conservatism* (Glencoe, Ill.: Free Press, 1963); and Weinstein, *Corporate Ideal.*

The "discovery" of corporate liberalism by Sklar and others was an interpretive breakthrough of major proportions, but one that ran into its own contradictions in Lustig's treatment of American social thought, where John Dewey becomes a corporate liberal. James Kloppenberg's *Uncertain Victory: Social Democracy and Progressivism in European and American Thought, 1870–1920* (New York: Oxford University Press, 1986) illustrates one way out of this dilemma. He styles the American intellectuals who hoped to construct a middle way between classical liberalism and Marxian socialism as "progressives," whereas the Europeans engaged in a similar effort come in as "social democrats." An attempt to reclaim the terms "progressive" and "progressivism" confronts two problems. First, there were irreducible differences among different types of "progressives," such as those between Herbert Croly and Dewey. Second, there is again the matter that, in important respects, corporate liberalism *was* progressive. In order to recognize the common ground among all the collectivists, while at the same time respecting essential differences among them, identifying a discourse and a political contest between two *different* types or variants of American new liberalism becomes essential.

This necessity is recognized elsewhere. To name just two examples, Montgomery, in *Fall of the House of Labor,* 176–8, identifies a pattern of "capitalist collectivism" that involved employers' associations and professional managers in rationalizing the corporate order, ably assisted by McKinley and Roosevelt Republicans; significantly, Montgomery also detects a "democratic collectivism," which democratic socialists and other reformers hoped for, that was realized to some extent through the efforts of Frank Walsh, the Commission on Industrial Relations, and the National War Labor Board (pp. 356–75). Sklar's recent study of the political economy of the trust question describes Theodore Roosevelt's approach as a statist variant (alongside William Taft's antistatist and Woodrow Wilson's regulatory visions) of corporate liberalism. See also Furner, "Knowing Capitalism," 241–6.

logic pattern of academic discourse that came into being as Gilded Age social scientists formulated alternatives to classical liberalism. Although the subject is social investigation, economics and economists are highlighted. The reasons for this emphasis become obvious when one considers that before the familiar modern division of labor in the social sciences was constructed political economy encompassed the entire range of social questions, including all those issues of social structure, social theory, and social welfare later assigned to other disciplines and professions. The very nature of the social problems, linked as they were to overproduction and recurrent economic depression, meant that the continued authority of economics in the knowledge culture of the day depended on the development of alternatives to discredited theories. The discussion here is concerned mainly, as were Gilded Age economists, with the labor, trust, and distribution questions. The remaining three sections explore the impact of national-level public inquiries on discussion of the social question and on the fashioning of political strategies for ordering a modern society.

ALTERNATIVES TO LAISSEZ-FAIRE: SOCIAL SCIENCE AND THE FORMATION OF A NEW LIBERALISM

Theories of distribution describe the way in which societies divide the wealth produced by industry among providers of the various factors—labor, land, capital, and entrepreneurial talent—needed to produce it. Among economists and informed participants in policy discussion generally, opinion remains divided as to whether distribution is governed by some automatic principle that ensures its fairness. Agreement is even lacking regarding what an optimal distribution would look like. Would it ensure the greatest equality of income, or would it reward unequal skill and effort with a correspondingly, even radically, unequal division of wealth? Which would be "fairer" in the short run, and which better for society over the long term? Modern distribution theories, which provide some orientation on these questions, originated in the Gilded Age, in the earliest forms of institutional and neoclassical economics, the two strands of analysis that have been most influential in the twentieth century.

The reconstruction of political economy can be dated from 1875. Francis Amasa Walker's famous assault on wage fund theory that year opened a new chapter in American economic theorizing. In the beleaguered classical system, the capitalist function of amassing a surplus to finance the next cycle of production was the basis for a putative harmony of classes. Observing the vast abundance produced by American industry and the rising conflict over division of income, Walker turned the classical picture on its head, concluding that wages as well as other income shares were actually paid out of present product. He accounted for profits as a rent of ability awarded by the price system to the employers capable of making labor efficient. When determinant shares were deducted for interest and land rent, he concluded, scarce labor collected what remained of industry's product, which meant that wages were governed by the productivity of labor.[11]

Except in the highly attenuated sense that survived in early productivity theory, the idea of labor as residual claimant did not endure. But an emphasis on the differing contributions of the various factors of production became the basis for theories of distribution that focused, following Walker's theory of profits, on marginal return. Over the next decade, Walker himself, Henry George, George Gunton, John Commons, John Bates Clark, and others (in conjunction with John Hobson and Sidney and Beatrice Webb in Britain) elaborated the Ricardian principle of the price-making marginal increment into a provisional general theory that accounted for all the income shares as economic rents determined by the difference between the more efficient producers and the most expensive portion of the necessary supply.[12]

The precise dynamics of this distribution according to a law of three rents took a variety of forms, whose minor differences need not detain

[11]The account of developments in economic theory that follows was first prepared for Mary O. Furner, "Liberty Versus Efficiency: The Industrial Transformation and American Social Thought," unpublished colloquium paper, Woodrow Wilson Center, 1982. For Walker's distribution theories, see Francis A. Walker, "The Wage Fund Theory," *North American Review* 120 (1875): 84–119; and idem, "The Source of Business Profits," *Quarterly Journal of Economics* 1 (1887): 265–88.

[12]Henry George, *Progress and Poverty* (New York: D. Appleton & Co., 1879), esp. book III, "The Laws of Distribution"; George Gunton, *Wealth and Progress* (New York: D. Appleton, 1887). Alfred Marshall, "The Theory of Business Profits," *Quarterly Journal of Economics* 1 (1887): 477–81, endorsed and extended Walker's rent of ability theory. See also Sidney Webb, "The Rate of Interest and the Laws of Distribution," *Quarterly Journal of Economics* 2 (1888): 188–208; John A. Hobson, "Law of the Three Rents," ibid., 5 (1891): 263–88; Clark, "Distribution as Determined by a Law of Rent," ibid., 288–318; Walker, "The Doctrine of Rent and the Residual Claimant Theory of Wages," ibid., 417–37; and John R. Commons, *The Distribution of Wealth* ([1893]; New York: Augustus Kelley, 1965), esp. chap. 3, "Distribution and Rent." George Stigler, *Production and Distribution Theories: The Formative Period* (New York: Macmillan, 1941), 317, credits Clark and Hobson with simultaneous formulation of the law of three rents.

us. What should be noted is the common thread of insight that distinguished George's castigation of land monopolists and the more general observations regarding rent-seeking contained in Commons's *Theory of Distribution* (1893) from Walker's approving description of profit-making entrepreneurs. A conventional Ricardian, Walker treated economic rents as the product of advantages (whether fertility of soil or managerial talent) that their possessors naturally *had*. By contrast, George and Commons argued that the prized locations that generated huge economic rents in industrial America were socially derived, monopoly advantages that their fortunate possessors actively (and often collusively) sought. Most such advantages, among them patents, franchises, and protective tariffs, were legally created. Another rent-making factor, control of transportation costs, was tolerated by the state. Even the closely guarded skills that leveraged scarcity wages for skilled workers depended on artificial rationing of admission to crafts, as recognized by capitalists keen to deny unions the protection of the law.[13]

Supported by everyday experience, the notion that elements of monopoly lurked everywhere helped to rekindle republican suspicions of wealth and the corruption of power that typically supported it. Ricardianism in this new form was an important factor in the antitrust discourse of the Gilded Age, and ways of dealing with monopoly rents remained a major policy question down through the 1930s.[14] More important, for its influence on the reconstruction of liberalism, an awareness of rent-seeking as ubiquitous, occasioned by the stresses and insecurities of a highly competitive and unstable market, provided a bridge to the great theoretical innovations made by this generation's economists— innovations that became the conceptual building blocks of modern economics and were often subsequently generalized to social theory.

Although the most important of these innovations, marginalism and neoclassical theory, looked to the marginal increment as the critical spot where value was determined, the two should not be taken as synonymous. Marginal theory is better seen as a neutral technique or method, opening up possibilities in two dissimilar directions. Economists such as Richard T. Ely, Commons, E. R. A. Seligman, Simon Patten, and Thomas Nixon

---

[13]Commons, *Distribution*, esp. chap. 4, "Monopoly Privileges and Legal Rights," and chap. 5, "Law and Rights."

[14]For example, in U.S. Temporary National Economic Committee, "Investigation of Concentration of Economic Power," Monograph No. 27, *The Structure of Industry*, 76th Cong., 3d Sess. (1941).

Carver, along with Alfred Marshall, Henry Sidgwick, and A. C. Pigou on the British side, constituted a "material welfare" school that dominated Anglo-American economics from the turn of the century until around 1930. In welfare economics, the concept of *diminishing utility* became the basis for an argument for redistributive state action—through progressive taxation, a minimum wage, or whatever—on the utilitarian grounds that the last dollars earned by millionaires added little to their pleasure, whereas, transferred to the poor, these same dollars added mightily to total welfare. If economics was concerned with maximizing society's welfare, in this reading it required statism.[15]

Given an opposite spin in the concept of *diminishing return*, marginalism opened the way to the full-blown productivity theory of factor shares that John Bates Clark and others developed into a formidable neoclassicism. In this version, marginal analysis suggested that, joined in production, mobile capital and labor would automatically receive their fair return, impartially determined by the value created by the final unit. Entrepreneurs' profits, which Clark considered "strictly temporary gains," were derived from mechanical or managerial innovations that temporarily disturbed the static forces distributing income. Their function was to provide the stimulus for further accumulation, shifting capital and labor to where they would be most productive and keeping the entire system progressive.[16]

On this reading of what happened at the margin, neoclassical purists counseled against the redistributive schemes of welfare economics. Labor and capital would earn their just rewards in any case, they argued, whereas any threat to profit would sap invention and shrink investment. The essential thing would be to maintain competition, which (in an economics unaware of the possibility of monopoly competition) could be counted on to satisfy consumers' proliferating wants at prices close to cost. Neoclassical economics was (and is) at best neutral, if not hostile to unions. Clark, for all his sympathy with labor, for example, held that

[15]On the "welfare school," see Herbert Hovenkamp, "The Political Economy of Substantive Due Process," *Stanford Law Review* 40 (1988): 437–8; and idem, "The First Great Law and Economics Movement," ibid., 42 (1990): 1000–8. On marginalism, see R. D. Collison Black, A. W. Coats, and Craufurd Goodwin, eds., *The Marginal Revolution in Economics* (Durham, N.C.: Duke University Press, 1973). On the British welfare economists, see Donald Winch, *Economics and Policy* (New York: Walker and Co., 1969), 37–46.

[16]John Bates Clark, "Possibility of a Scientific Law of Wages," *Publications of the American Economic Association* 4 (1889): 39–69; idem, "Profits Under Modern Conditions," *Political Science Quarterly* 2 (1887): 603–19; and idem, *The Distribution of Wealth* ([1899]; New York: Augustus Kelley Reprints, 1965).

union wages or a legislated minimum would raise the marginal cost of labor and cut employment, spreading misery among less fortunate members of the working class.[17]

As often happens, contradiction elicited critique. A chorus of historical and institutional economists[18] denied the alleged naturalness and fairness of neoclassical distribution. One of the keenest jabs was Thorstein Veblen's observation that labor's total product materially exceeded a mere multiple of the value created by the last worker hired. The residual claimant to the vast surplus between the wage established at the margin and the total value created by more productive workers further up the line was the capitalist. In addition, Veblen scorned what he perceived as the erroneous assumption that in a complex social process such as production, which was inevitably cooperative and interdependent, *any* individual's product could be separated from all others. Gunton and young Commons insisted that in the real world, where labor was immobile and often redundant, its total product determined not what workers *would* receive as wages, but the maximum that they could *possibly* obtain. Only vigorous unions, low unemployment, or a labor shortage would force employers to turn the surplus over to its creators.[19]

---

[17]Clark, *Distribution of Wealth*; Hovenkamp, "Law and Economics," 1009–13. At the same time, certain procorporate contemporaries, such as Arthur Hadley, considered conservative unions useful for raising general wage and consumption levels without threatening efficiency, and thought of labor as a structure of noncompeting groups. Hadley, *Economics: An Account of the Relations Between Private Property and Public Welfare* (New York: G. P. Putnam's Sons, 1896).

[18]The intention here is to broaden the definitions of historical and institutional economics, and to emphasize the continuity between them, so that this unified category includes all those in the last decades of the nineteenth century who either explicitly or implicitly, as attested by the assumptions, methods, and categories employed in their work, adopted a view of the economy and society as a historical process in which the forms and relations of production and distribution were mediated by, and developed relative to, the evolution of social institutions, including not only the systems and structures of business, but also law and government. Historical/institutional economists in the Gilded Age were evolutionists and stage theorists, oriented toward explaining economic development and crisis. Thus they had departed from classicism, with its emphasis on innate qualities of human behavior and an equilibrating market. They were critical of the idea of an equilibrium state, governed by what became known in neoclassical economics as economic statics, and in that sense neoclassicism was a reaction to the relativism and institutionalism of historical economics.

[19]Thorstein Veblen, "Professor Clark's Economics," *The Place of Science in Modern Civilization* (New York: Viking Press, 1919), 180–230, and "The Limitations of Marginal Utility," ibid., 231–51. These essays were originally published in 1908 and 1909. Veblen's observation pointed to the same type of disparity between price and value that Marshall referred to in his theory of consumer's surplus. Gunton, *Wealth and Progress*, 53–98; Commons, *Distribution*, 171–82, developed at much greater length in his *Legal Foundations of Capitalism* (Madison: University of Wisconsin Press, 1959), 282–312 and

Depending on which nascent distribution theory one adopted, Americans undergoing the trials or enjoying the triumphs of industrialization inhabited different narratives—one crammed with exploitation, and the other exuding equity and tending toward perfection. The persistence in American value theory of certain features of classicism (e.g., real-cost theory) and the potency of the institutional critique prevented neoclassicism from becoming the dominant tradition in American economics in the Gilded Age, or for that matter until well into this present "post-Keynesian" era. Thus, from the standpoint of tracking the development of a knowledge base for the new liberalism, the more significant differences were those that opened in the 1880s *within* the ranks of economists using essentially historical and institutional methods.[20]

This point requires attention, for it qualifies and supplements the view that the historical economists of this period were exclusively a prounion, anticorporate, proregulation element who formed the American Economic Association (AEA) to capture the discipline for laborism and statism. Accounts of the economists' controversy of the 1880s (including my own) have stressed disputes between German-trained, evangelical econ-

---

passim. Clark's response to Veblen argued that (1) all units of labor were interchangeable and (2) because the earlier workers had better machines, the difference in the value created further up the line was in fact a contribution of capital.

[20]I refer here to an important distinction between progressive and conservative historicists or institutionalists. Both types embedded economic motives and actions in historical context and evolutionary process. Progressive institutionalists stressed the capacity for purposeful guidance of social and economic development, often involving redistributive state action, whereas conservative historicists were both more optimistic about the undirected or autonomous tendencies of development, and more deterministic. Around the turn of the century, neoclassicism's market-based theories of subjective value and equilibrium began to offer a third alternative. The similarity in policy goals between conservative institutionalists and neoclassicists—plus the fact that corporate liberals relied increasingly on marginalist arguments to justify the institutions and distribution patterns of the emerging corporate order—obscured the differences between these two groups. Later, historical accounts structured debates in economics around an opposition between neoclassicism and institutionalism, in which the meaning of neoclassicism had been expanded to include economists who actually rejected some of its central assumptions. Conversely, the meaning of institutionalism was narrowed in histories of economic thought so that "institutional economics" referred exclusively to the radical institutionalism of Commons, Veblen, and Wesley Mitchell. Examples of this narrower definition of institutionalism are Allan Gruchy, *Modern Economic Thought: The American Contribution* (New York: Prentice Hall, 1947), and idem, *Contemporary Economic Thought: The Contributions of NeoInstitutional Economics* (Clifton, N.J.: Augustus M. Kelley Publishers, 1972). Something closer to the original meaning of institutionalism is captured in the so-called new institutionalism in political science (not economics), which holds that institutions not only reflect but affirmatively shape preferences, and determine the way in which individuals and groups, within contextual structures of language and meaning, construct their interests. See James G. March and Johan P. Olsen, *Rediscovering Institutions: The Organizational Basis of Politics* (New York: Free Press, 1989).

omists such as Ely, Edmund James, and H. C. Adams, and a conservative old guard composed of diehard individualists and antistatists such as William Graham Sumner and Simon Newcomb. Launched in part for rhetorical purposes and to some extent journalistically inspired, the American *Methodenstreit,* or methodological controversy, of the 1880s also drove a wedge between economists such as Arthur Hadley and Frank Taussig, whom we have thought of, following Joseph Dorfman's wise construction, as "younger traditionalists," and a "new school" that included Ely, Adams, the early Clark, and James.[21]

These battles illustrate tensions that powerfully shaped the intellectual climate and social authority structure of the 1880s, yet they may have obscured important areas of similarity, even congruence. Economists to the right and left of a political center fixed by issues such as gas and water socialism or the demands of the Knights of Labor could be found practically agreeing on methodological and even certain ideological questions of longer-term significance. Impressed by the ambiguities of their age and the contradictions uncovered by historical methods, key members of *both groups* had abandoned faith in a regime of unmediated competition and a number of the more important meanings of individualism. Both had begun sorting out what was defensible among the various collectivist perspectives on offer during the Gilded Age, and making their own sometimes tentative and conflicted collectivist contributions. Their different conceptions and applications of this dawning collectivism would take so-called traditionalists and the "new school" in opposing policy directions. But they had more in common, especially through their similar perceptions of the relation between law and economics, than either did with those pariahs whom Ely described as "men of the Sumner type."[22]

Both groups were essentially contextualists. The leading figures of the Adams-Ely group took an emphatically historicist view of law and economics. Defining economics as a dependent subset, along with juris-

---

[21] Furner, *Advocacy and Objectivity;* Ely, "Report of the Organization of the American Economic Association," *Publications of the AEA* 1 (1886): 5–46; A. W. Coats, "The First Two Decades of the American Economic Association," *American Economic Review* 50 (1960): 555–74; idem, "The Political Economy Club: A Neglected Episode in American Economic Thought," ibid., 71 (1961): 624–37; William Barber, ed., *Breaking the Academic Mould: Economists and American Higher Learning in the Nineteenth Century* (Middletown, Conn.: Wesleyan University Press, 1988); Adelstein, " 'Islands,' " 631–4; Leon Fink, " 'Intellectuals' v. 'Workers': Academic Requirements and the Creation of Labor History," *American Historical Review* 96 (1991): 395–421.

[22] Circumstances sometimes blocked unguarded expression of this historicism. On the constraints that confronted Hadley at Yale in the 1880s, see Furner, *Advocacy and Objectivity.*

prudence, of a comprehensive science of society being constructed to guide policy in the long-term social interest, Adams historicized property rights. Laws conferring special value on certain types of property were rooted in politics and custom, he insisted—not in nature. Such conventions did as much to shape the nation's economic life as the tendencies of human nature, which were themselves not irreducible but also shaped by institutions, a category that included not only organizational structures but culturally embedded ways of thinking. The key thing to recognize, in accordance with the most progressive thought of the age, was that law and economic institutions were both enmeshed in specific cultural contexts. "Lego-historical facts" such as private property, which seemed so rational and permanent, were in reality historically derived, creatures of positive or judge-made law. Economic theories were also relative—to the system of production going at the time. As Seligman—whose historicism led him to an economic interpretation close to Marxism—put it, the new institutionalism of the day was not a German movement but a "product of the age, of the *zeitgeist,* not of any particular country; for the underlying evolutionary thoughts of a generation sweep resistlessly throughout all countries whose social conditions are ripe for a change."[23]

Surprisingly, in light of their disputes over method, the "traditionalists" gave almost equal weight to context. To be sure, Arthur Hadley echoed the concern of his Harvard colleague Charles Dunbar for the future of a science in which runaway Baconianism entirely replaced deductive reasoning. Even so, Hadley's important contributions to theories of capital and competition were almost wholly concerned with institutions and development, within a relativist framework that explained events such as depressions in terms of social and cultural factors that precluded any possibility of a natural equilibrium. Hadley's seminal writings adopted the rough-and-ready language of evolution to describe and recognize as salutary a trend *away* from competition toward complexity, integration, and various forms of cooperation.

[23]For a different view of the importance of historicism in this generation of social scientists, see Dorothy Ross, *Origins of American Social Science* (Cambridge: Cambridge University Press, 1991). For examples of a historicist understanding in the texts of the 1880s, see Adams, "Economics and Jurisprudence," *Science,* Supplement, 8 (1886): 15–19; Hadley, "Economic Laws and Methods, ibid., 46–8; Adams, "Another View of Economic Laws and Methods," ibid., 103–5; Seligman, "Changes in the Tenets of Political Economy with Time," ibid., 7 (1886): 375–82, quotation at p. 382. See also Ely, "Ethics and Economics," ibid., 529–33; Richmond Mayo-Smith, "Methods of Investigation in Political Economy," ibid., 8 (1886): 81–7; and Seligman, *Economic Interpretation of History.*

But the main defense of any social form was here-and-now social efficiency. Hadley ascribed the rise of the corporate form to institutional selection, and advocated ratifying evolution by giving the full protection of the law to forms of combination generated experimentally in the marketplace. The major difference was that from the beginning the Adams-Ely-James contingent advocated institutional innovations by and within the state to counterbalance new centers of private power arising in society, whereas Hadley, Jeremiah Jenks, and others on the voluntarist side of the historical argument preferred to see spontaneously generated aggregations of private power offset, complement, and stimulate each other. For them, the "natural" space for social evolution, and the appropriate proving ground for institutional adaptations, was society, not the state.[24]

Thus the two sides in the economists' controversy converged on a relativistic, historicist epistemology. Democratic statists such as James and Ely recognized this new, radically contextualist vision of social knowledge as an argument for state intervention. Evolutionary naturalists such as Hadley also rejected competition and individualism but favored replacing traditional, now ineffective methods with associative forms of societal action that they saw evolving naturally. Following Lester Ward, Adams described a more deliberate process, in which legislatures guided progress toward a higher moral plane, expressing a uniquely human capacity for democratic social control and ethical improvement. Energized morally by the socialist critique but blocked politically and culturally from state socialism, the Adams-Ely group revived and modified collectivist elements in republicanism and social Christianity. They imagined achieving social democratic purposes without eliminating private property, by extending the meaning of property to include claims to subsistence, and socializing elements of its control.[25]

[24]Arthur Hadley, "Competition and Combination," *Andover Review* 2 (1884): 455–66, and idem, "Ethics as a Political Science," *Yale Review* 1 (1892): 301–67. See also, on Hadley's historicism, Sklar, *Corporate Reconstruction,* 57–61. For similar views from the new school, see Ely, *Studies in the Evolution of Industrial Society,* 2 vols. ([1903]; Port Washington, N.Y.: Kennikat Press, 1971), esp. vol. 1, 87–151. Ely argued, "Modern society itself establishes, consciously or unconsciously, many of the conditions of the struggle for existence, and it is for society to create such economic conditions that only desirable social qualities shall constitute eminent fitness for survival" (p. 140). The economists' theory of institutional selection had a parallel in turn-of-the century legal theory. See Herbert Hovenkamp, "Evolutionary Models in Jurisprudence," *Texas Law Review* 64 (1985): 645, and idem, "Law and Economics," 1013–31.

[25]On the search for an American middle way that avoided the extremes of classical liberalism and revolutionary socialism, see Kloppenberg, *Uncertain Victory.* Compare Dorothy Ross,

Conversely, and contrary to the social democratic view, Hadley, Taussig, and other conservative institutionalists argued for a distinction between a "science" that entitled economists to speak authoritatively and an "art" of politics that did not. This distinction was essentially a defense against statism, contrived by theorists awakening to a possible corporatist alternative. Important conceptually and rhetorically until the 1890s but abandoned when the immediate danger of social revolution seemed to have passed, it masked a preference for nonstatist intervention, to be orchestrated outside politics by the concerted, private actions of well-placed capitalists. Such corporate leaders, themselves no longer believers in laissez-faire and thus not attracted to neoclassicism, would voluntarily promote social efficiency and harmony while insulating their businesses from the vagaries of the market.[26]

By contrast, democratic collectivism was significantly more statist than any earlier variant of liberalism, and had different social purposes in view. Not content with merely promoting economic expansion, and morally offended by monopoly and dependency, they turned to government to ensure that republican and Christian values survived amid economic concentration. To that end, they formulated a larger regulatory role for a reinvigorated democratic government, complete with new administrative capacities and a broad, inclusive commitment to economic democracy and social protection.[27]

Corporate liberals opposed on principle such large-scale state involvement. Aware of an organizational revolution under way in civil society, they anticipated extending to new uses the theme of private, associative action, a hallmark of antebellum liberalism reinvigorated and redirected by innovative forms of business combination. A chaotic industrial capitalism could be ordered by increased cooperation, integration, and new types of bureaucratic management, improving efficiency and suppressing dangerous competition. Conservative trade unions showed potential for

"Socialism and American Liberalism: Academic Social Thought in the 1880s," *Perspectives in American History* 11 (1977–8): 7–79.

[26]By 1900, Hadley was advocating a more active, albeit an advisory or consultative rather than an overtly partisan role, for economists in government. See his AEA presidential address, "Economics and Political Morality," *Publications of the AEA*, 3d ser., I (1900): 45–61, and Commons's rejoinder, ibid., 63–80.

[27]On earlier uses of the state, see Louis Hartz, *Economic Policy and Democratic Thought, Pennsylvania, 1776–1860* (Cambridge, Mass.: Harvard University Press, 1948); Oscar Handlin, *Commonwealth: A Study of the Role of Government in the American Economy, 1774–1861* (New York: New York University Press, 1947); and Robert Wiebe, *The Opening of American Society* (New York: Alfred A. Knopf, 1984).

ordering labor markets and abetting cooperation between classes. Further developed, these spontaneous, voluntary methods of social ordering could sustain, control, and channel economic growth, raise living standards, and defuse conflict—leaving a minimal enabling function, not an intrusive moralizing or managerial role for the state.[28]

The beginnings of a collectivist idea of the capitalist future can be found in several key economics texts of the 1880s. "Economic Discussion" in *Science* magazine, a forum on economic laws and methods to which Adams, James, Ely, Hadley, Taussig, and Seligman all contributed, Adams's landmark essay, "Relationship of the State to Industrial Action," and several pieces by Hadley and Jenks that detected a natural tendency toward combination in industry all revealed the major points at issue. These texts are of special interest because they point up differences in the connections that the early architects of the two conflicting visions of new liberalism saw between legal and economic knowledge.

The differences are sharpest, and can be taken as emblematic, in the work of Hadley and Adams. Well known to contemporaries, the dialogue between them, which continued over many years, comes as close as any single discourse to establishing what Stefan Collini has termed, with respect to British new liberalism, the "context of refutation," or the arguments that had to be answered in this era of social inquiry. Employing virtually identical historical and institutional methods, both men identified a failure of competition as the root cause of the social question, and traced that failure to the special qualities of certain types of recently developed capital-intensive industries.[29]

There the similarities ended. Although both Hadley and Adams understood monopoly as an unexpected consequence of competition, they saw the social and political implications of market failure very differently. Adams's pathbreaking effort identified the greater efficiency of large operations as the reason why certain types of businesses tended naturally to monopoly and were not subject to market regulation. Ambivalent toward this new development, he concluded that the economic advantages of natural monopolies offset their inherent political dangers only

---

[28] Weinstein, *Corporate Liberalism;* Furner, "Knowing Capitalism"; and Sklar, *Corporate Reconstruction.*

[29] Arthur Hadley, "Overproduction," *Lalor's Cyclopedia of Political and Social Science* 3 (1884): 40–3; idem, "Competition and Combination"; Adams, "Relation of the State to Industrial Action," *Publications of the American Economic Association* 1 (1887): 465–549; idem, *Outlines of Lectures Upon Political Economy* (Baltimore, 1881); Collini, *Liberalism and Sociology,* 9.

if these giant concerns, conducting "low-tech," routine functions, were operated according to civil service principles and the norms of public finance, as they were in more statist societies such as Germany. Along with James, Adams was among the first to advocate extensive public control of transportation and utilities by the administrative agencies of a muscular, capable government.[30]

Significantly, because the question became critical in the antitrust debate, Adams detected no significant advantages to scale in manufacturing, beyond a size sufficient to reap the benefits of mechanization through a reasonable division of labor. Among the constant-returns industries, where he included manufacturing, monopoly occurred the old-fashioned way, through public or private corruption. Monopoly could be limited, and a socially beneficial competition among businesses of reasonable size restored, by the antitrust activities of a state intelligent enough to distinguish artificial from natural monopolies.[31]

By contrast, Hadley located a broader range of industries that were not only inherently monopolistic but dangerous, not for the political reasons that Adams raised but because they were the source of unprecedented economic instability. In their current, highly competitive state, these capital-intensive industries were destructive to all social groups, in Hadley's view. But they were especially so to the one indispensable engine of social improvement—capital. Hadley's pioneering analysis of trends in the railroad and pig iron businesses during the 1870s showed conditions—redundant investment, immobility of capital, and falling profits— that threatened the investment function, and thus the ability of capitalism to reproduce itself. If his analysis rather than Adams's was correct, and the same tendencies prevailed in manufacturing as in the major public utilities, a natural tendency to monopoly might in fact exist throughout the industrial core economy, justifying the headlong rush to combination in the era of pools, trusts, and mergers.[32]

---

[30]Developed before an adequate theory of competition existed, Adams's analysis of natual monopoly holds up admirably today. Joseph Dorfman, "Henry Carter Adams: The Harmonizer of Liberty and Reform," in Dorfman, ed., *Two Essays by Henry Carter Adams* (New York: Columbia University Press, 1954), 1–55.

[31]Adams, "Relation of the State." Compare Adelstein, " 'Islands,' " who erroneously includes Adams among economists who saw bigness as inevitable.

[32]Hadley, "On the Freedom of Contract," *Science*, Supplement, 7 (1886): 221–5, saw the same economies in manufacturing. See also idem, "Overproduction" and "Combination," and Furner, "Liberty Versus Efficiency." The best published account of Hadley's pathbreaking theory of capitalist crisis is Parrini and Sklar, "New Thinking About the Market," 559–78.

These generative texts framed the dilemma raised by the trusts as an opposition between what could be achieved through old-fashioned market methods and what required a collectivist solution, the latter to be achieved either through an extension of the regime of contract, which received a major refurbishing between the *Slaughterhouse* (1877) and the *Santa Clara* (1886) decisions, as a means of administering markets, or through state action. A segment of the *Science* series titled "How far have modern improvements in production and transportation changed the principle that men should be left free to make their own bargains?" addressed the legal position and prospects of the new forms of combination. Hadley conceded that wholesale adoption of the corporate form had drastically altered the several meanings previously attached to free contract. Personal responsibility had given way to dispersed, impersonal ownership and a relentless drive for profits. To make matters worse, Hadley knew from his work as Connecticut labor commissioner that the courts encouraged the trend toward sharp practice by validating as expressions of personal liberty the pernicious assumption-of-risk and fellow-servant doctrines. When freedom of contract sank to the base level of "a nominal freedom which does not correspond to the facts," desperate communities understandably retaliated by extending the police powers of the state. Thus Hadley joined a host of Gilded Age social critics who detected a dramatic, socially destabilizing decline in the moral level of competition that had set in along with industrial capitalism.[33]

Having exposed a fictitious legal individualism that masked an irresponsible collectivism, Hadley simultaneously warned against extensive state intervention, which "involve[d] the most serious dangers, both political and moral." If, as he and Adams both believed, excessive competition was the root cause of the problem, perhaps the answer lay in making private, collaborative methods more responsible. "Why not allow *voluntary* regulation of such competition within certain limits," he queried, "and hold the combination responsible for the abuses that may arise? An open, responsible, perhaps incorporated combination of capital or

---

[33] *Science,* Supplement, 7 (1886): 221–5. Concern for declining business morality was also evident in Adams, "Relation of the State," and in Ely, James, Clark, and Patten texts of the mid-1880s. It was part of a general preoccupation with competition as a social form in the mid-1880s, also evident in the works of sociologists such as Giddings and Small, and among the government scientists described by Michael Lacey in Chapter 4 of this volume. Discussion of competition changed dramatically in the 1890s. On the development of labor contracts in this period, see Haggai Hurvitz, "American Labor Law and the Doctrine of Entrepreneurial Property Rights: Boycotts, Courts, and the Juridical Reorientation of 1886–1895," *Industrial Relations Law Journal* 8 (1986): 307–61.

labor would in many respects be better to deal with than a secret and lawless one." As an alternative to the enforceable and legalized cartels already widely used in Europe, Hadley proposed essentially unchecked combination.[34]

For democratic statists such as Ely, Adams, James, and E. B. Andrews, the key deficiency in Hadley's program was its failure to recognize what they believed was an inescapable conflict between the private interest in immediate gain, which was no longer sufficiently restrained by moral values, and the public interest in ethical standards and long-term efficiency. As Adams put it, requiring "uniformity of action" by legislating the best moral sense of the community regarding such matters as child labor and factory conditions had nothing to do with the liberal bugaboo, " 'paternal government,' but is in perfect harmony with the idea of democracy."[35]

New thinking on the market provoked a corresponding growth of creative thinking on the state. Mixing the languages of commonwealth republicanism, German idealism, and historical relativism, James complained that knee-jerk antistatists had failed to consider the role of government historically, or in evolutionary terms. Instead of condemning specific abuses, they condemned state action as a general principle. Yet from James's perspective "historical investigation in this century" had proved "that the state, so far from being the source of innumerable evils, has always been not only the absolutely essential condition of human progress, but also one of the most important, if not, indeed, the most important factor in the economic evolution of society itself." James described the positive state evolving in his lifetime as nothing more than "a special form of associative action," especially useful for guarding society's weaker members and providing essential services, such as transportation, needed to spur individual effort and promote progress. "Associative action may be, and ordinarily is, the only means of securing such an end," he argued. "*Voluntary associative action* is generally precluded by the refusal of some individuals to take part whose cooperation is necessary to success. The only means left is *compulsory associative action through and by the state*." Thus, in the coming corporate order, the state could hardly be allowed to wither away. The total sphere of

---

[34]See Hadley, *Science,* Supplement, 7 (1886).

[35]Adams, "Economics and Jurisprudence," quotation at p. 17; Richard T. Ely, "Ethics and Economics," *Social Aspects of Christianity* (New York: Thomas Y. Crowell & Co., 1889), 115–32. On Ely's politics, see Kloppenberg, *Uncertain Victory,* chaps. 6–7, passim.

cooperative action would widen continuously with social progress; and essential energizing, moralizing forms of associative action would require bureaucratic methods of investigation, regulation, and administration.[36]

Statist collectivists blended elements of cultural determinism and free, democratic choice in their conception of the state. Adams's early reasoning along these lines centered on two points. He understood American democracy as a distinctive cultural type, fortunately lacking the authoritarian (French) ideal of a general will that overrode personal liberty, and incompatible with either radical (German) statism or radical (English) individualism, but capable of locating a middle way between these two extremes. And, like James, Adams took a historical view of American state forms in which the limits of state action varied, waxing and waning within the boundaries permitted by ingrained cultural traditions, relative to a political construction of the demands of particular historical situations, assessed on republican terms. In his book on the history of public finance, he recalled heroic traditions of public and mixed enterprise, prevalent in the early republic, that proved Americans were not born antistatist. He bemoaned the revulsion against internal improvements and hasty state withdrawal in the 1840s that had stunted commonwealth republican traditions, and he blamed the corruptibility of Gilded Age government on the subsequent weakness and vulnerability of the state. If the republic were to survive, he argued, the reform process ahead would center, initially at the local and state levels, on democratic state building.[37]

[36]James, "The State as an Economic Factor," *Science*, Supplement, 7 (1886): 485–8, 490. Quotation on p. 486. See also James, "Relation of the Modern Municipality to the Gas Supply," *Publications of the American Economic Association* 1 (1886): 47–122 (emphasis added). Ely framed the distinction similarly in a companion essay in which he juxtaposed "voluntary cooperation, possibly that of a corporation," against "the compulsory cooperation of the state." Ely, "The Economic Discussion in *Science*," ibid., 8 (1886): 3–6; quotation on p. 6. See his *Introduction to the Labor Problem* (New York: Harper Bros., 1886) for a fuller development of the distinction. Frank Taussig offered a rejoinder to James in *Science*, Supplement, 7 (1886): 488–90, which criticized, from a voluntarist, market-protecting perspective, *both* "the exaggerated laissez faire tinge of a generation ago" (as by Newcomb and Sumner in the *Science* discussion) and James's politically injudicious "general speculations about collective action and the sphere of the state" (p. 489).

[37]Adams, "Democracy," *New Englander* 40 (1881): 752–72; and idem, "The Position of Socialism in the Historical Development of Political Economy," *Penn Monthly* 10 (1879): 285–94. In the latter, Adams described the idea of "an economic state" as "the important historical idea of Socialism" and predicted it would give rise to "*two new schools of Political Economy*, the one of which incorporates the idea into its teachings and makes it the foundation of its system; the other, while admitting the ground to be tenable for which the interference of the State is demanded, will attempt a solution of the problem of just distribution upon the old *laissez faire* principle" (emphasis added). Here lies the distinction between democratic statism and corporate liberalism. "America must repudiate

Commons took this new type of "state talk" in a fully institutionalist direction. An Ely student whose greater debts in the domain of political thought were actually to Adams, Commons also defined the state historically and noted especially the weighty, historically contingent role of law and government in allocating economic advantages. In the current era, Commons argued, the state showered favors disproportionately upon capitalists. Yet, guided toward republican and social Christian ends, a further evolution of society and politics could yield a government capable of equalizing incomes and ensuring something like equal protection for labor.[38]

For Commons, both states and laws were cultural creations. His pioneering study of the sociological origins of sovereignty described the state as a historically evolving structure necessitated by the existence, growth, and changes in the form of property. The modern state was "not an ideal entity superimposed upon society, but . . . *an accumulated series of compromises* between social classes, each seeking to secure for itself control over the coercive elements which exist implicitly in society with the institution of private property." The most important function of states was the creation of rights, which in modern times normally occurred within the processes of politics and in response to pressure from enfranchised, organized groups. Propertied classes were the first to seek security in the state's protection. But as lower social groups forged a collective consciousness, they also grasped the value of sharing in the ongoing reconstruction of the political order, and insisted on their own, more democratic voice. In time, a progressive dispersal of power created rights for nonpossessors.[39]

the centralizing tendency of the German Economy," Adams continued, "because that tendency is opposed to the ideas upon which the government is founded; but, on the other hand, another century of private enterprise will itself contradict the theory of freedom, and destroy that government." Quotations on pp. 293, 294. See also his *Public Debts* (New York: D. Appleton, 1887); and idem, *Taxation in the United States, 1789–1816* ([1884]; New York: Burt Franklin, 1970).

[38]Commons, *A Sociological View of Sovereignty* ([1899–1900]; New York: Augustus Kelley Reprints, 1965). On Commons's political thought, see John Dennis Chase, "John R. Commons and the Democratic State," *Journal of Economic Issues* 20 (1986): 759–84; L. G. Harter, *John R. Commons: Assault on Laissez-Faire* (Corvallis: Oregon State University Press, 1962); Mark Perlman, *Labor Union Theories in America* (New York: Row, Peterson, 1958); and Furner, "Knowing Capitalism."

[39]As James Farr has recently noted, reinventing the state became a major preoccupation for founders of academic political science such as John William Burgess and W. W. Willoughby, who departed from earlier traditions that had stressed popular government and adopted an imported definition of the state as an abstract entity possessing absolute sovereignty. In academic circles, this approach found a challenge in the work of early

Starting close to Hobbes in his conception of the origins of states, Commons ended near what John Dewey would describe as the processes of politics. Democratic decision making could convert the law into an instrument for socializing private property without eliminating it, Commons calculated. Conceptions of justice would continuously be transformed, promoting the development of "working rules" to guide the conduct of private bargainers and public officials. As politics followed its normal course, conflicting claims could be settled in ways that offered increased protection to every group. Each accommodation described a kind of moving boundary, expressing new entitlements as ethical standards evolved. Commons imagined a time when government would lose its coercive character, expressed most disruptively in recent court decrees and armed assaults on strikers, and social investigation would be the basis for adjustment of class differences.[40]

Barred from regular academic work at the turn of the century and in close touch with advanced segments of organized capital and labor, Commons bridged the gap, pulled the two collectivisms together, and inched toward a description of changes in the form and processes of government that combined corporatist and statist elements. Working for the National Civic Federation, he watched bilateral negotiations in well-organized industries that struck him as "industrial parliaments" providing a new model for economic governance and for his version of industrial democracy. By providing specialized, credited facilities (such as those he later created in the Wisconsin Industrial Commission) for assessing data and devising legal remedies acceptable to all accredited parties, the state would help to institutionalize processes of social and political learning

historians of public administration such as H. C. Adams and Woodrow Wilson. From the standpoint of policy debates and developments, by far the more important students of the state were the new economists, for whom the state was a historical category, changing in form, capacities, and constituency, along with economic development and social evolution. See Farr, "The Estate of Political Knowledge: Political Science and the State," in JoAnne Brown and David K. van Keuren, eds., *The Estate of Social Knowledge* (Baltimore: Johns Hopkins University Press, 1991), 1–21. To measure the contrast between an idealist and a historicist point of view, compare W. W. Willoughby, *The Nature of the State* (New York: Macmillan, 1896), with Woodrow Wilson, *The State*, rev. ed. (Boston: D. C. Heath, 1896). Also see Daniel Rodgers, *Contested Truths: Keywords in American Politics Since Independence* (New York: Basic Books, 1987), esp. chap. 5, "The State."

[40] In Dewey's voluminous writings, the most accessible point of comparison is *The Public and Its Problems* (Chicago: Swallow Press, 1927), in which the discussions of the eclipse of the American state, the search for the Great Community, and the development of the methods of democracy—experimental inquiry, civic education, and public discussion—are strikingly similar to the Adams-Commons view.

designed to detect legitimate claims and settle differences on mutually advantageous terms. These agreements would take on a routine character, capable of expression in comprehensive contractual agreements that bridged the differences between classes, and in administrative law.[41]

Dialogues such as these among economists (and parallel ones in law, political science, sociology, and other fields) suggest that the American new liberalism had a special quality, compared with what developed in Britain in these years. It was the way in which the tension between an emergent democratic statism and corporatist voluntarism recapitulated a persistent dualism, present since the Revolution in American public discourse, between republican and liberal values. British new liberals converged on a statist response to the crisis of traditional liberalism in the pre–World War I years; only later, in the interwar period, did British new liberalism divide into left-liberal and centrist components. In the American case, two different conceptions of new liberalism were present from the beginning, constructed in the long progressive era that opened in the 1880s.[42]

Both versions addressed the new institutional forms of mature capitalism. The essence of democratic collectivism was the extension of popular sovereignty over corporations, a commitment rooted in historical and institutional analysis of the claims of property in relation to liberty. Once an undifferentiated category, property now existed in complex and hybrid forms, producing varied consequences, not all of them socially beneficial. Because most people could not expect to own productive property, conventional forms of proprietorship were not sufficient to protect the social interest; nor was the unlimited property right enshrined in classical liberalism a morally acceptable expression of individualism. Yet, despite the powerful attraction of the socialist moral critique, the democratic statists were unprepared to do away with property, linked as it was in republican tradition with political independence, preservation of civic virtue, and restraint of the state. Rather, they proposed extending the claims of citizenship, including entitlements and protections against

[41]Clarence Wunderlin, *Visions of a New Industrial Order: Social Investigation and Labor Reform Thought, 1879–1916* (New York: Columbia University Press, 1992). See also John R. Commons, *Labor and Administration* ([1913]; New York: Augustus M. Kelley Reprints of Economic Classics, 1964), 395–424; idem, "A New Way of Settling Labor Disputes," *American Monthly Review of Reviews* 23 (1901): 329–33.

[42]Michael Freeden, *Liberalism Divided* (Oxford: Oxford University Press, 1976), and Peter Clarke, *Liberals and Social Democrats* (Cambridge: Cambridge University Press, 1978). See also Chapter 9 by Barry Supple in this volume.

the pernicious insecurity of industrial modernism, among a new class of rights.

To the extent that democratic statists such as Ely and Adams developed a labor theory, it was also a historical one, in touch with republican producerism, social Christianity, and democratic socialism, which associated labor with virtue. Adams understood American labor relations as a case of delayed development, in which liberal virtues long practiced in the political realm had yet to be extended to industry. He considered class conflict inescapable in capitalism and essential to social progress. Thus, with Commons, his version of industrial democracy required equal organization on both sides, sustained adversarial relations, and collective bargaining, with the state encouraging worker organization while protecting the powerless unorganized and the community in general. In the 1880s, with union membership surging, capitalists relatively unorganized, and the judicial onslaught against labor only beginning, optimism in such matters was possible. Collectivist democrats anticipated the gradual formation, through struggle and accommodation, of a common law of industry, specifying socially approved entitlements. These proprietary rights, including job security, would make up an "industrial constitution," guaranteeing some measure of liberty for workers and independence for unions in an increasingly stratified society. To the disappointment of more radical contemporaries and subsequent labor historians, the democratic statists' laborism was qualified by their rejection of the identity of *any* private interest with the public interest.[43]

Meanwhile, emerging corporate liberals such as Jenks and Hadley had their own clear sense of social responsibility. Once again, the line of demarcation was the uses of the state. Whereas democratic collectivists believed voluntarism would favor those who were already powerful, the corporatists believed emerging functional groups were the natural structure of civil society. They encouraged responsible organization among all classes, and development, through education and increased consumption, of the capacities and aspirations of labor. But the corporation became their organizing principle, the truly defining institution in the new

---

[43] Adams, "Labor Problem," *Scientific American,* Supplement, 22 (1886): 8861–3; idem, "The Right of Employment," typescript, n.d. [circa 24 August 1893], Henry Carter Adams MSS, Michigan Historical Collections; idem, "What Do These Strikes Mean?" [March 25, 1886], ibid.; idem, "An Interpretation of the Social Movements of Our Times," *International Journal of Ethics* (1891): 1–19; and Perlman, *Labor Union Theories,* chap. 7.

industrial society—the source of continued progress and the appropriate method for social ordering.[44]

Corporate liberalism and democratic statism arose as elements in a common discourse[45]—as criticisms of an increasingly irresponsible, disruptive classical/neoclassical liberalism. Defining opposite ends of the spectrum of collectivist thought and policy, statism and associationalism were mirror images. Distinctive elements of a statist new liberalism were available in the 1880s—before the corporation assumed its modern influence and before corporate liberalism was fully elaborated around it.[46]

Corporate liberalism arose as a reaction not only to the visible menace to the emerging corporate order embodied in greenbackism, Populism, and socialism but also to less extreme and therefore more credible forms of statist collectivism, such as those in economics, sociology in the tradition of Lester Ward and Albion Small, and the early stages of legal realism, and in social democratic variants of the new sciences of public administration and social work, with their own state-building agendas. The case for private ordering and enabling structures for it came together rather slowly. Among other things that were lacking, the idea that economic management and a sizable chunk of social policy could be taken over by private governments required scientific justification—not available until the 1890s—for the contention that the price system contained guarantees against a fundamental conflict between the public and the corporate interests.[47]

[44]Hadley, *Economics;* Jeremiah Jenks, *Great Fortunes: The Winning, the Using* (New York: McClure, Phillips & Co., 1906); Parrini and Sklar, "New Thinking"; and Sklar, *Corporate Reconstruction.*

[45]On the history and analysis of discourses, see Quentin Skinner, "Some Problems in the Analysis of Political Thought and Action," *Political Theory* 2 (1974): 277–303, and Raymond Williams, *Keywords: A Vocabulary of Culture and Society* (1976; London: Fontana, 1983).

[46]I differ here from Weinstein and Lustig, who position corporate liberalism as a reaction to traditional, individualist liberalism. The latter, in Weinstein's formulation, includes both Populism and LaFollette progressivism.

[47]Furner, "Liberty Versus Efficiency" and "Knowing Capitalism." For other references to different forms of collectivism or new liberalism and a tension between them, see Roy Lubove, *The Professional Altruist: The Emergence of Social Work as a Career, 1880–1930* (Cambridge, Mass.: Harvard University Press, 1965); idem, *The Struggle for Social Security, 1900–1935* (Cambridge, Mass.: Harvard University Press, 1968); Michael B. Katz, *Poverty and Policy in American History* (New York: Academic Press, 1983), esp. chap. 3, "American Historians and Dependence"; Ellis Hawley, "Herbert Hoover, the Commerce Secretariat, and the Vision of an 'Associative State,'" *Journal of American History* 61 (1974): 116–40; idem, "Economic Inquiry and the State in New Era America: Antistatist Corporatism and Positive Statism in Uneasy Coexistence," *The State and Economic Knowledge,* 287–324; Christopher Tomlins, *The State and the Unions: Labor Relations, Law, and the Organized Labor Movement, 1880–1960* (Cambridge: Cam-

It was in the social sciences, and especially economics, that the new, statist and associative conceptions of modern liberalism were most clearly and consistently articulated. But to exert political leverage, these models for social ordering had to leave the academic setting and enter public discourse, where fertile ground for both was being prepared.

REDEFINING LABOR:
REPUBLICAN DREAMS AND INDUSTRIAL REALITIES

When modern democracies renegotiate the rules of their collective existence, their deliberations necessarily involve not only the representation of interests but also the introduction and diffusion of specialized knowledge and expertise. Thus the deliberations of government itself formed an important arena for the diffusion and further development of collectivist ideas developing among social scientists. Like public inquiries generally, congressional investigations of the labor question served more than one purpose. Initially, they were political responses that showed concern in times of crisis, placating angry constituents and buying time for evasion or for mature deliberation. They also contributed to a reassessment of inherited theories of enterprise and government, required in all societies facing industrial transformation. Along with other forms of social criticism, the congressional inquiries of the 1870s to the 1890s subjected the new industrial capitalism to a political and ideological fitness test. They located and publicized the new meanings that labor and capital were taking on as social categories, and oriented discussion of the implications of new forms of property and work relations for republican institutions and values, forcing conceptual and political change.[48]

Public investigation also affected the formation of the modern state. In particular, the Gilded Age labor inquiries provided settings in which initially inchoate criticisms of judicial repression of unions could be developed. They opened up lines of reasoning and experimentation through which theoretical warrant for alternative, associative, and bureaucratic methods of social ordering, incorporating function, interest, and class

bridge University Press, 1985); and idem, "The New Deal, Collective Bargaining, and the Triumph of Industrial Pluralism," *Industrial and Labor Relations Review* 39 (1985): 19–34.

[48] On the conceptual dimension of social investigation, see Terrence Ball, James Farr, and Russell L. Hanson, eds., *Political Innovation and Conceptual Change* (Cambridge: Cambridge University Press, 1989).

into the structure of representation, could be explored. Together, these investigations should be understood as the first phase of a process of political learning that culminated with the official adoption in the 1930s of measures that reflected conflicting collectivist approaches to the labor question: the associative model of voluntary collective action embodied in the Norris-LaGuardia Act of 1932, which lifted the threat injunctions posed to workers' collective efforts, and the (at least initially) more statist collectivism of Article 7a of the National Industrial Recovery Act and the Wagner Act.[49]

The Gilded Age labor question attracted the sustained attention of trained investigators who built professional or bureaucratic careers in whole or in part on the provision of useful knowledge for the public purposes of civic education and policy. Specialized labor bureaus, which appeared earliest in the United States and eventually in all industrialized countries, provided one type of expertise. In addition, as an expression of the growing cultural authority of academic knowledge, and to some extent as an antidote to the incorporation of more directly "interested" parties into policy discourse, professional social scientists became direct participants in official investigations of the labor question, displacing the dedicated amateurs and humanitarian reformers who had performed a similar, knowledge-bearing function in the antebellum era. Present at first sporadically as expert witnesses, by the turn of the century economists staffed and planned social investigations, bringing professional theories directly into the researches and recommendations of official bodies.[50]

Official investigation of the labor question disclosed a distressing fluidity in the meanings of the social categories that constituted the cus-

---

[49] An important literature exists on comparative development of welfare states in response to capitalist development and crisis—much of the best of it involving the works of Theda Skocpol and her collaborators. See, for example, "Why Not Equal Protection? Explaining the Politics of Public Social Spending in Britain, 1900–1911, and the United States, 1880s–1920," *American Sociological Review* 49 (1984): 726–50; Margaret Weir, Ann Shola Orloff, and Theda Skocpol, eds., *The Politics of Social Policy in the United States* (Princeton, N.J.: Princeton University Press, 1988). My main criticism of this excellent work is its lack of attention to specifically ideological factors changing over time. "Political learning" is Hugh Heclo's term for the process of "collective puzzlement" regarding what social conditions should be, and the resulting alteration of perspectives and institutional changes that leads to shifts in social policy, in his *Modern Social Politics in Britain and Sweden* (New Haven, Conn.: Yale University Press, 1974), chap. 6.
[50] Joseph P. Goldberg and William T. Moye, *The First Hundred Years of the Bureau of Labor Statistics* (Washington, D.C.: Bureau of Labor Statistics, 1985); James Leiby, *Carroll Wright and Labor Reform* (Cambridge, Mass.: Harvard University Press, 1960); Furner, "Knowing Capitalism," 246–68; and Tomlins, *The State and the Unions*, 44–52.

tomary language of social policy. A reconstruction of this language began between the House inquiry into the impact of the depression of the 1870s on labor and business, conducted in 1877–8, and the Senate hearings on relations between labor and capital held in 1883. In the earlier inquiry, continuity with the republican past was the dominant theme. Defining labor as a comprehensive category embracing all producers and as the source of all value, the call for hearings mandated a search for "liberal, just, and equal laws" to protect this fundamental social interest.[51]

Most of the witnesses were small proprietors, risen from artisan ranks, who adhered to the free-labor ideal. They traced the downturn in their fortunes to corrupt postwar financial policies favoring wealthy capitalists, and they sought relief in political remedies—such as the eight-hour day, land reform, public education, and currency inflation—designed to extend employment and preserve proprietorship. "We need laws to put a stop to overtowering corporations . . . [that] have now got it so that they can shake the United States government at their very will," a typical one snarled. Outraged, they sensed an imminent departure from the era of proprietary capitalism, yet their complaints and proposals were contained within a discourse of civic virtue and labor republicanism.[52]

A handful of witnesses departed from this producerist vision of a natural harmony corrupted by power and wealth to offer structural analyses of the depression. Radical labor leaders such as Albert Parsons, George Schilling, and Thomas Morgan espoused a view informed by European socialism, in which concentration of ownership was a progressive step, reflecting an evolutionary development and decay in capitalism that paved the way for socialism. Unsympathetic to small producers and scornful of bourgeois reform, they expected the emanci-

[51]U.S. House of Representatives, *Investigation by a Select Committee Relative to the Causes of the General Depression in Labor and Business,* House Misc. Doc. 5, 46th Cong., 2d Sess. (1879), 1. On the traditional meanings of labor, see Foner, *Free Soil;* Montgomery, *Beyond Equality;* William E. Forbath, "The Ambiguities of Free Labor: Labor and the Law in the Gilded Age," *Wisconsin Law Review* (1985): 767–817; idem, "The Shaping of the American Labor Movement," *Harvard Law Review* 102 (1989): 1109–1256; Leon Fink, "Labor, Liberty, and the Law: Trade Unionism and the Problem of an American Constitutional Order," *Journal of American History* 74 (1987): 904–25; Charles McCurdy, "Justice Field and the Jurisprudence of Government-Business Relations: Some Parameters of Laissez-Faire Constitutionalism, 1863–1897," *Journal of American History* 61 (1975): 970–1005.

[52]To sample the categories of opinion in this account, see the testimony of William Halley, Joseph Eastman, C. McAuliffe, George W. Dean, H. H. Bryant, David J. King, James McArthur, and Jonathan Y. Scammon for the small proprietors' view. *Investigation . . . Relative to the Causes of the General Depression.* The quotation is on p. 119, testimony of C. McAuliffe.

pation of labor to require more than mere legislation. They endorsed the eight-hour day on the grounds put forward by indigenous radicals such as the National Labor Union's intellectual leader, Ira Steward—that this particular reform would increase consumption, cause wage demands to rise, and ultimately eliminate profits, thereby ending capitalism.

Within a second group whose analyses also departed from republican thinking, economic journalists and academics summoned as expert witnesses, a split was evident. Horace White, Edward Atkinson, and William Graham Sumner offered what amounted to a classical liberal explanation that linked the 1870s slump to speculation in booming industries such as the railroads and telegraph. By contrast, three men—Lyman Gage, a Chicago banker; Carroll Wright, Massachusetts labor commissioner; and Charles Francis Adams, a Massachusetts railroad commissioner—identified overproduction as an endemic condition, structurally related to the new economy. In representative fashion for this group, Gage explained the worldwide slump as "mainly a reaction towards . . . normal relations that had been unnaturally disturbed by . . . the immense transfer of capital into fixed forms, such as ships, railroads, mines, manufactories, &c., out of due proportion to the then requirements."[53]

These three men understood the modern business depression as a form of market failure, occurring regularly in industrial economies, where productive capacity outstripped demand except in periods of peak consumption. As a remedy, all three advocated better private planning, not state action. Yet, in their recognition of a fundamental transformation in the structure of capitalism and capitalist society, and in the implicit collectivism of their views, they were closer to the socialists than to the republican small proprietors and classical liberals whose traditional categories and ideals dominated the hearings.[54]

By the mid-1880s, the context had changed dramatically as a reorganization of enterprise accelerated the proletarianization of American labor, fueling concern that the free labor system, defended so recently by force of arms and imposed by congressional enactment on the defeated South, was rapidly disappearing. Imported European doctrines as well as traditional American forms of republicanism and evangelical Chris-

[53]Ibid., quotation on p. 9.
[54]On Wright's original contributions to business cycle theory, see U.S. Bureau of Labor, First Annual Report, *Industrial Depressions* (1886); Furner, "Knowing Capitalism," 249–50; and Parrini and Sklar, "New Thinking," 559–78. On C. F. Adams's antistatist collectivism, see Thomas McCraw, *Prophets of Regulation* (Cambridge, Mass.: Harvard University Press, 1984), 1–56.

tianity informed an increasingly class-conscious reaction that denied the legitimacy of industrial capitalism. Labor reformers challenged legal doctrines long associated with artisan labor, such as liberty of contract, as inherently unequal when applied to the new forms of industrial employment, and defended the right to organize and strike as aspects of citizenship.[55]

In response to this alteration in social structure and consciousness, a series of more specialized congressional committees appeared. As part of a larger effort to modernize the intelligence-gathering function of government, these bodies subdivided and reassigned the labor question. Created in 1867, the House Committee on Education and Labor was divided in 1883 into separate committees, in view of the special need, identified by Cong. John O'Neill (D–Missouri), for "a committee in this House to which the representatives of the laboring element can submit their claims." "You do not want this terrible rumbling and uneasiness to culminate as it did formerly in the celebrated railroad strike," O'Neill admonished. "There must be some vent through which the feelings of that element can reach the law-making power." The Senate Committee on Education and Labor, formed in 1870, retained its dual focus, which reflected both the republican (and, in the days of Charles Sumner, the Republican) view that education was intimately related to the advancement of labor and an activist posture toward social policy that had been adopted during Reconstruction.[56]

Often largely composed of "friends of labor" such as Sen. Henry Blair (R–New Hampshire), who chaired the Senate committee from 1881 to 1891, Congressman O'Neill, and Cong. George Tillman (D–South Carolina), these committees drew their members from a nascent "labor group" in Congress that paid particular attention to the labor question and consulted with union leaders and labor reformers regarding threats

[55]Gutman, *Work, Culture, and Society,* 49–54, 272; Richard Schneirov, "Political Cultures and the Role of the State in Labor's Republic: The View from Chicago, 1848–1877," *Labor History* 32 (1991): 376–400; Linda Schneider, "The Citizen Striker: Workers' Ideology in the Homestead Strike of 1892," ibid., 23 (1982): 47–66; Charles McCurdy, "The Roots of 'Liberty of Contract' Reconsidered: Major Premises in the Law of Employment, 1867–1937," *Supreme Court Historical Society Yearbook* (1984): 20–33.

[56]For the O'Neill quotation, see *Congressional Record,* 48th Cong., 1st Sess. (1883), 194–95. On the history of labor committees, see *Records of the United States House of Representatives at the National Archives,* House Document No. 100–245, 100th Cong., 2d Sess. (National Archives and Records Administration, 1989), 125; *Records of the United States Senate at the National Archives,* ibid., 167; and Walter Stubbs, comp., *Congressional Committees, 1789–1982: A Checklist* (Westport, Conn.: Greenwood Press, 1982).

to labor's welfare.[57] Beginning with the first true freedom-of-contract decision, *In re Jabocs* in 1885, the greatest threat emanated from the courts, which by 1900 had struck down more than sixty labor laws. The Sherman Antitrust Act supplied additional danger, in the form of a new legal standard that outlawed labor unions' most indispensable concerted actions.[58]

In the face of this judicial activism, and in response to the rapid growth and politicization of the labor movement and an alarming rise in the size and frequency of strikes, congressional labor committees in the 1880s redefined the labor question so that it no longer referred to protecting propertied independence. Rather, the congressional version of the labor question referred to the living and working conditions of a class of wage earners apparently locked in perpetual conflict with an opposing class of employers. Skirting the argument raised in some quarters that the only real answer would be revolution, the labor committees assessed the justice or injustice of those conditions, and the possibilities presented by various methods, including legislative and administrative ones, for resolving the conflicts between classes before they tore the social fabric irretrievably.

In session after session, wrestling with bills designed to legalize unions, curb injunctions, and require arbitration, the labor committees recognized officially the inherent collectivism of modern industrial life. Hampered by partisan divisions and addressed to Gilded Age congresses that were either overtly probusiness or ill-disposed toward taking controversial positions, the efforts of these committees were halting and ambivalent, reflecting what labor and policy historians have viewed as a generally spineless attitude, in the face of capitalist opposition, that retarded the growth of the American welfare state. In reality, the main obstacle to more decisive action may well have been not business opposition, congressional conservatism, or a constraining federalism but divisions regarding goals within the working class[59] and the antistatism of a leading segment

---

[57]Members of the labor group also included Charles Boatner (D–Louisiana); Charles Brumm (R–Pennsylvania); Richard Coke (D–Texas); William H. Crain (D–Texas); Andrew Curtin (D–Pennsylvania); Zachariah George (D–Mississippi): Henry B. Lovering (D–Massachusetts); and James Tawney (R–Minnesota).

[58]Before 1897 elite jurists considered combinations of labor more harmful to consumers than combinations of capital, which they believed generally promoted productive efficiency. Herbert Hovenkamp, "Labor Conspiracies in American Law, 1880–1930," *Texas Law Review* 66 (1988): 919–65. See also Hurvitz, "American Labor Law and the Doctrine of Entrepreneurial Property Rights."

[59]On workers' confusion regarding political goals, see Fink, *Workingmen's Democracy*; Schneirov, "Political Cultures"; Bruce C. Nelson, *Beyond the Martyrs: A Social History*

of the labor movement, attributable to factors either external[60] or internal[61] to the working class, or to a combination of both.

Tunneling through a thicket of competing organizations and programs, the labor committees attempted to define policy in relation to what could be defended as the public interest. Discarding assumptions of classlessness embedded in antebellum liberalism, the Senate Labor and Education (Blair) Committee embarked on its investigations into the relations of labor and capital by adopting the premise that the United States was already, albeit in an as yet ill-defined sense, a class society.[62] A committee member reluctantly acknowledged a corrosive "antagonism and distrust instead of harmonious cooperation and mutual confidence" between labor and capital, which he believed stemmed from the "enormous growth of corporate power," "the aggregation of immense wealth in the hands of a few," and the consequent "reduction, comparatively, of the number of independent persons of small capital and the large increase of the number of those who derive their subsistence by wages paid, and too often dictated by employers."[63]

Inventing an investigative strategy to address these new realities, the Senate inquiry of 1883 allowed the heads of prominent national labor unions, rather than artisan proprietors or socialists, who had been prom-

of Chicago's Anarchists, 1870–1900 (New Brunswick, N.J.: Rutgers University Press, 1988); John Jentz, "Class and Politics in an Emerging Industrial Tradition: Chicago in the 1860s and 1870s," *Journal of Urban History* 17 (1991): 227–63; and the sources in notes 50 and 54 above.

[60] See especially Forbath, "Law and the Shaping of the American Labor Movement," which argues that judicial repression robbed mainstream labor of its ability to think in republican and/or collectivist terms and converted Samuel Gompers and the American Federation of Labor to a language of laissez-faire.

[61] See especially Richard Oestreicher, "Urban Working-Class Political Behavior and Theories of American Electoral Politics, 1870–1940," *Journal of American History* 74 (1988): 1257–86, which analyzes the impact of institutional constraints of the American electoral system on working class politics. See also Leon Fink, "The Uses of Political Power: Toward a Theory of the Labor Movement in the Era of the Knights of Labor," in Michael H. Frisch and Daniel J. Walkowitz, eds., *Working Class America* (Urbana: University of Illinois Press, 1983); Gwendolyn Mink, *Old Labor and New Immigrants in American Political Development: Union, Party, and State, 1875–1920* (Ithaca, N.Y.: Cornell University Press, 1986); and Richard L. McCormick, *The Party Period and Public Policy: American Politics from the Age of Jackson to the Progressive Era* (New York: Oxford University Press, 1986), 98–140.

[62] U.S. Senate, Committee on Education and Labor, *The Relations Between Labor and Capital*, 47th Cong., 2d Sess., 4 vols. (1883 [pub. 1885]). For a contrary view, which discounts the importance of class, see Morton Keller, "Regulating Labor," *Regulating a New Economy, 1900–1930* (Cambridge, Mass.: Harvard University Press, 1990), 114–47.

[63] On the need for a select committee, *Congressional Record*, 47th Cong., 1st Sess. (June 21, 1882), 5161–4. The quotation is from Sen. James George (D–Mississippi).

inent in the earlier hearings, to become the voices of labor. These witnesses confirmed the committee's perceptions by offering descriptions of
social conditions and industrial relations that were incompatible with
republican traditions. An early Knights of Labor platform referred to
"an inevitable and irresistible conflict between the wage-system of labor
and republican system of government." The American Federation of
Organized Trades and Labor Unions (AFOTLU) declared in its founding
document that the conflict under way in republican America was merely
the local version of "a struggle... going on in all the civilized countries
of the world, between the oppressers and the oppressed." As the major
spokesman for the wing of the trade union movement that explicitly
rejected the political goals of labor republicanism, Samuel Gompers
underlined for the Senate committee the view that industrial capitalism
was inevitably class society, that class relations were necessarily adversarial, and that these new realities entailed collectivism:

Modern industry evolves these organizations out of the existing conditions where
there are two classes in society, one incessantly striving to obtain the labor of
the other class for as little as possible, and to obtain the largest amount or number
of hours of labor; and the members of the other class being, as individuals, utterly
helpless in a contest with their employers, naturally resort to combinations to
improve their condition, and, in fact, they are forced by the conditions which
surround them to organize for self-protection. Hence trades unions.[64]

Gompers, Peter J. McGuire, Adolph Strasser, and Robert Layton of
the Knights could defend a class analysis in part because they had information regarding the standing of their constituency better than that
possessed by any other group. In addition to the wealth of experience
generated by their unions, an authoritative source of information on the
status and prospects of labor was the statistical and descriptive work
done by government scientific agencies devoted to tracking such matters.
By 1883, labor bureaus had been established in nine industrial states as
part of a political response to working-class organization and agitation.
Initially overtly partisan but gradually taken over by a new breed of
public statisticians such as Carroll Wright, the bureaus adopted class as
their unit of investigation; they collected information on workers' living
and working conditions, strikes, and labor legislation, arming trade union

[64]Ibid., Gompers testimony, 1:372–3. The Knights of Labor manifesto is quoted in Fink,
   Workingmen's Democracy, 4; "The Labor Congress," *The Samuel Gompers Papers*,
   Stuart B. Kaufman, ed., 3 vols. (Urbana: University of Illinois Press, 1986), 1:224.

chiefs with reams of statistics they could use to back demands for protective legislation.[65]

Information from the labor bureaus oriented congressional investigations both theoretically and ideologically. Studies such as Wright's classic report on the textile industry in Fall River disclosed working and living conditions so at odds with republican values that they invited intervention. So also did regular Bureau of Labor Statistics reports comparing America's emerging laissez-faire constitutionalism with the more protective official attitude toward labor and the more advanced methods of class bargaining evident in other countries. Avid consumers of the new labor statistics, union leaders referred constantly to "government figures" as evidence of hardening attitudes, unfair dealing, and repressive tactics by employers. Such evidence supported the collectivism of the view trade union leaders pressed on the committee—that nothing short of effective organization and judicious use of the strike weapon could secure just compensation and decent conditions for labor.[66]

More important, this evidence focused the investigators' attention on a revolution in judicial theorizing and practice under way in the mid-1880s that struck directly at the unions' legal standing and potential usefulness in social ordering. Under sympathetic questioning, the unrefuted testimony of trade union leaders did much to demonstrate that the main obstacle to the reformation of industrial capitalism was the courts. Targeting flagrant cases of judicial tampering with needed legislation, the hearings raised a specter of legal bias not accounted for in classical accounts of the governing process. By justifying unions as vital mechanisms in distribution and demanding at least a neutral posture toward them on the part of the state, the hearings gave currency to the view that individualism in labor relations was outmoded.[67]

Without explicitly attacking the new judicialism as strike investigation committees later would, the Blair committee attempted to discover what

[65]Gutman, *Work, Culture, and Society,* 269–71, 281–4, affirms the effectiveness of such investigations in his record of the legislative achievements of an Irish labor radical, Joseph McDonnell, who was New Jersey's first deputy factory inspector, served on the state's Board of Arbitration, headed the legislative committee of the New Jersey Federation of Organized Trade and Labor Unions, and orchestrated campaigns between 1883 and 1892 that secured dozens of labor laws in that state. On the timing of capitalist organization, see Hays, "Politics of Reform"; Weinstein, *Corporate Ideal;* and Sklar, *Corporate Reconstruction.*

[66]Leiby, *Carroll Wright,* and Furner, "Knowing Capitalism," 246–68. Wright's testimony before the Senate committee is in *Relations Between Labor and Capital,* 3:276–83, 418–36.

[67]For criticisms of the courts, see especially the testimony of Gompers and McGuire.

might be gained through positive legislation. The senators found, to their amazement, that unions' political demands on the national government were more modest than those presented by the labor republicans who had dominated the earlier House investigation, or than conditions seemed to warrant. Although the Knights often sought political goals in local electoral contests, this conservatism suggested that trade union leaders generally were conditioned to expect less from the state than from voluntary methods, and were already migrating toward collective laissez-faire. Judicial noninterference would at least place collective labor on an equal legal basis with combined, collective capital, allowing the two sides simply to slug it out in the marketplace.[68]

Despite important differences in goals and ideology, the Knights and AFOTLU had in fact compiled similar legislative agendas, aimed mainly at halting judicial attacks. Citing court rulings that effectively criminalized unions, McGuire and Gompers requested a federal legalization statute, modeled on recent British legislation aimed at quelling judicial harassment there, that would exempt labor organizations from criminal conspiracy actions and civil prosecution for restraint of trade. Their ambivalence regarding federal incorporation of unions stemmed from fears that vulnerability to civil damage suits might offset the advantages of greater protection for union property and the appearance of greater responsibility. Recognizing constitutional limitations, they did not imagine that the national government could regulate industrial working hours, but they insisted on strict enforcement of the eight-hour government day. They demanded an end to contract immigration. In part for informational purposes but also because a bureaucratic presence would help to offset political pressure from capitalists, they wanted a federal labor bureau.[69]

The Senate hearings marked the beginning of a congressional preoccupation with the potential of arbitration as a method of settling industrial disputes. Reflecting a generalized longing among middle-class Americans for an alternative to disruptive strikes, the committee's interest in arbitration also rested on the conviction, widely held in official and reform circles, and congruent with the statist turn in liberal policy dis-

[68]On the legislative programs, see *Relations,* particularly the testimony of W. H. Foster, general secretary of the Federation of Organized Trades and Labor Unions, 1:404; Frank Foster, 1:85–7; Gompers, 1:271, 377–9; John Jarrett, 1:1124; Martin Williams, 1:1172–3; McGuire, 1:328–34; Strasser, 1:461–2; Layton, 1:2, 10.
[69]Legislative programs adopted by AFOTLU between 1881 and 1884 called for all of these measures. See *Gompers Papers,* 1:220–9, 279–81. For references to British trade union laws, see the testimony of McGuire, ibid., 1:323–6; and of Gompers, ibid., 1:378–81.

course during the 1880s, that bureaucratic processes of investigation, negotiation, and expert judgment rather than contests of will and force could break the deadlocks over control of production and division of income. From this perspective, held by many in the rising academic and service professions, the public interest required an official presence in the determination of wages and thus in distribution. Contemporary discussion of arbitration shows that it carried several meanings, ranging from voluntary conciliation to more radical, statist proposals that contemplated removing resolution of labor conflicts to a novel institutional setting, a specialized administrative agency with quasi-judicial authority, empowered to weigh the claims of both parties in prolonged, serious wage disputes against a community standard of equity, and to subordinate the interests of workers and employers to the public interest in uninterrupted service from essential industries.[70]

Committee probing revealed a difference of opinion regarding arbitration between the more politically engaged Knights of Labor, for whom discussion centered on republican values and proprietary rights, and the more economistic posture of trade union leaders in the fledgling AFOTLU. The Knights were officially committed to substituting arbitration for strikes. McGuire and Gompers contended that arbitration would never work until employers were persuaded "by a class struggle, through a strike," that workers were their equals. Less apprehensive about voluntary mediation and yet fearful of compromising the strike threat, they stopped short of condemning arbitration, but they insisted on the workers' unencumbered right to fix the selling price of labor.[71]

By putting arbitration on the national agenda, the congressional labor group endorsed the principle—denied by the judiciary—that trade unions merited equal standing with combinations of employers in the resolution

---

[70]For discussion of arbitration in the Senate committee hearings, see, in *Relations,* the testimony of Gompers, 1:377; McGuire, 1:322; Frank K. Foster, 1:85–7; John S. McClelland, 1:139; and W. H. Foster, 1:404. For broad-gauged discussions of arbitration, see George E. McNeill, ed., *The Labor Movement: The Problem of Today* (New York: M. W. Hazen Co., 1887), 497–507 and passim; John D. Peters, ed., *Labor and Capital: A Discussion of the Relations of Employer and Employed* (New York: G. P. Putnam's Sons, 1902), 127–304, and the reports of the conferences on arbitration and conciliation held by the Chicago Civic Federation and the National Civic Federation, cited earlier.

[71]The quotation is in McGuire's testimony at p. 322. Gompers's statement in 1888 was typical; he believed in arbitration but not "between the lion and the lamb.... There can only be arbitration between equals. Let us organize." *Gompers Papers,* 2:87. Arbitration was frequently discussed in the AFL *Federationist* and other labor papers. Trade union witnesses before the Blair committee were familiar with the smallest details of European arbitration systems. See testimony of Gompers, *Relations,* 1:377–9.

of labor disputes. The Senate hearings signaled recognition in certain official circles as early as the Cleveland era that the new industrial system could only be described in a language of aggregates and functions. A system that treated corporate groups as individuals was sure to break down, the hearings suggested; a legal collectivism to match new social realities would become essential. This line of analysis opened the prospect, shared by a number of public officials, social scientists, and other middle-class reformers, that—at least with respect to strikes in vital industries— a politically accountable, inquiry-based process, capable of bringing statistical comparisons of profits and wages to bear on distribution, should take account of the social nature of both capital and labor, and subordinate class interests to a wider social interest in justice and stability.[72]

Although the Blair committee issued no formal recommendations, it bore a modest amount of legislative fruit. A national Bureau of Labor was established in 1884. Contract immigration was banned in 1885. In 1886, the O'Neill bill, a measure drafted by the American Federation of Labor (AFL), successor in 1886 to AFOTLU, permitting national incorporation of unions, was adopted, although a controversial provision explicitly legalizing unions was dropped in committee. Various versions of an arbitration bill, including one offered by President Cleveland, were under consideration when a Knights' strike against Jay Gould's Southwest railroad system provoked the first in a series of congressional strike investigations that extended the case for some effective nonjudicial means of accommodating class action to the public interest.[73]

Between 1886 and 1894, several major strikes cranked up pressure for official action. Responding to these challenges, the strike investigations served important intellectual as well as political purposes. One, which contributed to the development of a knowledge base for labor policy, was the purely sociological function of documenting social rela-

[72]For an influential congressman's review of thinking along these lines in the mid-1880s, see John J. O'Neill, "Arbitration," in McNeill, *Labor Movement*, 497–507.

[73]For a discussion of Senate Bill 1657 to legalize the incorporation of unions, see the Lovering Bill, H.R. 6084; the amended O'Neill bill, H.R. 7621; and the *Congressional Record*, 49th Cong., 1st Sess. (1886), 5447, 5565–6. On the appeal of arbitration in this era, see also Gerald Eggert, *Railroad Labor Disputes* (Ann Arbor: University of Michigan Press, 1967); Shelton Stromquist, *A Generation of Boomers: The Pattern of Railroad Labor Conflict in Nineteenth Century America* (Urbana: University of Illinois Press, 1987); Gerald Friedman, "Worker Militancy and Its Consequences: Political Responses to Labor Unrest in the United States, 1877–1914," *International Labor and Working-Class History* 40 (1991): 5–17; and Peter J. Coleman, *Progressivism and the World of Reform: New Zealand and the Origins of the American Welfare State* (Lawrence: University of Kansas Press, 1986).

tions in the affected industrial communities. Working on site, questioning hundreds of employees, trade union heads, industrialists, and community leaders, the investigators probed for the proximate causes of each disturbance. They also looked beneath immediate grievances to the underlying conditions of life and labor for industrial workers, and the employment, management, and investment practices of their employers. In so doing, they created an official record of these conflicts that laid the basis for an assessment of their causes and consequences. Second, at the level of constitutional analysis and institutional innovation, the strike inquiries exposed the contradictions of judicial theories, evolving from injunction to injunction in these years, which construed most forms of organized collective action against employers as violations of entrepreneurial property rights. And they extended the exploration of possibilities for linking bureaucratic methods with alternative constitutional theories and a responsible collectivism in industrial relations.

Chaired by Cong. Andrew Curtin (D–Pennsylvania), the House Select Committee Investigation of Labor Troubles in the Southwest established the first extensive record of a labor conflict involving primarily control issues. In the Southwest railroad strikes, the Knights, representing track and station hands outside the elite craft brotherhoods, demanded job security, union recognition, a voice in management, and arbitration. Connected historically with the republican ideal of independence, these references to proprietary rights for labor were explicitly at odds with the claim to an exclusive right to manage that the courts had recently attached to capital.[74]

The strike inquiries revealed social implications of an absolute property right not previously noted by the courts. Chaired by Cong. George Tillman, the House Select Committee Investigation of Labor Troubles in Pennsylvania, occasioned by a Knights' strike against the pooled, coal-hauling railroads that monopolized anthracite production, was the first official record of the desperate conditions endured by miners' families in isolated company towns. A "thick description" of life in these essentially

---

[74]U.S. Congress, House of Representatives, *Investigation of Labor Troubles in Missouri, Arkansas, Kansas, Texas, and Illinois* [hereafter *Labor Troubles in the Southwest*], House Report No. 4174, 49th Cong., 2d Sess. (1887). See also "Investigation of Labor Troubles," *Congressional Record*, 49th Cong., 1st Sess. (April 12, 1886), 3391–5, and President Cleveland's special message on the subject, "Labor Arbitration," ibid. (April 23, 1886), 3760–4. Compare Frank William Taussig, "The South-western Strike of 1886," *Quarterly Journal of Economics* 1 (1887): 184–223, which condemned the Knights' demands as an arrogant invasion of property rights. Taussig's father owned the St. Louis Bridge Company, which had an interest in a route shut down by the strike.

feudal settings exposed an unrepublican dependency, a corresponding sense of grievance against corporations that lacked legitimacy in the eyes of the community, and an imposed order dependent not only on brutal suppression of sporadic violence but on the wholesale corruption of community institutions, including politics and, most egregiously, the law.[75]

Their explicit focus on abuses of the law made the strike investigations important elements in the construction of a critical analysis not only of the new judicialism as it applied to labor, but of the crucial effect in labor disputes of law enforcement generally. As against specifically market forces, the investigating committees called attention to the role in class relations and distribution played by civil authorities—sheriffs and mayors, state governors and labor commissioners, and state and federal courts. Their findings invariably portrayed judicial handling of strikes as in violation of fundamental constitutional liberties, one-sided, and disruptive. A Knights' strike in 1885 had been settled, on terms favorable to the strikers, through mediation by state labor commissioners and state governors. By contrast, the Curtin committee pointed out, during the 1886 strike, railroads under court protection locked out the Knights, declined to meet with union spokesmen, and refused arbitration. Eventually, amid increasing economic disruption and escalating violence, law enforcement officials broke the strike.[76]

Because the strike reports focused on immediate crises, they revealed less about long-term trends in working conditions and living standards than the early labor bureaus' better studies did. Yet the congressional product was in important ways analytically superior to the more cautious reports of the bureaus, which depended on continued appropriations from a Congress that was less friendly as a whole to such initiatives than were its labor committees. The strike committee accounts—in their sympathetic reconstruction of working people's daily lives and motives; their attention to the effects of degrading conditions on health, character, and opportunity; their awareness of subtle as well as violent methods of social control; and their concern for defining the fundamental rights of citizens in relation to concentrated wealth—anticipated the redefinition of the public interest in the conditions faced by workers that defined legal realism and sociolog-

---

[75]U.S. Congress, House of Representatives, *Labor Troubles in the Anthracite Region of Pennsylvania, 1887–88,* House Report No. 4147, 50th Cong., 2d Sess. (1889).
[76]The best available account of judicial treatment of railroad strikes, Eggert, *Railroad Labor Disputes,* is dated and, especially with regard to the congressional side of the issue, unconvincing.

ical jurisprudence in the progressive era. Without intending to condemn capitalism per se, the strike investigators invariably attributed labor unrest to arrogant, exploitative management by monopolistic corporations, which lacked legitimacy in their eyes as well. Mingling inherited languages of virtue, corruption and rights, with a more modern vocabulary of class, dependency, and welfare, they decried an alienation of public functions that subjected large masses of citizens to unregulated private power. They exposed stock-watering, monopolizing, dictatorial control of company towns, corruption of justice, and evasion of legislative reform—all of which cast doubt on the argument developing in corporate and judicial circles that the corporate interest coincided with the public good.[77]

Two separate congressional inquiries reserved a special condemnation for the 1892 invasion of Homestead, Pennsylvania, by a private force of detectives—Pinkertons—spirited across state lines to break a union. In exquisite detail, these inquiries exposed the arrogant disregard for a bargaining tradition, the contempt for local law enforcement, and the secret preparations for outside help that Carnegie Steel officials had made when they decided to rid themselves of obstacles to maximum efficiency. In their conclusions, the House Judiciary Committee and the Senate Select Committee condemned the use of Pinkertons as an unrepublican "assumption of the State's authority by private citizens," urging the states to ban the practice. They exposed the insufficiency of existing methods for averting major strikes, denounced as flagrantly procapitalist the judge who handled criminal proceedings against the strikers, called for curtailment of private rights in the interests of distributive justice, upheld the strikers' claim to a right to bargain, and endorsed arbitration.[78]

Over a decade, the strike inquiries gradually articulated a pattern of legislative relief designed to curtail monopoly power and the judicial connivance that abetted it. When the Cleveland administration pressed

---

[77] *Labor Troubles in the Southwest,* xxii–xxv, xxvii–xxx; and *Labor Troubles in the Anthracite Region,* xx–xxxvi. See also Harold W. Aurand, "The Anthracite Strike of 1887–1888," *Pennsylvania History* 35 (1968): 169–85.

[78] Senate Select Committee, *Investigation of the Employment of Pinkerton Detectives,* Senate Report 1280, 52d Cong., 2d Sess. (1893), xv–xix. See also House Judiciary Committee, *Employment of Pinkerton Detectives,* House Report 2447, 52d Cong., 2d Sess. (1893). In grand jury proceedings, the presiding judge condemned the "agrarian doctrine that the employee may lawfully dictate to his employer the terms of his employment" and described the actions of a workers' advisory committee that took charge of the strike as treason. Ibid., xvi. See also *Congressional Record,* 52d Cong., 1st Sess. (1892), 5822–8, 5874–6, 7004–15; Edward W. Bemis, "The Homestead Strike," *Journal of Political Economy* 2 (1894): 369–96; Schneider, "Citizen Striker"; and David Brody, *Steelworkers in America: The Nonunion Era* (Cambridge, Mass.: Harvard University Press, 1960).

for voluntary arbitration of railroad conflicts, the Curtin committee declared voluntarism worthless and proposed enlarging the venue of the newly formed Interstate Commerce Commission (ICC) to include supervision of railroad labor. Attacking corporate arrogance and judicial connivance on a broad front, the more radical Tillman committee proposed to get at inequity in class relations by preventing railroads from owning coal mines, denying tariff protection to the anthracite monopoly, banning consolidation of competing lines, and prohibiting strikes and lockouts on the railroads. The report supported sweeping state-level restraints on corporate power. For example, the committee endorsed a New York ruling in the *Freight-Handlers* strike case of 1886 in which the Superior Court refused to issue an injunction against peaceful strikers whom the railroads were unable to replace at the wages offered, and threatened the New York Central and Erie railroads with writs requiring them to resume service or surrender their charters.[79]

When the Burlington strike in 1888 threatened a new crisis, members of the House and Senate labor committees formed a bloc that knitted the Tillman proposals into a five-stage bureaucratic process including (1) mandatory investigation; (2) mediation by a permanent commission composed of public experts; (3) compulsory arbitration, with unions recognized as parties; (4) a requirement (which would eliminate the excuse for an injunction) that workers stay on the job during and for a reasonable time after arbitration; and (5) a revocation of charter if the railroad failed to operate. In the face of ardent capitalist and union opposition, compulsory arbitration was dropped from the railroad mediation act of 1888. In subsequent years the scope of the injunction was expanded until at last, in the *Northern Pacific* case, a court forbade strikers to quit work in a body on the ground that their united action

---

[79]The *Freight-Handlers* ruling reasserted the republican principle that a railroad was an agency of the state. "The sovereignty of the state is injured whenever any public function vested by it in any person, natural or artificial, is abused," the court contended. "Such an injury wounds the sovereignty of the state and thereby, in a legal sense, the entire body-politic." Under pressure, the railroads rehired the strikers at higher wages. See *People of the State of New York* agt. *The New York, Lake Erie and Western and the New York Central and Hudson River Railway Companies*, 63 *How. Prac.* 291–7. Superior Court action was upheld by the New York Court of Appeals in *People* v. *N.Y.C. and H.R.R.R. Co.*, 28 *Hun.* 543–60. The quotations are from 28 *Hun.* 550, 558. The *Freight-Handlers* case was cited as a precedent in congressional debates, e.g., *Congressional Record*, 49th Cong., 1st Sess. (March 31, 1886), 2976; ibid. (April 1, 1886), 3008, 3016; and in numerous court cases between 1895 (in *Loader* v. *Brooklyn Heights R. Co.*, 35 *New York Supplement* 997) and 1960 (in *Sadow* v. *Long Island R. Co.*, 205 *New York Supplement*, 2d ser. 603).

was a criminal conspiracy to deprive the railroad owners of the use of their property, now defined as the right to an expected rate of return. Investigating the validity of this injunction, a Senate committee determined that the court had acted in collusion with railroad managers to destroy the union, and declared the injunction "a clear command to render involuntary service" that not only violated the Thirteenth Amendment but effectively outlawed unions, denying labor a right of combination extended freely to capitalists. Trade unions were vital to the workers' liberty, the committee argued. Thus an order not to quit work was "an invasion of the rights of American citizens and contrary to the genius and freedom of American institutions."[80]

Judicial handling of the Pullman strike in 1894 provoked an even more outraged response from proponents of bureaucratic methods for administering the railroad industry. The ICC condemned the injunction as a judicial attack on its administrative prerogatives and the congressional intention behind them. A classic in American social investigation, Carroll Wright's evenhanded strike report condemned George Pullman's refusal of arbitration, defined the General Managers Association's collusive uniform wage scale as "a usurpation of power" that invited union retaliation, chastised the American Railway Union for an unwarranted secondary boycott, and blamed the injunction and the presence of federal troops for inciting violence. Prounion, procorporate, proarbitration, and thus aligned with those who considered the direction of Gilded Age labor jurisprudence wrongheaded, Wright generally favored voluntarism. But he believed the special nature of the railroads' business and their peculiar ties to the state justified government control; the courts were simply the wrong forum. After considering state ownership, which union witnesses

---

[80]The Tillman bill was H.R. 12654, 50th Cong., 2d Sess. (1888), reprinted on pp. xxxvi–xxxviii in *Labor Troubles in the Anthracite Region.* Debate on several railroad arbitration bills rambles through the 49th and 50th congresses. See esp. *Congressional Record,* 49th Cong., 1st Sess. (March 31–April 6, May 11, and May 18, 1886); and 50th Cong., 1st Sess. (April 18–19, 1888). Reflecting the anticorporate animus of these measures, in response to a proposed amendment making union obstruction of interstate commerce a criminal conspiracy carrying fines or imprisonment, Senator Blair proposed one requiring employers to prove that they paid just wages and had redressed labor's grievances, or face the same penalties. U.S. Congress, House of Representatives, Judiciary Committee, *Receivership of the Northern Pacific Railroad Company,* House Report No. 1049, 53d Cong., 2d Sess. (1894). On the rise and effect of the equity injunction in labor disputes, see Edwin Emil Witte, *The Government in Labor Disputes* (New York: McGraw-Hill, 1932); Alpheus T. Mason, *Organized Labor and the Law* (Durham, N.C.: Duke University Press, 1925); and Felix Frankfurter and Nathan Greene, *The Labor Injunction* (New York: Macmillan, 1930).

before the U.S. Strike Commission universally favored, Wright discarded
the option as premature, though not inherently bad policy. Against the
advice of Gompers, Debs, and the Knights' leader, Robert Sovereign,
who considered state intervention under existing conditions inevitably
procapitalist, the commission endorsed compulsory arbitration by a permanent railroad labor commission possessing judicial and administrative
capacities, the latter housed in a crack statistical division able to track
costs and profits as a basis for wage determination. Attacking the fiction
of equitable contracts between the world's most powerful firms and individual workers, the strike commission urged that the parties to arbitration be collective bodies on both sides—corporations and "one or
more national unions."[81]

The strike-investigating committees did not consult academic social
scientists directly. Yet they were undoubtedly aware, as educated Americans were generally, of the sympathetic view of the labor movement held
by a number of the new economists. Ely, Adams, Commons, Edward
Bemis, and others wrote extensively on the labor question, connecting
workers' aspirations with Christianity, American republicanism, and the
moral ideals expressed in socialism. In touch with labor leaders and
familiar with their programs, they extolled the moral and social benefits
of unionization, advocated factory legislation, and, at considerable cost
to themselves in terms of professional advancement, warned that failure
to respond reasonably to labor's moderate demands for a voice in industrial government might lead to revolution. The AEA had been formed
in part to enlarge the state's role in reforming capitalism.[82]

In the 1890s, investigation of the labor question changed significantly,
making way for a new role for social scientists. In conjunction with
changes in the labor movement and in capitalist organization, forms of

[81]Interstate Commerce Commission, *Ninth Annual Report* (1895): 68–71, undoubtedly
written by H. C. Adams. United States Strike Commission, *Report on the Chicago Strike
of June-July, 1894* (Washington, D.C.: U.S. Government Printing Office, 1895), xv–xlvi,
and the testimony, especially of Eugene V. Debs, Gompers, James R. Sovereign, Everett
St. John, John M. Egan, Jane Addams, and Edward W. Bemis. Foreshadowing subsequent
railroad labor legislation, Wright proposed a ban on strikes during investigations, restrictions on quitting after the award, and a requirement that nationally chartered unions
expel members who resorted to violence; he urged railroad capitalists to grant unions a
broad and continuing voice in management.
[82]In the congressional session that considered the O'Neill arbitration bill, Congressman
O'Neill quoted remarks supporting arbitration by H. C. Adams, Clark, and James, which
originally appeared in a symposium on the labor question that ran in most issues of *Age
of Steel*, January–March 1886. For O'Neill's remarks, see McNeill, ed., *The Labor Movement*, 500–1.

investigation appeared that signaled a new stage in the reorientation of liberalism. Privately managed, corporative forms of investigation and mediation began appearing at the time of the Pullman crisis, as an associative response to social and economic instability. These new methods responded as well to the movement in Congress and official and reform circles more generally for compulsory arbitration, and to the official tilt toward statism embodied in Wright's report, which were increasingly credible alternatives to one-sided judicial intervention. Seizing the opportunities presented by these institutional innovations and withdrawing under pressure from direct appeals to public opinion, social scientists began gravitating toward consultative roles that offered more predictable, and for some of them more effective forms of influence.

One of the earliest institutional expressions of a corporatist approach to the labor question was the Chicago Civic Federation (CCF), which was organized to promote civic consciousness in the aura of the Columbian Exposition and transformed by the Pullman strike. Under the leadership of its first secretary and guiding spirit, Ralph Easley, the CCF and its successor, the National Civic Federation (NCF), lent their considerable prestige to efforts designed to achieve social and economic stabilization by promoting voluntary cooperation across class lines, and to combating statist initiatives. The CCF planned its first conference to shape the movement for an Illinois arbitration law fueled by George Pullman's arrogant refusal of mediation. Balanced, in that it represented unions and corporate capital equally, the conference did not present a full spectrum of views. Rather, as Henry Demarest Lloyd noted in a reference to "expensively managed 'Conferences' " staged to head off state intervention, it showed that "organized capital and organized labor stop fighting each other to fight side by side against compulsory arbitration."[83]

Managers of the new organization were intent on drawing a distinct line between union recognition, trade agreements, and conciliation—associative measures they endorsed heartily—and compulsory arbitration, a feature in two bills pending before Congress whose framers were

[83]Henry Demarest Lloyd, "Compulsory Arbitration," in Peters, ed., *Labor and Capital*, 189. On CCF, see Albion Small, "The Civic Federation of Chicago," *American Journal of Sociology* 1 (1895): 79–103; Green, *National Civic Federation*, 4–9; Eakins, "Development of Corporate Liberal Policy Research," 60–6; and Montgomery, *Fall of the House of Labor*, 257–62. On its role in the Pullman strike, see CCF, *Industrial Conciliation and Arbitration*, 94. On NCF attitudes toward arbitration, see Richard T. Ely, *Studies in the Evolution of Industrial Society*, 2 vols. (1903; Port Washington, N.Y.: Kennikat Press, 1971), vol. 2, 391.

also present, which they just as earnestly opposed. Wright appeared, Pullman report in hand, and was treated cordially. But the majority of the speakers were carefully chosen representatives of the construction industry and the metal trades, where traditional crafts predominated and organization of both labor and capitalists was well advanced. These people could demonstrate the efficacy of voluntarism by describing methods such as profit sharing, the sliding scale, and private settlement of disputes by joint boards chosen by employers and employees. There was some support for state assistance in the form of mediation services, investigation, and report, but very general resistance to compulsory features of the government plan.[84]

The CCF sought expert advice on the potential benefits of various forms of arbitration, an aspect of the labor question that divided historical economists along the lines suggested earlier, reflecting conflicting conceptions of the modern tendency to collectivism. E. R. L. Gould, an industrialist trained in economics at Johns Hopkins University, traced what he saw as an organic evolution in Europe and Australasia of statist methods for managing industrial disputes. He compared them with the voluntary, associative methods that seemed to work better in England and the American states, expressing a cultural preference in the Anglo-American setting for private action, which he equated with liberty. Gould neglected to mention the greater obstacles to voluntary collective action presented by the courts in the American case.[85]

The main dissenting voice was H. C. Adams's. Taking a different view of relations between institutions and political culture, Adams emphasized the radical discontinuity with the republican past and disruption of inherited values that came with capitalist industrialism. Stressing the loss of liberty he saw resulting from the judicial construction of property rights, Adams defended arbitration as a countervailing measure that

---

[84]Chicago Civic Federation, *National Conference on Industrial Conciliation and Arbitration,* passim. See especially M. M. Garland (president of the Amalgamated Association of Iron and Steel Workers), "Sliding Scales and Kindred Methods," 53–7; William H. Sayward (secretary of the National Association of Builders), "Arbitration and Conciliation," 78–84; Peter J. McGuire, "The Relation of Employer and Employee in the Building Trades," 84–9; Samuel Gompers, "The Necessity of Mutual Organization," 88–93. The arbitration bills were the Springer Bill and the Tawney Bill, proposed by William M. Springer (D–Illinois) and James A. Tawney (R–Minnesota). Except for vital industries such as the railroads, Wright himself favored only voluntary arbitration. On Wright's ideological evolution, see Furner, "Knowing Capitalism."

[85]Gould, "History of Industrial Conciliation and Arbitration in Europe and Australasia," ibid., 4–19. In 1894, twelve states had some form of mediation or conciliation services, ranging from mandatory investigation to voluntary, binding arbitration.

would aid in the deliberate social creation of "a new form of property, which from its very nature will diffuse itself among those classes who are now possessors of no property." One of a class of proprietary rights that necessarily included the right to organize and bargain, arbitration would promote the development of industrial democracy. Through a gradual expansion of the scope of labor contracts to include new entitlements and protections, property could be socialized to the greatest extent compatible with retaining, for those socially desirable purposes encompassed in entrepreneurship, the institution of private ownership.[86]

The benefits of arbitration would not be confined to labor or to the promotion of distributive equity. In Adams's view, arbitration signified a state role in industrial relations that would include policing possible conspiracies against consumers by monopolistic syndicates of capital and labor in organized industries, and generally supervising the powerful private associations that had begun to exercise the public function of governing the economy. Thus at one level arbitration would function as a flexible mechanism for legitimating unions and equalizing the bargaining positions of the two industrial classes. At another level arbitration would provide a bureaucratic method for protecting consumers, the unorganized, and nonmarket values from organized private interests.[87]

These conflicting views converged in their recognition of the need for alternatives to the individualistic language, concepts, and methods of the courts that reflected the technological and organizational realities of modern life. To a greater extent than has perhaps been recognized, legislation actually established bureaucratic alternatives to judicial intervention, in those areas that congressional action could reach, and thus reflected this collectivism. The Erdman Act of 1898 provided for federal mediation of railroad labor disputes by the ICC chair and the commissioner of labor. Under heavy pressure from the railroad brotherhoods, arbitration re-

---

[86] Adams, "Economics of Arbitration," in CCF, *Industrial Conciliation*, 63–8, quotation at p. 63.

[87] Adams, "An Interpretation of the Social Movements of Our Times," *International Journal of Ethics* (1891): 1–19. See also Bemis, "The Ethics of Arbitration," in CCF, *Conciliation*, 45–6, and his testimony to the Chicago Strike Commission (*Report*, 640–5), which held that private class bargaining would not protect the public interest. A member of the CCF and a citizens' panel that tried to mediate the Pullman strike, Bemis was an outspoken advocate of mandatory investigation of all major strikes, requiring access to data on profits in the case of strikes involving more than 500 employees, and compulsory arbitration of strikes in vital industries. See also Ely, *Studies in the Evolution of Industrial Society*, vol. 2, 381–90. Compare C. F. Adams's testimony, *U.S. Strike Commission Report*, 657; and Hadley, *Economics*, 399, which cautioned that compulsory arbitration would dampen investment in vital industries.

mained voluntary, but the act signaled a clear intention to prohibit railroad strikes. Through the Erdman ban on yellow-dog contracts, declared unconstitutional in *Adair* v. *United States* (1908), Congress sought in the only industry directly under federal supervision to remove one of the obstacles to unionization that the courts had been defining as expressions of corporate property rights and individual free contract.[88]

Compared with more aggressive patterns of state action developing in other countries, or with what had been imagined in the *Freight-Handlers'* precedent and proposals for ICC management of railroad labor relations, these were meager results. But as an element in the developing conflict between the new judicialism and an alternative view that subordinated traditional property rights to recognition of a public interest in collective action and a reasonable measure of industrial democracy, there was more to them. Viewed in this light, Erdman ranks with the Interstate Commerce Act as an event of some consequence in the formation of new liberalism and the construction of the modern state.

REDEFINING MONOPOLY:
MARKET FAILURE AND THE LIMITS OF STATE ACTION

Like the labor inquiries, congressional investigations of the problem of monopoly exposed the contradictions between inherited republican ideals and the social realities of the industrial age. A trio of investigations— hearings on railroad regulation by the Senate Select (Cullom) Committee on Interstate Commerce in 1885; a probe of the major trusts by the House Committee on Manufactures, which laid the groundwork for the Sherman Act; and an investigation by the United States Industrial Commission (USIC) of the new corporate economy at the turn of the century— made up an early, pattern-forming phase in a longer process of discovery and analysis directed at redefining relations between the liberal state and business. Taking stock of social and economic changes under way, these inquiries gave political meaning to a corporate reorganization of the

[88]The main congressional debate on the Erdman Act is at *Congressional Record*, 53d Cong., 3d Sess. (February 26, 1895). On the importance of Erdman, see Montgomery, *Fall of the House of Labor*, 366–67. See also McCurdy, "Role of 'Liberty of Contract.' " *Coppage* v. *Kansas* (1915) invalidated state-level anti-yellow-dog laws. Congress reinstated the ban on the yellow-dog contract in the Railway Labor Act of 1926, which in important ways anticipated the Wagner Act. Provisions for federal mediation of railroad labor disputes were strengthened in the Newlands and Adamson acts. For a view of yellow-dogs that portrays them as holdovers of an earlier economic individualism, see Daniel Ernst, "The Yellow-dog Contract and Liberal Reform, 1917–1932," *Labor History* 30 (1989): 251–74.

economy that largely eliminated from the central sectors of manufacturing the mythic figure of the small proprietor, previously associated with republican culture.

Official response to these changes was complicated by the fact that big business was linked with previously unimagined abundance, exciting new experiences for a rising class of urban consumers, new investment and employment opportunities, and rising productivity—developments that many in the new middle and managerial classes saw as gains that offset to some extent the trouble and pain among farmers, workers, and displaced entrepreneurs. To complicate matters further, the courts adopted a "natural entity" theory that entitled corporations to due process, protecting them against state-level regulation under economic rights conferred by the Fourteenth Amendment. By the turn of the century, judges were incorporating neoclassical economics into Sherman Act jurisprudence, which allowed them to define permissible restraints of trade more narrowly and establish new protections for competition.[89]

All these developments raised questions not easily answered by available forms of social knowledge. Were the new, monopolistic business forms simply heinous violations of liberty, unjustified in every case, or were at least the vertically integrated ones efficient and essentially beneficial? Should government protect endangered small producers, or were they simply inefficient, nostalgic reminders of a bygone age? Would a growth of regulation upset the delicate constitutional balance and impair equilibrating capacities still credited by many to the market? Conversely, were there values more important than perpetual economic growth? Could it be fairly said that liberty and state interference were opposed? Or did the rise of corporate power require a matching growth of government to prevent a new slavery? In a modern economic order, could the more statist position also be the more republican?

[89]On the history of legal thinking on the corporate form, in addition to sources already cited, see Morton J. Horwitz, *The Transformation of American Law, 1780–1860* (Cambridge, Mass.: Harvard University Press, 1977); idem, "*Santa Clara* Revisited: The Development of Corporate Theory," *West Virginia Law Review* 88 (1985–6): 173–222; Charles W. McCurdy, "The *Knight* Sugar Decision of 1895 and the Modernization of American Corporation Law, 1869–1903," *Business History Review* 53 (1979): 304–42; idem, "American Law and the Marketing Structure of the Large Corporation, 1875–1890," *Journal of Economic History* 38 (1978): 631–49; Herbert Hovenkamp, "The Classical Corporation in American Legal Thought," *Georgetown Law Journal* 76 (1988): 1593–1689; and William Letwin, *Law and Economic Policy in America: The Evolution of the Sherman Antitrust Act* (Chicago: University of Chicago Press, 1959). The indispensable source on the dominance of the corporate form is now Sklar, *Corporate Reconstruction.* Compare Chandler, *Invisible Hand.*

With the rise of monopoly capitalism, new theories of monopoly and competition were needed. The economists' response pointed in two directions. One strand of analysis eventually brought forth theories of perfect and imperfect competition, which became important touchstones in the twentieth century. Another body of work described monopoly historically and institutionally, attributing its appearance, as we have seen, either to the responsible pursuit of stability and efficiency by rationalizing capitalists, or to pecuniary motives, rent seeking, and simple greed. The strengths and shortcomings of both these analyses had their effect on what passed in those days for an industrial policy.

The congressional trust investigations provided a vital point of contact between theory and policy. At the most elementary level, at a time when business reporting was primitive and academics had little access to leading capitalists, the hearings generated vital, otherwise unavailable, information on the actual size of monopoly profits and the sources and extent of monopoly power. Reacting to the free-market tendencies of the new judicialism, institutionalists offered alternative and conflicting analyses of the causes and consequences of combination. Eventually, as these new insights acquired leverage in public discussion, they channeled policy talk away from the traditional view that competition was normal and generally desirable, toward a more complex and differentiated analysis that informed the corporate liberal and democratic statist variants of new liberalism.

Unfortunately, from the standpoint of policy needs, most of these developments reached a usable stage *after* the American pattern of antitrust policy had been established. Railroad economics was far enough advanced by the mid-1880s to have some influence in railroad regulation debates, but there was no authoritative explanation for the appearance of the manufacturing trusts, even within the discipline, at the time of Sherman. A decade later, exerts still disagreed on the costs and putative benefits of the manufacturing monopolies. But by that time conservative institutionalists could point to developments in price theory that argued persuasively for the procorporate view—that concentration in those industries was normal and desirable. These arguments, through their considerable influence on the deliberations of the USIC, shaped the political climate for antitrust revision.

H. C. Adams's version of natural monopoly theory opened the professional debate on the trusts. His pathmaking analysis preceded the development of a modern theory of competition, and contributed to it. Adams achieved his famous distinction between public utilities and industrial trusts by applying a crude version of marginalism to the question of economies of scale. Concluding that only a limited number of monopolies actually resulted from superior efficiency, he drew a line between the increasing-returns industries, where state action would be necessary, and "normal," constant-returns industries, among which he numbered virtually all manufacturing, where—providing special privileges and discriminations were eliminated—competition would regulate.[90]

This distinction between natural and unnatural monopolies seeped readily into political discourse. Even before the academics were directly involved, early state-level inquiries such as the important New York Hepburn investigation had focused on the special qualities of railroad rate making. Experts such as James, Ely, Seligman, and Hadley used their growing access to public and official opinion to build constituencies for the new conception. Their theoretical defense of natural monopoly was confirmed by the experience of hands-on mangers, among them experts such as Albert Fink and C. F. Adams, who had organized pools to shield the trunklines from ruinous competition. As the debate on national regulation heated up after the *Wabash* decision, congressional moderates such as Sen. Shelby Cullom (D–Illinois) mobilized the new thinking on monopoly, hoping to neutralize the radical antimonopolism embodied in a railroad bill before Congress in 1886.[91]

The dominant feature of that bill was a categorical ban on pooling and rate discrimination. Traditional theories that made the state responsibile for ensuring equal access to the market supported such bans. These old ideas ran directly contrary to the new thinking, which associated certain forms of discrimination with the social interest, and placed a favorable construction on price-fixing agreements, or pooling. Brought in prominently at the hearings, Hadley depicted higher charges for local service as a rational response to cutthroat competition elsewhere. Facing a perpetual depression in their competitive business, the railroads either had to cover

[90]Adams "Relation of the State," 98–114; idem, "A Decade of Federal Railway Regulation," *Atlantic Monthly* 81 (1898): 433–43.
[91]Stephen Skowronek, *Building a New American State: The Expansion of National Administrative Capacities, 1877–1920* (Cambridge: Cambridge University Press, 1982), chap. 5, contains an otherwise admirable account of the movement for railroad rate regulation that glosses over important theoretical differences among economists. See also Edward Purcell, Jr., "Ideas and Interests: Business and the Interstate Commerce Act," *Journal of American History* 54 (1967): 561–78.

their fixed costs by charging higher rates for local traffic or collude with or absorb their competitors.[92]

Furthermore, Hadley, C. F. Adams, and respected state commissioners contended that a simultaneous ban on discrimination and pooling would be both unenforceable and contrary to the public interest. By forcing rates down to the level of variable costs on competitive routes, a ban on pooling would in fact require discrimination. Conversely, a ban on discrimination would force the railroads to resort to pooling, criminal or not. These experts also argued that discrimination cut the prices of bulky necessities such as wheat and meat—actually helping the great mass of the American people and encouraging the development of new regions. As alternatives to "everlasting warfare among railroads provided for by statute," leading inevitably to further consolidation, the economics of the industry offered two choices: the statist alternatives of government ownership or European-style government-instigated cartels, and legalized, enforceable, voluntary agreements—from Hadley's antistatist perspective, the more culturally appropriate option.[93]

If the experts generally agreed on the theoretical issues in railroad economics, they nevertheless disagreed on the best method for ordering an industry that could not be regulated by competition. Procorporate voluntarists such as Hadley and C. F. Adams adopted a pluralist model that argued for legalizing cooperative self-regulation under the eye of a commission with advisory powers only. Statist new liberals such as H. C. Adams, Ely, and James favored a strong commission, like those already operating in midwestern states, which gave rate-making powers to a regulatory agency authorized to supervise the industry.

In defense of private ordering, the voluntarists offered a version of what later became known as capture theory, in which the railroads were not the villains. They opposed government rate making on the grounds that in a democratic polity shippers would inevitably dominate the commission, cutting returns on marginal capital and drying up investment. Their defense of permissive pooling was the argument underlying corporate-liberal thinking generally—that the corporate interest in max-

---

[92]U.S. Senate, *Report of the Select Committee on Interstate Commerce*, Senate Report No. 46, 49th Cong., 1st Sess., 2 vols. (1886). See also, for concurring views, T. M. Cooley, "State Regulation of Corporate Profits," *North American Review* 137 (1883): 205–17; E. R. A. Seligman, "Railway Tariffs and the Interstate Commerce Law," *Political Science Quarterly* 2 (1887): 223–64, 369–413.
[93]Ibid. Quotation is C. F. Adams, *Report*, 2:1204. Hadley's testimony is in ibid., 186–206.

imum earnings was identical with the social interest in adequate service at reasonable cost. A commission's role should be educational—promoting responsible behavior in the industry, restraining abuses through the power of public opinion, and cultivating public acceptance. To prevent undue politicizing of the marketplace, settlement of irreconcilable conflicts between opposing groups of capitalists should be left to the courts.[94]

The opposing argument for a strong commission was made by experienced regulators, political strategists, and the statist experts. Drawing on his New York experience, Commissioner John Kernan concluded that railroads shielded from competition would not restrict profits voluntarily. A veteran of regulatory wars in Illinois, which had identified a class of corporations "affected with a public interest," Sen. Shelby Cullom insisted that legalized pooling would require close monitoring by an independent body whose findings of fact should be accepted by the courts as prima facie evidence. Edmund James made the case for a broad extension of public authority. Reflecting his exposure to German idealism, James adopted an organic analogy in which the railroads figured as a social circulatory system, promoting communication and development. In this conception, transportation was no mere business, but an inherently public, moral function that encouraged striving, equalized competition, and promoted individual responsibility, while expressing and contributing to the increasing interdependence of an advanced society and the solidarity of its members. James denied the alleged identity between the railroad and the public interest. Like H. C. Adams, Ely, and Clark, he believed a modern order should blend elements of cooperation and competition, and of private and public social control. For Adams, by 1886, the missing element in the United States, to be supplied by a regulatory agency with a strong statistical arm, was a competent, credible performance by government. Ely, convinced that private ownership of powerful natural monopolies would lead to waste, exploitation of labor, and public corruption, held out for public ownership of all of them.[95]

---

[94]For Hadley's views, see the sources cited in note 28, above; Hadley, "The Prohibition of Railroad Pools," *Quarterly Journal of Economics*, 4 (1888–9): 158–71, and his testimony. See also *Report*, vol. 2, testimony of C. F. Adams, 1201–7; Albert Fink, 107–25; John D. Kernan, 3–23; John O'Donnell, 41–3; and Cullom, in the hearings and debates, passim.

[95]James testimony, *Report*, 2:493–506. See also James, "The State as an Economic Factor," *Science*, Supplement (May 28, 1886): 485–8, 490–1; and James, "Relation of the Modern Municipality to the Gas Supply," *Publications of the American Economic Association* 1 (1886): 53–122. For a more elaborate statement of the organic view of transportation, see Charles Horton Cooley, "The Theory of Transportation," in Robert Cooley Angell,

As the dialogue among the experts demonstrated, railroad economics was sufficiently developed by the mid-1880s to resolve important theoretical questions but not the ultimate ideological issue. A compromise measure designed to achieve broad support, the Interstate Commerce Act mingled aspects of collectivist thinking with more conventional approaches that had a stronger claim on public opinion, such as cost-of-service rate making, backed by antimonopolists. Despite Cullom's best efforts, even committee members who understood the economics of the industry recanted under pressure, and the law contained the dreaded ban on pooling. But the ICC was not prevented from experimenting with concerted rate making, which occurred under Judge Cooley's direction until Sherman Act enforcement cut off these efforts in 1897. The act also created potent new investigative capacities. Although a limited mandate and combat with the courts delayed the ICC's development, a small statistical staff headed from 1887 to 1911 by H. C. Adams began establishing informational control of the industry. The ICC won needed reforms, such as standard freight classifications, and advocated others, such as physical valuation, that ultimately made administrative supervision possible. The commission did not receive the unrestricted access to information, the control over railroad finances, or the immunity from judicial review that statist liberals sought. Nor did the act authorize the modes of private ordering that procorporate voluntarists favored. Yet, reflecting both the revival of a more statist interpretation of republicanism and modest concessions to an associative liberalism, the act was a significant step toward a collectivist reconstruction of the liberal state.[96]

The troubled state of theory prevented economists from contributing even this much to political learning on the trust question. Whereas the railroads had reached organizational maturity by the 1880s, the trusts were a hybrid, intermediate form, not destined to survive. More impor-

---

ed., *Sociological Theory and Social Research* (New York: Henry Holt & Co., 1930), Cooley's 1894 dissertation supervised by H. C. Adams at the University of Michigan. Ely's views on natural monopoly are in *Problems of To-day: A Discussion of Protective Tariffs, Taxation, and Monopolies* (New York: Thomas Y. Crowell & Co., 1888), chaps. 17–31; and idem, "Natural Monopolies and the Workingman," *North American Review* 158 (1894): 294–303.

[96]Financial reorganization of the railroad industry during the 1890s and legislation during the Roosevelt and Taft years completed some aspects of the statists' agenda. I. L. Sharfman, *The Interstate Commerce Commission: A Study in Administrative Law and Procedure,* 4 vols. (New York: Commonwealth Fund, 1931–7).

tant, debilitating gaps and inconsistencies cropped up in the various versions of competition and price theory then under development.[97]

Professional discussion revolved around three conflicting models: Adams's classification of industries by returns to scale; Hadley's analysis of the special vulnerability of high-fixed-cost industries; and the tentative glimpse that Clark's early neoclassicism provided of a form of market regulation, surviving even in the presence of monopoly, that might be trusted to control monopoly profits naturally, through the mechanism of potential competition. The democratic statists argued for state control of all true natural monopolies, but denied the existence of that form in manufacturing. Detecting no economies of scale beyond a size sufficient for a reasonable division of labor, Adams and Ely lumped all kinds of manufacturing into a rather crudely defined class of constant-returns industries, which could be market regulated so long as favors from government and control of transportation were not permitted.[98]

Adams's analysis of returns to scale in manufacturing was actually defective, in that it calculated the effects of the increasing size of a business on marginal cost, not marginal value. As Commons pointed out later, using a fuller application of marginal utility, expanding production would normally cause a drop in marginal value, or the price that could be charged for the last goods produced; extended far enough, expansion would *decrease* total return. Meanwhile, Hadley's recognition that companies continued producing at a loss during depressions, so long as their earnings equaled the variable costs of production, not only refuted neoclassical assertions regarding price making and equilibrium but also called into question Adams's distinction between natural and industrial trusts.[99]

[97] On the development of theories of competition and price, see George F. Stigler, "Perfect Competition, Historically Contemplated," *Journal of Political Economy* 65 (1957): 1–17, and the useful bibliography in George H. Webster, "Monopoly Theory in American Economic Thought, 1870–1910," Ph.D. Diss., SUNY, Binghamton, 1982.

[98] In addition to Adams's "Relation of the State," and idem, "Publicity and Corporate Abuses," *Publications of the Michigan Political Science Association* 1 (1894): 109–20, see, as representative of the democratic collectivist position, Ely, "The Nature and Significance of the Corporation," *Harper's Monthly* (1887): 970–7; E. Benjamin Andrews, "Trusts According to Recent Investigations," *Quarterly Journal of Economics* 3 (1889): 117–52; and idem, "Combination of Capital," *International Journal of Ethics* 4 (1894): 321–34.

[99] Commons, *Distribution;* Hadley, "Private Monopolies and Public Rights," *Quarterly Journal of Economics* 1 (1886): 28–44; idem, "The Formation and Control of Trusts," *Scribner's Magazine* 26 (1899): 604–10; Jeremiah Jenks, "Trusts and the People," *The Statesman* 6 (December 1889): 134–45; idem, "Trusts in the United States," *Economic Journal* 2 (1892): 70–99; idem, "Capitalistic Monopolies and Their Relation to the State,"

The issue in 1890 was whether the United States would be the only modern nation actually to *require* competition. At a crucial moment in the trust discourse, neither conservative nor progressive institutionalists could speak authoritatively about the market or social behavior of trusts. Unlike the railroad case, there were no experts in 1890 who simply *had* to be heard. Without the benefit of academic theories, the House Committee on Manufactures went searching for the origins and social consequences of manufacturing monopolies. Instructed to look at combinations that raised the prices of "the necessaries of life," the committee devoted its entire attention to two notorious horizontal combinations, the Standard Oil Trust and the Havemeyer Sugar Trust. These were precisely the cases most likely to support the classical notion that the solution lay in restoring the market, and least likely to disclose potential social gains from concentration. The committee heard at length the grievances of small proprietors these giants had ruined. Summoned to reply, H. O. Havemeyer and Standard Oil's J. D. Archbold and Henry Flagler laid no claim to any desire for efficiency, admitting their aim had been suppressing competition, pure and simple. Economies may have resulted inadvertently from closing antiquated plants, it was disclosed; but the trusts paid dividends on nearly all the equity of the combined companies, preventing savings to consumers.[100]

Questions of legal form rather than economic function dominated these proceedings, which revealed for the first time a standard pattern of trust formation contrived to circumvent conventions of the common law that rendered earlier forms of combination unenforceable, and there-

---

Political Science Quarterly 9 (1894): 486–509; and idem, "Recent Legislation and Adjudication on Trusts," *Quarterly Journal of Economics* 12 (July 1898): 461. See also Parrini and Sklar, "New Thinking About the Market"; and, on Jenks's work particularly, Wunderlin, *Visions of a New Industrial Order*.

[100]U.S. Congress, House of Representatives, *Report of the Committee on Manufactures on Alleged Combinations for Controlling Some of the Necessaries of Life [Investigation of Trusts]*, House Report No. 3112, 50th Cong., 1st Sess. (1888). Congressional debate can be traced in Earl W. Kintner, ed., *The Legislative History of the Federal Antitrust Laws and Related Statutes: Part I, The Antitrust Laws* (New York: Chelsea House, 1978). See also McCurdy, "The *Knight* Sugar Decision"; Hans Thorelli, *The Federal Antitrust Policy* (Baltimore: Johns Hopkins University Press, 1955), chap. 9; Sklar, *Corporate Reconstruction*, passim; Letwin, *Law and Economic Policy*. Compare Thomas McCraw, "Rethinking the Trust Question," in McCraw, ed., *Regulation in Perspective* (Cambridge, Mass.: Harvard University Press, 1983), 1–55. On the neorepublican, social democratic critique of monopoly that set the tone for the hearings, see John L. Thomas, *Alternative America: Henry George, Edward Bellamy, Henry Demarest Lloyd, and the Adversary Tradition* (Cambridge: Cambridge University Press, 1983); and Pollack, *Just Polity*.

fore useless for suppressing competition. Reflecting the producerite orientation of the outraged independent oil producers and small retailers called as witnesses, the committee decided to plug the gap between intention and performance by banning outright every combination in restraint of trade. The hearings disclosed that retail sugar prices rose only slightly when the Havemeyer trust controlled a mere 35 percent of domestic capacity, whereas Standard Oil, with a 75 percent share, controlled prices effectively. Yet, without a clear conception of monopoly competition, this indication that market share might be the major factor in market control did not invite suggestions for linking trust enforcement with an expert prior determination of the effect of prospective mergers and acquisitions on market share, or for continuous official monitoring of business practice through the processes of administrative law.[101]

When debate reached the Senate, a tough-minded John Sherman argued for subjecting manufacturing as well as trade to continuous national supervision. As Charles McCurdy has demonstrated, Congress opted instead for preserving the increasingly artificial distinction between matters involving commerce, or marketing, which fell entirely to Congress, and those involving structure, or the organization of business firms for production, which remained the province of the several states. Although Sherman understood that manufacturing inherently affected commerce, he believed the law that bore his name preserved the common-law distinction between reasonable and unreasonable restraints.

That distinction obviously evaporated in Supreme Court rulings of the 1890s. The court incorporated into the meaning of reasonableness a new theory of the market, arising in neoclassical economics and particularly in Clark's economic statics. It will be helpful to recall that classical liberals understood competition as a sort of freewheeling contest between all the buyers and sellers in society indiscriminately; preserving it by protecting freedom of contract would ensure that society would benefit from the productive energies of all. Applied to law, this view of competition permitted price-fixing agreements that helped to stabilize markets, so long as they did not coercively freeze out new competitors and deprive buyers of a choice among suppliers. By contrast, neoclassicism,

---

[101]For a committee description of the workings of trusts, see the statement by its chairman, Rep. Henry Bacon, *Congressional Record,* 50th Cong., 1st Sess. (July 30, 1888), 7038. On trust methods and price trends in combined industries, see especially the testimony of John E. Parsons, H. O. Havemeyer, Francis Thurber, Henry M. Flagler, J. D. Archbold, Henry Webster, Thomas W. Phillips, John Teagle, David Kirk, and James R. Goldsborough.

with its new focus on the diminishing utility of marginal increments, narrowed the study of competition to producers of the same product and expanded the meaning of coercion. Price-fixing agreements that had passed the common-law test of free-market access failed a new one, imposed by judges who adopted neoclassical thinking, in which anticompetitive agreements were ipso facto barriers to entry, depriving consumers of the benefits of competition. In this new mode, Sherman Act jurisprudence became a factor—along with economic necessity, returning prosperity, the maturing of securities markets, and promoters' greed—in a rush to tighter forms of combination during the great merger movement of 1898 to 1902.[102]

Whereas expert opinion in the railroad case had settled on an administrative solution employing associative or statist elements, the Sherman Act distinction between commerce and manufacturing precluded such a possibility. Meanwhile, under competitive pressure from New Jersey incorporators, other states did not rise to the challenge of closely supervising business structure and practice. The corporation emerged in its modern form under constant danger of prosecution, guided by lawyers, and described in lawyerly terms, but lacking official direction.

The USIC revisited the problem of industrial trusts ten years later, with very different results. Directed by Congress to diagnose problems of the emerging corporate order, this investigation was part of a flowering of liberal-corporatist thought and institutions in the McKinley years, which included the Indianapolis Monetary Convention, elite municipal reform, and the chamber of commerce and civic federation movements. Housed in structures that removed investigation from the immediacy of politics, this burgeoning corporate voluntarism temporarily eclipsed the tendency toward a more statist approach that had marked congressional inquiries, as well as public discourse more generally, in the 1880s and 1890s. Rationalizers in business and finance, an influential group of like-minded academics, and technocratic professionals united to extend the rationality and efficiency that characterized their corporate and professional environments. Mobilized by crisis, social conscience, the threat of

---

[102]McCurdy, "*Knight* Sugar Decision"; Thorelli, *Federal Antitrust;* Hovenkamp, "The Sherman Act and the Classical Theory of Competition," *Iowa Law Journal* 74 (1989): 1019–65; and idem, "The Political Economy of Substantive Due Process," *Stanford Law Review* 40 (1988): 379–447. Compare James May, "Antitrust in the Formative Era: Political and Economic Theory in Constitutional Antitrust Analysis, 1880–1918," *Ohio State Law Journal* 50 (1989): 257–395; and Tony Freyer, "The Sherman Antitrust Act, Comparative Business Structure, and the Rule of Reason: America and Great Britain, 1880–1920," *Iowa Law Journal* 74 (1989): 991–1017.

redistributive politics, a new president's indecision, and a number of antitrust bills in Congress, they sought associative methods for achieving economic stability, accommodation among competing capitalists, and class harmony. At the same time, they hoped to avoid aggrandizing the state in ways that might disrupt mechanisms of social control they considered essential and endanger an investment system they were only beginning to comprehend.[103]

An omnibus commission authorized to survey the whole field of social policy was initially the project of congressmen who spoke for small producers, but corporate liberals with privileged access to the McKinley White House made it their own and dominated its proceedings. Capitalist members of the commission expressed the needs of the large corporations and the fear of socialism; labor members were trade union chiefs hoping for recognition and relief from judicial interference; and public members were for the most part friendly to both corporations and conservative unions. The most comprehensive survey of American social conditions prior to the *Recent Social Trends* project commissioned by Herbert Hoover in the 1920s, the USIC produced nineteen volumes of testimony, investigative reporting, and expert analysis that surveyed the formation, influence, and legal standing of corporations; the living and working conditions of wage earners; the goals, organizational methods, and legal status of unions; and the special problems of the railroads and agriculture. The real work of the commission was to give meaning to an amazing acceleration of concentration that occurred while it was sitting. By the time the USIC issued its final report, a wave of mergers had utterly transformed control of American industry, concentrating nearly half the manufacturing assets in the hands of about three hundred corporations and reformulating the aspect of the social question that pertained to monopoly.[104]

The USIC marked a turning point in official consideration of the social question. In these deliberations, corporate liberalism gained coherence as a body of theory and policy, achieving official recognition as a com-

[103]USIC, *Report*, 19 vols. (Washington, D.C.: U.S. Government Printing Office, 1900–02). The best history of the USIC is Wunderlin, *Visions*. On trust bills pending during the USIC's tenure and congressional indecision regarding policy analysis, see also Thorelli, *Federal Antitrust*, 508–51.

[104]Ralph Nelson, *Merger Movements in American History* (Princeton, N.J.: Princeton University Press, 1959); Naomi Lamoreaux, *The Great Merger Movement in American Business, 1895–1904* (Cambridge: Cambridge University Press, 1985). By 1901 there was a billion-dollar corporation; and by 1902, when the commotion subsided, nearly 2,500 firms had disappeared into mergers capitalized at almost $7 billion.

prehensive strategy for coping with social and economic instability, and yet providing a credible alternative to statism. By assimilating the divisive, radicalizing labor question of the 1880s and 1890s to the newly defined corporations problem, corporate liberalism transformed the social question. In what became the USIC vision, the labor question was for all practical purposes a trade union question.[105]

For the first time, social scientists substantially controlled the content of a major public investigation. Under the commission's loose supervision, responsibility for designing research, organizing hearings, selecting witnesses, and drafting reports fell to Jeremiah Jenks, a former student of Ely, a Cornell professor and adviser to governors and presidents whose early studies of the pricing policies of industrial trusts laid the basis for monopoly price theory. Jenks's main assistants with the labor investigations were Commons and E. Dana Durand, a student of Jenks embarking on an important career as a government economist. All three economists were simultaneously employed by the NCF, where they orchestrated parallel investigations of combination and conciliation, maintaining communication and a degree of cooperation between the two corporatist policy groups.[106]

This convergence made Jenks's approach to the social question crucial. In professional and public forums, he and others had been attempting for a decade to engineer a reversal of public and official opinion regarding manufacturers' combinations, from what he perceived as the injudicious, theoretically unsupportable, but politically popular antitrust perspective that prevailed in the 1890s to a moderately procorporate position. Jenks laid an empirical basis for this reversal through a series of studies of the pricing policies of trusts begun in the late 1880s. In 1894, he challenged the validity of Adams's classification scheme. Denying an economic difference between the so-called natural monopolies and the industrial

---

[105]For an example of this transformation of the labor question in corporate liberal thinking, see the analysis provided by BLS economist William Frank Willoughby, in "The Concentration of Industry in the United States," *Yale Review* 7, old ser. (1898): 72–92. Having consigned proprietary capitalism, or free labor, to the dustbin of history, Willoughby concluded that concentration brought improvement in working conditions; worker safety, hours, and wages; steadiness of employment; and especially organization. In turn, certain labor organizations deliberately promoted the formation of pools or trusts, as in the case of bituminous coal, in order to steady and raise wages.

[106]The connection was often uncomfortably close, if not compromising. E.g., while Commons worked on the labor sections of the USIC report, NCF assigned him to help mediate the 1901 steel strike, and he traveled incognito in the steel towns to determine how much staying power the union had. On the operation of the commission and the role of the social science experts, see Wunderlin, *Visions*.

trusts, he proposed recognition of a new class of "capitalistic monopolies"—the large combinations in manufacturing—as equally natural and beneficial. He concluded that although the capitalistic monopolies probably did not enjoy increasing returns in the strictly mechanical aspects of manufacturing, substantial economies in management and marketing were available to them. Simply closing antiquated plants (the Whiskey Trust operated 12 out of 80) produced enormous savings.[107]

Did consumers (qua society) receive the benefits of those social savings? Not directly, Jenks conceded. In fact, his studies demonstrated that once competition was throttled, the new combinations raised their profit margins, shifting wealth to large capitalists. At a time when prices were generally falling, mergers boosted profits, forcing lower prices on their raw materials suppliers and denying consumers some of the savings from new technology. The fact that prices did not actually rise concealed these monopoly profits.

These tendencies were not excessive, Jenks contended, and they coincided with social benefits—the most important being elimination of the economic basis of overproduction. His arresting application of marginal analysis outlined the mechanism of entry pricing, converting to theory what corporate managers had long since learned when pegging their prices low enough to avoid attracting competition. By retiring inefficient works without disruption, by administering their markets and thus maintaining profits at reasonable levels, and by preventing the creation of new, redundant capacity, the new industrial giants would improve productivity, prevent depressions, encourage sustainable growth, and steady employment. Whether combination would also strike at what James Livingston describes as "the social basis of overproduction"—skilled workers' control of output—it was too soon to tell. Although combination foreclosed traditional opportunities for young men to learn self-reliance in an independent business, the new corporations provided ample scope for entrepreneurial talent, and predictable paths of career advancement

---

[107]On Jenks's developing understanding of monopoly, see, in addition to the sources cited in note 99 above, his "Trusts and Industrial Combinations," *Bureau of Labor Statistics Bulletin* 29 (1900), which contains a summary of his trust price and wage studies; idem, "The Trusts: Facts Established and Problems Unsolved," *Quarterly Journal of Economics* 15 (1900): 46–74; and idem, *The Trust Problem* (New York: McClure, Phillips & Co., 1900). The quotation is on p. 466 in "Recent Legislation and Adjudication on the Trusts." As evidence of Jenks's stature in the field, Gov. Theodore Roosevelt called on him in 1900 to write a New York State corporations law. G. Wallace Chessman, *Governor Theodore Roosevelt: The Albany Apprenticeship, 1898–1900* (Cambridge, Mass.: Harvard University Press, 1965), 158–76.

for a new, upwardly mobile middle class of technical specialists and professional managers.[108]

The capitalistic monopolies achieved market control simply by virtue of the enormous capital invested. To discipline their markets, they could deter competitors by keeping profits within reasonable bounds, eliminate them by intentional underselling, and even run deliberately at a loss for a time in their entire business. Conceding abuses but emphasizing the wastefulness and impermanence of competition, Jenks outlined a system for regulating industrial monopolies. He proposed a right of unlimited combination in all industries, publicity of corporate accounts, a ban on unfair competition, and a commission on corporations with authority to study the pricing policies of trusts and determine their reasonableness.[109]

The procorporate economists made no secret of their disdain for antitrust laws. Jenks's personal trial in the effort to discredit them came in 1897, when the New York State Senate (Lexow) Commission sought his expert testimony on the character and alleged benefits of capitalistic monopolies and then explicitly and resoundingly repudiated the whole Jenks system. Looking closely at the sugar, rubber, tobacco, and wallpaper trusts, the Lexow Commission concluded that capitalistic monopolies were far from natural. Intent on destroying competition, these mean-spirited giants closed factories that had operated for decades, displaced small employers, turned out labor, reduced quality of products once they had a clear field, and charged higher-than-normal prices. Through factors agreements, they controlled distribution and maintained retail prices. Their capitalization at inflated levels on the basis of expected monopoly profits required that management's attention be "directed toward maintaining earnings commensurate with the amount of stock issued, whether for live assets or for properties closed, abandoned, and dismantled."[110]

---

[108]Jenks, "Capitalistic Monopolies"; USIC, *Report*, 1 (1900), *Preliminary Report on Trusts and Industrial Combinations*. Jenks wrote the "Review of Evidence," 9–37, and "Industrial Combinations and Prices," 39–57, as well as the section, including recommendations, in the *Final Report* (1902) entitled "Industrial Combinations." His conclusions on trust prices are at USIC *Report* 1:39–57. On his authorship and role in the USIC, see Wunderlin, *Visions*, passim. See also Livingston, "Social Analysis," 87. Needless to say, combinations powerful enough to break unions could also foreclose the opportunity for a different method of combatting overproduction—through higher wages, promoting increased consumption.

[109]Jenks, "Capitalistic Monopolies," 505–9.

[110]State of New York, Senate, *Report of the Joint Committee of the Senate and Assembly Appointed to Investigate Trusts*, Documents of the Senate of the State of New York, No. 40, 120th Sess. (1897), 1–51. Quotation on p. 20. Compare Jenks, "Recent Legislation and Adjudication on Trusts."

The Lexow Commission concluded that the predatory creature Jenks called capitalistic monopoly should be exterminated, not excused. Yet its report showed the disparity between grievance and remedy so often apparent in Gilded Age reform efforts, reflecting the frustration of state legislators constrained by federalism and the courts. The commission favored strong measures—limits on capitalization, taxation of corporate profits, and licensing of corporations—but shelved them, fearing a judicial veto. Unable to control New Jersey corporations within their borders and unwilling to disadvantage their own state's companies or labor, the commission could only call for the authority to investigate, compel corporate testimony under immunity, and expose wrongdoing. Their caution proved warranted. An 1897 New York law against restraint of competition in the production of necessaries was judicially emasculated.[111]

With political pressure growing with each new merger, corporate liberals sought to break the impasse created by Sherman Act jurisprudence, placing Jenks in a position to put before official Washington a more positive construction of the merger movement. USIC reports he drafted presented the tidal wave of combinations as the result of market failure, and the modern corporation as a kind of savior. The product of evolutionary tendencies to greater size and integration, bigness was unavoidable but fortunately largely beneficial. The trust reports emphasized the social savings produced by bureaucratic management; the greater economic stability offered by administered markets; built-in restraints on abuses of monopoly power imposed by the desire for maximum earnings; and the likelihood, which experience so far indicated, that the trusts would provide steadier employment at higher wages. Surprisingly, despite union-busting policies at leading combinations such as U.S. Steel, and the potential in multiplant holding companies for shifting production to break strikes, there was labor support for this contention. Union leaders, repeatedly during the USIC inquiry and parallel NCF hearings on conciliation, displayed a generally positive attitude toward trusts, rooted in the expectation that large employers making adequate profits in administered markets would be easier to deal with than small ones plagued by ruinous competition.[112]

Regarding labor, the USIC research staff did little quantitative work

---

[111]Jenks, "Recent Legislation," 463–4; and Chessman, *Roosevelt*, 159.
[112]USIC, *Report* 19:595–649; ibid., vol. 13, *Trusts and Industrial Combinations* (1901), passim; Jenks, "How Trusts Affect Prices," *North American Review* 172 (1901): 906–18.

on wage and price trends or unemployment, which might have given clues to the conditions of the working class as a whole. Rather, in a period of rapid unionization and disruptive strikes, reflecting a common preoccupation among middle-class reformist elements with social conflict, Durand and Commons concentrated almost exclusively on locating equitable methods for settling industrial disputes. Their historical studies of labor legislation and their accounts of strikes in progress—including a national machinists' strike settled amicably in 1900 by mediation and a disastrous strike that badly weakened the Chicago construction trades—facilitated assimilation of the labor question to an associative vision.

In the various languages of labor reform employed since the 1880s, industrial democracy had shifting meanings. It meant proprietorship for some, syndicalism or socialism for others, and, for workers in the new mass production industries, a degree of worker control of shop floor management and output. The USIC promoted its own conception of industrial democracy, endorsed by AFL leaders who spoke for labor in these hearings. This model narrowed its meaning from joint management of production to collective bargaining on a narrow range of strictly economic issues. The USIC joined the NCF in touting national trade agreements as instruments for wage stabilization in competitive industries, modest redistribution, and general social and economic stabilization. To be workable, these agreements required recognition of unions as parties to contracts, which the courts had withheld; but they also depended on willingness of union leaders to enforce the agreements among the rank and file. Following AFL policy, the USIC endorsed strictly voluntary arbitration as a supplement to collective bargaining. Thus the USIC-NCF formula repudiated both government by injunction and the statist, bureaucratic alternative the congressional strike committees had been developing.[113]

As a courtesy to the lone defender of proprietary capitalism among its members, USIC's final report advocated strict enforcement of antitrust laws, a finding contrary to its general spirit that had dubious relevance to the corporate form in any case. Otherwise, the commission reoriented the trust debate by recognizing the failure of individualism and competition in both the capital and the labor markets. To fill the vacuum made by Sherman and the courts, and to shift enforcement from a legal to an

[113]USIC, *Report,* vols. 7, 8, 14, 16, and 17, deal with various aspects of the labor question and industrial relations. The final recommendations are in vol. 19. On the USIC and labor, see Furner, "Knowing Capitalism," 268–74; and Wunderlin, *Visions.* On NCF labor stabilization strategies, see Weinstein, *Corporate Ideal,* and Montgomery, *Worker Control.*

economists' discourse, the USIC called for administrative supervision of the corporate sector by a permanent, ICC type of trade commission authorized to monitor corporate behavior, compel disclosure of finances, and publicize capitalization and abuses.

In addition, initiating an important shift in the meaning economists and policymakers would subsequently attach to competition, the USIC recommended a ban on *unfair* competitive methods such as underselling, a graduated tax on corporate franchises, and a new study of the impact of the tariff on competition. As a political strategy, this proposed extension of the trust investigation was designed to placate old liberals who considered tariffs the mother of trusts. Such an extension would also improve the knowledge base for stabilization policy by determining whether the world's leading industrial nation might now be better served by tariff reduction through reciprocity, as President McKinley, procorporate economists, and major exporters contended. Finally, to escape problems of federalism, the USIC suggested that control of larger combinations might require federal incorporation of interstate businesses, a measure—popular with corporate leaders and lawyers—that would have nationalized control of the largest corporations, shielding them from hostile state-level regulation but holding them to a national standard to be worked out experimentally.[114]

The USIC endorsed no favorite policies of nineteenth-century republican liberals for keeping markets open to small producers. Instead, reflecting new learning about a market whose chronic failures produced recurrent economic and social crises, the commission depicted a new social order that assumed the permanence and desirability of corporately administered markets in the most advanced sectors of the economy. Rejecting the presumption in favor of competition embodied in Sherman Act jurisprudence, the USIC proposed resolving the social question through economic self-government within industries. A responsible, associative collectivism would be held to account, but not obstructed in its further development, by an associative state whose outlines the corporatist structure of the USIC anticipated.

A MORE STATIST FUTURE?

From the standpoint of social theory, the USIC vision represented a creative fusion of conservative historicist and neoclassical insights, supporting a voluntaristic conception of evolving cooperative arrangements

---

[114]USIC, *Final Report*, 649–52, followed by a lengthy dissent by Commissioner Thomas Phillips, 652–85.

for social ordering, created mainly in civil society. The USIC defended modern corporations as a product of institutional selection, invoking carefully selected applications of marginal theory (optimal earnings, entry pricing) to explain why this new capitalist life form was not only the fittest but, from the standpoint of all social groups, the best. The presumption of efficiency that Jenks, Hadley, and other conservative institutionalists attached to giant combinations was essential to this social vision, for the promise of ever expanding abundance provided the ultimate justification for choosing efficiency over republican liberty.[115]

This fusion of neoclassicism and conservative institutionalism proved to be unstable, and the heady illusion of corporate liberal ascendancy passed rather quickly. In the aftermath of the USIC, alternative intellectual traditions survived; lines of social criticism and protest developed that challenged the associative vision. Concurrently, events occurred in the Roosevelt years that revived the possibility of a more statist, more democratic future.[116]

Opposition to conservative institutionalist assumptions regarding the efficiency of the corporate order continued to arise on the other side of the economists' new liberal discourse. The tradition of progressive institutionalism extended down from Adams, Ely, and James to include, in the new century, Veblen's and Wesley Mitchell's early work on the business cycle, Commons in his Wisconsin period, and the host of Wisconsin and Johns Hopkins students who served with the Commission on Industrial Relations (1913–15), were industrial relations experts in the 1920s, and became the architects of New Deal labor policies in the 1930s. In touch with movements for a more statist approach to the labor question such as the American Association for Labor Legislation and women's reform, the stream of democratic collectivist thought also fed on currents arising within the law. Among these were the legal realism of Oliver Wendell Holmes, the sociological jurisprudence of Roscoe Pound, which attacked theories of property and corporate rights assumed by conservative institutionalists to be natural, and Louis Brandeis's empirically based denial of the efficiency of giant companies.[117]

---

[115]On the uses Jenks and Hadley made of marginalism, see above at 188, 230–2. Sklar, *Corporate Reconstruction*, 57–61.

[116]Compare Weinstein and Sklar, who argue that a corporate liberal synthesis achieved during these years set a lasting model for modern liberalism.

[117]Fisher, "Development of American Legal Theory," and Daniel Ernst, "Common Laborers: Industrial Pluralists, Legal Realists, and the Law of Industrial Disputes, 1915–43" (paper in the author's possession).

The story of this conflict in progressive era social theory is beyond the scope of this chapter. Yet, as an indication of how the economists' post-USIC discourse continued to flesh out contrasting conceptions of new liberalism, we might forecast the main outlines of the opposing argument. It focused on two main components that became essential to resolving the new version of the social question. The first was a microlevel response to the argument for economies of scale in integrated business firms such as those that engineered the merger movement. The second was a radical institutionalist view of the workings of the new market that shattered the very meanings of monopoly and competition—using marginalism in innovative ways to construct an early version of monopoly competition—and of the effects of this unexpected business strategy on society.

Aided by a new generation of progressive institutionalists, the Adams-Ely wing flatly rejected the Jenks idea of capitalistic monopoly. At a CCF trust conference in 1899, Adams challenged the procorporate view predominant there and offered a theory of "normal size of maximum efficiency." His rudimentary theory of optimum size in manufacturing anticipated one endorsed by later economists—and borne out by the late-twentieth-century floundering of behemoths like General Motors—that inefficiencies and diseconomies involved in managing a huge, multiplant company could rather quickly offset the alleged economies of scale. The policy implication of this line of argument was clear: confine monopoly to authentic public utilities that provided neutral access to the market, under public regulation. As for the appealing notion that combinations would moderate or even eliminate the dreaded business cycle, Adams invoked the "well wrought theory of socialistic writers." If depressions were caused by underconsumption, not overproduction, the trusts, with their tendency to concentrate income, would in fact become breeders of crises.[118]

---

[118]Ely, "The Future of Corporations," *Harper's Monthly* 74 (1887): 259–66, proposed an array of special requirements for corporations—including greater criminal and civil liability of promoters and directors, restricted access to limited liability for a term of years, and compulsory arbitration of labor disputes—as protections for shareholders, consumers, and labor. See also Adams, "Trusts," *Papers and Proceedings of the Sixteenth Annual Meeting of the American Economic Association* (1903): 91–107; Benjamin Andrews, "Trusts According to Official Investigations," *Quarterly Journal of Economics* 3 (1889): 117–52; idem, "Combination of Capital," *International Journal of Ethics* 4 (1894): 321–34; Ely, *Monopolies and Trusts* (New York: Macmillan Co., 1900), esp. chap. 3, "The Law of Monopoly Price"; and Veblen, "Industrial and Pecuniary Employments," *Publications of the American Economic Association*, 3d ser., 2 (1901): 190–235. Adams's Civic Federation address is in Chicago Civic Federation, *Conference on Trusts* [1899] (New York: Arno Press, 1973), 35–42. For the contemporary debate on economies of scale in manufacturing, see F. M. Scherer, "Economies of Scale and In-

Judged from this perspective, monopolies in manufacturing preempted resources, stifled innovation, and sabotaged production, not for efficiency but simply for monopoly gain. In an attempt to reconnect professional language with republican meanings, Ely sorted monopolies into his own set of categories. The main distinction was between those in increasing-returns industries that were genuinely natural and a whole range of "social monopolies" that were achieved by legislative favor (patents, franchises, etc.) or by collusion. Without contrived advantages, he saw no necessary connection "between mass of capital and monopoly force."[119]

In the event that society refused to tolerate the social monopolies (as in the Supreme Court rulings of the late 1890s), Commons had earlier glimpsed a mechanism that might reconcile the irreconcilables—monopoly and competition. As we have seen, he understood that from the standpoint of decreasing utility, every industry was subject to decreasing returns. He reasoned:

In this case, world prices are determined by world product, but inside the world product each entrepreneur has his especial range of customers. If he infringes upon the territory of his competitors, he can do so only by lowering [his own] prices, or by improving the quality of his product. In either case, he must soon reach a point of diminishing returns in values. And just as the industry as a whole may be subject to diminishing values, so each of its independent constituents may be subject to the same conditions.

What would prevent the few firms large enough to affect the others' destinies in this way from anticipating the actions of their market rivals and refraining from price competition?[120]

Monopolistic competition could be expected to erode the advantages to society of large-scale production rather quickly, either through the loss of scale economies involved in product differentiation or the return

dustrial Concentration," in Harvey J. Goldschmid, H. Michael Mann, and J. Fred Weston, eds., *Industrial Concentration: The New Learning* (Boston: Little, Brown, 1974), 16–54, and John S. McGee, "Efficiency and Economies of Size," ibid., 55–96. George J. Stigler, "Monopoly and Oligopoly by Merger," *Publications of the American Economic Association* 62 (1949): 23–34, contended that mergers generally occurred not for efficiency but for the possibility of capitalizing the expectation of monopoly profits, which could be sustained for a time even in conditions of free entry.

[119]Ely, *Monopolies and Trusts* (New York: Macmillan, 1900), chap. 4 (quotation on p. 177).

[120]Commons, *Distribution*, 131–2, and Joseph Dorfman's introductory note on Commons's insight, xii. The first fully developed theories of monopolistic competition came from the American economist Edward Chamberlain, *The Theory of Monopolistic Competition* (Cambridge, Mass.: Harvard University Press, 1938), and the British economist Joan Robinson, *The Economics of Imperfect Competition* (London: Macmillan, 1943).

of the allegedly repressed—excess capacity. As Edward Chamberlain worked out the scenario in the 1930s:

Such economies may develop, of course, under pure competition owing [as Hadley had earlier discovered] to miscalculation on the part of producers or to sudden fluctuations in demand or cost conditions. But it is the peculiarity of monopolistic competition that it may develop over long periods *with impunity,* prices always covering costs, and may, in fact, become permanent and normal through a failure of price competition to function. The surplus capacity is never cast off, and the result is high prices and waste. The theory affords an explanation of such wastes in the economic system—wastes which are usually referred to as "wastes of competition." In fact, they could never occur under pure competition, and it is for this reason that the theory of pure competition is and must be silent about them, introducing them, if at all, as "qualifications," rather than as parts of the theory. They are wastes of monopoly—of the monopoly elements in monopolistic competition.[121]

Without achieving Chamberlain's elegant conception, Commons described its most important social consequences in a language of "capitalized good will" and "unearned increments," while Veblen invented a language luxuriantly describing, from his uniquely non-Marxian socialist/Victorian standpoint, the social waste involved in "conspicuous consumption," "pecuniary emulation," capitalization based on the expectation of monopoly profit, and a conspiracy on the part of the "vested interests" to sabotage production in order to hold it to the point of maximum monopoly gain. Several younger economists, among them Edward Bemis, Maurice Robinson, and Edward Meade, echoed the view that the combinations had little to do with economic or social efficiency.[122]

Lacking a clear idea of how an undeveloped American state would regulate large numbers of corporations, progressive-institutionalists offered proposals that sometimes seemed arbitrary or visionary. Concerned primarily with the encroachment of corporations on republican values, Adams contended that the corporate form was inherently monopolistic. He proposed restricting its use to certifiable natural monop-

---

[121]Chamberlain, *Monopolistic Competition,* 146. See also Thomas C. Cochran, "Historical Aspects of Imperfect Competition," *Journal of Economic History* 3 (1943): 27–32; this passage is quoted on p. 29. Compare J. M. Clark, "Toward a Concept of Workable Competition," *American Economic Review* 30 (1940): 241–56, and Joe S. Bain, "Workable Competition in Oligopoly: Theoretical Considerations and Some Empirical Evidence," *Publications of the American Economic Association* 50 (1950): 35–47.

[122]Veblen based his *Theory of Business Enterprise* (New York: Charles Scribner's Sons, 1904) almost entirely on the USIC reports. See also Edward Meade, "Financial Aspects of the Trust Problem," *Annals* (1900): 1–59, and Charles Bullock, "The Variation of Productive Forces," *Quarterly Journal of Economics* 16 (1902): 473–513.

olies, to be run virtually as public companies. Ely's mature analysis convinced him that competition, not monopoly, was the permanent force in social evolution, and he concluded that investigation and publicity would regulate. Conversely, although J. B. Clark's neoclassicism sustained an expansive conception of the restraining influence of potential competition, he immediately began expanding his conception of the amount of regulation needed to restrict unfair competition, and blamed combinations for preventing the market from setting a natural, productivity-based rate of wages.[123]

In the years after 1902, alternative methods of political control took on greater reality. At President Roosevelt's urging, Congress created a Bureau of Corporations that proved less inclined toward trustbusting than conventional antitrusters had anticipated. In exchange for full disclosure, Roosevelt's hand-picked commissioners worked out cooperative relations with some of the largest corporations. But the meat-packing and Standard Oil inquiries took a more statist turn; publicity could be used to blackmail offending corporations. Meanwhile, Roosevelt's handling of the anthracite coal strike of 1902 blended associative and statist elements. The settlement did not compel union recognition, but it did shackle the trade agreement model to compulsory public mediation. It demonstrated Roosevelt's willingness to extend the railroad no-strike rule to essential manufacturing, and his government's intention to subject the private dealings of all organized interests to statist control.[124]

Gilded Age social investigation inspired a cycle of theoretical innovation and policy experimentation in which American social scientists

[123]Adams, Civic Federation paper; idem, "Trusts," *Papers and Proceedings of the 16th Annual Meeting of the American Economic Association* (1903): 91–107; and the discussion of it on pp. 108–37, where Bemis and Maurice Robinson supported the "optimum size" position. Ely, *Monopolies and Trusts,* passim; John Bates Clark, *The Control of Trusts* (New York: Macmillan, 1901). Compare idem, "Do Trusts Benefit Laborers?" *Labor and Capital,* 27–30, which contended that trusts raised their own workers' wages by restricting production but diverted extra labor to other employments, lowering the general rate of wages.

[124]On the Bureau of Corporations, see Jack M. Thompson, "James R. Garfield: The Career of a Rooseveltian Progressive, 1895–1916," Ph.D. diss., University of South Carolina, 1958, 95–139; Weinstein, *Corporate Ideal,* 69–70; Robert Wiebe, *Businessmen and Reform: A Study of the Progressive Movement* (Chicago: Quadrangle, 1968), 44–8. On the coal strike, see Anthracite Coal Strike Commission, *Report to the President on the Anthracite Coal Strike of May–October, 1902* (Washington, DC.: U.S. Government Printing Office, 1903); Peter Roberts, "The Anthracite Conflict," *Yale Review* 11 (1902): 297–307; idem, "The Anthracite Strike Commission's Awards," ibid., 12 (1903): 59–69; G. O. Virtue, "The Anthracite Combinations," *Quarterly Journal of Economics* 10 (1896): 317–23; and Robert Wiebe, "The Anthracite Strike of 1902: A Record of Confusion," *Mississippi Valley Historical Review* 48 (1961): 229–51.

described two possible futures. In the prosaic pages of scholarly journals and government reports, a struggle was under way for the soul of the new liberalism. As a statist collectivism evoked and then opposed an organizationally and philosophically enriched, antistatist, associative liberalism, the inherited ideologies found new leverage. In both law and economics, distinctive progressive and conservative variants of institutionalism challenged first classical and then neoclassical theories and social imagery. In the early, formative phase of "the era of distribution," a constructive discourse between two variants of new liberalism prepared the ground intellectually, inventing new vocabularies to describe industrial society and its social question, new policy categories, and new conceptions of what was politically and administratively possible.[125]

Political change depended on, was guided by, and was constrained within this process of conceptual innovation. The constraints were powerful. Gilded Age notions of entrepreneurial rights and neoclassical images of the market gave legal individualism new traction against the challenge of collectivist conceptions. The broadest constituency for social democratic ideas had initially been the labor movement; yet its most powerful segment, the AFL, abandoned politics, and prepared to conduct its struggle within the framework of legal individualism. Nonideological parties avoided polarizing issues, and bureaucrats were often timid or hamstrung. Yet, despite these limiting factors, in the interactions of economists and legislators investigating the social question, the groundwork was laid in the Gilded Age for a dialogue between statist and societal forms of social ordering that provided the ideological architecture for the politics of the twentieth century. The progressive era provided scope for legal realist, pragmatist, and institutionalist strands to come together; and they did so, in bodies such as the Commission on Industrial Relations, the War Industries Board, and the National War Labor Board. Then and later, in the New Era and the New Deal, whether democratic statism and liberal corporatism would countervail or mingle became the question.[126]

[125]Farr, "Understanding Political Change Conceptually."
[126]For suggestions regarding the possibilities both of continued opposition and of mingling of these forms as they reached full development, see Furner, "Knowing Capitalism"; Wunderlin, *Visions*; Steve Fraser, "From the 'New Unionism' to the New Deal," *Labor History* (1984): 405–30; and Larry Gerber, "Corporatism in Comparative Perspective: The Impact of the First World War on American and British Labor Relations," *Business History Review* 62 (1988): 93–127.

6

○■●○

The state and social investigation in Britain, 1880–1914[1]

ROGER DAVIDSON

The rise of social collectivism in late-Victorian and Edwardian Britain has been interpreted in a variety of conflicting ways. According to one viewpoint, a pluralistic social policy-making process after 1880 provided a powerful mechanism for effecting social change. Social legislation increasingly incorporated communal needs and values and represented an important extension of the social rights of citizenship, inspiring new levels of social awareness, aspiration, and solidarity.[1] In particular, under the influence of New Liberalism, welfare measures reflected a systematic program of social reorganization based on an informed awareness of the environmental reasons for individual hardship and of the structural determinants of social problems.[2]

In contrast, in recent years, a growing body of literature has interpreted developments in welfare ideas and provisions after 1880 primarily as a means of social control.[3] From this standpoint, social policy is viewed

[1]For an overview of this strand of welfare historiography, see R. Mishra, *Society and Social Policy: Theoretical Perspectives on Welfare* (London: Macmillan, 1977), chap. 1; V. George and P. Wilding, *Ideology and Social Welfare* (London: Routledge & Kegan Paul, 1976), chap. 4; J. H. Goldthorpe, "The Development of Social Policy in England, 1800–1914: Notes on a Sociological Approach to a Problem in Historical Explanation," *Transactions of 5th World Congress of Sociology* (Washington, D.C.: International Sociological Association, 1962), 41–2.

[2]See M. Freeden, *The New Liberalism: An Ideology of Social Reform* (Oxford: Clarendon Press, 1978); H. V. Emy, *Liberals, Radicals and Social Politics 1892–1914* (Cambridge: Cambridge University Press, 1973); P. Weiler, *The New Liberalism: Liberal Social Theory in Great Britain 1889–1914* (New York: Garland, 1982).

[3]For a review of the development and usages of the concept of social control, see A. P. Donajgrodski, ed., *Social Control in Nineteenth Century Britain* (London: Croom Helm, 1977), 9–15; F. M. L. Thompson, "Social Control in Victorian Britain," *Economic History Review* 34 (1981): 189–208.

fundamentally as a product of the values and interests of dominant elites within class society. Welfare legislation was accordingly designed to regulate the physical depreciation of Britain's work force, to increase workers' efficiency and receptiveness to new methods of manufacture, and to sustain industrial discipline and incentives. As one among many strategies of social control, "welfare bribery" was intended to contain class conflict and to furnish an antidote to the spread of socialism, without conceding any drastic changes in the structure of industry and society.[4]

This debate over the reasons for late-Victorian and Edwardian government growth is wide-ranging. Yet welfare historians of the period have largely ignored one of the more important factors shaping the rationale and scope of social legislation—the informational basis of welfare debate and the policy-making process. This is particularly surprising because historians and social scientists have typically discussed the impact of social investigation on policy within a similar framework of debate.

Many writers subscribe to the view that official inquiry has had a primarily conservative role. They argue that it has functioned as a means of social control to maintain a stable hierarchical society and to legitimate the capitalist social order by validating an existing range of policy options rather than by producing innovative policy perspectives. They maintain that the scope of official investigation has invariably been confined to descriptive accounts of social conditions rather than to an examination of structural, causative, probabilistic relationships, and that investigation has focused on "problems" that reflect the priorities of the political and industrial elite. According to this school of thought, even the techniques and methodology adopted by investigators have reflected the social and ideological needs of the state in capitalist society.[5]

Some historians of government growth have advanced a similar thesis.

---

[4]See, for example, I. Gough, *The Political Economy of the Welfare State* (London: Macmillan, 1979), chaps. 3–4; J. Carrier and I. Kendall, "Social Policy and Social Change: Explanations of the Development of Social Policy," *Journal of Social Policy* 2 (1973): 212–14; D. Wedderburn, "Facts and Theories of the Welfare State," *The Socialist Register* (1965): 137–9; J. Higgins, "Social Control Theories of Social Policy," *Journal of Social Policy* 9 (1980): 1–23; V. George and P. Wilding, "Social Values, Social Class and Social Policy," *Social and Economic Administration* 6 (1972): 236–46; J. Saville, "The Welfare State: An Historical Approach," *New Reasoner* 3 (1957–8): 5–25.
[5]See, for example, M. Abrams, *Social Surveys and Social Action* (London: Heinemann, 1951); P. Abrams, *Origins of British Sociology 1834–1914* (Chicago: University of Chicago Press, 1968); J. Irvine, I. Miles, and J. Evans, eds., *Demystifying Social Statistics* (London: Pluto Press, 1979), chaps. 1, 10; Radical Statistics, *Social Indicators: For Individual Well-Being or Social Control?* (London: Radical Statistics Collective, 1978).

For example, according to Eric Stokes, social investigation and analysis were essentially an ideational construct providing an important mechanism by means of which the official mentality constrained the pace and content of state intervention.[6] Similarly, according to Lubenow's incrementalist model of government growth, the primary aim of government inquiry is the preservation of the "fundamental structures and values of the old order"; official investigations serve to identify marginal shifts in policy necessary to avert social unrest and to monitor and interpret the social costs of industrialization by reference to traditional consensus-oriented criteria.[7]

According to yet another view of the relationship between empirical findings and the development of policy, social investigation has performed an innovative and contentious role by mobilizing public opinion and by revealing the disparity between government aims and objectives.[8] Some writers would argue that, in highlighting the divergence between the social problems as perceived by policymakers, on the one hand, and the reality and the structural relationships underlying the social problems on the other, social investigation by the state has helped to generate a fundamental reappraisal of welfare problems and strategies.[9]

Administrative historians have also emphasized the innovative effects, both intended and unintended, of official investigations. For example, in Oliver MacDonagh's celebrated model of self-sustained government growth, investigations play a vital role as propaganda. They expose the "intolerability" of the more excessive social costs of an unregulated industrial economy and provide the justification for a progressive shift from permissive to mandatory legislation and from reliance on local and voluntary initiatives to the establishment of an interventionist, centralized bureaucracy.[10]

[6]E. Stokes, "Bureaucracy and Ideology: Britain and India in the Nineteenth Century," *Transactions of the Royal Historical Society* 30 (1980): 131–56.
[7]W. C. Lubenow, *The Politics of Government Growth: Early Victorian Attitudes Towards State Intervention 1833–1848* (Newton Abbot: David & Charles, 1971), 26–9.
[8]See, e.g., A. B. Cherns, "Social Sciences and Policy," and H. C. Kelman, "The Relevance of Social Research to Social Issues," in *The Sociological Review*, Monograph 16 (1970), 53–75, 77–99.
[9]P. Ford, *Social Theory and Social Practice* (Shannon: Irish University Press, 1968), Part 2; I. Levitt, "The Use of Official Statistics," *Quantitative Sociology Newsletter* 22 (1979): 68–82.
[10]O. G. M. MacDonagh, "The Nineteenth Century Revolution in Government: A Re-Appraisal," *Historical Journal* 1 (1958): 52–67.

THE EFFECTS OF CONTEMPORARY PERCEPTIONS OF CRISIS

The expanding role of the state as social investigator after 1880 appears to have been primarily a function of the crisis perceptions of the late-Victorian and Edwardian governing classes. "Crisis" constituted a leit-motiv of the parliamentary papers and the political and industrial literature of the period.

During the 1880s and early 1890s, two strands of concern prevailed: first, concern at the breakdown of industrial relations, and second, concern at the apparent socioeconomic crisis of the urban (and specifically, metropolitan) economy. The sustained decline in commodity prices and profit margins after 1873 had engendered a more aggressive attitude on the part of employers toward wage costs and labor productivity. Meanwhile, a new and more militant trade unionism had emerged which condemned the consensus policy of the craft unions and challenged both the prerogatives of management and the conventional criteria of wage determination.[11] Not only did this militancy endanger social stability, but also it was regarded in government circles as a major obstacle to British economic growth.[12] Inevitably, this crisis in the social and economic relationships of production generated a rising demand in Whitehall and Westminster for information about the labor market; trends in the level of wage earnings and methods of industrial remuneration; the extent and motivation of unionization; and the causes, incidence, and repercussions of industrial unrest.

Meanwhile, there was increasing concern at the apparent failure of the market to avert the process of urban degeneration: the creation of inner-city areas of chronic male underemployment; female sweated labor and low-paid, irregular work in declining trades, with the associated problems of poor housing, pauperism, and ill-health; and the attendant threat of the "outcast" residuum (perceived as the congenitally unfit) to civic order and property and to the economic efficiency of the respectable working classes.[13] This alarm was duly reflected in the pressure from social scientists and politicians for an official program of investigation

[11]See especially K. Burgess, *The Challenge of Labour* (London: Croom Helm, 1980), chaps. 1–3.
[12]See R. Davidson, "The Board of Trade and Industrial Relations 1896–1914," *Historical Journal* 21 (1978): 571–91.
[13]See G. Stedman Jones, *Outcast London* (Oxford: Clarendon Press, 1971), chaps. 11–17; A. Sutcliffe, "In Search of the Urban Variable: Britain in the Later Nineteenth

into the extent and causes of urban underemployment, sweated labor, and low-income destitution, and into the adverse effects of the urban environment on the health, motivation, and efficiency of the work force.

Some of the most acute anxieties over the performance of the British economy were articulated at the turn of the century. The growth of competition from foreigners within markets traditionally dominated by Britain, the apparent "invasion" of alien products into the domestic market, and the continuing downward trend in the yield of domestic manufacturing investment generated fears of a real crisis in national enterprise and efficiency. These fears were fortified by the failure of Britain's human and material capital assets to respond effectively to the economic and military stresses of the Boer War.[14]

The upswing in demand for social and welfare data during the 1895–1905 period was dramatic. Investigation of wage rates and earnings was needed to establish the wage costs of British industry and the cost-effectiveness and productivity of the work force. The same rationale underpinned the quest for more systematic information about the housing, medical, and educational provisions available to labor. Meanwhile, data on working-class expenditure and costs of living were viewed by both right- and left-wing collectivists as vital to expose the insufficiency of wage earnings to maintain large sections of the work force at a level consistent with economic efficiency. Investigations into the extent of destitution and urban degeneration would, it was expected, illuminate the poverty debate produced by the local studies of Charles Booth and Seebohm Rowntree, by the findings of the Inter-Departmental Committee on Physical Deterioration (1904), and by the polemics of the national efficiency and eugenics movements.

Demand for information on foreign welfare provisions, particularly German social legislation, also was a logical outcome of contemporary crisis perceptions. The political elite of the efficiency school and the British business community shared a concern over the competitive threat of German industry in overseas and domestic markets, and this concern engendered a growing interest in the relationship between social collec-

Century," in D. Fraser and A. Sutcliffe, eds., *The Pursuit of Urban History* (London: Edward Arnold, 1983), chap. 12.

[14]D. H. Aldcroft, ed., *The Development of British Industry and Foreign Competition 1875–1914* (London: Allen and Unwin, 1968), 15–16; G. R. Searle, *The Quest for National Efficiency: A Study in British Politics and British Political Thought 1899–1914* (Oxford: Basil Blackwell, 1971).

tivism and labor productivity abroad.[15] The tariff reform controversy constituted another powerful strand of demand for welfare information, the debate over protection raising a variety of issues relating to British working-class incomes and purchasing power, the level and stability of employment, and the social depth of domestic demand.[16]

The 1905–14 period witnessed a further phase of crisis perception among the British governing classes. Although profit margins recovered sharply after 1905 and the finance and trading sectors of the British economy enjoyed remarkable prosperity, a combination of economic, legal, and institutional forces produced a major breakdown in industrial relations that threatened the competitiveness and continuity of industrial output and a major confrontation between labor and the state. The establishment press, cabinet memoranda, and political memoirs and diaries of the period convey an overriding impression of social conflict and concern at the breakdown of existing social and industrial controls.[17] Crisis of confidence in the adequacy of conventional social policy options was further undermined by the growing identification within the ideology of New Liberalism between economic and welfare issues. Social radicals such as J. A. Hobson argued that the crisis of Liberalism lay essentially in its failure to relate contemporary problems of economic inefficiency to social inequality, and in its failure to confront the shortfall in demand and economic performance by redistributing the power to consume and regulating the exploitation of human and material resources.[18]

Predictably, social and industrial politics after 1905 created further demands on the official machinery of welfare investigation. For example, from a radical viewpoint, it was essential to have systematic information on working-class income and expenditure patterns so that the social and economic costs of underconsumption might be confronted and welfare measures such as minimum-wage legislation and Poor Law reform justified. In particular, demand for cost-of-living data derived from the search for a defensible, scientific basis for a shift away from the conventional market determinants of labor remuneration. In government circles, standard-of-living statistics were increasingly valued as a means of ex-

---

[15]Roy Hay, "Employers and Social Policy in Britain: The Evolution of Welfare Legislation, 1905–14," *Social History* 3 (1977): 435–55.
[16]P. Cain, "Political Economy in Edwardian England: The Tariff-Reform Controversy," in A. O'Day, ed., *The Edwardian Age* (London: Macmillan, 1979), 35–59.
[17]Emy, *Liberals, Radicals, and Social Politics,* chaps. 5–7.
[18]Freeden, *The New Liberalism,* 19–21, 128–34.

plaining the escalation of industrial militancy and of establishing the relative significance of falling real wages and rising social expectations.[19]

The development of a national unemployment policy also required more refined information on the extent and incidence of the problem, the advantages and disadvantages of existing statutory and voluntary provisions, and the feasibility of a range of policy options designed to coordinate the labor market and insulate working-class living standards against cyclical unemployment.[20] Finally, an appraisal of overseas welfare legislation was viewed as essential in devising new strategies of "crisis avoidance." Faced with the social strains of a maturing economy and the unrest stemming from the erosion of traditional industrial relationships, British policymakers were eager to monitor overseas legislation (as in Canada and Australasia) designed to contain major industrial disputes and to maintain the continuity of essential services and output. They were equally eager to examine the use of welfare policy, as in Germany, to provide a positive response to socialism while sustaining industrial discipline, work incentives, and labor productivity.[21]

Reinforcing the impact of these various phases of crisis perception on the investigative role of the state was the strong thread of empiricism common to many contemporary political ideologies. Central to the collectivist theories of the national efficiency movement and Fabianism was the belief in the need for an efficient bureaucracy directed from above by a department of experts served by a comprehensive system of state inquiry. Although, in practice, Liberal imperialists made little attempt to investigate the social problems they identified, the rhetoric of social imperialism assumed a high degree of self-knowledge by the state. The role of the investigator qua expert was especially vital to the predictive and interventionist aims of the eugenics movement. Moreover, social investigation by the state was firmly embedded in the ideology of New Liberalism. As Michael Freeden has pointed out, underpinning its fusion of science and ethics and its fusion of biological and social theory was a commitment to systematic research into social phenomena and to the assumption by the state of an investigative role with which to regulate

---

[19]*Select Committee on Post Office Servants, Appendices to Minutes of Evidence,* Parliamentary Papers (hereafter P.P.) 1913 (268), 13, p. 2.

[20]J. Harris, *Unemployment and Politics: A Study in English Social Policy 1886–1914* (Oxford: Clarendon Press, 1972), chaps. 5–6.

[21]J. R. Hay, "The British Business Community, Social Insurance and the German Example," in W. J. Mommsen, ed., *The Emergence of the Welfare State in Britain and Germany* (London: Croom Helm, 1981), 107–32.

resources consistent with the optimum welfare of the community. Recent research on the Unionist Social Reform Committee suggests that even the "Radical Right" was disposed after 1909 to appreciate the need for a more rational and informed process of policy-making.[22]

THE EXTENT OF GOVERNMENT AND PRIVATE SOCIAL INVESTIGATION

The response of the British state to the data needs of crisis avoidance and social reform was duly reflected in the rise of government expenditure on the production and dissemination of social data over the period. It is impossible to assess precisely the financial outlay on social investigation; the annual accounts lack sufficient disaggregation. Moreover, important social information was often produced as part of commercial and industrial inquiries, such as the fiscal blue books. In addition, investigative expenditure was often subsumed within broader administrative budgets. Nevertheless, a rough estimate of government expenditure on social investigation can be obtained.

The graph on page 250 captures the dramatic increase in the establishment and operating costs of social investigation undertaken by late-Victorian and Edwardian government. It reflects the creation of specialist intelligence departments, the most notable being the Labour Department of the Board of Trade and the Office of Special Inquiries at the Board of Education, as well as the proliferation of investigative work undertaken or commissioned by Whitehall in general. However, the graph fails to capture two important areas of investigative enterprise. First, it excludes the vast amount of investigation undertaken by state agencies as a by-product of regulatory duties, especially the work of the inspectorates. Second, it fails to reflect the extent to which the state continued to rely on private research (both institutional and individual) for social information. Official inquiries regularly exploited the research of organizations such as relief agencies, trade unions, chambers of commerce, churches, and statistical societies. For example, government investigation

[22]Searle, *National Efficiency*, 81–6; H. C. G. Matthew, *The Liberal Imperialists: The Ideas and Politics of a Post-Gladstonian Elite* (Oxford: Oxford University Press, 1973), 136, 226, 294–5; B. Semmel, *Imperialism and Social Reform: English Social-Imperial Thought 1895–1914* (London: Allen & Unwin, 1960), 119; D. A. MacKenzie, *Statistics in Britain 1865–1930: The Social Construction of Scientific Knowledge* (Edinburgh: Edinburgh University Press, 1981), 56, 136; Freeden, *The New Liberalism*, 69, 75–6, 256; D. J. Dutton, "The Unionist Party and Social Policy 1906–14," *Historical Journal* 24 (1981): 881.

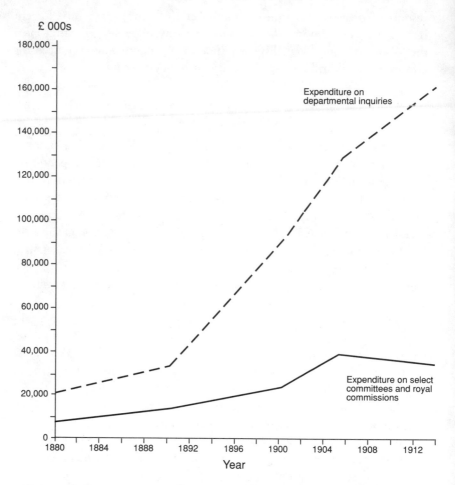

Estimated government expenditure on social investigation in Britain, 1880–
1913 (from *Parliamentary Papers Annual Civil Service Estimates*)

of working-class expenditure patterns depended on case studies provided
by the cooperative movement and by the London Economic Club. Trade
union information about unemployment benefits underpinned the government's employment index. The government's appraisal of trends in
the labor market strongly reflected local inquiries undertaken by chambers of commerce and employers' associations. And empirical studies of
sweated labor produced by the university settlement at Toynbee Hall in
the East End of London were incorporated into government reports on
the issue of low-income destitution.

The findings of individual social scientists and statisticians were an equally important resource for the government. Charles Booth and See-bohm Rowntree are but the most celebrated examples of "private enterprise" informing the social politics of the period. Others included Clementina Black (home work), A. L. Bowley (income distribution), W. Harbutt Dawson (vagrancy), H. Rider Haggard (rural housing and emigration), and Arthur Shadwell (physical deterioration).

Throughout the period, an important symbiotic relationship existed between social statisticians and investigators inside and outside Whitehall. They often had the same social and cultural background, emerging from the university settlement and extension movements of the 1880s and 1890s (established to bridge the gulf between rich and poor by means of social work and adult education lectures) or from involvement in the Charity Organization Society and other relief agencies. They also shared the same social science milieu at the Royal Statistical Society, the Economic Society, and the British Association for the Advancement of Science.

Moreover, although it operated very unevenly, a broad pattern of incorporation within state investigation can perhaps be discerned. In the first instance, private investigators would furnish briefing material or oral evidence to government inquiries. Thereafter, they might often be employed by Whitehall as subcommissioners for major royal commissions, such as the Royal Commission on Labour, in order to extend or to rationalize the data base of discussion. In addition, they might be appointed as fee-paid, part-time investigators to undertake specific areas of social research vital to the definition of government policy (e.g., the work of D. F. Schloss on profit sharing and cooperation in the 1890s and that of G. H. Wood, W. H. Dawson, and W. H. Beveridge on wages and unemployment in the 1900s). Meanwhile, professional statisticians might be temporarily engaged as consultants on the more ambitious government inquiries to advise on quantitative techniques (e.g., the input of A. L. Bowley and G. U. Yule to the cost-of-living inquiries after 1903). Finally, investigators of appropriate caliber and "temperament" might be given permanent employment as investigators within the civil service (e.g., Hubert Llewellyn Smith, Arthur Wilson Fox, and Michael Sadler).

In terms of motivation and operational philosophy, this investigative community can be grouped into three broad categories. First, there was a group of investigators and statisticians who viewed social inquiry from an orthodox Liberal standpoint. The most prominent member of this group was Robert Giffen, in charge of the government's major economic and social investigations throughout the 1876–97 period. After serving for a time with John Morley on the *Fortnightly Review*, Giffen had joined *The Economist* as assistant editor (1868–76) under Walter Bagehot. Following his appointment in 1876 as head of the Board of Trade's Statistical Department, he continued to write prolifically on a wide range of economic, financial, and statistical issues. In addition, he had played an influential role in the development of the Royal Statistical Society (as secretary and president between 1876 and 1884), the International Statistical Institute, and the Economic and Statistical Section of the British Association.[23]

In his social and economic beliefs, Giffen was a confirmed free-market Liberal individualist and a vigorous opponent of state intervention in industrial affairs. In particular, he resisted the tendency of government growth after 1880 to involve Whitehall in problems relating to the labor market. He thought that state arbitration and conciliation would distort the cost structure of British industry, that the provision of public works and other forms of job creation would divert funds from private enterprise, and that the more stringent regulation of working conditions might compromise the necessary prerogatives of industrial management. Giffen seriously questioned the severity of the so-called Labor Problem. He believed that the working classes were the major beneficiaries of economic growth, that pauperism was declining, and that, where pauperism persisted, lack of thrift rather than exploitation was the major determinant.[24]

Thus, although Giffen was a leading advocate of more extensive and systematic social investigation in the 1890s, he perceived its role as being primarily the containment of state intervention. In his view, it would further "efficient and economical" government. The fundamental community of interest between industrial management and the work force would be revealed and "irrational" conflict eliminated, voluntary effort would be focused more effectively on the crisis points of urban deprivation, and collectivist measures would be rendered unnecessary. Giffen regarded labor statistics explicitly as a means of discrediting "sensational politics and sociology" generated by the contemporary debate over the standard of living of the working classes and by "collectivist agitators" such as Henry George.[25]

---

[23]*Dictionary of National Biography, 2d Supplement*, vol. 2 (1912), 103–5; *Economic Bulletin* 3 (1910): 140–2.

[24]See, e.g., R. Giffen, "Depression Corrected," *Edinburgh Review* 182 (1895): 2–26; "The Gross and Net Gain of Rising Wages," *Contemporary Review* 56 (1889): 832–43.

[25]Ibid.; memo, "Board of Trade Labour Statistics and the Labour Commission," by R. Giffen, April 16, 1891.

Other senior investigators and statisticians within Whitehall who had similar views included A. E. Bateman, who succeeded Giffen as the government's chief commercial and industrial statistician; Dr. W. Ogle, superintendent of statistics at the Registrar General's Office; Alexander Redgrave, chief inspector of factories; and F. H. MacLeod, who, as senior investigator and principal for labor statistics after 1899, played a pivotal role in the investigatory work of the Labour Department.

A second, "labourist" group of social investigators can be detected in the machinery of government in the late nineteenth and early twentieth centuries. Typical was John Burnett. Apprenticed in a Tyneside engineering works, Burnett had provided the leadership of the Nine Hour Campaign of 1871–2 for shorter hours. In 1875, he had been elected as general secretary of the Amalgamated Society of Engineers (ASE) and for the next ten years directed the union's defense against increasingly aggressive management strategies designed to lower wage costs. However, by the mid-1880s, his leadership of the ASE, with its stress on stable bureaucratic control, industrial conciliation, and commitment to Gladstonian Liberalism, had come under mounting attack from rank-and-file militants. In 1886, Burnett relinquished his union responsibilities in favor of a career as a social investigator in the civil service.[26]

Several other investigators, such as C. J. Drummond and J. J. Dent, and many of the Board of Trade's fee-paid local correspondents, emerged from similar backgrounds and viewed social inquiry from their perspective as labor aristocrats who, faced with the emergence of a new and more militant trade unionism, had gravitated from labor politics to the security and prestige of public office.[27] Although advocating a range of social reforms, they also were hostile to socialist ideology and deprecated the divisiveness of New Unionism with its stress on industrial militancy. Their advocacy of welfare rights and measures was not identified with any support for an independent working-class political program, and they viewed the mechanism of social amelioration primarily as the growth of "wisely directed trade-unionism," with state intervention fulfilling only a residual role. In addition, they shared with Burnett a respect for hierarchy and a propensity to interpret the broader aspirations of labor in

[26]J. M. Bellamy and J. Saville, eds., *Dictionary of Labour Biography,* vol. 2 (London: Macmillan, 1974), 71–5.

[27]C. J. Drummond was a former Conservative Secretary of the London Society of Compositors; J. J. Dent was an apprenticed bricklayer who became prominent in London radical politics of the 1870s and 1880s. Dent was a leader in the Cooperative Movement, Workers' Educational Association, and Working Men's Clubs and Institute Union.

terms of the relatively structured and pragmatic motions of the Trades Union Congress (TUC).

Accordingly, this group of social investigators regarded the prime function of labor statistics as being to "educate" the labor movement, on the assumption that accurate data on employment, on the costs and benefits of strike action, and on the cost structure of British industry would rehabilitate the consensus tactics of mid-Victorian craft unionism and serve to preserve industrial peace. They also believed that more reliable and comprehensive labor market intelligence would enable the trade union movement to focus its energies on eliminating the more contentious aspects of the "Labor Problem," without recourse to legislative measures that might endanger the cost-efficiency of enterprise and the self-sufficiency and motivation of the laboring classes.

The motivation and operational philosophy of the third group of statisticians and investigators can most accurately be described as "progressive." Within this group a further distinction may usefully, though more arbitrarily, be drawn between "social innovators" and "technical innovators." The most prominent social innovators were Hubert Llewellyn Smith, Clara Collet, David Frederick Schloss, Arthur Wilson Fox, Michael Sadler, and Ernest Aves.[28]

The prime example is perhaps Llewellyn Smith, the first Labour commissioner. Born in 1864 to a middle-class Quaker family, Llewellyn Smith had been heavily influenced by the new Oxford Movement of the 1880s, with its concern over the condition of the working classes. Between university and public office, he had immersed himself in the world of late-Victorian progressivism. Initiated early on into the aristocratic, radical milieu of the Carlisles at Castle Howard, he had progressed to that mecca of social reformers and of future Labour Department personnel, the East End of London. There, at Toynbee Hall and later at Beaumont

[28]H. L. Smith was labour commissioner, 1893–7; deputy comptroller-general, Board of Trade, 1897–1903; comptroller-general, 1903–7; permanent secretary, Board of Trade, 1907–19. C. E. Collet was labour correspondent of Board of Trade, 1893–1903; senior investigator for women's industries, 1903–20. D. F. Schloss was personal staff, comptroller-general, 1893–9; investigator, 1899–1902; senior investigator, 1902–7; director, Census of Production, 1907–8. A. W. Fox was agricultural labour correspondent, 1895–7; assistant labour commissioner, 1897–1903; labour commissioner and deputy comptroller-general, 1903–7; comptroller-general, 1907–9. E. Aves was Home Office commissioner to investigate Australian and New Zealand wages boards, 1907–8; special investigator for Labour Department, Board of Trade, 1908–12; chairman of Trade Boards, 1912. M. E. Sadler was director of special inquiries, Education Department, 1894–1903.

Square, where he founded a subcolony called the "Swarm," he had participated in the university settlement movement. Meanwhile, in Charles Booth's inquiry into the life and labor of the people in London, at the British Association, the Royal Statistical and Economic Societies, at the Denison Club for Charity Organisation Society Workers, and in his travels as a university extension lecturer, he had made contact with the elite of social scientists and the leading statisticians of the day, both academic and government. In addition, his espousal of the New Unionism cause and his participation in London politics had made him the confidant of the labor leaders.[29]

Consistent with this background, Llewellyn Smith upheld an advanced radical view of the "Labor Problem." Deeply influenced by the works of Stanley Jevons, he condemned the Manchester school for its doctrinaire rigidity and cruel administrative complacency; welcomed the emergence of a more constructive, socially relevant economics; and sympathized with the cause of socialism. Given the absence of any other options, he preferred to be "wrong with Karl Marx than right with David Ricardo." Although Llewellyn Smith accepted the economic evils that socialism set out to remedy as "a just and valid cause for action," he was fundamentally opposed to revolutionary measures of social reform. Rather than endorsing the overthrow of the existing economic and social institutions and relationships, he advocated a "limited Socialism" that focused on "the breaking down of the barriers of class exclusiveness, the development of the spirit of class union and social sympathy" and "the education and moralisation of society."

Llewellyn Smith's brand of social and welfare philosophy was informed with the characteristic middle-class missionary perspective of late-Victorian social radicalism. In his view, social progress had to incorporate both the moral and the material advancement of labor, and this could be achieved only by maintaining overall social harmony during a process of gradual change. He argued that the value of government intervention in the labor market should be judged on purely pragmatic grounds, according to specific social priorities rather than doctrinaire theory, and

---

[29]Llewellyn Smith's early career is reviewed in detail in R. Davidson, "Llewellyn Smith: The Labour Department and Government Growth 1886–1909," in G. Sutherland, ed., *Studies in the Growth of Nineteenth-Century Government* (London: Routledge & Kegan Paul, 1972), 239–45. See also A. Kadish, *The Oxford Economists in the Late Nineteenth Century* (Oxford: Clarendon Press, 1982), 18–30, 70–5.

that self-reliance and associative effort on the part of the working class must remain the linchpins of social reform if the moral caliber and economic efficiency of the labor force were to be maintained.[30]

The investigative philosophy of the social innovators had been largely molded by their participation in the Booth inquiry and the university extension movement. Their primary concern was to provide a scientific exposé of the "Labor Problem"—a careful, minute, systematic observation of working-class life as affected by environment, heredity, and habit. This, they argued, would provide an impartial data base for debate on social issues, avoiding both "investigatory sensationalism" such as the pamphlet *The Bitter Cry of Outcast London,* which they regarded as "seriously deficient in the scientific sense," and superficial, socialistic, or autocratic legislative proposals that ignored the realities of the labor market and the complexities of social administration.[31]

Furthermore, this group of investigators shared the contemporary fear of the disintegration of society into the chaos of class war. They viewed social investigation as a means of cementing social relations and diverting working-class discontent into constructive channels. As Kadish concludes, "They felt certain that if the working man were given the correct knowledge as to the reasons for his condition . . . he would come to realise the fallacy of revolutionary socialism and adopt the right and best form of progress—gradual reform."[32]

The "technical innovators," led by Arthur Bowley, George Wood, and Udny Yule, were to play a crucial role in the series of inquiries into working-class income, consumption, and costs of living undertaken by Whitehall after 1902. They derived their inspiration from the rise of sociometrics and mathematical statistics at the turn of the century, associated in part with social Darwinism and in part with the more pragmatic demands for quantitative information generated by the tariff reform debate.

Their interest in social and industrial statistics was far from being purely technical or theoretical. For example, George Henry Wood was

[30]Davidson, "Llewellyn Smith," 240–3; Kadish, *Oxford Economists,* 72–3, 94–5, 100, 119.
[31]See H. Llewellyn Smith, *Methods of Social Inquiry* (Oxford, 1890), 4; Clara Collet Diary, 10 September 1876 to 20 August 1891, passim; D. F. Schloss, "The Road to Social Peace," *Fortnightly Review* 49 (1891): 255–6; Schloss, "The Reorganisation of our Labour Department," *Journal of the Royal Statistical Society* (hereafter *JRSS*) 56 (1893): p. 61.
[32]Kadish, *Oxford Economists,* 100.

a "radical with a strong impulse towards social reform" and a "great sympathy with the aims of the Socialists."[33] Bowley's social and economic views, although less explicit than Wood's, were in this period distinctly progressive. He was critical both of the Bismarckian paternalism of Conservative social policy and the indecisiveness of orthodox Liberals toward welfare issues. His sympathies in the early 1900s lay with the social radicals who were trying to alleviate chronic destitution, to rationalize the labor market, and to alter the level and incidence of social investment.[34]

Nonetheless, the overriding aim of the technical innovators was to refine the methodology of official statistics. They were concerned that the work of Adolphe Quetelet and other European statisticians had not produced a more progressive attitude within Whitehall toward statistical theory and methodology. In consequence, they thought, the British government did not produce "significant" information that was capable of testing the interdependence of social phenomena and of furnishing the type of quantitative data demanded by contemporary social and economic debate. Accordingly, they sought to permeate the production structure of social investigation undertaken by the state with more advanced techniques such as correlation analysis and sampling.[35]

LOGISTICAL AND IDEOLOGICAL CONSTRAINTS ON SOCIAL INVESTIGATION

Despite such patterns of resource allocation and recruitment, the scope and rigor of social investigation undertaken by British government after 1880 still fell far short of the needs and expectations of social scientists and reformers. Evidence would suggest that the role of the state as social investigator was seriously inhibited by a range of logistical and ideological constraints.

One of the more persistent constraints throughout the 1880–1914 period was undoubtedly Treasury control. The Treasury resisted the expansion of social investigation both as an issue of financial policy and as one of routine appropriation. Its attitude had been clearly articulated

---

[33]G. H. Wood Papers, unpublished biography, 1–12; *JRSS* 108 (1945): 485–7.
[34]R. G. D. Allen, "Arthur Lyon Bowley," in *International Encyclopaedia of the Social Sciences* 2 (1968): 134–6; Bowley Papers, "Socialism and Social Reform," unpublished address by A. L. Bowley, c. 1896.
[35]See, e.g., A. L. Bowley, "Address to the Economic Section of the British Association," *JRSS* 69 (1906): 540–54, and idem, "The Improvement of Official Statistics," *JRSS* 71 (1908): 469–77.

in a minute of 1882: "The collecting and digesting of public statistics is a duty that should be carefully watched and guarded in order that it may not degenerate into extravagance. There is a dangerous tendency to magnify work and extend functions beyond the limits required at once by economy and expediency."[36] Despite the economic and social crises of the period and the growing demand for an effective system of social investigation, the Treasury sustained this minimalist philosophy. In the Treasury's view, the provision of "routine 'administrative' rather than 'promotional' data" was entirely consistent with efficient government.

In effect, the Treasury imposed a catch-22 situation on late-Victorian and Edwardian social administrators. It expected Whitehall to demonstrate the cost-effectiveness of its measures, but resisted the deployment of resources by means of which both short- and long-term policy options and objectives might be evaluated and the social and economic repercussions of decision making monitored. Predictably, its resistance focused on "speculative inquiries" (i.e., investigation that might generate fresh areas of government expenditure) and on the appointment of professional statisticians and investigators who might foster such "departures."

Thus, the investigative inertia of the Local Government Board in its administration of pauperism, vagrancy, housing, health care, environmental pollution, and unemployment-related distress is partly attributable to the enervating effects of Treasury control. The head of the Statistical Department forcefully described his budget as "a public disgrace" and openly admitted his consequent inability to fulfill "any effective intelligence function" either for decision making within the board or for use in broader public and parliamentary debate. Treasury control seriously frustrated the development of an effective state medical service by its constraint on the board's research funding.[37]

British census authorities also lacked the staff and resources with which to address broader social and economic issues and the welfare implications of vital statistics. The Treasury refused to sanction the establishment of a senior administrative grade within the General Register Office. As a result, the staff were demoralized, lacked intellectual and statistical

---

[36]Public Record Office (hereafter PRO), H045/11787/B32589/2, Treasury minute, 21 April 1882.

[37]R. M. MacLeod, *Treasury Control and Social Administration: A Study of Establishment Growth at the Local Government Board 1871–1905* (London: G. Bell & Sons, 1968); PRO, MH78/1B, Local Government Board Committee, unpublished minutes of evidence, *Questions in Evidence* 2715, 2731–3; R M. MacLeod, "The Frustration of State Medicine 1880–1899," *Medical History* 11 (1967): 15–40.

caliber, and were incapable of undertaking the type of investigations advocated by many social commentators and administrators.[38] Similar financial constraints served to compromise the efforts of the Registry of Friendly Societies to monitor the savings and expenditure patterns of the working classes, their private welfare schemes, and the sickness and mortality experience of their membership. Attempts by the chief registrar to develop a broader investigative role in response to the welfare debates of the period were doggedly resisted by the Treasury as "departmental imperialism" wholly inappropriate to "a backwater of the Civil Service."[39]

In the case of labor investigation, the normal bureaucratic constraints of Treasury control were further reinforced by more personal, ideological prejudices. Most Treasury officials adhered to a conservative political and social ideology, and they viewed the extension of such intelligence as a populist strategy of social radicalism and the thin end of the socialist expenditure wedge. The Labour Department was perceived as a permanent conspiracy toward extravagance, and its efforts to fund the investigation of problems such as unemployment, industrial unrest, and low-income destitution were systematically frustrated.[40]

Industrial and community resistance to the inquisitorial role of the state also hampered the efforts of government to acquire social information. The opportunity cost to trade union officials and management of completing detailed schedules on a range of welfare issues was high. They could not be expected readily to appreciate the social benefits to be gained, the more so as the schedules issued by Whitehall departments generally reflected systematized bureaucratic expectations that hardly accorded with the often irregular and incomplete records compiled by union organizations and employers. Social investigators and administrators often made empirical demands that bore little relationship to the comparatively modest and pragmatic information flows required by manufacturers and the work force at the point of production.

Industrial resistance was not merely a function of logistics. It also reflected fairly deep-rooted ideological distrust on the part of both capital and labor toward the inquiries undertaken by Whitehall. For example,

---

[38]*Treasury Committee on the Census, Minutes of Evidence,* P.P. 1890 (C. 6071) 58, *Questions in Evidence* 10, 29, 34, 39, 57, 66; PRO, RG29/3 Registrar General to Treasury, 30 August 1905; *JRSS* 71 (1908): 477.

[39]PRO, T1/11705/27505.

[40]See R. Davidson, "Treasury Control and Labour Intelligence in Late Victorian and Edwardian Britain," *Historical Journal* 28 (1985): 719–26.

many union leaders objected to the disclosure of details about their financial resources for fear that such data would merely strengthen the bargaining position of employers and provide intelligence for any counterattack on the trade union movement.[41] A similar rationale—"of declining to enable the employers to know when to put the screw on"—underlay resistance to the provision of unemployment statistics.[42] Labor leaders were also apprehensive that data relating to working-class expenditure patterns and costs of living would merely provide an excuse for "middle class moralising" as to secondary poverty, and that this "stomach policy of the bourgeoisie" would obscure rather than illuminate the fundamental causes of destitution.[43]

In contrast, many industrialists feared that Whitehall would use information relating to employment, remuneration, and working conditions as a means of undermining private enterprise and business efficiency, by eroding market criteria of wage determination and by reinforcing left-wing demands for a range of welfare provisions such as countercyclical public works and minimum-wage legislation.[44] Accordingly, all the most vital social inquiries undertaken by the Board of Trade, whose Labour Department was staffed by former trade unionists and middle-class radicals, were seriously impaired by the refusal of employers to disclose information.[45]

Resistance from local authorities, especially in small urban centers and rural areas, further reduced the quality of information at the disposal of social policymakers. For example, sanitary authorities often failed to monitor industrial sanitation, in deference to vested interests in trade and property ownership.[46] Meanwhile, Poor Law guardians resisted pressure from Whitehall to provide additional information on poverty, unemployment, and local labor market conditions. They maintained either that its value was incommensurate with the additional work and cost involved or that "information in the public interest" should be funded by the Treasury and not constitute an additional burden on the rates.[47]

[41]See, e.g., *4th Report on Trade Unions*, P.P. 1890–91 (C. 6475), 92, p. 1.
[42]Trades Union Congress, *Annual Report* (London, 1893), 36.
[43]*Returns of Expenditure by Working Men*, P.P. 1889 (C. 5861) 134, p. 4; *JRSS* 56 (1893): 268, 290.
[44]See, e.g., *Reports of Chief Inspector of Factories*, P.P. 1897 (C. 8561), 17, p. 75; 1901 (Cd. 668), 10, p. 248; 1904 (Cd. 2139), 10, p. 227; *The Times*, 16 January 1902.
[45]See, e.g., PRO, LAB 41/186.
[46]See, e.g., PRO, MH15/91/112645/52(1907); MH15/91/7318/105(1904); MH78/46.
[47]PRO, TI/11110/21480.

Many school boards played a similar role in frustrating the efforts of the Education Department to gather and disseminate useful educational information. Such data as were produced by local authorities were frequently unreliable for the purposes of aggregate or regional analysis and worthless for cross-tabulation with other social indicators.

Moreover, evidence suggests that there was a broader societal resistance to the growth of government investigation to which Whitehall departments were sensitive in determining the scope of social inquiries. As compared with bureaucracies in other industrialized economies such as Germany, many areas of Whitehall were not armed with the investigatory powers of Roman law by which to compel the disclosure of information, and it is revealing that when statutory powers *were* sought to enforce public participation in major investigations, parliamentary debate raised fundamental issues of personal liberty and the inquisitorial rights of the state.

Thus, in 1906, members of Parliament were warned that, in sanctioning new social and industrial inquiries, "they were simply sacrificing their liberty to a gang of clerks in Downing Street" and "to oppression of every kind."[48] The association of social science inquiry with the more authoritarian schemes of social engineering advocated by social Darwinists and eugenists served to fuel public unease at the growth of state intervention, as did the "antiscience" sentiment existing, to a significant extent, in all classes of late-Victorian and Edwardian society. Public resistance to investigation in the 1880–1914 period was also part of a more general constitutional concern over the power of expertise and its threat to democratic process. The investigators/experts often lacked accountability (the more so after the rationalization of late-nineteenth century Whitehall insulated specialists from their professions and the public), yet they could play a decisive role in defining the objectives of government. This role threatened to obscure the dividing line between policy-making and administration central to the constitutional tenets of Liberalism and to provide an information base for autocratic government.[49]

[48]*Hansard*, 4th ser., 162, cols. 1171–3, speech by T. M. Healy, 1 August 1906.
[49]R. M. MacLeod, "Law, Medicine and Public Opinion: The Resistance to Compulsory Health Legislation, 1870–1907," *Public Law* (1967): 210–11; C. Denovan, "Attitudes For and Against the Application of Science in Social Policy, 1886–1914," unpublished master's thesis, Edinburgh University, 1980; S. Hynes, *The Edwardian Turn of Mind* (Princeton, N.J.: Princeton University Press, 1968), 156; R. M. MacLeod, *The Social Role of the Man of Knowledge: Expertise and the State in Nineteenth Century Britain*,

Despite the efforts of the technical innovators, another significant constraint was the failure of the methodology of social inquiry undertaken by Whitehall to keep pace with the data needs of contemporary welfare debate and with advances in quantitative techniques and statistical theory.[50]

For example, the time-series analysis relating to unemployment, pauperism, and sanitation, which was extremely modest, was employed more to form a basis for impressions than to differentiate systematically between long-term and short-term cyclical influences. The use of index numbers was equally simplistic; they were deployed to consolidate data rather than to isolate the main determinants of temporal shifts in economic and social phenomena. Despite extensive use of cross-tabulation, the methodology investigators used in their application of measures of association between social and economic variables also remained theoretically underdeveloped before 1914. Correlation and regression techniques were conspicuously absent from a whole range of welfare inquiries. Measures of central tendency and dispersion were equally unrefined, especially in the investigation of working-class incomes and expenditure. However, the most notable lag in the quantitative methods of Whitehall was its failure to assimilate random sampling techniques, despite the fact that many investigators were familiar with contemporary developments in sampling theory that could have radically transformed the state's ability to monitor social trends.

Several explanations can be advanced for this shortfall in the technical sophistication of welfare investigation. Where senior officials *were* anxious to improve the scope of information, they were more concerned with its relevance and coherence for use in policy briefings than with its methodological rigor and statistical refinement. This was particularly so after 1900, as these officials became increasingly preoccupied with an intensive program of industrial and welfare legislation.[51] In addition, career civil servants, including staff within the traditional inspectorates and statistical establishment, resented the adoption of new techniques as implicitly devaluing their specialist status and investigative skills.

Social Science Research Council Report (New York: The Council, 1978), 2–3, 11, 27–8, 38–42.

[50]For an extended treatment of this issue, see R. Davidson, *Whitehall and the Labour Problem in Late-Victorian and Edwardian Britain* (London: Croom Helm, 1985), chap. 10.

[51]See, e.g., *Transactions of the British Association for the Advancement of Science* (1910), 668–9.

Broader social determinants also constrained the methods of social inquiry undertaken by British government between 1880 and 1914. British empirical social research continued to lack the unified professional identity, institutional setting, and theoretical consensus necessary for the sustained diffusion of ideas and techniques.[52] As in other areas of scientific inquiry, such as criminology or epidemiology, no "professional" consensus existed as to the validity and application of the mathematical theory of statistics. "Ease of entry" meant that the investigation of social problems within social science organizations such as the Royal Statistical Society remained dominated by generalists. As a result, the "discipline" of quantitative investigation remained eclectic and fragmented, and its links with the machinery of government ad hoc and often informal, thus reducing the impact and status of new techniques. The prevailing norms and imperatives of social administration within Whitehall served merely to reinforce this tendency.

The power of the British state as social investigator was further eroded by lack of coordination within the information-gathering, analysis, and deployment functions of the government. As the Official Statistics Committee of 1879–81 revealed, the bulk of social information was agency specific and tangential to the broader welfare issues in public and parliamentary debate. The committee advocated "strong centralisation and control," but its recommendations for structural reform were tentative and ineffectual. In particular, the proposal for a central statistical office with which to coordinate the production and dissemination of economic and social information was rejected.[53] Moreover, subsequent attempts by the Board of Trade, in collaboration with the social science community, to press for a "department of civil intelligence" to undertake the planning and quality control of governmental investigative work also proved abortive.[54]

As a result, information was seriously lacking on a range of social conditions and problems that fell within the purview of more than one department of state. For example, although the Local Government Board provided information on pauperism and the Board of Trade monitored unemployment and low-income destitution, no department was respon-

---

[52]S. Cole, "Continuity and Institutionalisation in Science: A Case Study in Failure," in A. Oberschall, ed., *The Establishment of Empirical Sociology: Studies in Continuity, Discontinuity and Institutionalisation* (New York: Harper & Row, 1972), 73–129.
[53]*Report of Official Statistics Committee*, P.P. 1881 (39), 30, pp. xiv–xxxii, 56–8.
[54]Davidson, *Whitehall and the Labour Problem*, 198–200.

sible for investigating poverty per se. Hence it was left to the private enterprise of social scientists such as Booth, Rowntree, and Bowley to make good the omission. Similarly, the compartmentalization of official intelligence impeded the investigation of vital linkages between problems of education, employment, health, housing, and remuneration.

Finally, bureaucratic resistance within many departments of social administration represented a major obstacle to the growth of state investigation. Thus, the contribution of the Home Office to welfare investigation during the late-Victorian and Edwardian period was inhibited by the administrative philosophy of its permanent officials. As university-educated generalists, the majority of the senior establishment were career oriented rather than problem oriented, and they viewed social administration primarily as a source of income and professional status.[55] Consistent with this perspective was a minimalist attitude toward the role and utility of statistics. Whereas the bureaucrats acknowledged that, without statistics, administration might degenerate "into a blind mechanical process with no intelligent guide for its action," they did not perceive the Home Office as having an "investigative role," over and above the provision of routine administrative data sufficient to ensure the efficient enforcement of a code of industrial regulations.[56] This attitude was reflected in the limited status and resources allocated to investigative work by the Home Office and in its reluctance to employ the mass of welfare information possessed by its factory, mines, and workshop inspectorates in the determination of policy.

The Local Government Board's negative attitude toward social investigation also stemmed to a significant extent from the operational philosophy of its senior officials. As "professional" bureaucrats, they conceived of their role as the performance of prescribed duties rather than the creation of new ones, with the emphasis on the efficient application of rules or a "code" according to precedent.[57] This disinclination to innovate was strongly reflected in their attitude to investigative work. The board's senior officials viewed statistics as a routine adjunct of administration, not as a means of informing broader contemporary debate over poverty and efficiency. Indeed, they explicitly denied that the

[55] J. Pellew, *The Home Office 1848–1914: From Clerks to Bureaucrats* (London: Heinemann, 1982), 183, 190–1, 201–3.
[56] *Report of Factory Statistics Committee*, P.P. 1895 (C. 7608), 19, p. 19; Pellew, *The Home Office*, 108.
[57] K. D. Brown, "John Burns at the Local Government Board: A Reassessment," *Journal of Social Policy* 6 (1977): 158–63.

Local Government Board had an investigatory role to play, and any attempt by individual officers to undertake "original investigation" into contentious issues relating to social policy was firmly suppressed.[58]

Bureaucratic resistance to creative investigation also characterized the General Register Office. Until the appointment of Bernard Mallet and T. H. C. Stevenson as registrar general and superintendent of statistics in 1909, this office adopted a minimalist view of its functions as being those of enumeration and not investigation. Its overriding concern was to refine the accuracy of a narrow range of vital statistics rather than to bring such data to bear on the central issues in the social politics of the period. Even *The Times* was critical of its "sceptical turn of mind" toward the value of census data for identifying shifts in social structure and in the condition of the working classes.[59]

The history of the Office of Special Inquiries at the Board of Education furnishes the most revealing example of the prevailing tensions between generalist administrators and specialist investigators within Whitehall after 1880. The office was explicitly conceived as an "intelligence department" to undertake wide-ranging scientific inquiry into Britain's educational problems and to monitor the educational advances of its commercial and industrial competitors. However, senior officials were increasingly resistant to the innovative implications of its work and to the proactive philosophy of its director. As a result, the office was starved of resources and its terms of reference eventually were confined to informing the routine administrative work of the board.[60]

Moreover, even where, as at the Board of Trade, senior bureaucrats adopted an innovative approach to social and economic administration and clearly perceived the value of investigatory work to policy-making, the ideology of statisticians and investigators might still inhibit inquiry. They viewed the labor market from the standpoint of the labor aristocracy and middle classes, and to a significant extent their social status conditioned their attitude to their intelligence role. Although they believed that the provision of better information might help to erode the worst forms of labor exploitation, they were equally concerned to discredit idealistic schemes of social reconstruction. Their effort to identify and measure

[58]See especially PRO, MH19/203; MH10/59; T1/10224/12488; T1/8298A/6204.
[59]*The Times,* 22 September 1887; see also *Royal Commission on Labour, Minutes of Evidence,* P.P. 1893–4 (C. 7063), 39 Part 1, pp. 118–19; PRO, RG 29/19; RG 19/45.
[60]*Papers Relating to the Resignation of the Director of Special Inquiries and Reports,* P.P. 1903 (Cd. 1602), vol. 52.

the defects of the labor market was motivated as much by the fear that public ignorance and uncertainty might exacerbate social conflict and industrial unrest as by a positive commitment to social equity.

The investigative policy adopted by the board was also influenced by the economic philosophy of its staff. Although its more "progressive" statisticians and investigators rejected the wage-fund theory and orthodox economic assumptions, their overriding objectives remained the preservation of free enterprise, the security of capital, and the continuity and cost-competitiveness of industrial production. Despite their radical sympathies, they therefore perceived the aim of the department's labor investigatory work as preeminently one of "crisis avoidance."[61]

Accordingly, although traditional issues of hours and wage rates and working conditions (narrowly defined) received extensive coverage, the broader question of income distribution was evaded, as was the impact of technical and managerial innovation on the labor process.[62] In monitoring the process of unionization, Whitehall focused on trade-specific issues at the point of production rather than on more general economic and social factors. The government highlighted the conciliatory role of the trade union movement and its potential as a welfare agency rather than its more combative functions. Similarly, in investigating patterns of working-class income, expenditure, and standards of living, the Labour Department sought to demonstrate the normality of short-term fluctuations in wage rates according to market forces and the presumed long-term upward trend in real wages. Such data were expected to reduce labor unrest by illustrating the material "progress of the working classes," by revealing the high wage costs of production within British industry relative to those of Britain's competitors, and by deflating inflammatory claims about the extent of low-income destitution.[63]

Investigations of unemployment also were influenced by the crisis perceptions of investigators. A belief that disputes often originated in uncertainty about relative bargaining strengths at various stages of the business cycle inspired the Labour Department to construct an employment index. Other investigations stemmed from the fear that the perpetuation of a draconian Poor Law strategy toward the respectable

[61]See R. Davidson, "The Ideology of Labour Administration 1886–1914," *Bulletin of the Society for the Study of Labour History* 40 (1980): 29–31.
[62]See, e.g., *1st Report on Strikes and Lockouts*, P.P. 1887 (C. 5104), 89, pp. 7–9; *8th Report on Strikes and Lockouts*, P.P. 1896 (C. 8232), 93, pp. xv–xvi.
[63]See, e.g., *Memorandum on the Progress Made in Carrying Out the Arrangements for Collecting and Publishing Statistics Relating to Labour*, P.P. 1888 (433), 107, p. 4; PRO, LAB2/1555/L1099/1903.

unemployed would not only alienate them from the existing industrial system but also provoke their alliance with the casual "residuum" within the depressed inner-city areas and cause trade grievances to escalate into generic social unrest. The Board of Trade therefore sought to identify different categories of unemployed workers and unemployment, so that a package of measures could be implemented to mitigate the impact of cyclical unemployment on the incomes of deserving workers, while the undeserving idle were separated out for more deterrent measures.[64]

SOCIAL INVESTIGATION AND WELFARE POLICY

The nature and the extent of the impact of social investigation on late-Victorian and Edwardian social policy were shaped by the impulses and constraints that have been outlined. Serious methodological problems arise in any attempt to monitor the flow of information through the decision-making hierarchy and to evaluate its impact upon welfare policy,[65] because information was only one of the several resources that policymakers used in reaching a decision. Moreover, single reports regarding welfare issues were typically not used or applied in themselves. Officials accumulated evidence concerning a particular aspect of the problem, summarized it, and sent a report based on the compiled evidence to a policymaker. Rarely did a cabinet memorandum, a legislative proposal, or administrative guidelines directly draw on or quote an empirical study.

Nevertheless, the sequence of minuting on departmental files furnishes an excellent indicator of the extent to which investigative reports relating to welfare problems penetrated policy-making circles. The registration and preservation procedures of Whitehall departments also provide invaluable insight into the subsequent use of this information, briefing papers relating to policy issues being docketed together in sequence. Where the original data base is absent, the identity can often be extrapolated from policy memorandums. Such evidence reveals that, despite gaps, official welfare information fulfilled a formative role in defining policy options. This role was highly ambivalent. Although it served to enlighten social politics and to advance the more systematic treatment

[64]See, e.g., *Report on Agencies and Methods for Dealing with the Unemployed*, P.P. 1893–4 (C. 7182), 82, pp. 407–9.
[65]For a general discussion of the methodological problems involved, see R. F. Rich, *Social Science Information and Public Policy Making* (London: Jossey-Bass, 1981), 111–28.

of social problems, its primary effect was to ensure that policy initiatives were consistent with the needs of economic efficiency and social stability. The evolution of unemployment and minimum-wage policies during the 1880–1914 period furnish prime examples of this.

Between 1886 and 1906, state investigation of unemployment discredited a range of measures advocated by socialist, labor, and radical groups. Labor market information furnished by Whitehall to policymakers and the press served to counteract the image of unemployment fostered by such groups in their pursuit of the state regulation of employment. Official information regularly discredited left-wing estimates of the level of unemployment and the extent of the associated distress.[66] In briefing ministers and the cabinet, civil servants often "massaged" the information in order to present the most optimistic view of the state of the labor market.[67] Moreover, rather than furnishing the data base for a range of innovative, preventive measures, investigations such as the Select Committee on Distress from Want of Employment underscored the normality of cyclical unemployment in a maturing economy and provided a wide-ranging critique of proposals for public employment schemes.[68]

The majority of such measures were revealed to be irrelevant to the paramount needs of the "competent victims of trade fluctuations" or to be positively counterproductive. British and overseas relief schemes were portrayed as being patronized predominantly by occasional rather than year-round workers, thoroughly cost-ineffective, and a potential source of pauperization. Meanwhile, evidence derived from monitoring government-funded employment programs in New Zealand and New South Wales clearly indicated their minimal impact on the labor market and their propensity to erode work incentives and industrial discipline within the private sector.[69] Although official investigations did much to reveal the economic determinants of unemployment, implicit within their evaluation of demand-oriented strategies, such as counterdepressive public works, was the fear that they would endanger the investment fund and destabilize the capital market for private enterprise.

At the same time, social investigation served to discredit the more

[66]See, e.g., PRO, CAB 37/38; LAB 2/1478/L210/1903.
[67]See, e.g., PRO, LAB 2/1597/L117/1905.
[68]See the evidence of H. Llewellyn Smith to the *Select Committee on Distress from Want of Employment*, P.P. 1895 (365), 9, pp. 47–84.
[69]See, e.g., *Report on Agencies and Methods for Dealing with the Unemployed*, P.P. 1893–94 (C. 7182), 82, pp. 407–9; PRO, LAB2/213/L156/1904.

provocative and coercive schemes advocated by right-wing authoritarian ideologies aimed at segregating the unemployed from the normal labor market. Investigations into the causes of unemployment and the efficiency of existing agencies for dealing with the unemployed indicated that schemes such as regimented labor colonies could have at best only a peripheral effect on the level of employment and could provide no permanent solution to the aggregate problem of urban unemployment.[70] In particular, their rationale was shown to assume a degree of social engineering that lacked a sufficient empirical base. Social administrators emphasized that, in the absence of systematic data on the social incidence of unemployment and the industrial history of the unemployed, it was impossible to establish the existence and dimensions of an unemployed "class" or to differentiate between the so-called residuum (the congenitally unfit) and the respectable unemployed. Without such a distinction, evidence suggested that there was a real danger of using administrative procedures that, from Continental experience, were appropriate only to the suppression of vagabondage and vagrancy and would further politicize the unemployed as a movement and precipitate social unrest.[71]

Within the context of unemployment policy-making, official investigations during the 1886–1906 period therefore underscored the need, in the short term, to avoid drastic and contentious measures in favor of marginal innovations designed to widen the repertoire of relief provisions in the dispensation of local authorities. This strategy was broadly adopted in major guidelines issued by the Local Government Board in 1886 and 1892, the 1902 Labour Bureaus (London) Act, and the Unemployed Workmen Act of 1905. However, official investigation also indicated that, in the long run, the overriding aims of economic efficiency and social consensus would be best served by a policy option in which the regimentation *and* the welfare of the unemployed might be combined.

Welfare and labor market investigation played a vital role in realizing this option after 1906. Previous investigations had served to redefine the role of labor bureaus in unemployment policy. Official reports and ministerial briefings had consistently dismissed their potential for job creation. Detailed analyses of the performance of existing bureaus in Britain and overseas indicated that their net impact on unemployment during periods of generalized cyclical depression was minimal and that, given

[70]P.P. 1893–94 (C. 7182), 82, p. 407; P.P. 1895 (365), 9, questions 4977–8, 4992.
[71]See, e.g., PRO, LAB2/1555/L1099/1903.

the immobility of the labor force due to factors such as social and cultural ties, skill specificity, and the interdependence of family income, their ability to alleviate local pockets of structural unemployment also was slight.[72] In contrast, the potential of labor registries for conducting manpower surveillance and for providing systematic information about the composition and level of unemployment, on which selective welfare expenditure might be based, was increasingly identified in Whitehall and by a growing body of managerial opinion.[73] A national network of labor exchanges was explicitly viewed as an extension of the intelligence functions of Edwardian government by means of which the deserving, bona fide unemployed might be distinguished from the voluntarily idle and unemployable, and the supportive and coercive elements of welfare measures varied appropriately.

In particular, bureaucrats of the New Liberalism, such as Llewellyn Smith and Beveridge, viewed the data generated under the Labour Exchanges Act of 1909 as critical in regulating statutory measures of social insurance in accordance with the need for industrial efficiency.[74] By monitoring the demand for labor and the industrial record of welfare recipients, such data were designed to ensure (1) that work incentives and motivation were sustained despite the increasing security of working-class incomes provided by unemployment insurance; (2) that inefficient and disruptive patterns of industrial behavior or employment were identified and penalized; and (3) that the eligibility of beneficiaries was calculated primarily by reference, not to any criterion of social need or to any welfare right of citizenship, but to the recipients' conformity to the work ethic.

Social investigations undertaken by the state fulfilled a similar role in defining the scope of minimum-wage policy during the late-Victorian and Edwardian period. First, they greatly understated the extent of low-income destitution. The problem was identified as an anomaly of certain "diseased" and "parasitic" trades rather than as a general feature of the unskilled and secondary labor market. For both ideological and logistical reasons, the real dimensions of the mass of urban destitution resulting from low and irregular earnings remained uncharted, despite the constant demands from socialist and social radical groups for more detailed in-

[72]P.P. 1893–4 (C. 7182), 82, p. 406; PRO, LAB2/1477/L1294/1894.
[73]Hay, "Employers and Social Policy," 443.
[74]See Llewellyn Smith's Presidential Address to Section F of the British Association for the Advancement of Science, in *Transactions* (1910): 9–17.

formation. In collating wage and earnings data, Whitehall assiduously adhered to the traditional focus on average levels of pay rather than on inequalities within the pattern of industrial remuneration.

Minimum-wage campaigners viewed the limitations of official data as both sinister and inhibiting. At the height of the campaign for wage board legislation in 1907, Charles Dilke devoted his presidential address to the Royal Statistical Society to the lack of an empirical basis for the British welfare debate.[75] As the Anti-Sweating League pointed out, this omission had a vital impact on policy-making. By identifying low-income destitution as a problem specific to certain sweated occupations that were characterized by home work, female employment, and outdated technology, and were atypical of the general labor market, the government's investigators effectively restricted application of minimum-wage legislation before 1914 to a few isolated trades and diverted public policy from the general demand for a statutory minimum applicable to the work force as a whole.[76] Further, by demonstrating the abnormality of the labor market within such trades, Whitehall was able to dissociate the introduction of selective measures such as the 1909 Trade Boards Act (which provided machinery for fixing minimum rates of pay for chain making, paper box making, and garment making) from more general demands for a national minimum. In the context of minimum-wage policy, empirical and ideological constraints were therefore integrally linked.

The scope of minimum-wage policy was also confined by Whitehall's analysis of the causes of "sweated" labor. Rather than evaluating it as part of the broader exploitative relationships inherent in the production structure of British industry, official investigations interpreted it as primarily a function of localized imperfections in the machinery of collective bargaining, which produced levels of exploitation inimical to the efficiency of the work force and to the stability of wage levels within the urban labor market. The logic of such an approach was that the remedy for "sweating" lay in identifying and filling the more acute gaps in industrial organization rather than making any fundamental innovation in the criteria of wage determination, and it was precisely this order of priorities that shaped British minimum-wage legislation of the period.[77] The overriding objective was to underpin working-class associative effort

[75] *JRSS*, 70 (1907): 553–82.
[76] See, e.g., PRO, LAB2/19/TB2677/1914; National Anti-Sweating League, *Sweating and Wages Boards* (London: The League, 1909).
[77] Ford, *Social Theory and Social Practice*, 139.

either (as in the implementation of the Fair Wage Resolutions) by furnishing the trade union movement with data relating to traditional areas of low pay, such as public sector employment,[78] or (as in the formulation of the 1909 Trade Boards Act) by providing "surrogate" collective bargaining machinery for selected trades.[79]

In its provision of commercial and social information, Whitehall effectively resisted any broader terms of reference for government intervention in labor costs. It discredited the concept of statutory minimums as an alternative means of wage determination, provided a critical appraisal of overseas legislation, and denied welfare debate any rigorous assessment of wage norms necessary to ensure the physical efficiency and the subsistence of the work force. Although official inquiries often exposed the diseconomies of sweated labor and demonstrated the inability of even organized labor adequately to protect its purchasing power against irregular earnings, they did not sustain a radical critique of market forces. Whitehall's more interpretative labor statistics suggested that, as far as possible, factor costs should remain flexible if profit margins and investment incentives were to be sustained, and that any attempt to impose social rather than commercial criteria on wage determination might seriously undermine the viability of British enterprise. Broader considerations, such as fluctuations in the cost of living, might legitimately play a role in wage regulation only if they did not significantly disturb the vital nexus between wage levels and the value of output, and were not permitted to exert a ratchet effect on labor costs.[80] According to the Board of Trade's investigation of overseas labor legislation, it was precisely these conditions that Australasian minimum-wage measures failed to observe. Indeed, British official welfare information was in marked contrast to the mainstream contemporary welfare literature, typified by the works of Pember Reeves, in focusing on the deficiencies rather than the virtues of the measures taken overseas.

Meanwhile, in addressing issues of industrial remuneration, official statisticians and investigators refused to provide any official poverty line or to establish a data base on which national or regional minimums might be constructed. To a limited extent, they were prepared to furnish a

---

[78]PRO, LAB2/1479/L2343/1893.

[79]H. A. Clegg, A. Fox, and A. F. Thompson, *A History of British Trade Unions Since 1889, Vol. 1: 1889–1910* (Oxford: Oxford University Press, 1964), 404.

[80]See especially P.P. 1913 (268), 13, p. 11; Davidson, "The Board of Trade and Industrial Relations," 584–7.

profile of existing working-class income and consumption patterns but not to extend their analysis to identify a subsistence or living wage that might form the basis of statutory regulations. Indeed, they remained remarkably resistant to constructing any authoritative index of real wages with which to illuminate the minimum-wage debate.[81]

MANAGED REFORM

It is evident that, for logistical and ideological reasons, welfare debate and policy formation between 1880 and 1914 lacked the informational basis for systematic social engineering consistent with the more coercive strategies of social control. Nor does this study support a simple conspiracy theory of social legislation as being purely a function of the values and perceptions of the financial and industrial elite within market capitalism. The ambivalence or active resistance of that elite to government inquiries has been demonstrated, reflecting a policy-making process that incorporated a range of competing elites, including bureaucratic and professional groups whose status and aspirations were less directly and less critically dependent on the imperatives of the market. Nonetheless, an analysis of the rationale and scope of civil intelligence in late-Victorian and Edwardian Britain clearly registers the need to recognize the more elitist and manipulative aspects of social reform.

First, the ad hoc, fragmented pattern of investigation and its lack of focus on the structural causes and context of welfare problems were inconsistent with any substantive program of social reconstruction. The data base of policy-making was not designed to address the systemic problems of exploitation and deprivation produced by the social relationships of production. Instead, it reflected the overriding concern of the policymakers to contain social unrest, to reestablish industrial consensus, and to secure a stable environment within which the vitality of the British economy might be restored. Thus, the empirical basis of legislative initiatives was more compatible with a static, restorative concept of reform than with a dynamic, regenerative ideology of state intervention. It was essentially a reactive empiricism engendered by the "crisis" perceptions of the governing classes.

Second, official investigation did not conform to a "progressive" model of social reform, because the issues addressed, the phenomena and re-

[81]See, e.g., *Select Committee on Post Office Pay, Minutes of Evidence*, P.P. 1913 (268), 12, p. 1437.

lationships monitored, and the framework of the analysis adopted were primarily oriented to the market rather than to welfare. They frequently reflected a concern with the competitive needs of industry rather than with the social needs of the working classes; a concern with the cost and efficiency of labor as a factor of production rather than its welfare rights of citizenship. Welfare investigation mirrored a government perception of the "Social Problem" as preeminently a problem of market imperfections rather than of social deprivation; intellectual and welfare historians have signally ignored the degree to which, throughout most of the late-Victorian and Edwardian period, official investigations subordinated social politics to industrial and commercial issues.

Even when official investigators did confront the distributional aspects of the "Social Problem," they evaded the more contentious welfare issues of income inequality, focusing instead on the industrial and fiscal implications of the patterns and elasticities of working-class demand. Investigations were clearly not designed to establish any normative welfare values of income and consumption with which existing levels of working-class remuneration and expenditure might be compared. Data on wage earnings and costs of living and on housing, health, and education were symptomatic of government concern with the efficiency of human capital stock rather than indicative of any programmatic commitment to the minimum wage as an exercise in redistributive justice.

This focus of social investigation on economic rather than welfare concerns was also indicative of the disciplinary and regulatory aspects of social reform. Many investigations, such as those relating to labor unrest, pauperism, vagrancy, and unemployment, while clearly motivated in part by a commitment to monitor areas of social distress and destitution, reflected also a strong concern to identify groups within society for whom the normal controls of the work ethic and industrial discipline were either unacceptable or inoperative. Similarly, considerations of productive efficiency as well as of social amelioration appear to have underpinned government inquiries into such problems as underemployment, sweated labor, and physical deterioration, reflecting an overriding concern of policymakers with the impact of the residuum on the equilibrium of the urban labor market and hence the earnings potential and motivation of the regular skilled and semiskilled work force. To the extent that attention was directed at the social rather than economic repercussions of idleness and low-income destitution, the categories of analysis retained strong overtones of conventional middle-class individualism, echoing Whitehall's intention to preserve within welfare measures the moral and economic sanctions of "less-eligibility."

Furthermore, the rationale and scope of welfare investigation did not indicate a pluralist structure of social policy-making, incorporating the popular demands and aspirations of organized labor. It clearly reflected the paternalism of prewar social administration in which labor was perceived and treated as a problem amenable to administrative solution imposed unilaterally from above, rather than as a "class" whose aspirations required a fundamental shift in the ideology and personnel of social policy-making.

This study suggests that, during the 1880–1914 period, the investigatory response of British government to social problems had significant limitations. There were several reasons: (1) logistical and institutional constraints (for example, problems associated with financial accountability and with bureaucratic resistance to the refinement and centralization of official data), (2) broader societal resistance to the provision of information and to the inquisitorial role of the state, and (3) the social and operational philosophy of policy-makers and their advisers. During a period of economic and social crisis, or perceived crisis, welfare investigation was viewed largely as a means to present social problems as "manageable" within the existing framework of social theory and administration. As a result, official investigation often failed to address the more structural issues underlying the welfare debate. Thus, although the investigative role of the state undoubtedly provided a dynamic element in late-Victorian and Edwardian government growth, it also acted in some important respects to constrain the content and outcome of social politics.

Part III

Pluralism, skepticism, and the modern state

7

Think tanks, antistatism, and democracy:
the nonpartisan ideal and policy research
in the United States, 1913–1987

DONALD T. CRITCHLOW

Because of the complexity of advanced industrial systems, all modern
governments require an enormous range of specialized knowledge and
administrative expertise with which to order their affairs. This dependence of government on knowledge is recognized by leading students of
the structure and processes of modern states. For Gianfranco Poggi, for
example, a vital stage in modern state development was the "rationalization of rule," in which governments gave up the claim to rule by right
and made knowledge the recognized basis not only of specific policies
but of the very claim to sovereignty.[1]

Uniformity in demand has not produced uniformity in the character
and organization of the supply of knowledge for government purposes.
There are significant variations, linked to diverse cultural traditions, in
the sources and methods of applying expertise. In Western Europe and
Japan, for example, central government bureaucracies directly provide
many more sources and opportunities for the development of policy
expertise and administrative personnel than they do in the United States,
which relies heavily on private research organizations operating outside
government bureaucracies for functional expertise. As the federal role in

The author wishes to thank Ellis Hawley, Mary Furner, and Robert Cuff for their help
and advice.

[1]Gianfranco Poggi, "The Modern State and the Idea of Progress," in Gabriel Almond, ed.,
Progress and Its Discontents (Berkeley, 1982). See also Robert Lane, "The Decline of
Politics and Ideology in a Knowledgeable Society," *American Sociological Review* (October
1966): 649–62; and Martin Bulmer, ed., *Social Science Research and Government* (Cambridge, 1987).

economic and social policy expanded in the post–World War II era, increased federal funding did not produce a commensurate increase in the size of government. Instead it strengthened the complicated network of relationships among the federal government, state and local governments, and private groups, including nonpartisan research institutes. As Hugh Heclo has shown, federal employment increased less than one-fifth from 1955 to 1980, while federal spending rose from $22 billion to $167 billion, principally for federal payments to individuals for Social Security, health care, veterans' pensions, unemployment insurance, and public assistance. To implement these programs, following a characteristic pattern of devolution, the federal government operated indirectly, through intermediary organizations in state and local government, and in civil society.[2]

The think tanks, as the independent research institutions that have provided much of the needed policy advice are popularly known, are a peculiarly American social invention, and an understudied one. To suggest the scope and variety of institutions of this kind and to establish context for the discussion that follows, the accompanying table details the founding dates and subjects of interest for a selection of twenty of the more prominent Washington area policy research institutes.[3]

The think tanks fulfill a variety of functions. They provide intellectual underpinnings for policy, they equip and train pools of experts available for government posts, and they offer holding environments for those unlucky enough to lose office. Hugh Heclo, among recent commentators, portrays the entire American policy process as dominated by fluid networks of policy specialists, who operate in and between government and the private sector, identifying policy issues, generating "solutions" to policy problems, and overseeing and evaluating the implementation and administration of policies within their specific areas of competence. Although the think tanks are ostensibly nonpartisan, in some instances they function as extensions of state power, coming into and falling out of

[2] Hugh Heclo, "Issue Networks and the Executive Establishment," in Anthony King, ed., *The New American Political System* (Washington, D.C., 1980), 87–124.

[3] For studies on the think tanks, see James A. Smith, *The Idea Brokers: Think Tanks and the Rise of the New Policy Elite* (New York, 1991); Paul Dixon, *Think Tanks* (New York, 1971); Joseph G. Peschek, *Policy-Planning Organizations: Elite Agendas and America's Rightward Turn* (Philadelphia, 1987); David W. Eakins, "The Development of Corporate Liberal Policy Research in the United States, 1885–1965," Ph.D. diss., University of Wisconsin, 1966; Guy Alchon, *The Invisible Hand of Planning* (Princeton, N.J., 1985); and Donald T. Critchlow, *The Brookings Institution, 1916–1952: Expertise and the Public Interest in a Democratic Society* (De Kalb, Ill., 1985).

Prominent think tanks in the Washington, D.C., area

Institution	Date founded	Research areas
American Enterprise Institute (AEI)	1943	Government regulations; economics, health, energy; foreign affairs; voluntary organizations and intermediary institutions; religion and politics; constitutional studies
Brookings Institution	1916	Economics, domestic and international; U.S. social policies and programs; government and political institutions; regulation; trade and industrial policy; regional studies of United States; U.S. relations with Soviet Union, East Asia; Middle East
Carnegie Endowment for International Peace	1910	International affairs and U.S. foreign policy; Middle East; U.S.-Soviet relations; South Africa; arms control; international law and organization; nuclear proliferation
CATO Institute	1977	U.S. public policy, foreign and domestic; economics; international trade and regulations; education; banking policy; U.S.-Soviet relations
Center for Judicial Studies	1982	Roles and activities of federal judiciary, problems of judicial policy-making, courts and social policy; issues of constitutional law; evaluation of federal judges
Center for National Security Studies (affiliated with American Civil Liberties Union)	1974	Secrecy, classification, intelligence agencies, national security institutions and policies; administration of Freedom of Information Act and related statutes
Center for Strategic and International Studies (CSIS)	1962	Energy; international economics and business; international resources; maritime studies; crisis management; arms control; political-military affairs; regional studies
Economic Policy Institute	1985	Trade and fiscal policies; trends in wages, income, and prices; analyses of privatization proposals; productivity, labor market problems; rural and urban policies; state-level economic strategies
Environmental Law Institute (ELI)	1969	Administrative, economic, scientific-technical aspects of environmental policy; regulatory enforcement and reform; air and water pollution control; toxic substances, hazardous wastes; wetlands management
Ethics and Public Policy Center	1976	Analysis of public policy activities of Protestant, Catholic, and Jewish institutions and organizations; business-government relations; business ethics; government educational policy and practice; military and foreign policy
Free Congress Research and Education Foundation	1977	Educational, social, and family policy; judicial reform; ballot initiatives; electoral behavior and theory; public opinion
Heritage Foundation	1973	U.S. public policy, foreign and domestic; social policy, economics; regulation; education; environment; judiciary; privatization

Prominent think tanks (continued)

Institution	Date founded	Research areas
Institute for International Economics	1981	International economic issues; international trade, investment, and monetary policies; exchange rates; international debt; interaction of economic and foreign policy goals
Institute for Policy Studies (IPS)	1963	National security; foreign policy; human rights; international economic order; knowledge and politics; domestic reconstruction; arms control and disarmament; women in developing countries; transnational corporations; race and class; science and technology
International Law Institute (ILI)	1955	American and international antitrust law; trade agreements; investment policy and problems; comparative studies of corporation and labor law; economic development; technology transfer; arbitration
Joint Center for Political Studies	1970	Politics and public policy; with special reference to impact on minorities and disadvantaged people; social and economic conditions of African Americans; political participation of minorities; problems of elected minority leadership
National Women's Law Center	1972	Policies and practices in both public and private sectors as they affect women; women's legal rights; employment, education; income security, child support, public assistance; Social Security, pensions, and taxes
Overseas Development Council	1969	International trade and industrial policy; international investment and finance; development strategies; U.S. policy toward the third world; World Bank policies and programs; U.S.-Mexican relations; Soviet activities in the third world
Resources for the Future (RFF)	1952	Social science aspects of problems associated with development, conservation, and efficient use of natural resources; land, water, minerals, air; environmental quality; energy policy
Urban Institute (UI)	1968	Domestic social and economic affairs; health policy; housing and community development; human resources; income security and pensions; public finance; productivity, employment, and training; women and family policy; minorities and social policy; demography

Source: Adapted from information in *Research Centers Directory*, 17th ed. (Detroit, 1993), a guide to 12,000 university-related and other nonprofit research organizations established on a permanent basis and carrying on continuing research programs.

influence with changes in governments and shifts in the ideological climate of the country. In other cases the think tanks function more independently, questioning and monitoring state strategies and structures. For example, the Rand Corporation of the 1940s and 1950s was designed to strengthen the programs of the U.S. Air Force, whereas in the 1960s the Institute for Policy Studies (IPS) was a major center of criticism of U.S. foreign policy and of domestic social programs and policies in the areas of civil rights and poverty, among others.[4]

Often the ideological orientation of the tanks has reflected changes in the historical context and political climate, as indicated by the dominant trends in high and popular culture, changes in voting behavior, and shifts in political leadership such as occurred between the cold-war consensus of the 1950s and the crisis and breakup of centrist liberalism that accompanied the emergence of a polymorphous counterculture in the 1960s, when left-oriented institutes such as the IPS appeared on the scene. Between those days of rage and confrontation and the "Reagan revolution" of the 1980s, a new ideological climate opened the way to influence for think tanks—such as the Heritage Foundation—that denied the efficacy of regulation and welfare programs and offered a rationale for deregulation and privatization.

As indicated later, research groups such as the Brookings Institution and the American Enterprise Institute have gone through various incarnations over the decades, reflecting a capacity to adopt different attitudes toward the role of government and toward specific policy issues at different times in their history. Contemporary institutions also reveal that there is space in the knowledge-policy continuum for very different commitments along the political spectrum, currently stretching from the democratic socialism of the IPS to the free-market conservatism of the Heritage Foundation.

World War II, and the postwar continuation of a large defense program as well as expansion of New Deal social programs, was obviously a watershed in the evolution of the American think tank. As Nelson Polsby has observed, at the end of the war Americans made a political decision to have government train, subsidize, and regularly consult a sizable population of civilian experts on such issues as defense, welfare, health, and

[4]Heclo, "Issue Networks," passim. See also Jack Walker, "The Diffusion of Knowledge, Policy Communities, and Agenda Setting: The Relationship of Knowledge and Power," in John Tropman, Milar Dlahey, Roger Lind, eds., *Strategic Horizons of Social Policy* (New York, 1973).

economic stability. Yet, as the preceding table indicates, not all of the Washington area think tanks originated after World War II. An explanation of their origins and the patterns of their growth, and particularly of their peculiarly private-public character, requires appreciation of a number of historical traditions, which are explored in this chapter.[5]

The factors that have encouraged the development of think tanks include the entrepreneurial origins of American philanthropy, buttressed by tax laws that allow the preservation of large fortunes in forms that permit and even encourage patronage of activities with policy consequences, so long as they are not overtly partisan; and the constitutional fragmentation of power, which provides the legal setting for a porous and conflicted governmental system and encourages efforts at penetration. There are also policy traditions of a more nebulous kind that flow from American political culture—above all, a deeply entrenched distrust of centralized state power, which had its origins in Revolutionary-era republicanism and classical nineteenth-century liberalism, and which has helped to preclude the federal government's taking an activist planning role and to encourage the government's abandonment of such a role after it has appeared in times of national emergency, such as World War I. And there are the presumptions in the American tradition of wisdom inhering in the people, of the primacy of civil society over the state, and of the virtues of voluntarism.[6]

Some historians and social scientists have interpreted the evolution of think tanks as a fairly obvious instrument of corporate social control—a means of removing issues from the arena of electoral politics, shrouding them in expertise, and promoting corporate capitalist hegemony.[7] This

[5]Nelson Polsby, "Tanks But No Tanks," *Public Opinion* (April–May 1983): 14–16, 58–9.

[6]The link between the absence of active state planning and think tanks must be qualified, not only because some agencies (e.g., the Tennessee Valley Authority, the Department of Agriculture, the Atomic Energy Commission, the National Aeronautics and Space Administration, and the Department of Defense) have long had planning roles, but also because other countries currently without central state planning, such as Britain, have far less of a think-tank tradition. Canada also has no significant think-tank phenomenon, even though it possesses a comparatively strong party history, a minority democratic socialist strain, and a public enterprise tradition. It is also necessary to specify what state planning means. Certainly Japanese bureaucrats at the Ministry of International Trade and Industry claim that Japan is not a "planning state"; it may be a "developmental state," but only if a fiercely competitive business system is allowed into the definitional mix.

[7]For various views of the connections between corporate capital and state power, see G. William Domhoff, *The Higher Circles: The Governing Class in America* (New York, 1970); Nico Poulantzas, "Political Power and Social Classes," translated by Timothy O'Hagen (London, 1973); Fred Black, "The Ruling Class Does Not Rule: Notes on the Marxist

chapter suggests that although foundations and corporate donors have indeed figured prominently in the financing of think tanks, the complexity of their motives, as well as those of other advocates for and inhabitants of the tanks, including the academics and professionals who staff them, precludes any such simple cause-and-effect equation. At least at the start, the think tanks can better be related to a persistent distrust of the state, expressed in various ways by different groups of Americans, that has resulted in the placement of a large portion of policy analysis and initiatives in the private sector. Along with antistatism, a related and equally potent factor has been a persistent antipathy to party politics, rooted in a republican conception of civic virtue as the capacity to rise above self-interest and the spirit of faction. To reinforce this connection, one need only reflect on the fact that the first think tanks appeared during the progressive era, when large numbers of educated Americans, horrified by a party system that seemed hopelessly mired in corruption, identified superior government with the nonpartisan ideal.[8]

THE BROOKINGS INSTITUTION

There is no clearer embodiment of this central theme, linking the suppression of partisanship and the cultivation of expertise, than the Brookings Institution, founded in 1927 as a successor to the Institute for Government Research (IGR). Robert S. Brookings was one of a group of reformers who had been involved in establishing the IGR in 1916 as a mechanism to argue the case for extracting the national budget-making process from log-rolling congressional politics and turning it over to nonpartisan experts in the executive branch. Part of a larger movement for efficiency and economy in government, the IGR was modeled on the independent municipal research bureaus that proliferated during the progressive era as vehicles for an assault by progressive capitalists and middle-class reformers on the inefficiency and corruption associated with

Theory of the State," *Socialist Revolution* (May–June 1977): 6–28; and Theda Skocpol, "Political Response to Capitalist Crisis: Neo-Marxist Theories of the State and the Case of the New Deal," *Politics and Society* (1975): 155–99.

[8] Woodrow Wilson noted a "reaction against democracy" and called for the development of "expert organization, if our government is to be preserved." "Democracy and Efficiency," *Atlantic Monthly* (March 1901), in *Selected Literary and Political Papers of Woodrow Wilson* (New York, 1925), vol. 1, 112. See also Stephen Skowronek, *Building a New American State: The Expansion of National Administrative Capacities, 1877–1920* (Cambridge, 1982). On depoliticization, see Walter Dean Burnham, *Critical Elections and the Mainsprings of American Politics* (New York, 1970), 71–90.

boss rule. As cochairman of the War Industries Board, Brookings recognized that efficient government and responsible economic oversight during postwar reconversion depended on the availability of basic information concerning industrial resources and capacity, aggregate output, and manpower. "Practically all of the problems which have been submerging the world since the signing of the Armistice are economic problems," he contended, "more or less poisoned by political traditions." In 1922, with a $200,000 grant from the Carnegie Corporation, Brookings established two sister organizations to the IGR, the Institute of Economics and a graduate school bearing his name. The mission of these bodies was to produce a cadre of scientifically trained recruits to enter government service and bring new expertise to bear on public policy.[9]

That Brookings saw the need for an economics research institute in the nation's capital indicates the visionary qualities of this rather eccentric entrepreneur from St. Louis. A progressive businessman who made a fortune in the dry goods trade and in the building of Cupples Station—in its day, the most modern freight station in the country—Brookings showed a strong distaste for business and a distrust of most businessmen. A cultured man who once forsook business for a career as a concert violinist, a bachelor who never smoked or drank, Brookings stood as an outsider to most business circles. His closest friends were philanthropists such as Andrew Carnegie, who shared his ambition to build new institutions that might reshape the capitalist system, preserving the opportunity that had allowed the rise of self-made men such as themselves even in the new world of corporate capitalism.

Brookings had essentially a corporatist vision of economic cooperation between classes and a reduction of partisan controversy. Seeking rationalization and accommodation of conflicting interests, he advocated profit sharing, election of workers to the boards of their companies, agricultural cooperatives, and a common trading market for Europe. Although he considered the development of the modern corporation inevitable and largely beneficial, like many progressives he favored federal incorporation laws and a trade commission with access to corporate books, on the

[9]Charles Thomson, *The Institute for Government Research* (Princeton N.J., 1956); Martin T. Schiesl, *The Politics of Efficiency: Municipal Administration and Reform in America, 1890–1920* (Berkeley, 1977); Herman Hagedorn, *Brookings: A Biography* (New York, 1937), passim, quotation at p. 261; and "Proposal to the Carnegie Foundation," Minutes of the Institute of Economics Board of Trustees, January 5, 1922, in Brookings Institution Files (hereafter BIF), Washington, D.C.

ground that only "intelligent public supervision" would serve "to protect the public and trade alike from grasping intractable minorities." Here again, as with the newly founded institutes, reliable information on social and economic conditions was expected to provide the basis of efficiency and harmony.[10]

To head the new Institute of Economics, Brookings recruited Harold G. Moulton, a young economist from the University of Chicago who had gained a reputation as an innovator in banking theory. Moulton accepted the post only after he was assured that the new institute was not intended as a partisan businessmen's lobby on the order of the National Industrial Conference Board. Until his death in 1932, Brookings shielded the institute's research programs from trustee interference.

In 1927 he disbanded the graduate school, which had not succeeded in sending its graduates into government service, and merged the IGR and the Institute of Economics to form the organization bearing his name, the Brookings Institution. Under Moulton, who retained the presidency until 1952, the Brookings Institution renewed its commitment to non-partisanship, based on a nineteenth-century faith in disinterested research and scientific objectivity that Moulton maintained, in the face of rising philosophical relativism, as the best defense of the general interest against the special interests of party and class, the frequent disruptions of electoral politics, and the excesses of democracy.[11]

There is evidence for this nonaligned position in the subjects the Brookings Institution investigated and the enemies it made. In the 1920s, Brookings economists tackled the knotty problems of international trade and finance and, to the consternation of the Hoover-era Republicans, recommended a general reduction of tariffs and a scaling down of war debts. Isador Lubin's study of wages and profits in the coal industry provoked some red-baiting by the coal magnates. And a study of government assistance to Native Americans was denounced by the Bureau of Indian Affairs.[12]

[10]Robert Brookings, *Economic Democracy: America's Answer to Socialism and Communism* (New York, 1929); and idem, *Industrial Ownership: Its Economic and Social Consequences* (New York, 1928).

[11]Minutes of the Institute of Economics Board of Trustees, April 21–22, 1922, BIF; Moulton to Brookings, January 11, 1924, ibid.; and Charles B. Saunders, Jr., *The Brookings Institution: A Fifty-Year History* (Washington, D.C., 1966).

[12]On foreign economic policy, see Harold G. Moulton and Leo Pasvolsky, *World War Debt Settlements* (New York, 1924); Harold G. Moulton, *America and the Balance Sheet of Europe* (Washington, D.C., 1924); Moulton and Pasvolsky, *The French Debt Problem* (Washington, D.C., 1925); and Moulton, *War Debts and Prosperity* (Washington, D.C.,

The consistent theme in Brookings social criticism became apparent in the 1930s, when the institution became increasingly critical of New Deal liberalism, as Roosevelt's policies shifted toward Keynesianism and the managerial state. Ideals such as nonpartisanship and scientific objectivity were compatible with Moulton's belief that "in the long run decisions of the market place are the truest guide to economic production and development," and with his fear that deficit spending would politicize economic policy, tempting politicians to court interest groups, and bring on inflation. Brookings studies criticized the National Recovery Administration, the Agricultural Adjustment Administration, securities regulation, Roosevelt's proposals for government reorganization, and New Deal labor policy.[13]

Even in the midst of these controversies, the Brookings Institution tried to avoid becoming directly involved in partisan politics. For instance, Moulton delayed the publication of Edwin Nourse's critical study of the Agricultural Adjustment Administration and New Deal farm policy until after the election of 1936 to avoid the appearance of siding with Roosevelt's political opponents. Yet by 1937 the institution's criticisms of New Deal policies provoked the resignation of Frederic Delano, FDR's uncle, as chairman of the Brookings board of trustees. Moulton warned in his annual report that the "federal budget situation will present perhaps the most important single problem" for the nation; castigated Keynes for failing to understand "the basic principles of economic reasoning"; and counseled fellow economists, many leaning in that direction, to beware the "New Economics."[14]

Moulton carried his crusade against the New Deal into the war by refusing to relent in his attacks on deficit spending and the theory behind

1932). On the coal industry, Walton Hamilton and H. Wright, *The Way to Order in the Bituminous Coal Industry* (Washington, D.C., 1928); Isador Lubin, *Miners' Wages and the Cost of Coal* (New York, 1924); Director of the Institute of Economics, "Report to the Board of Trustees" (1924), in BIF. On the Indian administration question, see Lewis Meriam et al., *The Problem of Indian Administration* (Washington, D.C., 1927); and G. Lindquist to Charles A. Burke, December 12, 1929, Papers of the Indian Administration, National Archives.

[13] Moulton, "Economic Problems Today" (June 1931), BIF; Moulton, *Recovery Problem in the United States* (Washington, D.C., 1937); Saunders, *Brookings Institution*, 43–62.

[14] Edwin A. Nourse et al., *Three Years of the Agricultural Adjustment Administration* (Washington, D.C., 1937); and Brookings Institution, "President's Annual Report, May 22, 1936," BIF. On Keynes, personal communication of James C. Nelson to the author, February 10, 1975; and Moulton, "Economic Essentials Today," speech to the Union League Club, January 31, 1939; and Moulton, "The National Debt—Retrospect and Prospect," speech to the Citizens' Conference on Government Management, Estes Park, Colorado, June 17, 1940, BIF.

the policy. A principal target became the National Resources Planning Board (NRPB), an agency established in the early 1930s to oversee the effects of New Deal policies on the nation. Although the NRPB never really developed into a central planning agency, for businessmen and members of Congress who opposed the New Deal it represented a symbol of Roosevelt's intent to establish a planned economy. In 1943 the NRPB further alienated anti-Roosevelt forces when it proposed that the federal government provide minimum security for all Americans through the establishment of national health insurance, an extensive public works program to maintain full employment, and the extension of the Social Security system to farm and domestic workers, disabled persons, and dependents.[15]

This threatened comprehensive and permanent reliance on an interventionist state mobilized opponents of government planning. Moulton contributed to the attack, both on the NRPB, which he saw as "a vicious body, a menace to the American people," and on those members of the economics profession such as Alvin Hansen who had forsaken "sound" economics for Keynesian doctrine. Brookings investigations provided fodder for conservative opponents of New Deal statism. Moulton's widely circulated assault on the NRPB won praise from one Republican congressman for revealing the "dangerous infiltration of our government by these enemies of our American way of life for the purpose of undermining and destroying this government of ours."

In the immediate postwar years Moulton became a frequent speaker before civic groups, business conventions, and professional conferences, warning repeatedly that the government had drifted into "uncharted seas, if not state socialism," and calling for an end to "regimentation." During the Truman administration the institution opposed wage and price controls, national health insurance, extension of Social Security, and other social programs on the ground that they would eliminate the discipline of the market and undermine the character of the American people.[16]

---

[15]Moulton, *Controlling Factors in Economic Development* (Washington, D.C., 1949); Moulton and Schlotterbeck, *Should Price Controls Be Retained?* (Washington, D.C., 1945); George W. Bachman and Lewis Meriam, *The Issue of Compulsory Health Insurance* (Washington, D.C., 1944); and Lewis Meriam and Karl T. Schlotterbeck, *The Costs and Finances of Social Security* (Washington, D.C., 1950).

[16]Moulton, *The New Philosophy of the Public Debt* (Washington, D.C., 1943); *Congressional Record*, 78th Cong., p. 1212; A 108, 1146; and Moulton speeches, "Government and Postwar Business Policy," November 17, 1943, "Government Finance and Economic Development," November 18, 1943, and "Economic Potentials and Requirements," November 3, 1929, BIF.

While the basic welfare programs of the New Deal were not undone, the advance of government planning was halted, and in that sense the institution's efforts, along with those of other conservative agencies, were successful—but at a price. Increasingly, academics doubted Moulton's claims to objectivity, criticized the centralization of power at the institution in his hands, and questioned the quality of Brookings personnel and the value of Brookings research. Liberals who favored further reforms called Moulton a mouthpiece for corporate interests, and conservatives who commended the institution's stands on domestic social policy were repelled by its liberal-internationalist views in foreign policy.

By the early 1950s the Brookings Institution appeared to have gone gray. Moulton offered to resign in 1948 but remained in office, while the research program languished, until, in 1952, Robert Calkins, head of the General Education Fund at the Rockefeller Foundation, finally agreed to head the institution.[17]

In the three decades since Moulton had come to Washington in 1922, the world of policy had changed in two significant ways. First, Republicans, by accepting the basics of the New Deal program, the Social Security system, parts of the welfare and regulatory state, and internationalism in foreign affairs, allowed a broad policy consensus to be reached. The period from the 1950s through the 1970s would be characterized by the politics of incrementalism, exemplified in the broad bipartisan support for extension of Social Security. Both parties agreed on the need for automatic stabilizers and some discretionary spending through transfer payments and defense expenditures. Moreover, both Democrats and Republicans discovered that discretionary spending through increases in transfer payments or defense appropriations could be politically beneficial.

A second significant change from the 1920s was the greatly increased demand for expertise in policy innovation and program evaluation engendered by the growth of government activity stemming from this incremental politics. Crucial political decisions such as the defeat of the NRPB limited government's ability to undertake systematic or long-term planning; as a result, as noted earlier, government bureaucracy expanded much more slowly than government spending. Yet the alternative system of delivering social programs through intermediary organizations created

---

[17]Joseph H. Willits, "Memorandum Concerning Jerome Greene," May 9, 1947, Brookings File, Rockefeller Foundation Archives [hereafter RFA]; Saunders, *Brookings,* 76; Milton Lehman, "Oracle of Lafayette Square," *Nation's Business* (May 1950).

a demand for expertise in those organizations and encouraged professional groups, lobbyists, lawyers, and others to form around the differential effects of various social programs. As policy questions became increasingly technical and complex and professional groups multiplied, a splintering process occurred in which a specialized subculture, composed of highly knowledgeable policy watchers, or to use Hugh Heclo's phrase, "policy networks," was created. With the emergence of this highly differentiated market for policy specialists, the Brookings Institution found new opportunities in the world of policy analysis at the same time that it experienced increased competition from new think tanks.[18]

In response to this new environment and the reluctance of foundations to fund an institution they perceived as ineffective or out of touch, Calkins rebuilt the Brookings in the early 1950s, bringing it into the ideological mainstream. He reorganized the institution into three separate research divisions: Economic Studies under Calkins, Government Studies under Paul David, and Foreign Policy Studies under Robert W. Hartly. He cut the staff in half, easing out conservative holdovers from the Moulton era and recruiting people with liberal credentials and government experience. Economists such as Walter Salant and Joseph Pechman exemplified the new effort to transform the institution into a major policy research center operating within the assumptions of the liberal consensus. Salant was a Keynesian who had served as a staff economist with the Roosevelt Commerce Department, the Truman Council of Economic Advisers (CEA), the North Atlantic Treaty Organization, and the Committee on Economic Trade Policy. Pechman also brought extensive government experience, at the Treasury (1946–53), as a member of the CEA (1954–6), and as an economist for the Committee for Economic Development.[19]

Moving in and out of public service as situations demanded their expertise, these people and others like them at the new Brookings established close ties with government, and, unlike the devotees of the earlier nonpartisan ideal, aligned themselves closely with presidential administrations. For the incoming Kennedy staff, the Brookings Institution drafted a series of transition papers, not disclosed to the press or public, that aided in a smooth transfer of power between opposing parties.

---

[18]Heclo, "Issue Networks," 87–124.
[19]Joseph H. Willits to Robert Calkins, January 18, 1952, RFA; Robert Calkins to Dr. Gow, October 29, 1953, BIF; Robert Calkins interview with James Farrell, November 15, 1976, Washington, D.C.; and Kenneth Thompson memorandum on H. Field Haviland, March 11, 1953, RFA.

Extending these ties, Calkins established a Conference for Federal Executives to offer senior career executives a chance to discuss a wide range of policy issues with experts; a similar Advanced Study Program was offered to corporate executives.

By 1965, when Calkins retired, the Brookings Institution was representative of mainstream economic thinking, and its growing influence was reflected in renewed foundation support, including a Ford Foundation grant of $14 million, $10 million of which was to be used for endowment purposes. In the subsequent Kermit Gordon era (1965–76), Brookings's reputation as a liberal Democratic think tank became further entrenched. In a surprise appearance on Brookings's fiftieth anniversary, Lyndon Johnson reinforced the impression when he declared, "You are a national institution, so important to, at least to the Executive branch— and I think to Congress and the country—that if you did not exist, we would have to ask someone to create you."[20]

Between the mid-1960s and the mid-1970s, the institution was both a major research center and a holding area for policy experts who were temporarily out of office. Gordon recruited Gilbert Steiner from the University of Illinois to head the Government Studies program and enticed Henry Owens to leave the State Department to reorganize and expand the Foreign Policy Studies program. Among the leading scholars in residence were Arthur Okun, George Perry, Henry Aaron, Charles Schultze, and Alice Rivlin in economics; Herbert Kaufman, Martha Derthick, and James Sundquist in government; and A. Doak Barnett, C. Fred Bergsten, Lawrence Kraus, William Cline, and Joseph Grunwald in foreign policy.

The institution also expanded into new areas of research. Okun and Perry initiated the *Brookings Papers on Economic Activity,* and Schultze edited *Setting National Priorities,* which analyzed the president's budget and suggested alterations. In 1967 Henry Owens expanded the Foreign Policy Studies program to include a Defense Analysis Group, which produced fifteen major studies from 1971 to 1976; other researchers targeted the social and economic problems of Asia and Latin America. Reflecting the priorities of the expanded welfare state, the institution produced studies on revenue sharing, health care, housing, education, welfare, and taxation. Yet, illustrating the institution's capacity for breaking new ground in policy studies, Brookings researchers also did important work

---

[20]Saunders, *Brookings,* 98–9; Theodore Sorenson, *Kennedy* (New York, 1965), 229–30; "The Gordon Years," *The Brookings Bulletin* (Fall–Winter 1976). The Johnson quotation is in Dickson, *Think Tanks,* 316.

on deregulation in this period, including pioneering studies by Ann Fried-lander on the economic effect of railroad regulation, studies by Charles Schultze and Allen Kneese on the effects of environmental regulation, and a dozen more.[21]

Despite these departures from liberal orthodoxy, as divisions over foreign and domestic policy opened cracks in the liberal consensus in the early 1970s, many observers saw the Brookings Institution as isolated from large segments of business and from elements in the Nixon admin-istration, where there was even talk of firebombing the institution on the assumption that Daniel Ellsberg's Pentagon Papers were being held there. The image of Brookings as a scholarly way station for Democrats eager to return to government seemed to have some basis in fact when Charles Schultze, Karen Davis, C. Fred Bergsten, Henry Owens, Barry M. Blech-man, and other Brookings people migrated into the Carter administration after 1976.[22]

The secure claim to influence that these appointments might have signaled was illusory. By the later 1970s, indecision at the center, attacks on the "establishment" from left and right, widespread voter apathy and disillusionment with government, and the onset of problems such as "stagflation" that discredited existing economic policies and suggested that the system might be ungovernable, along with shrinking corporate funding, compelled another redefinition of Brookings's politics and re-direction of its efforts.

This time the trustees selected Bruce MacLaury to head the institution. A Princeton- and Harvard-educated former regional Federal Reserve banker and Treasury official acceptable to business, MacLaury, over the next five years, successfully courted business support, increasing corpo-

---

[21]"The Gordon Years"; Leonard Silk, *The American Establishment* (New York, 1980), 154–6; Morton H. Halperin, *Bureaucratic Politics and Foreign Policy* (Washington, D.C., 1974); Arthur M. Okun, *Equality and Efficiency: The Big Trade-off* (Washington, D.C., 1975); James Sundquist, *Dynamics of the Party System: Alignment and Realignment of Political Parties in the United States* (Washington, D.C., 1973); Alice Rivlin, *Systematic Thinking for Social Action* (Washington, D.C., 1971). Typical Brookings works on reg-ulation include Roger G. Noll, *Reforming Regulation: An Evaluation of the Ash Council Proposals* (1971); Roger Noll et al., *Economic Aspects of Television Regulation* (1973); Stephen B. Bryer and Paul W. MacAvoy, *Energy Regulation by the Federal Power Com-mission* (1974); George W. Douglas and James C. Miller III, *Economic Regulation of Domestic Air Transportation* (1974); Almarin Phillips, ed., *Promoting Competition in Regulated Markets* (1975); Allen Kneese and Charles Schultze, *Pollution, Prices, and Public Policies* (1975). For a full list of books published in the Gordon years, see the *Brookings Bulletin* (Fall–Winter 1976): 21–3.
[22]Brookings Institution, *Annual Reports, 1976–8.*

rate representation on the board of trustees and giving the trustees increased power over selection of research subjects. Another important policy shift, dropping restrictions on contract research, increased government support of the institution as well; the trade-offs were a change in the style of research, toward shorter reports targeted on specific, immediately current policy questions, and an increased necessity to maintain cordial relations with the party in power.

In 1981 the institution hired a public relations expert, Roger Semerad, a former fund-raiser for the State University of New York system and executive director of the Republican National Platform Committee, who sought greater institutional visibility with a new quarterly magazine, the *Brookings Review,* and through television and radio interviews, press conferences, and luncheons with corporate executives and donors to publicize Brookings reports and authors. A gratifying rise in corporate support, from $95,450 in 1978 to $1.6 million in 1984, and increased foundation funding, including large grants from Ford and the Carnegie Endowment, permitted MacLaury to expand the research program and recruit new staff. Alice Rivlin returned from the Congressional Budget Office to head Economic Studies; Paul Peterson, a political scientist from the University of Chicago, took over Government Studies; and John D. Steinbruner took charge of Foreign Policy Studies.[23]

The significance of this second reorientation of Brookings strategy, in which the institution moved away from its Democratic linkages toward a more moderate ideological stance, could be read in part in the criticisms of it. There were charges of trustee interference, of a devaluation of genuine scholarship in favor of short-term policy research, of staff appointments going to Republicans to achieve political balance, and of a forced consensus in the formation of an institutional perspective when it came to writing such studies as *Economic Choices 1984.* Most important, these charges signaled the abandonment, or at least the fundamental transformation, of the nonpartisan ideal, with its perhaps naive assumption that social scientists could stand above the political fray and act in the public interest, which had motivated Robert Brookings and other progressive era architects of independent research institutes. Their zeal for objectivity and efficiency and their distrust of politics, embodied in nonpartisanship, gave way to the very different conception that political knowledge was somehow inseparable from fundamental values,

[23]Brookings Institution, *Annual Reports,* 1977–84.

and thus—in the Brookings case—to a quest for ideological balance. As one MacLaury-era Brookings official put it, "There is no such thing as 'nonpartisan' research. At best research can only be bipartisan."

This change in the meaning of nonpartisanship can be attributed in part to a change in the political mood of the country, toward a new conservatism and a more aggressive business consciousness in which the social programs of the New Deal and the Great Society were viewed as increasingly hostile to the interests of conservatives and business. For the first time in its history, the Brookings Institution confronted competition from another major policy research institution, the American Enterprise Institute for Public Policy Research, which was perceived in most business circles as a strong defender of the market economy.[24]

THE AMERICAN ENTERPRISE INSTITUTE

The American Enterprise Institute (AEI), which was founded in 1943 as the American Enterprise Association (AEA), illustrates the experience of a conservatively oriented research institution that shared, although with deep ambivalence, the post–World War II policy consensus. The AEA was moderately critical of the liberal state established during the New Deal, but most of its criticism was directed toward effecting incremental changes and not toward fundamentally challenging the programs themselves. The AEA called for a greater emphasis on market solutions in the field of public policy, but not for the complete dismantling of the liberal state. Moderate in its approach to current public policy issues and suspicious of government involvement in the economy, the institute has displayed a vitality that has allowed it to move into new areas of public policy, including deregulation and the role of religion in American society.

In its early years, the AEA expressed a sentiment common among enlightened corporate leaders, that business could accept the basics of the New Deal program while remaining critical of too much government intervention in the economy. The key figure behind the establishment of the AEA was Lewis Brown, chairman of Johns-Manville Corporation. Having come of political age during the Great Depression, Brown had no longing to return to a golden age of laissez-faire capitalism. He realized that the New Deal had changed the political environment for business

---

[24]"Double Think Tank," *Regardies* (April–May 1983): 56–61.

and, although he expressed some anxiety about the level of government intervention, he accepted much of the New Deal program.[25]

Brown's outlook was essentially corporatist, as was much of the New Deal. Like Brookings before him, he favored cooperative, collaborative solutions to the problems that pitted Americans against each other across class and interest lines. He believed that the organization of labor should be recognized as legitimate; that business, labor, and government should cooperate in economic matters; and that capital should recognize labor's legitimate goals, including collective bargaining. Labor, in turn, must learn to understand the problems of industry and recognize the prerogatives of management.[26]

Brown's views on industrial relations were shaped in large part by his experiences as president of Johns-Manville, a leading supplier of asbestos and building materials. To improve employee relations within his own company, he initiated an extensive education program that provided workers with annual reports summarizing corporate expenditures and pamphlets explaining company policies on wages, hours, and working conditions. While he objected on principle to the closed shop, he accepted collective bargaining. Perceiving his own role as that of "scientific manager," he hired industrial relations experts for each plant; and, to ensure that the company fulfilled its promise of public accountability, he had Walter A. Jessup, president of the Carnegie Foundation for the Advancement of Teaching, elected to the board.

Brown considered most businessmen "antediluvians," stubborn, self-centered, and supremely individualistic. The success of the Johns-Manville program led him to attempt to convert others to his version of industrial statesmanship. A group of progressive businessmen that he organized to promote industrial cooperation sought "to break down class consciousness and the battle spirit," and Brown urged his colleagues to

[25]"Lewis Harold Brown," *Current Biography, 1947* (New York, 1948), 68–70. For a view of Brown as a sharp departure from unenlightened management, see Virgil Jordan to J. D. Rockefeller, Jr., June 8, 1944; John Spargo to William Allen White, June 29, 1938; and John Spargo to George Houston, July 15, 1938, RFA.

[26]On Brown's career and views as a manager, see "Johns-Manville and Its Workers," *Business Week* (July 16, 1938): 30–1; "Seeks Code for Management," *Business Week* (October 22, 1938): 22; Brown, "America's Future," *Vital Speeches* (March 1, 1942): 308–11; idem, "New Cooperation in Industry," *Atlantic Monthly* (November 1939): 635; and "Medalist," *Time* (November 6, 1939): 67. For an excellent discussion of new attitudes among managers toward industrial relations, see Howell John Harris, *The Right to Manage: Industrial Relations Policies of American Business in the 1940s* (Madison, Wis., 1982).

recognize their wider responsibilities to "labor, the government, and the farmer, and the public generally."

Yet Brown cautioned against undue paternalism. While he praised Roosevelt for acting swiftly and decisively in a slump that could not be cured by private efforts alone, and commended the more conservative New Deal measures such as unemployment insurance, Social Security, and minimum wage, he warned against the liberal idea that "government should enter into direct competition with its citizens, and that the government of a representative democracy [can] do everything for everybody." By 1943, like Moulton at the Brookings at the same time, Brown began to espouse "the American way of life and private enterprise... predicated upon incentives that develop enterprise and stimulate people to work." Condemning redistributive programs and deficit spending, he urged his country to pursue policies based on the "multiplication of wealth, not the division of wealth." He warned that America could not possibly "reconcile the principle of democracy, which means cooperation, with the principle of government omniscience under which everyone waits for an order before doing anything. In that way lies loss of freedom and dictatorship." A properly balanced cooperation among labor, business, agriculture, and government, on the other hand, would lead to "a new America," "the Eldorado of a whole new world."[27]

This faith in American economic and political potential remained central to Brown's vision for the world. Imbued with a deep commitment to serve his country, he became increasingly aware of the need for an association to educate the public concerning matters before Congress. In 1943, working with government and business advisers, Brown organized the AEA to provide Congress and the public with objective summaries and analyses of current legislation and legislative proposals.[28]

From the start, the AEA reflected a conservative bias. As one early publication declared, the "public interest" should be judged against the following criterion: "Will it strengthen or weaken the individual enterprise system?" AEA trustees, personally recruited by Brown, reflected strong corporatist leanings. Among the advisory board members responsible for overseeing AEA publications were economic journalist Henry

[27]Brown, "Using Business Agencies to Achieve Public Goals in the Postwar World," *American Economic Review*, Supplement (1943): 71–81; and idem, "How to Get the Country Back to Work," *Vital Speeches* (March 15, 1946): 342–5.

[28]"The Brown Plan," *Business Week* (October 25, 1947): 25; and "Preface" to the Brookings National Economic Problems series.

Hazlitt; economists John V. Van Sickle and Leo Wolman; Charles C. Abbott, dean of the Harvard Business School; James E. McCarthy, dean of the University of Notre Dame Business School; legal scholar Roscoe Pound; and a representative from Metropolitan Life, John Hohams.[29]

With a staff of four based in New York and Washington, the AEA conducted two kinds of research—legislative analyses and broader studies of national economic problems. In each research area, AEA publications tried to present both sides of an issue, with legislative analyses usually conducted by junior members of five or six law firms associated with Johns-Manville Corporation. The National Economic Problems series generated hundreds of pamphlets by well-known conservative scholars on a range of questions, including fiscal policy, antitrust issues, farm price supports, natural resources, social welfare, and Social Security. Economic analyses were frequently critical of New Deal programs, but suggestions for reform were usually moderate. AEA pamphlets opposed full-employment legislation and favored private development of atomic energy. In general, authors showed "a strong personal leaning in favor of reliance upon private enterprise."[30]

In its early years the AEA acted less as a think tank than as a clearinghouse for moderate conservative thought, and Lewis Brown's death in 1951 further threatened its growth. By 1954, the AEA was virtually defunct. That year, however, Charles Abbott persuaded A. D. Marshall, head of General Electric, to assume the presidency. Marshall, a man with a remarkable ability to spot talent, immediately hired William Baroody, Sr., and W. Glenn Campbell, both staff economists at the U.S. Chamber of Commerce, to head the research program at the AEA. Under their guidance, AEA was gradually built into a modern research institute.[31]

The son of a Lebanese immigrant and an economist by academic training, William Baroody brought to the institution a strong belief in

---

[29] The quotation is from John V. Van Sickle, *Industrywide Collective Bargaining in the Public Interest* (New York, 1947), 5.

[30] Representative studies in this series are Paul F. Wendt, *The Role of the Federal Government in Housing* (1956); Jules Blockman, *Regulation of Prices During the Reconversion Period* (1945); Wilhelm Ropke, *The Economics of Full Employment* (1952); Robert A. Freeman, *Federal Aid to Education: Boon or Bane?* (1955); and Joseph H. Ball, *Where Does Statism Begin?* (1950). The quotation is from Wendt, *Role of the Federal Government*, v.

[31] Nick Thimmesch, "The Right Kind of Think Tank at the Right Time," *Human Events* (October 7, 1978): 12–21; Tom Bethell, "The Rewards of Enterprise," *New Republic* (July 16, 1977): 17–19; and "The New Conservative Idea Men," *Dun's Review* (April 1976): 39–41, 81.

conservative values, a suspicion of centralized institutions, faith in the ability of the marketplace ultimately to solve most social problems, and intellectual tenacity in defending his belief in the "competition of ideas." Baroody believed conservatism would triumph if traditional values were given a hearing, but he also valued a diversity of views. "A free society can tolerate some degree of concentration in the manufacture of widgets," he contended. "But the day it approaches a monopoly in ideas and information, that is its death knell."[32]

A Melchite Catholic, and a conservative one by the standards of the 1960s, Baroody maintained a deep religious faith and worried about the social implications of Vatican II, which he felt released "a nihilism of criticism in the church" led by Catholic progressives. These "shrill voices" who disclaim "almost hysterically against centralized authority in the Church are the loudest in clamoring for increased centralization of political authority in the secular sphere," he observed. Baroody expressed particular concern that the church was developing a "social line" that declared that for a "Catholic to espouse a conservative position . . . or to support a conservative candidate for political office is gravely sinful." As a consequence, liberal Catholics had developed an orthodoxy regarding "labor unions, the United Nations, disarmament, the Dominican Republic, 'extremist groups,' and a host of other issues." Such people sought to exclude other opinions from entering political discussion, he warned, thereby reducing "the rationality of the discussion that does exist."[33]

Like his predecessor, Lewis Brown, Baroody emphasized the social significance of economic enterprise and its centrality in American values. The typical American asks only that "the state erect no artificial barriers to his progress, impose no unnecessary burden," Baroody insisted; the American wants "the state to leave him alone as much as possible." And behind this request lay "a confidence that America truly is the land of opportunity, the confidence that within this Continent real failure is the exception not the rule." For people who did fail, Baroody counseled, Americans had traditionally offered "cooperative action in social and economic life not as action coerced and imposed by political authority [but] through voluntary cooperation. No society has formed more clubs,

[32]"The Conservative Brookings Institution," *Dun's Review* (April 1976): 43; and American Enterprise Institute, *Annual Report, 1977* (Washington, D.C., 1977).
[33]William J. Baroody, Sr., "Erosion of National Debate: The Authority of Church and State," *Vital Speeches* (September 1965): 720–4.

societies, mutual aid societies." In this way Baroody reiterated Brown's belief in the cooperative society, based on individual incentive, free enterprise, and the reciprocity of class interests.[34]

Baroody shaped the institution to these values. As Robert Bork, an AEI legal scholar later nominated to the Supreme Court, observed, "If it is ever true that an institution is the shadow of a single man, it is true of the AEI and Bill Baroody." The first years of growth for the AEA were slow; by 1960 it employed only twelve full-time people and had an annual budget of $230,000 drawn largely from such conservative bodies as the Falk, Earhart, Kresge, Pew, and Sloan foundations. Baroody attracted a group of well-established scholars and strengthened the publications review process. As opportunity expanded, he pressed for a broader intellectual and research perspective, and in 1961 he persuaded the board of trustees to change the name to the American Enterprise Institute, although they balked when he proposed that "Enterprise" be dropped as well because the term seemed too value laden.[35]

The AEI's reputation as a conservative think tank changed slowly. Its legislative analysis series, running at about twenty a year in the early 1960s, enjoyed some success as balanced, objective summaries of pending legislation, but some AEI critics suggested that the institute's choice of subjects reflected a conservative bias. The election campaign of 1964 raised further questions concerning the nonpartisan character of the institute when Baroody took a leave of absence to participate in Barry Goldwater's race for the presidency. And a subsequent investigation by Sen. Wright Patman (D–Texas) of tax-exempt foundations, in which Patman finally gained access to AEI financial records, seeking—unsuccessfully—to document a connection to the Goldwater campaign, raised further doubts concerning AEI impartiality, especially among liberals. Baroody's desire to have the AEI perceived as a well-respected policy institute, dedicated to scholarly objectivity, remained unfulfilled as the decade drew to a close.[36]

A crucial turning point in the AEI's reputation came in 1972, when the Ford Foundation finally awarded a $300,000 grant to the institute. The Ford Foundation was eager at the time to show its own nonparti-

---

[34]Quotations ibid., 723.

[35]*William J. Baroody, Sr., Remembered by Paul McCracken, Robert H. Bork, Irving Kristol, and Michael Novak* (Washington, D.C., 1981).

[36]William A. Rusher, *The Rise of the Right* (New York, 1984), 157; and "Institute Quizzed on Political Tie," *Washington Post* (April 15, 1965). See also Lou Cannon, *Reagan* (New York, 1983).

sanship, and although a grant from a major foundation not associated with the political right conveyed important recognition, it contributed little to the AEI's overall budget. Principal support still came from the Lilly Endowment; the Scaife, Earhart, and Kresge foundations; and from corporate sources such as General Motors, U.S. Steel, Republic Steel, Mobil, and Standard Oil. The Republican connection was underlined, though the institute's reputation was further enhanced when the Nixon administration called a number of AEI associates to government positions, including Paul McCracken to head the CEA, Murray Weidenbaum at Treasury, Robert Bork at Justice, and Robert Pranger at Defense. Baroody took pride in the AEI's association with the Republican administration, but he continued to insist that AEI did not hold to a Republican "policy line." He claimed that the institute made a sharp distinction between partisan politics and policy research.[37]

By 1977, the AEI had clearly come to rival the Brookings Institution, if its publications and their effect on legislation were any indication. The institute's policy of "disseminating its product," as one AEI official observed, had widened its influence; so had a $1.6 million expenditure on public outreach programs. The AEI was able that year to produce 118 publications received by 400 universities, and to send its public affairs broadcasts to 700 television stations. According to *Dun's Review,* the AEI was "adept in getting its studies into the hands of people who mold opinion, make laws, and set policy." AEI supporters claimed that the institute had helped defeat Nelson Rockefeller's "emergency" energy program, challenged the FDA's power to withhold safe and effective drugs, contributed to the defeat of a proposed Consumer Affairs Agency, and helped Robert Packwood and Daniel Moynihan in writing a tuition tax credit bill.[38]

The AEI also emerged as a successful proponent of deregulation. In 1975, it published Murray Weidenbaum's influential *Government Mandated Price Increases: A Neglected Aspect of Inflation.* The following year, Irving Kristol, editor of *The Public Interest* and dean of the neoconservative movement, joined the institute to help direct AEI studies on deregulation. Furthermore, two AEI economists, Marvin H. Kosters and

[37]See Bethell, "Rewards of Enterprise," 18; and Thimmesch, "Right Kind of Think Tank," 19.
[38]"Conservative Brookings," 43; Emily Yoffe, "The Domains of Eminence: Great Minds Do Not Always Think Alike," *Washington Journalism Review* (November 1980): 30–1, 33; and Thimmesch, "Right Kind of Think Tank," 13.

James C. Miller, former staff economists to the CEA, emerged as major critics of economic regulation. Their work sought to bring to the field, they explained later, a "careful, substantiated analysis" that looked at the costs and benefits of government regulation. In pursuing regulation studies through cost-benefit analysis, AEI reflected a growing trend in economics toward looking at efficiency on a microeconomic level, thereby placing questions of equality within a larger context that weighed economic costs against economic rewards.

Much of AEI's work in deregulation, although within the mainstream of economic thought, still took on, in the excitement of the times, a crusadelike character that seemed to go beyond dispassionate cost-benefit analysis. James Miller, an AEI scholar who later headed the Federal Trade Commission and still later directed the Office of Management and Budget (OMB) in the second Reagan administration, told the conservative journal *Human Events* that the "next realization will be that *all* regulation" is "not a free lunch." Liberals attack economic agencies for being controlled by the special interests, he declared, but want "to keep those social regulatory agencies (those dealing with civil rights, affirmative action, etc.)." Conversely, conservatives want to "rid us of all regulations—economic and social."[39]

By 1977, after spending nearly a quarter-century at the AEI and feeling certain that he had achieved much of what he had set out to accomplish, William Baroody, Sr., decided to retire. His son, William Baroody, Jr., took over the presidency of the institution. A graduate of Holy Cross who had briefly prepared for the priesthood, William Baroody, Jr., had been in government service since his graduate student days in political science at Georgetown University. He brought to the AEI experience and connections earned as an aide to Melvin Laird both in Congress and at Defense and as a special assistant and liaison person with business groups in the Nixon and Ford administrations. He also had a strong sense of AEI tradition, and his principal goal was to ensure the continued independence of the institution by developing new foundation and corporate support. In 1976 the institute received 25 percent of its revenues from 200 corporations. Under its new head, AEI expanded its support to include 500 corporate donors which provided 57 percent of its revenue.

---

[39]"Baroody Looks at the Presidency," *Government Executive* (February 1982): 13–16; Thimmesch, "Right Kind of Think Tank," 19; and Murray L. Weidenbaum, *Government Mandated Price Increases: A Neglected Aspect of Inflation* (Washington, D.C., 1975).

By 1982 the institute's budget had approached $11 million, supporting a staff of 140.[40]

The research program was expanded to encompass legislative analysis, seminar programs, health policy, government regulation, legal policy, tax policy, and foreign and defense policy. In 1978, the AEI also initiated four new periodicals aimed at the scholarly and policy communities: *AEI Economist, AEI Defense Review, Regulation,* and *Public Opinion.* The institute's continued insistence on exploring new approaches to policy was evident in the development of the "Mediating Structures Project" headed by a sociologist of religion, Peter Berger, and a clergyman, the Reverend Richard John Newhaus. The project was designed to examine new ways in which mediating structures (i.e., those that stand between the individual and the state)—including family, civic groups, churches, and voluntary associations—could deliver health, education, welfare, housing, and law enforcement, with the intention of reducing bureaucratic centralization and restoring local control.

To improve its standing in the academic community, the AEI assembled an impressive staff of scholars and public figures, many of them with experience in government, including Gerald Ford, Melvin Laird, William Simon, Robert Bork, Carla Hills, Michael Novak, Herbert Stein, and William Fellner. Among the academic scholars, Norman Ornstein and Austin Ranney came to the AEI, along with fifty other academics associated on an adjunct basis. Throughout his tenure, William Baroody, Jr., remained concerned that the AEI continued to be widely viewed as a Republican or conservative think tank. He reminded the press that the AEI had "a number of people who would fit slots in any administration," and he emphasized that the institute's staff included Democrats, as well as "some liberals." Furthermore, he argued that the AEI's research approach to problems did not always fit the conservative agenda. Herbert Stein, for example, emerged in the early 1980s as a major critic of the "so-called supply-side economics," a term he had in fact coined in criticism, and other AEI fellows expressed concern about the budget deficits and tax policies.[41]

---

[40]*William J. Baroody, Sr., Remembered;* Baroody, "The Man for Businessmen to See," *Business Week* (March 9, 1974): 114–16; "A Way to Tell Your Business Story to President Ford," *Nation's Business* (August 1975): 28–9; and "The Shadow Cabinets—Changing Themselves As They Change Policy," *National Journal* (February 25, 1978): 297.

[41]Baroody Looks at the Presidency," 10–12; "At 40, a Think Tank Sets Out to Win Dollars and Scholars," *Washington Times* (December 8, 1983); and Herbert Stein, *Presidential Economics* (New York, 1982).

The tenure of William Baroody, Jr., as president ended in the summer of 1987, when an increasingly restive board of trustees forced his resignation. During the decade of his leadership, the AEI had expanded dramatically, and in the eyes of some critics, haphazardly, with seemingly little oversight of costs and revenue. Baroody was criticized for poor administration and planning. Despite the large number of AEI staffers who held appointments in the Reagan administration (thirty left the AEI to join the administration in its first two years alone), members of the New Right, suspicious of a drift toward the center, occasionally voiced bitter criticism of the AEI. The movement of funds away from the AEI to more conservative institutes such as the Heritage Foundation exacerbated the organization's financial problems, and many observers felt that any restoration of the AEI's long-term financial position must come from conservative sources, thus requiring a sharper conservative profile.

Baroody's successor, Christopher DeMuth, came to the AEI with strong New Right credentials. A former associate director of OMB under David Stockman, DeMuth had established a reputation as a hard-liner on deregulation and a fiscal conservative. Almost immediately he instituted sharp staff and payroll reductions, cutting the budget to $7.5 million, only slightly more than half its level in the previous year. He eliminated research programs in education, health, and the Middle East, often centers critical of the Reagan agenda. DeMuth bolstered the conservative orientation of the institute by bringing on board several former Reagan administration officials with strong rightist reputations, among them Richard Perle, former assistant secretary of defense; Alan Gerson, a former Justice Department counselor; and Constantine Menges, a former special assistant to the president for national security.[42]

On December 8, 1988, the fruitfulness of relations between AEI and recent Republican politics and policy was celebrated in an institute-sponsored dinner for 1,600 in honor of the achievements of the Reagan administration. In his speech before the group, which in a curious way echoed the remarks of Lyndon Johnson before a Brookings Institution gathering twenty-two years earlier, President Reagan saluted AEI for its work in bringing to "intellectual fruition" the ideas of contemporary conservatism. "The universities," he said, "once the only real home for American scholarship, have been particularly unresponsive" to conser-

[42]Edward Sussman, "Conservative Think Tank Comes Back from the Brink of Financial Disaster, Leaning More to the Right," *Wall Street Journal,* September 3, 1987.

vative ideas. "And so," observed the president, "it became necessary to create our own research institutions.... And your institution's remarkably distinguished body of work is testimony to the triumph of the think tank."[43]

THE INSTITUTE FOR POLICY STUDIES

In the decades when AEI was emerging to challenge the Brookings Institution as Washington's preeminent think tank, the liberal consensus was coming apart. The first signs of this disintegration appeared in the debates over foreign policy precipitated by the Vietnam War. By the 1970s the liberal commitment to an incrementalist domestic policy was also subjected to attacks from both the left and the right, and an increasing polarization in policy debate allowed formerly excluded groups to exert significant influence by raising questions that challenged the fundamental premises of the liberal state.

Concurrently, and obviously as a related phenomenon, the idea of objective, nonpartisan research in a scientific institution outside and above politics and dedicated to the public interest yielded to a different conception. A number of the policy research institutes, or think tanks, came to be viewed as an integral part of the political order—each one amassing and interpreting specialized information and theory from a particular perspective in a policy process that mingled an older style of interest conflict with new state capacities and a new politics of information and expertise. The increased importance of knowledge-generating elements in public discourse reflected expansion of the political agenda beyond the old distributive questions to include the newer, and often highly technical, "quality of life" issues, as well as many more international concerns.

In this new policy system, competing think tanks were linked with segments of political parties, congressional committees, executive agencies, citizens' lobbies, political action groups, and the educational arms of traditional interest groups in political coalitions, often devoted to single causes but sometimes agreed on a broader reform agenda. Advocacy and commitment on the part of scholars were accepted as appropriate, even necessary, within limits that preserved the canons of scholarly integrity in social investigation and research. With the center falling apart, and

---

[43]Marjorie Williams, "Cheering the Chief on His Big Day—But at Think Tank Dinner There's Confusion on What It All Means," *Washington Post*, December 8, 1988.

expanded roles for policy intellectuals and institutions emerging, new policy institutes appeared to represent positions on the left and the right of the political spectrum. On the left came the Institute for Policy Studies (IPS); a decade later, the Heritage Foundation became a major center for policy thinking on the right.

The IPS emerged in the turbulent 1960s and became a permanent center of left policy analysis and political activity, offering a consistently radical critique of liberalism. By virtue of its passionate distrust of partisan politics within the established party system and its cynical estimation of government's role in protecting the "public interest," the IPS presents itself, much as the early Brookings did, as an institution that stands above party, for reform, democracy, and the public interest. Yet the IPS is not opposed to politics or state activism per se. It simply dismisses debate between the two major political parties as self-serving and ultimately misleading, and perceives federal involvement in the economy as promoting the continuation of the military-industrial complex. According to IPS policy analysts, U.S. political leaders have no real interest in democracy; political divisions based on interests, groups, and goals defined in the New Deal no longer reflect political realities, nor can they mobilize people around their real social and economic interests. IPS spokespersons characterize the two-party system as a "binary affair, shaped like an idiot's brain," and contemporary political debate as moved by "imaginary interest and fantasies." In this formulation, the IPS was styled as an independent academy, challenging "the myths and assumptions of state power" and constructing new issues and a new politics that accurately reflect social problems and actual social divisions. Thus the initial purpose of the IPS, as Marcus Raskin, a cofounder along with Richard Barnet, later explained, was to create "an institution outside the government that could identify and critique these underlying assumptions [concerning imperialism and inequality] and the policies they produced, and offer alternative directions."[44]

Today, the IPS perceives itself as playing a unique role in the policy arena. While the Brookings Institution serves technocratic-bureaucratic interests, the American Enterprise Institute corporate interests, and the Heritage Foundation Sun Belt entrepreneurial interests, Raskin argues,

[44]Gore Vidal, "Introduction," and John Friedman, "Preface," in Friedman, ed., *The First Harvest: An Institute for Policy Studies Reader, 1963–1983* (Washington, D.C., 1983); *IPS Annual Report, 1983: The Twentieth Year*, 2.

the IPS represents the concerns of the poor and the disfranchised in the United States and the world. Thus the IPS advocates "a longer and deeper struggle, a struggle underlying the principles and future direction of political culture itself." The IPS envisions its role as finding "new approaches and programs" that people will be working to implement twenty years from now. Robert Borosage, director of the IPS, explains: "Our job is to expose the moral and political bankruptcy of the ideas and assumptions now governing America, and to work with citizen groups and popular movements to make that vision a reality."[45]

Affirming this moral vision, IPS researchers perceive themselves as "public scholars" actively trying to change the world. Research is combined with activism, knowledge with political power. This emphasis on knowledge as political struggle entails an explicit denial of "objective," scientific, nonpartisan research, and even of the independent, objective existence of data. Raskin explains, "Facts are manufactured entities that are mediated through individuals. Most people mediate facts through social roles." Thus social investigation is never "objective" in the sense adopted by late-nineteenth-century social scientists; instead of being "out there" to be discovered, social phenomena are constructed, perceived, and imbued with meaning amid the expectations, symbols, and values of the moment. At best, Raskin concludes, all one can hope for is "individual accountability and responsibility" in conducting research.[46]

The IPS and similar, ideologically based think tanks have attracted and been shaped by people with career patterns quite different from those of Robert Brookings or Lewis Brown, who moved from private business careers through philanthropy to public policy. Members of the new breed often started their careers in government, became disillusioned, resigned, and forged a backward linkage to public policy through private foundations and institutes. Both of the men who guided the IPS from its founding in 1963 through its first twenty years began as young members of the Kennedy administration. Marcus Raskin, a New Yorker, attended the University of Wisconsin before coming to Washington as an aide to Cong. Robert Kastenmeir and then serving as a White House aide to McGeorge Bundy. Richard Barnet attended Boston Latin School, Harvard as an undergraduate, and Harvard Law School before serving as an

---

[45]Ibid., 6.
[46]Marcus Raskin, interview with the author, Washington, D.C., December 3, 1984.

aide to John J. McCloy at the State Department. (He later completed his studies at Harvard's Russian Research Center and the Princeton Center for International Relations.)

The idea of forming an independent research center, as Raskin and Barnet tell the story, came out of a meeting in 1963 between members of the State and Defense departments to discuss disarmament. Attending this meeting, the two men simultaneously realized that they did not belong there. Disarmament would come neither from academics, who were too close to government because of defense contracts, nor from politicians, who found compromises too easy to make. What was needed, they agreed, was a new institution, dependent neither on government nor on partisan interests, an advocate for social justice and international peace.

In the months that followed, Barnet and Raskin raised money from various sources closely connected to the Democratic party. Initial funding came from Philip Stern, heir to the Sears fortune; from James Warburg, an international banker; and later from the Samuel Rubin Foundation, founded by the owner of Fabergé. The Rubin Foundation continued as a major funding source for the institute, and Peter Weiss, the son-in-law of Samuel Rubin, served as chairman of the board. This support enabled the IPS to open in the fateful fall of 1963, with a budget of $200,000. Organized like an academic department, with resident fellows receiving an equivalent of tenure and associate and visiting fellows serving as junior faculty, the IPS placed an early emphasis on education. The first resident fellows included Barnet and Raskin, as well as Gar Alperovitz and Arthur Waskow, who had served with Raskin as aides in Kastenmeir's office. Also joining the resident staff were Milton Kotler, an urban sociologist from the University of Chicago, and Christopher Jencks, a young protégé of David Riesman's. From the outset, the IPS emphasized establishing seminars to introduce members of Congress, legislative aides, and civil servants to the best thought concerning public issues. During these years, IPS provided a forum for such notable thinkers as Hans Morgenthau, Hannah Arendt, Paul Warnke, Leo Szilard, and left libertarian Paul Goodman.

Despite its distrust of politics, the IPS initially sought to use the Democratic party's commitment to the Great Society as an instrument for reform. For example, Raskin and Jencks helped to establish the Model Schools program and the Teacher Corps. But the growth of the civil rights movement and America's involvement in Vietnam turned the IPS in a more radical, activist direction. As Arthur Waskow later described its mood, the IPS became not just an ordinary research center. Because of "its commitment to the ideal that to develop social theory one must be involved in social action and in social experiments," the IPS became a focus of civil rights and antiwar organizing activity.[47]

During these years, IPS fellows figured prominently as radical activists. In 1965, Raskin and journalist Bernard Fall collected documents relating to the war in the *Vietnam Reader,* which became an indispensable source for antiwar teach-ins. Raskin and Waskow wrote "Call to Resist," inviting massive opposition to the draft, and Raskin was eventually indicted, along with Benjamin Spock, for organizing draft resistance. In 1968, having completely broken with the Democratic party, Raskin attempted to organize the New Party, which called for the complete dismantling of the military establishment.[48]

Other IPS fellows gained notoriety in radical causes. Arthur Waskow played a prominent role in organizing the radical Federal Employees for a Democratic Society, Jews for Urban Justice, and antiwar and anti-Nixon demonstrations in Washington. Milton Kotler proposed a model neighborhood-government program for Cleveland, which was later organized by IPS associate Ivanhoe Donaldson, a civil rights activist. During these same years, the IPS helped organize neighborhood projects and co-ops in Washington, including Drum and Speak Bookstore and the New Thing Art and Architectural Center.

The IPS also helped to establish activist institutes in other regions. In 1970, the IPS organized the Institute for Southern Studies in Atlanta, codirected by Julian Bond and an IPS fellow. The Southern Institute, operating on an annual budget of $150,000, targeted examination of regional poverty programs as its major focus and undertook an oral history project studying the development of working people in the South. The Bay Area Institute, inaugurated shortly after the Southern Institute, focused its research on Latin America and the entire Pacific region. Like the IPS in Washington, the Bay Area Institute established an alternative school that became an important activity of the center.[49]

Although the IPS appeared to be more activist than research oriented, it produced influential scholarly work. Gar Alperovitz's *Atomic Diplomacy,* which argued that the United States had used atomic weapons in

[47]See Garry Wills, "The Thinking of Positive Power," *Esquire* (March 1971): 98–101.
[48]Joshua Muravchik, "The Think Tank on the Left," *New York Times Magazine* (April 27, 1981): 36–48, 106–9, 121–2.
[49]Wills, "Thinking of Positive Power," 100.

Japan during World War II primarily to intimidate the Soviet Union, had a major impact on early cold-war revisionism. Richard Barnet's *Intervention and Revolution: The United States in the Third World* (1968) and *Economy of Death* (1969) challenged America's military-industrial complex and condemned intervention in Greece, Lebanon, Vietnam, the Dominican Republic, British Guiana, Iran, and the Congo. Arthur Waskow's *Running Riot: A Journey of Official Disasters and Creative Disorder in American Society* (1971) articulated New Left concerns relating to neighborhood control of city resources and the police. The following year, Marcus Raskin's statement of political philosophy, *Being and Doing*, described the "colonization" of American society by the military, corporations, the school system, and the mass media.[50]

Yet, perhaps because of its diverse and sometimes frenetic activism, the IPS by 1971 seemed to some observers to have lost its way. Garry Wills, later a trustee, commented that the institute seemed to be going off in all directions, a problem he attributed to "the failure to stake out an area, work persistently at it, and achieve widely recognized results." The IPS still attracted a good deal of attention, both from the right and within government. Between 1968 and 1972 more than sixty agents from the FBI and other agencies infiltrated or acted as informers on the IPS. The Internal Revenue Service examined the IPS in 1967, following Raskin's indictment for draft conspiracy, and an investigation of its tax-exempt status was instigated in 1970 by Sen. Strom Thurmond, who insisted, "By giving a tax exemption to an organization like the Institute for Policy Studies our government is allowing tax exemption to support revolution."[51]

In 1973, the IPS attracted further attention, especially from the right, by establishing an international program called the Transnational Institute, with centers in Amsterdam and London devoted to research and advocacy on behalf of the poor nations of the third world. Two years later, the IPS invited Orlando Letelier, the former foreign minister of Chile under the Allende regime, to direct the Transnational Institute. Letelier had spent less than a year in this new position before he was

[50]Gar Alperovitz, *Atomic Diplomacy: Hiroshima and Potsdam* (New York, 1965); Richard Barnet, *The Economy of Death* (New York, 1969); idem, *Intervention and Revolution: The United States in the Third World* (New York, 1968); George McGovern, "The Economy of Death," *New York Times Book Review* (December 28, 1969), 6; "Running Riot," *Christian Century* (July 1, 1970): 824; Marcus Raskin, *Being and Doing* (New York, 1972).
[51]Wills, "Thinking of Positive Power," 101; Thurmond quoted there.

assassinated by Chilean-paid agents in Washington, along with IPS fellow Ronnie Karper Moffitt.[52]

The assassination precipitated a crisis in the IPS over its future political direction, a crisis that exposed an underlying conflict between research and activism. Marcus Raskin proposed that the IPS should undertake a long-term project, the writing of an "Encyclopedia of Plans and Practices for an Alternative Society," to serve as a guide for the creation of new social institutions, ranging from government to family relations. A more activist-minded contingent headed by Arthur Waskow sought to take the IPS into more community-organizing activities. Tensions between these two groups were further exacerbated by a dispute over the status of resident fellows and associate fellows. During the IPS's first decade, such well-known figures as Irving Goffman, Hannah Arendt, Herbert Marcuse, Angela Davis, and Hans Morgenthau had been turned down as resident fellows in institutewide votes. With each vote, a struggle developed over whether the IPS should promote from within, which meant that staff and associate fellows could become resident fellows, or whether the IPS should look outside to recruit the best minds possible. Matters came to a head in 1977 when dissident staff members tried to organize a union. After an acrimonious confrontation between union and founders, the IPS finally agreed to award $300,000, about one-third of its endowment, to the splinter group to form the Public Resources Center.[53]

After the turmoil of 1977, the IPS sought to regain its sense of direction. In 1978, Robert Borosage, a graduate of Yale Law School and former director of the liberal Center for National Security Studies, was appointed director. Borsage sought to resuscitate the IPS by initiating a publications program, an active visiting scholars program, and an alternative school offering courses on such subjects as the media, macroeconomics, health and safety, and control of nuclear weapons—all of which proved quite successful. He expanded the research effort, organized into four major programs: Domestic Reconstruction, International Economics and Human Rights, National Security and Foreign Policy, and the Washington School. New projects were initiated, including the Third World Women's

---

[52]For an account of the Letelier assassination, see John Dinges and Saul Landau, *Assassination on Embassy Row* (New York, 1980).

[53]"IPS Faces Life," *New Republic* (August 6, 1976): 17. Len Rodberg, a physicist speaking for the dissidents, claimed, "we were fired.... Our politics weren't welcome at the institute. Dissidents were concerned with organizing citizens' groups," he added, while Barnet's work "shows up as a book, but a lot of what we do does not appear in writing. So we are attacked for not doing anything."

Project," headed by Isabel Letelier and Jill Gay, and project "Women and the Economy," directed by Barbara Ehrenreich. Rebuilding its staff, the IPS added Roger Wilkins, a former assistant attorney general under Lyndon Johnson and vice president of the Ford Foundation, to the Domestic Studies group in 1984; three others joined the IPS the same year: Jorge Sol, former executive secretary of the International Monetary Fund; John Cavanaugh, a Princeton-trained economist; and Chester Hartman, a specialist in urban affairs. By 1984, the IPS had twenty full-time staff members, supported by a $1.7 million budget.[54]

The IPS became more visible in policy circles when Marcus Raskin undertook a study of the federal budget at the request of sixty members of Congress in 1983. To conduct this project, Raskin recruited Chester Hartman; Roger Wilkins; Leon Keyserling, former head of the Council of Economic Advisers; Francis Fox Piven; Edward Herman of the Wharton School; and Bertram Gross of the City University of New York. The IPS team developed an alternative budget that offered full employment and extensive cuts in defense spending. The budget was presented at a day-long seminar that drew a large audience from Capitol Hill. IPS fellows also reached a wider, general audience through their books and contributions to major newspapers and journals of opinion.[55]

In the mid-1980s, the IPS came under increasing attack from the conservative and right-wing press. Articles appeared under such titles as "Moscow's Friends at the Institute of Policy Studies," "They Run America," "Gambling with Subversion," and "The Institute for Policy Studies: Empire on the Left." These attacks replaced legitimate differences over policy with rhetoric and intimidation.[56]

The institute's critique of the liberal state reflects ideological assumptions concerning the efficacy of the marketplace and the state far different from Harold Moulton's or Lewis Brown's criticisms of New Deal liberalism. Yet by dismissing New Deal liberalism for failing to address the social and economic problems that arose in the 1960s and 1970s, the IPS participated, albeit from the left, in a general attack on postwar

[54]IPS, *The Washington School Catalogue, 1984–85;* IPS, *Report, 1983.*
[55]Muravchik, "Think Tank on the Left," 46. For a complete bibliography of IPS writings during these years, see IPS, *Report, 1983.*
[56]Aryeh Neir, "An Open Letter to the *Times* Magazine," *Nation* (May 30, 1981): 660–2; Rael Jean Isaac, "The Institute for Policy Studies: Empire on the Left," *Midstream* (June–July, 1980): 7–18; John Rees, "Moscow's Friends at the Institute for Policy Studies," *American Opinion* (November 1983): 30–41, 45–7, 51–4; and Susan L. M. Huck, "Gambling with Subversion," *American Opinion* (May 1977): 9–14; 91–9.

liberalism. With the breakup of the liberal consensus, ideological polarization inevitably occurred within the policy research establishment, contributing to a proliferation of think tanks.

THE HERITAGE FOUNDATION

The Heritage Foundation represents a conservative counterpart to the IPS. Founded in 1973 by Edwin Feulner and Paul Weyrich to provide rapid and succinct legislative analysis on issues pending before Congress, the Heritage Foundation sought to promote conservative values and demonstrate the need for a free market and a strong defense. The Heritage Foundation's articulation of conservative values in social policy, education, and government activities placed it in the forefront of New Right activity. Edwin Feulner, president of the Heritage Foundation, described it as an "activist version of the Brookings Institution." Heritage's strongest assets have been its forceful presentation of the conservative cause in matters of policy and its ability to turn out policy pieces within twenty-four hours. "Our concept," Feulner stated, "is to make marketing of the product an integral part of it. Our role is trying to influence the Washington public policy-making community . . . most specifically the Hill, secondly the Executive branch, and thirdly the national news media."[57]

The Heritage Foundation's commitment to conservative economic theories and social values allows the institution to be critical of both Republicans and Democrats. Although sympathetic to the Reagan wing of the Republican party, the Heritage Foundation showed a willingness to criticize the Reagan administration for its failure "to live up to its mandate." Also, the Heritage Foundation on occasion alienated business elements by its attacks on steel import quotas, synthetic fuels development studies, and certain military procurements, and by its support for deregulation. In this way, the foundation remains "nonpartisan" while it continues to advocate specific ideological positions. Its mission remains, Feulner explained, to play "a positive and constructive role in the [policy] process by mobilizing intellectual resources and support for conservative policymakers and, perhaps as important, providing constructive criticism and prodding when needed." Within the framework of conservative values, the Heritage Foundation sees itself as an independent organization.

[57]"Issue Oriented Heritage Foundation Hitches Its Wagon to Reagan Star," *National Journal* (March 20, 1982): 504.

Because of its support for a free-market, free-trade ideology, Stuart Butler argued, Heritage was "neither a tool of big business, nor a tool of the Reagan administration."[58]

The founders of Heritage, Feulner and Weyrich, like Barnet and Raskin before them, came out of government. The founders of both the IPS and the Heritage groups perceived, although in fundamentally different ways, that the system had failed because it was based on erroneous, if not altogether dishonest theories; and a fundamental change in the political order, based on a new ideological approach, was needed. The specific occasion for the founding of the Heritage Foundation occurred shortly after a congressional battle over the supersonic transport aircraft, when Weyrich and Feulner, then congressional aides, received an AEI analysis of the bill *after* the vote in Congress. The two decided there was a need for an organization that would do more timely research on subjects before Congress. Their success in finding backing reflected the high standing of Weyrich and Feulner in conservative Washington circles: Feulner had served as assistant to Melvin Laird and to Rep. Philip Crane before becoming director of the conservative Republican Study Committee. And Weyrich, a former broadcast journalist, was press secretary to Sen. Gordon Allott of Colorado. Wealthy conservative Joseph Coors made an initial donation of $250,000 to create such an organization; another $900,000 came from John Scaife, a scion of the Mellon family, and other contributions came from the Noble Foundation, the John Olin Foundation, and corporate sources.[59]

The Heritage Foundation remained relatively small in its early years. Its involvement in policy matters was largely confined to Congress, although in 1974 Heritage sent its attorney, James McKenna, to West Virginia to help a "profamily" group of parents protesting textbooks used in the local schools. From this experience Heritage organized the National Congress for Educational Excellence, which attempted to bring conservative "profamily" educational groups together into a national organization.[60]

In late 1975 the budget of Heritage was only $750,000. That year

---

[58]Ibid., 502; Richard N. Holwell, ed., *The First Year* (Washington, D.C., 1981); "Building a Heritage in the War of Ideas," *Washington Post* (October 3, 1983); and Charles L. Heatherly, *Mandate for Leadership: Policy Management in a Conservative Administration* (Washington, D.C., 1981).
[59]"The Mystery Angel of the New Right," *Washington Post*, July 12, 1981.
[60]Alan Crauford, *Thunder on the Right: The New Right and the Politics of Resentment* (New York, 1980).

Weyrich resigned as president of Heritage to form a political lobby group, the Committee for the Survival of a Free Congress, and Jerry Preston James briefly succeeded him. The following year, a turning point in Heritage's history, Frank J. Walton, former secretary of transportation for California under Governor Reagan, became president, and immediately introduced the technique of direct mailing. Within a year the institution had developed a core of 100,000 supporters. Finally, in 1977, steady leadership came to the foundation when Edwin Feulner resigned his post at the Republican Policy Study Committee to take over from Walton.[61]

Under Feulner, the Heritage Foundation developed into a full-fledged policy institution. The board of trustees was strengthened with the election of Joseph Coors and former secretary of the Treasury William E. Simon, and the staff was increased. Heritage updated its two public policy briefs, *Backgrounders* and *Issue Bulletins,* and Feulner initiated a quarterly journal, *Policy Review,* for longer Heritage pieces. He brought in young researchers to undertake the work of supplying Congress with up-to-date analyses.

Feulner realized, as had other policy institute directors, that scholarly respectability enhanced the reputation of an institution. Therefore, he established a distinguished scholar program, which brought in such important figures as Russell Kirk, Stephen Haseler, Ernest Van den Haag, and Walter E. Williams, and began to acquire a list of highly visible academics associated with the institution, including Russian historian Richard Pipes of Harvard; Bernard Sheehan of Indiana University; economists Thomas Sowell of the Hoover Institution and Gordon Tullock of George Mason University; George Gilder; and foreign affairs specialist Ernest Le Fever. The Heritage Foundation further extended its ties to academe through the creation of an academic resource bank containing the names of more than 1,000 conservative scholars and researchers to be enlisted for research, congressional testimony, conferences, and commencement addresses. This burst of activity created excitement in the conservative community, and by 1979 the annual budget of Heritage exceeded $3.5 million.

The election of Ronald Reagan brought further challenges and rewards to the institute. Before the inauguration, the Heritage staff prepared a transition program, *Mandate for Leadership,* a detailed 3,000-page study that took a year to write and cost $100,000. The task of dissecting the

[61]Morton Kondrake, "The Heritage Model," *New Republic* (December 20, 1980): 12.

federal government fell to 250 contributors who examined the entire federal bureaucracy, focusing special attention on thirteen cabinet-level departments, the principal regulatory agencies, the Office of Management and Budget, the National Endowments for the Arts and Humanities, and Action, a poverty program. "Our strong feeling," Feulner commented, "was that the people who came into the Administration should have some source of information and guidance other than what you get from the incumbents you replace."[62]

A carefully orchestrated publicity campaign ignited conservative enthusiasm for the document, and it was equated, in the minds of many, with the Reagan agenda. If Reagan strayed from its recommendations, it appeared, he strayed from his own mandate. The impression that the president supported the recommendations of the *Mandate* was given legitimacy by Reagan's subsequent appointment of many of those who had worked on the Heritage project, including James Watt as secretary of interior; Norman True as Treasury under secretary on tax policy; and Charles Heatherly, the editor of *Mandate,* to the Department of Education. Over the next three years an estimated twenty Heritage people were appointed to middle-level positions in the administration.

Heritage became a major source of policy information for a young Congress with many new conservative members. As one congressional aide later described those first hectic days of the Reagan administration, "Information was power; and they [Heritage] had a flow of information. It was just indispensable. We could have everything at our fingertips." The Republican Study Committee, which served close to 150 conservative representatives in the House with a staff of only fourteen to summarize and evaluate pending legislation, relied heavily on Heritage. In turn, the foundation stressed its ties with the administration. In a fund-raising letter to a select group of conservatives, presidential adviser Edwin Meese called the Heritage Foundation "a vital communication link" to the White House and to those who supported the Reagan program. Feulner reportedly visited the White House once a week.[63]

In its early years the Heritage Foundation operated as a cross between an ideological lobby and a conservative think tank. The institution defined its basic role as the activist one of keeping Reagan "honest," which in

---

[62] Andrew C. Seamans, Sr., "Heritage Study Sets Firm Foundation for Reagan," *Human Events* (January 10, 1981): 10, 16–17.
[63] "Heritage," *Washington Post,* October 3, 1983; "Meese Helps Group to Raise Funds," ibid., January 20, 1982.

practice meant freeing the economy from undue regulation and strengthening national defense. This sense that conservatism must be protected from possible pragmatic turns by the Reagan administration allowed the Heritage Foundation to remain critical of some of its actions. The foundation's *First Year Report* offered "frank assessments and occasionally strong criticism of the administration." The basis of this evaluation, the report declared, was the recognition that President Reagan's goal was to "change the course of government from an expansive to a devolutionary trend." While disappointed with some of the president's appointments and actions, Heritage judged the administration to have been 62 percent successful in addressing the issues raised by *Mandate for Leadership*.[64]

Citing its influence on the Reagan administration, the Heritage Foundation claimed a share of credit for this success, in general by helping to create a receptive climate for "supply-side" economics, and specifically through its efforts in promoting or defeating concrete measures. Heritage fellow Owen Harris, former Australian ambassador to UNESCO, played a key role in changing American policy toward that agency; Heritage's Asia Center, endowed in 1983, encouraged President Reagan's movement toward establishing closer ties with Japan and Korea; and, through its working luncheon group, Heritage helped to defeat the Law of the Sea Treaty, which had been many years in preparation. The proposals in Heritage's *Agenda 83* provided a guideline and a defense for much of what followed as the administration's first term in office drew to a close. Heritage officials claim to have influenced the gas deregulation proposals put forth by the Department of Energy, the changes in Medicare subsequently adopted by the Department of Health and Human Services, and the debate over the Clean Air Act. Heritage proposals for free-enterprise zones, initially made by Stuart Butler, as well as for privatized air control, a voluntary social security program, and the sale of public housing to the poor, have all entered the policy discourse.[65]

This success in the policy arena must be attributed in some part to effective use of the media. The foundation developed an extensive public relations organization. With a budget exceeding $10 million in 1983, the institution allotted approximately 20 percent to public information. This budget allowed Heritage to publish some 150 booklets each year. The foundation developed close relations with a large number of reporters

[64]"Heritage Foundation Gives Reagan a Passing Grade," ibid., November 22, 1981; and Holwell, ed., *The First Year*.
[65]Heritage Foundation, *Agenda 83* (Washington, D.C., 1983).

and newspaper editors, and each week Heritage officials met to target a core list of 350 reporters throughout the country with a variety of policy sheets, selected to meet each paper's needs. These policy sheets were written to be placed immediately in newspapers without alteration. Often a letter accompanied the material, personally signed by a key Heritage staff member. Furthermore, Feulner wrote a weekly column that was distributed to 1,500 daily and weekly papers. The Heritage Feature Syndicate also provided commentary pieces and cartoons to 130 subscribing newspapers, which reached an estimated 15 million newspaper readers each week.

Aiming for short, timely pieces containing information and analysis, the Heritage Foundation has developed a variety of formats to reach different audiences. Its *Issues Bulletins* on pending legislation and *Backgrounders* on current domestic international issues were intended for members of Congress and their staffs who have limited time for reading. Heritage also published two journals for longer, interpretive pieces, *National Security Record* and *Policy Review,* which have gained respect in certain policy circles.

Well organized, efficient, and well financed, the Heritage Foundation had an established niche by the mid-1980s. Its *Mandate for Leadership II,* released in December 1984, received widespread publicity. Its agenda for policy changes suggested a continued effort to "privatize" the economy by turning over many government tasks to private enterprise. Heritage also called for a strong defense through increased military expenditures and a cautious approach to changes in Soviet foreign and domestic policies under Gorbachev. Heritage urged closer ties with friendly countries in the Pacific region and proposed to shift American policy away from Europe toward the East. Plans calling for a common market in the Pacific basin were undertaken.[66]

By the mid-1980s, the financial base of the Heritage Foundation rested in large part on 120,000 persons who contributed more than $3 million a year (34 percent of the institution's annual budget). Heritage had gained increasing foundation and corporate support from conservative groups, and its officials planned to create an endowed fund.

The Heritage Foundation's growth and success reflected the collapse of the liberal center and the consequent widening of public discourse to

---

[66]Stuart M. Butler, Michael Sanera, and W. Bruce Weinrod, *Mandate for Leadership II* (Washington, D.C., 1984).

include elements of a revival both of conservative values, broadly based in the citizenry, and of conservative theory in several academic disciplines. The foundation was able to exploit discontent among conservatives with economic performance, civic morality, and American standing in world politics that prepared a significant fraction of working- and middle-class voters and their political representatives for a departure from liberal strategies for ordering the economy and society.

The Heritage Foundation played an important role in the Reagan administration. Yet many of its proposals were challenged by the AEI, the Brookings Institution, and to a lesser extent the IPS, as well as other policy institutes. Especially in the Bush years, the "supply-side" economics espoused by Heritage has been criticized by both Brookings and AEI economists, most notably Herbert Stein. Disputes among think tanks have occurred over defense, energy, transportation, health care, and a host of other policies. The relations of these institutions to one another, to the state and private groups, and to the process of social and economic investigation remain fluid, multidimensional, and complex.

PARTISANSHIP AND EXPERTISE

For the purposes of this volume, the most obvious and significant development concerning the major Washington think tanks is the gradual transformation of the nonpartisan ideal that gave purpose to the early ones into an outlook that accepted ideological commitment, and sometimes even partisan linkage, as a prominent feature of research institutes. This more recent conception assumed that the think tanks populated a policy-investigation universe that might (without confronting all the philosophical implications) be termed pluralistic, meaning one in which a wide range of contemporary political and ideological perspectives are represented by different and competing institutions, and in which the particular slant of each institution's work might be adjusted periodically, reflecting changes in context, issues, and personnel. The change in the ethos of think tanks has been related here to a breakup of the liberal consensus; to a reassessment, based on heightened ideological tension, of the classical notion of scientific objectivity, a recognition of social pluralism, and philosophical relativism; and to the appearance of a new type of think-tank promoter who came out of government disillusioned with a particular policy line and determined to marshal information and theory to support a comprehensive shift in direction. It was possible for

Robert Brookings and Lewis Brown to equate nonpartisanship with non-alignment, as has been noted, but the tensions between advocacy and commitment and the claim to evenhandedness were all too apparent in the Moulton era, when the New Deal forced recognition of an antistatist-entrepreneurial bias at Brookings, and even more so in the Barnet-Feulner era, when ideological polarization swept the country, demanding commitment everywhere and fragmenting the institutions of knowledge and power.

In ways that can only be suggested here as avenues for future research and reflection, this change in the ethos and program of the think tanks might also be related to other developments. In the first instance, the change undoubtedly had something to do with theoretical developments within individual disciplines. American economists have never agreed that there is only one paradigm, and a breakdown of operational consensus in the discipline has sometimes occurred prior to, or irrespective of, a breakdown of consensus in the wider political order. Then, too, the nonpartisan ideal was never accepted universally. There was ideological conflict aplenty among experts even during the progressive era, when the attraction of nonpartisanship was strongest. In the 1960s, liberal Keynesianism confronted major shifts in the political climate, but it was also challenged by practical operational problems such as the energy crisis and stagflation, which it did not effectively address, and by theoretical developments within the discipline that forced economists to re-evaluate the Keynesian system and weakened Keynesian influence on policy.

The decline of the nonpartisan ideal can also be linked to changes in the political system that reflect a more complicated pattern of political mobilization by a larger and more diverse array of interests and groups, many of them unwilling to link their destinies to a single political party. While business groups have shown a heightened political consciousness in recent decades, so have dozens of others, most notably the new-style "public interest" groups addressing social justice concerns, energy-environmental issues, and foreign policy causes in which the role of government has been seen as increasingly problematic. This increased politicization of the society as a whole has produced a fragmentation of politically effective knowledge and a demand for specialized data and targeted expertise that the institutional characteristics of policy-research organizations—their ability to tap private funds efficiently, their flexibility of program and personnel, and their quasi-public character—ideally suited them to satisfy. In a sense, the decline of the nonpartisan ideal might be linked with a far-reaching, as yet only dimly understood, redefinition of the political order that also encompassed politicization of new ethnic and other minority groups, geopolitical changes that culminated in the end of the cold war, changes in the nominating process, the rise and decline of the "moral majority," the loss by union leadership of control over rank-and-file members, political action committees, negative campaigning, and the tendency of Americans to want a president from one party and Congress and the statehouses in the hands of another.

A few implications of these changes in the ethos and activities of the think tanks can be suggested. Perhaps most obviously, research institutions with clearly recognized policy agendas and ideological inclinations may be held in a certain sense *more* accountable, their research more directly subject to informed evaluation, than those without such clear identities. Heritage Foundation or IPS research is automatically on the defensive, and therefore its authors on the alert, because the burden of proof that a policy predilection has not unduly colored the research falls on its producer. In addition, the proliferation of think tanks marshals expert against expert, testing the credibility of each and enriching the information environment in which the policy discourse occurs and decisions are taken.

On the one hand, this openness to many comers has democratized the policy process. The think tanks provide a vibrant, permeable institutional setting, paralleling the congressional one, in which specialists in policy research who are insulated from at least some of the perils faced by elected officeholders bring their expertise to bear on the issues. On the other hand, the process is not equally open to all comers. Access to financing is one limitation, access to those in power another, and the two are not necessarily reciprocal.[67]

Finally, the proliferation of expertise that has arisen in response to the demand for more policy inquiry has not necessarily improved the information base on which important political decisions are made. More is not necessarily better. Science mingles with hype, as public relations experts manage delivery of information and massage data. On highly technical issues, opposing experts—those few who really understand the complexities—may cancel each other. Competition for attention to re-

---

[67]Thomas Byrne Edsall, *The New Politics of Inequality* (New York, 1984). See also Michael Useed, *The Inner Circle: Large Corporations and the Rise of Business Political Activity in the United States and the United Kingdom* (New York, 1983).

ports places heavy demands on the time and attention of lawmakers, who are left ultimately, in a universe where all data are value laden, to decide what information counts for them on the basis of their own values. A widespread acceptance of relativism, embodied institutionally in the think tanks, has irrevocably altered the process of social investigation and the uses of social knowledge.

8

Social investigation and political learning in the financing of World War I

W. ELLIOT BROWNLEE

"Class politics," Thomas Sewell Adams told the American Economic Association in 1927, "is the essence of taxation." In his presidential address to the association, the Yale professor described the process of making tax policy as he had experienced it during a decade as an adviser to the Department of the Treasury. He told the economists that "tax-making in its most characteristic aspect is a group contest in which powerful interests vigorously endeavor to rid themselves of present or proposed tax burdens." Consequently, he warned, tax making "is, first of all, a hard game in which he who trusts wholly to economics, reason, and justice, will in the end retire beaten and disillusioned."[1]

Adams's assessment, made more than sixty years ago, seems to support currently fashionable accounts of federal taxation and its history. Political scientist John Witte, for example, recently argued that the history of the federal income tax reveals an incremental political process in which "*no one* controls tax policy" and politicians confer "as many benefits on as many groups as is politically feasible." The consequence of the process, he concluded, is "a tax system of enormous complexity, which may have reached the limits of legitimacy, the capacity to meet revenue demands, and the capability of reform." Significant tax reform, for Witte, can come only if the process is first reformed—perhaps by insulating the tax system from politics.[2]

---

[1] Thomas Sewell Adams, "Ideals and Idealism in Taxation," presidential address delivered at the Fortieth Annual Meeting of the American Economic Association, 27 December 1917, *American Economic Review* 18 (March 1918): 1.
[2] John Witte, *The Politics and Development of the Federal Income Tax* (Madison: University of Wisconsin Press, 1985), 21 and 23.

Adams, however, went on to soften his harsh verdict on the character of tax politics. He advised his fellow economists that they could *learn* from the political process, just as he had. "Contest and class politics," he had found, "are indispensable elements in discovering what is truth and sound policy in matters of taxation. For each sound principle of taxation laid down by the economist or statesman, the taxpayers themselves, in bitter struggle, have brought to light half a dozen." Economists could learn not only about economic factors previously ignored but also about the influence of "collateral factors," such as "education, the progress of democracy, the acquisition of political finesse and tax technique" by political spokesmen. Influential among these noneconomic factors was concern for the social implications of taxation, or, as Adams put it, "regard for the general welfare and for sound public policy," which he found "frequently exercises a powerful influence." Moreover, on many tax issues "a majority of legislators and voters are unaffected and disinterested; they may cast their votes as a more or less disinterested jury." And "in the adoption of tax legislation there come zero hours, when the zeal of the narrowly selfish flags."

The challenge that Adams proposed was for experts to take advantage of these openings. "There are thus many important tax problems," he declared, "which may be settled on the broad basis of equity and sound public policy, if one is wise and ingenious enough to find the right solution." The right solution would result from the combination of "patient research and the disinterested mind."[3]

Adams did not disclose the winners and the losers in the tax politics he had witnessed at close hand, so his comments shed little light on the debate over whether tax politics has conformed more to a middle-class pluralism or a corporate elitism.[4] Adams did, however, direct attention

[3]Adams, "Ideals and Idealism in Taxation," 1–7.

[4]Drawing on John Witte's study, two other political scientists, Carolyn Webber and Aaron Wildavsky, *A History of Taxation and Expenditure in the Western World*, have summarized the pluralist view: "The truth is out: As Pogo might have put it, we—the broad middle and lower classes—have met the special interests, and 'they is us.' " Webber and Wildavsky, *A History of Taxation and Expenditure in the Western World* (New York: Simon & Schuster, 1986), 531. The best summary of the corporate "elitist" interpretation is that of political scientist Ronald King, who stresses the importance of a "hegemonic tax logic" that gathered force during the 1920s. Ronald Frederick King, "From Redistributive to Hegemonic Logic: The Transformation of American Tax Politics, 1894–1963," *Politics and Society* 12, no. 1 (1983): 1–52. Historians have, by default, left the modern study of tax institutions largely to political scientists and economists, despite the importance of taxation for the study of a wide variety of historical topics, including progressivism, wartime mobilizations, the twentieth-century state, and the development of the modern

to the importance of what, nearly fifty years later, political scientist Hugh Heclo called "social learning." In the political process as described by Adams, conflict over taxation was severe, and the outcome was uncertain; taxation was up for grabs. But in such turbulent politics, to borrow Heclo's phrasing, financial policy "was not created by the bumping of impenetrable billiard balls of power, but by men who could learn and whose viewpoints could change."[5] Adams suggested that, as part of the learning process, deliberate social investigation plays a role in resolving crises, even though these, too, may have been shaped and modified within the conflict.

Adams's observations covered the years of World War I, during which American taxation and, more generally, public finance underwent dramatic transformations. Between 1917 and 1920, the federal government raised U.S. $13.5 billion in war revenues, primarily from progressive taxes on incomes and profits, and in the process ended its reliance on import duties. Of the remaining U.S. $38 billion required for the war effort, slightly less than two-thirds (about U.S. $24.5 billion), was borrowed from the American people. In the process, the federal government revolutionized the techniques of debt finance. The history of how these changes in public finance were accomplished reveals a process of social learning that confirms the validity of Adams's insights. Moreover, it suggests an approach to the history of public finance in the United States that subsumes the debate over the nature of class conflict.

THE BACKGROUND FOR WARTIME FINANCIAL POLICY

Wartime financial policy in the administration of President Woodrow Wilson was set within a process in which Secretary of the Treasury William G. McAdoo enjoyed a great degree of administrative control but remained deferential to the prerogatives of a Congress and its Democratic party

political economy. No historian has written a comprehensive history of federal taxation since Sidney Ratner's *American Taxation: Its History as a Social Force in Democracy* (New York: Norton, 1942), which argued that the main theme of tax history during the twentieth century was the victory of social democracy through the adoption and elaboration of progressive income taxation. Ratner's book was republished in an expanded edition, but with no shift in interpretation, as *Taxation and Democracy in America* (New York: Wiley, 1967).

[5]Hugh Heclo, *Modern Social Politics in Britain and Sweden: From Relief to Income Maintenance* (New Haven, Conn.: Yale University Press, 1974), esp. 304–26.

leadership.[6] In 1917, McAdoo and Congress knew that they faced wartime financial requirements of unprecedented scope and that they had to meet those requirements rapidly and with largely untested and unstudied monetary and fiscal systems. Their limited information about incidence of taxation, about its effects on economic and institutional structures, and about the probable behavior of taxpayers set the stage for social investigation and for innovation. The substantial body of information produced by more than a generation of professional investigation in public finance pertained largely to state and local governments.[7] They knew little with certainty about the prospects for borrowing. Assistant Secretary of the Treasury Oscar T. Crosby, who had responsibility for "fiscal bureaus" at the onset of the war, recalled the pressures:

The thing that comes back as dominant on all occasions, was the absolute necessity for haste.... Are you a political economist? Then you would like to carefully study the delicate questions connected with...tax exemption. Are you an active banker? Then you would like to have time to feel the pulse of your fellow bankers throughout the country to determine the rate of interest and the maturity of the loans which you are to negotiate. Are you both a political economist and a banker? Then you would like to get together and analyze a lot of statistics to determine how large a bond issue the country can absorb. Are you a bond seller? Then you will want to make long and careful plans for bringing out your issue, and a nice determination as to the length of time that is to elapse between its announcement and the closing of subscriptions. Important and fascinating are all these inquiries. But meantime the Germans with thundering gain are straining forward toward Paris.[8]

---

[6]By autumn 1915, McAdoo had succeeded in establishing independence from Colonel House, in staking out a leadership role in supervising the carrying of administrative bills, and in insulating Treasury Department matters from the incursions of other cabinet members. And, during 1916, as Wilson's attention turned even more toward foreign policy, McAdoo's power further expanded. On the issue of McAdoo's power, see John J. Broesamle, *William Gibbs McAdoo: A Passion for Change, 1863–1917* (Port Washington, N.Y.: Kennikat Press, 1973), 138ff. McAdoo's independence is a good example of the "discretionary space" for entrepreneurship that Wilson extended to senior executives in order to attract risk takers to public office. See Jameson W. Doig, "Woodrow Wilson and the Public Authority Tradition," in Jack Rabin and James F. Bowman, eds., *Politics and Administration: Woodrow Wilson and American Public Administration* (New York: Dekker, 1984). For emphasis on party government in Wilson's career as a "state builder," see Stephen Skowronek, *Building a New American State: The Expansion of National Administrative Capacities, 1877–1920* (Cambridge: Cambridge University Press, 1982), esp. 174–6.

[7]For a survey of the prior work of economists with a special interest in public finance, see Clifton K. Yearly, *The Money Machines: The Breakdown and Reform of Governmental and Party Finance in the North, 1860–1920* (New York: State University of New York [SUNY] Press, 1970), esp. 167–92.

[8]Oscar T. Crosby, "War Finance," undated but probably written during the early 1930s, Oscar T. Crosby Papers, Library of Congress.

Compounding the difficulty of the financial decisions were the demands for social justice by the progressive movement, which was just then reaching its high-water mark. Americans were becoming increasingly insistent that the state play a role in humanizing the terms of industrial life. At the same time, the organization of financial and managerial capitalism was maturing through the flowering of large, multidivisional, hierarchical corporations.[9] Even without wartime mobilization, the federal government would have had to play a major, and expanding, mediating role between a variety of social groups and the new corporations to maintain social order. The war effort made this mediation even more difficult, because the federal government needed to acquire the resources for a massive, capital-intensive war effort. This meant that, in the mobilization for war, the administration could not escape addressing a new, and potentially raw, distributional issue—how the huge costs of war would be allocated, or "who should pay."

Wilson, McAdoo, and the progressives in Congress approached the allocation of war costs with only a brief experiment with a federal income tax as background. Before intervention in World War I, they had moved cautiously in enlarging the tax, enacted only in 1913, to meet emergency needs. Contributing to their caution were the opinions of public finance economists who, like Edwin R. A. Seligman, a professor at Columbia University, found progressive income taxation to be a highly equitable mode of taxation but had reservations about the ability of the government to define clearly the concept of income and to administer the tax effectively. Moreover, Seligman favored a balance of income taxes and customs duties.[10]

In 1914, the cautious Wilson administration responded to the first major weakening of tariff revenues not by expanding income taxation but by passing the Emergency Revenue Act of 1914. This act installed, for one year, a set of regressive taxes on consumption and transactions. By mid-1915, however, the Treasury had acquired two years of experience in collecting progressive income taxes, and McAdoo had become

---

[9]Alfred D. Chandler, Jr., finds that the integration of American industry was complete by World War I. "By the second decade of the century," Chandler concludes, "the shakedown period following the merger movement was over." The result was that "modern business enterprises dominated major American industries, and most of these same firms continued to dominate their industries for decades." Chandler, *The Visible Hand* (Cambridge, Mass.: Harvard University Press, 1977), 345.

[10]For his reservations about income tax administration, see Edwin R. A. Seligman, *The Income Tax* (New York: Macmillan, 1911).

guardedly optimistic about the department's administrative ability to raise substantial new revenues through increasing both the individual and corporate components of the tax.

ENACTING RADICAL TAX REFORM

The Treasury's informed optimism encouraged the Wilson administration to cooperate with a powerful group of insurgent Democrats who opposed preparedness but whose preoccupation with the social implications of taxation led them to champion supported redistributive taxation. These insurgents, led by Cong. Claude Kitchin of North Carolina, who chaired the House Ways and Means Committee and served as majority leader of the House, held on to nineteenth-century antimonopolist, redistributionist traditions. Focusing on taxation issues, they merged Populist and single-tax hostilities toward the concentration of wealth. As a consequence of the collaboration, they enacted a potent measure of tax reform, the Revenue Act of 1916.

This act, in one stroke, broke the dominance of the tariff over the federal revenue system; transformed the experimental income tax into the foremost instrument of federal taxation; introduced federal estate taxation; imposed the first significant taxation of corporate profits and personal incomes; and introduced the concept of taxing corporate "excess-profits" (applying it to munitions manufacturers) and the concept of taxing corporate surpluses and undistributed profits.[11] And, finally, the act provided something of a dress rehearsal for the creation of a wartime fiscal program in 1917. Experience gained with the act helped the Wilson administration and Congress link the existing income tax system of 1913, one that the editors of the *Journal of Political Economy* described in December 1915 as "little more than an ornament," with the later wartime measures.[12]

Confident that taxation of corporate profits and the incomes of wealthy individuals could now raise large revenues, the Wilson administration continued to work with Kitchin and the other congressional insurgents during the revenue crisis of 1917. "Soak-the-rich" taxation became an even more important part of Woodrow Wilson's program of

[11]For an account of the Revenue Act of 1916, see W. Elliot Brownlee, "Wilson and Financing the Modern State: The Revenue Act of 1916," *Proceedings of the American Philosophical Society* 129 (1985): 173–210.
[12]*Journal of Political Economy* 23 (December 1915): 1001.

party government. Less than a year after the enactment of the Revenue Act of 1916, the Revenue Act of 1917 rejected both high taxes on domestic consumption and a mass-based income tax—one falling most heavily on wages and salaries because of low exemptions and high rates on the lower income brackets. Instead, the 1917 act dramatically advanced progressive personal and corporate income taxation by raising the rates on personal income to a maximum of 67 percent (on incomes over $1 million) and, most important, by expanding the taxation of excess profits.

In contrast with Britain, which taxed "war-profits" with a tax on the excess of wartime over peacetime profits, the United States, through the Revenue Act of 1917, imposed a graduated tax on all business profits earned above a "normal" rate of return on invested capital of between 7 percent and 9 percent. Also, the act set the tax rates in a range from 20 percent to 60 percent, the maximum applying to net incomes providing more than a 33 percent rate of return. The goal was to tax the profits accruing to monopoly power. As one Treasury staff member put it, the excess-profits tax had "the manifest advantage...of becoming a permanent part of the Government's revenue system, and can be used, if need be, as a check upon monopolies or trusts earning exorbitant profits."[13]

The adoption of excess-profits taxation was, by any measure, a radical step. For one thing, it constituted a sharp break with historical experience. No state in the union had ever experimented with the tax. The federal government had less than one year's experience with the tentative version enacted in 1916. Among the other belligerents, only Canada had employed the excess-profits base. Claude Kitchin, the chairman of the Ways and Means Committee, took comfort from the advice of Sir Thomas White, Canada's minister of finance, who assured him that the administration of excess-profits taxation was feasible, but neither the Ways and

[13]I. J. Talbert, Head of Law Division, Commissioner of Internal Revenue, to George R. Cooksey, Assistant Secretary of the Treasury, 8 August 1917, Papers of William Gibbs McAdoo, Library of Congress (hereafter MPLC). The best survey of excess profits taxes, and related taxes, during World War I remains John R. Hicks et al., *The Taxation of War Wealth* (Oxford: Clarendon, 1942). As a result of the Revenue Acts of 1916 and 1917, various income and estate taxes produced 79 percent of federal tax revenues in fiscal 1918. The corporate and individual income taxes accounted for 86 percent of the $2.9 billion increase in tax revenues over fiscal 1917; of the $2.8 billion collected in income and excess-profits tax, more than two-thirds, about $2 billion, came from corporations. Commissioner of Internal Revenue, U.S. Office of Internal Revenue, *Annual Report for the Fiscal Year Ended June 20, 1918* (Washington, D.C.: U.S. Government Printing Office, 1918), 98–9.

Means Committee nor the Treasury had time for a systematic investigation of the Canadian tax.[14]

Business was virtually united in opposition to excess-profits taxation. Even small manufacturers, who might have seen the tax as a means of penalizing big business, vigorously registered their hostility to it.[15] The Wilson administration's own business supporters opposed the tax, as well as the administration's general emphasis on income taxation. Wilson's Princeton classmate and largest campaign contributor, Cleveland H. Dodge, who had been silent throughout deliberations over the Revenue Act of 1916, minced no words in 1917. Revealing his own concerns with the social implications of taxation, he warned McAdoo against "schemes of taxation which would kill the goose which lays the golden egg." He also argued that, if the tax bill was "too radical," it would "militate against the ability of the people to subscribe to the bonds as they are issued," and made it clear that he preferred "war-profits" taxation to "excess-profits" taxation.[16]

Another Wilson backer, Jacob Schiff, the senior partner in the investment banking house of Kuhn, Loeb & Co., told McAdoo that heavy reliance on income taxation for financing the war would "curb the push and ambition which is at the bottom of all material progress and development." He singled out the excess-profits tax as "a measure which is economically unsound and which will strike at the very foundation of ... prosperity."[17]

Among the Republican businessmen who were most strenuously opposed were the investment bankers Otto Kahn (another partner in Kuhn, Loeb & Co.), J. P. Morgan, and Morgan's partners. They hoped to replace the excess-profits tax with a combination of war-profits taxation, a mass-based relatively flat income tax, and a variety of consumption taxes. However, they expressed their views cautiously for fear of further arousing anticorporate passions. Morgan appealed privately to McAdoo, while

---

[14] Alex M. Arnett, *Claude Kitchin and the Wilson War Policies* (Boston: Little, Brown, 1937), 263.

[15] The North Carolina textile and furniture manufacturers, for example, strenuously opposed the excess-profits tax. See J. F. Taylor, president of Kinston Cotton Mills, to Kitchin, 2 May 1917, and Fred N. Tate, president and treasurer, the Continental Furniture Co., to Kitchin, 3 August 1917, Kitchin Papers. Thus there is no evidence that Kitchin regarded excess-profits taxation as a means of favoring the southern textile industry.

[16] For Dodge's views, see Dodge to McAdoo, 10 April 1917, and 16 April 1917. For the opinion of other business leaders, see W. P. G. Harding, Governor of Federal Reserve Board, to McAdoo, 3 May 1917, and attachment ("Recommendations by the Federal Advisory Council to the Federal Reserve Board," 18 April 1917, MPLC.

[17] See Jacob Schiff to McAdoo, 12 April 1917, with enclosure, MPLC.

his partner Thomas Lamont worked through the senior Republican on the Senate Finance Committee, Henry Cabot Lodge.[18]

Finally, reflecting an ingrained concern for the accumulation function and a reluctance to engage in "social engineering," most of the nation's professional economists opposed the excess-profits tax. Their preference, like the leaders of business and the Republican party, was for greater reliance on consumption taxes and on income taxes that reached middle-class families. They argued that consumption taxes and mass-based income taxes would fight inflation and promote investment more effectively because they would fall more heavily on the middle classes, thereby discouraging consumption and encouraging investment. Representative of the majority of economists was Edwin R. A. Seligman, who supported "war-profits" taxation but warned the public against "excess-profits" taxation because "excessive taxes on industry will disarrange business, damp enthusiasm, and restrict the spirit of enterprise at the very time when the opposite was needed." Seligman remained an advocate of shifting taxation more heavily to progressive income taxation and declared, "I should be the last to deprecate the fiscal aspects of social reform." Nonetheless, he warned that a fiscal war policy "predicated primarily on principles of social reform will be likely to lose the war."[19]

In fact, the hostility to excess-profits taxation of Seligman and the other distinguished economists of his generation who held senior positions in the nation's leading universities went far beyond opposition to the tax on the ground that it was an ineffective wartime instrument. They had established their professional reputations during the 1880s and 1890s by eschewing or attacking severe policies of redistribution and by championing "scientific" reform programs as against the radical proposals made by "amateur" economists. In 1890, at the annual meeting of the American Social Science Association, Seligman, who was not yet thirty years old, had dramatically faced an aging Henry George and declared

---

[18]For J. P. Morgan's views, see Morgan to McAdoo, 27 April 1917, MPLC. Morgan held back in mobilizing other campaigns which might give tax legislation an even more radical tone. Thus, in April 1917, he discussed with Benjamin Strong the possibility of organizing an effort to repeal the Clayton Act, but confided to Strong that the time was not right "when we are all being threatened with financial catastrophe by the imposition of enormous taxes on the top of large bond issues." J. P. Morgan to Benjamin Strong, 23 April 1917, in *Hearings Before the Special Committee Investigating the Munitions Industry*, 10,428.

[19]Edwin R. A. Seligman, "Our Fiscal Policy," in *Financial Mobilization for War: Papers Presented at a Joint Conference of the Western Economic Society and the City Club of Chicago, 21 and 22 June 1917* (Chicago: privately printed, 1917), 10, 12.

that no professional economist would embrace single-tax ideas. In that confrontation and after, Seligman charged that George and his followers sought reform inspired by nothing more than moral imagination, whereas he and the other young economists were developing, through slow but steady experimentation, institutions that could reduce inequality without destroying the capitalist engine of productivity.

Twenty years later, just before World War I, Seligman relived his confrontation with George, as he intensified his attack on the single-tax movement, which, despite the hostility of most economists, was gaining momentum once again. For Seligman, the contest over wartime taxation was yet another episode in the continuing struggle on behalf of a "progressive capitalism" that was threatened by radical single-tax principles and amateur, unscientific reformers.[20]

Seligman energetically promoted his ideas in 1917. He pressed them upon his Wall Street friends—his brother, Isaac N. Seligman (the senior partner of the investment banking firm of J. & W. Seligman & Co.), Jacob Schiff and his son Mortimer Schiff (the most active lobbyist among the Kuhn, Loeb partners), and Otto Kahn.[21] And he sought out powerful congressmen. On the Ways and Means Committee, Cong. Cordell Hull consulted closely with Seligman, as he had since 1913. He was sympathetic with Seligman's concerns over excess-profits taxation and the failure to establish a broader income tax, but kept his counsel in the face of Claude Kitchin's power on the committee.[22]

[20]For Seligman's full evaluation of Henry George's ideas, see Edwin R. A. Seligman, *Essays in Taxation* (New York: Macmillan, 1921), 66–97. Discussions of the significance of the 1890 clash between Seligman and George are found in Steven B. Cord, *Henry George: Dreamer or Realist?* (Philadelphia: University of Pennsylvania Press, 1965), 29–33, 81–92, and John L. Thomas, *Alternative America, Henry George, Edward Bellamy, Henry Demarest Lloyd and the Adversary Tradition* (Cambridge, Mass.: Harvard University Press, 1983), 324–6. For analysis of the emergence of the modern economics profession, see Mary O. Furner, *Advocacy and Objectivity, A Crisis in the Professionalization of American Social Science, 1865–1905* (Lexington: University of Kentucky Press, 1975). For suggestions of the importance of the single-tax movement to the development of federal income taxation, see Brownlee, "Wilson and Financing the Modern State: The Revenue Act of 1916," 183ff.

[21]Mortimer L. Schiff to Seligman, 26 April 1917; Isaac N. Seligman to Edwin R. A. Seligman, 15 May 1917; and Jacob Schiff to Seligman, 7 June 1917, Edwin R. A. Seligman Papers, Butler Library, Columbia University.

[22]See Edwin R. A. Seligman to Cordell Hull, 1 May 1917, Seligman Papers. On Seligman's relationship with Hull, see Seligman to Hull, 9 March 1916, Cordell Hull Papers, Library of Congress; Seligman to Hull, 22 January, 10 April, and 4 May 1917, Seligman Papers. An important intermediary between Congress and Seligman was Middleton Beaman. He had helped organize the Columbia University Legislative Drafting Bureau between 1911 and 1916. In 1916 the Ways and Means Committee hired him to assist Hull in drafting the Revenue Act of 1916, and broke precedent by allowing him to participate in private

On the Senate Finance Committee, both the Democratic chairman, Furnifold Simmons, and Henry Cabot Lodge worked with Seligman and Robert R. Reed, who was counsel for the Investment Bankers Association of America, to modify the 1917 legislation.[23] Seligman made his connection with Lodge through the good offices of Thomas Lamont. In May, Lamont had called Lodge to introduce Seligman and to urge him to take Seligman's advice in redrafting the pending revenue legislation. Lamont wrote that "it seemed to us that members of the Committee even though they themselves might be most experienced in taxation problems, would welcome having before them the layout of some constructive scheme for producing revenue in adequate volume and yet not doing it in a way to cripple our industries and dry up the sources of taxation's blessings." Lamont told Lodge that "we are asking" Seligman "to give up temporarily his work at Columbia in order to render this possible service to his country."[24]

Seligman's criticisms had less effect on the Revenue Act of 1917 than they might have had, in part because the Wilson administration found its own professional economist—Thomas Sewell Adams—to respond to at least one of the objections of Seligman: that the excess-profits tax could not be administered. The Treasury had hired Adams, an economist on the Yale University faculty, as an adviser in drafting the Revenue Act of 1917. Adams was superbly qualified, having a well-earned reputation for his ability to untangle the knotty, and critical, administrative problems inherent in income taxation. He had served on the Wisconsin Tax Commission (1911–15) during the formulation and implementation of Wisconsin's personal and corporate income tax; had acquired the reputation for having made the Wisconsin tax an administrative success; and, along with Seligman, had advised New York State on the introduction of its income tax in 1916. Moreover, Adams had experience as an investigator

---

drafting sessions. In 1919, Beaman became the first legislative counsel of the House and served in that position until 1949. See Cordell Hull, *The Memoirs of Cordell Hull*, vol. I (New York: Macmillan, 1948), 80; and *New York Times*, 18 September 1951.

[23] Furnifold M. Simmons to Seligman, 19 May 1917 and 4 June 1917; Henry Cabot Lodge to Seligman, 5 June 1917; Robert R. Reed to Seligman, 22 June 1917, Seligman Papers.

[24] Lamont did not suggest retention by the Finance Committee, which the Democrats controlled, but asked Lodge to accredit Seligman personally "to enable him to secure from the Treasury Department such information as may be necessary for his studies." Thomas Lamont to Henry Cabot Lodge, 12 May 1917. Lamont also introduced Seligman to a third Morgan partner, Harry Davison, who was in Washington as chairman of the Red Cross War Council. Lamont explained that he and Dwight Morrow, another Morgan partner, "regard Seligman's ideas as very sound." Lamont to Davison, 22 May 1917, Thomas Lamont Papers, Baker Library, Harvard University.

with a broad range of economic and industrial problems. He had also worked in the Census Bureau with Wesley C. Mitchell, served as assistant treasurer of Puerto Rico, and acted as an investigator for the Bureau of Labor Statistics. In addition, he had held professorial appointments at the University of Wisconsin, Washington University, and Cornell University before joining the Yale faculty in 1916.

In 1917, Adams was a major academic figure in the field of public finance and had cooperated professionally with Seligman. Nonetheless, there were important differences between them—differences that indicated Adams's greater sensitivity to the concerns of the Wilson administration and of Claude Kitchin. Adams had been trained at Johns Hopkins University by Richard T. Ely, and at Wisconsin he had come to know John R. Commons well, both of whom were more willing than Seligman to accept the influence of class issues on institutional development. In 1905, Adams was coauthor, with Helen L. Sumner, of a widely used textbook, *Labor Problems,* in which they wrote that the demand for equality in wealth distribution "is not only a sound social ideal, but, properly understood, it is the only sound ideal." And, in accepting the pioneering challenge of administering the Wisconsin income tax, Adams had chosen to confront public finance orthodoxy, particularly with regard to the taxation of corporate income. His work in Wisconsin had successfully belied the dismal predictions of Seligman.

Even so, Adams also initially approached excess-profits taxation with serious reservations about the penalties the tax might attach to productivity and efficiency. In June 1917, however, even while expressing such reservations, Adams publicly asserted that "the government's claim to ...war profits is so strong as almost to justify the statement that the stockholder has no claim to them until the government has released them." He proposed a graduate corporate income tax based "upon the excess of the earnings in any particular year above the normal rate required to attract to the industry in question a socially sufficient amount of capital," and claimed that there was no theoretical conflict "between the pre-war and invested-capital bases." Either basis, properly applied, would produce "normal" rates of return. What was needed to implement the law, he asserted, was "a maximum of administrative discretion." The creation of a "board of referees" could "recognize *normal rates of profit* for different classes of business."[25]

[25]There is no biography of Adams. The best summary of his career is Joseph Dorfman,

Adams failed to win support for his concept of a completely flexible standard for normal profits, but, endorsed by McAdoo and Cordell Hull, Adams's proposal for the creation of a "board of referees" gained acceptance as a means of resolving congressional concerns over the objections of business leaders and the economists. In the deliberations over the Revenue Act of 1917, McAdoo asked Congress to give him "power to adjust inequalities," and Congress responded by calling on the Treasury to write an elaborate set of regulations implementing the legislation. McAdoo subsequently created an Excess Profits Advisory Board and a committee of legal advisers to assist in administering the excess-profits tax. And he named as the board's chairman and vice chairman, respectively, Cong. Cordell Hull and Thomas S. Adams.[26]

Most important, however, in explaining the willingness of Wilson and McAdoo to gamble on a radical departure in tax policy was the fact they were, indeed, closer to Henry George than to Seligman in their emphasis on taxation as an instrument for achieving social justice. To some extent they shared Claude Kitchin's ideal of using taxation to restructure the economy according to nineteenth-century liberal ideals; they presumed that the largest corporations exercised inordinate control over wealth and that a "money trust" dominated the allocation of capital. For Wilson and McAdoo, the tax program, with its promise to tax monopoly power, seemed to constitute an attractive new dimension to his "New Freedom" approach to the "emancipation of business."[27]

The Economic Mind in American Civilization, vol. 4 (New York: Viking, 1959), 214–21. On the positions of Seligman and Adams on the Wisconsin tax, see W. Elliot Brownlee, *Progressivism and Economic Growth, The Wisconsin Income Tax, 1911–1929* (Port Washington, N.Y.: Kennikat, 1974), 47, 50–2, 61, 125. On Adams's initial statements regarding excess-profits taxation, see his "Defects of the Excess-Profits Tax," *The Annalist* (4 June 1917): 750, 756; "The Income and Excess-Profits Tax," *Financial Mobilization for War*, 110–25; and Adams to Seligman, 30 March 1924, Seligman Papers. Privately, Adams advised that with a proper definition of "normal" net profits and clear specification of the deductions to be allowed in determining current profits, the excess-profits tax would be "the least burdensome" of all modes of wartime finance. See Adams manuscript, "The Fundamentals of War Finance," July 1917, in Thomas Sewell Adams Papers, Sterling Library, Yale University.

[26] McAdoo to Benjamin Strong, 27 September 1917, MPLC.

[27] Wilson and McAdoo's belief in the strength of monopoly power was based in part on the results of social investigation in two important pieces of government-sponsored social investigation: the report of the Pujo Committee, the special House committee that investigated "The Money Trust" in 1913, and Louis Brandeis's 1913–14 exposé, *Other People's Money*. The Pujo Committee report reinforced Woodrow Wilson's New Freedom campaign and established the committee's controversial counsel, Samuel Untermyer, as an influential adviser to Wilson and McAdoo. McAdoo used Treasury Department information to provide Brandeis with answers to ten complicated questions on business

Wilson, McAdoo, and Kitchin all tended to favor the "benefit" principle of tax distribution that Henry George had popularized in promoting a "single-tax" on land. This principle presumed the existence of a sharply delineated class structure based on special privileges. Applying this principle meant distributing taxes according to the "special privileges," such as monopoly power or the private ownership of what George called the "site value" of land. (In contrast, Seligman favored a version of the "ability to pay" theory that justified a broad, albeit progressive, spreading of tax burden.) Both Wilson and McAdoo entertained explicit "single-tax" ideas. In February 1917, McAdoo asked the attorney general for a ruling on the constitutionality of a direct federal tax on land. And McAdoo seriously considered proposing a constitutional amendment to allow "direct" taxation of land without apportionment according to population. In May 1917, Wilson suggested that McAdoo consider the proposal of George L. Record, a leading single-taxer from New Jersey, for a federal tax on "the value of land." Wilson told McAdoo that Record was "a man of somewhat erratic temper but of very clear grasp of some fundamental things." Moreover, McAdoo's close and influential friend, Oscar T. Crosby, who served as assistant secretary of the Treasury in charge of fiscal affairs until October 1917, was a self-proclaimed "single-taxer." Although single-taxer Warren Worth Bailey complained that Wilson's cabinet focused on income taxation, he noted that "these chaps are all land value taxers."[28]

Wilson's and McAdoo's willingness to allow class issues to shape tax policy was part of their larger strategy for mobilizing in a way that would be consistent with a war waged on behalf of democracy. Thus, they saw taxation for social justice as necessary for the effective prosecution of the war. Without such taxation, class issues would be more likely to blunt the war effort, just as they had threatened to do before the Revenue Act of 1916. Moreover, they regarded their tax policies as the ones required to maintain party government. Wilson and McAdoo knew they could have easily engineered passage of a much less progressive tax system—one relying more heavily on consumption taxes and mass-based

corporations and capital for *Other People's Money.* See Brandeis to McAdoo, 7 October 1913, and the editorial note in Melvin I. Urofsky and David W. Levy, *Letters of Louis Brandeis,* vol. 3 (Albany: SUNY Press, 1973), 189–90.

[28] T. W. Gregory to McAdoo, 1 March 1917; Record to Wilson, 3 May 1917; Wilson to McAdoo, 8 May 1917, MPLC. On Crosby's views, see his "Letter to the Editor," *New York Evening Post,* 27 June 1911. Warren Worth Bailey to William M. Reedy, 24 July 1917, Warren Worth Bailey Papers, Seeley G. Mudd Library, Princeton University.

income taxes—in cooperation with Republicans and a minority of conservative Democrats; but they also knew that, if they did so, they would have betrayed the heritage of and program of their political party—a party with strong traditions of representing the disadvantaged, of hostility to a strong central government as the instrument of special privilege, of opposition to the taxation of consumption, and of support for public policies designed to widen access to economic opportunity.[29] Without a highly progressive and "reconstructive" tax program, they would have bitterly divided their party, spoiled their opportunities for attracting progressive Republicans to their party, and destroyed Wilson's strong partnership with congressional Democrats—a partnership both leaders regarded as necessary for the effective advancement of national administration.

MINIMIZING THE BORROWING

The Wilson administration and congressional Democratic leaders also felt confident that they could impose the radical tax program without damaging the nation's basic economic infrastructure because of the second major aspect of their wartime financial policy: minimizing the borrowing used to finance wartime expenditures. This policy would be not only the equitable course, as the congressional progressives led by Claude Kitchin suggested, but also the efficient course, in that limiting borrowing would restrain the inflationary effects of wartime finance.

Wilson and McAdoo managed to fund the initial program of preparedness with no borrowing at all, through the Revenue Act of 1916. In March 1917, McAdoo discussed ways to finance the war with Colonel Edward M. House, Wilson's closest adviser, and they agreed that "a large part of the war's cost should be met by taxation." In April 1917, after America's entry into the war, they decided to limit wartime borrowing to no more than one-half of expenditures. In June 1917, after the success of the first Liberty Loan and a substantial increase in their estimates of the costs of war, they somewhat loosened their restraint on borrowing, raising their planned borrowings to two-thirds of expenditures. But even this higher level left a degree of reliance on taxation that was a substantial

---

[29] For discussion of the importance of hostility toward special privilege to the culture of the Democratic party, see Robert E. Kelley, *The Transatlantic Persuasion: The Liberal-Democratic Mind in the Age of Gladstone* (New York: Alfred A. Knopf, 1969).

departure from historical practice, and was greater than the level of any of the other World War I belligerents.[30]

The Wilson administration had no time to conduct a careful study of how to achieve the proper balance of taxation and borrowing. Nonetheless, the administration did rely heavily on the advice of economists, whose expertise more readily applied to this traditional public finance issue than to the unanswered empirical questions surrounding the social effects of excess-profits taxation. Through their reading of a rapidly growing professional literature, Treasury staff, such as Assistant to the Secretary George R. Cooksey, Cong. Cordell Hull, and the staff of the Ways and Means Committee became familiar with the Civil War experience and the borrowing programs of the other belligerents.

Cooksey, who in the early months of the war was McAdoo's closest adviser, paid particular attention to historical information gleaned from Davis R. Dewey's *Financial History of the United States.* A professor of economics and statistics at the Massachusetts Institute of Technology, Dewey offered his historical judgment that "the weakest element in the financiering of the Civil War was the delay in applying effective taxation" and had placed the blame for that delay with Secretary of the Treasury Salmon P. Chase, who "took no leadership" despite the fact that "the country was impatient to contribute."[31]

A few other economists, most notably Seligman and Harvard University's Charles Bullock, disagreed. Seligman argued that in early stages of the war "very much greater sums ought to be raised by loans than by taxes" and that, overall, no more than one-third of wartime expenditures should be financed through taxation. But McAdoo was more impressed by Dewey and a large group of economists organized by E. Dana Durand of the University of Minnesota. This group included economists ranging from Oliver H. Sprague, who advocated the 100 percent "conscription

---

[30]On McAdoo's discussion with House, see Edward M. House, "The Diary of Edward M. House," vol. 10, 28 March 1917, Papers of Edward M. House, Sterling Library, Yale University. From 1917 through 1920, the 36 percent of the costs of the war paid through taxation in the United States was higher than the level reached by any of the other belligerents. The best general discussion of comparative war finance remains Seligman, *Essays in Taxation*, 748–82.

[31]Davis R. Dewey, *Financial History of the United States* (London: Longmans, Green, 1915), 299–300. McAdoo had asked for historical background on wartime finance and Cooksey responded by sending him a copy of Dewey's book, noting the appropriate pages and commenting that "if you have the time, on the train for instance, I hope that you will be able to read what he has to say about Civil War financing." Cooksey added, "I am sure it will show you what a hodgepodge Civil War financing was." Cooksey to McAdoo, 22 March 1917, MPLC.

of wealth," to the conservative Irving Fisher of Yale University. They telegraphed McAdoo that "the public interests demand rapid increase of taxation ... till taxation ultimately provides much the greater part of expenditures," and they volunteered their services to the Treasury.[32]

The importance of the economists' advice to McAdoo is suggested by the fact that McAdoo turned his back on the advice of the business community, which had traditionally assumed major responsibility for managing the public debt. The most powerful investment banker, J. P. Morgan, had recommended that only 25 percent of expenditures be financed through taxation, and the Federal Advisory Council of the Federal Reserve Board recommended an even lower share, 20 percent.[33] Among the business supporters of the Wilson administration, only Benjamin Strong, governor of the Federal Reserve Bank of New York, favored heavy reliance on taxation. An expert on financial history and a close follower of European public finance, Strong suggested that because "this country has more than twice the wealth of Great Britain ... it should certainly be possible, by an equitable distribution of taxes, to meet a large proportion of our share of war expense by that means, rather than by permanent borrowings."[34]

FLOATING LOW-INTEREST, LONG-TERM LOANS

The third element in the program of war finance was to float long-term loans at interest rates consistently below those available on relatively risk-free investments, even with the tax benefits available to federal bond holders. (By the fourth Liberty Loan, the Liberty Bond interest rate was no more than half the rate available on comparable municipal or corporate bonds.) This decision, which ran contrary to the best information

---

[32]Edwin R. A. Seligman, "Loans Versus Taxes in War Finance," *Financing the War, Annals of the American Academy of Political and Social Science* 75 (January 1918): 52–82; Durand et al. to McAdoo, 17 April 1917, MPLC. Seligman, supported by Columbia professor Robert M. Haig and Harvard professor Charles J. Bullock, engaged in an extended debate with the members of the Durand group. The central statements are found in a widely circulated piece by Oliver M. W. Sprague, "Loans and Taxes in War Finance," *American Economic Review* 7 (March 1917): 199–223, in *Financial Mobilization for War*, and in the *Financing the War* 75 (January 1918).

[33]J. P. Morgan to McAdoo, 27 April 1917; W. P. G. Harding to McAdoo, 3 May 1917, and attachment, "Recommendations by the Federal Advisory Council to the Federal Reserve Board," 18 April 1917, MPLC.

[34]Strong to McAdoo, 11 April 1917, MPLC.

available to the Wilson administration, was very much McAdoo's personal decision, one made in the hectic and uncertain early days of the war. Virtually all commercial and investment bankers pressed for substantially higher rates. Investment bankers did not believe the public would buy subpar issues in great quantities, and commercial bankers disliked the downward pressure on interest rates. Even Benjamin Strong, who favored a long-term strategy of offering submarket rates, urged the Treasury to set a premium for the first Liberty Loan in order to guarantee its initial success. And, as on the excess-profits tax, the economists generally agreed with the business leaders. After the first Liberty Loan, Seligman wrote, "It is unreasonable to suppose that we shall be able to do what no country in the world has ever been able to do, that is, to compel people to lend money at what is really less than money's worth."[35]

McAdoo ignored this advice on borrowing not because he had better information but because his own experiences, his democratic ideals, and his ambitions for the Treasury and the federal government all dictated a different answer. For one thing, McAdoo wanted to limit the future, and especially the postwar, burden of interest payments on the federal government. Confronting an ambitious, capital-intensive military effort of unpredictable duration, and potentially great pressures on existing capital resources, McAdoo knew that the long-run interest charges to the federal government could cripple future or postwar federal initiatives. This would be particularly so if, as McAdoo expected, postwar deflation were to force the federal government to pay back its huge war debts with dollars that had increased enormously in value. A closely related objective was to keep the federal government from becoming dependent on wealthy creditors. McAdoo feared that if the Treasury did not reduce dependency on the wealthiest borrowers, the scale of borrowing required to fight the war might be so great that control of the state would pass to a small class of wealthy capitalists, and that there would be a massive redistribution of wealth favoring the wealthy few. McAdoo was certain that "in a democracy, no one class should be permitted to save or to own the nation."[36]

Finally, McAdoo feared most the monopoly power of financiers. His fear was based not on systematic investigation but on his own experience

---

[35]Strong to McAdoo, 26 March 1918, MPLC; and Edwin R. A. Seligman, "Our Fiscal Policy," 6.
[36]"Memorandum in Explanation of the Proposed War Loan Bill," August 1917; McAdoo to George Cooksey, 22 October 1917, MPLC.

in promoting railroads in New York and New Jersey, and on his observations while secretary of the Treasury. In May 1918 he described for the president how J. P. Morgan had recently exacted a monopolistic interest rate from the New York Central Railroad when it wanted to borrow $6 million. "The old idea of some of the financial bosses of Wall Street still exists," McAdoo told Wilson. McAdoo was concerned about the ability of merchants and smaller manufacturers, particularly those still specializing in civilian goods, to raise capital, and about the effects of taxing and borrowing on these manufacturers and on the railroads, who had to finance their needs in competition with those of the federal government and the more profitable wartime sectors of the economy.[37]

McADOO'S "STATIST" APPROACH TO MOBILIZING CAPITAL

McAdoo's break with the market-dominated approach to war finance included, as well as low-priced bonds, a fourth element, which might be described as a "statist" or administrative, rather than market, approach to converting capital to the conduct of the war. Early in 1919, Benjamin Strong described the decision confronting the Treasury as a choice between "one school," represented presumably by Edwin R. A. Seligman, "believing that economy could and should be enforced and inflation avoided through establishing higher [interest] rate levels" and "the other school, which included the writer," believing "that economy must be enforced through some system of rationing, or by consumption taxes, or by other methods more scientific, direct, and equitable than high-interest rates." McAdoo's plan relied on the second approach: to borrow capital at low rates and then develop new government machinery that would guarantee American business adequate access to the resources for maintaining health and productivity into the postwar period.[38]

In implementing this fourth policy element, McAdoo led a Treasury effort to gain control of the nation's capital markets, and, outside the Treasury, he pressed Wilson, other members of the cabinet, and Congress to increase the federal government's control over prices and the allocation of capital, and to coordinate and centralize all wartime powers. In August 1917, Colonel House commented on McAdoo's program: "When you

---

[37]McAdoo to Woodrow Wilson, 31 May 1918, MPLC.
[38]Benjamin Strong to Russell C. Leffingwell, 6 February 1919, in U.S. Senate, 74th Cong., 2d Sess., *Hearings Before the Special Committee Investigating the Munitions Industry*, (Washington, D.C.: U.S. Government Printing Office, 1934–43), 9567.

sum up, it means he would be in complete control of the Government," and, "taking his demands as a whole, it would leave him as arbiter not only of the United States but of the European nations as well."[39]

McAdoo's most important statist initiatives began late in 1917, when he became concerned about the difficulties that the railroads and other utilities were having in financing wartime expansion.[40] Working closely with the members of the Federal Reserve Board, particularly Benjamin Strong and Paul Warburg, he devised proposals to block any capital expenditures that did not advance the war effort and to give priority to the capital needs of railroads and the Treasury. In November 1917, McAdoo proposed that Congress empower him to appoint a commission to review "all applications for new capital expenditures" and to impose a 10 percent tax on those expenditures if they were not appropriate for the war effort. This proposal led to the formation of the Capital Issues Committee of the Federal Reserve Board.[41] One month later, in December 1917, he proposed, with the support of the Federal Reserve Board, creating a War Emergency Finance Corporation funded with $500 million. This led to the creation of the War Finance Corporation. McAdoo attached great importance to both organizations, seeing them as instruments for rationing scarce capital resources, providing public capital for critical private needs unserved by the marketplace, and enhancing confidence in the banking system.

In addition, McAdoo used the issues of war finance to advance his campaign to take over the railroads. On 10 December 1917, he wrote

[39]Centralization of the budget process was a high-priority item for McAdoo, and he even urged the creation of a Central Bureau of Intelligence. On these and other initiatives, see McAdoo to Claude Kitchin, 25 January 1917; McAdoo to Woodrow Wilson, 12 May 1917; McAdoo to Woodrow Wilson, 16 and 30 April and 16 May 1917; McAdoo to Newton D. Baker, 6 July 1917; Benjamin Strong to McAdoo, 15 February 1918; McAdoo to Strong, 19 February 1918; McAdoo to Wilson, 19 February 1918; MPLC. For Colonel House's comments, see "The Diary of Edward M. House," vol. 11, 7 August 1917. An excellent introduction to McAdoo's planning interests is Dale Norman Shook, *William G. McAdoo and the Development of National Economic Policy, 1913–1918* (New York: Garland, 1987).

[40]McAdoo was worried that the railroads could not, because of a critical Interstate Commerce Commission decision in December, raise their rates; that the Revenue Act of 1917, through a provision which established high rates of taxation on holding companies, further compounded their problems; and that these problems of finance threatened the stability of bond and stock markets and the ability of the government to raise taxes. McAdoo received details of these troubles from a wide assortment of investment bankers, including J. P. Morgan, Thomas Lamont, and S. R. Bertron. Most urged McAdoo and the president to declare, as Bertron put it, "that no further war taxation need be enacted in the near future." Bertron to McAdoo, 7 November 1917, MPLC.

[41]McAdoo to Leffingwell, 5 November 1917, MPLC.

to the president, "The railroad situation is inextricably bound up with the vital and major problem of Government finance," adding that "we shall have to handle these two problems with very great care and skill" and that "future financial operations of the Government will be seriously affected by your action, and whoever you may choose to direct this operation should work in the most harmonious relationship with the Treasury Department." Four days later, he wrote again, this time confidentially, warning Wilson of the demoralization of New York security markets and urging him to "take action in the railroad matter at the very earliest possible moment" because if "a panic would set in, grave injury would result and the financial operations of the Government would be seriously imperilled." Within less than a week, Wilson had decided to name McAdoo the director general of the railroads.[42]

MAXIMIZING THE SALE OF BONDS TO THE MIDDLE CLASS

McAdoo's interrelated desires to keep interest rates down, reduce government dependence on the wealthy, and increase the capital available for problem industries led to the fifth element of the Treasury's financial program: maximizing the sale of bonds to middle-class Americans. Among the five elements, this one was most clearly the Treasury's responsibility; Congress left the marketing procedures almost entirely to Treasury discretion. Free to act, McAdoo attempted to persuade middle-class Americans to change their economic behavior: to reduce consumption, increase savings, and become creditors of the state. After the conclusion of the war, he hoped, the bond holders would be repaid by tax dollars raised from corporations and the wealthiest Americans.

Selling the high-priced bonds directly to middle-class Americans on a multibillion-dollar scale required sales campaigns of unprecedented scope. In the course of the four Liberty Loans, McAdoo and the Treasury expanded the federal government's, and the nation's, knowledge of the social basis of capital markets. Largely through trial and error, they formulated a vast array of state-controlled national marketing techniques, including the sophisticated analysis of social sources of national income and savings. McAdoo and his staff were particularly interested in developing the capacity to identify and target particular categories of bor-

---

[42]McAdoo to Woodrow Wilson, 10 and 14 December 1917, MPLC. On the timing of Wilson's decision, see "The Diary of Edward M. House," vol. 12, 18 December 1917.

rowers. There was no time to develop systematic information for the first Liberty Loan in the spring of 1917, but in the autumn, as the collective pressures of the war effort tightened the supply of capital, McAdoo and the Treasury commissioned an analysis of savings by Melville W. Thompson, the senior member of Thompson & Black, a firm of Wall Street accountants.

Two findings of the Thompson study were particularly influential. First, it rendered an optimistic verdict with regard to the availability of capital. It estimated that in 1917 the economy would generate $18 billion of savings and be able to sustain $10 billion of federal taxes and borrowing. Second, the study found attractive, untapped capital resources—some $3.5 billion of farm savings—within the agricultural community. And, to restrain inflation, the report recommended that "the forthcoming loan be placed primarily with the farmer." The study pointed out that these savings would not normally flow into industrial "investment centers," and warned that they might "be dissipated in doubtful and unnecessary enterprises unless conserved by the government."[43]

Persuaded by the Thompson study, McAdoo set the goal of the Second Liberty Loan at $3 billion (versus the $2 billion of the first), and worked hard to shift bond sales to farmers. He ordered "every Internal Revenue Collector and Revenue Agent to exert every effort" to solicit loans from farmers and "to make every deputy an active agent in the field for this purpose." In addition, he telegraphed to the presidents of the Farm Loan Banks that he wanted "the Farm Loan Banks to make a special effort ... to get every farmer to buy some of these bonds no matter how small the amount." After the end of the second loan, working directly with the postmaster general, McAdoo acquired the means to reach directly into farm households. He acquired a mailing list of more than 2 million farms throughout the United States and sent more than 1.2 million of them a propaganda package. In addition, the Post Office Department, through its fourth-class post offices, delivered 7 million unaddressed copies of a special pamphlet aimed at farmers. Meanwhile, in preparation

[43]Contributing heavily to the Thompson & Black study was David Friday, a young economist who had joined the firm. "Memorandum from M. B. Clagett for the Secretary," 7 September 1917, MPLC. M. W. Thompson, "The Supply of Capital and the Next Loan," September 1917. Thompson joined the War Department, where he continued his analysis of capital accumulation and war finance as president of the War Credits Board. See M. W. Thompson to McAdoo, 28 March and 4 April 1918, MPLC.

for the Third Liberty Loan, McAdoo commissioned Thompson & Black to update its analysis of savings.[44]

Informed by systematic investigation and armed with modern techniques of mass communication, the Treasury succeeded in placing the Liberty Loans deep in the middle class. In the Third Liberty Loan campaign (conducted in April 1918), for example, more than 18 million people, accounting for nearly 18 percent of the American population and probably representing at least half of all American families, subscribed.[45] Consequently, the borrowing stimulated a substantial degree of voluntary saving, just as McAdoo had hoped. The estimates of savings on which McAdoo relied in late 1917 turned out to be remarkably accurate. Personal savings, the crucial component for McAdoo's borrowing strategy, nearly doubled between 1916 and 1917, increasing from $5.56 billion to $10.07 billion; they increased further in 1918, to $12.69 billion. Most, and perhaps nearly all, of these increases were a consequence of investments in U.S. government securities. And, because of these investments, personal savings as a share of gross national product increased from about 12 percent in 1916 to 17 or 18 percent in 1917–18.[46] This increase in the savings rate, coupled with the high level of taxation, contributed to what should properly be seen as a relatively low rate of inflation during the World War I period.[47]

[44]Telegram, McAdoo to Presidents of Federal Loan Banks, 20 October 1917; McAdoo to George Cooksey, 18 October 1917; McAdoo to Brice Clagett, 4 November 1917. The mailing list of farmers was suggested by the collector of internal revenue in Raleigh, North Carolina, who proposed that the solicitation be limited to farmers with incomes over $1,000. J. W. Bailey to McAdoo, 29 October 1917. See also Frank R. Wilson, Director of Publicity, War Loan Organization, to McAdoo, 25 May 1918, MPLC. David Friday also prepared the new analysis. See David Friday, "War and National Savings: A Study in the Supply of Capital," March 1918. Adams Papers.

[45]Secretary of the Treasury, *Annual Report on the State of the Finances for the Fiscal Year Ended June 30, 1918* (Washington, D.C.: U.S. Government Printing Office, 1918), 8.

[46]For the data on savings, see Bureau of the Census, *Historical Statistics of the United States, Colonial Times to 1970* (Washington, D.C.: U.S. Government Printing Office, 1975), 224 and 262.

[47]Some economists have criticized the Wilson administration for contributing to inflationary pressures by inadequately taxing consumption and lower incomes, and by adhering to an excessively easy monetary policy. Charles Gilbert, in the only extended history of World War I finance, has made the most elaborate statement of these criticisms. See Charles Gilbert, *American Financing of World War I* (Westport, Conn.: Greenwood Press, 1970), esp. 117, 197, and 236. (I admit to having contributed to such criticism; see *Dynamics of Ascent: A History of the American Economy* [2d ed., 1979; reprint, Belmont, Calif.: Dorsey Press, 1988], 375–7.) However, during mobilization, the annual rate of increase in wholesale prices actually declined—from about 18 percent per year (June 1914 through March 1917) to about 12 percent per year (March 1917 through November

ADMINISTRATION FOR WARTIME TAXING AND BORROWING

For success, the complex and ambitious program of taxing and borrowing required a vast expansion of the administrative capacity of the Treasury. During the war, Congress increased the number of assistant secretaries from three to five and created a sixth position of comparable status, the special commissioner to the Inter-Ally Council, who supervised the complex economic relations between the United States and the Allies. The three areas of responsibility overseen by the first three assistant secretaries had been "fiscal bureaus," customs, and "public buildings and miscellaneous." As a result of the demands of new wartime activities, the "fiscal bureaus" area became "fiscal matters." One of the new assistant secretaries took over supervision of both the Bureau of Internal Revenue and the Bureau of War Risk Insurance. The second new assistant secretary supervised the Foreign Loan Bureau and the War Loan Organization, which, under a director, supervised the sale of Liberty bonds and war-savings certificates.[48]

During the first few months after the United States entered the war, McAdoo made no important changes in Treasury personnel. But after the completion of the first Liberty Loan, McAdoo began to assemble a new management group, one that was more appropriate to meet the severe demands of the wartime financial crises and to serve his ambitions. The most important of McAdoo's new managers was Russell T. Leffingwell, whom McAdoo first appointed as special counsel for Liberty Loan matters in May and then, in October 1917, named as assistant secretary of the Treasury in charge of the most powerful administrative

1918). After the armistice, the rate fell further, to well under 10 percent through May 1919; it subsequently increased to a rate of 21 percent (over the period through May 1920). Moreover, the 12 percent inflation rate was substantially less than the 25 percent during the Civil War. And the 16 percent annual rate of increase during the entire wartime period (August 1914 through May 1920) was surprisingly close to the 9 percent annual rate at which prices increased during the comparable World War II years (September 1939 through 1948). The World War I record was more impressive because much of World War II mobilization took place during a period of high unemployment and depressed demand and because in World War II price controls and rationing had greater force. Milton Friedman and Anna J. Schwartz, *A Monetary History of the United States 1867–1960* (Princeton, N.J.: Princeton University Press, 1963), 206–7, and Milton Friedman, "Price, Income, and Monetary Changes in Three Wartime Periods," *American Economic Review* 42 (March 1952): 612–25.

[48]No adequate history of the Department of Treasury exists, but see Lloyd Milton Short, *The Development of National Administrative Organization in the United States* (Baltimore: Johns Hopkins University Press, 1923), 269–98, and Carroll H. Wooddy, *The Growth of the Federal Government: 1915–1932* (New York: McGraw-Hill, 1934), 5–46.

zone in the Treasury: "fiscal matters," including the Treasury's borrowing and debt management policies.[49]

Leffingwell was well suited to make the most of the opportunity. In addition to having a strong grasp of the technical issues of finance, Leffingwell was a long-time friend of McAdoo's, a Republican, and a former partner in the well-connected New York law firm of Cravath & Henderson (representing major firms, including both J. P. Morgan & Company and Kuhn, Loeb & Company).[50]

Leffingwell proved expert not only in organizing the borrowing activities and manipulating the complex array of short-term debt instruments but also in managing congressional relations, anticipating shifts in revenue needs, and overseeing personnel. Soon, and particularly after April 1918, when a new assistant secretary relieved him from the Liberty Loan and foreign loan responsibilities, Leffingwell began functioning, de facto, as an under secretary of the Treasury. He supervised all Treasury affairs and assumed management of the department during McAdoo's numerous absences on Liberty Loan promotions, tours of railroad facilities, vacations, and sick leave. Largely as a consequence of his success, Congress created the office of the under secretary of the Treasury in 1921.

A major tool for success in fulfilling the Treasury's new responsibilities was the Federal Reserve Board. In fact, the board functioned during the war as an arm of the Treasury, working in close harmony with Leffingwell's borrowing and debt management operations. This control over the Federal Reserve developed in part because McAdoo had been successful in cutting off a movement to establish a council of bankers that would advise the Treasury.[51] McAdoo essentially directed the Federal Reserve

[49]Leffingwell replaced Oscar T. Crosby, who became president of the Inter-Ally Council on War Purchases and Finance (1917–19) and special commissioner of finance (1918–19). In these positions, Crosby represented the Treasury and American financial interests in Europe and ranked with Leffingwell and Roper in McAdoo's management team. However, consideration of the foreign dimension of Treasury policy lies outside the scope of this essay. The best discussion of this topic is Kathleen Burk, *Britain, America and the Sinews of War, 1914–1918* (Boston: George Allen and Unwin, 1985).

[50]McAdoo to Wilson, 28 October 1917, MPLC. In 1911 and 1912 Leffingwell represented Kuhn, Loeb & Co. in the proposed six-nation $300 million loan to the Chinese government, and, along with Paul Cravath himself, most of the Kuhn, Loeb bond issues. Leffingwell does not appear to have ever represented McAdoo, but the Cravath firm did handle the refinancing of McAdoo's Hudson & Manhattan Railroad in 1912 and 1913. See Robert T. Swaine, *The Cravath Firm and Its Predecessors, 1819–1948* (New York: privately published, 1948), 108–9, 113, 119, 130–2.

[51]In March 1917, Comptroller of the Currency John Skelton Williams described this movement "to devise plans for raising such funds as may be necessary in the event of war with

Board's policy by cultivating a solid relationship with Benjamin Strong, the powerful chairman of the New York Federal Reserve Bank, and by maintaining control over three of the Wilson appointees to the Federal Reserve Board: Boston lawyer Charles Hamlin, Birmingham banker Warren P. G. Harding, and McAdoo's close friend John Skelton Williams (serving ex officio as comptroller of the currency).

To support the administration's program of mass-marketing bonds, the twelve Federal Reserve banks coordinated the Liberty Loans in their districts, and the Federal Reserve Board and the Treasury devised innovative techniques for federally sponsored installment credit.[52] In addition, McAdoo used the Federal Reserve System as a source of national information gathering. The Federal Reserve Board and John Skelton Williams kept McAdoo supplied with reports on corporate bank balances, particularly those of the munitions, steel, iron, and coal companies, for the purposes of monitoring the tax-paying capacity and capital needs of corporations. The centralized collection of business information on a national scale gave the Treasury enhanced ability to respond to and shape economic change.[53]

The third major Treasury domain—after "fiscal matters" and the Reserve Board—was the Bureau of Internal Revenue, which was directed by the commissioner of internal revenue (serving under the general supervision of an assistant secretary).[54] The bureau experienced the most dramatic augmentations and reorganizations of any Treasury agency, and between 1913 and 1920, its personnel increased from 4,000 to 15,800, largely to assess and collect taxes on incomes and profits.

Over this essentially new empire presided Commissioner Daniel C. Roper. His political career, which had begun as a member of the Farmers'

Germany" as "an effort on the part of the super-bankers . . . to arrogate to themselves . . . the responsibilities of the Administration and the Treasury Department." Williams noted, "We have a better organization today than ever before for the distribution of Government loans, through Federal Reserve Banks and member banks, and the help of the Federal Reserve Board." Williams to McAdoo, 23 March 1917, MPLC.

[52] Milton Friedman and Anna Schwartz have described the Federal Reserve during the war as becoming "to all intents and purposes the bond-selling window of the Treasury." Friedman and Schwartz, A Monetary History of the United States, 1867–1960, 216.

[53] See, for example, Williams to McAdoo, 13 September 1917, MPLC.

[54] No adequate history exists for the Bureau of Internal Revenue (Internal Revenue Service after 1953), but see Laurence F. Schmeckebier and Francis X. A. Eble, The Bureau of Internal Revenue (Baltimore: Johns Hopkins University Press, 1923); and John C. Chommie, The Internal Revenue Service (New York: Praeger, 1970), 3–29; Lilian Doris, The American Way in Taxation: Internal Revenue, 1862–1963 (Englewood Cliffs, N.J.: Prentice-Hall, 1963); and Daniel C. Roper, Fifty Years of Public Life (Durham, N.C.: Duke University Press, 1941), 172–84.

Alliance, had led him to become a seasoned bureaucrat and an influential figure in the national Democratic party. By the time he joined the Treasury, he had served as a clerk for the Interstate Commerce Commission, a researcher on textiles for the Bureau of Census, a clerk of the House Ways and Means Committee, first assistant postmaster general, head of the Bureau of Organization for Wilson's 1916 campaign, and vice-chairman of the Tariff Commission. Appointed in September 1917, Roper immediately conducted an extensive analysis of the bureau, reorganized it along multifunctional lines with clear specifications of responsibilities and lines of authority, and assembled what he called his "cabinet"—key assistants, including John E. Walker, Roper's successor as clerk on the Ways and Means Committee, and former associates from the Post Office Department and the Tariff Commission.

A critical new element in Roper's Bureau of Internal Revenue was the Excess Profits Advisory Board. McAdoo welcomed and exploited the board's creation as an opportunity to enhance the power of the Treasury over taxation, to enlarge the Treasury's administrative apparatus, and to reconcile corporations disenchanted with the Wilson administration. Consequently, the Revenue Act of 1917 marked the first significant shift of tax policy away from Congress, and toward the executive branch. And, most important, the Advisory Board institutionalized a process of learning in which experts in the Treasury Department would interact with taxpayers.

The Treasury's area of freedom for making administrative rulings under the excess-profits tax was broad, but McAdoo wanted the tax to work as Congress had intended. By appointing Samuel Untermyer, who had been counsel for the Pujo "Money Trust" Committee in 1913, as one of the three legal advisers, McAdoo left no doubt about his intentions. Untermyer devoted himself to fending off what he described as "a concerted movement of the big industrial interests to discredit" the tax; these enthusiasts, he said, were "looking to the discarding of the present law and to the inevitable chaos that will result from the substitution of a new method of taxing excess-profits."[55] In fact, McAdoo allowed no compromise on fundamental issues. For example, he overruled the Advisory Board's recommendation that corporations under financial stress be allowed to defer their payments of taxes due in 1918. He argued that the army should bail out any war contractors who were pinched, and that

[55]Untermyer to McAdoo, 10 December 1917, MPLC.

other corporations could find relief from the commercial banking system reinforced by the War Finance Corporation.[56]

The Treasury did attempt to make the new corporate tax law, which was extremely ambiguous on critical definitions, work fairly and consistently, and to increase allowances for capital investment, which reduced corporate tax assessments. More than twenty years later, Roper recalled that his administration of the Bureau of Internal Revenue had been based on the concept of "the Government in partnership with business."[57] Especially appreciative of this policy were the numerous smaller corporations and partnerships whose capitalizations, rates of return, and rates of taxation would have been much higher without favorable Treasury rulings. Many of these smaller corporations drew on Treasury expertise to apply modern accounting practices with regard to the valuation of capital investment and depreciation, and many corporations recruited the Treasury experts for their own accounting departments. Perhaps ironically, the Treasury, in acquiring the information and methods necessary to enforce the excess-profits tax, contributed to the diffusion of knowledge of modern accounting practice and enhanced the efficient operation of financial markets. Both the Treasury and the corporations learned from the exercise.[58]

Crucial to developing and maintaining this interactive process were Cordell Hull and Thomas S. Adams, the leaders of the Advisory Board. They had just the right balance of detachment and commitment on excess-profits taxation for McAdoo's taste. Both men were known to have had serious reservations about excess-profits taxation, but both were also enthusiastic about progressive income taxation. Both also had well-deserved reputations for technical expertise in taxation and for conscientious respect for the law. Hull had training in tax law and had drafted the initial House version of every major piece of tax legislation since

---

[56]McAdoo received vigorous support in his opposition to deferred installment payments from Leffingwell, who explained this policy to the bankers. Leffingwell to McAdoo, 7 December 1917; Leffingwell to Benjamin Strong, 22 April 1918; Leffingwell to Paul Warburg, 23 April 1918; Leffingwell to McAdoo, 23 April 1918, Russell C. Leffingwell Papers, Library of Congress (hereafter LPLC).

[57]Roper, *Fifty Years of Public Life*, 177.

[58]Ibid., 181. H. Thomas Johnson has highlighted the importance of return-on-investment accounting in multidivisional corporations, but no one has explored the precise contribution of the Treasury to the diffusion of the techniques. See H. Thomas Johnson, *A New Approach to Management Accounting History* (New York: Garland, 1986), 13–34 and 142–5.

1913. Adams had become an enthusiastic supporter of excess-profits taxation, advertising the work of the Advisory Board as an experiment that was designed to try to make the excess-profits tax work, and one that might make "tax paying and tax gathering . . . different and far more wholesome things" by promoting "cooperation between those who pay and those who collect taxes." The tax itself, he said, offered promise as "a liberal and democratic financial policy during the reconstruction period which must follow the war," particularly in a period of rising tariffs and price regulation. It might "promote individualism and private industry," recognizing that "not only land sites, as Henry George emphasized, but other commercial and industrial opportunities differ enormously." The test would be, Adams suggested, whether the Treasury could solve problems of capital valuation and could establish "a practicable and reasonably equitable determination of normal capital value."[59]

As a tax expert, Adams played a role at the Treasury Department far beyond his service, however important, on the Advisory Board. His appointment to the board followed service as a technical adviser to the Treasury on the drafting of legislation and on the organization of the Bureau of Internal Revenue. His contributions to the latter were so important that Robert M. Haig, a Columbia University economist and close student of British wartime profits taxation, later compared Adams's accomplishments with those of Sir Josiah Stamp in the British Inland Revenue. But whereas "Stamp had at his command a corps of trained tax administrators which was the pride of the British Civil Service," Haig wrote, "Adams had nothing. He had to build from the ground up."[60]

And perhaps most important, Adams enhanced the long-run capabilities of the Treasury by developing a rapidly growing research enterprise based in the Bureau of Internal Revenue. Much of the bureau's research was directed toward monitoring the operation and effects of excess-profits taxation, but it gradually encompassed all aspects of the new programs of taxation. Adams mobilized a wide range of professionals—

[59]Thomas S. Adams, "Principles of Excess Profits Taxation," *Annals of the American Academy of Political Science* 75 (January 1918): 147–58, and "Federal Taxes upon Income and Excess Profits," *American Economic Review* 8 (March 1918): 18–26.
[60]Robert M. Haig, "Tribute," in George A. Boissard, ed., *In Appreciation of Thomas Sewell Adams* (Madison, Wis.: privately published, 1933), 8.

often co-opting economists, accountants, and lawyers from other work in the Treasury—to analyze proposed tax legislation and to make projections of revenue needs and tax yields.

The latter investigations fell largely to David Friday, an economist who joined the Treasury as a consultant in 1918 after he was recognized for his work on the Thompson & Black analysis of national savings and income. Friday, who had been a student of Henry C. Adams at the University of Michigan and had worked with Adams for a number of state commissions, had developed expertise in accounting and had joined New York University as head of the Department of Economics in 1915. Friday's work not only proved invaluable to the planning of tax policy within the Treasury but also advanced the nascent study of national income, led by economists such as Wesley C. Mitchell and Willford L. King. However, Friday's work on the national income was less effective than the work of his counterparts in Britain because the British tax, with its low exemption, reached more people and generated more complete data on national income. Moreover, Friday had no interest in basing his career purely on economic measurement. However, he did draw on his Treasury research during the 1920s when he went on to become one of the most important innovators in applying a microeconomic understanding of the firm to an understanding of macroeconomic behavior.[61]

No formal organization existed to provide a sharp focus for the research activity of the Treasury. In 1866 a Bureau of Statistics had been created in the Treasury Department but, as the revenue system stabilized around the tariffs, the bureau languished until 1903, when it was transferred to the new Department of Commerce and Labor. McAdoo chose not to reestablish such a bureau. He preferred to use Thomas S. Adams in a highly flexible, informal fashion, drawing on his organizational talents as crises emerged. In a sense, the absence of

---

[61]See notes 44 and 45 above. Friday's academic contributions, based heavily on his Treasury research on incomes, included "The Course of Agricultural Income During the Last Twenty-Five Years," *American Economic Association* 13 (March 1923): 147–58; "The Taxable Income of the United States," *Journal of Political Economy* 26 (December 1918): 952–69; "The War and the Supply of Capital," *American Economic Review* (March 1919); and *Profits, Wages, and Prices* (New York: Harcourt, 1920). For a biography of Friday, see Dorfman, *The Economic Mind in American Civilization,* vol. 5, 403–14. On the advantages that British students of national income had as a consequence of fuller tax data, see Don Patinkin, "Keynes and Econometrics: On the Interaction Between the Macroeconomic Revolutions of the Interwar Period," *Econometrica* 44 (November 1976): 1091–123.

a formal organization testified to Adams's importance to the Treasury. However, after the war, the influence of the kind of research that Adams had led was recognized in the creation, in 1920, of the Section of Statistics, which gathered together all the activities in the Treasury related to economic research.[62]

The leadership team McAdoo had established proved to be exceptionally capable, in part because of the "businesslike" methods fostered within the Treasury by gifted administrators like Roper and Leffingwell, but also because of its intellectual flexibility, entrepreneurship, ambition, and institutional diversity. Leffingwell, for example, who had the breadth of vision and technical expertise required to supervise all aspects of Treaury operations, turned out to be a gifted negotiator with Congress and had connections with the most powerful elements of the business community.[63] Benjamin Strong helped McAdoo achieve de facto control of the Federal Reserve System and establish excellent communications with the largest commercial bankers. John Skelton Williams helped maintain McAdoo's ties with more radical antibusiness progressives, and made McAdoo seem, by contrast, conservative and reasonable to business leaders. Roper had experience in political and administrative problems across a wide range of federal agencies and linked McAdoo with the Southern textile industry, which he had studied and come to know well in the Census Bureau and on the Tariff Commission. Thomas S. Adams had experience in legislative consultation, implementing radical forms of progressive taxation, and conducting economic investigations. He became the leader in the drafting of legislation, tying together the process of administering old laws with the formulation of new ones. And Cordell Hull brought to the service of the Treasury his own expertise in tax law and the respect he commanded on the Ways and Means Committee. Moreover, both Adams and Hull had strong ties with economists and economic expertise outside the federal government.

Lacking a formal civil service presence adequate for his ambitions for the Treasury, McAdoo had fashioned within the Treasury what Hugh

---

[62]In 1927 the Treasury renamed it the Section of Financial and Economic Research.

[63]For example, McAdoo delegated to Leffingwell the task of persuading Thomas Lamont to support the War Finance Corporation. The "mere existence of the Corporation," Leffingwell explained to Lamont, "with power to give relief in case of necessity will have the effect of restoring confidence to such an extent as to make financing through the ordinary channels of the banks and banking houses possible, which is not now possible." Leffingwell to Lamont, 21 February 1918, LPLC.

Heclo has called an "informal political technocracy," or a "loose grouping of people where the lines of policy, politics, and administration merge in a complex jumble of bodies." This was an early example of what would become a typical expression of America's unique form of a "higher civil service." In the Treasury, McAdoo's group, advising him continuously in both formal and informal ways, developed a significant degree of autonomy and served as the Wilson administration's primary instrument for learning about financial policy and its social implications, shaping the definition of financial issues and administration programs, and mobilizing support for those programs. That group was the necessary means for McAdoo to form and dominate networks linking together competing centers of power within the state and linking the state with civil society. If he had not formed such a group, McAdoo would have been unable to design and implement a coherent financial policy with clear social objectives. Without McAdoo's leadership, the Treasury would have fallen under the control of competing centers of power within the state and of groups outside the state and into the disarray, described by Robert Cuff, that characterized much of the Wilson administration's mobilization apparatus.[64]

CORPORATE REACTIONS TO NEW TAX POLICIES

Corporations, as well as Treasury officials, were learning from the operation of the new taxes, particularly the excess-profits tax. Some corporations, to be sure, fought it in every way possible: evading it, impeding its collection, challenging assessments, exhausting legal appeals, and sometimes delaying payments for more than a decade. For example, a dispute between the Bureau of Internal Revenue and the Phelps-Dodge Corporation over the valuation of invested capital and depletion allowances dragged on until its settlement in 1929.[65] But much of the delay resulted from a slowdown in the collection process during the administration of Secretary of the Treasury Andrew Mellon;

[64]Hugh Heclo, "The State and America's Higher Civil Service," paper delivered at "Wilson Center Conference on the Role of the State in Recent American History," 23–4 October 1982. For suggestions on the importance of "policy communities" in shaping social policy in the twentieth century, see Jack L. Walker, "The Diffusion of Knowledge, Policy Communities and Agenda Setting: The Relationship of Knowledge and Power," in John E. Tropman et al., eds., *New Strategic Perspectives on Social Policy* (New York: Pergamon, 1981), 75–96.

[65]"Exhibit No. 1721," *Hearings Before the Special Committee Investigating the Munitions Industry* (Washington, D.C: U.S. Government Printing Office, 1934–43), 6528–9.

on the whole, corporations decided that they should and could cooperate with the McAdoo program for assessing and collecting taxes. Most corporations were eager not to jeopardize the war effort and were willing and able to pay their taxes, assuming that they were doing so on an emergency basis.

Corporations applauded the appointment of the Advisory Board, although they were disappointed that McAdoo had broken his promise to the Investment Bankers Association to appoint "nine of the most prominent business men of America." They believed that the members of the board he did appoint tried, as McAdoo had charged them, to apply the excess-profits law "in the fairest and most equitable manner to the business of the country," and the quasi-independence of the board from McAdoo's authority encouraged business acceptance of their decisions. Most agreed with Robert Murray Haig who wrote, in 1919, "In spite of the fact that they were Internal Revenue officials they could be counted upon to take a large, unbiased view of the taxpayer's problem." And the corporations tried to maintain good relations with McAdoo, whom they believed to have acted fairly in administering a bad law. In August 1918, Russell C. Leffingwell, McAdoo's assistant secretary who was closest to the large corporations, noted, "The Secretary of the Treasury has managed to make himself an advocate of huge taxes without antagonizing, but on the contrary has gained the confidence of the taxpayers."[66]

Nonetheless, despite the success of McAdoo and the Treasury in their mediation between progressive social and political goals and the profit-maximizing goals of the corporations, the Wilson financial program, especially the excess-profits tax, posed significant long-term threats to corporate interests. Most important, its proponents intended it to become permanent or at least prevail through the postwar period for the payment of the war debts. And the combination of redistributional and significant "state-building" components in the Treasury's financial program constituted a substantial strategic threat to the nation's corporate infrastructure. Most severely threatened were the large corporate hierarchies who believed their financial autonomy to be in jeopardy. Probably no other single issue aroused corporate hostility to

---

[66]McAdoo, "Address to Investment Bankers Association," Baltimore, 14 November 1917, MPLC; Robert Murray Haig, "British Experience with Excess Profits Taxation," *American Economic Review* 10 (March 1920): 11; and R. C. Leffingwell to George R. Cooksey, 23 August 1918, MPLC.

the Wilson administration as widely or as deeply as excess-profits taxation.[67]

In 1918, corporations found an opening for a counterattack on wartime tax policy, progressives in Congress, the Wilson administration, and, most important, the Democratic party because of the convergence of dramatic new revenue needs for the war effort and the congressional elections. By December 1917, McAdoo knew that the war effort in the next two years would require massive revenues beyond the capacity of the Revenue Act of 1917 (which, as yet, had not produced any tax collections). His careful Treasury studies revealed that unless taxes were increased and tax collections accelerated at the same time (through advance "installment" payments), they would cover only about 16 percent of the U.S. $25 billion of wartime expenditures required in fiscal 1919. The federal borrowing, which would have to accelerate in 1918, would sharply drive up interest rates and crowd out private borrowers or, if monetary policy was eased, produce enormous inflation. Taxes could be imposed retroactively on incomes in fiscal 1919, but this action, too, could have disruptive effects on capital markets. As McAdoo put it, "the community is entitled to be informed, and informed promptly, if increased taxes are to be levied."[68]

Congressional Democrats, however, worried more about the elections of 1918 and feared that Republicans might be able to persuade many voters in the Northeast who had supported Wilson in 1916 that Democratic policies, including the tax increases, had caused wartime inflation and other economic disruptions.[69] Moreover, the chairman of the House Ways and Means Committee, Claude Kitchin, had become a favorite target for ridicule in editorials and cartoons as a result of his populist rhetoric and his successful championing of a dramatic increase in second-

[67]The conventional wisdom with regard to corporate tax burdens has been summarized by Alfred D. Chandler: "Taxes remained low until the war (II) and had a minimal impact on the direction and growth of the modern managerial enterprises and the sectors they administered." See Chandler, *The Visible Hand*, 494–5. Even without a systematic and comprehensive study of the history of corporate taxation and corporate tax burdens, this wisdom neglects the various threats of tax policy to corporations and the importance of the politics of taxation to corporate managers and investors.

[68]McAdoo, "Tax Legislation," internal Treasury memorandum, 20 May 1918, and McAdoo to Wilson, 23 May 1918, MPLC.

[69]For example, Cong. Henry T. Rainey of Illinois reminded McAdoo "that nothing wins in elections so easily as a campaign of protest against taxes," and advised him "you cannot find a single Democrat in the North who would consider his place in the House secure if another tax bill is passed at this session." Henry T. Rainey to McAdoo, "Personal," 21 May 1918, MPLC.

class postage rates—amounting to a tax of 5 percent on the gross advertising receipts of newspapers and magazines.[70] Much of the northeastern urban press portrayed him as a narrow-minded, class-conscious southerner—someone who was playing sectional politics with taxation—and this argument reinforced the attack on the Wilson administration by business and Republicans. In October, an organizer for the Democratic National Congressional Committee told McAdoo that the Republicans "in many places are building their hopes on the notion that the Revenue Bill is designed to tax the north for the benefit of the south."[71]

THE WILSON ADMINISTRATION'S INVESTIGATION OF TAX OPTIONS

The Wilson administration attempted to resolve the tension by conducting an extensive investigation of tax options, and of the operation of excess-profits taxation. The investigation, which was unprecedented for its depth and range, surveyed a broad sweep of tax options, all redistributional in content and some having a radical constitutional potential: the taxation of land values, the taxation of the income from state and municipal bonds, and even the unification of state and federal tax systems, including the creation of a U.S. commission for the collection of state taxes. And, following the suggestion of John Skelton Williams, the Treasury considered taxing away all the interest collected on money loaned at rates over 6 percent.[72] In its deliberations, the Treasury also addressed the problem that, according to McAdoo, "terrible frauds are being practiced in the matter of income and corporation tax returns."[73]

The critical part of the investigation was scrutiny of the excess-profits tax led by Adams. All the conclusions reinforced the concern of the members of the Excess Profits Board about the administrative complexity and fairness of the excess-profits tax. First, the Treasury analysts found

---

[70]This was one element of Kitchin's approach to revenue raising from which McAdoo consistently dissented. See, for example, McAdoo to Frank P. Glass, 9 May 1917, MPLC.
[71]James K. McGuire to McAdoo, 31 October 1918, MPLC.
[72]T. W. Gregory, attorney general, to McAdoo, 7 January 1918; Richard Weed, "Memorandum for Mr. Leffingwell," 27 February 1918; McAdoo to Thomas S. Adams, 11 May 1918, and John Skelton Williams to McAdoo, 2 May 1918, MPLC. The "antiusury" tax appealed to McAdoo as a means of maintaining the price of Liberty Bonds, but he concluded that increasing the normal income tax, focusing it on "unearned" income, and maintaining interest deductibility would have the same effect.
[73]McAdoo to George Cooksey, 4 June 1918, MPLC.

that the difficulties of accurately determining capital investment and rates of return on capital had actually contributed to "profiteering" through tax avoidance. Most important, some corporations had increased their capital issues to reduce their rates of return and slip into lower tax brackets under the excess-profits tax. Corporations also increased their salary and advertising costs to reduce current rates of return.

Second, the analysis by Adams of the distribution of excess-profits taxes by size of company demonstrated rather conclusively that the highest rates of return on capital, and thus the highest tax rates, were earned by the smallest corporations. Third, the Treasury concluded that numerous war contractors were earning large rates of return, yet were taxed at relatively low rates under the excess-profits tax.[74]

The results of the study of the excess-profits taxation were discouraging and embarrassing to Kitchin and McAdoo, who remained committed to redistributional ideals that focused on restraining monopoly power. They had discovered from this analysis that the excess-profits tax seemed to have exactly the opposite effect: rewarding bigness. The Adams study did, however, suggest a solution to the problem of effectively waging a fight against monopoly and, at the same time, raising huge war revenues: The Treasury should adopt a "dual-basis," under which corporations would pay the higher of an increased excess-profits tax or the British-style war-profits taxation. Adams, who had begun the war with a preference for the British-style tax before he endorsed excess-profits taxation, had now changed his mind for the second time, and he had persuaded McAdoo to abandon his loyalty to the excess-profits tax. The new tax, McAdoo decided, would place a relatively heavier burden on the largest corporations. In May, after complaining to the president about the monopoly power of J. P. Morgan and "the financial bosses of Wall Street," McAdoo told him, "A proper war-profits tax will have a salutary effect upon these gentlemen."[75]

McAdoo hoped to focus attention during the 1918 congressional campaign on war "profiteering" through the tax issue. As he put forward his tax program, he worked with Sen. William E. Borah, who was launch-

[74]Russell C. Leffingwell to Paul Warburg, 7 April 1918, LPLC; Thomas S. Adams, "Table Showing 7899 Representative Corporations Classified According to Amount of Invested Capital and Ratio of Net Income to Invested Capital," 1917, MPLC.

[75]Adams later recalled that at the beginning of the drafting of new legislation in 1918, he had opposed the views of both McAdoo and Kitchin. T. S. Adams to Edwin R. A. Seligman, 20 March 1924, Seligman Papers. McAdoo to Woodrow Wilson, 31 May 1918, MPLC.

ing an attack on "war profiteers," attempting to hold up to public scorn those corporations that had exploited the war and were not paying their fair share of taxes. The Treasury agreed to produce a list of all corporations that had earned more than 15 percent on their capital stock in fiscal 1917. In July, in little more than a month, Adams and his staff had produced an extensive compilation of critical data on more than thirty thousand corporations. McAdoo wrote to his friend Cong. John Nance Garner that "indefensible profits are being earned in various lines of industry, and when the facts are made public, as they must before [the tax] bill is passed, every man who had the courage to stay in Washington and fight to remedy these conditions will strengthen himself with the American people and with his own constituency particularly." In August, during the final stages of House deliberations on the new legislation, McAdoo placed on the record more of the Treasury's analysis—the estimates by Adams that the 80 percent tax on war-profits would bear more heavily on a great many of the largest corporations, including all the steel companies (producing $100 million more in revenues from U.S. Steel alone) and the Standard Oil group ($60 million more). Six years later, Adams recalled that he had changed his mind again because to have provided tax relief for Standard Oil and the Ford Motor Company "would have been absurd."[76]

Gaining confidence from the Treasury investigations and recognizing the scale of the fiscal crisis, Wilson broke from his customary adherence to party government.[77] Rather than simply deferring to congressional Democrats and abstaining from seeking any tax increases until after the November elections, Wilson, spurred on by McAdoo, asserted presidential leadership over tax policy. What followed was Wilson's unprecedented congressional appearance on May 27 in which he proposed the specific form the new tax legislation should take and proclaimed, "Politics is adjourned."[78] McAdoo followed with recommendations to Congress

[76]McAdoo to John Nance Garner, 3 June 1918, George R. Cooksey to McAdoo, 6 June 1918; McAdoo, "War Revenue Act, Memorandum, August 14, 1918," MPLC; U.S. Senate, 65th Cong., 2d sess., *Corporate Earnings and Government Revenues, Senate Documents,* vol. 15, no. 259 (5 July 1918); Thomas S. Adams to Edwin R. A. Seligman, 30 March 1924, Seligman Papers.

[77]The best account of the congressional politics of this episode is Seward W. Livermore, *Politics Is Adjourned: Woodrow Wilson and the War Congress, 1916–1918* (Middletown, Conn.: Wesleyan University Press, 1966), 123ff.

[78]Woodrow Wilson, "An Address to a Joint Session of Congress," 27 May 1918, Arthur

for *doubling* federal taxes in fiscal 1919 by raising the normal income tax on "unearned income," imposing high luxury taxes, and, most important, by shifting corporation taxation from an excess-profits to a "dual-basis." McAdoo suggested raising the rates to a flat rate of 80 percent, the rate employed by Britain.

A COMPROMISE

Kitchin and his followers in the House, however, refused to entertain a complete break with excess-profits taxation. As in 1916, Kitchin remained focused on the postwar world, and he was convinced that improving the implementation of the excess-profits concept, even with its flaws, was the best way to deal with *long-run* distributional issues. In August 1918, two individuals played crucial roles in breaking the deadlock. Wilson personally intervened again, pressing the case for war-profits taxation on Congress, and in the hearings before the Ways and Means Committee Adams was able to persuade Kitchin that accepting the "dual-basis" compromise would not prevent excess-profits taxation from becoming permanent and would, in fact, be a more effective means of taxing corporate profits. At the conclusion of Adams's testimony, Kitchin remarked that "I used to think I was a radical until we got on this bill, but now I find I am a conservative."[79]

Kitchin finally accepted the compromise, but his wrangling over it prolonged the House consideration of the bill through August and allowed Republicans to turn attention on his personal role in shaping the legislation. The compromise itself, with the retention of excess-profits taxation and the high rates of war-profits taxation, failed to satisfy corporate opponents. They carried their opposition into the Senate, hoping to delay consideration of the new tax bill until after the November elections, when they hoped to have greater strength in Congress. Meanwhile, a group of corporate leaders sponsored their own investigation, agreeing

S. Link, ed., *The Papers,* vol. 48 (Princeton, N.J.: Princeton University Press, 1985), 162, 165.

[79]Wilson's intervention was arranged by Leffingwell, who, while McAdoo was on a Liberty Loan speaking tour, explained the principles of war-profits and excess-profits taxation to the president and Joseph Tumulty. Leffingwell to Tumulty, 31 July 1918, Leffingwell to Wilson, 2 August 1918, and Leffingwell to McAdoo, 3 August 1918, LPLC. For the crucial exchanges among Adams, Kitchin, and the Ways and Means Committee, see U.S. Congress, House of Representatives, *Hearings Before the Committee on Ways and Means on the Proposed Revenue Act of 1918* (Washington, D.C.: U.S. Government Printing Office, 1918), 87–119.

to finance an ambitious study on the impact of the excess-profits tax in Britain and the United States—a study that Edwin R. A. Seligman would lead as chairman of the American Economic Association's War Finance Committee. Seligman had continued actively to criticize excess-profits taxation, even publicly ridiculing Adams for his shift of position.[80]

The controversy deterred the Senate from acting on the legislation until after the congressional elections, which brought Republican control of Congress. The Democratic defeat was widely viewed as a consequence of Republican success in linking Democratic tax policy with economic distress.[81] McAdoo, more than a decade later, after he had abandoned his presidential ambitions, attributed the Democratic loss of Congress in 1918 to the "unpopularity of the proposed legislation, with its proposal to increase taxes generally and to bear heavily on large corporate and individual incomes." Acutely aware of historical contingency, McAdoo was confident that "if the Armistice had occurred a month earlier...the Democrats would have won the election and...the history of the next two years would have been vastly different."[82]

POSTWAR CONSOLIDATION

Acknowledging the 1918 defeat, being spared a fiscal emergency by the armistice, and perhaps trying to build conservative support for a Democratic coalition that he might lead in 1920, McAdoo quickly moved away from even war-profits taxation. Immediately after the armistice, McAdoo called for the elimination of all excess-profits and war-profits taxation (after the collection of those taxes on incomes earned in calendar

---

[80]Seligman attracted attention with a "Comment" on Adams's support of excess-profits taxation, *American Economic Review* 8 (March 1918): 42–45. Beginning in May 1918, a group of businessmen in New York and Boston, led by Jesse I. Strauss of R. H. Macy & Co. and including Thomas Lamont and other investment bankers, organized to support Seligman "in his plan to make a study of the results of the Excess Profits Taxes and Income Tax here, and...a study of the success of the British and French methods of war finance." The group raised a fund designed to cover any deficit up to $50,000 incurred by Seligman and the War Finance Committee of the American Economic Association. Professor Robert Murray Haig of Columbia University headed the Columbia delegation to Britain, but passport difficulties delayed their trip until 1919 and the publication of a research volume until 1920. Strauss to Lamont, 1 May 1918; Seligman to Lamont, 5 June 1918; Lamont to T. DeWitt Cuyler, 6 June 1918; Lamont Papers. The result of the British study was Robert Murray Haig, "The Taxation of Excess Profits in Great Britain: A Study of the British Excess Profits Duty in Relation to the Problem of Excess Profits Taxation in the United States," *American Economic Review* 10 (December 1920).
[81]See, for example, *New York Sun*, 8 November and 26 December 1918.
[82]McAdoo, *The Crowded Years* (Boston: Houghton Mifflin, 1931), 412.

1918 or on contracts entered into during the war). In November 1918, assessing the new conditions, McAdoo warned of the possibility of a postwar depression and urged Congress "to look ahead to the future of American business and industry." Taxation, he told Congress, "should be devised as to encourage and stimulate rather than to burden and repress them."[83]

The same month Daniel Roper reinforced McAdoo's message, telling the Business Men's Club of Cincinnati that the system of taxation "must become a stimulus to redoubled activity and effort and the motive for attaining the highest possible degree of productiveness and efficiency." And Roper underscored the Treasury's movement away from industrial reconstruction by adding that "cooperative and constructive competition is rapidly gaining universal acceptance." Finally, Roper suggested leniency in the settlement of disputes over wartime taxes: "It must also be recognized that the interests which the taxpayer and the Government have in common greatly exceed in importance any differences which may arise as to the adjustment of the tax burden."[84] Nonetheless, Congress, in passing the Revenue Act of 1918 (in February 1919), maintained the main element of the Adams-McAdoo compromise—the hybrid "excess-profits" and "war-profits" tax.

After the destruction of the congressional base that was necessary for effective Wilsonian party government, McAdoo quickly left the Treasury. Looking to the 1920 elections and putting party victory as the highest priority, he urged Wilson to return the railroads to private control and to stake out the leadership of the Democratic party on behalf of tax reduction and the reduction of prices.[85]

After McAdoo's departure, the essential elements of the financial organization he had created in the Department of the Treasury remained intact. In part, this was so because McAdoo's two key aides, Roper and Leffingwell, stayed on in their positions through 1919 and into 1920 and 1921, respectively. They provided continuity to financial planning through the Victory Loan and the complex issues of reconversion, as did McAdoo's successor as secretary, Carter Glass, who kept in close touch with McAdoo. The third Treasury secretary of the Wilson administration,

---

[83]McAdoo to Furnifold M. Simmons, 14 November 1918, MPLC.
[84]Daniel C. Roper, "Address of Daniel C. Roper, Commissioner of Internal Revenue, Before Business Men's Club of Cincinnati, Ohio, November 20, 1918." Roper had given McAdoo an opportunity to review his text. Roper to McAdoo, 19 November 1918, MPLC.
[85]McAdoo to Wilson, 31 July and 6 August 1919, MPLC.

David Houston (secretary of agriculture until 1920), was more conservative on taxation issues than his predecessors, but he had professional training in business and finance, had been chancellor of Washington University, had a deep faith in the benefits of systematic knowledge, and worked to consolidate the expansion and reorganization of the Treasury achieved by McAdoo.[86]

In mobilizing capital for war, McAdoo and his supple Treasury organization had accomplished a prodigious financial feat. Its scale and significance for the development of American institutions in the twentieth century should be acknowledged in scholarly efforts to discern the social and class structures shaping modern politics, to assess contemporary fiscal and monetary policy, and to understand the role of the state in modern life. Two of the most important wartime accomplishments were the emphasis of the U.S. tax system on progressive equity and the commitment of the Treasury to analyzing public finance and its social *and* economic setting systematically. These accomplishments became infused into the massive and permanent augmentation of the financial power of the U.S. federal government resulting from the war. Representing the continuing importance of these two elements was Adams, who survived the transition to the administration of Secretary of the Treasury Andrew Mellon and served in the Treasury as its principal tax adviser until 1933.

Adams intended to be an agent of institutional learning and political change. He retained his faith in the power of systematic information and in his ability to perceive politic moments of opportunity—ones in which his powers of analysis and persuasion might enhance tax equity. Beginning in December 1919, this faith led him to play a critical role in the

---

[86]McAdoo supported either Glass or Bernard Baruch as his successor and then was heavily involved in the selection of the successor to Glass, who entered the Senate in 1920. McAdoo preferred Roper while Glass favored Leffingwell, but Wilson, apparently wishing to avoid appointing a secretary associated with either Wall Street or southern interests, settled on Houston instead. In 1920 Roper became president of Marlin Rockwell Corporation, a manufacturer of ball-bearings that had produced rifles; he maintained an active political career, acting as floor manager for McAdoo in his presidential campaign of 1924 and serving as secretary of commerce, 1933–8. Leffingwell rejoined the Cravath firm after resigning his Treasury post and, in 1923, became a partner in J. P. Morgan & Company with major responsibilities in the financing of foreign governments. In 1948, Leffingwell became chairman of the board of the House of Morgan. Houston aspired to a corporate career and, after leaving the Treasury in 1921, became vice-president of Bell Telephone Securities Company and board chairman of the Mutual Life Insurance Company of New York. McAdoo to Edward M. House, 29 November 1918, MPLC; McAdoo to Carter Glass, 8 December 1919; Glass to McAdoo, 11 December 1919; McAdoo to Glass, 13 December 1919; and Colonel House to Glass, 15 December 1919; Carter Glass Papers, University of Virginia Library.

effort to kill excess-profits taxation, which Congress did in 1921. Adams justified what was his third change of heart on the merits of the tax on the grounds that the tax had failed to accomplish its objectives and that pruning the tax created a political opportunity to strengthen the rest of the progressive income tax. His role in the subsequent politics of taxation remains untold, but the progressive income tax did survive the 1920s and was, in effect, sanctioned by the Republican administrations. Later, in the mid-1930s, when progressive redistributive taxation again rose to the top of the nation's political agenda, the focal point was a tax, like the excess-profits tax, highly threatening to the large corporations—a tax on their undistributed profits. Such a tax had been first proposed as a central part of the tax system in 1919, as a replacement for excess-profits taxation, by Thomas S. Adams.[87]

[87]For a suggestion of the importance of the Treasury advisers from the Wilson administration whom Mellon retained, see Benjamin G. Rader, "Federal Taxation in the 1920s: A Re-examination," *The Historian* (May 1971): 419–21. On Adams's third change see his "Immediate Future of the Excess Profits Tax," *American Economic Review* 10 (March 1920): 15–18; "Should the Excess Profits Tax Be Repealed?" *Quarterly Journal of Economics* 35 (May 1921): 363–93; and "The Economic and Social Basis of Tax Reduction," *Proceedings of the American Academy of Political Science* 11 (March 1924): 24–34. See also Adams to Edwin R. A. Seligman, 30 March 1924, Seligman Papers.

9

The state and social investigation in Britain between the world wars

BARRY SUPPLE

This chapter considers a number of general questions in terms of the specific experience of Britain between World War I and World War II:

1. Where does the impulse to social investigation come from and what determines its focus?
2. Why do states or ostensibly private groups of people gather, devise, or invent information about economic and social conditions?
3. Is it useful to distinguish general principles from "pragmatic" responses when considering the evolution of government intervention?
4. To what extent does the information generated by social investigation transcend the purposes, and even the data, encompassed by the investigators?

Because this chapter derives from research on the vicissitudes of the British coal-mining industry, my perspective appears to be narrow. Yet the parochialism is more apparent than real. After 1918 the principal characteristics of coal mining were chronic economic stagnation and profound social decay. These characteristics made coal mining a fertile breeding ground for the sorts of innovations in the role of the state, and the object of the type of social inquiry, that were generally characteristic of the period.

There are several reasons why such a prolonged and painful episode in the industrial history of private enterprise is relevant to the theme

I wish to express my gratitude to the participants in the Conference on the State and Social Investigation held at the Woodrow Wilson International Center for Scholars, and particularly to Michael Lacey and Martin Bulmer for their useful comments on my chapter.

under consideration. First, coal mining was intrinsically important in economic and social terms: around World War I it employed more than 1 million men (about 10 percent of the total male labor force), so bitter industrial strife or rates of unemployment in excess of 20 or 30 percent among such a determined and large proportion of the population were bound to excite dismay and attention in the rest of society. In the event, the coal industry was the most enduring setting for "crisis management" in the history of modern political economy in Britain.

At the same time, the fate of the coal industry and of coal mining communities could be taken as symptomatic of developments in a mature capitalist society. The economic context that helped explain their decline, the resulting economic pressures and social tensions, the instability of markets, and the waste of resources and capacity could all be seen in a much longer perspective. The debate about the performance of the coal-mining industry was, in effect, one installment of the debate about capitalism, business cycles, and economic stagnation. More specifically, there were general principles as well as short-term practical reasons for the canvassing of social or collective control in the industry, and for the marshaling of information relevant to its condition and the explanation of its problems.

More prosaically, the decline of the coal industry was the first and most dramatic indication of the passing of an economic era. By the late 1920s it was clear that the extraordinary industrial prosperity, the relatively tranquil operation of the international economy, and the unquestioned reliance on more or less individual private enterprise, all of which had characterized Britain's world before 1914, had gone for good. "Everything being now relative," wrote Galsworthy, "there is no longer absolute dependence to be placed on God, Free Trade, Marriage, Consols, Coal or Caste."[1]

This situation, in turn, meant that, for practical and immediate reasons, people began to explore the possibilities of a new, or a newly emphatic, role for cooperative, collective, or state action in the economic sphere. The coal industry was notoriously fragmented, individualistic, and even anarchic in its structures and decision making. As a result of the coal industry's demoralization, even proponents of private property and enterprise (as well as opponents who relished the thought of their

---

[1]John Galsworthy, *A Modern Comedy* (London, 1929), quoted in Arthur Marwick, *The Deluge: British Society and the First World War* (London, 1965), 237.

decay) were now moved to advocate the centralization of action, and therefore of knowledge, in the cause of structural reform or economic and social stability.

Finally, the collapse of large parts of the coal industry, which was demographically the most concentrated of all the staple industries, generated that sadly typical problem of the interwar years: the "derelict," "special," or "depressed" areas ripe for investigation, whether by journalists or private individuals, voluntary associations or government commissioners. Of course, none of this was new: the modern social survey, particularly the statistical survey, had originated a hundred years earlier in a concern with urban poverty and deprivation. But it was to flower with the heightened visibility of social distress and political leverage in the coalfields of Britain in the 1920s and 1930s.

But if historical research on one industry and a particular set of socioeconomic problems is offered as my necessary empirical credential, it is by no means the only basis of this chapter, For one thing, the experience of coal mining obviously lay at the heart of a number of general issues of shifting economic structures, mass unemployment, community decay, overcapacity, and industrial strife. And it was these general phenomena that did most to excite change (if indeed change there was) in the role of the state and the purposefulness and range of social investigation in interwar Britain. Managing economic decline, or encountering social pathology, is obviously a much more potent incentive to social inquiry and action than are prosperity and harmony.

Of course, it is possible to look at the problem in a longer-term intellectual perspective. The debate about economic and social conditions between the world wars was itself part of a more enduring intellectual and political tradition. After all, the period between 1919 and 1939 was hardly the first to experience the maladaptation of socioeconomic systems, threats to community health and material welfare, the strains of industrial change and social immobility, or anxiety about the uneven distribution of wealth and income and power. Nor was it the first to have the conviction that systematized information needed to be gathered and used (whether scientifically, morally, or politically) as the basis for the pursuit of public policy. All these phenomena were surely familiar aspects of Britain's nineteenth-century economic heyday as well as its twentieth-century disappointments. And the associated outlook is a symptom of the intellectual and emotional reaction to modern industrial society that has virtually coexisted with that society.

It follows, therefore, that the specific economic problems and social dislocations that generated so much inquiry between the world wars were perceived and rationalized, at least in part, by people who derived their outlook from a broader and older tradition. This was most obviously the case, if for demographic reasons alone, in the 1920s. Thus, to anticipate one example, in 1919, in response to an urgent political crisis, the Lloyd George coalition government appointed what turned out to be an influential Royal Commission on the coal industry. The Sankey commission's charge was to appraise not only the miners' wages and hours claim, but also the arguments in favor of outright public ownership of coal mining or workers' control in the industry. In some respects the commission was a characteristic child of the turbulence of postwar society; and yet its extensive statistical inquiries and controversial hearings were heavily influenced by its fairly traditional radical membership—by Sidney Webb, R. H. Tawney, and Leo Chiozza Money, each of whom had important connections and experience with systematic, empirical social inquiry and critical scholarship harnessed to reform. A similar example occurred six years later when yet another industrial-relations crisis in the coal industry led to the appointment of yet another Royal Commission. The new one was chaired by Sir Herbert Samuel but dominated by William Beveridge, who, again within a quasi-official framework, brought to bear his own more "professional," if no less provocative, brand of vigorous inquiry, one that was derived from a now-conventional framework of public service and social investigation directed toward policy prescription.

The Sankey and Samuel commissions were dramatic examples, but still only examples, of the public engagement of individuals, nurtured in a variety of related traditions of civic consciousness, factual discovery, social reform, managerial adjustment, and collective intervention. Inquiry was changing the basis of state action, and state involvement (however reluctant) was establishing the basis for further inquiry.

AMBIGUITIES

The convergence of intensely perceived and newly threatening social problems and a longer tradition of intellectual concern raises a number of questions and ambiguities about the creation of the knowledge base in the interwar years. As I have suggested, not only the personnel but frequently the issues they identified would have been familiar to those who dealt in social inquiry and reform in Edwardian or even late-Victorian Britain, and the framework of political attitudes involved also contained important strands of continuity. (In fact, as is discussed later, some of the social investigation of the interwar years was a virtual replication, in a changed setting, of inquiries between 1880 and 1914.)

There can be little doubt, however, about the decisiveness of some of the changes in social response as a result of interwar developments. Prolonged mass unemployment and the stagnation of staple industries and many communities generated new concerns, theories, and modes of inquiry. The emergence of Keynesian economics was perhaps the most obvious example of the intellectual departures; even if it had little direct influence on the government policy, it was associated with shifts in practical thinking and advocacy. And the phenomenon was general. Thus, in 1934 the Conservative minister of labor, Oliver Stanley, asserted that "we are all planners now"; and a few months later Harold Macmillan argued that laissez-faire had been relegated to "the limbo of forgotten things."[2] Both may have been somewhat premature, but they were responding to a new tide of events that made the formulation of an industrial and regional policy inescapable. Both were contributing to parliamentary debates following the exposure of atrocious economic and social conditions in the depressed areas first by private, and then by official, surveys. Moreover, the minister was actually introducing legislation—feeble, but a vital departure in principle—to create commissioners for the special areas, who would, in effect, generate even more systematic information about the problems of interwar Britain and intensify pressure on the state to take more effective action. As in so many other cases, the political elements of the problem of depressed areas were inextricably connected to the investigative.

Clearly, then, the intellectual response to conditions in the 1920s and 1930s, and the general state of social inquiry and analysis at the time, had distinctive as well as "traditional" characteristics. How far and why did the experience of these years (institutionally and socially, as well as in terms of social attitudes and advocacies) differ from that of the Victorian and Edwardian world?

First, Britain's economic failures and distress coincided with rapid growth in total national income, the emergence of new and prosperous industries and occupations, the proliferation of consumption patterns,

[2]*House of Commons Debates,* 3 December 1934 and 3 April 1935.

and improved living standards. Such diversity and imbalance of experience had doubtless always characterized industrial Britain, but the resulting heterogeneity appeared to present new problems after 1918.

Second, the evolution of the role of the state, whose roots were still to be found in the experience before World War I, was both startling and superficial in relation to the problems it purported to tackle. The startling aspect of its character was a rapid increase in the level of public expenditure; an extension of health services and social security payments (unemployment and poor relief, old-age and widows' pensions); purposeful industrial, regional, and tariff policies; a measure of "corporatism" and a larger degree of market and structural control in particular industries; and an effective program of state ownership and management in a number of strategic areas.

In many fields the unthinkable had become common political currency. And yet, when viewed alongside the issues being addressed, the intrusion of government was minimal. Market forces still reigned supreme over structural change and regional decay; politicians and civil servants, when considering general problems or macroeconomic policy, still adhered to strict canons of budgetary propriety and financial rectitude; official presumptions were still in favor of decentralization, individualism, and the market. Altogether, the state asserted itself and yet managed to continue to stand aloof.

The contrasts exemplified within economic experience and within the realm of state activity were also associated with divergent modes of thinking about social facts and the nature of social operations. Of course, such divergence is characteristic of all periods of history, but what seems relatively new about the interwar decades was the extent to which erstwhile heretical or dissident thinking was debated not simply in the orthodox political arena, but also in the context of investigative commissions and official encounters. Moreover, alternative views of the role of information and state agencies were to be found within those agencies themselves (historical views of the interwar civil service that concentrate on the Treasury are responsible for an altogether excessively monolithic interpretation of bureaucratic attitudes). At the same time, of course, and especially by the 1930s, there was an unprecedented intensity of discussion and organization by eminent figures in public life.

As a result, although most policy changes took place in piecemeal fashion and had immediate, practical origins, the slow tide of opinion increasingly introduced "managerial" and unorthodox economic ideas into public discourse. By the 1930s, although concepts of "planning" were still imprecise and nonoperational, some version of the "middle way," embodying important new assumptions about the necessity of systematic inquiry and coordinated social management, had become commonplace, even while neoclassical interpretations of economic and social behavior remained widely influential.

VARIETIES OF MOTIVE

The impulse to social investigation and state intervention in the interwar years was obviously derived from more than one direction, embodied in more than one form, and mediated by more than one type of thinking.

The first distinction that needs to be made is between the "pragmatic" and the "theoretical" or "principled." Certainly, much interwar intervention was "pragmatic" in the sense of being a response to immediate economic or social problems or the need for "crisis management." There is, of course, ambiguity and imprecision inherent in the very concept of pragmatism when applied to explanations of government actions. On the one hand, it contributes nothing to an explanation of why a social or an economic situation comes to be identified as a "problem" or "crisis" in one period, whereas in another age it is assumed to be beyond the scope of action or even of systematic inquiry. On the other hand, even ostensibly ad hoc and unconnected interventions must themselves reflect a set of assumptions about the possible and desirable. All policy reflects some view of the way society works and some set of theoretical and political preferences. Pragmatism cannot be divorced from ideology, nor can ideology be separated from theory.

Nevertheless, when all this has been acknowledged, there must surely be a special term, and *pragmatic* seems as good as any, to describe the basis of government policy during the 1920s and 1930s. For one thing, determinedly held views (on the iniquity of industrial subsides, for example, or the moral hazards of social security payments, or the virtues of competition) were changed with great speed, with little attempt at theoretical or even ideological adjustment, and quite patently in the face of immediate circumstances. Pragmatism in this sense typifies not so much a peculiar British virtue as a practical accommodation to political forces, and a posture based on a newly refined perception of facts, even if that perception is not accompanied by any very radical reassessment of the overall workings and moral worth of economic and social systems.

Intervention along lines such as these had rather special relationships with social knowledge. At one level, it was almost invariably stimulated by the "politicization" of information or by a manifest threat to stability. (Interwar examples range from the inquiries into particular industries or regions to the threat of political upheaval in the face of new rates of unemployment benefits in 1935.) At another level, the intervention itself generated knowledge.

First, and most obviously, it created data bases. This was most clearly the case with the unemployment insurance scheme, which (as will become evident) enabled measurements to be made that could, in turn, be used as the raw material for further policy departures.

Second, even intervention based on the most blatant or unprincipled political cynicism demanded the appearance of rationality. The resulting commissions of inquiry or primitive regulatory responsibilities became independent nodal points of new knowledge and advocacy. This was most notable with respect to the coal industry, but it also occurred elsewhere. For example, in the mid-1930s the commissioner for special areas (England and Wales), who had been appointed in an attempt to undertake minimal tasks in relation to regional policy, nevertheless successfully mustered influential arguments in favor of more active and interventionist policies.

Third, intervention created interest groups (bureaucrats, businessmen, employees) that became unavoidably committed to the refinement and extension of intervention, and thereby concerned with the gathering of information and the generation of "theories."

But if much of the knowledge base for and from social action was the more or less direct product of an interventionism that may usefully be defined as "pragmatic," it is still necessary to take account of the more principled or systematic origins of state activity and social knowledge. For, in the twentieth as in the nineteenth century, much apparently theoretical knowledge and practical inquiry, irrespective of their intellectual roots, cannot be dissociated from the perception of manifest imperfections in the economy whose character and workings they were attempting to explain.

This was obviously true of the interwar surveys of poverty and health, which not merely illuminated the problem of depressed areas but also contributed to the discussion of social class in industrial Britain. It was equally the case with apparently new theoretical models of economic processes, such as Keynesian economics. Moreover, quite apart from the "practical" origins of such theories of economic and social mechanisms, they (like the more old-fashioned social statements) tended to generate policy prescriptions that were then contested by the authorities. And in the process of that contest (e.g., the controversy concerning the health of the unemployed or the debate about the countercyclical value of public works expenditure)[3] those who denied or resisted the "new knowledge" were themselves obliged to ponder and develop "counterknowledge"— facts that purported to demonstrate the frailty of radical descriptions or proposals, or alternative hypotheses about the workings of economic and social institutions.[4]

VARIETIES OF EXPERIENCE

What, then, can be said about the ways in which practical policies and new theoretical knowledge, civic inquiry, and official investigations were organized? The principal issues were those already suggested: mass unemployment, industrial decline and structural change, depressed areas and derelict communities, and the health and welfare of the population.

Unemployment—even prolonged and large-scale unemployment—was no doubt a widely familiar fact of life in nineteenth-century Britain; but it did not become truly "visible" as a political and analytical problem (a continuing and chronic aspect of economic life rather than a temporary aberration) until the 1920s and 1930s. Then, the fact that society was ill-equipped with usable "knowledge" (whether about macroeconomic theory or about the institutional workings of labor and capital markets) meant that even those who had inherited the view that economic dislocation was remediable by state action and institutional reform were hard-pressed to propound a systematic solution. (Hence the extraordinary ineptitude of much of the Labour party's thinking on social and economic problems until the mid- to late 1930s.) The problem of worklessness, however, did give rise to action or "knowledge broking" at three levels.

First, as already suggested, information was generated by the extension of the unemployment "insurance" scheme. This was done largely under the pressure of political necessity at the end of World War I, although its roots were firmly sunk in the social inquiries and reforms of pre-1913

---

[3] For the debate about health, see notes 9 and 12, below. For countercyclical public expenditure, see Roger Middleton, *Towards the Managed Economy: Keynes, the Treasury and the Fiscal Policy Debate of the 1930s* (London, 1985).

[4] *Memorandum on Certain Proposals Relating to Unemployment* (Cmd. 3331. 1929).

Britain. In any event, the extension, and perhaps equally the prolonged entitlement, of insurance transformed its indirect utility as well as its social significance from the early 1920s.

For example, the insurance records ultimately made it possible to assess the duration, age composition, nature, and industrial and regional distribution of unemployment. Admittedly, some of the potential of these data (for example, their use for the measurement of labor mobility or the distinction between long- and short-term unemployment) was not fully appreciated for some time. Furthermore, although official inquiries into the operation of the insurance scheme were common, they tended to be motivated primarily by anxieties about the fiscal consequences of departures from sound actuarial principles. Nevertheless, the state's attempts to tackle the consequences (if not the causes) of unemployment through benefit payments, precisely because they involved the management and oversight of a bureaucratic system, produced a vast and varied effort to record and understand social processes. Indeed, in some ways the statistical information, once fully analyzed, actually demonstrated the chronic nature of the unemployment crisis, and therefore the economic crisis, for the first time. Paradoxically, the response to the problem of unemployment was, in effect, a prerequisite of its identification and assessment.

The second level at which mass unemployment was related to social knowledge was through the evolution of macroeconomic theory and debates about economic policy. Of course, these were not always mediated through the state. Keynes, for example, developed most of his central ideas while working independent of officialdom. Yet he necessarily devoted much effort to trying to persuade officialdom of the validity of his ideas, and he was inevitably drawn into the state network, through private contacts, public controversy, and his membership on committees of inquiry. Keynesianism did not become an orthodoxy until the 1940s, but the extension of its influence, and the resulting elaboration of systematic knowledge about modern economies, could hardly have occurred without the legitimation of the discussion of unemployment in the context of the state and state action.

The third relevant aspect of the response to unemployment, which overlaps with the Keynesian debate, concerns the controversy about public works and the feasible role of government. Partly in pursuit of "safe" policy innovation but principally because of the unexpectedly urgent need to justify traditional official skepticism about public expenditure as a tool of employment policy, civil servants and politicians had to reexamine facts and analyses. Too often, perhaps, the result was a reiteration of conventional truths, but occasionally it was the accumulation of "knowledge" of a sort. The "Treasury view"(that public works would and could not effectively raise the total demand for labor in the economy)—often represented as blind ideological prejudice—was in fact an evolving body of "theory" about political economy and the complexity of political and administrative decision making.[5]

Industrial stagnation was associated with the issue of worklessness. Again, the result was inexorable pressure on government, from the political perception of events as well as the arguments of interest groups and unofficial observers. Industrial disputes, idleness of factors of production, market and structural imperfections—all attracted a breadth of attention and an intensity of government intervention that had been largely absent in the previous century.

It must be acknowledged that this shift in attitude had only limited effect. Admittedly, there were important policy innovations: industrial subsidies, compulsory restructuring, protectionism, and extensive mediation in disputes. Yet their economic impact was still fairly limited by 1939, and those who advocated a "middle way" (most commonly, if always imprecisely, a "planned" middle way) for economic decision making remained grievously disappointed. Nevertheless, it is important to avoid too modern a perspective. The departures from the orthodoxy of Victorian and Edwardian Britain were substantial. Perhaps more important from the current viewpoint was the much greater "brokerage" role for state institutions with respect to social knowledge.

If the practical results of intervention were relatively small, there was equally little resolution of theoretical issues concerning (for example) protection, the economies of scale, the costs and benefits of compulsory industrial closures, the advantages of cartelization, or the improvement of factor mobility. And to that extent, too, there must be some doubt about how advanced the knowledge of the workings of the industrial system actually was.

Yet here, as well, the change was far from insignificant. Attention was more keenly and extensively focused on the "facts" of Britain's industrial

[5]Peter Clarke, *The Keynesian Revolution in the Making, 1924–1936* (Oxford, 1988); and G. C. Peden, "The 'Treasury View' on Public Works and Employment in the Interwar Period," *Economic History Review*, 2d ser., 37 (1984): 167–81.

performance and organization, and on vitally important conceptual issues relating to industrial and social economics. The impetus of political
anxiety and pressure groups, together with the resources of public investigation and regulatory agencies, made a significant difference
to the informed discussion of industrial institutions—a difference that,
as Paul Addison has shown, when compounded with the experience
of World War II, was probably decisive in producing the modern mixed
economy.[6]

COAL MINING: A CASE STUDY

The coal mining industry provides a critical example of these developments. Even before 1913, the political perturbations that had accompanied the miners' campaign for shorter hours and minimum wages had
brought the government into the affairs of the industry. During World
War I itself, coal mining had been continuously scrutinized and controlled
by the state, and in 1919 (again as a result of the assertion of bargaining
power by the miners' union) the industry became the object of national
controversy and public scrutiny.

The Royal Commission of that year (the Sankey commission), even
though it has been interpreted as a cynical ruse to deflate the miners'
militancy, proved to be an important vehicle of social "knowledge" and
action. It generated a vast amount of factual data concerning the social
conditions in and economic operations of the industry, as well as intense
debate about the determinants of efficiency, the industrial-relations system, the advantages and drawbacks of public ownership, and the economics of large-scale mining. It harnessed public sympathy to the miners'
social aspirations and grievances. It established a momentum toward a
residual state responsibility for the industry which, although it came to
little in the short run, was to prove irresistible within a decade.[7]

Significantly, too, the Sankey commission verged on constitutional
innovation. Partly because of the political circumstances of its creation
and partly because of the political and publicity skills of the miners and
their allies on the commission, it almost seized the policy initiative from
the Lloyd George government and thrust it willy-nilly into the course of

---

[6]Paul Addison, *The Road to 1945: British Politics and the Second World War* (London,
1975), chap. 1.
[7]See Barry Supple, *The History of the British Coal Industry*, vol. 4: *1913–46: The Political
Economy of Decline* (Oxford, 1987), chaps. 6 and 8.

public ownership. As Beatrice Webb confided to her diary, the commission was being transformed into a "revolutionary tribunal," and its proceedings were emerging as "a state trial of the coal owners and the royalty owners, culminating with the question, 'why not nationalise the mines?'"[8] No doubt that was a rare moment of emotional euphoria for the mature Beatrice. But the commission did give some people a fright, and in Parliament there were those who warned against the apparent delegation of government power to an irresponsible commission.

Such anxieties, as well as Beatrice Webb's hopes, were, of course, hopelessly premature. The Lloyd George government never had any intention of abrogating its role or its prejudices, and the miners, in their ultimate disappointment, assumed a grievance they were never to relinquish.

Even after the immediate controversy of 1919 had subsided and government had finally abandoned its formal control of the industry in 1921, coal mining remained at the center of social and political controversy. In line with Keynes's prophecies, it was the principal victim of the return to the gold standard in 1925, the focus for political crisis in 1926, and the casualty of chronic slump in 1927–8. At each stage, the state was obliged to play an explicit role—most often in spite of itself. And its discussions and inquiries, along with the accumulating responsibilities and experience of the Ministry of Mines (established in 1920), meant that official mediation played a dominant role in the entire interwar consideration of Britain's largest industry. More than this, the "raw material" provided by the problems of the coal-mining industry (social judgments as well as social facts) was extensively used as critically important information about the nation's industrial and regional problems.

Direct state intervention in the coal industry's private affairs arose through its involvement in national disputes (in 1919, 1921, 1925–6, 1930–1, and 1935–6); through occasional subsidies; through legislation to impose cartel arrangements on the industry and thereby stabilize its markets and prices and employment (in 1930, 1934, and 1936); through regulatory attempts to enforce structural concentration and mergers; and through the Coal Act of 1938, which greatly augmented administrative powers to override private property rights and provided for the nationalization of all coal reserves.

[8] *The Diaries of Beatrice Webb*, edited by M. I. Cole (London, 1952), 152–3 (March 12, 1919).

All these constituted a spectacular set of innovations concerning the role of the state, but they also resulted from and helped reproduce new or newly significant knowledge about the industry. Such knowledge had always been available (for, even in the nineteenth century, coal mining had been the object of official oversight for safety reasons). However, the transformation of the industry's political and social position in the twentieth century meant that social and economic data now became part of the ordinary currency of social debate and that far more systematic and deliberate data was collected. Both aspects were exemplified in the committees that unceasingly pored over the industry's affairs, and in the controversies that raged in newspapers and the trade journals.

As has already been emphasized, however, the coal mining industry's problems did not raise merely "technical" or purely economic problems. Because it was so large and so concentrated, and because its problems were so severe, it also became the focus for much broader issues of action and investigation—concerning labor migration, the depressed areas generally, and individual and community health.

Thus, the Industrial Transference Board of 1928 grew out of the government's need to be seen to be doing something about the problem of mass unemployment. Having identified and, for the first time, officially acknowledged the staple industries' problems of chronic overcapacity and excess labor supply (which the market would never resolve), the board subsidized retraining and migration of men and women without work in the depressed areas.

Soon after, publicity about the apparent threat to health posed by regional stagnation and concentrated unemployment led to official inquiries into the condition of the people in South Wales and Durham— the prelude to a long series of investigations of nutrition, maternal and infant mortality, and class differences in mortality and morbidity. Despite public reassurances, the state itself could not avoid an intermittent concern with such inquiries, and both formal investigations and general reports from the chief medical officer at the Ministry of Health continued to throw a wavering light on the relationship between unemployment and health in the early 1930s.[9]

[9]See *Report on Investigation in the Coalfield of South Wales and Monmouth* (Cmd. 3272. 1929); *Annual Report of the Chief Medical Officer of the Ministry of Health for the Year 1932*, 16–41; also *Annual Report of the Chief Medical Officer of the Ministry of Health for the Year 1933*, 206–21; *Report on an Investigation into Maternal Mortality* (Cmd. 5422. 1937); *Report on Maternal Mortality in Wales* (Cmd. 5423. 1937); *Report of an Inquiry into the Effects of Existing Economic Circumstances on the Health of the Com-*

More significantly, however, such preoccupations were taken up, as they had been initiated, by unofficial agencies. *The Times,* for example, sent a correspondent to South Wales in 1928 and published a series of articles entitled "A Stricken Coalfield," which referred to a "social disaster," to "men and women starving; not starving outright but gradually wasting away through lack of nourishment." Six years later *The Times* published a similar series of articles on the Durham coalfield ("Places Without a Future") and concluded that "it is no longer a question of saving an industry, but of saving the people from a desperate plight."[10] Such investigative journalism was reinforced by a growing body of medical and sociological inquiries—of which R. M. Titmuss's *Poverty and Population* in 1938 was perhaps the best known to historians.[11]

With the advantages of a longer perspective and more comprehensive statistics, modern historians have taught us that the issue of health in the Depression is more complex and subtle than was imagined at the time. Indeed, there is a case for arguing that health standards actually improved (owing to the effects, across the generations, of very long-run improvements in living standards).[12] Yet no one would really claim that standards of health, environmental quality, and nutrition were particularly good in the depressed areas of the early 1930s; and the discovery and reiteration of these characteristics became social "facts," with their own potent role to play in the evolution of social reform and attitudes, and the health service and welfare state.

Finally, at the most general level of all, the concern with regional stagnation again obliged the state to intervene (however hesitantly) in

munity in the County Borough of Sunderland and Certain Districts of County Durham (Cmd. 4886. 1935).

[10]*Times* (London), March 28—April 3, 1928; March 20–22, 1934.

[11]R. M. Titmuss, *Poverty and Population: A Factual Study of Contemporary Social Waste* (London, 1938). See also V. A. Demant, *The Miners' Distress and the Coal Problem* (London, 1930); Hilda Jennings, *Brynmawr: A Study of a Distressed Area* (London, 1934); Thomas Sharp, *A Derelict Area: The South-West Durham Coalfield* (London, 1935); C. E. McNally, *Public Ill-Health* (London, 1935) and G. C. M. M'Gonigle and J. Kirby, *Poverty and Public Health* (London, 1936); John Newsom, *Out of the Pit: A Challenge to the Comfortable* (Oxford, 1936); *Fact*, November 15, 1937 ("Portrait of a Mining Town"); Pilgrim Trust, *Men Without Work* (Cambridge, 1938); and D. M. Goodfellow, *Tyneside: The Social Facts* (Newcastle-upon-Tyne, 1940).

[12]See J. M. Winter, "Infant Mortality, Maternal Mortality and Public Health in Britain in the 1930s," *Journal of European Economic History* 8 (1979): 439–62; and "Unemployment, Nutrition and Infant Mortality in Britain, 1920–50," in Jay Winter, ed., *The Working Class in Modern British History: Essays in Honour of Henry Pelling* (Cambridge, 1983), 232–56. But also see the opposing view of Charles Webster: "Healthy or Hungry Thirties?" *History Workshop* 13 (Spring 1982): 110–29; and "Health, Welfare and Unemployment During the Depression" *Past & Present* 109 (November 1985): 204–30.

the operations of markets and private property, and was associated with extensive reports that themselves became forces for change. These reports, Harold Macmillan warned, were the result of "a visit from Whitehall to the Passchendaele of Durham and South Wales"; they contained "passages ... of an explosive and even revolutionary character." The images of war and revolution were perhaps sufficient indication of the relative novelty of the problems and the approaches to them.

In such an atmosphere, the government could not resist legislation, and so, in 1934, it passed the Special Areas Act. This was innocuous enough, given the huge scope of the problem and the limited powers and restrictions on the budget and initiative of the two commissioners, but it began a process that assumed a momentum of its own. Once the Commissioner for England and Wales had published reports on the extent of the problem of regional stagnation, drawing attention to the constraints on his autonomy and the desirability of a more positive policy (more direct encouragement of local investment, for example), further government intervention became inevitable. In 1937 an amending act greatly extended the Commissioners' powers, and in the same year the creation of the Royal Commission on the Distribution of the Industrial Population pointed toward a greater breadth and vigor of policy once the dimensions of the problem had been officially explored.

The evolution of a policy toward the depressed areas exemplified two important points about the process of state action and social knowledge. First, while the origin of intervention was straightforwardly political, in that publicity transformed the political calculus, the knowledge that was deployed to secure a change in policy was both "objective" and "politicized." (In other words, the social and economic problems were real, and information about them was effectively "managed.") Second, the beginning of intervention (irrespective of its mild and unpurposeful nature) led to the creation of an institutional framework and mechanisms of oversight and inquiry that established the basis for more information and further action.

VEHICLES OF SOCIAL CHANGE AND INVESTIGATION

The policies of the 1930s evolved piecemeal, and their consequences were limited and uncertain. But, combined with the increasingly elaborate inquiries and the intensification of public discussion, they led to a diffused acceptance of the legitimacy of a significantly more "forward" role for the state. Despite inhibitions, this was even the case with macroeconomic policy and substantial extensions of health and welfare services, as well as with policies concerned with the operations of individual industries and regions.

From one viewpoint the origins of all this, and of the associated extensions of social theory and argument, lay in the aggravated problems of British society and in the intensified intellectual, moral, and political perceptions of those problems. New knowledge and new attitudes were, in the last resort, produced by uneven and unsatisfactory levels of employment, environmental health, medical care and nutrition, and living standards.

Yet an "explanation" in these terms, as with the use of the concept of "pragmatism" in describing the array of government action, can be misleading. Even if Britain's social and economic problems were entirely new (and they were clearly not), it would still be important to understand why they provoked new responses; and in the more likely circumstance that the perceptions (as well as the things perceived) were new, it would also be necessary to consider the history of ideas and institutions that embodied them. Where, then—from what people and organizations— did the impulse to knowledge and action come?

The most obvious formal framework for structural and policy reform between the wars was at the level of political argumentation. From the present viewpoint, that argumentation began to take shape with Lloyd George's new version of the Liberal party that evolved from the discussions and publications of the summer schools of the mid-1920s; was advanced by the advocacy of extensive state intervention in the Liberal Industrial Inquiry's *Britain's Industrial Future* (1928); and began to take more systematic shape in the 1930s with the more diffused advocacy of public works, and with the Labour party's reformulated policies, embodied in *Labour's Immediate Programme* (1937). In the case of both Lloyd George and the Labour party a crucial role was played by political defeat (Lloyd George's fall from power in 1922 and the Labour party's electoral defeat in 1935). But the changes were also critically influenced by academic, or at least intellectual, thinking—efforts to understand the workings of a capitalism that appeared incapable of adequate performance if left to itself.

Of course, neither program was based on much new empirical knowledge, but both ultimately involved the acceptance of substantial innovation in economic theory and, therefore, reasoned advocacy. Certainly, once fully articulated, these apparent alternatives to Conservativism embodied radical departures from the positions adopted by the Liberal and Labour parties of the prewar decade. War, depression, and political ambition in the face of a powerful adversary were responsible for departures which, powerless as both parties turned out to be in these years, marked important stages in the evolution toward a different sort of society.

During the interwar years there was an alternative "political" mode of inquiry and action, which has led some political scientists and historians to argue that a new form of political organization—"corporatism"—came to prominence in public affairs.[13] This hypothesis is hardly acceptable if it is taken to mean that the conventional modes of political decision making and negotiation on economic and industrial affairs were abandoned in favor of new consensual arrangements that "incorporated" and subdued mass opinion through the cooperation of power brokers representing government, employers, and the unions.[14]

The idea of a "corporatist tendency" is much more persuasive if it is designed to remind us of the greater private and official readiness to discuss general issues and industrywide matters and policies. The plethora of committees and commissions; the extension of government agencies with economic functions and, therefore, with a need to consult with businessmen and unions; the growth of economic legislation that necessarily involved continuing monitoring; the impossibility of government agencies' tackling, let alone resolving, crises in the absence of direct contact with those involved in those crises—all inescapably meant that new vehicles of information gathering and policy formulation were being created throughout these two decades. Government had assumed the task of interest-group mediation and had, incidentally, itself become an interest group. War and postwar developments had extended, solidified, and formalized a new layer of political action.

Outside the formal political arena, there was also a more familiar, and more influential, mode of social inquiry. This was the "sociological survey," derived from a solidly continuous tradition, with roots in the anxiety about urban health and poverty in Victorian Britain. As in the

---

[13]The most detailed historical statement is Keith Middlemas's *Politics in Industrial Society: The Experience of the British System Since 1911* (London, 1979).

[14]For a discussion of the concepts of "corporatism" and "industrial politics" in the context of the coal industry, see Barry Supple, "Problems of the British Coal Industry: Aspects of Industrial Politics, 1914–45," in Gustav Schmidt and Karl Rohe, eds., *Referate und Diskussionsbeitrage der 1. Jahrestagung Arbeitskreis Deutsche England,* vol. I (Bochum, 1982).

nineteenth century, the resulting investigations were largely dependent on private philanthropic institutions and even more on individual initiative (through such men as Seebohm Rowntree, Arthur Bowley, Caradog Jones, Boyd Orr, Richard Titmuss). Indeed, as has already been emphasized, personnel, location, and even (at least in part) methodology were in some instances relatively unchanged.

Thus, in the 1930s Seebohm Rowntree repeated his surveys of poverty in York (as he was to do after World War II); in the 1920s Bowley replicated his earlier statistical study of poverty in five towns; Llewellyn Smith, who as a young man in the late 1880s had been one of Charles Booth's team of investigators in London, and subsequently joined the Board of Trade, supervised the New London Survey in the late 1920s, which combined Booth's original methods with the more systematic sampling techniques pioneered by Bowley. From the late 1920s such models were being imitated and adumbrated by a host of investigators firmly located in this proto-sociological tradition—although not all concentrated on poverty, and some simply analyzed existing quantitative data.[15]

Considered in terms of its effects on economic and social policy, much of this abundant effort appears to have been deficient in various important respects. Particularly insofar as it was concerned with poverty, it was based on rather vague concepts of both "poverty" and "class"; was confusing as to the nature of "cause"; and was unilluminated by any use of correlation techniques, which would have been indispensable to an effective statistical analysis of survey data.[16] (The effort also seemed to have little direct connection with the multicompartmentalized world of academic sociology.) Its lack of a clear framework of thought and the lack of precision in its concepts and methods seriously limited the use and practical influence of its "conclusions."

The best-known examples of interwar social inquiry did not, therefore, readily or persuasively point the way to detailed policy prescriptions or shed much light on the workings (as distinct from the general state) of society. Nevertheless, there are two reasons why they are of considerable importance in the present context.

First, their "political" effect—the extent to which they dramatized

---

[15]Raymond Kent, "The Emergence of the Sociological Survey, 1887–1939," in Martin Bulmer, ed., *Essays on the History of British Sociological Research* (Cambridge, 1985). See also R. A. Kent, *A History of British Empirical Sociology* (Farnborough, Hampshire, 1981).

[16]Kent, "The Emergence of the Sociological Survey," 56–66.

issues and excited the public conscience—was enormous. The contemporary and, even more, the subsequent history of state intervention in social affairs and industrial and regional policy was intimately related to widespread perceptions and presuppositions stimulated by the insistent inquiries of the 1930s. As with the parallel surveys of unemployment and depressed areas, inquiry into poverty and health reinforced the growing mood of social expectation: that economic and social problems were, indeed, just that (and not simply the outward sign of personal failings), and that a collective trauma needed some collective action. It was in these respects, then, that the twentieth-century followers of Booth and Rowntree had a distinctive role: for them the scale of the issues and the likely scope of the answers were much more extensive. Their professional and middle-class origins no doubt help explain their continued adherence to moderate reform and constitutional stability; but in the context of their time their findings were sufficiently radical, their advocacy (where they permitted themselves that luxury) sufficiently critical.

Second, the continuing history and influence of "sociological surveys" demonstrate how easy it is to exaggerate (or mislocate) the role of the state in the evolution of knowledge gathering at the initial stages of "modernity." Detailed survey work and social investigation remained heavily dependent on initiatives, researchers, and funds outside the realm of direct government activity. They therefore remained rooted in the combination of conscience and guilt, disinterest and political hopes, the ambition for knowledge and the desire for action, which had always been so influential in these matters. This is not to say that the official machine was irrelevant to the knowledge base of the modern state. On the one hand, its encounter with mass unemployment and prolonged depression obliged it (through committees of inquiry or such advisory bodies as the Economic Advisory Council and its Committee of Economists) to sponsor investigations into the workings of the economic system that were directly instrumental in the evolution of new doctrines and new policies. On the other hand, even where formal social investigation was not an explicit purpose of government initiatives, the *indirect* outcomes, in terms of new empirical information, were of increasing importance. The significance of the two major royal commissions (of 1919 and 1925–6) concerned with the coal mining industry have already been mentioned. But these were merely examples of a host of administrative and exploratory activities that generated information in a mounting flow and that still has not been fully explored.

Returning to the question of private investigation, it is also well to remember that "traditional" sociological surveys were not the only devices for gathering information. And in other respects, therefore, there was genuine innovation in approach and method. Mass-Observation, for example, was one departure; the Sociological Society (which had very little to do with academic sociology) was another. More influential in the present context were those highly systematic but much more explicitly "committed" inquiries that were specifically designed not simply to enlighten but also to engender new policies. On the whole, these were characteristic of the 1930s, rather than the 1920s—no doubt because it was not until the latter decade that the issues appeared to be sufficiently endemic (especially after the searing experience of the "economic blizzard" of 1929–32) to warrant more drastic thinking. For example, the centrist and left-of-center businessmen, academics, professionals, and politicians who were responsible for the founding of Political and Economic Planning (PEP) in the spring of 1931 subsequently spoke of it as a response to "a world apparently on the point of falling apart."[17] In any event, PEP was perhaps the most important and influential representative of the new movement toward a special mode of social inquiry. And its influence, which was as much empirical as ideological or political, was based on a distinctive form of "research."

PEP is generally thought of as a nonpartisan research organization devoted to the advocacy of planning, and certainly that is how it was born and presented itself. The fact is, however, that it undertook or sponsored little original research (it had few field investigators). Rather, it was a "fact-finding," or, more accurately, a "fact-mobilizing," institution—an action-oriented group of people assembling and publicizing often readily available material to present in coordinated, systematic, and argumentative ways. On the spectrum of social inquiry, it was far more propagandistic than academically "objective"—although it was commendably empirical and its propaganda proved acceptable to many people. At the same time, however, its relationship with "planning" was always ambiguous and involved serious internal tensions.[18] For, quite apart from the conceptual problem of exactly what was involved in the process, much actual and even more potential support for PEP came from

[17] Max Nicholson, in John Pinder, ed., *Fifty Years of Political and Economic Planning: Looking Forward, 1931–1981* (London, 1981), 5.
[18] Ibid., 5–13.

people who found the idea of planning too redolent of central direction and administrative power.

Despite these caveats and its private status, PEP had an extraordinarily influential role—even if most of its influence was realized only in the next two decades. Its numerous broadsheets and substantial reports on individual industries and particular aspects of British society (housing, health services, social services) were the most authoritative pronouncements on what was wrong with, and what might be done about, British economic and social institutions and policies. And although formal planning was not at the forefront of its ideas and prescriptions, its predilections, as was increasingly the case within the private and public spheres, were toward nonmarket action, coordination, and intervention. Vague as was the concept of the "middle way," vaguer still as was the contemporary idea of "planning," the main thrust of the new modes of thought was readily apparent: It was toward centralization, cooperation, and the enlightened use of detailed information.

A much more overtly "political," or at least exhortatory, version of the new trends was the Next Five Years group, formed in 1935 to consider a program of reform that might feasibly be achieved within the five-year term of a Parliament. Like PEP it was heavily influenced by men and women already well established in public life and drawn from a wide, although by no means complete, spectrum of political opinion. And, equally like PEP, it is not to be thought of as a marginal or dissident grouping. Admittedly, neither was able to muster many spokesmen from the left, but both echoed increasingly widespread opinion (and practice) within government as well as outside. When the Next Five Years group published its statement of aims and means, G. D. H. Cole expressed intense socialist skepticism. He ridiculed what he took to be "the 'Lib-Labs', the Progressives, come back hopefully to life after being out of action ever since 1914." Yet even he had to acknowledge that they were "prepared to be a great deal more 'socialistic' now than most of them were twenty or thirty years ago." It may have been significant that although he tried to dismiss the Next Five Years, along with Lloyd George's advocacy of extensive public works as a means of tackling unemployment, Cole's argument implicitly acknowledged that there had been a shift in radicalism. The signatories, he wrote, were "prepared to re-draft Liberalism in terms of post-war problems, and not afraid of a dash of Socialism." Even more significant, however, was his acceptance that the programs probably matched the private opinions of the leaders of the

Labour party and accurately reflected "the collective mind of the British electorate."

In fact, Cole's argument tacitly demonstrated the movement of opinion. Writing of the Next Five Years and of Lloyd George's latest statement, he said: "There is in them nothing new, nothing that has not been said many times before.... There is in both much sense, but it is common sense, drawn out of a stock of ideas that is already common property." Yet Cole seems to have missed the significance of his own generalization—just as he was wrong in implying that the "unoriginality" of the policies would mean that they would lead nowhere. He was, however, accurate in prophesying that if the manifestos ever were put into effect it would be "under the name and aegis of Labour," which would act in the spirit of the Next Five Years and call its action "Practical Socialism."[19]

This anticipation of consensus serves as a concluding note. The convergence of attitude and implicit doctrine to which Cole drew attention, like the change in the role of government and the objective of private social inquiry, came less from integral developments in the history of political and social thought than from the nature of what Cole called "post-war problems." Indeed, as far as the general motive, and in many respects the actual form, of direct investigation were concerned, the prevailing characteristic was continuity rather than novelty. Change, when it came, was frequently embodied in indirect channels (and produced knowledge as a by-product of pragmatic action), and most frequently derived from the role of the state itself, that is, from the immediate necessity for official response to social and economic problems. These problems were new in their incidence and drama and in terms of their effects on the minds of contemporaries. There was no doubt a logical progression from pre-1913 to post-1918 thinking, but differences in degree ultimately do become differences in kind, and by the late 1930s both the armory of argument and the contexts of inquiry, whatever the inheritance from the prewar decades, had been altered beyond recognition.

[19]G. D. H. Cole, "Chants of Progress," *Political Quarterly* 6 (1935): 534–5, 540.

10

War mobilization, institutional learning, and
state building in the United States, 1917–1941

ROBERT D. CUFF

National defense remains a major component of contemporary American
life, even after the end of the cold war. By their continuous demand for
weapons, supplies, and expertise, national security agencies support a
significant, if shrinking, network of aerospace contractors, military bases,
materials producers, scientists, engineers, consultants, and local communities throughout the nation. In fiscal year 1990, for example, national
defense outlays of U.S. $309.1 billion accounted for 5.7 percent of the
gross national product (GNP) and funded 74 percent of all goods and
services purchased by the federal government.[1]

It was not always so. In 1940, for example, a year before the United
States entered World War II, military outlays stood at U.S. $1.7 billion,
less than 2 percent of GNP, and totaled only 18 percent of federal expenditures. After World War II, however, by virtue of its size, durability,
and power, the national defense establishment altered the very context
in which Americans discussed such enduring issues as the balance of
power in a federal state, the optimum relation of state and civil society
in a democratic polity, and the proper mix of plan and market in a free
enterprise economy.

Few of the civilian or military participants in the early stages of these
developments would have dared to predict the powerful set of institutions
that the economics of defense would produce. America's first experience
with mobilizing a modern industrial economy for war in World War I,

---

[1] *Economic Report of the President February 1991* (Washington, D.C.: U.S. Government
Printing Office, 1991), 286, 381; *Historical Table, Budget of the United States Government
FY 1989* (Washington, D.C.: U.S. Government Printing Office, 1988), 39.

after all, took place against a background of nineteenth-century liberal attitudes toward the role of the state and the military, and the planning function of government; and the isolationist impulse of the interwar years subsequently impeded widespread appreciation of the Great War's lessons for industrial preparedness. And yet elements of social learning did occur as military institutions experimented with the means during World War I and after to link themselves to the private industrial economy on which so many of their modern functions had come to depend. An examination of this process of institutional experimentation and learning as it developed between 1917 and 1941 reveals elements of both continuity and discontinuity in the early stages of the evolving U.S. defense system.

WILSON'S MOBILIZATION

In the broadest terms, the dominant nineteenth-century American political tradition opposed both an active federal government and a permanent military establishment. Although Adam Smith, the great prophet of English liberalism, included defense as a necessary duty of the state in his seminal speculations on the wealth of nations, his intellectual heirs— particularly those in the United States of the late nineteenth century— were often forgetful that he did so. In fact, resistance to developing the professional military and civilian components of national defense was probably stronger in the United States than in any other major industrial country in the world.

There were many reasons for this attitude, including a suspicion of standing armies born of a revolutionary heritage, a powerful belief in the myth of the citizen soldier, a strong tradition of states' rights, the unhappy Reconstruction experience of recent memory, and continuing hope for protection by a vast ocean expanse. State builders in the United States, in contrast to their counterparts in Germany or Japan, could not appeal convincingly to impending threats to national security as a motive for action.[2]

[2]For important studies on pre–World War I state building in the United States and on attitudes toward it, see Richard F. Bensel, *Yankee Leviathan: The Origins of Central State Authority in America, 1859–1877* (Cambridge: Cambridge University Press, 1990), passim; Barry D. Karl, *The Uneasy State: The United States from 1915 to 1945* (Chicago and London: University of Chicago Press, 1983), chaps. 1–2; Morton Keller, *Affairs of State: Public Life in Late Nineteenth Century America* (Cambridge, Mass.: Belknap Press, 1977), passim; and Stephen Skowronek, *Building a New American State: The Expansion of National Administrative Capacities, 1877–1920* (Cambridge: Cambridge University

In his pioneering essay on public administration in 1887, Woodrow Wilson, then a youthful academic reformer, cited Prussian administration, which owed so much to military experience, as exactly the model that American innovators had in future to avoid. European practices would have to be adapted "to a complex and multiform state, and made to fit highly decentralized forms of government. If we would employ it, we must Americanize it. . . . It must learn our constitutions by heart; must get the bureaucratic fever out of its veins." Wilson went on, "If it came to a choice, is better to be untrained and free than to be servile and systematic."[3] In 1887 Wilson shared the general optimism among middle-class liberals that the United States could find a way through this dilemma. He was equally optimistic in April 1917, when the United States declared war on Germany, for he believed then, as he had thirty years before, that the United States, because it was more free than other countries, could make a uniquely systematic response to an organizational challenge.

In many respects, Wilson, both as youthful state builder and wartime president, reflected the deep ambivalence that middle-class Americans felt about war and the state during the first two decades of the twentieth century. And that ambivalence pervaded the country's response to the European war from August 1914 to its entry in April 1917. The nation's military institutions, fragmented by interorganizational rivalry and the politics of federalism, had never seriously considered the implications of large-scale industrial mobilization for warfare, for example, and Wilsonian diplomacy after 1914 limited their opportunities to learn. As General Douglas MacArthur later recalled, "At the beginning of the World War we had no major plan, we had no ramifications of that plan. Everything was indefinite and inchoate."[4]

Press, 1982), passim. See also Samuel P. Huntington, *The Soldier and the State: The Theory and Politics of Civil-Military Relations* (New York: Knopf, 1957), chap. 9; and James L. Abrahamson, *America Arms for a New Century: The Making of a Great Military Power* (New York: Free Press, 1981), 145–6. On Adam Smith and defense, see Gordon H. McCormick, "Strategic Considerations in the Development of Economic Thought," in Gordon H. McCormick and Richard E. Bissell, eds., *Strategic Dimensions of Economic Behavior* (New York: Praeger, 1984), 4, 10–12, 13.

[3]Woodrow Wilson, "The Study of Administration," *Political Science Quarterly* 11 (June 1887): 202. See also Robert D. Cuff, "Wilson and Weber: Bourgeois Critics in an Organized Age," *Public Administration Review* 38 (May/June 1978): 240–4; James W. Doig, "If I See a Murderous Fellow Sharpening a Knife Cleverly . . . : The Wilsonian Dichotomy and the Public Authority Tradition," ibid., 43 (July–August 1983): 292–304; and Raymond Seidelman and Edward J. Harpham, *Disenchanted Realists, Political Science and the American Crisis, 1884–1984* (Albany: State University of New York Press, 1985), 40–59.

[4]*War Policies Commission Hearings* (Washington, D.C.: U.S. Government Printing Office

Nor could the federal government's civilian departments be expected to consider mobilization tasks before 1917, given the president's policy of neutrality. Moreover, the tasks themselves, even if they had been brought into government view for prior consideration, demanded a range of competencies well beyond the reach of regular departments. Every belligerent was compelled to create special wartime agencies and recruit private specialists for government service after 1914. By these means alone could states at war administer the unprecedented human and material resources they required. In the United States, a weak civil service tradition, compounded by the long-standing habit of political recruitment to top policy-making posts, made even more likely a proliferation of special agencies and wartime volunteers in Washington, once the decision for war was taken.[5]

The trend was evident well before April 1917. Business and professional groups responded early to the economic and scientific problems revealed by a deepening war crisis abroad and its growing impact at home. Private planning preceded public planning. Allied war orders, for example, gave financial and manufacturing firms such as J. P. Morgan and the Du Pont Corporation a firsthand look at the financial, technical, and labor requirements of munitions production. In addition, between 1914 and 1917 a remarkable number of American professionals, motivated by a mixture of patriotism, professionalism, and political opportunism, turned their attention to the specialist requirements of modern war. In this way they established reputations as independent authorities and thus identified themselves as potential recruits for wartime service.

Herbert Hoover, a mining engineer and self-made millionaire, is a good example. He gained a reputation for expertise in the administration of war food supplies with his extraordinary work for the Commission for Relief in Belgium between 1914 and 1917. Similarly, Bernard Baruch, by means of prewar preparedness activity, transformed himself from a wealthy Wall Street speculator into an authority on raw materials policy. Drawing private authorities such as Hoover and Baruch into government service became a central principle of American war administration. As a

1931), part II, 379. See also Abrahamson, *America Arms for a New Century*, 158–71. For the general failure among all belligerents to anticipate the economic dimensions of the war, see Gerd Hardach, *The First World War 1914–1918* (Berkeley and Los Angeles: University of California Press, 1977), chap. 4.
[5] For an interesting parallel example of organized private business activity in another war effort, see Lewis H. Siegelbaum, *The Politics of Industrial Mobilization in Russia, 1914–17: A Study of the War-Industries Committees* (London: Macmillan, 1983), passim.

result, state administration after April 1917 became to a remarkable degree the application of private knowledge to public problems.[6]

The Wilson adminstration's first major entry in the field, the Council of National Defense and Advisory Commission (CND-AC), established in late 1916, reflected the trend. Composed of six cabinet officers and seven volunteer advisers who reported to the cabinet officers, this administrative arrangement served a liaison function linking government departments to prior, private mobilizations among professional, business, and conservative labor organizations. In this way government departments could tap private data and personnel in the formulation of public policy. The advisory commissioners focused on problems that private investigators, not government policymakers, had identified as significant. For example, in cooperation with the nation's major engineering societies, Howard Coffin, an auto-parts manufacturer and chairman of the Committee on Production, had in 1915 conducted a private survey of the country's munitions capacity, and he regarded his Advisory Commission membership as an opportunity to expand this work under council auspices.

The CND-AC is also significant from another perspective. Although the experiment was designed to draw private experts into public service, it was also intended nevertheless to retain a clear line between advisers in quasi-official positions and government officials with statutory authority. Private volunteers would advise, cabinet officers would formulate and execute policy, or so the theory held. The CND's original name, the "Executive Council of Information," reflected this intention much better than its final designation. Tensions between advisers and cabinet officers were inevitable, of course, and part of the administrative story of American mobilization involves the displacement of regular executive departments and civil servants by wartime agencies and their private staffs, some of which originated under the Advisory Commission. Moreover, the lines between policy-making and advisory roles collapsed as the mobilization proceeded; so did the distinctions between government and nongovernment interests that such lines were supposed to demarcate.[7]

[6]Kathleen Burk, *Britain, America and the Sinews of War 1914–1918* (London: George Allen & Unwin, 1985), chaps. 1–5; Alfred D. Chandler, Jr., and Stephen Salsbury, *Pierre S. Du Pont and the Making of the Modern Corporation* (New York: Harper & Row, 1971), chap. 13; and Robert D. Cuff, *The War Industries Board: Business-Government Relations During World War I* (Baltimore: Johns Hopkins University Press, 1973), chap. 1.

[7]For an interesting discussion of the CND-AC as part of a wartime search for "a substitute

The CND-AC structure also reflected two fundamental assumptions widely held at the time: (1) that a clear distinction could and should be drawn between conditions of war and of peace and (2) that this distinction could and should find organizational form in two different kinds of government administration: the "emergency" and hence temporary, on the one hand, and the "normal" and hence permanent, on the other. By this definition, departures from peacetime norms gained legitimacy only in the context of the crisis itself. As the editors of the *New Republic* explained in May 1917, "These institutions, designed for the war, must be so organized that they will serve efficiently their purpose, and disappear upon the return of peace. Otherwise personal liberty is at an end." All the more reason, then, to draft personnel from the private sector for public duty. In contrast to permanent officials, who would inevitably seek to perpetuate their wartime power, "A war service organized by business men, according to the principles of active private business, may easily be discontinued upon the return of peace."[8]

Woodrow Wilson, like the *New Republic* editors, similarly recognized the value of including private business executives in his emerging war administration. But he also worried about the prerogatives of his cabinet colleagues, at least in the early stages. He searched for a unique combination of private and public power through which corporate executives could serve the state without dominating it.

Wilson did not instinctively share the impulse toward specialized techniques and academic expertise that the *New Republic* editors and Washington technocrats so enthusiastically cultivated. As an educator and university administrator, Wilson had championed the ideal of liberal culture against advocates of technical and specialized academic training and research. The educational philosophy he demonstrated as president of Princeton University had embraced a search for an organic, cultural homogeneity; for a unity that could somehow bridge the gaps among disciplines, among faculty and students, among graduates and undergraduates. He expanded this search for communitarian wholeness during

for the modern state," see Ellis Hawley, "The Great War and Organizational Innovation: The American Case." Liberal reformers argued against using traditional departments: "It might as well be recognized now as later that modern war cannot be waged through the peace establishment assisted and advised by outsiders." "Reorganizing War Administration," *New Republic* 11 (May 12, 1917): 40–1. See also A. N. Holcombe, "New Problems of Governmental Efficiency," *American Economic Association, Supplement* 8 (March 1918): 271–80, which emphasizes the investigatory role of the Advisory Committee system.
[8]"Economic Dictatorship in War," *New Republic* 11 (May 12, 1917): 37.

the war to include not only the American nation but the entire world. Wilson's *personal* search for wartime political and social order, in other words, stemmed far more from an ideal of organic culture than from a commitment to the goals of superior administrative management. In the context of state building, therefore, the president served as a restraining force over his more pragmatic, specialized advisers, in the early stages of the war at least, and over his more enthusiastic technocrats in the immediate postwar period.[9]

Nevertheless, wartime requirements compelled enormous administrative expansion in the short period between April 1917 and November 1919. And as the CND-AC relationship suggests, much of the impetus originated with private managers close to the operational realities of war enterprise.

Administrative growth responded to the perceived need not only for more specialized data but for the government authority and administrative organization required to assemble and apply it. The expansion of the War Industries Board (WIB), for example, was propelled in part by a growing demand among business bureaucrats for greater access to information on military industrial requirements. It was this kind of pressure that established the context for a new organizational structure that in the spring of 1918 finally brought military purchasing officers and WIB commodity supervisors together in single administrative units.[10]

As a cultural phenomenon, Wilsonian mobilization rested heavily on voluntarism as a major principle of social action, and the moral suasion and appeals to altruism that that principle implied clearly exerted a powerful social force. Voluntarism established a supportive context for nationwide regulations and for potential social cooperation across the boundaries of a complex federal state. It encouraged political cooperation among a wide range of economic interest groups. But such appeals offered mobilization managers no practical guide to administrative action. The Wilsonian call for voluntarism and patriotic duty might motivate corporate lawyers, social workers, statisticians, and others to come to Wash-

---

[9]An argument developed in Robert D. Cuff, "We Band of Brothers—Woodrow Wilson's War Managers," *Canadian Review of American Studies* 5 (Fall 1974): 135–48. For evidence of these cultural themes in Wilson's pregovernmental career, see John M. Mulder, *Woodrow Wilson: The Years of Preparation* (Princeton, N.J.: Princeton University Press, 1978), passim.

[10]For a description of this process from the perspective of a key army representative, see John Kennedy Ohl, *Hugh S. Johnson and the New Deal* (Dekalb: Northern Illinois University Press, 1985), chap. 3.

ington, but such sentiments could not tell them what, exactly, they were supposed to do. Nor could Woodrow Wilson be expected to know. Concrete, administrative action required specialized information and specified behavior. National mobilization, in turn, required hierarchical controls and policy planning, as those who supervised the technical tasks of pricing war materials, assessing labor costs, measuring shipping requirements, and conducting army personnel policy could appreciate. Federal state agencies grew in range and power because voluntarism, without central direction and power, proved insufficient as a mobilization instrument.[11]

In the course of administrative evolution, government agencies appeared in haphazard fashion, a result of executive orders in some cases, of congressional legislation in others, and of informal arrangement in still others. Administrative differentiation also occurred within the regular federal establishment. The War Department passed through a series of reorganizations, for example, as its central administrators struggled to discipline the army's competitive, decentralized, supply bureaus. As part of this process, military institutions also drew corporate and academic personnel into their managerial ranks.[12]

A number of important boards appeared in the spring and summer of 1917, including the Committee on Public Information, the Emergency Fleet Corporation (created by authority of the Shipping Act of 1916), the Food and Fuel Administrations, the War Industries Board, the Aircraft Production Board, and Capital Issues Committee. But administrative expansion and reorganization reached its most feverish pace during the winter of 1917–18, when for a moment it seemed as if the entire war machine had ground to a halt. In December, the government took over

---

[11]On the importance of the voluntarist theme, see David M. Kennedy, "Rallying Americans for War: 1917–1918," in James Titus, ed., *The Home Front and War in the Twentieth Century, The American Experience in Comparative Perspective* (Washington, D.C.: U.S. Government Printing Office, 1984), 47–55. For an example of evolution toward greater bureaucratic power in a specific policy area, see Valerie Jean Connor, *The National War Labor Board: Stability, Social Justice, and the Voluntary State in World War I* (Chapel Hill: University of North Carolina Press, 1983), passim. And for an example of the theme in the context of federal-state relations, see William J. Breen, *Uncle Sam at Home: Civilian Mobilization, Wartime Federalism, and the Council of National Defense, 1917–1919* (Westport, Conn.: Greenwood Press, 1984), esp. chap. 1.

[12]See, for example, Daniel R. Beaver, "The Problem of American Military Supply, 1890–1920," in Benjamin Franklin Cooling, ed., *War, Business, and American Society* (Port Washington, N.Y.: Kennikat Press, 1977), chap. 5; and James E. Hewes, Jr., *From Root to McNamara: Army Organization and Administration, 1900–1963* (Washington, D.C.: Center of Military History, 1975), 21–50.

the railroads, and major administrative networks appeared for the first time in the international realm, a result of conferences among the United States and the Allies over the military and material needs of coalition warfare.

External administrative expansion pressured Washington, in turn, for interagency coordination, and in March, Wilson, in an attempt to head off congressional and business pressure for a munitions ministry, elevated Bernard Baruch to the WIB chairmanship and simultaneously created an industrial cabinet composed of the heads of his key wartime agencies. It was through this "fragmentalized system of bureaus," as Robert Wiebe has described America's wartime government, that the United States raised the troops, built the cantonments, acquired the funds, and got the 2 million–strong American Expeditionary Force to Europe.[13]

There were as many lessons to draw from the experience as there were people willing to draw them. At the most fundamental level, the mobilization seemed to confirm the ancient verities: that is, civil society, in characteristically American fashion, had come to the rescue of the state. Citizens had left their plows and sprung to arms. In the more narrowly defined administrative realm, the assumption seemed to be that the war effort succeeded, or lagged, insofar as regular government departments accepted, or resisted, civilian volunteers. Such occasions as there were to celebrate wartime government activity, it seemed, derived more from the innovations created during the emergency itself than from the work of regular departments.

Even the obvious false starts and chaos of the process produced benefits, according to this view. Walter Gifford, who, as a young American Telephone and Telegraph (AT&T) executive, served with Howard Coffin and the CND during the war and remained active in public life thereafter, claimed in the mid-1920s that

the informal pragmatic growth of the organizations at Washington was the healthiest, most efficient and quickest way to get the nation organized. If individuals

---

[13]Robert Wiebe, *The Search for Order, 1917–1920* (New York: Hill and Wang, 1967), 300. For a recent survey of the American war effort, see David M. Kennedy, *Over Here: The First World War and American Society* (New York: Oxford University Press, 1980), passim. On the evolution of war administration, see William F. Willoughby, *Government Organization in War Time and After* (New York: Appleton, 1919). The author's portrait of Wilsonian mobilization, and the chapter as a whole, draw on Robert Cuff, "American Mobilization for War, 1917–1945: Political Culture vs. Bureaucratic Administration," in N. F. Dreisziger, ed., *Mobilization for Total War* (Waterloo, Ont.: Wilfrid Laurier University Press, 1981).

had been given power at first, even the best of them would have made lots of costly mistakes. Everyone was overflowing with pet ideas and new schemes for winning the war, and if they had had power, everything would have been upset. As it was these men butted into others who had other pet ideas and each picked flaws in the other's plans. Progress seemed blocked, and when the best solution was found it went. What seemed like unnecessary delay was really healthy seeking of right steps to take, and with all the mistakes which were made we were usually free of bad blunders as compared with other nations.[14]

This positive assessment about the intelligence of American democracy in crisis did not mean, however, that the genius of the enterprise had originated with the people of democratic myth, although that conventional wisdom remained a powerful cultural current. For some political theorists, indeed, the crisis demonstrated just the opposite. The popular illusions and blind patriotism of a democracy at war revealed just how irrational and easily misled the citizenry could be under the stimulus of wartime propaganda. By this account, the capacity for effective social action lay essentially with professional and business leaders, the kind of people Gifford had in mind. In the view of many intellectuals and administrators alike, the mobilization proved what could be achieved not by the citizenry but on behalf of the citizenry by private, public-spirited, professional and business groups in cooperation with a state sympathetic to their private voluntary activities.[15]

This interpretation fueled postwar optimism among those private technocrats, who, like Walter Gifford, moved between business and government institutions. Because they collectively believed that the war had demonstrated how to forge a uniquely American combination of state-society relationships, they sought to apply the lessons to peacetime problem solving. As Ellis Hawley has described so well, Herbert Hoover tried to put this insight into practice. First as secretary of commerce and then as president, Hoover attempted to convert to peacetime uses the techniques of private-public cooperation he had fashioned in wartime, but

---

[14]"Memo of conversation with Walter S. Gifford, Nov. 8, 1926," in the Papers of Edwin F. Gay, Hoover Institution, Stanford, California.

[15]"During the First World War the army had given intelligence tests to more that 1,700,000 enlisted men. The results startled many people, for they apparently showed that 60 to 70 per cent of the soldiers had a shockingly low level of intelligence." Debate over the reliability of the tests followed. From Edward A. Purcell, Jr., *The Crisis of Democratic Theory* (Lexington: University of Kentucky Press, 1973), 98. See also Robert H. Ferrell, *Woodrow Wilson and World War I, 1917–1921* (New York: Harper & Row, 1985), 19–21. On the war's diverse impacts on American liberal intellectuals, see Stuart I. Rochester, *American Liberal Disillusionment in the Wake of World War I* (University Park: Pennsylvania State University Press, 1977).

without the coercive element of state-based power, which, as food administrator, he had also required.

A significant part of Hoover's task was to develop the specialized data required for rational decision making among professional and business elites, for the war had revealed just how thin the knowledge base for economic and industrial management really was. In terms of the overall civil society–state duality, however, the war had caused neither Herbert Hoover nor middle-class Americans in general to fear the state less. It had caused them rather to admire their civil institutions, and the people who directed them, all the more.[16]

INSTITUTIONAL LEARNING BETWEEN THE WARS, 1919–1939

Mobilizing a modern industrial economy for war had been an unprecedented task that had posed new social problems and had generated new organizational forms. It had raised awareness about the managerial requirements of an interdependent economic system and had served as a seedbed for postwar experiments in national social and economic management.

But what did the war mean for industrial mobilization as a newly discovered issue in its own right? How did the state and society approach that "problem" in the postwar years? After all, it had been in response

---

[16]For an introduction to these themes and to recent work on Hoover and the 1920s, see Guy Alchon, *The Invisible Hand of Planning, Capitalism, Social Science, and the State in the 1920s* (Princeton, N.J.: Princeton University Press, 1985), passim, and Donald T. Critchlow, *The Brookings Institution, 1916–1952: Expertise and the Public Interest in a Democratic Society* (Dekalb: Northern Illinois University Press, 1985), chaps. 1–4. Among works by Ellis Hawley, see "Herbert Hoover, the Commerce Secretariat, and the Vision of an 'Associative State,' 1921–1929," *Journal of American History* 61 (June 1974); and "Three Facets of Hooverian Associationalism: Lumber, Aviation, and Movies, 1921–1930," in Thomas K. McCraw, ed., *Regulation in Perspective, Historical Essays* (Cambridge, Mass.: Harvard University Press, 1981), 95–123. See also Samuel P. Hays, "Political Choice in Regulatory Administration," in McCraw, ed., *Regulation in Perspective*, 124–54.

   The founding of the National Bureau of Economic Research (NBER) in 1920 was one institutional result of the war-induced quest for greater economic knowledge. As Wesley C. Mitchell, its research director, recalled, "[NBER] was organized the year after the war closed . . . by a group of economists, most of whom had shared in the wartime mobilization and learned from hard experience how inadequate was their equipment for dealing with the problems put up to them. They wanted to increase knowledge of the sort the war had demanded, for they believed that it would be valuable also in peace." Wesley C. Mitchell, *Economic Research and the Needs of the Times*, NBER, Twenty-fourth Annual Report April 1944, 11. See also William J. Barber, *From New Era to New Deal: Herbert Hoover, the Economists, and American Economic Policy, 1921–1933* (Cambridge: Cambridge University Press, 1985), passim.

to the imperative to mobilize an entire society and economy for war that Hoover, Baruch, and other state builders had learned so much about the nation's institutional strengths, and, more important, about its institutional weaknesses, weaknesses they sought to overcome by expanding the nation's knowledge base and trying to improve the competence of the nation's managers in the postwar years.

Mobilization issues dropped off the national agenda in subsequent years. In a fundamental sense, the objective problem went away, and the public mood was generally one of "good riddance." Disarmament and isolationism dominated the nation's military policy; U.S. Army personnel fell from 846,198 in 1919 to 131,959 in 1923, to remain well under 200,000 until 1940. But industrial mobilization did remain as a "problem" for study and learning. War demands had introduced the issue; the postwar period offered time to study it. In the crisis, action preceded planning; now there was an opportunity to ensure that planning, based on codified knowledge, would guide action in the next crisis.

As a public issue in the 1920s and 1930s, industrial mobilization found a sympathetic, if narrow, holding environment among a small web of organizations and individuals, both public and private, that retained an appreciation of its ultimate significance. Cleveland manufacturer Frank Scott, the first WIB chairman, and Bernard Baruch, Scott's successor, had taken up the topic in prewar preparedness activity. Others testified on the subject before congressional committees during the war, and, as administrative veterans of the emergency crisis, they testified again during the interwar period, before the War Policies Commission in 1930 and the Nye Committee in 1934. The Army Ordnance Association, a group of military contractors and army officers incorporated in 1919, also possessed a natural interest, and many of these people kept in touch as members of the business advisory committees that linked military suppliers to the Ordnance Department's geographically decentralized procurement districts. In fact, the very interlocking nature of military and business personnel interested in munitions production became one of the most shocking discoveries of the Nye Committee's congressional investigation into the munitions industry in the 1930s.[17]

---

[17]The following account draws on Terrence J. Gough, "Industrial Mobilization in Its Relation to Military Manpower Mobilization," in *U.S. Manpower Mobilization for World War II* (Washington, D.C.: U.S. Army Center of Military History, Histories Division, September 1982); Paul A. C. Koistinen, "The 'Industrial-Military Complex' in Historical Perspective: The Inter-War Years," *Journal of American History* 56 (March 1970): 819–39; Marvin A. Kreidberg and Merton G. Henry, *History of Military Mobilization in the*

From the point of view of institutional learning and state building, however, a more significant development occurred in 1920. In that year, Congress responded to business criticism of the army's wartime procurement activity, authorized creation in the War Department of an Office of the Assistant Secretary of War (OASW), and charged it with responsibility for procurement and industrial mobilization planning. As a result, industrial mobilization as an issue acquired a permanent location inside the military bureaucracy for study and policy promotion. Information gathering, which before the war rested on private investigation, as is evident in Howard Coffin's prewar munitions survey, had now become the public responsibility of a segment, albeit a small one, of the state's military arm. This change reflected a widely held view that "the lack of an inventory and catalogue of American resources ... was the most serious lack which the war industrial program faced at the beginning, and the factor of most delay."[18] According to one enthusiast, "This statute embodies the experience of the World War and, for the first time in our history, gives legislative recognition of the economic factor in war."[19]

The OASW became official custodian of the records of the Council of National Defense, the War Industries Board, and the Committee on Public Information—and, in a certain sense, of the industrial mobilization experience itself. It established a Planning Branch to consider both procurement and industrial mobilization planning; that branch created a series of commodity committees along WIB wartime lines ("to collect, collate, and evaluate all information that is pertinent to the commodity assigned to it");[20] and in 1924, OASW established an Army Industrial

United States Army, 1775–1945 (Washington, D.C.: Department of the Army, November 1955), chaps. 12–15; Jordan A. Schwarz, The Speculator: Bernard M. Baruch in Washington, 1917–1965 (Chapel Hill: University of North Carolina Press, 1981); Harold W. Thatcher, "Planning for Industrial Mobilization, 1920–1940," Historical Section, General Administrative Services Division, Office of the Quartermaster General, 1943; and Harry B. Yoshpe, "Economic Mobilization Planning Between the Two World Wars," Military Affairs 15 (Winter 1951): 199–204; and Military Affairs 16 (Summer 1952): 71–83. On the Nye Committee investigation, see John E. Wiltz, In Search of Peace: The Senate Munitions Inquiry, 1934–36 (Baton Rouge: Louisiana State University Press, 1963); and Wayne S. Cole, Roosevelt and the Isolationists, 1932–45 (Lincoln and London: University of Nebraska Press, 1983), chap. 11.

[18] From Benedict Crowell and R. F. Wilson, The Giant Hand: Our Mobilization and Control of Industry and Natural Resources, 1917–1918 (New Haven, Conn.: Yale University Press, 1921), 13, quoted in Government Purchasing—An Economic Commentary (Washington, D.C.: U.S. Government Printing Office, 1940) [Monograph No. 19, TNEC], 44.

[19] Irving J. Carr, "The Army Industrial College," Army Ordnance 9 (November–December 1928): 167.

[20] Annual Report of the Secretary of War, 1925, 27.

College to provide the supply branches with a continuing source of procurement specialists.

Creation of the OASW reflected the general postwar view that management functions in government and in industry, and especially in the relationships between them, deserved far more systematic attention. From the management point of view, industrial mobilization had raised one challenge more than any other: to avoid future breakdowns and bottlenecks like those that had plagued the nation's short-lived production effort. For OASW, this meant an obligation to cultivate continuing access to information on advanced corporate management practice, to devise more effective ways to coordinate military requirements with industrial supplies, and to ensure that mobilization management schemes were formulated and understood by top policymakers before the next war.

Although the OASW contributed a base in the state for thinking about the economics of defense management, its subsequent activities, like those of its post–World War II successors, evolved in combination with private organizations. The connection between the OASW and the Harvard Business School (HBS) exemplifies the pattern.

The navy's wartime need for cost accountants had brought the military services into their first contact with the HBS, but army interest followed in 1923, when OASW decided to send supply officers to "keep the work abreast of progressive business practice." The assistant secretary of war tried initially to have the HBS accept army officers for less than the two-year minimum, but the HBS dean held firm. The Planning Branch also sought to turn the HBS to its own uses by getting it to incorporate into its curriculum a number of cases of particular relevance to army planners. And Harvard did concede that point in the early stages: army officers could satisfy HBS requirements with summer research papers written on topics assigned by the Planning Branch.[21]

The first eight army officers attended HBS in 1924 and, by 1929, forty officers had completed the two-year course. A few of these graduates then joined the Army Industrial College faculty and designed a curriculum along HBS lines, incorporating War Industries Board records and other information produced during the war years as basic data for student studies of industrial mobilization problems. These studies, in turn, pro-

---

[21]*Annual Report of the Secretary of War*, 1928, 18; Dean W. B. Donham to Assistant Secretary of War Douglas [*sic*] F. Davis, September 4, 1923, and April 21, 1924, both in Wallace B. Donham Papers, Harvard Business School Archives, Baker Library, Harvard University Business School (hereafter Donham Papers).

vided an empirical base for the Planning Branch's attempts to formulate synoptic Industrial Mobilization Plans.

As for the Army Industrial College's (AIC) basic educational function, the assistant director concluded:

> It does not seem probable that the college will ever develop into an Army school of business. Its task of training officers for their proper work in procurement planning is so great that it does not appear either practicable or desirable that the course of the college should take the place of the instruction which certain officers of the supply branches are now receiving from such institutions as the Harvard School of Business Administration, the Babson School and others.[22]

With that division of educational labor clearly established, AIC proceeded about its self-defined tasks and, by 1940, had graduated approximately eight hundred officers.

But the OASW-HBS connection was only one method by which the Planning Branch learned about best business practice. It also studied developments in corporate administration at first-hand and had corporate executives lecture at the AIC. The assistant secretary noted in 1929: "Business firms in the United States have become so large that the volume of their operations frequently exceeds those of the War Department... and the problems met and solved by them are often of the same character." Control and purchasing systems possessed special interest, and departmental representatives looked closely at how to devise "statistical methods for controlling and coordinating procurement... with the co-operation of some of the larger corporations of the country. In this field the opportunities for statistical analysis are practically unlimited."[23]

---

[22]Carr, "The Army Industrial College," 170. The AIC's founders first referred to it as the "Army School of Business Administration." See Dwight Davis Assistant Secretary of War to Wallace B. Donham, May 5, 1924, Donham Papers. By 1939, the army had sent 135 men to the HBS, and the navy had sent 55. Ties between the HBS and the War Department had become so close by the end of the 1930s that the school expected the relocation of the Army Industrial College to Soldiers Field for the war years. See Jeffrey L. Cruikshank, *A Delicate Experiment: The Harvard Business School 1908–1945* (Boston: Harvard Business School Press, 1987), 209–10.

[23]*Annual Report of the Assistant Secretary of War*, 1919, 36–7. For an example of the kind of innovations in corporate management that entranced military planners, see Donaldson Brown, General Motors vice president, *Decentralized Operations and Responsibilities with Coordinated Control* (n.p.: American Management Association, 1927). More precise information was essential for institutional control in this system. "As a fundamental requisite in the world of coordination, it should be remembered that the bringing of men's minds together in connection with a given problem can always be greatly facilitated through a presentation of the facts. Disagreements fade away in proportion to the degree to which facts may be substituted for opinion.... Questions of policy are clarified; and through the operation of these several committees a means is provided of gaining a widely diffused knowledge and understanding of corporation policies, and a

Establishment of the AIC may be interpreted as an example of the routinization of specialized activity in the state, a result in part of discovering a new kind of problem for which Congress, under pressure from wartime business veterans, made the OASW responsible. Yet its founding link with the HBS is also characteristic of the view that a close, continuing connection with a private institution, in this case the country's leading private school of business management, was required to fulfill this novel state function.

The public-private pattern was also evident in munitions production. It was a basic policy assumption of interwar industrial planning that private producers, in the future as in the immediate past, would be the major source of army munitions in another major conflict.[24] Army arsenals could contribute between 5 and 10 percent of estimated military requirements. In terms of overall responsibility for eventual industrial mobilization, this basic institutional fact necessarily made the army ultimately dependent on major industrial corporations and on the private managerial advances they devised, which they hoped the state could turn to military use during a mobilization. The logic of this position led OASW officials to establish as many collaborative relationships as possible.

In the postwar years, OASW planners sought ways to have wartime manufacturing skills retained in peacetime. They also advocated a program of "educational" munitions orders, under which private manufacturers, identified from army surveys as likely to convert to munitions production in a future conflict, would take small orders to update their production techniques. But a number of peacetime statutes barred the way. A section of the OASW charter itself restricted the manufacture of supplies to government-owned facilities unless production could be

---

sympathetic compliance with them as they may bear upon the immediate problems of divisional management" (16–17). See also Alfred D. Chandler, Jr., *Strategy and Structure* (Garden City, N.Y.: Doubleday, 1966), esp. 177–99.

[24]"The policy of the Ordnance Department at present does not contemplate, in case of emergency, an extensive expansion of government owned plants, but on the contrary, a production, in excess of present arsenal capacity, by private manufacturing concerns, in accordance with our industrial war plans. These plans are based, as far as practicable, on the utilization of existing private establishments and their equipment." C. L. H. Ruggles, Acting Chief of Ordnance to Maj. Townsend Assistant Secretary of War, Planning Branch, National Archives, Washington, D.C., Box 18 (hereafter Planning Branch Records). The situation was more complicated for relations between the navy and private aircraft manufacturers. See William F. Trimble, "The Naval Aircraft Factory, the American Aviation Industry, and Government Competition, 1919–1928," *Business History Review* 60 (Summer 1986): 175–98.

achieved more economically elsewhere. Larger production runs enabled government arsenals to produce specialized military articles at lower prices than commercial firms, so the army found it difficult to place orders for special equipment with commercial firms. Strict enforcement of competitive bidding also prevented distribution of "educational orders." That requirement threatened to make the department dependent on one firm or group of firms "who get a start on Government orders through patent ownerships, development activities, or otherwise, and can therefore usually underbid all other firms that might be interested. Most reliable manufacturing establishments make it a point to absorb development costs in bids."[25] These were the kinds of legislative barriers army planners wanted Congress to eliminate in the 1920s and 1930s.

At the urging of the OAWS, the U.S. Chamber of Commerce endorsed an educational order proposal in 1927, and the first bill came before Congress that year, but without effect. Subsequent bills met a similar fate. In the early 1930s, when government relief funds made current procurement a live issue, the program's supporters cast the proposal as an anti-Depression measure. If undertaken on sufficient scale, the educational order program might provide "the spark that will ignite the whole body of commercial enterprise and start it on the way to normal operation."[26] But the arms buildup implied by this kind of proposal had to wait until impending war in Europe altered the domestic political context. In 1938, Congress granted $2 million a year for each of five years beginning in fiscal 1939, and in January 1939, Franklin D. Roosevelt recommended a $32 million expansion. By that time, however, the educational order program, whose origins could be traced to Howard Coffin's pre–World War I campaign, had begun to merge with the enormous surge of defense contracts that preceded American entry into World War II.[27]

[25] Annual Report of the Assistant Secretary of War, 1929, 54. See also John W. Weeks, Secretary of War, to Senator James W. Wadsworth, December 22, 1922; and "Conference with Major Wesson, O. D. March 5, 1923," both in Planning Branch Records, Box 43; R. R. Nix, "Procurement of Noncommercial Material in Time of War," Army Ordnance 9 (November–December 1928): 158–9; and A. B. Quinten, Jr., "War Planning and Industrial Mobilization," Harvard Business Review 9 (1930–1931): 8–17. For a discussion of these and other problems in the case of the aircraft industry, see Jacob A. Vander Meulen, The Politics of Aircraft: Building an American Military Industry (Lawrence: University of Kansas Press, 1991), 55–82.

[26] Benedict Crowell to General Douglas MacArthur, April 12, 1933, Planning Branch Records, Box 43.

[27] Col. James H. Burns, "Production Is Preparedness," Army Ordnance 22 (July–August 1939): 114–16; Col. Harry K. Rutherford, Director of the Planning Branch, "Educational

As the foregoing example suggests, the Planning Branch encountered major barriers to its activities, and there is no intention here either to minimize their effect or to exaggerate the OASW impact on interwar events outside or inside the military. Within the services, the navy, which controlled much of its own supply through navy yard construction, held aloof from the educational order campaign and from industrial mobilization planning in general. It also withheld initial support from the Army-Navy Munitions Board, an agency formed under the OASW in 1922 to coordinate logistics requirements between the two services.

Obstacles also existed within the War Department itself. As a co-ordinating agency, the OASW and its Planning Branch depended on the technical supply services—the Ordnance Department, Signal Corps, and the rest—for a variety of resources, including the amount their respective budgets devoted to planning and the quality of officers they assigned to the AIC. In 1927, only fourteen officers worked on industrial mobilization planning in the Planning Branch, for example, but ninety worked on full-time procurement planning in the branches. Skepticism about the entire enterprise within the Army General Staff proved even more threatening. General Eisenhower recalled the "rather isolated atmosphere" when, in 1929, he joined the Planning Branch under Brigadier General Van Horn Moseley. "Indeed, the Chief of Staff of the Army . . . forbade any General Staff officer to go into the office of the Assistant Secretary of War."[28]

As it turned out, the atmosphere improved soon after Moseley and Eisenhower arrived, and OSAW planning for industrial mobilization got under way in earnest. General Douglas MacArthur, appointed army chief of staff in 1930, provided more sympathetic support at the top, navy cooperation picked up, and, most important of all, critical congressional interest forced planners to crystallize their recommendations for public inspection. A joint congressional-executive body, the War Policies Commission, set up in 1930 to study how to take the profit out of the war,

Orders, Peace Time Training for Industry in Arms Manufacture," ibid., 20 (November–December 1939): 162–6; and Ernest T. Trigg, "Industry and the National Defense, The Preparedness Role of the U.S. Chamber of Commerce," ibid., 11 (November–December 1930): 107–9.
[28] Dwight D. Eisenhower, *At Ease: Stories I Tell to Friends* (Garden City, N.Y.: Doubleday, 1967), 212. See also "Discussion of Strategic Commodities, Etc." June 2, 1934, "Conferences on the Work of the Planning Branch . . . ," Planning Branch Records, Box 7; and Allison W. Saville, "The Naval Military-Industrial Complex, 1918–1941," in Cooling, ed., *War, Business, and American Society*, 105–17. Terrence J. Gough provides a detailed description of constraints on industrial mobilization planning in "Soldiers, Businessmen and U.S. Industrial Mobilization Planning Between the World Wars," *War and Society* 9 (May 1991): 63–98.

requested a plan, and the Nye Committee, a special Senate committee established four years later to investigate the munitions industry, continued the pressure for revision and review. As a result, a series of Industrial Mobilization Plans appeared during the 1930s, all based on a close reading of the wartime experience, and all revised in response to congressional and sympathetic private critics, most notably Bernard Baruch, who with his talent for self-promotion had become the best-known and most highly regarded private spokesman on the issue. Baruch proved so adept as a policy entrepreneur in industrial planning that no investigation on the problem during the interwar years, whether by Congress, the military, or other government commissions, was complete until his views had been heard.

Army planners possessed statutory and professional responsibility for the industrial mobilization planning function, and that was a real gain over pre–World War I days. However, by the early 1930s, the OASW was only one of many groups in Washington that cultivated the planning impulse and found administrative models to emulate in World War I. By 1932, with the country in the depths of the Depression, pressure mounted for government action, and FDR, who took up the reins of power in 1933, responded with "a period of central state building."[29] As a former assistant navy secretary during World War I, Roosevelt had his own war memories; and the planners' former wartime colleague, General Hugh Johnson, brought wartime precedents to bear during the National Recovery Administration (NRA) experiment between 1933 and 1935. Planning Branch officials assigned nineteen officers to various industrial code authorities and five to Johnson's office to see what the NRA had to teach.

Administrators in a variety of policy areas, from labor to welfare, turned to the prior mobilization experience for inspiration and guidance. They also attempted, as in wartime, to increase the state's capacity both to describe and to regulate civil society. The Temporary National Economic Committee, set up in mid-1938 to investigate economic concentration, was simply one of the most extensive of the many inventories

---

[29]Margaret Weir and Theda Skocpol, "State Structures and the Possibilities for 'Keynesian' Responses to the Great Depression in Sweden, Britain, and the United States," in Peter B. Evans et al., eds., *Bringing the State Back In* (Cambridge: Cambridge University Press, 1985), 133. On the general theme of state expansion in the United States, see William E. Leuchtenburg, "The Pertinence of Political History: Reflections on the Significance of the State in America," *Journal of American History* 73 (December 1986): 585–600.

that an invigorated and expanded state took of civil society during these years.[30]

Needless to say, by the end of the 1930s, industrial mobilization planners confronted in civilian departments and agencies, both "normal" and "emergency," an expanded administrative capacity that altered dramatically both the organizational environment in which they operated and the range of activities that civilian departments and New Deal agencies believed themselves competent to undertake. This meant that as the threat of European war mounted, army industrial planners who might have expected to occupy secure positions of leadership on the issue encountered a proliferation of potential competitors. They were challenged on the technical quality of their recommendations—on such problems as price and production controls, war finance, and strategic materials acquisition—as well as on their administrative schemes for overall wartime government.

The confidence evident in the Department of Agriculture was typical among civilian agencies. When queried about their capacity to respond to a wartime challenge in September 1939, departmental officials emphasized that the basic statutory authority and administrative organization was firmly in hand:

Most of the score or more of programs assigned to the Department . . . for Administration in the last six years were authorized to meet emergency conditions. . . . The Department commands an educational organization extending into every agricultural county. It maintains a vast fact-finding network which can supply other Departments of Government, better than in any other way, the most complete information on agricultural matters. It maintains inspection services in all markets and at all points of entry into the United States. It has at its disposal credit facilities . . . authority for storing, handling, and marketing huge quantities

---

[30]On the NRA-military connection, see Bradish J. Carroll, Jr., to W. H. Bagley, June 1, 1934; C. A. Bishop, executive assistant, NRA Division of Research and Planning, April 28, 1934, Planning Branch Records, Box 55; and *Annual Report of the Assistant Secretary of War*, 1934, 28. And for the pioneering article on the WWI–New Deal connection, see William E. Leuchtenburg, "The New Deal and the Analogue of War," in John Braeman, Robert H. Bremner, and Everett Walters, eds., *Change and Continuity in Twentieth-Century America* (New York: Harper & Row, 1966), 81–143. Johnson emphasized the differences between the NRA and the army's Industrial Mobilization Plan. "The Industrial Mobilization Plan is indeed industry control. Both impulse and direction proceed from Government. The National Industrial Recovery Act, on the other hand, contemplates the least amount of industrial control, either in the sense of impulse or direction." Johnson to Harry H. Woodring, Secretary of War, June 22, 1933, Planning Branch Records, Box 55. For a detailed analysis of Johnson's views and for references to the role of wartime precedents in this area, see Ohl, *Hugh S. Johnson and the New Deal*, chaps. 6–11.

of agricultural produce. It is experienced in the administration of regulatory laws. . . . It is skilled in specialized research techniques.[31]

Mobilizing food during World War II would require no Herbert Hoover.

In some respects, military industrial planners had learned their wartime administrative lessons too well. In their view, mobilization required civilian superagencies outside the regular departments—agencies such as the Fuel Administration, the Food Administration, the Committee for Public Information, the War Industries Board, and so on, of World War I. That had been one of the basic axioms of interwar planning. More than that, these agencies would necessarily be staffed largely, although by no means exclusively, by business volunteers. This would be especially true of what army planners eventually envisaged as the central coordinating body of emergency war government, a War Resources Administration, modeled along the lines of Bernard Baruch's War Industries Board. The war had taught as much, and subsequent study had reinforced it. In 1930, the army made the same argument for superseding regular cabinet departments in a future conflict that the New Republic had made in 1917: "Emergency organization would automatically terminate after the war. If these controls were exercised by a cabinet department, they might be continued after the end of the war to the great detriment of the country."[32]

The Hoover White House might have approved this line of argument in 1930, but the scene had changed dramatically with Roosevelt in 1933. Successive editions of the Industrial Mobilization Plans created administrative space for new state agencies. The Securities and Exchange Com-

---

[31]Mastin G. White, Memorandum for the Secretary, September 5, 1939, in Record Group 225, Records of the Army-Navy Munitions Board, Special and Confidential Correspondence, 1922–1945, National Archives, Washington, D.C., Box 1. "The economists and the professional men brought in to man the emergency agencies, many of them recent graduates from the professional and graduate schools of our leading universities, had their own ideas as to proper methods of instituting economic controls, which did not always coincide with those of the Industrial Mobilization Plan." Thatcher, "Planning for Industrial Mobilization," 302. It was not until September 1939 that OASW created a Statistics Branch. Moreover, Planning Branch work on both procurement and mobilization of industry "included few important statistical studies." See Richard O. Lang, "Problems of Statistical Control—Military Aspects," Journal of the American Statistical Association 36 (March 1941): 13.

On the planning impulse in general during the New Deal, see Otis L. Graham, Jr., Toward a Planned Society: From Roosevelt to Nixon (New York: Oxford University Press, 1976), chap. 1. And for a broader discussion of "The New Deal and the Idea of the State," see Alan Brinkley's essay of that title in Steve Fraser and Gary Gerstle eds., The Rise and Fall of the New Deal Order, 1930–1980 (Princeton, N.J.: Princeton University Press, 1989), 85–121.

[32]Annual Report of the Secretary of War, 1931, Appendix A, 61.

mission of 1934 joined the list of agencies expected to cooperate with the plan's Price Control Commission in the 1936 version, for example, and the 1939 revision proposed "to use existing Government agencies to their fullest extent."[33] But OASW officials never fully grasped the administrative and political changes that swirled around them from 1933 to 1939. In 1940, *Fortune* magazine caught the implications in an article titled "War and Peace": "The people of the United States, over a period of years, have created a powerful war organization," it observed. "It is not the navy. It is not the army. It is the Executive Branch of the Federal Government."[34] By that point, the OASW was only one of several administrative-political groups who competed for "pieces of the action" offered by the defense buildup.

THE DEFENSE PERIOD, 1939–1941

Expanded government capacity and a suspicion of corporate interests among many New Dealers were among the factors that help to account for the strong resistance to superagencies evident among civilian administrators in Washington during the partial mobilization of 1939 to 1941, a resistance without parallel in the comparable period before World War I. But increased self-confidence among a rising group of professional public administrators associated with New Deal experiments was equally significant. The defense crisis did not simply afford them an opportunity to vindicate public planning experiments such as the Tennessee Valley Authority; it also opened the way, they hoped, to demonstrate a more general point: that neither business institutions nor business executives had a lock on administrative competence. According to one of their number, "As the defense program got underway, a great philosophical argument on the theory of administration ran through the Washington scene. The point at issue was this: Do you give defense functions to existing agencies, or do you create new agencies to deal with specific phases of defense work?"[35]

---

[33] *Annual Report of the Assistant Secretary of War,* 1939, 20.
[34] *Fortune* 22 (November 1940): 65.
[35] "Memorandum of conversation between Mr. Herbert Emmerich and Sidney Hyman, Washington, D.C., May, 1949," Papers of Louis Brownlow, John F. Kennedy Library, Boston.
  One brief for the regular departments put it this way: "New agencies should be established to carry forward emergency work only where this is absolutely necessary because of a discovered gap that is clearly present in the programs, work, or potential activities of existing organizations. Such cases will unquestionably be comparatively rare

The OASW had a ready answer. After all, in contrast to the pre–World War I period, industrial planners now had a place in government from which to press their claims. Moreover, as a result of interwar planning, their office possessed a professional staff as well as guidelines for technical and administrative action; and in Assistant Secretary Louis Johnson, their political chief, appointed in 1937, they also had an aggressive administrative leader. And Johnson made the issue his own. He pressed his statutory authority to the limit; he campaigned across the country; he supported private studies intended to shape public debate; he engaged the Brookings Institution, a nonprofit research body, to study wartime price control; and he lobbied Roosevelt vigorously for approval of the Industrial Mobilization Plan, which by this point had come under the direction of the Army-Navy Munitions Board.

As a result, the OASW could provide Roosevelt with recommendations for industrial mobilization drawn from a serious effort to codify useful principles from prior experience. Moreover, because of the plan's joint sponsorship under the Army-Navy Munitions Board, it possessed the combined support of both services. Wilson had none of this available to him in 1917. According to the plan, indeed, in event of a sudden decision for war, the board would carry the administrative burden until civilian superagencies got into place.[36]

As early as 1937, Assistant Secretary Johnson pressed Roosevelt to establish an "Advisory Board for Industrial Mobilization," a group of

today as compared to the situation a quarter of a century ago—particularly in the defense emergency. During the period 1916–1918, it was necessary for the federal government to create many new agencies to assume responsibilities for meeting acute problems arising from World War I. Many of them proceeded with programs that were not as closely integrated with the national effort as they might have been, partly because they were new and partly because the President did not have adequate staff aid or an appropriate administrative device for supervising their activities.... Today we are better prepared." William H. McReynolds [Liaison Officer for Office of Emergency Management], *Public Administration Review* 1 (Winter 1941): 133–4. See also Herbert Emmerich, *Federal Organization and Administrative Management* (Tuscaloosa: University of Alabama Press, 1971), 71–2; and Theodore J. Lowi, *The Personal President: Power Invested, Power Unfulfilled* (Ithaca, N.Y.: Cornell University Press, 1985), 52–5.
[36]Charles O. Hardy's *Wartime Control of Prices* (Washington, D.C.: Brookings Institution, 1940) was undertaken at the War Department's request. Harold J. Tobin and Percy W. Bidwell's *Mobilizing Civilian America* (New York: Council on Foreign Relations, 1940) also reflected the private-public mix, with initiative in this case coming from the Council on Foreign Relations, with War Department cooperation. The military planners, who demonstrated a lack of political insight in so much of their activity during the 1930s, did it again by turning to Brookings for economic research. Under the leadership of economist Harold Moulton, that institution had aligned itself against every major New Deal initiative—"government reorganization, deficit spending, and national planning." Critchlow, *The Brookings Institution, 1916–1952*, 106.

leading citizens who would not only study and approve the Industrial Mobilization Plan, but who would also provide the nucleus for a War Resources Board, the central coordinating authority of wartime mobilization.[37] Roosevelt held off Johnson for two years. The issue was complicated not only by the domestic debate over foreign policy that raged among isolationists and interventionists during these years. There was also a bureaucratic dimension: Johnson and his superior, Harry Woodring, the secretary of war, feuded on all major issues, and the politics of industrial mobilization planning was no exception. However, in the summer of 1939 it suited Roosevelt's purposes to yield to Johnson's request, and on August 9, 1939, while Woodring was out of town, Johnson and Assistant Secretary Charles Edison, with the president's approval, announced the formation of a War Resources Board.

The original composition of the board was as follows: Edward Stettinius, Jr., chairman of the board of the United States Steel Corporation; Karl T. Compton, president of the Massachusetts Institute of Technology; Walter S. Gifford, president of AT&T; Harold G. Moulton, president of the Brookings Institution; John Lee Pratt, a director of the General Motors Corporation; and General Robert E. Wood, chairman of Sears, Roebuck and Company. John Hancock, an investment banker and crony of Bernard Baruch, was added later in an effort to rectify the omission of the country's leading statesman of industrial preparedness. Three of these men—Gifford, Wood, and Hancock—had been deeply involved in the first mobilization, and all seven typified the kinds of private sources of expertise and management that had begun to converge on preparations for the second. More than that, they represented exactly the kind of business and academic professionals from private life who had provided a major support for the Wilsonian war effort. The board took testimony from administrative veterans of the World War I effort, surveyed inventories of key industries, blessed the basic plan, and volunteered to serve as the central agency envisaged by Army-Navy Munitions Board planners.[38]

---

[37]Louis Johnson, Memorandum for the President, December 4, 1937, Papers of Louis Johnson, University of Virginia Library, Box 84.

[38]Among questions that Johnson addressed to the board were the following: "What bottlenecks will be encountered in supplying equipment for the armed forces in the time and quantity required? Is the cooperative basis of the plan sound or should some more positive method be adopted? To what extent should legislation be enacted in peace to permit prompt setting up of the control necessary in war? Are the essential needs of the civilian population adequately provided for?" Johnson to Edward R. Stettinius, Jr., August 10, 1939, Papers of Edward R. Stettinius, Jr., University of Virginia Library, Box 74. See

But that was not to be. Labor and agriculture representatives protested their exclusion from the board. Liberal New Dealers opposed the encroachment of powerful industrial and investment banking interests (which, in their view, Stettinius, Pratt, and Hancock represented) on government. And isolationists, as well as those who mistrusted Roosevelt's planning instincts, saw in the Industrial Mobilization Plan a "Blueprint for Fascism."[39]

More important, Roosevelt had his own reservations. He could not afford politically to alienate organized labor, a major source of his political support; nor, in a generally isolationist country, could he be seen to be preparing the nation for war. The fact that the conflagration began in Europe within four weeks of the appointment of the members of the War Resources Board served only to dramatize the connection between the plan, the board, and possible U.S. intervention.

But there were institutional prerogatives as well. In 1939, Congress created an Executive Office of the President, and Roosevelt began to provide himself with the instruments of a managerial presidency. The new legislation allowed him to appoint seven administrative assistants, and it transferred the Bureau of the Budget from the Treasury Department to the White House. The move by the Budget Bureau, created in 1921 as an offshoot of the World War I effort, was an important development because the Bureau of the Budget officials shared Roosevelt's determination to forge the managerial instruments of modern presidency. Roosevelt intended to use them, moreover, to ensure that he remained "kingpin"[40] in any defense organization. From the start, the president and

also Harold G. Moulton to Stettinius, August 14, 1939; Frank B. Jewett to Stettinius, August 17, 1939, ibid. See also *Report of the War Resources Board* in Record Group 179, Records of the War Production Board, File #011.28 R, National Archives, Washington, D.C.

  Board members wrote: "Final responsibility for policies and for the coordination of the war program must be vested in the President" (p. 4). But they also emphasized, "We recommend that wartime powers be vested in specially-created wartime agencies which will be automatically demobilized when war is over. Should wartime powers be granted to existing executive or quasi-judicial agencies of the government, it will be next to impossible at the end of the war to separate the wartime from the peacetime functions of the government" (p. 7).

[39] Albert A. Blum, "Birth and Death of the M-Day Plan," in Harold Stein, ed., *American Civil-Military Decisions: A Book of Case Studies* (New York: Twentieth Century Fund, 1963); and "Roosevelt, the M-Day Mess, and the Military-Industrial Complex," *Military Affairs* 36 (April 1972): 44–6; and Jordan A. Schwarz, *The Speculator* (Chapel Hill: University of North Carolina Press, 1981), 356–63.

[40] Diary of Harold Smith, Budget Director, Roosevelt Library, Hyde Park, New York, vol. 23, May 23, 1940. See also Emmerich, *Federal Organization*, 68, and Richard E. Neustadt, "Approaches to Staffing the Presidency: Notes on FDR and JFK," *American Political*

Budget Bureau officials alike aimed to protect the presidency from military managers, on the one hand, and from industrial managers, on the other. The Industrial Mobilization Plan seemed to combine both threats in a single proposal. In its final recommendations of November, the review panel, sensitive to the president's wariness, downgraded the War Resources Board from a controlling to a coordinating superagency. But it was too late; Roosevelt thanked the board, buried its report, and never called again.

After almost a decade of political struggle amid a burgeoning set of administrative fiefdoms, Roosevelt could appreciate, far more than Wilson ever could have, the administrative dimension of a prospective war mobilization, and, as the foregoing example suggests, the political intrigue required to manage it. FDR also had available a greater range of bureaucratic instruments by which to pursue elements of mobilization, before an official declaration of war. And, given his commitment to the Allies, he intended to use them.

The Reconstruction Finance Corporation (RFC) was characteristic. Created under the auspices of the Hoover administration early in 1932 and modeled essentially on the old War Finance Corporation of World War I, the RFC became a central factor in the escalation after it gained congressional authority to lend money for defense purposes, to own defense plants, and to negotiate contracts. This allowed the administration to begin a prewar acquisition program for strategic materials such as OASW planners had recommended, and to inaugurate a capital investment program of historic proportions. By means of subsidiary creations, such as the Defense Plant Corporation established in August 1940, the RFC undertook a direct investment program that would ultimately equal in expenditure more than half the dollar value of the nation's entire manufacturing plant as of 1939.[41]

Science Review 57 (December 1963): 855–8. Richard Polenberg, *Reorganizing Roosevelt's Government 1936–1939* (Cambridge, Mass.: Harvard University Press, 1966), and Barry D. Karl, *Executive Reorganization and Reform in the New Deal* (Cambridge, Mass.: Harvard University Press, 1963), describe Roosevelt's effort to reorganize the presidency. See also Karl, *Uneasy State*, 155–65. On the Budget Bureau, see Larry Berman, *The Office of Management and Budget and the Presidency, 1921–1979* (Princeton, NJ.: Princeton University Press, 1979), 3–29. See also Don K. Price, *America's Unwritten Constitution, Science, Religion, and Political Responsibility* (Baton Rouge: Louisiana State University Press, 1983), 99–109; see esp. 102–3 for a suggestive comment on the military contribution to the development of the presidency as an institution.

[41] Jesse H. Jones, *Fifty Billion Dollars: My Thirteen Years with the RFC (1932–1945)* (New York: Macmillan, 1951), part II; Gerald D. Nash, "Herbert Hoover and the Origins of the Reconstruction Finance Corporation," *American Historical Review* 46 (December

Similarly, the investigative capacity of the state, exercised through such agencies as the National Recovery Administration (NRA), the Securities and Exchange Commission, the National Resources Planning Board, and the Temporary National Economic Committee, provided the government with far greater specialized knowledge than the Wilsonians had ever possessed. In the interwar years, private agencies such as the Brookings Institution and the National Bureau of Economic Research had few competitors as sources of applied economic research. "Until the National Resources Planning Board undertook its major studies of consumer incomes and expenditures in 1938," for example, "the Brookings capacity studies remained the major guide to the economy for policy makers, liberal and conservative alike."[42]

Washington took on more federal workers in the 1930s than during the preceding three decades combined, and among them were a cadre of government-based specialists determined to employ research on behalf of their view of the public interest. Leon Henderson is an interesting example. A consumer-oriented economist with the Russell Sage Foundation, Henderson had first joined the New Deal in 1933 as head of the NRA's Research and Planning Division. He had then participated in major economic debates within the administration as an adviser to the Works Projects Administration, as a member of the National Resources

1959): 455–86; and Gerald T. White, *Billions for Defense: Government Financing by the Defense Plant Corporation During World War II* (Tuscaloosa: University of Alabama Press, 1980), passim.

[42]Critchlow, *Brookings,* 123. For an example of the reach of the federal government's research in one policy area, see Sanford Schwarz, *Research in International Economics by Federal Agencies* (New York: Columbia University Press, 1941). The entire SEC enterprise rested on access to and specialized analysis of private financial information. See Thomas K. McCraw, *Prophets of Regulation* (Cambridge, Mass.: Harvard University Press, 1984), chap. 5.

The Army Engineers had opposed the NSRB from its inception. Byrd L. Jones, "A Plan for Planning in the New Deal," *Social Science Quarterly* 50 (December 1969): 526.

The continuity between the NSRB and wartime economic planning efforts can be illustrated in the careers of Ralph Watkins, Glenn E. McLaughlin, and Thomas C. Blaisdell, Jr. The three economists moved from the NSRB to the War Production Board's Planning Committee. Watkins, a specialist on natural resources, subsequently headed the Plans and Programs Division of the National Security Resources Board, the greatly transformed, post–World War II analogue to OASW. Marion Clawson, *New Deal Planning, The National Resources Planning Board* (Washington, D.C.: Resources for the Future, 1981), 70, 122, 153, 159ff.

For a survey of NSRB's war-related studies, prior to its dissolution in 1943, see Philip W. Warken, *A History of the National Resources Planning Board 1933–1943* (New York: Garland, 1979), chap. 5. They included studies of railroad transportation, stockpiling, electrical and coal supplies, and of industrial location factors. As part of their work, the research studies gave special attention to the effectiveness of controls under World War I agencies (p. 142).

Committee, and in 1938 as executive secretary for the Temporary National Economic Committee. In this latter capacity he commissioned a total of forty-three research monographs on various dimensions of the American political economy and launched his own mini-hearings on wartime price controls. There were many other professionals with New Deal commitments like Henderson who shared his conviction that they deserved a central role in the defensive buildup. They also supported Henderson's determination to base any prospective government fight against wartime inflation on nonbusiness sources of expertise from both government and universities, and to ensure that operational posts in any price control system be headed not by business executives but by accountants, engineers, lawyers, and especially economists.[43]

Roosevelt proved sympathetic. In May 1940 he revived the Council of National Defense and Advisory Commission, which was still on the statute books and with which in 1916 the Wilson government had made its initial administrative response to the private preparedness groups that clamored for action, and he made Henderson head of the Price Stabilization Division. But there was a characteristically Rooseveltian twist. Under Wilson, as mentioned earlier, the seven advisory commissioners had reported to the council, which consisted of six cabinet members. Under Roosevelt, the commissioners reported directly to the president. And if the arrangement functioned as Bureau of the Budget officials

---

[43]Soloman Fabricant, *The Trend of Government Activity in the United States Since 1900* (New York: National Bureau of Economic Research, 1952), 29. But in 1940, the 1 million federal civilian workers still accounted for only 22 percent of all government workers, when state and local government workers are added.

   Andrew H. Bartels, "The Politics of Price Control: The Office of Price Administration and the Dilemmas of Economic Stabilization, 1940–1946," unpublished Ph.D. diss. Johns Hopkins University, 1980, chaps. 1–2; Ellis Hawley, *The New Deal and the Problem of Monopoly* (Princeton, N.J.: Princeton University Press, 1966), chaps. 20–21 and 24; and Hugh Rockoff, *Drastic Measures: A History of Wage and Price Controls in the United States* (Cambridge: Cambridge University Press, 1984), 86–90.

   For a list of National Bureau of Economic Research staff who entered government service or served as consultants during the buildup, see *Economic Research in War and Reconstruction*, Twenty-second Annual Report of the National Bureau of Economic Research, 1942, 13–15. They included Simon Kuznets, who in 1942 would play a significant role in policy debates over the economic feasibility of proposed military programs. Winfield W. Riefler, "Government and the Statistician," *Journal of the American Statistical Association* 217 (March 1942): 1–11, offers an interesting overview of the interwar expansion of governmental statistical services and of the contributions of statisticians to the advancement of economic knowledge. Examples of TNEC work related to defense issues include Monograph No. 19, *Government Purchasing—An Economic Commentary* (Washington, D.C.: U.S. Government Printing Office, 1940), which includes a survey of the World War I mobilization effort; and Monograph No. 20, *Taxation, Recovery, and Defense* (Washington, D.C.: U.S. Government Printing Office, 1941).

intended, "This would provide an over-all planning group with most of the execution falling into normal administrative channels with the Chief Executive making the decisions upon the basis of advice carefully sifted for him."[44]

In yet another effort to strengthen White House control, Roosevelt also changed the rules on the military industrial planners. He shifted the Army-Navy Munitions Board from its reporting chain of command through the assistant secretary of war to a position in the Office for Emergency Management (OEM), which he had created by executive order on September 8, 1939. Roosevelt wanted to change the Army-Navy Munitions Board from an administrative agency of the War Department to an agency directly responsible to the chief executive. More generally, he used the OEM as a device "to take executive action to create necessary administrative machinery without waiting for the approval of Congress."[45] As a result of these measures, by the end of 1940, some observers believed Roosevelt had "pocketed the portfolio of national defense."[46] But of course, FDR could not pocket the portfolio of national defense. No one person could have handled this job, given the enormous collective enterprise that mobilization for total war was destined to become for the United States after December 1941. The scene in 1940 was set for administrative struggle, not central control.

Perspectives differed. The ANMB had two main goals. The first goal was to recover the administrative ground the services thought had been theirs before the president struck down IMP and embarked on his ad hoc approach to constructing a war administration. The second goal was to ensure that no civilian agency interfered with the statutory authority of the services to place defense contracts. The board ultimately succeeded on both counts. In the eighteen months from June 1940 to the attack on Pearl Harbor, December 7, 1941, the War Department, the biggest military spender, acquired $36 billion from Congress, a sum larger than

---

[44]Smith Diary, vol. 3, May 19, 1940. See also vol. 4, May 24 and 25, 1940. The seven members of the Advisory Commission, including Henderson, and their specialties were Edward R. Stettinius, Jr., industrial materials; William S. Knudsen of General Motors, industrial production; Sidney Hillman, labor leader, employment; Chester C. Davis, former Agricultural Adjustment Administration head, farm products; Ralph Budd, railroad executive, transportation; and Harriet Elliott, consumer advocate, consumer protection.

[45]In the opinion of Louis Brownlow, as reported in "Conference with Brownlow, Levi, Atkinson, June 19, 1944," in Papers of V. O. Key, JFK Library, Box 24, "Wilson lacked such machinery and was greatly handicapped." For a description of OEM, see William H. McReynolds, "The Office for Emergency Management," *Public Administration Review* 1 (Winter 1941): 131–8.

[46]"National Defense: The Sinews," *Fortune* 22 (October 1940): 58.

combined War and Navy Department spending during World War I, and placed contracts worth nearly $13 billion in less than a year. It also obtained the right to negotiate all defense purchases under new appropriations and to make awards directly to allocated or desired facilities without advertising and competitive bidding. And it successfully fought off civilian attempts to control its allocation procedures. Well before 1942 it was clear that the military services during World War II would prove to be a far more imposing set of institutions than they ever had been during World War I.[47]

From the perspective of New Dealers such as Leon Henderson, however, battles remained to be fought with corporate executives whom Roosevelt, like Woodrow Wilson before him, felt compelled to place in top policy-making and administrative positions in both civilian and military agencies. As a colleague recalled, "Leon had just come from long, hard months of work on the TNEC hearings, where the operations of the cartel builders were stripped bare. He was naturally suspicious when he saw the same men whose financial manipulations he had been studying suddenly appear in positions of great Government trust."[48] Military personnel also posed problems. In 1940, Henderson believed that "the War Department . . . is paralleling the Defense Commission with experts on powder, airplanes, machine tools, etc., and is moving into territories which, by all logic, belong to the Commission. . . . My guess is that the War Department is organizing its own version of a War Resources Board."[49] In the competitive struggle for position and power in wartime Washington, it behooved each group to possess not only its own lawyer, but also its own economist, accountant, statistician, and the rest.[50]

---

[47]R. Elberton Smith, *The Army and Economic Mobilization* (Washington, D.C.: U.S. Government Printing Office, 1959), 219–21.

[48]"Memorandum of conversation between Mr. Emmerich and Sidney Hyman, Washington, D.C., May, 1949," Brownlow Papers.

[49]Henderson to Roosevelt, October 14, 1940, Papers of Franklin D. Roosevelt, OF 813A, Franklin D. Roosevelt Library, Hyde Park, New York.

[50]In early October 1940, Secretary of War Henry Stimson made an interesting diary entry on the bureaucratic politics of statistics: "Then at 12:00 o'clock General Crowell [Benedict Crowell, WWI Assistant Secretary of War, and an architect of the OASW] came in and I had a good long talk with him—and Colonel Leonard P. Ayres of Cleveland, who has come down to head the Statistics Branch of Patterson's office and to try to straighten out our statistics. This brought up the question of the relations between the Defense Advisory Commission across the way and our own munitions branch of the War Department. Crowell warned me that the Defense Commission was likely to try to absorb the whole work of being the munitions branch of the Government, and he told me how that had happened before in the last war. It is beginning now by their attempting to get into our statistics, and the appointment of Colonel Ayres to reform and strengthen our statistical

In the meantime, FDR used the political appointment process to build an administrative coalition of interest groups. In 1940 he invited senior Republicans to head the War and Navy departments. They in turn recruited their own staffs of corporate lawyers and business managers. Labor, agriculture, scientists, and other groups also would find a place, with varying degrees of power and influence, in the welter of agencies that followed. The federal government in 1939 possessed far greater administrative capacity than it had in the spring of 1917, and under Roosevelt's leadership it administered an unprecedented experiment in peacetime mobilization. By the fall of 1941, some observers argued that national defense policy was "taking hold of the economy, regardless of events in Europe. It has become a driving force all by itself."[51]

Despite such gains in reach and ability, however, the U.S. government still required a range of skills that only private institutions could provide. Washington had to enlist the production efforts of private business corporations. A central question of the defense period became how to per-

branch is a good way of blocking off their encroachment.... The statutory responsibility is on us and we have got to stand up to it." October 11, 1940, Stimson Diaries, vol. 31, Yale University Library. As chief of the Statistics Branch of the Army General Staff during World War I, Ayres compiled the official statistical survey of U.S. military preparation and action. See Leonard P. Ayres, *The War with Germany, A Statistical Summary* (Washington, D.C.: U.S. Government Printing Office, 1919).

The Defense Commission's Bureau of Research and Statistics was the unit that worried Stimson. Created in June 1940, it was headed by Stacy May, formerly assistant director for social sciences at the Rockefeller Foundation, who, like Henderson with price controls, staffed his agency with nonbusiness statisticians and economists from government departments and academe. The Bureau of Research and Statistics would produce the analysis with which proexpansionist New Dealers battled corporate spokesmen and military leaders on defense estimates, production goals, and industrial capacity. See Civilian Production Administration, *Industrial Mobilization for War, History of the War Production Board and Predecessor Agencies, 1940–1945, vol. I* (Washington, D.C.: U.S. Government Printing Office, 1947), 36–8.

[51] *Business Week* (October 4, 1941): 13. That same year, TNEC researchers concluded that in the light of the percentage of the federal budget spent on national defense (including veterans' pensions and benefits and interest on debt from previous war borrowing) it was difficult to distinguish war and peace economies at any time. "In 1915 almost 44 percent of the Federal Budget went for military activities, and even in the greatly enlarged Budget of 1939, 20 percent was so spent. There is no such thing as an economy whose efforts are devoted singly to peace or war, for the activities of both overlap, coincide, or are superimposed one on the other. But national policy can determine which sector of the economy shall have the go-ahead signal, and which shall be subordinated to the other" (p. 237). See also Harold G. Vatter, *The U.S. Economy in World War II* (New York: Columbia University Press, 1985), 11–31.

On the argument that FDR's use of special war agencies, and appointments to them, was driven "by the quest of national unity," see Wayne Coy, "Federal Executive Reorganization Re-Examined: A Symposium, I," *American Political Science Review* 40 (December 1946): 1127.

suade or coerce private producers such as General Motors and United States Steel to shift fully from private to public markets at a time when rising military expenditures boosted consumer spending.[52] As in the case of World War I mobilization, anxiety over collapsing lines between private and public functions had to yield before the necessity of forging the institutional mechanisms required to combine private and public purposes on behalf of national war enterprise.

BUREAUCRATIC LEARNING

The managerial capacity of the U.S. government expanded dramatically between 1917 and 1939. The Wilsonian mobilization unintentionally contributed much to that development. It introduced for the first time a great number of private professional and business elites to the problems of social and economic management on a national scale. It provided them with an opportunity to test such skills and concepts as they had developed, and, more important, to experiment with new kinds of organizational and managerial devices.

It also left a legacy of unresolved policy issues such as Allied war debts, overcapacity in the coal industry, agricultural surpluses, a swollen national debt, a subsidized merchant marine, expanded Veterans Administration activities, the politics of government-owned nitrate plants, and governmental reorganization issues, as in the case of the army, all of which required increased attention to national management techniques and to the kind of statistical bases for the administrative decision making such management required. The war also provided a historical reference point for subsequent policy debates over how best to fashion instruments for national management, including management of the executive branch itself, an issue of great personal significance to President Roosevelt.

Although it was the bureaucratic expansion and learning that these managerial tasks required on the civil side of government that most

[52]Barton J. Bernstein, "The Automobile Industry and the Coming of the Second World War," *Southwestern Social Science Quarterly* (June 1966): 22–33; Richard A. Lauderbaugh, *American Steel Makers and the Coming of the Second World War* (Ann Arbor, Mich.: MI Research Press, 1980), passim; Kim McQuaid, *Big Business and Presidential Power: From FDR to Reagan* (New York: William Morrow, 1982), chap. 2; and Vatter, *The U.S. Economy in World War II*, 24–8. For a critical look at these and subsequent wartime events, see Paul A. C. Koistinen, "Warfare and Power Relations in America: Mobilizing the World War II Economy," in Titus, ed., *The Home Front and War in the Twentieth Century*, 91–110, 231–43. See also Jeffery M. Dorwart, *Eberstadt and Forrestal: A National Security Partnership, 1909–1949* (College Station: Texas A&M University Press, 1991), chaps. 1–3.

interested contemporaries,[53] the military sector also tried to learn such lessons as the war had to teach, and as it turned out, in the longer run of history, those institutions emerged as far more important to national management than contemporaries before 1939 could ever have imagined.

In the process of learning about national economic management for war on the army's behalf, the OASW Planning Branch was given an impossible task, both conceptually and organizationally. Conceptually, industrial mobilization as a problem required the analytical capacity of a wide range of both government and nongovernment organizations. Consequently, it made little sense to allocate responsibility for a national problem to the military bureaucracy alone, and to a small, underfunded segment of it at that. The OASW struggled along under adverse circumstances, and the extent of its isolation (not just political, but intellectual as well) became clearer as the results of its studies came under attack in the late 1930s.

In contrast to the civil side of government, the army had developed little contact with the social sciences in the interwar years. For example, it had made no systematic effort to provide itself with continuing sources of current economic research, for which Herbert Hoover and his research committees on economic changes and social trends were the great exemplars in the 1920s, and for which the National Resources Planning Board may be taken as exemplary in the 1930s. World War I had taught military planners the necessity of taking business practice into account; as a result, they established characteristic patterns of public-private interpenetration, as the examples of the OASW-HBS and educational order campaign suggest. Lack of institutional memory was certainly not a problem in the OASW, but intellectual and political isolation was. Some academics, such as Harold Moulton of Brookings, lectured at the Army Industrial College in the interwar years, but it would take World War II and the cold war to bring the military into a full embrace with the social sciences.[54]

---

[53]Carroll H. Wooddy's important reference work *The Growth of the Federal Government 1915–1932* (New York: McGraw-Hill, 1934) contains nothing on the military, including the Veterans Administration (VA), although the VA constituted "the greatest single source of increasing governmental expenditure since the period of the World War" (p. ix).

[54]On the social sciences during the war, see Peter Buck, "Adjusting to Military Life: The Social Sciences Go to War, 1941–1950," in Merritt Roe Smith, ed., *Military Enterprise and Technological Change, Perspectives on the American Experience* (Cambridge, Mass.: MIT Press, 1985), chap. 5. In general, and "largely as a result of the criticism directed at the military during the 1930's regarding its alleged joint responsibility with the 'munition makers' for American involvement in World War I," U.S. military leaders during

The rapidity with which military organizations could and would adjust was already clear in the defense period, however, much to the consternation of New Deal professionals such as Leon Henderson. The military industrial planners encountered a traumatic defeat when FDR turned down the Industrial Mobilization Plan. But a loss in that early bureaucratic battle did not mean that military institutions would lose the bureaucratic war. The subsequent wartime alliance between major industrial suppliers and their military buyers was one example of successful adjustment.

Much had changed in the relationship between the state and civil society in the United States between 1917 and 1941. The feverish period of government expansion in the 1930s had pushed government politics and administration to new levels of institutional and intellectual complexity. As public officials discovered during those years, economies of scale existed in government as in business, and management of both institutions required new kinds of expertise. The defense buildup, in turn, previewed an even more labyrinthian bureaucratic world. James Burnham's *The Managerial Revolution: What Is Happening in the World,* published in 1941, for all its exaggeration, did strike a chord of recognition among informed contemporaries.

Yet that older ambivalence over the relationship between state and society by no means disappeared. On the contrary, increased popular suspicion paralleled increased state growth. Among conservatives, this sentiment found an outlet in congressional pressure against the expansion of New Deal government and in a mounting, even irrational, fear for traditional American values in a world of Fascist and Communist states. The burden of justification, as ever, remained on government officials. But liberals also had reasons for concern. They, too, were eager to draw sharp distinctions between the United States and the country's totalitarian enemies abroad; they also were determined to ensure that U.S. military professionals remained subordinate to civilian power. Many of them, like Leon Henderson, looked to a liberal in the White House to save government from capture by oligarchies of both business and military power.

In this respect, New Deal liberals shared another strand of the Wilsonian legacy. After all, in peacetime and wartime, President Wilson had

World War II "had a certain distrust of the intellectual, the scholar, and the academician." Moreover, military planners themselves had little or no training in the social sciences. See Perry McCoy Smith, *The Air Force Plans for Peace, 1943–1945* (Baltimore: Johns Hopkins University Press, 1970), 11.

aimed to protect the government and civil society from domination by oligarchies of undemocratic power. He had preached a New Freedom. Historians still debate the outcomes. What is not debatable, however, is that, in pursuing that goal, Wilson had one luxury his successors in the 1940s and after would never have: that is, he could honestly believe, as he did in 1919, that he could save government from its enemies by simply dismantling much of it once the war crisis had passed.

Obviously World War II and the continuing cold war transformed that historical context, and informed observers understood from the outset how a heightened concern for national security could threaten the customary institutional balance in the United States. In 1941, for example, social scientist Harold Lasswell predicted that the trend was away from the dominance of the businessman toward the supremacy of the soldier in a "garrison state." Political scientist Clinton Rossiter, who also speculated on the meaning of this new world, particularly for executive-congressional relations, described the outcome as a "Constitutional Dictatorship." Still others pondered the impact of defense on the "scientific estate" called into being by the need to readjust state-society relations in the light of cold war demands. In January 1961, President Eisenhower brought together a number of common themes in his farewell address. He warned that under conditions that required "an immense military establishment and a large arms industry new in the American experience," it was imperative to recognize that "the potential for the disastrous rise of misplaced power exists and will persist."[55]

And the controversy continues. In the 1960s and 1970s, much of the academic debate over the subject was rooted in opposition to the Vietnam War. For one thing, that war demonstrated the extent to which the state had acquired an administrative capacity to manage military escalation without a major mobilization of civil society. Moreover, executive agencies administered that effort in ways that challenged conventional understandings of the liberal state, not least of which was the government's

[55]Harold D. Lasswell, "The Garrison State," *American Journal of Sociology* 46 (January 1941), reprinted in Leon Bramson and George W. Goethals, eds., *War* (New York: Basic Books, 1968), 317–27; Clinton Rossiter, *Constitutional Dictatorship* (Princeton, N.J.: Princeton University Press, 1948); Dwight D. Eisenhower, "Farewell Radio and Television Address to the American People, January 17, 1961," *Public Papers of the President of the United States, Dwight D. Eisenhower, 1960–61* (Washington, D.C.: U.S. Government Printing Office, 1961), 1035–40. For a recent and very helpful study of the impact of World War II on the U.S. national security state, see Gregory Hooks, *Forging the Military-Industrial Complex: World War II's Battle of the Potomac* (Chicago: University of Illinois Press, 1991).

persistence in goals that sprang from no apparent fundamental need in civil society. The state possessed more autonomy than liberal theorists would, or Marxist critics could, admit. For some time, indeed, it appeared as if the executive branch, in the thrall of its own peculiar logic, was hell-bent on pursuing internally generated goals, irrespective of their devastating effects on the civil society whose interest the state, theoretically at least, was intended to secure.

The government's ability to manage the logistics of the effort without the emergency agencies of previous major war efforts was characteristic of its new-found administrative capacity. Leaving aside the issue of comparative resource use and the issue of how best to engage civil society in war enterprise, the point is that by the 1960s the executive branch could call on an array of institutional and technical routines to manage in peacetime a substantial war enterprise short of total mobilization. Some of the techniques were of comparatively minor significance in the general scheme of things, yet they were of considerable importance to the management of a limited war effort.

For example, for the first time in its war history the United States undertook a major military enterprise with stockpiled surpluses of strategic materials, most of which had been contracted for during the Korean buildup of the mid-1950s. The problem of critical materials for munitions production, an important policy issue in the pre–World War II years, had been largely "solved" by the 1960s, at least for purposes of limited war. The state also had a range of managerial instruments that could be used to coordinate the flow of critical materials such as steel, aluminum, copper, and nickel without the drama and crisis occasioned by the production efforts of previous escalations.

By the 1960s, moreover, the techniques required to manage a political economy for war had become in many respects indistinguishable from those required to manage a political economy at peace. Some argued, in fact, that Washington after World War II pursued a new kind of "military Keynesianism," finding in defense spending a tool for macroeconomic management. Such circumstances led economist John Kenneth Galbraith to conclude, "I don't think that anything much happens in war that doesn't happen in peace except there is more of it."[56] Galbraith, a former

[56]Quoted in Craufurd D. Goodwin, ed., *Exhortation and Controls: The Search for a Wage-Price Policy, 1945–1971* (Washington, D.C.: Brookings Institution, 1975), 397. The Economic Stabilization Act under which President Nixon imposed wage and price controls in August 1971 had been passed by Congress as an amendment to the Defense Production

price controller during World War II, made this point in the context of price control policies, but the comment may be taken to have general relevance.

The comparatively cost-free security the United States enjoyed in its earlier history had constrained the development of professional military administration, in particular, and government bureaucracy, in general. Conversely, the subsequent projection of military power, especially after World War II, transformed those underlying conditions and the scope and power of defense management along with them. External changes compelled internal adjustments. Max Weber, the German theoretician of bureaucracy, had made the point, if in exaggerated fashion, before World War I. "The United States," he wrote then, "still bears the character of a polity which, at least in the technical sense, is not fully bureaucratized. But the greater the zones of friction with the outside and the more urgent the need for administrative unity at home become, the more this character is inevitably and gradually giving way formally to the bureaucratic structure."[57]

In view of the growth in national defense, it is not altogether surprising that commentators in the 1980s and early 1990s should find in that sector one area where the United States might in future pursue industrial policies in ways analogous to those of the Japanese. After all, military bureaucrats and mobilization experiences contributed significantly to the foundations of the role of government that guided the Japanese economic miracle of the post–World War II years sometimes called the "developmental state." But more than that, it is the parallel interest that U.S. defense managers have in coordinating and developing resources on behalf of the nation's security that suggests the potential overlap between the Japanese approach to industrial policy and the technocratic management system in U.S. defense.[58]

Act (DPA). Originally enacted in 1950, DPA had served as the legal charter for much of the Korean mobilization. See Harvard Business School reprint, Arnold R. Weber, *In Pursuit of Price Stability, The Wage-Price Freeze of 1971* (Washington, D.C.: Brookings Institution, 1973), 6.

[57] Quoted in H. H. Gerth and C. Wright Mills, eds., *From Max Weber: Essays in Sociology* (New York: Oxford University Press, 1974), 211.

[58] Chalmers Johnson, *MITI and the Japanese Miracle: The Growth of Industrial Policy, 1925–1975* (Stanford, Calif.: Stanford University Press, 1982), esp. chaps. 4 and 5. On the Pentagon-MITI analogy, see Michael Y. Yoshino and Glenn R. Fong, "The Very High Speed Integrated Circuit Program: Lessons for Industrial Policy," in Bruce R. Scott and George C. Lodge, eds., *U.S. Competitiveness in the World Economy* (Boston: Harvard Business School Press, 1985), chap. 4. See also Clyde V. Prestowitz, *Trading Places: How*

Since the turn of the century, then, the federal government has gained enormous power to collect and manage human and material resources for military purposes. It has created a national management system for defense. That system has grown episodically; it has emerged by means of an intensely political process. It is not simply the product of some inevitable bureaucratic drift.

But if creation of a defense management system has been a political process in which groups struggle over the uses of government power, it has also been a process of learning. In Hugh Heclo's terms, "If states power, they also puzzle,"[59] and the evolution of power in the defense realm has also been the occasion for continuing intellectual and administrative effort devoted to solving the problems that acquiring and managing those resources have imposed.

We Allowed Japan to Take the Lead (New York: Basic Books, 1988); and "The Calls for an Industrial Policy Grow Louder," *New York Times*, July 19, 1992, F5.

[59] Hugh Heclo, *Modern Social Politics in Britain and Sweden, From Relief to Income Maintenance* (New Haven, Conn.: Yale University Press, 1974), 305.

About the authors

W. ELLIOT BROWNLEE is Professor of History at the University of California, Santa Barbara. His publications include *Dynamics of Ascent: A History of the American Economy* (2d ed., 1979) and "Woodrow Wilson and Financing the Modern State: The Revenue Act of 1916," *Proceedings of the American Philosophical Society* (June 1985). He is a former Fellow of the Woodrow Wilson Center.

DONALD T. CRITCHLOW is Professor of History at St. Louis University and editor of the *Journal of Policy History*. His publications include *The Brookings Institution, 1916–1952: Expertise and the Public Interest in a Democratic Society* (1985). Editor of *Socialism in the Heartland* (1989), (with Ellis Hawley) *Poverty and Public Policy in Modern America* (1989), and (with Ellis Hawley) *Federal Social Policy: The Historical Dimension* (1989), he is a former Guest Scholar at the Woodrow Wilson Center.

ROBERT D. CUFF, Professor of History and Administrative Studies, York University, Toronto, is the author of *The War Industries Board: Business-Government Relations During World War I* (1973), and coauthor of *Canadian-American Relations in Wartime* (1974) and *American Dollars/ Canadian Prosperity: Canadian-American Economic Relations, 1945– 1950* (1978). He is a former Guest Scholar at the Woodrow Wilson Center.

ROGER DAVIDSON, Professor of History, University of Edinburgh, is the author of *Whitehall and the Labour Problem in Late Victorian and Edwardian Britain* (1985).

MARY O. FURNER is Professor of History at Northern Illinois University. The author of *Advocacy and Objectivity: A Crisis in the Professionalization of American Social Science, 1865–1905* (1975), Furner contributed to and coedited (with Barry Supple) *The State and Economic Knowledge: The American and British Experiences* (1990). She is a former Fellow of the Woodrow Wilson Center.

LAWRENCE GOLDMAN, Fellow and Tutor in Modern History, St. Peter's College, Oxford, is the author of "A Peculiarity of the English?: The Social Science Association and the Absence of Sociology in Nineteenth Century Britain" in *Past and Present* (1987).

MICHAEL J. LACEY is Director of the Division of United States Studies at the Woodrow Wilson Center. He is the editor of *Religion and Twentieth Century American Intellectual Life* (1989), *The Truman Presidency* (1989), and, with Knud Haakonssen, *A Culture of Rights: The Bill of Rights in Philosophy, Politics, and Law—1791 and 1991* (1991).

BARRY SUPPLE is Professor of Economic History at the University of Cambridge. His publications include *The Royal Exchange Assurance: A History of British Insurance, 1730–1970* (1970) and *A History of the British Coal Industry, 1913–1946* (1987). He contributed to and edited, with Mary O. Furner, *The State and Economic Knowledge: The American and British Experiences* (1990). He is a former Guest Scholar at the Woodrow Wilson Center.

DONALD WINCH is Professor of the History of Economics at the University of Sussex. His most recent books are *Adam Smith's Politics* (1978); *That Noble Science of Politics: A Study in Nineteenth Century Intellectual History* (1983), written in collaboration with Stefan Collini and John Burrow; and *Malthus* (1987).

Index

429